BORN TO SHOP

FRANCE

*The Ultimate Guide for
Travelers Who Love to Shop*

4th Edition

WILEY

Wiley Publishing, Inc.

For KVF, who gave me Provence and taught me how to use it: with love and thanks.

Published by:

Wiley Publishing, Inc.
111 River St.
Hoboken, NJ 07030-5774

ISBN 0-7645-5691-6

Editor: Leslie Shen
Production Editor: Bethany André
Photo Editor: Richard Fox
Cartographer: Elizabeth Puhl
Production by Wiley Indianapolis Composition Services

For information on our other products and services or to obtain technical support, please contact our Customer Care Department within the U.S. at 800/762-2974, outside the U.S. at 317/572-3993 or fax 317/572-4002.

Wiley also publishes its books in a variety of electronic formats. Some content that appears in print may not be available in electronic formats.

Manufactured in the United States of America

5   4   3   2   1

CONTENTS

MAP LIST

ABOUT THE AUTHOR

Suzy Gershman is a journalist, an author, and a self-confessed shopping goddess who has worked in the fashion and fiber industry for more than 25 years. The *Born to Shop* series celebrated its 20th year in 2004 and has been translated into eight languages, making Gershman an international expert on retail and trade. Her essays on retailing have been used by the Harvard School of Business; her reportage on travel and retail has appeared in *Travel + Leisure, Travel Holiday, Travel Weekly,* and most of the major women's magazines. Gershman currently writes for *Air France Madame.* When she's not in an airport, she can be found in Paris, Provence, or Texas.

TO START WITH

While Paris may have been the co-star in the final episodes of *Sex and the City*, it is France that's the real star of this edition— making it clear that on the one hand there's Paris, and on the other, France. The two are very, very different.

This edition will be most helpful for those who plan to drive around the French countryside. With the TGV fast train and the fact that I now own a house in Provence, I have loaded down these pages with notes from research trips, with a heavy slant toward Provence and the rest of the south of France.

If you're going to just be in Paris or if you think you will confine your serious shopping to Paris, you'll find that *Born to Shop Paris* is more for you. The Paris chapter in this book is for people who will be in and out in a day or two and who have already had the opportunity—or will soon have the opportunity—to shop in the countryside.

Thanks go to everyone who has helped me learn about France and feel comfortable here, especially Karen Fawcett of Bonjour Paris (www.bonjourparis.com); her husband, Victor Kramer; all my hotelier friends who have whispered tips and updates in my ears; and all the friends who have sent me magazine articles and so forth.

Special thanks go to Alexander Lobrano, who first took me to Marseille and showed me its hidden wonders. Alec and I are eating our way through all the new and rotated chefs in the south of France as you read this; I'm the fat one. The tourist boards in many cities went out of their way to understand my bad accent and to point me toward the best in town; particular thanks to Nathalie Steinberg in Marseille.

Chapter One

....

THE BEST OF FRANCE AT A GLANCE

CRÈME DE LA CRÈME

Paris is a special place unto itself. Far more than just the City of Light, it has many wonderful and beautiful things to see, to eat, and to buy—but it is not France. In many ways, it is the opposite of the rest of France.

You will find passion and fashion and style by the mile in Paris, but you will not find the soul of France. Therefore, I have devised this quickie overview chapter to give you a fast look at what I consider to be some of the best bets in the French countryside. Nearly everything listed below is outside Paris; for specifics on the best of the City of Light, see chapter 4.

Obviously, I haven't been to every village in France, and this book does not cover the entire country. What you have here are some highlights that might help you flash forward to the best addresses if you are in a mad rush. *Vite, vite!*

Who knows, you could be between screenings at the Cannes Film Festival. Or you could be between couverts. Straighten your black tie, fluff up your bosom, put on your Ray-Bans, and get out your highlighter pen.

1

Best Overall Makeup & Perfume Shop

SEPHORA
Stores in Paris and the provinces.

There are Sephora stores all over France, and each varies, depending on the real estate. The flagship on the avenue des Champs-Elysées is probably the best one, but there are good branches in most major cities.

Many Sephora stores are on two levels and come complete with a kiddie play area. Merchandise is organized by color in the front of the store and by brand around the sides of the store, with fragrance in a different area. Fragrance is alphabetized, and no one line has more space or adverts over any other line: It's very democratic. There are tons of testers and paper strips, so you can spritz until you cease to breathe.

The house line of bath products not only is fabulous, but also comes in miniature sizes that are perfect for travel or gift-giving. Sephora provides an electronic *détaxe* (VAT refund) at the cash register if you qualify (see "Détaxe," in chapter 2).

Best Overall *Parapharmacie*

PARASHOP
Stores in Paris and most French cities.

A *parapharmacie* like Parashop specializes in beauty and pharmaceutical brands, often from the same companies that make designer products. While best for *les soins* (treatments), it sometimes has color cosmetics as well. You'll also find bath products, soaps, health and beauty aids, and more.

Best Monday in France: Cannes & Nice

This is a double-header for true flea-market devotees: You can do the half-hour between the two cities on a train. Monday flea markets are held year-round, so there's none of this closed-on-Monday business.

Although the Cannes Monday *brocante* market (Marché Forville) isn't very big or splendid, it is very nice and funky, and prices are good. Combine it with the 250-odd dealers at the cours Saleya in Nice, and you'll have yourself a fine day.

Best Tuesday in France: Vaison-la-Romaine

Vaison-la-Romaine is a small city in northern Vaucluse, in Provence. The market rambles all over the city and will bring you much joy.

Best Fruit & Flower Market

COURS SALEYA
Nice.

Any day of the week except Monday, the cours Saleya in Nice is awash with striped awnings and tables heaving with locally grown fresh produce. You can buy flowers, candies, olives, honey, and more.

Best Factory Store

PORTHAULT
19 rue Robespierre, Rieux-en-Cambrésis (near Lille).

The Porthault factory sells goodies at a fraction of their retail price. It's very hit or miss, and you must pay in cash; but this is not only worth the drive—it's worth a trip to France.

Best Factory-Outlet Mall

LA VALLEE VILLAGE
Marne la Vallée, outside Paris.

Though more and more outlet malls open all over Europe, this one, 40 minutes outside Paris and just 5 minutes from Disneyland Paris, is the best because it offers more upscale brands than the others. That it's adorable and clean and next to a regular mall and has an outdoor nursery makes it even better. The only bad news: no dogs. La Vallée's outlets are open on Sundays, although note that the adjacent Auchan store and shops in the mall are not. For more info, call © 01-60-42-35-00 or go to www.lavalleevillage.com. You can arrive by RER or take the Cityrama shuttle bus from Paris every Tuesday, Thursday, or Sunday (✆ **01-44-55-60-00** for reservations).

Best Annual Sale Event

LES OLIVADES
Chemin des Indienneurs, St-Etienne-du-Grès.

I get all sweaty just thinking about this one—a factory sale that's in an actual factory, with products set in a jumble on tables or falling out of open cartons, and yard goods sold right off the bolt. There's clothes, there's home style, there's fabrics. There's delightful chaos at rock-bottom prices. See p. 220 for more.

Best Secret Sales

CATHERINE MAX
17 av. Raymond Poincaré, Paris.

Catherine Max has a most un-French concept and is doing business like gangbusters: Her private club allows members entrance to either or both of her Paris showrooms, where she hosts a rotating array of big-brand sample sales. Normal admission is by invitation and for members only; readers of *Born to Shop* may gain one-time entrance without membership by showing a copy of this book at the door. Go to www.espacecatherinemax.fr to find the dates and brands that correspond with your visit to Paris.

Best Way to Look French (for Men)

VILEBREQUIN
Stores in Paris and major French cities.

This men's bathing-suit line (which also makes boxer shorts) is de rigueur beachwear, especially in the South of France. There are free-standing shops in Cannes, Monte Carlo, and St-Trop. The suits have a very identifiable style of print—much better than a logo.

Best Way to Look French (for Women)

Wear high heels without stockings, be tan, and buy everything a size too small. Cleavage is good.

Best Nautical Looks

Coco Chanel and Pablo Picasso made the striped French fisherman's T-shirt an icon of fashion. Today there are several firms, with distribution in both department stores and free-standing shops, that have reeled in most of the market due to their quality: **St-James** and **Amour-Lux.** These little babies are not cheap (about 45€/$52), but last forever, even after many washings. You will also see copycats out there, as stripes are always in style.

Best Soap

Savonnerie Marius Fabre
148 av. Paul Bourret, Salon-de-Provence.

My friend Alain Ducasse turned me on to this brand; it's a small firm that's been in business since 1900. You don't have to go to Salon-de-Provence to buy it; there is distribution in most Provençal-style shops, especially in the area between Nice and Cannes. You can also find it elsewhere in France, but you have to be looking hard.

Best Multiple

L'Occitane
Stores throughout France—and now the rest of the world.

L'Occitane (www.loccitane.com) now has shops everywhere—not just in France. It carries an enormous line of soaps, bath products, beauty products, and household scents such as candles, incense, and room sprays. I like the little tins of soap. The shea butter is good for very dry hands, and the orange-cinnamon home-ambience oil is delightful. This is a great place for doing all your gift shopping in one swoop.

OLIVIERS & CO.
Stores throughout France.

This is the latest creation of the marketing genius Olivier Baussan, who also created L'Occitane. The first stores were named O&Co., and you still sometimes see signs written that way. They specialize in Mediterranean olive products—essentially olive oils and olive-based foodstuffs, but also things made of olive wood, chocolates shaped like olives, books, and so on. A few of the stores have food bars as well.

Best Cookies

MERE POULLARD
Mont St-Michel and most French supermarkets.

These simple butter cookies from Mère Poullard will slay you. They are nationally distributed throughout grocery stores in France; I buy mine in Paris at any grocery store.

TUILES CITRON
Most French supermarkets.

Lu, the largest maker of cookies and biscuits in France, now has a Taillefine line of low-cal cookies. Its *Tuiles Citron* (lemon wafers) are to die for . . . and to diet for.

Best Chocolate

JOEL DURAND
3 bd. Victor Hugo, St-Rémy; 46 rue Victor Hugo, St-Paul-de-Vence.

I'm not sure if I've fallen for the gimmick, the beauty of the man, or the taste of the chocolates, but who cares? This young choco-latier has me hooked. He makes 26 flavors of chocolate, each named for a letter of the alphabet. You use a chart to figure out what's inside. I am addicted to L—chocolate and lavender.

RUNNER-UP

BERNACHON
42 cours Franklin Roosevelt, Lyon.

Okay, so it's no surprise that Bernachon would end up on my list—he's on everyone else's list, too. For chocolate candy, Joël (see above) gets my vote, but when I'm thinking of a rich, creamy chocolate éclair, then it must be from Bernachon.

Best Confiture Shop

MAISON DE LA CONFITURE
Gassin (outside St-Tropez).

Note that I didn't say Maison de la Confiture has the best confiture in France—that would be too hard to pick—but it does have the best shop. Maison de la Confiture has many wild, weird, and wonderful flavors and combinations, and all the jam jars are topped with little squares of Provençal fabric. My fave is the blood-orange confiture. The store also sells some antiques and gift items. *Note:* No credit cards.

Best Cooking Classes

ECOLE RITZ ESCOFFIER
15 place Vendôme, Paris.

Learn how to ritz a dish. Classes are offered in both English and French. For info, call ☎ **800/996-5758** from the U.S. Local phone ☎ 01-43-16-30-50. www.ritzparis.com.

LA VARENNE
Château du Feÿ, Villecien.

La Varenne is the most famous—they've been doing it to rave reviews for the longest time. Call ☎ **800/537-6486** from the U.S. Local phone ☎ **03-86-63-18-34**. www.lavarenne.com.

Le Jardin des Sens Atelier de Cuisine
36 bis av. St-Lazare, Montpellier.

The most famous twins in France. Call ✆ **04-99-58-38-38** or go to www.jardin-des-sens.com.

Best Ever

Just to make sure you remember you're in France now, I'd like to inform you that this is the country that teams a nutritionist and a three-star Michelin chef to plan the menus in its prison system.

BEST BETS FOR GIFTS

You're Going to Buy Only One Thing in France

- A house in Burgundy.
- An Hermès tie or scarf (check out the newest model, a tribute to Salvador Dalí).
- A bottle of scent not yet introduced in the U.S.

You Only Have Time for One-Stop Shopping

Try any branch of Monoprix or a *hypermarché,* the French version of a modern dry-goods store.

Best Kitsch Outside Paris

This wasn't meant to be funny, and not everyone thinks it is (kitsch has that problem), but personally, I think this is just the best little giggle in France: You can buy Joan of Arc (Jeanne d'Arc) coffee in Rouen, the city where Joan was burned at the stake. It's French roast.

Best Gifts Under $5

- Latest edition of a French magazine, preferably *Elle,* which costs about 2.60€ ($3).

- *Calissons* (candy-covered almonds), sold everywhere in Provence for about 4.35€ ($5) a box.
- Savon de Marseille, about 4.35€ ($5) for a 400g block (the bigger-size square soap).
- A *gant de toilette,* the French version of a washcloth (like a terry-cloth mitt), which can be teamed with soap if you're a big spender.
- Something from the grocery store (see below).

Best Gifts from the Supermarket

- Coffee—my friend Ken swears by **Carte Noire** brand, found at any supermarket for around 2.60€ ($3). Pay attention to the packaging, as this comes in ground or whole-bean form, freeze-dried, instant, and so on.
- Cookies, such as the two types listed earlier in this chapter, the Belgian cinnamon cookies called Speculoos, or the Petit Sables Normands brand of orange-flavored butter cookies are all wonderful choices.
- *Confiture* (jam), especially if you can find unusual flavors such as rose.
- Tea—the British may be famous for theirs, but there are several French flavors that you rarely find outside of France. Try Red Fruits *(les fruits rouges),* a blend sold by various brands. I think the Monoprix house brand's is the best.

Best Serious Gifts

- A bottle of wine from a meaningful vintage year (for example, when a child was born or when you were married—you get the idea). Conversely, choose a wine that will be at its peak on a special date (a 21st birthday, a 50th birthday, and so on). Remember, non-vintage Champagne cannot keep more than 3 years.
- A selection of beauty products from **Caudalie,** which are available in the U.S. but are easier to find in France. Made from grape seed and straight from a vineyard in Bordeaux,

these products can be gathered together and given in a basket—you can even add a small bottle of wine.

- Jewelry from one of the famous French crystal houses such as **Baccarat** or **Lalique.** It's less expensive in France, with greater savings if you qualify for *détaxe.* I like the new slide bracelet from Lalique (you buy the crystal charm and the bracelet separately)—drop-dead chic at a fair price (about 175€/$200).

- A candle with an exotic scent, such as one from **Mariage Frères** in Paris, about 43€ ($50). There are less expensive candles at other shops; department stores have a large selection, as does Sephora. I'm big on **Diptyque,** a brand with almost cult status in the U.S.—about 26€ ($30) per candle at Printemps in Paris or the Diptyque shop on the Left Bank.

- A **Longchamp** folding shopping bag or weekend tote; prices range with size and style. These are sold all over the world and are not unique, but they are so French and so important to *le look* that they make a great gift.

- A white blouse from **Anne Fontaine,** a chain found in every major city in France and several in the U.S. . . . the point is that nothing is more French than a fabulous white blouse. Prices begin around 65€ ($75).

Best Gifts for Kids

- Monoprix has a small toy selection, but it is well stocked with Legos and often has models that are not available in the United States.

- Little girls (and big girls, too) love perfume miniatures and samples, as well as makeup and small-size toiletries. Hoard the ones you get free, buy miniatures if they are well priced (some are collectors' items and cost a fortune, so watch out), and stop by Sephora for its adorable bath and fragrance collection in tiny sizes.

- Books in French, especially storybooks that you already have in English, make wonderful gifts for children. All Disney stories are available in French. Do not buy videocassettes,

as they are in Secam format, not NTSC, and will not be com-
patible with your VCR.

- Build-it-yourself paper cutouts of French landmarks can provide hours of entertainment.
- Try to find a souvenir with the child's name on it in French. If you can't get an exact match, find a similar name and give the child a French pet name. You can even pick a saint to go with it and then celebrate the saint's name day with the child.

Chapter Two

....

FRENCH DETAILS

BIENVENUE

....

Although the shopping in Paris may be quicker and easier than in any other city in the country, you don't really get an accurate picture of France if you stick to the City of Light. You can be in Paris and not really be in France. And you don't get the real shopping treats you deserve.

So get out of town, even if only for a day or a weekend. If you're looking for a price break, you'll want to go to some of the out-of-the-way places and even to a few factories—things are cheaper outside Paris. *C'est vrai!*

But no matter how the dollar dances, this is also where you'll create memories so priceless that money no longer matters. Once out of Paris, you can experience charming old towns, geraniums in window boxes, luxury hotels, perfume buys and beauty programs, Provençal fabrics, heaps of raspberries nestled into little handmade *paniers* (baskets), and people who are willing to listen to your attempts to speak French. Welcome to a country that will fill your senses with wonder and wash your soul in passion.

So *bienvenue*, my friends. Grab hold of your map and hit the road, Jacques. France and all its bounty await. And no, the French don't hate Americans, they don't forget who died on D-Day (or why), and yes, *mais oui*, they really want you to visit. Just don't mention the war.

KNOW BEFORE YOU GO

If you want to have plenty of money for shopping, you have a fair amount of homework to do before you set foot in France. The bargains are not just lying around; you're going to have to work for them. The cost of living in France is high, so you have to live French-style in order to save. Also remember, there are deals for tourists and deals for locals, and you need to know when you should be which.

The French Government Tourist Office (www.france tourism.com), which has offices in various U.S. cities, offers some super materials, and I have been knocked out by the brochures, maps, and paperwork sent to me by local tourist offices throughout France. All are available in English. Don't be shy about writing or faxing directly to France and to each *département* for information.

Print Information, Please

Club France is a service offered by the French Government Tourist Office. A single membership costs about $95; call © 800/881-5060, ext. 27, for information or to join. Membership entitles you to a discount card and a bulletin filled with tips and coupons for complimentary drinks and other goodies.

France Today is a great newspaper published in the United States in English. I'm not sure which I enjoy more—the editorial content or the ads, which often have specific travel and trip info. There's also a classified section you can use if you want to rent a house or get personal in French. A 1-year subscription is about $40 in the U.S., $50 outside the U.S. Call © 800/999-9718 for more information.

FUSAC is a local freebie handed out in Paris but hard to find elsewhere. It's mostly ads—great for finding long- or short-term rentals, swaps, cars, and services. You can get a subscription in the U.S. or have a friend in Paris mail it to you. Check out www.fusac.fr for info; there are 6-month subscriptions available if you are just using it to help prepare for a trip.

Electronically Yours

Hotels, airlines, and travel agents all have their own websites, often offering glimpses of properties, special deals, or more. Many stores have websites as well. Each issue of *France Today* has a column called "Web Watch," which highlights some of the best websites on France. One site I like is Bonjour Paris (www.bonjourparis.com), which actually covers more than just Paris.

Also remember to look up generic U.S. travel sites and bulletin boards that have information on many places, including France.

As you know, websites come and go at a rapid pace, but here are a few you might want to check out (note that any site that ends with "fr" is most likely to be in French):

www.bonjourparis.com (best overall English-language site on France)

www.culture.fr (wisdom from the French Culture Ministry)

www.champselysees.org (updates on news from the 'hood)

www.hotelweb.fr (hotel-booking site for French firms like Sofitel, Novotel, Mercure, and Ibis)

www.info-france-usa.org (French Embassy in the U.S.)

www.meteo.fr (French weather reports)

Seasonally Yours

The biggest secret to eating, sleeping, and shopping in France is simply seasonal. The prices on most items change with the climate; if the dollar ratio has you down, think off season.

Most destinations have two seasons: in and out. Summer is traditionally thought of as "in season." Everyone who travels knows that winter is "out" and thus always cheaper than summer. However, France does not play by the same rules.

In France there are four seasons, and almost all hotels have four different price categories for the same room: high, very high, low, and shoulder.

In Cannes, there is an extra season, called festival, which means there are five seasons on the Riviera. During festival, which covers the Film Festival in May and all large conventions, rooms are actually scalped and prices are raised sky-high. Summer's high season is a respite compared to festival prices.

As much as I don't like to talk about it, I must also point out that there is what I call tragedy season. This happens when some weird act of God or other terrible thing (for example, a bombing, a hijacking, a strike, or a hoof-and-mouth disease outbreak) occurs, and people refrain from traveling, thus pressuring hotels and restaurants to drop their prices. Tragedy seasons can be terrible things—but the chance of anything happening to you is usually small, and the bargains to be had are usually large.

Besides the fluctuation in hotel rates, menu prices also change with the season. Similarly, if prices in stores aren't raised outright during peak seasons, at the least your bargaining position with the proprietor varies according to the flow of tourists.

Please note that by *tourists* I don't just mean just Americans. During the French school holidays, when families travel to resorts, the prices are raised for French tourists as well. It's good to know when French school holidays fall, as they will affect your freedom to travel and find deals. The French Government Tourist Office prints a free wallet-size card that lists all school vacations; any French calendar will also list school breaks by zone.

Note: Seasons in resort towns vary by region. When it's in season in Cannes, it may still be out of season in Deauville. When rooms are top dollar in Cannes, with surcharges up the wazoo, prices are dirt-cheap in Paris, where they'll throw in everything but the hotel's Porthault bathrobe.

Big cities traditionally have low room rates in July and August, and on weekends throughout the year. Also note that the French celebrate many holidays (try getting any work done in the month of May). During these times, hotel rooms in big cities go begging, while resorts are sold out. Plan your travel accordingly.

The British Are Coming

Along with the American tourists and the French, you must also take into account the local British population and how it affects prices and transportation. In specific parts of France (mostly Normandy and the southwest), the British population is so strong that specialty stores selling English foodstuffs have popped up, and real-estate brokers say their clientele is 90% Brit. Real-estate prices have gone so high in some areas that only Brits can afford to buy. French is now a second language.

These communities seem to pop up near transportation centers—especially low-cost airline hubs or train routes that are near ferries or Eurostar. If you travel to Europe through London, you may be able to take advantage of some of these affordable fares to reduce the cost of getting to France.

GETTING THERE

From the United States

Here are a few of the tricks I've discovered:

- Get on the e-mail subscriber lists for all airlines and have them send you their special fares. You'd be surprised what can turn up.
- If you're traveling from the United States to a city in France other than Paris or Nice, you need to connect. Consider your connections and price the legs of your trip carefully. When you buy an Air France transatlantic ticket, you're entitled to specific programs and passes that may lower your fare. When you buy a Delta ticket, you get the entire Air France network as part of a code share. Ask!
- British Airways is working very hard to promote and maintain London as a hub for European travel. You can often buy a ticket to a French destination by way of London, with a free layover . . . you may even get a couple free nights in a hotel.

The Regions of France

- Yeah, the guys at British Airways are nice, but they aren't promoting London just to be nice. They're faced with stiff competition from the Eurostar train and low-cost carriers that fly into dozens of small French cities (as well as Belgium). Depending on your flexibility and your wallet, you may want to fly to London and wing it (so to speak) from there.

- Delta has a fabulous nonstop flight from New York to Nice, which is superb for getting to the Riviera or Provence (or even northern Italy). During the summer season, this flight is so popular that it is often full or blacked-out for upgrades with frequent-flier mileage. Book now!

- Speaking of miles: Note that during the off season, various airlines discount the number of miles you need to cash in for a ticket. You may also want to consider mileage promotions when you book your tickets: British Airways customers recently earned triple mileage points on flights from the United Kingdom to France.

- If you think you can just book arrival in one airport and departure out another, and then pick up easy or inexpensive transport between cities, I beg you to think twice and to read the "Getting Around France" section, below. France isn't a very big country, but it's plenty big when it comes to driving or taking the train from Nice to Paris or Lyon to Bordeaux or Marseilles to Biarritz. And it's plenty expensive when it comes to buying a one-way plane ticket between cities. Try every trick you can think of when you price fares.

From the United Kingdom

Travel from Great Britain to France has always been a breeze, and the opening of the Chunnel has made it even breezier. This is the case not just for the obvious reason, but also because of the demand factor: Airlines and ferries are now engaged in price wars and promotional deals geared to woo travelers away from the convenient new train services, Le Shuttle and Eurostar, both of which are booked through **Eurail** (© 888/382-7245). With all these deals, there are more and more options, and price possibilities, for easy, affordable connections from the United Kingdom.

The Chunnel offers two types of service: Eurostar, which is regular passenger service on a deluxe train, and Le Shuttle, which allows you to bring a car to France. Several car-rental companies even have packages that allow you to rent a car in Britain and drop it off in France. There are three kinds of service on the passenger train, at three different prices: economy, first, and premium. (Premium means you have a first-class seat and a taxi waiting for you at the station.) There are also promotional fares, especially in winter.

If you prefer to fly, the discount airline **Ryanair** (www.ryanair.com) offers service from London-Stansted to Paris, but may land at Beauvais airport (1 hr. north of Paris) or Orly. Ask before you get a surprise. Most of the low-cost carriers originate in the United Kingdom, but not all (see below).

From Other European Locales

Using a point of entry outside France, even for travel mainly within France, can be attractive if your trip includes other international destinations or if you are bargain-hunting and like the looks of some of the other Euro airlines or code shares. With the merger of Air France and KLM, you get a lot of extra options.

EasyJet (www.easyjet.com) flies from various European destinations to Paris, Marseille, Toulouse, Lyon, and Nice. **Basiq Air** (www.basiqair.com) flies from Amsterdam to Bordeaux, Nice, and Marseille; and from Cologne to Paris and Nice. Remember, discount airlines go in and out of business rather quickly—and the airports they serve can also change—so use this information only as a jumping-off point.

GETTING AROUND FRANCE

By Plane

Air France has passes for unlimited travel that work much like train passes. Le France Pass allows you any seven flights in a 1-month period. Keep in mind that you can purchase these passes only when you also purchase an Air France transatlantic ticket.

Student and youth passes are also available.

Note that it costs less to fly on certain days of the week than on others, and that airlines offer all sorts of promotions. Look through French magazines and newspapers, even if you can't read French; if you see a travel ad with good prices, get your hotel concierge to translate. Also, because France is in the middle of various airfare wars, the newspapers often post price comparisons between Air France and its latest rivals. For example, if you compare the best prices offered by Air France (which you might not get) and EasyJet, it looks something like this:

PARIS–NICE

| Air France | 165€ | ($190) |
| EasyJet | 82€ | ($94) |

PARIS–TOULOUSE

| Air France | 155€ | ($178) |
| EasyJet | 76€ | ($87) |

Be sure to know what airport you are using—especially with low-cost airlines, which often use alternative airports. For more on low-cost carriers, see "Getting There," above.

Tricky parts: Certain intra-France tickets must be booked in the U.S. before you take your transatlantic flight. But there are also deals for locals that are available only once you get here, so you might not want to book ahead. It's a game of nerves . . . with some French culture thrown in.

By Car

Car rentals that are pre-arranged in the United States are usually cheaper than any on-the-spot rentals you'll find in France. All major car-rental agencies have competitive deals for day-, week-, or month-long stays.

Tips: Don't assume that mileage is unlimited, that your car has automatic transmission, or that the price quoted includes tax or value-added tax (VAT). Ask and compare. Do not assume you and your luggage will fit into a Type A car—or even a Type B. Make sure you get the help-line phone number for the country or regions where you will be driving, and find out if English-language assistance is available.

Picking up (and returning) rental cars at major French airports can be much easier than using car-return offices at French train stations. Finding the train station in a major city can ruin your vacation. The bigger the city, the more train stations it

Parking Tips

Parking is almost never included in the price of a hotel room—even a hotel in the boonies. In Cannes, parking at a major hotel costs 30€ ($38) or more a night; in Bordeaux, it's a mere 10€ ($12). It is usually very difficult to park in resort cities. Should you be so lucky as to find a space, note that there are different types of spaces with different systems for paying. Make sure you understand the rules (see p. 45 for further details).

has, which means the more parts of town you have to drive through, the more one-way streets, the more chances to get lost, and the more stress. In one city, we actually hired a taxi driver to lead us to the train station.

When you pick up a car in France, do not congratulate yourself if you are upgraded to a larger car free of charge. The larger the car, the less easily it will make the corners in medieval towns.

ADA (www.ada.fr) is the biggest secret discovery I've made while living in France. This French car-rental agency is said to be the least expensive. It has an American partner, but is not called ADA in the States, and thus works as a co-op situation much like that of Kemwel. There are over a dozen ADA bureaus in central Paris, including locations at all major train stations.

I also like **Kemwel** (© 800/576-1590; www.kemwel.com), which uses Citer in France. Note that cars must be booked in the U.S. There is a 3-day minimum, but don't let that slow you down—sometimes its 3-day rate is less expensive than a single day with another firm.

You can often find fly-and-drive packages that include airline tickets and car rental, as well as fly-train-drive packages that include airfare, a certain number of days of train travel, and car rental. With a fly-train-drive package, you can use the train to get out to the countryside and then pick up the car for the good stuff and the wonderful back roads.

Car-Rental Companies at a Glance

ADA	✆ 08-36-68-40-02 in France; www.ada.fr
Auto Europe	✆ 800/223-5555; www.autoeurope.com
Auto France	✆ 800/572-9655; www.auto-france.com
Avis	✆ 800/331-1084; www.avis.com
Budget	✆ 800/527-0700; www.budget.com
Eurodollar	✆ 800/800-6000
Europcar	✆ 877/940-6900; www.europcar.com
Hertz	✆ 800/654-3001; www.hertz.fr
Kemwel	✆ 800/576-1590; www.kemwel.com
National/Citer	✆ 800/227-7368; www.citer.fr
Renault Eurodrive	✆ 800/221-1052; www.renault-eurodrive.com

By Train

Train passes are incredibly convenient and easy to use. That ease may be worth dollars and cents to you. I've learned to never knock convenience, even if you have to pay for it. However, train passes equal their cost or save you money only if you use them on long hauls or if you plan your travels carefully.

Having a train pass that's good for 5 days of travel is downright stupid if it's used only for day trips from Paris or short hops to places such as Versailles, Chartres, Reims, or even Lyon. The pass costs far more than the individual legs would if you just walked into a French train station (or travel agent) and bought the tickets.

If you are undecided as to which offers better value—a train pass or a few single-leg tickets—try to get some idea of the fares on big-haul trips. Note that the really cheapo fares usually go to locals who buy 30 days in advance. Also remember that train passes and/or tickets in France pay for passage, but do not guarantee a seat! Even with a pass, you'll still need to make a reservation for a seat on the specific train you want; it's required for all TGV and fast trains. You can get reservations in Paris, usually at 5€ ($5.75) a clip. (And yes, your dog needs one, too.)

Finally, no matter what type of ticket you use for a train in France, make sure you *composter* (validate) your ticket before you get on board. There is a hefty fine for not doing so, and playing "dumb American" will not work. *Composter* is such a perfect verb for this act that it is hard to translate; I guess it means "punch your ticket with an electronic hitching post." Near the entry to each train platform is an electronic post, painted bright yellow or orange. You place your ticket, with the magnetic strip up, into the slot. The machine automatically chomps on the ticket, punching an electronic nick, and spits it out. Congratulations, you have composted.

By Bus

Regional buses are a great option in places such as the south of France, where the cities aren't very far apart and the buses are cheap, frequent, and offer scenic rides. Consider, for example, taking the bus when traveling from Nice to Cannes, or from Avignon to Tarascon. There is no train service between St-Raphael and St-Tropez, so a bus is a handy idea there.

Also consider getting to airports by bus. If you can handle it, this will save you a lot of money, especially in the Nice area, where the taxis from the Nice airport to nearby cities are outrageously expensive.

By Boat

Be it cruise ship, yacht, or barge, there's no better way to get around France than boat, because you don't have to park the sucker yourself and you aren't stuck in a train station looking for a porter or a trolley.

I have developed a travel rule, which states that the amount of pleasure afforded by a specific destination in France is directly proportional to the difficulty of finding a parking space or negotiating the traffic jams there. When you travel by boat, you usually arrive in—or are taken by the boat to—the cute part of town. I call it The Cute.

Aside from the cruise ships that regularly call in the south of France, some companies also offer a schedule of French Atlantic ports of call, such as an itinerary from Lisbon to London with four stops in France. The *Queen Mary 2* calls at Cherbourg.

Some 200,000 people per year barge around France, choosing to arrive in various cities by water and often eliminating the crowd problem by stopping at ports that are less congested than the Cote d'Azur. Barge trips move slowly, often feature a good chef, and are almost always sold as inclusive packages with air, land, meals, and so on. Shore excursions and tips are extra. Some barge trips specialize in antiquing, with itineraries that involve barging all night and shopping all day. They can also arrange to ship home your purchases. These trips take place most often in Burgundy, where prices on furniture are the best.

PHONING AROUND

Rather than using any of the U.S. telephone companies' direct-dial deals, which have fees attached to them, I simply buy a France Telecom phone card at any *tabac* (tobacco shop; pronounced ta-bah) or news kiosk and use pay phones, even to call the United States.

If you don't mind dialing a lot of code numbers, there are other phone cards that can be used from any telephone and offer big savings over hotel rates. These cards can also be bought at *tabacs*.

Another good bet is to buy a U.S. phone card (with AT&T or MCI service) at a place like Wal-Mart or Sam's Club. You can use these cards to call home from Europe.

Note: Your U.S. mobile phone will not work in France unless it is a three-band phone.

HOTEL DEALS IN FRANCE

Here are a few tips on getting hotel deals:

- The easiest way to book rooms for a multi-destination trip is through any of the hotel associations or chains that have properties all over France. Get it all done in just one phone call.
- The best ways to get a deal? Contact the general manager of the hotel directly and ask for the best price available. Or book through the chains and associations, asking if they have prices frozen in U.S. dollars and/or any promotional deals that offer extras or discounts. Once you know the national reservation system's best offer, you can sometimes get a better rate by then calling the specific hotel directly. Many small establishments do not have toll-free numbers or booking agencies in the U.S.—another reason to contact the hotel yourself.
- Inquire about hotel extras that may range from full breakfast (a better value than continental breakfast) to airport transfers to one free night for every so many nights you pay for. Express, for example, is very aggressive about getting its hotel partners to offer perks to guests who book and pay with Amex cards.
- Do not expect your travel agent to know every trick in the book or to be responsible for saving you money. Travel agents can be terrific—use a good one—but be willing to do some legwork yourself by using online sources, toll-free numbers, and brochures (one picture may save you from a mistake).

Hotel Chains in France

Almost every hotel offers a promotional rate on weekends. Paris hotels usually discount in July and August, while resort hotels may add surcharges in August or throughout summer.

If you're traveling with children, you might want to stick to modern hotels, which are usually bigger and provide more beds and space in each room. Some hotels have lofts so that three or four can sleep in one unit. It is difficult to find a château room that fits a family of four.

Several hotel chains now specialize in "well-being" *(bien être)*—which means they have spas or offer spa packages. If you have serious work to do on your *forme,* you can even book packages for a week or 10 days.

ACCOR   Accor is the holding company that owns six international hotel chains. The ones you will want to know about are the more upmarket properties, including **Sofitel** and **Mercure.** These usually four-star hotels are often cute, older places that were taken over and offer great location and some charm. Of course, there are modern high-rise hotels, too, but with those you almost always know what you are getting. Take a look at individual properties at www.accorhotel.com, www.sofitel.com, or www.mercure.com; call ℂ **800/221-4542** for reservations.

CHATEAUX & HOTELS DE FRANCE   Do not confuse this brand with Relais & Châteaux (see below). This is an association of more than 500 hotels and restaurants. Most are the small and charming kind, but not all properties are equal, and sometimes the photos are better than the real thing. Check out www.chateauxhotels.com; call ℂ **800/553-5090** for reservations.

COMPAGNIE DES HOTELS DE MONTAGNE   This is a tiny, family-run chain, but it's extremely luxe and just may have all the hotels you need to book. There are several properties in the mountain town of Megève—hence the name—with other hotels dotted around in Lyon, outside St-Tropez, and smack in the middle of Provence. For more information, go to www.c-h-m.com.

CONCORDE HOTELS   This chain has changed a lot and I am no longer sure what's going on . . . but you can contact the U.S. offices (ℂ **800/888-4747;** www.concorde-hotels.com) and ask. Concorde owns the Crillon and other nice Paris hotels, as well as several properties dotted all over France.

HILTON   There are six Hilton hotels in France, so this chain makes the most sense if you are visiting France and the surrounding area: Brussels, Barcelona, and Geneva. Indeed, if you look at a map, Geneva is almost in France, making it a practical solution for some overnight visits. The most exciting development is the gorgeous new Hilton Arc de Triomphe, which offers the best value for the money in Paris and comes complete with many Hilton benefits. All Hiltons in France are modern or post-modern; two are located at Paris's airports. Call © 800/HILTONS or go to www.hilton.com.

INTER-CONTINENTAL   The Inter-Continental (© 800/327-0200; www.interconti.com) is one of my secret ways to afford a luxury hotel in Paris. This chain doesn't have a lot of properties in France, but if you're only going to Paris and Cannes, you may be quite happy with one phone call.

LEADING HOTELS OF THE WORLD   Leading Hotels (© 800/223-6800; www.lhw.com) is my main squeeze and frequently the only place I need to call anywhere in the world. This group has the fanciest and best hotels, although they do tend to be the large, flashy kind. If the prices are over your budget, check out corporate plans, promotional deals, or seasonal specials.

LE MERIDIEN   This world-famous chain has a French name but British management. Never mind. It often has good promotional deals, and while Le Meridien (© 800/543-4300; www.lemeridien.com) doesn't have heaps of hotels across France, it does have properties in key cities such as Paris, Nice, and even Juan-les-Pins on the Riviera (right near Cannes).

RELAIS & CHATEAUX   These fine châteaux with wonderful chefs are a dream come true. Many people consider the Relais & Châteaux (© 800/735-2478; www.relaischateaux.fr) catalog to be their bible for planning a trip to France; indeed, it could even be sold as a coffee-table book. Its member hotels are more consistently uniform than those in larger associations. Note the various spa packages available.

MONEY MATTERS

As we go to press, the euro is unusually strong and the dollar terribly weak, making prices seem painful. If you are visiting many E.U. countries in one trip, you will save money by not having to repeatedly exchange currency; but for the simple transaction between $ and €, it's not a pretty sight.

Currency Exchange

To get the best rate of exchange, you should use a credit card rather than cash, and withdraw what cash you need from an ATM. Here are some other tips:

- Buy traveler's checks in euros if you don't expect the dollar to gain dramatically.
- Don't walk around with tons of cash on you, but remember that you are paying a fee each time you use an ATM (unless your bank card allows for free international withdrawals). Your bank and the bank whose ATM you're using usually charge a total of $5 per transaction; nonetheless, an ATM is still often the best way to get cash.
- Shop rates at money changers and *cambios*—they aren't all the same. If you find a good rate, stick with the winner. A good *cambio* can be better than a bank for changing money.
- Avoid those cute foreign machines that look like ATMs but ask you to insert cash (U.S. dollars or currency from the last country you visited) in order to receive the local currency.
- After you return home, keep watching your credit card bills for accurate charges and refunds. Don't be alarmed if it takes a while for stores in smaller towns to post your charges with the credit card company—it can get quite laid-back in the French countryside. One May I bought a dress at Galeries Lafayette in Nice; it appeared on my January bill the next year. Now there's a float.

- If the dollar gains strength after you've made prepayments on your trip expenses, don't beat yourself up over the fact. Let it go, and have a good time anyway.

Détaxe

If you are making a big purchase, you'll want to get a value-added tax (VAT) refund. VAT is called TVA in France, and it's a whopping 19.6%. You are entitled to a refund of approximately 12% to 13% if you spend about 175€ ($201) or more in one day in the same store. This refund is called *détaxe*.

Some stores let you accumulate receipts from their various departments, as long as you spend the total in one day in one store (a reason why you might want to shop in department stores).

The refund is granted only to visitors who live outside the E.U. and who take the goods out of the country within 3 months of purchase. You must show the goods to Customs officials when you depart the E.U.; if you travel beyond France to another E.U. country before returning to the United States, you claim the refund in the last country you visit—even if you didn't buy anything there.

Although the refund can be given to you in cash at the airport, if you go this route, you will probably lose money on the exchange rate. The best way to get a refund is to have it put directly onto your credit card. Simply mark the appropriate box on the refund forms.

Major French department stores have offices that handle the refund papers at the time of purchase. Allow at least 20 minutes (much longer in summer) to complete the paperwork. Outside Paris, retail staff may not speak English and may not be familiar with the paperwork. Stores that sell luxury goods (including perfumeries) are very familiar with the refund process and can usually supply the papers—and a lesson in how to fill them out, if needed—in a minute or two.

Warning: You might decide to make a purchase based on the fact that you think—or the salesperson convinces you—that you will get an almost 20% discount, by getting the entire 19.6% TVA back via *détaxe*. However, this rarely happens. Very few retailers refund the entire amount of the tax. Big department stores tell you up front that all you get back is 12% because of the fee charged for doing the paperwork; other firms may keep it more hidden that they take a commission.

Tipping Tips

In France, you basically tip the same number of euros that you'd give in dollars back in the U.S. Because times have been tough here, people are more dependent on tips than they were in the past, and in some cases—especially in Paris, in resort destinations, and at luxury hotels—the amount expected for a tip has doubled in the past couple years. Here are the basics of tipping in France:

- Tip 2€ ($2.30) per bag to the bellhop who handles the luggage in a luxury hotel, 1€ ($1.15) in a lesser property.
- Give 1€ ($1.15) to a doorman for hailing a taxi.
- Round up your taxi fare to add a little bit. I don't give a percentage, but I never give less than .50€ (60¢).
- Give a few euros extra at the hairdresser for cut or color. The shampoo person gets 2€ ($2.30).
- In restaurants, I usually leave 5€ ($5.75) cash as an additional tip on a dinner bill for two people in a fancy place with stellar service. If it's just a snack, coffee, lunch, or not a big deal, 1€ to 3€ ($1.15–$3.45) will do, depending on the size of the bill and how long you sat there.

U.S. Customs & Duties Tips

To make your re-entry into the United States as smooth as possible, follow these tips:

- Know the rules—and stick to them!
- Don't try to smuggle anything.

- Be polite and cooperative (up until the point when they ask you to strip, anyway).

Also remember the following:

- You are currently allowed to bring home $800 worth of merchandise duty-free. Each member of the family is entitled to this amount, including infants. You may pool within a family.
- You pay a flat 10% duty on the next $1,000 worth of merchandise.
- Duties thereafter are based on a product-type basis. This varies tremendously per item, so consider each purchase and ask storekeepers about U.S. duties.
- The head of the family can make a joint declaration for all family members. Whoever is the head of the family, however, should take the responsibility of answering any questions the Customs officers may ask. Answer questions honestly, firmly, and politely. Have receipts ready, and make sure they match the information on your landing card. Don't try to tell a story that won't wash under questioning. If the Customs officers catch you in a little lie, you'll be labeled as a fibber, and they'll tear your luggage apart.
- Have the Customs registration slips for your personally owned goods handy in your wallet or otherwise easily accessible. If you wear a Cartier watch, be able to produce the registration slip. If you cannot prove that you took a previously owned French-made item out of the country with you, then you may be forced to pay duty on it.
- The unsolicited gifts you mail from abroad do not count in the $800-per-person rate. If the value of a gift is more than $50, the recipient pays duty when the package arrives. You're allowed only one unsolicited package per person, and you can't mail gifts to yourself.
- Do not attempt to bring any illegal food items back to the U.S.—dairy products, meats, fruits, or vegetables (coffee is

okay). Generally speaking, if it's alive, it's verboten. I also shouldn't need to tell you that it's tacky to bring in drugs and narcotics.

- Antiques must be at least 100 years old to be duty-free. Provenance papers help you get the item through Customs, and so does permission to export the antiquity, since it could be an item of national cultural significance. Any bona fide work of art is duty-free, whether it was painted 50 years ago or just yesterday; the artist need not be famous.

- Dress for success. People who look like hippies get stopped at Customs more than average folks. Equally suspicious are those women who look like a million dollars, dragging their fur coats and Gucci handbags and luggage with first-class tags—but who declare they have bought nothing.

- Laws regarding ivory are new and improved—for the elephants, anyway. You may not bring any ivory into the United States. Antique ivory must have provenance papers to be legally imported.

Chapter Three

....

FRENCH LESSONS

HOW TO BE FRENCH

Okay, you don't really want to be French. You just want to know enough to not make a fool of yourself, to have a good time, and to prevent being cheated, laughed at, or scorned.

Although you would have to live in France longer than a week or two to get into the cultural differences and to begin to understand French thinking, you can learn some of the most basic facts of life by taking my crash course.

You'll find that French people aren't rude, but they do live by a series of rules and social codes that are very different from American (and even British) rules and codes. When we don't know their rules, French people are offended—or amused. If they are offended and show it, we then assume they're rude. If you plan to sail through France without interacting with the people, you might do fine. Otherwise, I suggest you *bonne* up.

Below is a brief dictionary of French life and style. It includes some important French lessons, such as how to tell the difference between the menu and *la carte,* among other things.

Once you know how to act, you'll be ready to shop, so this chapter also includes an alphabetical rundown of the major French boutiques and chains.

GUIDE TO FRENCH LIFE & STYLE

A/R (ALLER/RETOUR) This means round-trip and usually appears after the price for a plane or train ticket. Do not assume that a one-way fare is half the cost of a round-trip fare.

AUCTIONS The basic auction business has been changed by new French laws and is no longer a government-run monopoly. France has a tradition of accessible auction houses that are not nearly as intimidating as Christie's and Sotheby's, which is great if you prefer the small-country kind of auction or funky merchandise.

Of course, there are other sorts of auctions. Among the most famous is a wine auction held on the third weekend of November in the town square of the medieval town of Beaune, in Burgundy. The annual event, celebrated since 1859, raises funds for the local hospice and serves to set the regional wine prices for that year's harvest. It's a big mob scene of tasting and touring, and you don't have to bid in order to join the party. Call © **03-80-26-21-30** for details.

AUTOROUTE France is connected by a series of toll highways, autoroutes, which are the closest thing to an American freeway, a British motorway, or a German autobahn. Some autoroutes offer only one lane in each direction, but in most cases the roads are similar to American highways. Autoroutes are designated by the letter *a* before their route number, and they also can be marked *peage,* which means toll road. The tolls, which are very steep, can be paid in cash or by credit card.

A VOLONTE All you can eat. Certain dishes (often the oysters and the chocolate mousse) are priced at a flat rate, and you can just keep shoveling it in.

BCBG (BON CHIC BON GENRE) This means preppy and is usually used to describe a style of clothing.

BEAUJOLAIS NOUVEAU This is a brilliant marketing plan to get people to drink young wine. The new wine is uncorked on the third Thursday of November, usually around the 15th.

The exact date, which varies each year to add to the fun, is announced and celebrated throughout France. Festivities begin around 5pm the night before the big day, with official sales beginning as the clock turns to midnight. (So if the third Thurs of Nov is the 15th, then the party starts on Wed the 14th and lasts until midnight, at which time the stores open and the party continues.)

The event has become international in the world of spirits and is even big in Paris. It's not unusual to spot *le nouveau est arrivé* signs here and there—even in New York.

BIDET   If Mother told you it was for washing your socks, she lied. Even if Mother told you the truth, she probably didn't tell you how to use it. I mention this because I was shocked by one of the finer details: You stand facing the wall. The rest is pretty basic.

BOURJOIS   This is a dime-store brand of makeup sold at every Monoprix and department store in France. The line also has some international distribution (it's sold in Sephora stores in the United States). Bourjois is not low-cost, but is affordable (and less expensive in France than elsewhere). Plus it comes with its very own secret: Chanel makeup is made in the same factories. There are differences between the two brands, of course, but they aren't as big as the price difference.

BROCANTE   There is an enormous difference between a *brocanteur* and a person who sells antiques, so heads up, everyone. An antiques dealer sells *antiquités,* which are important pieces from previous times. *Brocante* is junk. It is usually sold at flea markets or during the *brocante* day at the local *marché* (market). It is sold by anyone and carries no particular provenance or value.

CAPOTES ANGLAISES   Slang for condoms.

CARRELAGE   French for tile.

CARTE   We all know that a la carte means off the menu— or at least that's what it means to an American. To the French, the menu is the list of the set meals for the day, and the *carte* is the rest of the offerings. In short, what you think is the menu is really the *carte!*

CENTRE VILLE You'll often see this on signs; it means downtown. Sometimes it's written as VILLE PROPRE.

CHAMPAGNE Mere alcohol doesn't thrill me at all. But start singing about the night they invented Champagne, and let me sing along, off-key, and explain it all in simple terms.

First, Champagne is a *département* of France—a very particular part of the French map and some very specific real estate. If the grapes aren't grown in this zip code, then the bubbly they make just ain't champagne.

The word has become synonymous with the type of sparkling wine made in the Champagne region, but no wine can legally claim to be "champagne" unless the grapes grew to maturation in Champagne. Thus, you have scads of champagne-like drinks that aren't really champagne; rather, they are made with the *méthode champenoise.*

CHARIOT French word for the luggage handcart or trolley at train stations, airports, and grocery stores. Sometimes they are free, and sometimes they cost 1€ or 2€ ($1.15–$2.30) (horde coins in these amounts—you can never find one when you need one). The big grocery stores charge for use of their shopping carts; you get your money back only when you return the cart to the line and click it back in place. You forfeit your money if you leave the cart in the parking lot.

COCA-COLA Just ask for *un coca*. But if you're on a budget, forget it. The average price of a Coke at a bar in any decent hotel in France is 5€ ($5.75)—and it can go higher. You can buy a six-pack of Coke in any grocery store for about 2.50€ ($2.90).

COOKING CLASSES For gastronomy classes at **Le Cordon Bleu,** in Paris, call © 800/457-CHEF in the U.S., or go to www.cordonbleu.net.

The **Ecole Ritz Escoffier** (www.ritzparis.com), at the Hotel Ritz in Paris, has its own cooking classes and even offers a program for kids. One look at the brochure, and you'll be in heaven. There are also lectures and events; this is not just a ladies' thing. Call © 800/996-5758 in the U.S.

A number of French food-related tours are organized in the U.S. **Annemarie Victory** (© 212/486-0353) is a travel agent in New York who specializes in a wide range of international deluxe specialty tours, including a variety of top-flight gourmet food and wine-tasting tours in France. **France in Your Glass** (© 800/578-0903) specializes in wine tours but also offers some cooking and eating tours. A variety of options are available, including day trips, weekends you can add to your own trip, and even kitchen visits. **European Culinary Adventures** (© 800/852-2625 or 508/535-5738) offers country kitchen tours, which range from a barge trip and stays at local inns to visits to farms and vineyards.

COPPER (CUIVRE)   French cooking is widely associated with copper pots, which have been used locally for centuries because of the evenness of the heat conduction. Villedieu-les-Poêles, a small town near Mont-St-Michel, is known for the best copper pots in France, but you can find fabulous copper for sale at any *brocante* in France.

When buying copper pots, judge the quality of the pot by how thick the copper is, and make sure the copper is the same thickness all over. Check to see if the pot or pan has been patched or repaired. Look to see how the handles are attached and if the rivets go into the inside of the pot (which is bad). Also remember that it takes more than a little elbow grease to clean up an old copper pot.

COUCHETTE   If the first phrase you ever learned in French was *"Voulez vous coucher avec moi?"* (Will you go to bed with me?), then you haven't booked an overnight train in France. Yes, a *couchette* is a bed, but in train parlance, it's a bunk bed, and there are usually six—stacked three and three—in each train. A wagon-lit is a real bed in a real sleeping car.

CREPES   To an American, any French pancake is a crepe. Actually, there are two types: meal crepes, which are usually made of buckwheat flour, and dessert crepes, which are made of white flour.

DEGRIFFE   A *griffe* is a signature, or label, in France. Clothes sold without labels, à la Loehmann's, are sold *dégriffé;* the stores that sell them are also called *dégriffé.* This is another way to spell "bargains" in French. Not by a long shot do all *dégriffé* shops sell designer names. Every now and then, though, you'll find one that advertises itself as *haute*—this means it sells designer clothing.

DEGUSTATION   Most fancy restaurants have a *menu dégustation* (tasting menu) whereby you are served many courses and get to experience the many talents of the featured chef. Beware that these events usually take forever and offer far more food than a human was ever intended to eat. Furthermore, you can wait up to an hour between courses if you get unlucky. I'm not saying don't do it; I'm saying watch out and have plenty of time on your hands. Elastic waistbands also help.

DEPOT-VENTE   This is a used-clothing store, often specializing in designer resale. A handful of resale stores in Paris, Cannes, and the bigger cities of France will make you swoon with their selection and fair prices. Others specialize in antiques.

DUTY-FREE   Paris has a slew of duty-free makeup and perfume stores that offer great discounts (a total of about 35% off) to non-E.U. residents. More traditional are the general duty-free stores at airports and the duty-free offerings made on airplanes. Intra-European duty-free sales were outlawed in 1999, but if you are leaving the E.U., you can buy duty-free goods at the airport.

ELECTRICITY   There's no shortage of electricity in France (nuclear power!), but there is a shortage of people who have recovered from their post–World War II deprived childhood. Don't be shocked if the lights are off in the hallway. Feel around to find the switch, and voilà—you have limited lighting on a timer.

EURO   At press time, 1€ equaled about $1.15, but this will fluctuate. Note that euros are used only within the euro-zone countries, which means that many members of the E.U. still do not use euros.

FAIENCE   Hand-painted ceramic earthenware identified with country France. Some regional painting styles are more famous than others, especially those made in Marseille in the 1860s. The designs mostly consist of flowers on a white background. French faience is decidedly different from Italian faience and is usually simpler, with a larger portion of white background. There is a museum of faience in Marseille.

Expect to pay approximately 17€ to 39€ ($20–$45) for a new faience plate. Antique wares are considerably higher.

Because they are earthenware (clay, not porcelain), they break easily, so pack with care or carry by hand.

The major French faience cities are Rouen, Nevers, Gien, Nîmes, and Moustier-Ste-Marie. Salernes is thought of as the capital of tiles, whether earthenware or hand-painted. However, deepwater trade to Brittany also affected local pottery there, so northwestern Atlantic France has its own regional faience and pottery styles, which are best known to Americans through Quimper.

As for basic design points: Moustier is mostly known for storytelling pictures; Quimper has peasant figures; and Rouen features Arabic-influenced lace-edged patterns with arabesques and elaborate borders. Note that Gien faience is not earthenware but white paste, similar to English bone china. Gien patterns are very elaborate and are partially transferred by copper engraving (like English Staffordshire) and then hand-painted. This gives a much more sophisticated image than what you get when a local artisan paints a cock in the center of a plate.

FESTIVAL INTERNATIONAL DU FILM (FIF)   Held in Cannes for 2 weeks in the middle of May (the dates vary slightly each year), the FIF takes over the town. Although it is virtually impossible to get a decent hotel room in Cannes during the festival, you can write ahead for movie tickets and get a room in Nice. Write **International Film Festival,** Service d'Accreditation, 99 bd. Malesherbes, 75008, Paris, France; or fax 01-45-61-97-60 (www.festival-cannes.fr). It's virtually impossible to get into the official competition screenings, but there are so many other screenings that it's worth a shot. Don't forget your tux and dark glasses, darling.

FEVE   The word in French actually means "bean," but shoppers know this as a collectible that's best found in a French flea market. To celebrate Epiphany, French bakeries make *galette des rois,* cakes in which an ornamental bean is placed. If you get the piece of cake with the *fève,* you are the king or queen and get to wear a paper crown. The *fève* itself represents life and death. It's a symbol that stands for fertility, goodwill among humankind, happiness, and peace.

Not only is this popular with French children, but various firms also market different types of *fèves* for promotional purposes. Tiny porcelain *fèves* can be bought at flea markets and are collectors' items.

FRENCH LETTERS   More condoms.

FRENCH MAGAZINES   To subscribe to French magazines in French (from France!) at your home in the United States, call **Express Mag** (℡ 800/363-1310). French *Elle,* which comes out weekly, costs about 175€ ($200) per year. The women's supplement to *Le Figaro,* called *Madame Figaro* (also weekly), is over 350€ ($400) a year, exactly what it would cost you to buy it every week in France—you just don't get the Saturday newspaper that comes with it.

FROUFROU   This is a legitimate style in France, and it means just what you think: overbearingly decorated with swags, bows, ribbons, ruffles, and the like.

FRUITS CONFIT   Close, but you're wrong—this is not *confiture* (jam) made of fruits. Fruits confit are essentially jellied fruit, a regional specialty in the south of France. Instead of being dried, the fruits are soft and a little gooey—often covered with a sprinkled-sugar crust. Their natural liquids have been drained and they have been immersed in fresh sugar water for about a month. Nonfattening, of course.

GALETTES   Galettes literally means cookies. Each region of France has its own specialty galette. An important part of your research as you travel will be to test them all. The differences in taste are usually related to the proportion of butter in the dough, which ranges from about 18% to 35%.

GAS   If you are driving across France, you will do well to watch the fuel gauge and start thinking about where you can fill 'er up when you have a quarter of a tank left. This will allow you to be a little bit choosy and to plan your course to include a stop at the gas station of a *hypermarché.* You will usually need to follow signs to get to one, which will be off the autoroute but not sufficiently far as to be avoided. Unleaded gas is called *sans plomb;* it is sold in either 95 or 98 proof. Few cars need 98. If your car needs diesel fuel, buy *gaz.*

GIBIER   This means game, as in game season in late fall and early winter, when restaurants feature game and stores may even get into the act, with either promotions or window displays. I once saw a store window filled with stuffed rabbits wearing clothes! These were real dead rabbits, not plush toys. The entire concept of game season takes France by storm, especially in the northern regions.

GITE   This is a small cottage, the home of a real person, or a funky place that you can rent in lieu of a hotel. There are agencies in France that rent them to Americans, although you are taking a blind chance. There are approximately 60,000 properties offered for rent, and the French government does not regulate them or the listing firms. *Bonne chance!*

GRANDS MAGASINS   No, this isn't a particularly thick or overly fancy issue of *Vogue.* The big department stores are called *les grands magasins.* Sometimes ads don't list specific suppliers but simply say *les grands magasins.* Mostly this means Galeries Lafayette and Au Printemps.

H2O   It's water, and in France when you drink it from a bottle, it can either be *plate* (flat), which is also called *sans gas,* or *avec gas,* which is the bubbly kind. Many people order bottled water by brand name to indicate that they know the terrain and the types. Say Evian or Vittel to indicate that you like flat water. Say Badoit or Perrier, and you'll get bubbly water. If the house does not carry those brands, the waiter will counter with the brands the house offers. To get tap water (which is perfectly safe to drink), request *un carafe d'eau*.

HERBS DE PROVENCE   Sold in bundles, jars, or even glass containers, these spice gift packs are a mixture of the indigenous herbs of Provence and include rosemary, thyme, bay leaves, and savory—often crushed and blended but sometimes sold as dried twigs.

HONEY   Provençal honey is considered the best in France because the bees buzzed around lavender before they made their little combs. Look for the label MIEL DE LAVANDE. Labels marked LABEL ROUGE are the best quality.

HYPERMARCHE   Americans may have supermarkets and even warehouse clubs, but no one has *hypermarchés* like the French do: Think of a Super Wal-Mart combined with a Super Target—the clerks are on in-line skates and there are usually a hundred checkout counters. They sell everything for the home, the office, the fashion freak, and the gourmet. A handful of French *hypermarchés* tried to make it in the United States and failed. To this day, I do not understand why.

These giant supermarkets rival the original concept of a general store, but are all modern convenience without a bit of French charm. Part of the *hypermarché* is a grocery store, part of it is a hardware store, and part sells dry goods, such as clothes and linens and household equipment. There's always a gas station outside, and usually a car and tire center as well.

To buy fruits, veggies, or anything that has to be weighed, place your choice in a plastic bag and then go to a nearby weighing station with a clerk. He or she will weigh your purchase, staple the bag closed, and mark the price. Goods are not weighed at the checkout lane as in America.

JOKER   A highly discounted type of train ticket, which even applies to Eurostar trains. (See "Getting Around France," in chapter 2, for train information.) The ticket is very restricted, but if you can plan ahead, you'll save a heap.

LAGUIOLE   A type of deluxe knife, far more chic than a Swiss Army knife. Laguiole is not a brand name or a trademark, it's simply a type of knife. That's one of the reasons so many variations are available—pocketknife, carving knife, even the new Lady Laguiole and a very chic corkscrew—and why new ones keep coming along. Even Philippe Starck has created one. Some of the knives are made in the town of Thiers and some in Laguiole.

LAMPES BERGER   Think of a chic oil lamp, and you've got the idea—only this version doesn't burn oil, it burns scent. It wipes out odors caused by smokers, pets, humidity, and so on. Every French home has one or more. The firm has its own flagship store in Paris, and Galeries Lafayette carries a huge selection as well. Genevieve Lethu has her own designs in each of her shops all over France. Fancy design and home-furnishings stores in resort towns also carry some versions. The lamp itself, which comes in lots of styles, costs anywhere from 35€ to 87€ ($40–$100). There are 20 different scents. It's illegal to bring the fluid on a plane, but you can order it in the United States by calling ✆ 800/321-0020.

LAVENDER   The patron flower of Provence, lavender has a soothing scent and is thought to help induce sleep. It grows in abundance in the Luberon region, where it is harvested the first week in August. Tourists are regularly harvested of their souvenir budget in every town in the south of France—actually, lavender is sold in TTs (tourist traps) all over France, where the most common form is a cellophane-wrapped string of lavender-filled cotton sachets. Note that there is a technical difference between *lavande* and *lavandin*—the latter is produced at lower altitudes and is more plentiful (it's what most of us think of as lavender). Real lavender is more expensive and lasts longer.

MARCHE   A *marché* is almost always a fruit and vegetable market at which regional foodstuffs (such as honey, jam, and olive oil) are also sold. A supermarket is never called a *marché*.

MARCHE AUX PUCES   A flea market. There may be some vendors selling cooked foods, crepes, or soft drinks, but there are no fruit-and-veggie stands.

MAXI CHOCOLAT   A giant *pain au chocolat* (see below), easily measuring 5 by 7 inches, if not more.

MICHELIN   A tire company that got the brilliant idea to promote driving around the countryside by writing books about nice places to stop to eat. Its system of awarding stars to the best chefs has become such an important commentary that the announcement of each new annual edition is a major news story. Stars range from one to three, and there are fewer than two dozen three-star chefs. When chefs are mentioned along with the number of stars they have earned, those stars are only from Michelin. No one else's really count. (Gault Millaut gives toques; they do count.)

MIMOSA   A small yellow polka dot of sugar, about the size of a saccharine tablet, used to sweeten coffee or tea in the south of France. Mimosas are usually served by spoon from a sugar bowl, and they may also be served mixed with candied violets. I just bought a jar of them, marketed by Fauchon, in a Paris grocery store for 8.70€ ($10). Great gift item.

MINITEL   This is a French information service. Minitel addresses are listed in phone books, on ads and billboards, and even on business cards, telling you where to go online (for a fee) to receive more information. Theater tickets, train tickets, airline tickets, and so on can be booked online via Minitel. With increasing Internet use, Minitel is now used less frequently— but the access codes remain printed in ads and the phone book.

NOUGAT   Candy made from caramelized honey with nuts and/or dried fruits added. Each region of France and each maker has a slightly different variety, based on what types of nuts, seeds, or fruits are grown locally. The candy is often sold from stalls at markets or roadside stands in the south of France. Many makers also sell their own honey.

OLIVE OIL   Olive oil is serious stuff in Mediterranean regions. The best kind is extra-virgin. You may also be given a choice between one that is *douce* (sweet) or regular. Americans often prefer the sweet one. You can buy it directly from the *moulin* (mill); it's cheaper if you bring your own container. High-quality extra-virgin olive oil is expensive.

PAIN AU CHOCOLAT   This is an envelope of light and flaky croissant dough filled with melted chocolate.

PANIER   Technically this means a basket. When you go to a store and want one of those plastic shopping baskets for your things, it's called a *panier*.

PARADOX   Also sometimes referred to as the French Paradox, this is the noted phenomenon that French people eat a lot of rich foods and drink wine yet don't die of heart attacks at a higher rate than anyone else. Supposedly this is because the tannin, or something or other, in red wine cuts through the cholesterol or the fat cells or something. Can't drink? *Pas de problem*—there are Paradox pills. Honest.

PARAPHARMACIES   These large discount drugstores are the latest trend in Paris and are also spreading to the provinces. They sell an enormous selection of drugstore-brand makeup, skin-care, health, diet, and beauty products at 20% off.

PARKING   Parking lots are marked with the letter P. There's usually an electronic message board out front that tells you whether the lot is *complet* (full) or exactly how many spaces are available. Rather ingenious.

In traditional parking lots, you take a ticket as you enter. You usually pay for the ticket before you get back in your car to leave; few lots in France have drive-out tellers as in the United States. If there is a long line at the *caisse* (cashier), see if there is a machine on a nearby wall that allows you to insert your ticket, pay for it, and have it canceled. You show the canceled ticket as you leave.

To pay for street parking, first park your car and then find the ticket machine attached to a nearby wall. Buy a ticket for the amount of time you estimate you will need. Return to your car and attach the ticket inside your car on the driver's side of the windshield. Then lock your car. Note that because clever thieves have learned how to rob these machines, there is a new trend toward electronic smart cards, which you must buy ahead of time; this is annoying for tourists. Parking is expensive in France—expect to pay 1€ ($1.15) per half-hour at a metered space.

When a French presidential election approaches, jokers run wild. It is tradition for the incoming president to excuse all parking fines and tickets. Locals, who park just about anyplace under normal circumstances, have a wild time.

Speaking of parking fines, I have decided that the police can identify a rental car by the code in its license plate, and that you are much more likely to be ticketed if you have this type of plate. I actually paid one of my parking tickets just to be able to tell you how to do so, should you feel compelled to do the same.

To pay a ticket:

- Go to a *tabac* (tobacco shop) and present the ticket.
- Pay the fine to the salesperson, who will give you two sets of stamps.
- Fix half the stamps to one page of the ticket and half the stamps to the other page.
- Mail the part that is addressed to be mailed, and keep the other part as proof that you have paid the ticket.

PASTIS This liqueur is the most disgusting beverage I've had in a long time, but there's a resurgence in interest in this local French drink—considered a spring and summer drink by some—and there's even an "in" brand: Henri Bardouin. It starts out clear; then you add water, and it turns cloudy.

PERFUME Perfume accidentally came to France via the glove industry. It seems that in the Middle Ages, M'lady always kept her hands in kid gloves, but the tanning process produced fine kid gloves that smelled yucky. In order to make life bearable for Madame, the glove makers (conveniently located in the town of Grasse, near Cannes) created floral essences that would blot out that nasty waxy yellow buildup. Before they knew it, the perfume industry was born. Grasse remains the industrial center of the industry, although the best buys in terms of discount and duty-free stores are in Paris.

People have written whole books on this subject, but I'll just pass on a few tidbits you might not know:

- Why does French perfume of the same brand smell different in Europe than in the United States? French perfume has a different chemical composition than the U.S. version; it is made with potato alcohol, which is organic. Supposedly this produces a cleaner version of the scent that wears better than the U.S. version, which is made with synthetic alcohol.
- If you can't afford true perfume, which is which after that? Perfume is very pricey because of the ingredients and because of all the money they have to pay Shalom Harlow to be in the ads. All the derivatives move away from the original scent in a matter of generations. *Parfum* is the most concentrated, then comes *eau de parfum,* then *eau de toilette,* then *voile de toilette.* Prices decrease in the same order.
- Are there any bargains out there? Well, 100ml of a fragrance does not cost much more than 50ml—a marketing ploy that makes it smart for you to buy the larger bottle and get twice as much for less than twice the price.
- Where should you buy your perfume in France? The duty-free store at the airport is one of your worst choices, friends. Very best is any of the big-time discounters in Paris, which offer 25% to 30% off list price regardless of how much you buy. Then, if you qualify for *détaxe,* you get another 15% off. Airport discounts are usually 13% to 15%, so even in the south of France, where there aren't too many discounters, if you find someone who will give you 20% off (not counting *détaxe*), you'll do better than at the airport.

PILLS The French seem to think there's a magic pill for just about everything. It's common practice to self-prescribe homeopathic remedies galore. You can find pills for getting a suntan, pills to prevent wrinkles (Catherine Deneuve takes them), pills to banish cellulite, and so on. The pills Deneuve takes are called Oenobiol capsules and are sold in every pharmacy. However, Oenobiol makes a variety of pills for a variety of beauty flaws, so read the package carefully.

POCHETTE   This is a pocket square worn in a men's jacket. Hermès makes them.

POISSON D'AVRIL   For years I have wondered why chocolate fish are sold in France in the spring. First I thought it was a beach gimmick or maybe a religious thing. No, it's just Poisson d'Avril, April Fish—the French equivalent of April Fool's Day, also celebrated on April 1st.

POMMEAU   You know that metal hose spritzer thing attached to the taps in French bathtubs that you hate? You may call it the telephone type of shower. It's technically called a *pommeau*.

PONT   *Pont* is the French word for bridge. Also, what Americans call a long weekend is known as a *pont* to the French, and it can affect restaurant and store openings, especially in May.

POTERIE   Although hand-painted ceramics are an art form in France—as they are the world over—local shops that carry *poterié*, especially in the south of France, usually sell simple, monochromatic earthenware that is glazed brown, blue, green, or ochre—the colors of the region. Painted *poterié* is called *faience*.

RED FRUITS   You will frequently, especially in summer, be offered desserts, or even teas, *aux fruits rouges*, which is a composition of strawberries, raspberries, red currants, and blueberries. Those are considered the four red fruits, and they always come in that combination, unless otherwise stipulated on the *carte*.

RESERVATIONS   You know to make a reservation for dinner, possibly even for lunch, but don't forget to make one for the train. Train fares are much lower if reservations are made in France rather than in the United States.

ROND POINT   Although you may know this as a particular spot in Paris, at the beginning of the Champs-Elysées, actually any roundabout (or rotary) on any French road is a *rond point* and is referred to as such on signs.

RUDE   They're not rude—you don't speak French.

SANTON   Close your eyes and picture a traditional Christmas crèche. Okay, those little figures of the wise men, the sheep, and the baby Jesus are what the French call *santons*. The craftspeople who make these have put a regional spin on the art by adding local characters from any village to the basic nativity bunch.

The tradition is basically from Provence, although *santons* are sold all over the south of France. *Santons* are made of brightly painted clay or wood; some are embellished with fabric and even twigs or dried fruits. Prices vary with size, quality of carving, and detail of painting. Most popular *santons* are only about 2 inches tall and cost 8.70€ to 16€ ($10–$18) each. A basic crèche may be sold as a set.

Note that aside from the traditional figurines in a crèche, there is nothing religious about the rest of the figures—they are purely simple village folk, from the woman who comes to market with her cauliflower in hand to the glazier who uses a trumpet to attract customers.

Marcel Carbonel is perhaps the most famous *santon* craftsman; his workshop is in Marseille (see "Provençal Crafts," in chapter 7). A small paperback guide to his creations also serves as a common dictionary of the characters now thought to compose an entire collection. This book costs about 13€ ($15) and is in French and English; it's sold in many tourist shops and bookstores.

SAVON DE MARSEILLE   Traditional French soap, usually sold in a square cube measured by the gram. When comparing prices, make sure you have noted the differences in size. The soap should be composed of 72% oil, which may be imprinted (in French) on the cube.

La Compagnie de Provence, located in Marseille (see chapter 7), is one of the national heroes of soap making. Others located in Provence include L'Occitane (whose factory is at 21 rue Grande, Manosque) and Savonnerie Marius Fabre (whose factory is at 148 av. Grans, Salon-de-Provence).

SERVICE COMPRIS   This means the service (that is, the tip) is included in the cost of a meal, as is the tax. Therefore, the price listed on the bill is the price you pay, totally inclusive. However, it is common, especially in fine restaurants or when service has been attentive or personal, to leave a few extra euros in cash on the table.

SOLDES   This means sales. French stores tend to have only two sales a year. Traditional spring sales usually begin the last week in June and extend through the first week in July. Traditional winter sales are at the end of January, after Epiphany. Sales are usually advertised in newspapers, including the *International Herald Tribune.* Hard times have moved the seasons ahead, so nowadays anything goes.

Some deluxe brands have special sale events once or twice a year, such as the Hermès sales in October and March, when people line up for hours before the store opens.

SOULEIADO   The south of France is known for a specific type of cotton fabric that is printed in bright colors with swirls of paisley, flowers, and arabesques. The designs are created with wood blocks using the same style of fabric printing that has been done in India for centuries.

These fabrics originally entered France through the port of Marseille, hence their association with the south of France, where they became known as *tissus Indiennes* or even *tissus Nîmes,* Nîmes being another major textile center in the south (and the home of denim—de Nîmes).

The fabric has been made locally for centuries, but Charles Démery, a craftsman who began a fabric firm known as Souleiado, revived it in Provence in the late 1930s. Souleiado became popular in the United States in the 1980s through a firm called Pierre Deux, which at that time carried exclusive rights to sell Souleiado in America. Souleiado recently went bankrupt, but was bought and reorganized. Pierre Deux stores in the United States now carry the Les Olivades brand.

Of all the many firms making *tissus Indiennes,* Souleiado has the highest quality of screens and fabric and by far the highest prices.

STAR A word with many meanings in French and in Franglish: If it's a star in the sky, it's *l'etoile;* if it's the place in Paris where the Arc de Triomphe is located, it's *L'Etoile;* if it's a movie star, even a French one, he or she is a star (so *les stars* hang out in Cannes for the Film Festival). When a foodie refers to a chef and his stars, he is referring to the chef's *Michelin Guide* ranking.

SVP This is an abbreviation for *s'il vous plait* (please), used frequently in print advertisements and directions.

TABAC This is a tobacco shop where newspapers, magazines, cigarettes, gum, and the essentials of life are sold, including stamps and phone cards. It's also where you pay parking tickets.

TAMTAM This is the French version of a pager.

TAPENADE This is a specialty food item from the south of France, where olives are the mainstay of life. Tapenade is essentially a spread made from mashed-up olives with a few spices, some olive oil, and other ingredients—some makers chop up an anchovy or two into the mix. The combination of spices used and the texture of the mashing make for the variety of styles. Olives have quite a piquant taste, and tapenade is very full bodied. Each maker prepares tapenade differently, so you can taste your way across the south of France.

You can buy tapenade in jars in most markets in the south of France. Surprisingly, Brand X from the guy at the market in Nice is no more or less expensive than the version Roger Vergé sells in his boutique in Mougins. The going price for a small jar is usually about 4.35€ ($5).

TELECARTE This is an electronic phone card that not only makes calling home, or calling anywhere, an affordable breeze, but also leaves you with a collectible.

You can buy phone cards at any *tabac* or news kiosk. The smallest denomination is 6€ ($6.90) for 50 units. This will go surprisingly far, especially if you are calling within France. If you plan to call the United States, you should buy a card with a large number of units as soon as you arrive. The more units to the card, the more savings.

Although you can still find telephones that use a *pièce* (coin), they are more popular in the boonies than in big cities.

Here's how you use a *télécarte:*

- Locate a modern-looking phone booth or one that has a horizontal slot in it for the phone card.
- Lift the phone off the receiver and insert the *télécarte.*
- Read the computer display on the phone, which gives instructions in French. Don't read French? Not to worry. Anyone can figure this out. For example, "please wait" is written *"patience, svp."* Easy as *un, deux, trois!* And you didn't know you spoke French.
- The units will click away electronically and visually. When you are down to the last few units, a beeping noise ensues. Time to say *au revoir.*

TGV TGV stands for *Train à Grande Vitesse,* if you insist on knowing. As far as I'm concerned, it's Trains-R-Great-4-Vous. TGV is one of the oldest high-speed train networks in the world; its trains go up to about 300kmph (186 mph). More and more TGV track is laid each year, so you can get to more and more regions of France quickly.

THALASSOTHERAPIE The French, who are great believers in spa treatments for improving or maintaining health, have recently gone bonkers over *thalassotherapie,* which means spa treatments related to seawater. Major spas are located on the French Atlantic coast, although Prince Rainier in Monte Carlo has recently opened a spa there to capitalize on the trend and to make his life easier—now he doesn't have to travel out of town to get treatments.

A key part of the treatments involves soaking in seawater or seaweed-enhanced bathwater, the theory being that seaweed will rebalance the impurities in your body. For proper treatment, your soak should be at body temperature, to encourage osmosis. This is rather cool—a nice hot bath is traditionally 103° to 106°F (39°C–41°C), not a lowly 98.6°F (37°C). So don't be shocked if you're asked to pay 35€ ($40) to sit in a cold bath of smelly brown water for a mere 15 minutes.

TIRE-BOUCHON   This is a corkscrew. You'd be surprised how many styles there are; corkscrews are a serious collectible.

TISSUS INDIENNES   French Provençal-style fabrics (see "Souleiado," above).

TRAVERSIN   How adorable: Your traditional French bed has a *traversin* (bolster) and you and your loved one are about to count *moutons* (sheep) and count your blessings for having found such a cute little French inn. But you need to know that the bolster does not move and is not adjustable. Call for pillows before you try to make it through the night.

USINE   A *usine* is a factory. *Magasins d'usine* are factory-outlet shops.

As in every other part of the world, there are real factory shops and fake factory shops. Watch out for some of those factory-direct perfume shops in the south of France. Even some of the real factory shops, such as the Souleiado shop in Tarascon, offer no bargains.

But wait: There is a new trend in France toward American-style outlet malls. The city of Troyes, about an hour from Paris, has been the outlet capital of the country since the early 1990s. There's also a really chic and jazzy outlet mall called La Vallée, located just outside Paris next to Disneyland (p. 3).

Paris is dotted with factory-direct stores that sell old stock, much of it from big names such as Cacharel and Sonia Rykiel. Note the use of the word *stock* in the names of such shops.

VO   Movies with the original voice (VO) have subtitles in French. You can see any American or British flick in a French theater and not only understand the whole thing but also teach yourself French while reading the subtitles. VO movies are most common in the big movie theaters along the Champs-Elysées in Paris, but they play elsewhere as well.

WINE If you say no to wine, you say no to France. If you think I'm going to go beyond that, you're nuts. There are books and books and books about all this. Study them; subscribe to the mags.

In the United States, call © **800/522-WINE** for a free booklet on French wine and wineries that are open to visitors. Or check out the website: **www.frenchwinesfood.com.**

GUIDE TO BOUTIQUES & CHAINS

What follows is a sampling of some of the big names in French retail. Some are well-known designers, while others are multiples (chain stores) with numerous branches all over France.

AGATHA Whimsical costume jewelry at moderate prices. Some stores are found in the United States.

AGNES B Upscale casual wear for men and women, often in separate shops. Hip, but not too *outré*.

BLANC BLEU BCBG looks with a nautical edge and a Ralph Lauren feel; excellent quality and status for those in the know. Men's, women's, and children's lines.

CAMIEU Cheapie version of Sweden's H&M for inexpensive fashions; worth a look, especially for teens and tweens.

CARRE BLANC For bed and tabletop. It's a good source for duvet covers, which are hard to find in abundance in the United States.

CHACOK Status design firm known for bright colors, ethnic inspiration, lots of knits for winter, and floating cotton for summer. It also has sensational looks for the south of France, where dash and flair really count. Prices are equal to those of American designer bridge lines.

CHIPIE Chipie carries blue jeans and casual clothes with French chic.

COMTESSE DU BARRY This large chain of gourmet food stores carries packaged goods with the house label.

DESCAMPS   These stores carry bed linens, bathrobes, great baby gifts, and a wonderful line of scented rocks. Its freestanding stores were closed in the United States, but it's alive and quite well all over France.

FLORIANE   Expensive, but adorable, kiddie clothes. Young and hip meets traditional.

FNAC   This chain of book and music stores is a great place to meet young people. It has slightly better prices than regular record shops as well as a huge selection. It also sells tickets to events.

GENEVIEVE LETHU   This Provençal designer has hundreds of tabletop boutiques all over the country as well as a few outside France. The colors are great and the style vibrant and contemporary, while still a little traditional.

HABITAT/THE CONRAN SHOP   These are two totally different firms, although each was begun by Sir Terrence Conran, and they sell very similar goods: items with country flair and clean contemporary lines for the home. As impossible as this seems, the designs are at the same time very French and very English. Habitat is a major multiple located throughout France. The Conran Shop is only in Paris.

LACOSTE   The world's most knocked-off alligator (called *le crocodile* in France) is alive and well and living in France in major department stores and freestanding boutiques. Here's the catch: The goods are often less expensive in the United States. But there are styles in France that are not exported to the U.S.

MARINA RINALDI   This is an Italian brand of large-size fashions from Max Mara, sold throughout France in freestanding stores and in Max Mara boutiques. It's the leading line of European plus-size fashion.

MONOPRIX   This chain of dime stores, owned by Galeries Lafayette, is a great place to shop for affordable everything. Many of these stores have grocery stores attached. There is a branch of Monoprix in almost every French city; be sure to check out the ones in fancy suburbs and good neighborhoods—they have the best supply of chic for the price.

PIMKIE   For cheapie teenage fashions with cutting-edge style, look no further.

REDOUTE   This major catalog company, sort of like JCPenney, has now also opened its own retail shops.

REPETTO   This traditional ballet house is known for first introducing ballet slippers into mainstream fashion. It now makes slippers (and mocs) in a variety of colors and skins.

SEPHORA   This chain sells all kinds of makeup and fragrance brands, as well as some hair accessories, its own line of bath products, and every other beauty treatment you can imagine.

TROIS SUISSES   This is a major catalog company that basically sells cheap clothes, but guest designers make seasonal offerings. It even offers Vivienne Westwood.

Chapter Four

....

SHOPPING PARIS

WELCOME TO PARIS

When you leaf through French magazines, you'll notice that in ads, the addresses for branch stores are written as "Paris" and "provinces." Not *Provence;* that's *provinces.* You see, even to the French, it's very simple: There's Paris, and there's the rest of France. Even to the French, if you're not in Paris, you're in the provinces.

Paris is indeed the City of Light. It is the beginning and the end of a certain kind of light. For a shopper, Paris means serious shopping. There is no comparison between the energy—yes, even shopping energy—that vibrates off the streets of Paris and what goes on in the countryside. Maybe that's my point: Paris is about energy, whereas the countryside is about the luxuries of time, space, sunflowers, wine, slow meals, and slow shopping.

The provinces are also less expensive than Paris. At a time when the dollar isn't as strong as it used to be, prices count. You may want to use your time in Paris for a special meal, a memorable experience, or a neighborhood that just makes your soul smile. Sometimes the kind of shopping you do in Paris isn't to buy things—it's to gain insight.

Paris at a Glance

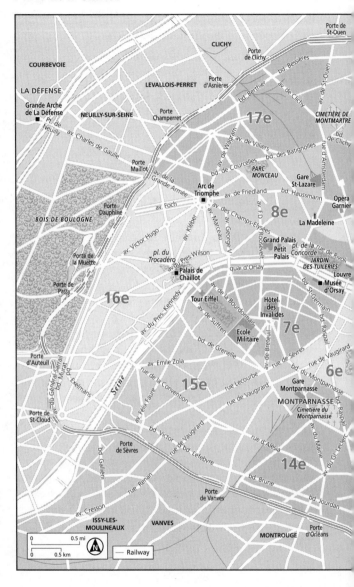

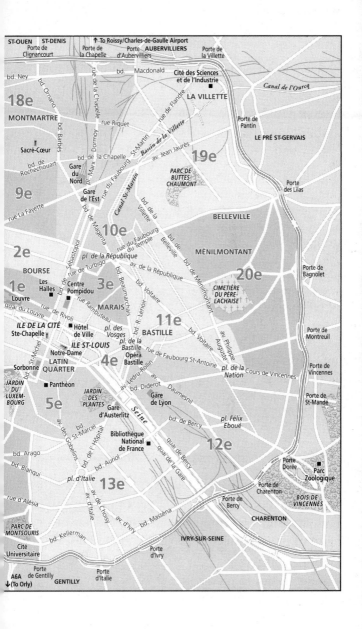

Planning Paris

Shoppers don't need to come to Paris at all—but if you are planning to include Paris on your trip and aren't certain of the details, hear me out.

Paris represents intense shopping. Note that it's only after you've been through France and done the country bit that you'll know what you still need for your at-home use or for your own psychic rewards. It's also silly to shop in Paris first and fill your suitcases with items that you will then have to schlep in and out of a series of hotels.

If you don't know Paris well, the number of shopping services available can be downright overwhelming; so rather than getting a headache and heart palpitations or making a shopping boo-boo, seek Paris as a last resort—in all senses of the word. Paris is different from all the rest of France—and although you can buy many of the same things in other parts of France, there's only one Paris, and that's why it's Paris.

The Lay of the Land

Paris is composed of 20 *arrondissements* (districts; see the map on p. 58). The name of the arrondissement is usually included in an address, either as simply the arrondissement number (for example, 1er, 17e) or as part of the zip code (for example, 75001 equals 1er, 75017 equals 17e).

Born to Shop Paris

If you're going to be in Paris for more than a day, I suggest that you check out *Born to Shop Paris*, as the book you are holding was created specifically for those who have only a day to shop in Paris, or possibly even just a few hours.

This chapter gives an overview of Paris and some ideas on how to best use the small amount of time you have here. It is by no means comprehensive.

Part of your job in selecting a hotel for a short stay is to study the lay of the land and get nestled into an arrondissement that will serve as many of your needs as possible, so you don't have to schlep all over in a mad dash.

Also make sure you have good Métro connections, as that will be your best way of getting around—and shopping around. You will be less tempted to take taxis if you have good public transportation—and every taxi fare saved is another gift bought.

Getting Around Paris

Paris is a great city for walking. You can spend your days staring at the architecture, the stores, and the people. If you want a quicker method of transportation, you can use the Métro, which connects every part of town and costs 1.30€ ($1.50) per ride. To save money and time, buy a *carnet,* a book of 10 tickets for 10€ ($12). These tickets can be used on both the bus and the Métro. If you're in Paris for just a day, you may want a 1-day card; or perhaps you have chosen your hotel and shopping goals so that everything is at hand.

Taxis are expensive (flag drops at 2€/$2.30) and often have surcharges for luggage, extra passengers, and so on. Please note that it is against the law for a taxi sedan to carry five adults. Therefore, if you are a group of four people and one of you does not drive a taxi, you may need to call **TaxisG7** (© 01-41-27-66-67), which operates special vans. If you call a taxi, the meter drops the minute they accept your address.

If you need a private driving service (with vans) for groups or for airport transportation, try **Paris Millénium** (© 01-30-71-93-03; parismillenium@wanadoo.fr). This is my regular service; the drivers speak English and will help you with luggage or the details, and even with reservations and touring information. This company also rents by the hour for a drive around Paris or for day trips.

SLEEPING IN PARIS

The Palace Hotels

Hotels in France are rated from one to four stars. Thus there are no five-star hotels, but there are four-star deluxe hotels (written ****D), which are classified in the French manner as "palace hotels."

FOUR SEASONS GEORGE V
31 av. George V, 8e (Métro: George V).

This hotel is all about style and location and customers who can't get enough—the flowers have become one of the latest sights to see in Paris, so much so that even those who aren't staying here come by to gawk. Many rooms have Eiffel Tower views; the spa-cum-pool is luxury itself; the chef has three stars; and the shopping location is excellent, especially for upmarket goods.

Although rack rates start at over 600€ ($690), promotional deals can be available—especially out of season. Some include a spa treatment; others provide dinner in the famous restaurant Le Cinq. For reservations in the U.S., call © **800/332-3442**. Local phone © 01-49-52-70-00. Fax 01-49-52-70-10. www. fourseasons.com.

HOTEL DE CRILLON
10 place de la Concorde, 8e (Métro: Concorde).

Located at the base of the Champs-Elysées, the Crillon is an old-fashioned mansion with a low-key luxury lobby where even Madonna feels at home (no autographs, please). It boasts the first Guerlain spa located in a hotel, it has a fancy gym for guests, and it has redone all rooms—even the dining room (where it recently poached one of the most famous chefs in town). The location is sublime—just a block from Hermès and the other big names on the rue du Faubourg St-Honoré.

Rates start at 600€ ($690), but can vary with promotions (for example, a free fourth night when you pay for the first 3 nights). Book in the U.S. through Leading Hotels of the World (© **800/233-6800**). Local phone © 01-44-71-15-00. www.lhw.com/decrillon.

HOTEL MEURICE
228 rue de Rivoli, 1er (Métro: Tuilleries or Concorde).

Forget anything you may remember of the old Meurice. The hotel has undergone an enormous renovation to welcome it to the Dorchester Group, and is now fancier than the Ritz. Talk about a gilt trip: It's got a two-star chef, one of the best shopping locations in town, and even various promotional deals. Check out the bar scene, where you'll see me sipping a cocktail called a Meurice Millennium. This is certainly the place for those who want as much old-fashioned glamour as they can stand.

Official rack rates are over 600€ ($690), but ask about special deals. Leading Hotels of the World has promotions offering one free night; call © **800/223-6800.** Local phone © 01-44-58-10-10. www.meuricehotel.com.

Good Finds

CONCORDE ST-LAZARE
108 rue St-Lazare, 8e (Métro: St-Lazare).

The lobby is drop-dead gorgeous, historical, and protected by French law, and it's also in a well-priced hotel with the best location for shoppers. It's particularly great for those who are in town for just a day or two, as everything you really need is within 5 minutes.

There are all sorts of good rates, but expect to pay about 280€ ($320) with a promotional deal. In the U.S., call © **800/888-4747.** Local phone © 01-40-08-44-44. Fax 01-42-93-01-20. www.concordestlazare-paris.com.

LE WALT
37 av. de la Motte Picquet, 7e (Métro: Motte Picquet).

I consider this hotel one of my greatest finds: It's chic, has a wonderful location, and isn't too expensive. It also offers its own shopping promotion that includes a limo ride to an outlet mall. Le Walt is located on the Left Bank in a neighborhood that feels residential, not touristy; but it's still just a few meters from the famous food markets of rue Cler. The Métro stop is right out the front door; there's also several good bus lines.

The hotel has only 25 rooms, and yes, those rooms are a bit small . . . as are all hotel rooms on the Left Bank. Nonetheless, they're gorgeous and outfitted with all the modern luxuries you'd expect—two phone lines, modem, cable TV, and so on. The backdrop to each bed is a hand-painted copy of a masterpiece, so you'll feel like you're sleeping in a museum while spending less than 300€ ($345) per night.

Note: If you can't get into Le Walt, ask about Le Marquis, in the 15e, which is owned by the same family. The feeling of that neighborhood is different; I prefer to send you to the 7e. Local phone © **01-45-51-55-83**. www.inwoodhotel.com.

PLAZA PARIS VENDOME
4 rue du Mont Thabor, 1er (Métro: Tuileries).

If you crave fancy but don't want to spend 600€ ($690) per night, check out this hotel, which is right behind the Meurice and offers a different kind of luxe at closer to 300€ ($345) per night. There's a pool and health club, a restaurant founded by a multi-star chef, and 99 rooms done in neutral moderne flourishes that will cushion you from the real world. Local phone © **01-40-20-20-00**. www.plazaparisvendome.com.

SHOPPING HOURS

You're in the big city now, so forget everything you might know about provincial shopping hours. In Paris, shopping hours are usually 10am to 7pm. Some big stores stay open until 9pm or even 10pm. Most stores are open during the lunch hour; all big stores are open on Monday mornings.

The large department stores tend to open at 9:30am, while the dime stores (such as Monoprix) open at 8:45 or 9am, depending on the time of the year. Gourmet Lafayette is open until 9pm, as are some of the other dime stores. The Monoprix on the Champs-Elysées is open until 10pm in winter and until midnight in summer.

Sundays aren't dead in Paris. They never really were, thanks to the flea markets and antiques business, but now more and more districts' stores are fighting government regulations about Sunday openings. Currently, in order to open on Sunday, an area must be designated a tourist zone—both the Marais and the Champs-Elysées are designated thus. Flea markets and antiques "villages" are also allowed to open on Sunday. Museums and their gift shops can open on Sundays; the mall in the Louvre is hopping on Sunday, as is La Vallée, the outlet mall near Disneyland Paris (p. 3).

There are also "exceptional openings." By French law, stores can be open five Sundays a year. So each store picks its five most valuable Sundays, which are usually before Christmas. Some stores do an opening on Easter Sunday or Mother's Day or even the first day of the sales.

SNACKING & SHOPPING

For those in search of a light meal that's convenient to shopping yet not too expensive or time-consuming, here are a few ideas:

- All the big department stores have restaurants, cafes, or take-out food—try the new **Lafayette Maison.**
- Many specialty stores now have restaurants—from **Armani Caffé** to **Etam** to **Colette.** All of these choices offer a chic crowd and good eats. Even though Etam is a mass-market

store, the food is good and the cafe is a delight. Try the flavored iced tea with lunch.

- **Paul** is a national chain of bread shops that originated in Lille and is expanding like mad all over Paris. There is even one on boulevard de la Opéra, right across from the new **Starbucks.**

- **Toastissimo** is a chain of fast-food eateries that serve *panini* (toasted Italian sandwiches) and salads; there's one just about everywhere, particularly in the 1er and 8e.

- **Oliviers & Co.** is a chain of gourmet olive-oil shops located all over France; some of the stores now have small restaurants. There's one in Paris on the rue des Levis, 17e (Métro: Villiers).

- Food palaces and gourmet grocery stores have restaurants and snack bars right inside them—try **Fauchon, Hédiard, Lafayette Gourmet,** and **La Grande Epicerie,** which is part of Le Bon Marché.

- Museum cafes are being upgraded to an art form. **Georges** (Pompidou Center) is the fanciest of the lot. Others are less well known, such as the cafes at the **Musée Jacquemart-Andrée** and **Gare d'Orsay,** which are both so wonderful that you will dine out on the decor for days.

SHOPPING STRATEGIES

- Organize your day way before you even get to Paris. Have a map and a plan of attack if you want to cram a lot of specifics into one day.

- If spending 175€ ($201) takes some doing on your part but you want to take advantage of the tax refund *(détaxe)* in France, plan ahead of time where you think you're most likely to spend that kind of money and get the refund. Then allow time for the paperwork.

- Consider doing all your shopping within one department store so that your total purchases meet the minimum required for the *détaxe* refund. Don't buy a little here and a little there if you think you can save money by using a strategy. Remember, you must spend the 175€ ($201) in the same store on the same day to get the refund.

- Note that real life in Paris is expensive. You'll do best if you splurge on one fabulous something or limit yourself to small gifts, food items, and souvenirs in the $5-to-$10 range.

- If you plan to shop in any of the big department stores, try to get there around 10am or earlier, when they open. By noon, they are very crowded.

- When you shop in small stores, remember your French manners; see "How to Be French," in chapter 3.

- Consider making one big haul of the same item as gifts for everyone, or stocking up on gifts for use throughout the year once you're back at home. With luck, you'll buy enough to qualify for *détaxe*. I do this with candles from L'Occitane, Diptyque, or Mariage Frères. French luxury candles are not cheap, so buy one that lasts a long time (the burn time is listed on the package) and represents a status brand; you'll pay at least 30€ ($35) for the aforementioned brands.

- Wear comfortable shoes and a handbag that can either fit across your body or be worn under your coat. Paris is no more dangerous than any other big city, but when you're jumping on and off the Métro and bustling around, you want to make sure you aren't an easy target.

- If you plan to try on clothes, wear something that is easy to get in and out of.

- As you plan your day, figure out where you want to end up for lunch. If your time is limited, your shopping will be much more successful if it's planned properly. Even if you just want fast food, know which neighborhood to hit at lunchtime and the type of meal that will best fulfill your fantasies. Also plan a proper tea or coffee break for around 4pm. You might also want to work in a drop-off point to get rid of your packages.

- If time is truly a worry, consider splurging on professional help for a day. Some shopping services take you out and about with car and driver. Paris traffic can be terrible, but you won't have to do any thinking or read any maps on your own. *Note:* Don't go to a flea market in a limo.

- Keep receipts to declare your goods when you return home. Don't try to run anything past U.S. Customs officers; nothing screams out like a new handbag or a pair of *ooh la la* shoes.

- Allow at least a half-hour at the airport for reclaiming your tax refund if you're leaving the European Union from Paris. (If it's the height of the summer season, allow 1 hr.) If you're going on to another country in the E.U., no sweat—you claim your refund only as you depart the E.U. for good.

ONLY ONE HOUR IN PARIS?

If you have only an hour to shop, you might want to try a place like the flagship **Galeries Lafayette,** as it has everything you can imagine (and then some). **Au Printemps,** the neighboring department store, is smaller than Galeries, although beauty and home style are in one building and fashion is in another (Métro: Havre-Caumartin or Chaussée-d'Antin).

If, however, you have the kind of nerves that fray in crowds or under pressure, spend your hour somewhere peaceful—like a museum shop (try the store attached to **Musée des Arts Décoratifs,** 109 rue de Rivoli; Métro: Louvre or Palais Royal) or even the stores in the galleries that surround the Palais Royal. You won't find lots of cheap gifts at the Palais Royal, but you will glimpse a hidden part of Paris and feel what it's like to have shopping in your soul. You can also fit in a stop at the gift shop at **La Comedie Francaise,** which does have classy souvenir gifts; it's right in front of the Palais Royal Métro station in the outside arcade.

Personally, if I had just an hour, I'd take the Métro to Sèvres-Babylone and spend my time at the grocery store that's part of Le Bon Marché, **La Grande Epicerie.** Foodstuffs make great inexpensive gifts, and I swoon for food dreams. With any leftover time, I'd walk up the adjacent rue St-Placide, where there are a few discount shops (try **Vidna,** 9 rue St-Placide, for discounts on the Nitya brand) and a fabulous Arts-and-Crafts store called **Crea,** at 55 rue St-Placide. To make this a total hat trick, I'd lunch at **Delicabar,** a wildly inventive restaurant upstairs from L'Epicerie. You'll be telling the folks at home about it for days.

BEST SHOPPING NEIGHBORHOODS

Because you're on a tear, I've listed below the best streets and neighborhoods for finding a lot of stuff, the new and hot stores, and the unusual items on offer.

Street of Brands

Most of the stars of international design have shops on the **rue du Faubourg St-Honoré.** This is a strolling and window-shopping street with a few affordable options as well as many of the world's fanciest art galleries, antiques shops, and designer flagships. (Start at the Concorde Métro station and walk west.)

While new stores do keep opening up, and this remains an important shopping area because of its image, it might not be on your must-do list unless you're really into big-time labels such as **Gucci** (no. 2), **Hermès** (no. 24), **Versace** (no. 62), and **Sonia Rykiel** (no. 70). Perhaps all you can afford to do on this street of dreams is eat a burger. If so, check out **Café Bleu,** inside the **Lanvin** men's store (no. 15).

Note, however, that this street connects magnificently to other, more realistic shopping spots. It's only 2 blocks from department-store heaven (see below), 1 block from place Vendôme (more fancier-than-thou shops), 2 blocks from the Opéra, and just down the street from a marvelous and relatively inexpensive shopping street, **rue St-Honoré,** which is an extension of rue du Faubourg St-Honoré.

So don't necessarily get hung up on the hype that accompanies the name Faubourg St-Honoré. I'm big on the adjacent area, including the rue Royale, which leads to place de la Madeleine, rue St-Honoré, rue de Castiglione, and great stores with great addresses that aren't directly on the Faubourg. Incidentally, several new shops have opened at place de la Madeleine on the avenue des Malsherbes side of this area (Métro: Madeleine).

Best Fancy Shopping Street

For the world's biggest names and fanciest digs, get a look at **avenue Montaigne.** (Take the Métro to Alma Marceau; then walk east.) You'll pass every big name from **Bulgari** (no. 27) to **Ungaro** (no. 2). Hmmm, make that **Valentino** (no. 17) and **Vuitton** (no. 22), with **Dior** (no. 30) and **Max Mara** (no. 31) thrown in for good fun. Oh, and don't forget **Emilio Pucci** (no. 36) and **Celine** (no. 38). Eat an affordable but ever-so-chic lunch at the cafe inside **Joseph** (no. 14). If you're loaded with euros and want something to remember for the rest of your life, lunch in the courtyard at the **Hotel Plaza Athénée** (no. 25), where you'll dine on custom-made Porthault linen, replete with red geraniums. There's more shopping, of course. **Porthault** (no. 18) is right across the street, so you can buy your own $1,000 linens . . . and then there's **Chanel** (no. 42), which has expanded and also added an **Eres** shop.

Best Born-Again Shopping Street

I used to detest the **Champs-Elysées,** but I am finally impressed. (Métro: Ch.-de-Gaulle Etoile to start at the top of the Champs-Elysées.) Now you'll find the **Louis Vuitton/Marc Jacobs** (no. 101) stuff at an LV temple to retail, an **FNAC** (no. 74) to compete with **Virgin Megastore,** the tea salon **Ladurée** (no. 75) for a snack, and **Sephora** (no. 70–72) for perfumes and beauty aids. Touch base with the new Paris at **Le Drugstore** (no. 131), with its bookstore, boutiques, pharmacy, news kiosk, fantasy toilets, and brasserie with Alain Ducasse menu—and all this open on Sundays. You'll come across many other branch stores, from **Lacoste** to **Gap** and the **Disney Store** (oy) and also a good **Monoprix** (yay) . . . and at the far end, a new **Cartier** (no. 154). You may not be in the market for a car, but the auto showrooms are a treat, and some have art galleries and even restaurants inside. Most of the movie theaters in this area have English voice tracks.

Best of the Left Bank

To the tourist, the heart of the Left Bank is the area surrounding **St-Germain-des-Prés.** Obvious designer stores are on the boulevard, but the back streets in this area are sublime. Various nooks and crannies of the neighborhood are devoted to shoes or fabrics or antiques. The best little streets are rue Dragon, rue Cherche Midi, rue de Seine, rue de Buci, rue Jacob, and the tiny place de Furstemburg. To see, and feel, the spirit of the Left Bank, you must leave the boulevard St-Germain and get medieval. Don't miss **place St-Sulpice!** (Métro: St-Germain-des-Près.)

Best of the Marais

Hidden away in an almost medieval part of Paris, the Marais features a large square surrounded by an arcade of stores and a series of small back streets. This area is home to a lot of the funky designer shops that are the backbone of Paris style. Many of the stores in the Marais are open on Sunday.

Outside the Marais, but only 2 blocks away, is the **Village St-Paul** (rue St-Paul), a small antiques district between the Marais and the Seine. The 50 stores here are open on Sunday.

In the other direction from the river, back toward the small streets, is the **Picasso Museum.** As you make your way, you'll pass more and more tiny shops featuring the latest cutting-edge ideas in fashion. (Métro: St-Paul.)

Best of the Louvre/Rue de Rivoli

The back end of the Louvre stretches along the rue de Rivoli for several blocks. Inside there may be art treasures, but outside there are stores. In fact, there are even stores underneath.

Check out **Carrousel du Louvre,** an American-style shopping-mall. It has a food court on the mezzanine level and is attached to the Louvre through a gallery lined with museum gift shops and a row of stores, including **Sephora, Lalique,** and **Virgin Megastore.** Everything is open on Sunday, so if you need a shopping fix when Paris seems closed, this is the place.

Across the street is a building filled with antiques dealers, **Le Louvre des Antiquaires.** One block over is the **Palais Royal,** which has a hidden garden filled with arcades of tiny, wonderful shops. This is one of my favorite spots in all of Paris. Don't miss **Shiseido,** if only to gawk; it's a gorgeous makeup and perfume shop. A few doors away is **Le Prince Jardinier,** which is no ordinary garden shop.

Meanwhile, the 2-block parade along rue de Rivoli across from the museum is door-to-door tourist traps (TTs), selling every imaginable T-shirt, ashtray, and lighter, plus a few perfume and scarf shops. One block away, discreetly tucked behind that gold statue of Joan of Arc, is a **Monoprix.**

Don't miss the opportunity to eat lunch at **Café Marly,** which faces the courtyard of the Louvre—what a crowd. (Métro: Palais-Royal or Louvre-Rivoli.)

Best Department-Store Street

This could be department-store heaven or hell, depending on the time of year and how you feel about crowds. The two most famous *grands magasins* (large department stores) in Paris, **Galeries Lafayette** (no. 40) and **Au Printemps** (no. 64), are side by side on the boulevard Haussmann, in the 9e. If you're in a hurry, you might find that visiting a department store is the answer to all your prayers. These places are huge, carry a little of everything, and offer a flat 10% discount to foreigners (pick up free vouchers at the store's information desk), plus a *détaxe* refund if your purchases qualify.

The snazziest store to hit Paris in decades is **Lafayette Maison,** the home-style branch of Galeries Lafayette. Meanwhile, Galeries Lafayette's men's store houses **Lafayette**

Gourmet, a fancy grocery store with a new wine shop and two restaurants.

Au Printemps has three parts: Printemps Maison (my favorite), Printemps Mode, and Brummel, which is also called Printemps Homme (the men's store). Part of the so-called home store was just renovated and has a rich panoply of luxury brands. There is also a knock-your-socks-off two-level beauty department.

On the curb in front of these stores are stalls and hawkers, selling promotional merchandise from inside the stores. Buy a crepe and munch and stare. (Métro: Havre-Caumartin.)

Best Weird, Little-Known Shopping Destination

Get on the new no. 14 Métro line and hop off at Cour St-Emilion to get to Bercy Village, a rather American-style shopping-mall experience created out of a series of wine ·warehouses in the 12e. The stores are interesting, but it's the ambience of the whole place and the no. 14 that make the trip worthwhile—not the actual stores. Come to think of it, the stores aren't bad, either. You'll find Sephora's White Store, of which there are only a handful in the world; Résonances, a gift shop (it has also opened up at place de la Madeleine); a very cute Club Med vacation store; and Truffaut, a gardening and flower store. There are also cafes and bars and snack places, so you sit outside and stare at the fun young crowd.

RUNNER-UP

A runner-up in this category, giving you an option that's easier to get to (Bercy Village is sort of out there) is **Marché Saint Honoré,** a small square off the rue St-Honoré, 1er. Now, remember that I said rue St-Honoré, *not* Faubourg St-Honoré; we're talking around the corner from the Meurice. The highlight, retail-wise, is the **Castelbajac Concept Store,** but there's some awfully interesting architecture in the square itself, as well as a Belgian baker, **Le Pain Quotidien,** that makes a great stop for a snack, brunch, or lunch. You'll also find a few hidden discount stores and all sorts of stuff that you would not see if you weren't looking. This district is a mere sneeze from a main tourist street, yet remains enough off the beaten path to avoid feeling touristy. (Métro: Tuileries.)

NEWSMAKERS

Best New Department Store

LAFAYETTE MAISON
*35 bd. Haussmann, 9e (Métro: Havre-Caumartin
or St-Lazare).*

Galeries Lafayette has its flagship store, and then it has the men's store next door, with a gourmet grocery store upstairs from that. Now it has opened the first new department store in Paris in 35 years—and *ooh la la!* Of the five floors, the best are the ground level (get takeout food here) and the basement (look for cooking demonstrations). The entire place is all modern, with tiny beams of electric lights blinking out the names of brands in graffiti style. The ground floor looks a bit like a fancy Target (heaps of colorful merchandise), but Paris has not seen this much energy since the French Revolution.

Best New Concept Store

LE DRUGSTORE
131 av. des Champs-Elysées, 8e (Métro: Ch.-de-Gaulle Etoile).

The street level is far, far better than the lower level, and the ladies' room is perhaps best of all, but this store stays open on Sunday, borrows its origins from Colette and some U.S. marketing ideas, and offers a lot of energy, a great crowd, and the usual suspects in terms of design and artsy objects—plus a wine shop, a great news kiosk, a small food section, and, of course, the pharmacy.

Runner-Up

Le Carre des Simples
22 rue Tronchet, 8e (Métro: St-Lazare or Madeleine).

Medicinal plants, forgotten cures, secrets of the ages, essential oils—you name it, it's here. The location is easy to get to and near the major department stores.

Best New Ethnic

Shanghai Tang
76 rue Bonaparte (Métro: St-Sulpice).

Shanghai Tang is not a new brand, nor is the Maison la Chine new to Paris or the place St-Sulpice . . . but the store's arrival has brought a blast of fresh air and a whole new way of looking at things, of adding Zen to your French attitude.

Best New Makeup/Beauty Store

Au Printemps
64 bd. Haussmann, 9e (Métro: Havre-Caumartin).

This department store has totally redone its beauty floors to add not only drop-dead chic, but also wide aisles and lots of play space—you can try all sorts of makeup. There's also a *parapharmacie* (large discount drugstores) and a slew of brands not found elsewhere. Don't forget to ask at the information desk for your tourist discount card.

Best Shoe News

This is a doubleheader, as the designer is the same man working under two different labels. The '60s iconic brand **Roger Vivier** has come back to life with a new store at 29 rue du Faubourg St-Honoré, 8e (Métro: Concorde). The man designing the shoes is named **Bruno Frisoni,** who has also opened his own shop at 34 rue de Grenelle, 7e (Métro: Ecole Militaire). Fans of sensible footwear need not apply.

Meanwhile, the **Charles Jourdan** brand, which has all but disappeared in recent history, is also being revived—by none other than Canadian Patrick Cox, known for his Wannabe line of shoes in London. There's a big Jourdan shop on the Champs-Elysées, at no. 86 (Métro: Franklin Roosevelt).

PARIS ICONS

Best Existing Ethnic

MIA ZIA
4 rue Caumartin, 9e (Métro: Havre-Caumartin).

This store hasn't been around forever, but it has taken its place as almost a French classic in terms of drama and importance in style. Here, Northern Africa meets the Mediterranean meets international chic in just the right colors to make you feel like a gypsy nomad without looking like you're ready for Halloween. There are stores in several big French cities.

Best Hidden Store

ASTIER DE VILLATTE
173 rue St-Honoré, 1er (Métro: Palais Royal).

Astier de Villatte is one of the smallest shops I've ever been in; the medieval home turned store is hidden in plain sight and you would walk right by if you didn't know it was there. It sells many gift and tabletop items, but mainly it sells style. Astier de Villatte's handmade white porcelain serving pieces are sold in the U.S. for twice as much, and redefine chic as well as minimalist pleasure. Eat that, Armani Casa.

Best Food Markets

Sunday mornings, real foodies and gourmands should head to **rue Cler**, 7e (Métro: Latour Marbourg). Also on Sundays is an organic *bio* (pronounced bee-oh) market that is fabulous, but a tad esoteric: **boulevard de Raspail,** 6e (Métro: Sèvres-Babylone).

Best Weekly Flea Market

Close to central Paris, **Puces de Vanves,** 14e (Métro: Porte de Vanves), is a tag sale sort of thing. This Saturday and Sunday market is the real insider's place to get a bargain. On Sunday, there's also a fruit and food market one street over. Note that the market is over by 1pm.

Best Marketing Notion

LITTLE BLACK DRESS
125 galerie de Valois, Jardin du Palais Royal, 1er (Métro: Palais Royal).

Didier Ludot became famous in Paris about 20 years ago as the majordomo of important vintage clothing. His business has grown and expanded, as has his reputation. Now there's Little Black Dress, which carries new little black dresses inspired by the vintage clothing he sells. The shop is in the Jardin du Palais Royal, on the opposite side from Ludot's vintage business. Dresses cost about $150 to $200; they are also sold from his shop in the department store Au Printemps.

PRODUCTS WITH A TWIST

TOILETTE INTIME   All cultures have feminine cleansing products, but the French invented the bidet and a staggering number of products to go with it. The Roger Cavaille brand offers three different hygienic cleansers, each adapted to the needs of the modern woman. (Could I make this stuff up?)

LE STRING   You may know scanty undies as a thong, but in France, it's *le string* because it really is only a string in there—these have been banned in high schools to prevent

Monica Lewinsky–like behavior. Buy them at specialty stores or department stores' lingerie sections; prices start at 6€ ($6.90).

EASY CREDIT   Colette is a gallery-cum-store which for 10 years has offered *outre* products to the French. The latest fad is a credit card holder (in alligator) that you wear around your neck so you don't have to tire yourself out searching through your handbag for the plastic.

Chapter Five

....

SHOPPING THE WINE REGIONS: CHAMPAGNE, BURGUNDY & BORDEAUX

CHAMPAGNE

....

Champagne is a French *département* and the name of a very particular drink. By law, if the grapes for this sparkling wine aren't grown in this region of France, the bubbly ain't champagne. If it is champagne, then officially it's capitalized, (making it Champagne).

If you look closely at a map, you'll realize that the *département* of Champagne is shaped like the letter *C;* most of the famous bottlers are to the north, while some are more in the south. There are factory outlets in the south, in and around the town of Troyes (pronounced *trois,* like the number 3).

Locals take day trips from Paris to either northern or southern Champagne; there are also tourist overnights and fancy tours that go to Troyes for the shopping and then to Epernay for the tasting.

Charm Warning

Before you get all excited about Reims, the capital of the Champagne region, or start wondering how many bottles of bubbly are on the wall, let me warn you that if you are thinking romantic, if you are thinking beautiful, you might want to sit down now and try to cope before you are off, running, and daydreaming.

Reims is not adorable. It was bombed in World War I (although the vineyards weren't), and although it has a very nice Gothic cathedral (bombed but not ruined), there is not a lot of quaint charm to win over your heart and head. That said, Reims is a terrific place to have some fun, tour a few caves, buy champagne, and eat gourmet meals. And if you want charm, you can go to Troyes. Epernay is more charming than Reims—and closer.

Reims & Surroundings

You might not be able to spell it (I thought there was an *h* in there somewhere) or pronounce it (say *Rance*), but you do know this town as the heart of the French Champagne district.

GETTING TO REIMS

Most of the big-brand champagne houses are within the city limits of either Reims or Epernay, but Reims is on the main train line, while Epernay, which is technically closer to Paris, is not. The smaller brands tend to be in smaller towns along the Route du Champagne.

Catch the train at the Gare de l'Est in Paris; it's a 90-minute trip. You can buy tickets ahead of time through **Rail Europe** in the U.S. (© **877/456-RAIL;** www.raileurope.com/us). When the TGV-East opens in 2007, Reims will be one of the stations, accessible via Lille or Marseille.

Driving from Paris to Champagne is very easy: Just head out past Disneyland Paris on the A4, pay a few tolls (by credit card, if you like), and pick your exit depending on the houses you wish to visit. As you drive, you can see the new TGV-East tracks and stations as they are being built.

GETTING AROUND REIMS

The train station is alongside downtown Reims; you can walk just about everywhere in the downtown area, but the cathedral

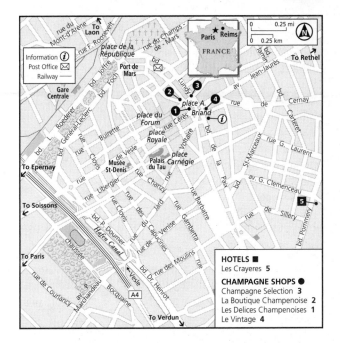

is across town. There are taxis waiting at the train station, and some drivers will make a deal for a day of sightseeing. To call a taxi 24 hours a day, dial © 03-26-47-05-05.

If you're going for a simple overnight and a little sightseeing, eating, and sleeping, you do not need a car. If, however, you want to really see the area and the vines, you do need to drive.

SLEEPING IN REIMS

Most of the famous kitchens in Reims also have rooms, since people like to linger over a gourmet dinner or want to drink.

LES CRAYERES
64 bd. Henry Vasnier, Reims.

Not only is this the number-one choice for all discriminating visitors, but it is often named one of the top five hotels in the world. Although the formal name of this restaurant and hotel is Les Crayeres, most people call it Boyer, in honor of the famous chef who is now retired from the kitchen.

Located across the street from the Pommery château and almost in the heart of town, this manor house is set in a small park and comes complete with so many luxuries, you'll have to pinch yourself to make sure it's all real.

Rates begin at 265€ ($305) and go up to about 500€ ($575). And that doesn't usually include breakfast. Book in the U.S. through **Relais & Châteaux** (© **800/735-2478**). Local phone © 03-26-82-80-80. Fax 03-26-82-65-52. www.relais chateaux.com.

ROYAL CHAMPAGNE
Champillon-Epernay.

Royal Champagne is for those who prefer to be closer to Epernay than to Reims, more out on the Route du Champagne; it's also a tad closer to Troyes. (Troyes is slightly more than an hour from Epernay.)

This lush property was created from a former post house. The rooms are huge and really nice—and each has a sweeping view of the vines. The feel is not as grand manor house as Boyer, but it is very, very nice and quite plush, with decorations in the local rustic style. Again, there's a famous chef and good eats to be had here.

There are 27 rooms; rates begin around 250€ ($288), but there are promotional deals. From the U.S., call **Relais & Châteaux** (© **800/735-2478**). Local phone © 03-26-52-87-11. www.relaischateaux.com/royalchampagne.

SHOPPING IN REIMS

SHOPPING HOURS   Most stores in Reims are open from 9am to noon and 2 to 7pm. The *hypermarchés* (modern dry-goods stores) are open nonstop until 9pm. (Frankly, though, they don't have that much good champagne, and their prices aren't much lower than anyone else's.) Some stores open at 10am and remain open during the lunch hours. Monday mornings are slow.

REAL-PEOPLE SHOPPING   In keeping with the feel of the town, the real people's "downtown" shopping district isn't very cute, either. The main drag is Victor Hugo, where there's a decent branch of **Galeries Lafayette** (with supermarket). You'll find more commercial shopping and mass-market brands (and **Monoprix**) at place d'Erlon.

MARKETS & FAIRS   Markets are open in Reims from 6am to 1pm every day except Sunday. On the first Sunday of every month, except in August, there is a flea market from 8am to 7pm at the Parc des Expositions. **Galerie Jamin** (6 rue Jamin) is open Monday and Friday from 2 to 7pm, Saturday and Sunday from 10am to 7pm.

FINDS   Because most people go to Reims partly to see the incredible cathedral, it's important to know that you can gawk, worship, and then go shopping all in the same space. There are a handful of excellent wine shops here that sell many, many brands and offer great gifts.

Almost all the shops sell chocolate champagne corks, which make a super gift. I'm also big on small bottles of champagne for the folks back home, so that they can taste a range of bubblies, and I love the fact that a few houses (Moët in particular) make six-packs of small bottles. Another novelty item comes from Pommery—it's a small (200ml) bottle of champagne called Pop. It was designed for teens and tweens, to be drunk with a straw and to teach them the taste of fine champagne.

CHAMPAGNE SELECTION
Face à la Cathédrale.

This store does not sell champagne. Rather, it makes custom champagne corks, so you can get ones that announce the baby or celebrate a big birthday. You can provide a photo of the celebrant to be imprinted on the metal top that goes over the cork. The minimum order is 250 pieces, which costs about 87€

($100). A bottle can be personalized in 2 minutes. Other novelties are available as well.

LA BOUTIQUE CHAMPENOISE
5 place du Cardinal Luçon.

This isn't as cute or elegant as other shops in the area, but it's jammed with merchandise and has probably the best prices.

LA VINOCAVE
45 place Drouet d'Erion.

This store is toward the end of the pedestrian shopping street that leads from the Reims train station toward downtown and the cathedral. You'll recognize it by the 3-foot-tall bottles of champagne standing outside. Inside, the large selection includes both big-name and little-known makers. The helpful staff speaks English.

LE PARVIS
Place du Cardinal Luçon.

This shop has a large selection of bottles and a helpful staff.

LES DELICES CHAMPENOISES
2 rue Rockefeller.

How can you not love a champagne store that's open daily? It sells all brands, big and small.

LE VINTAGE
1 cours Anatole France.

Located directly across from the rear of the cathedral, this store has a huge selection of champagne, including small-size bottles of the *grandes marques,* which make great gifts. I never knew there were so many choices. I paid about 14€ ($16) for a half-bottle of Bolly to bring home. This is the best of the several boutiques around the cathedral.

About Those Cookies

You can buy biscuits de Reims in any grocery store in France, but if you want the real thing from the real source, check out **Fossier**, 25 cours Jean-Baptiste-Langlet, Reims, which opens Monday through Friday at noon. The point of the biscuit is that you don't get drunk and they get dunked. Fossier is the most famous brand, and the *rose* is preferred.

Touring the Champagne Houses

Many of the champagne houses have two (or more) addresses, since each has both a showroom and an actual château out in the fields, where the grapes are grown. Most often, the château is used for private functions or can be visited only by appointment.

A few of the big houses own several brands, so the addresses are the same. Don't worry.

Call before you drive any great distance, as there may be a closer address for what you want to see, taste, or buy.

SIPPING HOURS

Most champagne houses follow the same hours as local retail shops: They open at about 9:30am and close for lunch around noon. Many close at 11:30am so that the final groups are out by noon; one or two actually close at 11am. After lunch, they reopen, usually at 2pm. Champagne houses close for the day at various times—some at 3:30pm, some at 7pm. Anything in between is also possible. Hours may vary with the season.

Believe it or not, most champagne houses are open on Sunday! However, some of them are closed on Monday and Tuesday.

MONEY MATTERS

Many châteaux have elaborate visitor centers and tours (even train rides). Most of them charge a fee for the tour, usually from

5€ to 10€ ($5.75–$12) per head (it can be more—ask). The price of admission includes a glass of champagne at the end of the tour. If you just want to buy, you can usually be admitted directly to the shop without taking the tour.

You can also buy champagne at many stores in town or even at Carrefour, the *hypermarché* right outside town at the junction of RN31 and BP7. Carrefour may be slightly cheaper, but only by about a buck a bottle. I went, hoping to find God, but was disappointed: The selection was not very good, and the savings weren't worth the trouble.

Do not expect factory-outlet prices at the factory. In fact, prices will be only slightly lower than in Paris—and may be similar to prices at home. In some cases, prices are even better at home. Forget about airport duty-free prices in the United States or France; you'll do better on the street.

For the luxury visitor, there are package tours and day trips from Paris that include a tour of a cave and lunch at Les Crayeres. The price can be 200€ ($230) per head or more, but this is actually a bargain—and you don't have to drive, so you can drink.

RENDEZ-VOUS, SVP

It is best to have an appointment for a tour; at some houses, you will be seen only with a private appointment. Many of the houses advertise, especially in French food, wine, and cooking magazines; they also have roadside signs. Please note that just as in Bordeaux, there are a lot of mixed messages and conflicting sources of information out there.

If there is a house you'd like to visit, but someone tells you, "Oh, no, they are not open to the public," call or fax the house yourself. Also note that there is a difference between the showroom and the château, so there may be a difference in how happy one or the other is to see you.

Brace yourself for a wide discrepancy in style at the various houses. At Bolly, I found the selection terrible and the attitude even worse. At Pommery, they were prepared for princes and kings and treated me as if I were both; the selection there is bountiful, well displayed, and easily accessed.

Also brace yourself for cultural differences and know your French manners. There's a huge difference between the big commercial houses and the tiny family houses. There are also many houses in between. I wanted to buy directly from one such house in Reims, and when I called for an appointment, it was easy and well done. When I called later to tell the house we were running late, which I thought was incredibly polite, they denied that I had an appointment and didn't know what I was talking about. Another house tried to trade me over to a sister firm, one that I had no interest in. In such situations, don't be so polite that you end up wasting your time.

MATTERS OF TASTE

It took only a few hours in Champagne for me to begin to suffer from Belgian Chocolate Syndrome, which I acquired doing research and which left me sick at the very sight of chocolate. (I have since recovered.)

BETTER BRANDS

Why does each house make several kinds of champagne, and are the more expensive cuvées worth it? You might not be able to afford it, but the difference in taste between nonvintage and vintage grande cuvée is enormous. You can pay 26€ ($30) or 56€ ($65) for a bottle of champagne, but you will be able to taste the difference. Nonvintage champagne is for those who aren't willing to spend the money to learn that there is a difference.

Note that prices of important vintages and brands can be lower in the United States than in France, especially if you luck into a year-end promotional event. Know your stuff before you commit to a big-ticket item in France. The shopping in Reims is really best for brands or vintages you can't get in America.

THE MAGIC FLUTES

The following are the big-name champagne houses in Reims and the surrounding region.

CHAMPAGNE BILLECART-SALMON
Château: 40 rue Carnot, Mareuil-sur-Ay.
✆ 03-26-52-60-22

CHAMPAGNE BOLLINGER
16 rue Jules Lobet, Ay.
✆ 03-26-53-33-88

CHAMPAGNE KRUG
5 rue Coquebert, Reims.
✆ 03-26-84-44-20
Château: Le Clos du Mesnil, Mesnil-sur-Oger.
✆ 03-26-57-51-77

CHAMPAGNE LAURENT-PERRIER
Tours-sur-Marne.
✆ 03-26-58-91-22

CHAMPAGNE LOUIS ROEDERER
21 bd. Lundy, Reims.
✆ 03-26-40-42-11

CHAMPAGNE MOET ET CHANDON
18–20 av. de Champagne, Reims.
✆ 03-26-54-71-11
Château: Abbaye d'Hautvillers, Rue Cumières, Hautvillers.
✆ 03-26-59-42-67

CHAMPAGNE MUMM
34 rue du Champs de Mars, Reims.
✆ 03-26-49-59-70
Château: Moulin de Verzenay, Verzenay.
✆ 03-26-49-59-69

CHAMPAGNE PIPER-HEIDSIECK
51 bd. Henry Vasnier, Reims.
✆ 03-26-84-43-44

CHAMPAGNE POMMERY
5 place du Géneral Gouraud, Reims.
℡ 03-26-61-62-55

CHAMPAGNE RUINART
4 rue des Crayères, Reims.
℡ 03-26-77-51-51

CHAMPAGNE TAITTINGER
9 place St-Niçaise, Reims.
℡ 03-26-85-45-35
Château: Château de la Marquetterie, Pierry.
℡ 03-29-54-04-53

CHAMPAGNE VEUVE CLICQUOT PONSARDIN
1 place des Droits de l'Homme, Reims.
℡ 03-26-89-53-90

MAISON PERRIER-JOUET
26 av. de Champagne, Epernay.
℡ 03-26-53-38-00

MAISON PHILIPPONNAT
Château: Le Clos de Goisses, 13 rue de Pont, Mareuil-sur-Ay.
℡ 03-26-52-60-43

POL ROGER
1 rue Henri Le Large, Epernay.
℡ 03-26-55-41-95

THE LITTLE-KNOWN HOUSES

Of course, a champagne need not be world famous to be good. Without a big advertising budget, a house may remain little known. Part of the glory of champagne shopping in Reims is that you can uncover your own finds and fall in love.

There are thousands of little champagne houses; you can drive around and taste for years. I bought just a few specialty bottles that were suggested by the wine stores in Reims or by experts. Most of these brands are carried in the stores in downtown Reims; few bottles are exported to the United States.

Please note that most of the wines I tested were vintage, top-of-the-line cuvées. It does make a difference. A nonvintage wine from the same house will not be the same. The following list mentions by name each bottle that I found so special, just to steer you toward the right taste, although you might find other vintages more appropriate when you shop:

- Clos des Goisses 1986, **Champagne Philliponnat** (13 rue de Pont, Mareuil-sur-Ay; ✆ 03-26-52-60-43)
- n.v., **Champagne Ployez-Jacquemart** (Ludes, Rilly-la-Montagne; ✆ 03-26-61-11-87)
- Les Mesnil 1983, **Champagne Salon** (Mesnil-sure-Oger; ✆ 03-26-57-51-65)
- Grande Cuvée 1985, **Champagne Alain Theinot** (4 rue des Moissons, Reims; ✆ 03-26-47-41-25)
- n.v., **Champagne Vilmart** (4 rue de la République, Rilly-la-Montagne; ✆ 03-26-03-40-01)

Troyes

If you want a totally different area of the *département* Champagne, where you can sip the bubbles, see an adorable town, and get to factory-outlet stores, then perhaps Troyes should be your destination. (**Note:** This is a lot to do in a day.)

Troyes has a fine Museum of Modern Art, marvelous architecture, and, of course, plenty of cute places to stay and eat. There are not as many American tourists here as in Reims, so you'll feel more of a sense of discovery. The problem is that you pretty much have to decide if you've come for the outlet shopping or for the other tastes of France.

I've been to every outlet in Troyes, and seeing them all is really a 2-day proposition (as long as you have the strength and the financial backing). Otherwise, you can visit for a day and pick and choose. Because the outlets are owned by different companies, they are in different parts of the city, often in towns or suburbs that are not technically called Troyes. The city center is filled with posters, signs, and billboards to guide you. Note that none of these outlet villages are cute.

Boyer's Babies

I asked three-star chef Gérard Boyer, still the biggest star in Reims despite retirement from the stove, for his list of favorite small houses. Here are his choices (Boyer says you can use his name as a reference):

- Christian Busin, Verzenay
- Diebolt-Vallois, Cramant
- Pierre Gimonnet, Cuis
- Lasalle, Chigny-les-Roses
- Lilbert, Cramant
- Monmarthé, Ludes

GETTING TO TROYES

The outlets are about 1½ hours from Paris, south toward Dijon. If you do not go on an organized tour, you'll need a car. To get there, head south on the A5 and get off at exit 21 (Epernay). For directions or specifics, call the outlet center (✆ 03-25-82-00-72) or the Troyes tourist office (✆ 03-25-73-00-36).

SLEEPING IN TROYES

HOTEL DE LA POSTE
35 rue Emile-Zola, Troyes.

This four-star hotel is a member of Best Western France; it has 32 rooms. It is also right in the center of Troyes and 2 blocks from the cathedral. Rooms cost about 87€ ($100) per night. ✆ 03-25-73-05-05.

EATING IN TROYES

LE CLOS JUILLET
22 bd. du 14 Juillet, Troyes.

Most foodies agree that not only is this the best table in town, but it's also reason enough to visit Troyes. For reservations, call © **03-25-73-31-32**. It's closed for dinner Sunday and all day Monday.

SHOPPING THE OUTLETS

BELGRAND
5 rue Belgrand et 55 bd. du 14 Juillet, Troyes.

This small center bills itself as the "downtown" factory-outlet mall; I can't get too excited about it except that it has Rodier.

MACARTHUR GLEN
Zone Nord, voie du Bois, Pont-Ste-Marie.

This is a lot less cute than it used to be, but then maybe you don't care about cute. MacArthur Glen has an international array of outlets, including Armani, Calvin Klein, Versace, Nike, Mephisto, and, of course, McDo (which is what locals call McDonald's). It's open Monday from 2 to 7pm, Tuesday through Friday from 10am to 7pm, and Saturday from 9:30am to 7pm.

These guys have a *navette* (shuttle-bus) service that runs between Paris and the mall. For information, call (toll-free in France) © **08-00-80-92-43**; the pickup point in Paris was once place Concorde, and then it moved to Bastille, so be sure to check. Also note that the bus goes to only this mall; the other outlets are too far away to make walking between them possible.

MARQUES AVENUE
114 bd. de Dijon, St-Julien.

Marques Avenue (www.marquesavenue.com) was one of the first outlet malls in France and remains very French in style. This is the largest and most famous outlet mall; the brands are the most well known in France, short of being Lacroix, Balmain, or St-Laurent.

Some 800m (2,624 ft.) from the five-building Marques Avenue complex is a separate part of the mall, called Marques Avenue Maison & Decoration, with 30 shops devoted to home style.

Rue Danton, Pont-Ste-Marie.

This is the most low-end of the outlet malls; it's also the smallest. (It's not really a mall, but more a grouping of stores and freestanding buildings.) But it does have Etam stock (inexpensive high-fashion clothes for teens and tweens)—so if you're an Etam fan, you may have fun.

BURGUNDY

Perhaps most Americans knew about wines from Burgundy before they learned their Bordeaux, but face it—the Bordeaux has quite a run as the snob's choice. These days, of course, international wines are the rage and French wines are being re-thunk, especially by Americans. Suddenly the Burgundy region has become more and more interesting, not only for the wines and the vines but also because it's not considered as touristy or overwrought as Provence.

The Burgundy region is closer to Paris, and though the weather may not be as good as in the south or in Provence, there's a whole lot of wine going on. The small area between Dijon and Lyon is now ripe for discovery.

Dijon

I recently read that *Dijon Vu* is the fear of mustard you have already seen. Dump those fears, as this is not going to be the problem when you get to Dijon—there are so many unusual mustards that you will consider buying a hot-dog stand. But wait, the subject was roses . . . and the vineyards that go with the roses. (When you start touring the vineyards, you will note that each row of vines has its own rose bush, an early warning sign for the detection of pestilence.) Dijon is the start of a visit to Burgundy and the capital of the region.

So welcome to Dijon, where the shopping is easy, the food is fun, and the architecture will fill your soul with the wonders of wandering France. This is one of the most user-friendly cities in the country; you will love to shop and stroll . . . and snack.

And yes, you can do Dijon as a day trip from Paris, and without a car—you won't get much feel for the grape, but you can have a nice day out and see a few brands of mustard you might not otherwise find in Paris.

GETTING TO DIJON

Take a TGV train from Paris—the ride's a little more than 2 hours—or drive (about 3 hr.). The Dijon station is technically within walking distance of town, but not really—especially if you have luggage.

If you want to really see the countryside, you will need a car, but then, if you really want to drink, you will need a designated driver.

THE LAY OF THE LAND

Dijon is the Queen of Burgundy, so a visit here incorporates not only an adorable medieval town, and all that mustard, but also the regional foodstuffs and wines of the entire area.

Like most medieval French cities, the downtown area is restored and charming; malls and big-box stores are located outside of town.

Various cutie-pie towns are located downriver from Dijon, as is the Burgundy wine district. If you have a rental car, head south on the N74, the road right through the Côte d'Or and more vineyards (called *domaines*) than you can imagine. For specifics on Beaune, see later in this chapter.

If you are on a barge tour, you will probably use Dijon as your turn-around city and then get to many of the small villages via river.

GETTING AROUND DIJON

Although Dijon has more to it than a fancy high street, everything in city center is pretty much within walking distance and is well organized.

SLEEPING IN DIJON

HOTEL SOFITEL LA CLOCHE
14 place Darcy, Dijon.

This is *the* hotel in town—it's a four-star and it's a Sofitel. Furthermore, it's within walking distance of everything. The hotel is not a grand palace, but it is classified as a national monument. Interiors have some charm: Some of the rooms have the original beams; there are apartments as well. Rates are about 150€ ($173) per night. ✆ **03-80-30-12-32.** www.hotel-lacloche.com.

A BRIEF HISTORY OF THE DUKES

Since this part isn't often taught in American grade schools, it's easy to get confused about the part wherein Burgundy was a separate country and then part of Italy before it ended up in France. This enormously rich real estate brought much power to the dukes of Bourgogne, who were major players in medieval times. There were four dukes, ruling from 1342 to 1477 but setting the seat of power for centuries to come. Today, many historical references and parts of Dijon date back to the 14th century.

Along with this wealth and history came a very specific type of architecture, *faience* (painted, glazed, monochromatic earthenware), furniture (big, heavy, carved), and food—after all, where do you think *boeuf bourguignon* came from? And who invented the drink called a Kir? (M. Kir was once mayor of Dijon, folks.) Cassis is another regional foodstuff, a fruit very similar to the grape but with its own uses in wine or baking.

And because this is a short history of the Middle Ages, I am not even going to mention Alesia, which shoppers know as the name of a street in Paris with many stock shops. Historians know it as a battlefield in the Burgundy region where the Romans defeated the local thugs (played by Gérard Depardieu in the movie version) and took France. Hail Caesar.

A BRIEF HISTORY OF MUSTARD

This has nothing to do with Colonel Mustard, and much to do with shopping in this part of France, so pay attention. You can thank not only Marco Polo for bringing mustard to Europe, but also the medieval pharmacists' guild for making this seed the germ of big enterprise. By the 13th century, Dijon had developed a reputation and even supplied the king's court with its mustards. Thereafter, all aristocratic banquets served mustard from Dijon. But Grey Poupon did not rest—by 1740 there was a mustard war between Paris and Dijon, and flavored or aromatic mustards were invented. In 1742, the house of Maille was founded—and the rest is, well, history.

BEST BUYS

Okay, so you think I'm an idiot—you have fancy mustard available in the U.S. and you know you'll visit other French cities that undoubtedly have mustard. Hell, you even see it at French train stations and airports. But wait—Dijon has a downright shocking number of flavored mustards that you simply cannot find anyplace else. Some are outright strange (violette?), which makes them the perfect gift. The price is right, too: A small jar of mustard usually costs less than 2.60€ ($3), and designer mustard rarely costs much more. Note that a selection of mustards in a cute package is usually more expensive than individual jars.

Dijon is also famous for its *pain d'épice,* which translates as "spiced bread" and is somewhat like gingerbread. But this product also comes in assorted flavors, many of which may be totally new taste sensations. Don't have the preconceived taste of American gingerbread in mind before you nibble. The most famous maker is **Mulot et Petitjean,** with three shops in Dijon and one in Beaune.

Also try the local candy that's called a *Jacqueline,* sold at **A. Michelin,** 18 rue Lusette. It was first created in 1926 and represents the tears of a woman named Jacqueline.

SHOPPING NEIGHBORHOODS

MAIN STREET   The high street with most French brands and multiples, and even McDonald's, is called rue de la Liberté. There's a famous mustard shop here (**Maille,** no. 32), near a bakery famous for *pain d'épice* (**Mulot et Petitjean,** no. 16).

BEHIND LIBERTE   If you're walking on rue de la Liberté with the Sofitel La Cloche to your back, then at midpoint on the right side is a small mall and an entirely hidden shopping area, anchored by **Monoprix.** Go out the other side of Monoprix and you'll be on rue Piron, a secondary high street with brands such as **Marina Rinaldi** and **L'Occitane,** as well as stores you may have never seen (try **Fruits & Passion,** no. 25, for bath products) and many local mom-and-pop shops.

HIDDEN LUXE   Nestled between these two streets, in a far corner, is a tiny alley—no through traffic—called the rue Amiral Roussin, only a block long and filled with big-name stores. Perhaps the best store in Dijon is here: **Les Appartements de JuJu** (no. 39), which sells women's fashion brands such as Yohji and Dries.

DOWNTOWN CROSS STREETS   Running on a grid system between rue de la Liberté and the market hall are a series of small pedestrian streets devoted to shopping ops, cafes, and the like. They have names like rue François-Rude, rue de Godrans, and rue du Bourg. There are some brands in here, but also local heroes—plus most of the city's best food suppliers (see below). Closer to the main Poste, at place Grangier, you'll find a small, freestanding branch of **Hermès** (no. 12). Not far away is home-style guru **Geneviève Lethu** (15 place Grangier).

MARKET   **Les Halles Centrales** is the covered market building made of wrought iron in a style you thought was lost when Britain's Brighton Pier sank last year. This building is the center of an entire market district that goes on for blocks and weaves its way all over the heart of town.

To Market, to Market

Market days are Monday, Thursday, and Friday mornings and all day Saturday. The market in Dijon is so wonderful that it deserves a special trip—plan your visit to include one market day, even in winter. Inside the market building, you'll find the usual suspects along with plenty of surprises, including a dealer who specializes in food supplies from Vietnam. Yet the Market Hall is just a small part of the show. Out on the streets, you can buy everything from fashion to copies of medieval tapestries. There's also a small flea market at place Grangier. Yawn.

Department Stores

Galeries Lafayette
41 rue de la Liberté.

Not only is this a larger than average branch of the famed department store, but it also has a fabulous gourmet grocery store in the basement. (**Note:** Much of the gourmet merchandise is also sold at Monoprix for a few cents less.) The store itself carries many fashion brands and offers tax refunds for those who spend 175€ ($201).

Monoprix
11 rue Piron.

One of the best Monoprix in any city center, this one has a good-size supermarket upstairs (with an excellent selection of mustards and *pain d'épice*) and the best prices in town. You can also buy clothes for the family, home style, makeup, books, maps, and more.

Foodie Finds

Au Parrian Genereux
21 rue du Bourg.

The local master chocolatier.

BOURGOGNE SAVEURS
14 rue Musette.

Local foodstuffs in a fancy setting—pick from wines, jams, mustards, and more.

CASSIS VEDRENNE
1 rue Brossuet.

This firm also has a shop in Beaune. It's devoted to showcasing the local fruit champions in liqueurs and confitures.

LE CHALET COMTOIS
28 rue Musette.

Cheese heaven. Enough said.

MAILLE
32 rue de la Republique.

Located in the old Grey Poupon shop, this store sells its mustards as well as other foodstuffs and ceramic mustard jars. It doesn't have nearly the range of flavors you would imagine, but does have some worth snapping up, including Provençal (coral-colored and spicy), cassis, and honey. The shop in Paris (place de la Madeleine) is actually cuter and better stocked with non-mustard merchandise.

MAISON AUGER
61 rue de la Liberté; 21 place Darcy.

Along with Mulot et Petitjean, the other king of *pain d'épice*.

SPÉCIALITÉS YAZQUEZ
Rue Musette and rue Quentin.

This is the most exotic of the small food markets and the most Mediterranean in terms of product range and choice. Much is sold from outside, including a very wide selection of mustards in unusual (some very unusual) flavors. I paid 1.30€ ($1.50) and 1.40€ ($1.60) for various jars, only to find the same brand for less at Monoprix. Still, this place is charming and adorable and everything you dream of in a market-souk movie set.

YVES NICOT
48 rue Jean-Jacques Rousseau.

This is one of the most famous *caves* (wine cellars) in the area and a great place to start for those interested in local wines, partly because of the knowledge of M. Nicot himself.

Beaune

Say the name of this town the way you feel about it (in French, of course): *Bon.* After you've mastered that, get your hotel reservation: This is a major tourist destination and is mobbed the minute the weather gets good—as well as during special events and wine auctions. And no, the famous *Hospices* is not a hospital.

Beaune is simply one of those adorable, cutie-pie towns that is perfect in every detail except its popularity—it can be mobbed. If you drive here, park or leave the car at your hotel; if you come by boat—lucky you. The town is medieval in its layout, which means it's somewhat circular and snail shaped, so you can just wander until lost and found.

This is not really shopping paradise—there are a few French multiples and many, many wine shops selling souvenirs, carafes, decanters, and postcards. You will have no trouble finding wine by the bottle or the case, and will be swamped with wine-inspired gift items. *Caves* for tastings are in and outside of town.

The town is located only a half-hour south of Dijon. To get here by train from Paris, you must change to a regional train in Dijon. If you're driving, you'll pass through many of the most famous names in wine. There are taxis and shuttles from Dijon into the nearby villages.

If you're spending the night, you want to stay within walking distance of the action. My first choice is **Hôtel de la Poste,**

5 bd. Clémenceau (© 03-80-22-08-11), where rooms begin at 100€ ($115) for a single. Right down the street is **Le Cep,** 27 rue Maufoux (© 03-80-22-08-11), which is also nice and charges similar rates. Both of these are four-star hotels. Hôtel de la Poste has its own parking area.

Note: For my first overnight in Beaune, I chose a place to stay from a guide of cute hotels. I verified the information by phone when I booked. When I got there, I was shocked by what the owner defined as "in town" and canceled my reservation. I was lucky to find something much better for my needs. Be warned that this is high tourist territory; anything goes.

If you have a car and prefer to be tucked away in your own château at night, there are several deluxe ones in the area that take guests. **Hostellerie de Levernois** is a member of Relais & Châteaux; go to www.levernois.com for details.

For guides to the nearby châteaux, winery visits, or cooking classes with local chefs, get a list at the tourist office. You can even arrange a visit to **La Moutarderie Fallot** (www.fallot.com), a mustard-making factory with museum and shop. The mustard tour costs 10€ ($12) per person.

MARKET DAYS

All markets are held in the mornings only. The Beaune gourmet market is on Wednesday; the main market and *brocante* are on Saturday. Meursault is on Friday. Nolay is on Monday. And Savigny les Beaune is on Sunday.

BORDEAUX

Ah Bordeaux, I blush, I laugh, I giggle, I seethe when I realize it's time to fess up. I hate Bordeaux because every time I've been here, I've been lost. That's not a very good excuse, I know, I know. I wholeheartedly welcome you to the Bordeaux area . . . and the rest, well, welcome and we'll figure it all out together.

I love the areas around Bordeaux and recommend them—from various domains to the wine spa in Martillac (Les Source de Caudalie), even Arachon, a beach area that has a nearby wealthy community that has everything to do with money and not much to do with wine. I've recently become interested in the wines of the Blaye district, which is nearby—so yes, I'd go there, too.

But metro Bordeaux? Forget it! I was once so lost that I had to hire a taxi so I could follow it to my hotel. I'll admit that it's easier if you arrive by cruise ship and don't have to deal with the sprawl of this town.

The Lay of the Land

Where there's wine, there's rivers, so this area feeds off the Gironde and the Garonne rivers and nestles into a bicoastal niche formed off a peninsula jutting into the ocean.

Many of the nearby domains and/or châteaux are so famous, they're brand names. The various areas do take on their own personalities, but you'll have visitors who like certain mini-regions because of their preference for the wine of those areas.

My late husband and I did one of those driving trips where we thought we'd just poke along the roads, take in the villages, and stop at various châteaux. For the most part it was a bust—few of the châteaux take walk-ins, and things didn't always go smoothly even when we had appointments. Out of a hand-ful of visits, only one was a truly wonderful experience.

On the other hand, I went on a bus tour of the St-Emilion area and found it delightful—often the vineyards are geared toward tour groups, and they sure get more friendly when there are 30 people hanging around.

Surely, my best visit to the area involved arrival at the Bordeaux train station with pickup from the wine spa, a drive through the vines that I didn't have to navigate, and a luxuri-ous few days—tour of château included—at Les Sources de Caudalie on the property of Château Smith Haut-Lafitte.

Obviously this area offers many, many choices—having the wine experience does not necessarily mean a trip into downtown Bordeaux. You may want to work with either your favorite wine-tasting towns or a well-known hotel chain (such as Relais & Châteaux) to find choices that are outside of downtown Bordeaux.

The *grands crus,* and therefore the basic wine-growing areas, are:

- Médoc
- St-Emilion
- Pessac-Leognan
- Graves
- Sauternes
- Barsac
- Pomerol

DOWNTOWN BORDEAUX

Alas, I let my obsessions about getting lost get in the way. Bordeaux is a large town set within a huge ring road. In fact, there are actually two ring roads. What you really want is Old Bordeaux.

In reality, Bordeaux is not only a great town but also one that keeps getting more interesting, partly because of M. Alain Juppe, the controversial mayor and president *manqué* of France. As France's provinces have stopped being provincal, Bordeaux has taken a lead among the most interesting of the cities headed into new futures.

This is a city famous not as a medieval shrine (although there are parts that date back into the 1500s), but more as an artistic and business center from the 17th century on. This is a city that has considered itself sophisticated for many centuries.

As for the joys of Old Bordeaux, there's a nice bunch of historic buildings, a lot of good museums, and the thriving wine business, as well as much interest in contemporary art and home design. Shopping is secondary to pure visual delight in the historic parts of town. If you stick to the main shopping districts listed below, you can walk everywhere and you won't get lost.

Getting Around Bordeaux

If you stick to the main areas and the *quais,* you can walk to most places of historic and shopping interest. Bordeaux also has a rather unique tram system that is part of the new technology and will have some 84 stations by 2007. (It now has 50-odd.)

Sleeping in Bordeaux

RADISSON SAS GRAND HOTEL BORDEAUX
2–5 place de la Comédie.

This was originally built as *the* grand hotel of Bordeaux, but over the course of time fell into a state of disrepair and had to be shut down. New ownership has now decided to extend and convert the existing structure into an international first-class property, to be reopened in early 2006. It will have 150 rooms, two restaurants, a lobby bar, a wine-tasting bar, meeting facilities, and a health club. The hotel has a superb location, right in the heart of the city center. From the U.S., call © 888/201-1718. www.radisson.com.

Eating in Bordeaux

BRASSERIE LE NOAILLES
12 allées de Tourny.

The *in* place, with a great location and local heroes to stare at. For reservations, call © 05-56-81-94-45.

CAFE DU MUSEE
CAPC Museum, 7 rue Ferrère.

The cafe in this contemporary art museum was created by Andrée Putman. The food is by Gregory de Lepinay, who also has his own bistro called Chez Greg.

Shopping in Bordeaux

SHOPPING NEIGHBORHOODS

QUAIS DES CHARTRONS   The harbor, along with the old warehouses for merchants and wines. Follow your nose away from the *quais* along rue du Faubourg des Arts and you'll pass the home-style and -decor district. There are also some antiques stores right on the *quai;* try **Espace Antiquites** (no. 56).

COURS CLEMENCEAU   Main street for luxury shopping, with all the big names you expect to find in any world-class shopping city. Don't miss **Jean Vier** (no. 40), a shop selling its own brand of Basque textiles. The area between here and the Opéra is called the *Triangle d'Or* (Golden Triangle) because all the big brands and luxury labels have their stores here.

OPERA   Don't miss the Opéra itself while you're looking for the stores; it inspired the Opéra Garnier in Paris (so they say). There are many luxe stores dotted into the allées de Tourny, including **Cadiot-Badie,** a fancy, old-fashioned chocolate shop known for its truffles. There's also the **Parfumerie de l'Opéra,** which carries many hard-to-find fragrances (stop here if you're not going to be shopping in Paris). Among my favorites in this allée is **Compagnie Française de l'Orient et de la Chine,** which sells clothes and home style from China.

COURS DE L'INTENDANCE   The third stroke of the triangle, with more big names and big brands. This runs east–west.

PLACE GAMBETTA   Transitional landmark for shoppers moving between the Golden Triangle and the antiques district. There are several big-name stores here as well, including **Hermès.**

GALERIE DES GRANDS HOMMES   It's a minimall with many brand names, right at the place des Grands Hommes in the center of the Golden Triangle.

RUE STE-CATHERINE   This pedestrian street is more commercial, with the department store **Nouvelles Galeries** (no. 50–60), a division of Galeries Lafayette. Rue Ste-Catherine runs north–south, heading into the Golden Triangle at a perpendicular angle. It's the heart of a pedestrian shopping district between the Bourse and place Gambetta.

BOUFFARD   A district of antiques stores, with the rue des Remparts running alongside. Note that shops may open late in the day (say, 11am or noon); most are closed entirely on Mondays. Don't miss **Passage Saint-Michel,** 14 & 17 place Canteloup (© **05-56-92-14-76**), with some 50 *brocante* dealers of all styles and prices. There's also rue Nôtre Dame and **Le Village Notre Dame.**

REAL-PEOPLE SHOPPING

You won't have trouble meeting personal needs in any *pharmacie,* Galeries Lafayette, or shopping mall. To find the pharmacist on duty on Sundays, call © **05-56-01-02-03.** If you need a hairdresser, there's a branch of **Jacques Dessange** right at 20 cours Clémenceau (© **05-56-44-74-91** for appointments).

THEME SHOPPING

Obviously you expect to find wine stores here, and the usual big names and chains, but there's also an interesting connection with British brands due to the centuries-old trade across the sea, directly between Bordeaux and the U.K. Brands such as **Penhaligon's,** 14 cours Clémenceau, have outposts here, and a store called **Covent Garden,** 52 cours Clémenceau, specializes in Brit brands.

With the proximity to the sea, there are also many products with nautical themes.

WINE STORES

AMOUR DU VIN
10 cours de Verdun.

The Sam's of Bordeaux vineyards.

LA VINOTHÈQUE DE BORDEAUX
8 cours du XXX Juillet.

This one is my favorite—it reps several hundred local vineyards.

L'INTENDANT
2 allées de Tourny.

This store is amazing to look at from all aspects, with over 15,000 bottles.

Chapter Six

....

SHOPPING THE TEXTILE CITIES: LYON, LILLE & BIARRITZ

WELCOME TO THE FRENCH TEXTILE CITIES

France has been famous for the quality of its textiles for centuries. The northern, more industrial part of France still houses factories—some of which are working factories, while some have been turned into our favorite kind of store, factory outlets. Of course, many factories have closed, as is the way of the modern world.

Lyon, which is south of Paris and on the road to Provence and the Côte d'Azur, has long been the silk center of France and is where Hermès makes its scarves (sorry, no outlet store). As science and technology have advanced, Lyon has become a center for cottons, knits, and especially bathing suits and lingerie. Several international textile trade fairs are held in Lyon each year.

Lille is cotton land, where most of the textiles for bed linen are made. There are tons of outlet stores here, including one in the Porthault factory. Not familiar with Porthault? This old French firm is considered by many to make the best and most luxurious linens in the world. If you buy in one of its tony retail stores, you will pay more than 870€ ($1,000) for a king-size sheet. At the outlet, I bought sheets for 87€ ($100) each. (*Note:* American beds tend to be larger than French beds by a few inches, so note the measurements when you buy sheets for use in the U.S. Duvet covers will work just fine.)

With its proximity to Spain, Biarritz is a wonderful city for finding Basque textiles. Basque linens come in two shades— either bleached hard white or natural unbleached beige, with stripes of color woven through the final inches of fabric, usually toward the selvage.

Garmentos also know that the word denim comes from *de Nîmes;* Nîmes is a city in Provence and is covered in chapter 7. *Les tissus Indiennes,* the Provençal fabrics made from woodblocks first brought from India, are also covered in that chapter.

A Weekend Away

Any of the textile cities makes an excellent weekend away. All have more to them than shopping, including great museums and very fine chefs. Several rental-car agencies and hotels offer 2-night stays as part of their packages. Some of the better luxury hotels (usually in the countryside) require a minimum 2-night stay, especially during the season. These cities also participate in a weekend program that offers two hotel nights for the price of one.

Trains to the Textile Cities

Paris has different train stations to serve rail lines heading to various destinations. If you're going to Lyon, you want Gare de Lyon (which also serves the south and Provence); for Lille, you want Gare du Nord; and for Biarritz, you want Gare Montparnasse.

Lyon now has three train stations and Lille has two, so have your brain turned on while traveling. TGV trains depart from and arrive at specific stations, which are marked on the schedule. (*Note:* Lyon St-Exupéry is the airport, not downtown.)

LYON

Originally, I thought I could do Lyon as a day trip, sort of a shop-and-see mission with lots of eating thrown in. I don't mean that I felt that I could get to know a city in a day. I thought with TGV service at a mere 2 hours, I could go, do a little looking around, have lunch at one of the famed multi-star tables, sample Bernachon's chocolates, and call it a day trip. Silly *moi*.

I stayed for 3 days on my first visit and started babbling about moving there. I have been returning to Lyon regularly ever since. Lyon has a lot more to offer than you might think; the recent addition of a truly world-class luxury hotel has also made a big difference.

So welcome to Lyon, the perfect place to go for a day, a week, or maybe a lifetime. Welcome to Lyon, one of France's biggest towns, offering industry and commerce as well as daily food markets, a picturesque Old Town, a serious food and wine tradition, and all sorts of shopping. Shopping for chocolates? Dreaming of a town that's famous for its chocolate shops? Did someone say let's spend the day eating chocolate?

That means that Lyon has the dual personality of a food and fabric town. Much fabric manufacturing takes place in and around Lyon—and yes, where there are factories, there have to be outlet shops. And jobbers, too.

This is also a cultural kind of a place, with a gorgeous rehabbed opera house downtown. There are plenty of designer clothes to buy, as well as resale shops to survey. Most of the French majors have stores here, so you can also revisit your favorite chains. The only problem is the sprawl—you'll never have the time or the energy to see it all.

To get information about Lyon online, try www.mairie-lyon.fr or www.voilalyon.com.

Location, Location, Location

When you check your map, you'll note that Lyon is quite near the Beaujolais country. It's on the way to Geneva, and it is also

Lyon

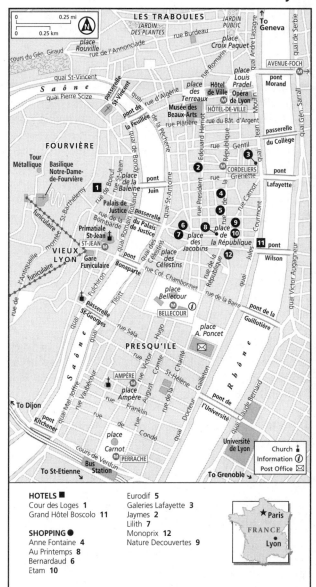

HOTELS ■
Cour des Loges **1**
Grand Hôtel Boscolo **11**

SHOPPING ●
Anne Fontaine **4**
Au Printemps **8**
Bernardaud **6**
Etam **10**

Eurodif **5**
Galeries Lafayette **3**
Jaymes **2**
Lilith **7**
Monoprix **12**
Nature Decouvertes **9**

Church ♦
Information ⓘ
Post Office ✉

★ Paris

FRANCE

Lyon

on the way to the south of France. While you're driving around the area, you'll see signs for the Alps and the famous ski resorts. Lyon is the center of the real France.

Getting to Lyon

BY PLANE Nonstop service to Lyon from the U.S. comes and goes with the fashions and traffic. Major carriers have offered and then discontinued the route, so ask your travel agent. Lyon is a great gateway to ski resorts or to the south of France, so if you can get a nonstop from the U.S., grab it. As we go to press, there are no nonstops; you can take a TGV train from the Paris airport into either Lyon or the Lyon airport.

BY TRAIN TGV fast trains for downtown Lyon depart Paris's Gare de Lyon every hour; the trip takes 2 hours. Beware of faster trains that may put you at the airport instead of going into town.

Lyon's modern Part Dieu train station is mostly flat and has handcarts and access for serious passenger traffic. Perrache Station is older, has no handcarts, and is not built for getting around easily.

Die-hard shoppers may want to note that Part Dieu adjoins a commercial center (a giant shopping mall), with branches of just about every French multiple as well as an office tower with Le Meridien hotel located in the middle of the tower. Go upstairs to check in.

It's technically possible to spend your day trip to Lyon at the train station and just pop out to dine in one of the famous restaurants and make a quick tour to Bernachon before heading back to Paris. Of course, that's cheating.

The Lay of the Land

Lyon is huge; the most central area is divided by the convergence of two rivers, La Saône and Le Rhône. The city is divided into *quartiers;* there are also *arrondissements* (districts), just like in Paris, but in this chapter I pretty much ignore them. Within the central core, there are good parts on both sides of the two rivers; the heart of the city lies on a small peninsula between them called Presqu'île. To sum up, you have three main portions of downtown; let's call them:

- Old Town (Vieux Lyon)
- Midtown (Presqu'île)
- New Town (where the two main train stations are)

Note that it is possible for a tourist, especially a day-tripper, to not realize how big Lyon is and to visit only one part of the town, missing a great deal of what's available. Sticking to one part of town simplifies things if you're on a day trip, but it doesn't give you much of an understanding of Lyon or a good overview of what's available.

The Part Dieu train station, where you will probably arrive if you take the TGV from Paris, is on the farthest bank of the Rhône in the part I have named New Town. A taxi to Vieux Lyon (Old Town), on the far side of the Saône, costs about 10€ ($12). Presqu'île is where most of the shopping and tourist sights are located.

NEARBY

Not to confuse the issue, but Lyon also has scads of interesting suburbs—even some of the most impressive restaurants are in suburbs rather than Lyon central. You may also find nearby towns of interest, from Vienne, known for its Roman ruins, to St-Etienne, which has been getting press for its chefs and its decorative-arts museum, to Romans, an hour south and the town where shoes are made. It's filled with shoe factory outlets (p. 217) as well as an American-style outlet mall.

Getting Around Lyon

For a day trip to Lyon, you'll probably want to cab it. For real life, I use a combination of cabs, Métro, bus, and old-fashioned foot power. The city is far too big, and the train stations are too far away, to be able to consider this a mere stroll-and-shop kind of town. Finding a parking place for your car is too difficult to contemplate for exploration purposes. If you are just in town for a few hours, find a central parking lot on Presqu'île.

BY TAXI I admit that in some of my explorations of the town, when I was really in the further patches of tourist land, it was not easy to find a cab or even a taxi rank. Therefore, you might need to call **Allo Taxi** (© **04-78-28-23-23**). It has daily 24-hour service and some 300 radio taxis.

BY METRO The Métro here is great, but it is not extensive enough to completely serve you, especially if your time is limited. It's a new, modern train with clean stations and easy-to-use directions that are posted everywhere. The 1-day Ticket Liberté allows you unlimited access to the Métro; you can buy one at the tourist office, handily located in place Bellecour (© **04-72-77-69-69**).

BY BUS The bus is pretty easy to use once you have an idea of what's where or if you're staying at Le Meridien and want to get to the other shopping districts. The only problem is the one-way streets—this means you will not get back on the bus to return "home" where you got off. Bus fare is 1.30€ ($1.50); you can buy a ticket onboard.

Weekend en Ville

Lyon is one of several major French cities participating in a weekend promotion coordinated through **SNCF** (www. sncf.com), the French high-speed train system. You can get a discounted TGV ticket as well as two hotel nights for the price of one at zillions of participating hotels, including most of the best accommodations (though I don't think the Relais & Châteaux properties are included). Breakfast, tax, and so on are included in the promotion. Each participating city has free brochures at the tourist office. Another promotion, called Weekend Lyon Festival, offers 2 nights in a hotel, a 2-day city card, and tickets to an event. For more information, go to www.lyon-france.com.

Sleeping in Lyon

Lyon does a large convention business, so be certain you know where your hotel is located. For example, Hilton customers may be thrilled that there's a Hilton in Lyon, but this one is next to the convention center and not near anything of much charm.

COUR DES LOGES
6 rue du Boeuf, Old Lyon.

For years, Lyon has had nice accommodations—but not a single drop-dead, fancy-shmancy hotel. All that changed with the arrival of Cour des Loges, created from the marriage of four medieval buildings in the heart of Old Lyon.

A member of the family of Compagnie des Hôtels de Montagne (begun in Megève), this is a small, family-run operation that is all elegance and high style. The rooms are done in a medieval-moderne style, with either Renaissance Italian or contempo French savoire faire—plus Philippe Starck bathrooms. Amenities include a pool, sauna, private gardens, restaurant, and large breakfast buffet.

Rates are about 250€ ($288) per night, though they vary by season and day of the week. *Note:* Once you have a reservation, ask the concierge to fax you an access map—this includes the code for the otherwise pedestrian-only street. Without the code, you can't get the barrier down. Local phone ✆ 04-72-77-44-44. www.courdesloges.com.

GRAND HOTEL BOSCOLO
11 rue Grolée.

I've stayed at this four-star hotel for years because of its location and mid-range prices; it is by no means luxe—but it's practical. The lobby has been modernized and the rooms have been renovated, but there are still old-fashioned wide corridors, high ceilings, and enormous French doors leading to balconies overlooking the Saône. You're right in the core of the city and can walk to just about everywhere in town; a Métro stop is a block away. This may not be a five-star, drop-dead-chic hotel, but you can't beat the excellent location and great prices.

The out-of-season rate of 110€ ($127) includes a buffet breakfast. This hotel participates in the Bon Weekend program, so you can get 2 nights for the price of one. From the U.S., call © **888/626-7265.** Local phone © 04-72-40-45-45. Fax 04-78-37-52-55. www.boscolohotels.com.

Le Meridien Part-Dieu
129 rue Servient.

I have a love-hate thing for this place simply because I hate modern, high-rise hotels that lack the least bit of charm. On the other hand, if views are your thing, then this is the right place. The hotel is situated in a tower and is said to be one of the highest up in all of France . . . so you do get a view, as well as various promotional rates. I also admit that I love sneaking over to the 260-store Part-Dieu mall next door several times a day (for a peek, go to www.partdieu.com). The hotel is next to the main train station and just a block from the main market, a kind of indoor food hall. Right outside the front door, you can catch a tram or bus to Presqu'île or other shopping destinations. You won't feel like you're in a cutie-pie town, but it is a convenient enough location. It's also great if the weather is bad, thanks to the ease with which you can get to the mall.

Rooms are about 150€ ($173) with a good deal. *Note:* When you arrive, you'll see a desk on the ground floor, but then you'll have to take an elevator for check-in, way up in the clouds. Local phone © **04-78-63-55-20.**

Eating in Lyon

Entire books have been written about food in Lyon, so you will have no trouble driving yourself nuts with the various choices and possibilities. *Note:* I have had enough experience with the wander-and-choose-one method of dining out to warn you that you will most likely suffer if you do this—I've had some disastrous meals in the two major cutie-pie restaurant districts in Old Town and Presqu'île.

BERNACHON
42 and 46 cours Franklin Roosevelt.

Bernachon—one of the world's most famous chocolatiers—has its own restaurant and tearoom, called **Bernachon Passion** (no. 42). If you prefer food to go, try **Bocuse & Bernachon** (no. 46). This neighborhood, the 6e, is not far from the city's indoor food market—you can walk if you aren't carrying too many chocolate bars.

BRASSERIE LE NORD
18 rue Neuve, Presqu'île.

Paul Bocuse owns several bistros around town, each bearing the name of a direction. Le Nord is smack in the heart of Presqu'île and is one of my regulars—I can't help but love the traditional bistro decor, the waiters in their long aprons, the *carte* of traditional foods, and the fact that prices are not high. Call © **04-78-28-24-54** for reservations.

CAFE DES NEGOCIANTS
1 place Françisque Regaud, Presqu'île.

This is the central hangout for just about everyone—and a good spot for a crepe, a coffee, or a meal. It's right off the main drag of Presqu'île, rue de la République, and near Monoprix.

CAFÉ EPICERIE
8 rue du Boeuf, Vieux Lyon.

This is by far the best cafe in Old Lyon, especially if you're looking for comfy-trendy. The crowd is hip, the Mediteranean-inspired *carte* is not too expensive, and the presentation looks like a design magazine's spreads. Entrees are served in canning jars and the like. For reservations, call © **04-72-77-44-44**.

DEBEAUX
16 rue de la République, Presqu'île.

This is one of those old-lady tearooms in France that actually feels quite chic rather than old-lady. It's good for a light lunch or snack during your shopping adventures.

Shopping in Lyon

Lyon has everything and every kind of store—they just may be harder to find than in other tourist towns because the city is so spread out. As much as I believe in wandering the streets and as much as I hate the concept of an American mall on foreign shores, you may enjoy the **Commercial Centre Part-Dieu** (across the street from the Part-Dieu train station) if you're in town for just a short period of time or if the weather is foul. Guests at Le Meridien can access the mall through a downstairs door and bridge. Part-Dieu has one of every major chain as well as a good-size supermarket where you can buy foodstuffs for picnics or gifts.

BEST BUYS

FOOD   Lyon and food are synonymous, not only to the French, but also to food lovers everywhere. Many make the pilgrimage to Lyon just to eat and buy food. There is an indoor food hall not far from the Part-Dieu mall and train station (see below). You can munch on chocolate all day, although I will admit outright that after visiting a few chocolate shops, my eyes began to cross and my stomach went into knots. I found that the most heavenly chocolate was in pastry form, not candy form. Still, I bought candy bars from Bernachon as gifts for many friends.

SECONDS, OVERRUNS & ODD LOTS   Lyon is surrounded by fabric mills and clothing manufacturers. I was delighted to bump into two different jobbers who specialized in unloading cheap clothing. I extended my wardrobe threefold for a mere 50€ ($58). Lyon manufacturers are particularly big on underwear and bathing suits, so these are good items to find at jobbers.

About Those Silks

I'd like to tell you that I was impressed with the silks I inspected and that the silk legend is true. But I found the silk shops in Old Town very touristy, and the silk factory in the silk district downright embarrassing. I must have been in town during cocoon season.

And since I know you want to know, here's the skinny on Hermès: Yes, the factory is in Lyon. Yes, you can take a tour if you have a VIP group or make arrangements ahead of time. But no, there is not a shop. Employees buy Hermès at any store with an employee discount. Although the style of silk screening that Hermès made famous is of a type that originated in Lyon and at one time was thought of as a citywide style, there are no other silk makers in Lyon that make anything near what Hermès does.

Shopping Hours

Stores usually open at 9:30am and close at 7 or 7:30pm. In the big shopping mall, Commercial Centre Part-Dieu, the stores are open from 10am to 7pm, 6 days a week.

Thankfully, you're in the big city now, so not that many stores close for lunch. Even though part of your day trip will involve eating at one of the famous Lyonnaise restaurants, it's nice to know that many stores are open when you want them to be. You can also have pizza for lunch (I often do) and spend more time exploring the city.

Just about everything is closed on Sunday, except in Old Lyon or the usual neighborhood food stores throughout the rest of town. But there is a big business in antiques here, especially on Sundays, and a big crafts market is also held on Sundays.

As for other markets, there is an antiques village, with fancy stuff, and one of the best flea markets I've ever been to in France, along the canal (see below). The food market along the Saône River is especially good on both Saturday and Sunday; don't miss it.

Most stores are closed on Monday mornings; some are closed all day Monday. The Part-Dieu mall and most of the large stores in Lyon are open Mondays.

SHOPPING NEIGHBORHOODS

Lyon is enormous. These shopping neighborhoods have been organized according to what makes sense to me—thus may mean little to a French person. Study your map as you read this to get a better understanding of the lay of the land and which parts of town you'd like to visit if you're on a limited schedule. I have included just the main shopping parts of town—no out-of-the-way finds.

MIDTOWN PRESQU'ILE   Presqu'île is the name of the peninsula that juts between the two rivers. It is home to the central part of Lyon and much of the main shopping district in terms of department stores, boutiques, French multiples, and so on. Although different parts of this peninsula have different names, the heart of it, where the main shopping is located, is what I call "Midtown." On a map, this is basically the area to the right of the place Bellecour (if your back is to Part-Dieu and you are facing the Saône) and the place de la Bourse.

This area is a grid, with all the streets packed with stores. The main shopping street is rue de la République, a pedestrian mall near the place Bellecour. The commercial and mass-market brands are located here, as well as McDo and some cinema houses. For more upmarket shopping, don't overlook rue du Président Edouard Herriot, rue de Brest, or any of the streets that radiate outward from the place des Jacobins.

DELUXE PRESQU'ILE   The fanciest stores and the most deluxe French names are primarily located on the rue Gasparin and the rue Emile Zola, which run parallel and are each only about a block long. Both begin at the place Bellecour and stretch toward the place des Jacobins.

FANCY ANTIQUES   Leading away from the major park in the center of Presqu'île (place Bellecour) lies the very small rue Auguste Comte, which is home to a few designer shops and many upscale antiques and interior-design shops.

VIEUX LYON   The Old Town part of the city is on a hill overlooking the Saône. You must first cross the river; then wander around, exploring and going up and down steps and deciding how high you want to go. Most of the shopping is lower rather than higher, thankfully. There are no big-name stores here; this is boutique land. Note that stores in this neighborhood don't open until 11am and are closed on Mondays. It's very lively on Sundays.

CROIX ROUSSE   This is the part of town where the silk weavers used to hang out; supposedly the houses were built to allow maximum light. I found only one silk factory here— it was a bust, and I think you can pass on it. This area is north of the Opéra and can be reached by public transportation. It is beginning to be known for its shops of up-and-coming designers. Check out the passage Thiaffait, rue St-Polycarpe, and place des Terreaux.

FDR/THE 6TH   Lyon does have arrondissements like Paris; I'll take the 6e. I came to know the 6e only because I had to have a taste at the famous chocolatier **Bernachon,** located on the cours Franklin Roosevelt (no. 42). How was I to know that this street is a main thoroughfare in a rich little nook of Lyon with several designer boutiques as well as a branch of **Souleiado** (no. 54), just an éclair's throw away from Bernachon? Note that cours Franklin Roosevelt changes its name to cours Vitton. Therefore, the **Lacoste** shop, which is only a block from Souleiado, is located at 1 cours Vitton. You can take the Métro to this area.

PART-DIEU   It's a bird, it's a plane, it's a train station, it's a mall, and it's even the home of Les Halles—the indoor food markets of Lyon. This isn't a cute area—it's all tall buildings and modern urban renewal—but there are sidewalks and buses, and you can easily find your way to many good things to eat and take home.

TETE D'OR   This area is where the **Cité des Antiquaires** is located—it's technically called Villeurbanne. *Warning:* You will never find a cab when you are ready to leave, and there isn't much in terms of public transportation. You can walk over to the Museum of Contemporary Art and maybe find a taxi, call **Allo Taxi** (© 04-78-28-23-23) for one, or try taking bus no. 59 or 70.

FINDS

CASANOVA
56 cours Franklin Roosevelt.

This is an old-fashioned leather and saddle shop in the 6e, the likes of which are not often seen in this century. It sells luggage and handbags, as well as everything else you and your horse may need.

COTELAC
6 rue Emile Zola, Presqu'île; 18 rue Auguste Comte, Presqu'île

Cotélac is a multiple that has stores in Paris as well. It's somewhat unique and special—the clothes are hip and a tad whimsical.

JAYMES
25 rue de Brest, Presqu'île.

Jaymes is a jobber that sells big-name clothing and lingerie and all sorts of things from nearby French mills. The store is stocked with men's, women's, and children's clothing; it's especially packed with fabulous and otherwise very expensive baby and toddler clothes from some of the best French brands. You may or may not find leather goods, towels, bathrobes, and other treats. You just never know.

LES HALLES DE LYON
102 cours Lafayette.

This indoor food hall in the 3e is neither old-fashioned nor quaint, but if you're a fan of food markets, you will have a great time picking and choosing from the local specialties. Note that it's not the most exciting food market in the world, so if you are of the school of seen-one-sausage-seen-'em-all, you will not be knocked out. Les Halles is not far from Part-Dieu and can be reached by public transportation.

NATURE DECOUVERTES
58 rue de la République, Presqu'île.

This is the French branch of the Nature Company. There is one in Paris, in the Carroussel du Louvre, so you do not need to jump on a train and come all the way to Lyon just for this store. However, if you have never seen one, it is a total joy, especially if you are familiar with the American cousin. There are lots of inexpensive gifts and great gadgets for kids.

Lyon Resources A–Z

BIG NAMES & BRANDS

What follows are some of the big designer boutiques and trendy multiples in Lyon.

ANNE FONTAINE
49 rue Edouard Herriot, Presqu'île.

BERNARDAUD
15 rue des Archers, Presqu'île.

CHRISTIAN DIOR
87 rue Edouard Herriot, Presqu'île.

DIESEL
29 rue Edouard Herriot, Presqu'île.

ETAM
67 rue de la République, Presqu'île.

FAÇONNABLE
30 rue Edouard Herriot, Presqu'île.

LILITH
3 rue des Archers, Presqu'île.

LONGCHAMP
32 rue Edouard Herriot, Presqu'île.

MAX MARA
85 rue Edouard Herriot, Presqu'île.

MUJI
29 rue Edouard Herriot, Presqu'île.

PLEIN SUD
8 rue des Archers, Presqu'île.

PUMA
38 rue Edouard Herriot, Presqu'île.

SEPHORA
66 rue Edouard Herriot, Presqu'île.

SONIA RYKIEL
62 rue de Brest, Presqu'île.

TARA JARMON
10 rue des Archers, Presqu'île.

VENTILO
42 rue de Brest, Presqu'île.

ZAPA
49 rue Edouard Herriot, Presqu'île.

BOOKS & MUSIC

FNAC
Rue de la République, Presqu'île.

This branch has three floors of books (including some in foreign languages), music, computer gadgets, and tickets to events all over France.

CHOCOLATES & FOODSTUFFS

BERNACHON
42 cours Franklin Roosevelt.

This chocolatier in the 6e is the most famous in town. The éclairs are worth 9 hours on a plane—better than sex. Looking for a great gift for a fellow foodie? You can get 500 grams of cacao here for about 8.70€ ($10).

Les Halles de Lyon
102 cours Lafayette.

See p. 122.

Malleval
11 rue Emile Zola, Presqu'île.

In Lyon since 1860, Malleval is known as a purveyor of gourmet foodstuffs, wine, and champagne.

Monoprix
33 rue de la République, Presqu'île.

This Monoprix has a grocery store that's a good enough resource for food items, picnics, and edible gifts.

DEPARTMENT STORES

Au Printemps
42 place de la République, Presqu'île.

Right in the heart of downtown, next to the place des Jacobins, this is the department store you want, where you want it.

Galeries Lafayette
6 place des Cordeliers, Presqu'île; C C Part-Dieu, 6e.

There are two Galeries Lafayette stores: one a few blocks from the main shopping streets on Presqu'île, and the other inside the mall at the Part-Dieu train station. The downtown branch is nice enough if slightly off the beaten track, right near the river—you have to look for it.

Monoprix Grand Bazaar
31 rue de la République, Presqu'île.

This is one of the strangest sights in French retailing: The storefront looks like a regular department store, named Grand Bazaar, which it must have been at one time. From the outside, it's quite dramatic. Inside, however, it's rather ordinary. It does have several levels, so it pays to poke around a bit. This is where I found Provençal-style contact paper in the housewares department. There's a grocery store, too.

DISCOUNTERS

EURODIF
43 rue de Grenette, Presqu'île.

This is a branch of Bouchara and one of the famous discount clothing stores in France. The best buys are teen-style hot fashions and accessories.

JAYMES
25 rue de Brest, Presqu'île.

See p. 122.

HAIR & BEAUTY

CHRISTINE MARGOSSIAN CENTRE DE BEAUTE
9 rue Grolée, Presqu'île.

This is not only a beauty salon for hair, makeup, and treatments, but also a well-being center that offers the latest in French cures. It's near the Grand Hôtel Boscolo and is one of the fanciest salons in town.

EURO SANTE BEAUTE
Place de la République, Presqu'île.

This French chain of *parapharmacies* (large discount drugstores) has an excellent selection of pharmaceutical brands and good prices. It's right near the center of town, on the side of the main place.

MARKETS & FAIRS

There's a very nice—though rather simple—daily fresh-food market that stretches along the quay side of the Saône at *quai*

St-Antoine. Weekends are heavenly: The colors are beautiful, and some of the regional produce is unique. This market is thin on weekdays, though, and doesn't have as much energy as I would like. Foodies like to visit in the early hours, with hopes of spying one of the area's famous chefs. There is also an indoor market on *quai* Tilsitt.

The regular weekend *brocante* market, **Puces de Canal,** is held on the canal. This is in the middle of nowhere, and you might be frightened on first approach. Please don't fret—it's fab. The market is very funky, with an indoor part and an outdoor part and lots of tag-sale types of vendors and tables. It's a local market superb for buyers and market sophisticates. However, if you speak no French and like your markets sugarcoated, this might not be for you. It's open Sunday (the best day, with 400 dealers) from 6am to 1pm; Thursday and Saturday (when there are only 60 dealers) from 8am to noon. You can get here via bus no. 37 or 7.

Cité des Antiquaires, 117 bd. Stalingrad (© 04-72-44-91-98), is very clean, neat, and upmarket. The architecture is a little strange, and the design of the building may lead you to think it is closed. It has clean bathrooms and a good selection of shops, though most are fancy. This is just past the Tête d'Or park and a little out of the way from other shopping. It's open on Sundays until 1pm.

Saturday and Sunday are the best days for old papers and books along the *quai* des Bookinistes, on the left bank of the Saône, where about 20 book and ephemera dealers open their stalls. A few dealers are open during the week, but most of the action is on weekends.

On Sunday from 8am to 1pm, there's a crafts fair on *quai* Romain Rolland, which is in the heart of Old Lyon along the Saône. I find it sort of like your average high-school bazaar with paintings, sculpture, and the usual suspects—but it's still fun. And it's right across the bridge from the book, fruit, flower, and veggie markets—so all in all, do 'em and enjoy the day out.

Every June (usually the third weekend), there's a giant antiques salon, the **Brocante du Vieux Lyon.** And on the first

Thursday of October, the antiques shops on rue Auguste Comte hold open house until 11pm.

The nouveau Beaujolais is released at midnight on the third Wednesday in November. People all over France get together to drink and celebrate, but the goings-on are particularly festive in Lyon.

LILLE

And now to bed. In Lille. After all, Lille is famous as the heartland of French bed linen, the home of Porthault and Descamps, and the address for zillions of outlet stores.

It is also the capital city of northern France, and it turned around to new celebrations of life, art, and tourists when the Eurostar picked Lille as its turnaround city. Trains through the Chunnel all connect in Lille—they turn right to go to Paris and left to go to Brussels. Furthermore, there are whispers that the mayor of Lille wants to be president of France, so she's making sure that everything's up-to-date and working great.

Lille has a kind of architecture you won't see in many other French cities: It has a lot in common with Brussels and gives you more than a little chance to think about the cultural differences between the French and the Flemish. Traditionally speaking, because of the manufacturing, Lille and the rest of the north have been rich cities, and locals have not been shy about showing off their wealth. The architecture here is embellished and even the middle class is into designer clothing. The beer is good, the food flavorful, and the shopping simply super.

Also note that, culturally speaking, Lille is no backwater factory town. In 2004, the city (and surrounding area) became the European City of Culture. The people of Lille not only painted the town red to celebrate, but also turned the inside of the train station pink. Lille has tons of energy and many arts programs in theaters, in opera houses, and even on the street; it also represents a large metro area with villages that actually stretch across the border into Belgium.

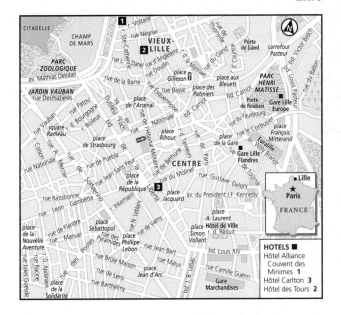

Location, Location, Location

Lille is a mere 10 minutes from the Belgian border and a short distance from Calais. It's slightly northeast of Paris and directly north of Reims. It is equidistant to both Antwerp and Brussels. Thanks to this location, and the connections created by the Eurostar, TGV, and Thalys trains, Lille is one of the most international cities in Europe, with 100 million European citizens living within a 320km (200-mile) radius of the city. Because of the proximity of the U.K., many of them speak English. However, few American tourists visit Lille.

Getting to Lille

If you're coming from Paris, you do not take the Eurostar to Lille. This train takes on passengers, *but does not allow them to disembark*. Instead, take the **Thalys** train, also from Gare du Nord. There are discounted TGV train tickets for a day of shopping from Paris to Lille in the Pret-à-Partir group of pro-motions. The train ride from Paris to Lille is 1 hour.

If you want to drive (not a bad idea), it takes about 2½ hours from the north of Paris to Lille. If you want to do the factory outlets, it's better to have a car. Getting into Lille itself is easy; expect to get lost once you start looking for the outlets.

The Lay of the Land

Like Lyon, Lille is an enormous city with a great spread and many suburbs. If you're on a day trip, you probably won't get to know these suburbs; if you have a car and get to outlets, you'll soon know many of the names of the nearby towns.

The heart of Old Lille (Vieux Lille) is rather small, is eas-ily walked, and can be enjoyed in hours—just be sure you look at all the buildings and their pretty colors before you start lick-ing the store windows.

The center of Lille (a short walk from Old Lille) is the Grand Place, and the nearby Old Bourse is a must-see for its archi-tecture. Don't miss the book market, with its shortcut into the heart of the shopping district in Vieux Lille. Because of the medieval nature of the city, it takes a little longer to get your bearings in the old part of Lille. I suggest repeated shopping forays and patience with a map. I have often been delightfully lost.

The old (pre-Eurostar) train station is named **Gare Lille Flan-dres;** it forms the end of the shopping and central downtown district at one side of town. If you have a choice of train sta-tions for your visit, arrive at this one. Take a nice hard look at the train station—it happens to be an old friend. It was moved, brick by brick, from Paris, where it originally housed the Gare du Nord, the connecting link from Paris to Lille. The pink ceil-ing will be painted out eventually.

From the Grand Place, numerous streets form the spokes of retail: The big chains (even the **Disney Store**) are on rue Neuve, while the department stores (including a good branch of **Au Printemps**) are on rue Nationale. You can take other spokes from the Grand Place, such as rue de la Grand Chaussée, toward the place du Lion d'Or to get deeper into the little medieval streets and hit some of the linen stores.

Away from the center of town, but not far from the original train station, is a double-header: an American-style mall (**Centre Euralille**) and, a block away, the "big" train station built for the arrival of Eurostar, **Gare Lille Europe** (which is noted as *LE* on train schedules). This station is in a contemporary building that's not at all old-fashioned or charming.

Outside town are endless suburbs and connecting cities—more than 100 of them in the metro area. Shoppers will want to remember (even if they can't pronounce) **Wazemmes,** the site of the Sunday-morning flea market. (You can get there on the Métro.) **Roubaix** is a neighboring town, now being renovated; it's home to many outlet stores (and a museum in a swimming pool).

Getting Around Lille

You can do the city center on foot. If you want to give up treks to Porthault and big-time outlets and just go to the outlet mall in Roubaix, you can take public transportation or make a deal with a taxi driver to drop you off and pick you up a few hours (or weeks) later. If you've come to Lille with a car, you'd do best to park in pay lots. Street parking is hard to find.

Sleeping in Lille

HOTEL ALLIANCE COUVENT DES MINIMES
17 quai du Wault.

This four-star hotel, now a member of the Golden Tulip chain, was created from a 12th-century convent. The architecture is grand and the space comfortable enough, though neither glam nor deluxe. It's about a 5-minute walk to the Grand Place. The hotel has 91 units and a restaurant in the cloister; rates are about 125€ ($144) per night, including buffet breakfast. Local phone ✆ **03-20-30-62-62.** Fax 03-20-42-94-25.

Hotel Carlton
3 rue de Paris.

The Carlton has been spruced up and offers a fabulous location, a block from the Grand Place and within walking distance of all the shopping. This four-star hotel is small and not chic or fancy, but it's considered one of the nicest in town. (Johnny Hallyday stays here.)

Rates vary by time of year and promotion; expect to pay from 200€ ($230) on up. The Carlton participates in the two-for-one weekend deal. For dollar rates and promotional deals, call Concorde in the U.S. at © **800/888-4747**. Local phone © 03-20-13-33-13. Fax 03-20-51-48-17. www.concorde-hotels.com.

Hotel des Tours
27 rue des Tours.

If you're fine with three stars, then you'll like this hotel—it has a fabulous location in the heart of Old Town. The property is new; everything is clean, modern, and low-key; and there are mezzanine rooms for families. Rates are about 100€ ($115). Local phone © **03-59-57-47-00**. Fax 03-59-57-47-99. www.hotel-des-tours.com.

Eating in Lille

You'll have no trouble finding cafes and other places to snack and shop—waffles and *frites* (fries) are sold in stands on the streets and in shopping areas, including the factory outlets at Roubaix. In cafes, try local dishes made with a Flemish touch or cooked in Belgian beer.

Le Coq Hardi
44 Grand Place.

This is one of the many cafes on the Grand Place. I like the prices (low), the food (excellent), the regional-style cooking (like that smelly cheese tart), and the location in the heart of everything. Employees here speak English.

L'Huitriere
Rue des Chats Bossus and rue Basse.

This is a very fancy Michelin-starred restaurant and grocery store in the medieval part of town, not far from the place du Lion d'Or. The specialty here is oysters. Don't miss the decorative tiles outside or the decorative touches inside.

Meert
27 rue Esquermoise.

This traditional old-fashioned tearoom for waffles, pastries, chocolates, and the like was established in 1761.

Paul
8 rue de Paris.

Paul is a national chain with many cutie-pie locations around France, but this is where it all began. The flagship cafe is a must-do, and because it's across the street from Hôtel Carlton and in the center of town, it should be an easy assignment. Paul also runs the cafe in the Palais des Beaux Arts, which is fine and nice, but don't miss the attractive sit-down opportunity in town, with wooden beams, tiles, charm, and good stuff to eat any time of the day. It's open daily from 6:30am to midnight.

Shopping in Lille

Lille sees few American visitors, and while it does have a strong tourist business among Brits and other Europeans, the shopping style is very real-people oriented. The outlets are mobbed by both locals and visitors, and locals traditionally make the rounds at their off-price resources once a month or whenever possible, since outlet shopping can be so hit or miss.

There are a few local chains and jobbers that have branches only in northern France. My favorite find is **Fantastik,** a jobber right off the Grand Place that has designer goods being dumped at low, low prices.

Lille also has a blend of established designer names (**Hermès, Lancel,** and so on), new-to-me names, and French multiples and outlet stores. In Old Town, a good bit of the retail is hidden in plain sight—most stores don't have numbers posted, and the streets wind around in an adorable fashion that makes shopping here a treasure hunt. Everything you could want is right within walking distance, allowing you to wander the cute and charming streets.

OUTLETS

There are a lot of outlet stores and many malls in the Lille area, stretching from town all the way to the sea and Calais. If you want to get to some of the outlets, I suggest you have a plan of attack—work with a map and form a basic schedule—before you come to town. Outlet shopping requires a lot of juggling and a good amount of driving, depending on how many stores you're hitting, so start with a basic plan and then be somewhat flexible. Any French bookstore sells guidebooks to the outlets.

On most of my trips to Lille, the Porthault factory—about an hour's drive from downtown Lille—is my number-one priority. Because it is so off the beaten track from everything else, all my plans have to be coordinated with this trip. If you're driving from Paris, this outlet is midway between Paris and Lille, so it makes a great first stop.

Note: I've found that after a certain number of outlets, I begin to crack up. Make your plans based on your known tolerance for this kind of shopping.

In the section "Lille Resources A–Z," below, I've listed the specifics of shopping at those outlets I've personally visited. I found that the opportunities I had more than wiped out my credit rating and my stash of euros. In the end, despite the fact that I had pages of outlet addresses, there wasn't enough time, energy, or money in a weekend to hit much more than Porthault, Old Town, and the big outlet in Roubaix. But there are hundreds of other outlets in the Lille area, so you could spend a month here to shop them all. If you're serious about this pursuit, get one of the outlet books mentioned above.

MARKETS & FAIRS

The Friday edition of the local newspaper has an *On Chine* section listing all nearby flea markets, *brocante* markets, and tag sales.

On the first weekend in September, Lille hosts a giant flea-market street fair called the **Braderie,** which is based on a medieval tradition whereby home owners allowed the servants one day a year to clean out the attic and sell off the master's old junk. Now thousands of vendors line the streets, people eat mussels and drink beer, and they shop way into the night. The market goes on for 24 hours and lasts for 2 to 3 days, so many night owls prefer to shop in the middle of the night. Hotel rooms book up months in advance, so find out the exact dates and book early.

A small antiques and used-book market is held daily in the courtyard of the Old Bourse, right near the Grand Place.

Every Sunday, there's a flea market in the suburb of **Wazemmes,** at place de la Nouvelle Aventure. This one is a winner. *Important note:* To get here, take the Métro from Rihour (downtown) in the Wazemmes direction—but get off at Gambetta. Do *not* get off at Wazemmes.

Because of Lille's location, there are many organized tours that go to flea markets, art markets, and the like. People think nothing of a day trip to the United Kingdom, even all the way to London, or a trip to Maastricht or Bruges or Brussels (which is a great market town). There are even Christmas markets in Germany to think about—you can take an all-day tour to the Christmas market in Cologne. There are also some organized tours to outlets. Ask at the tourist office, 6 place Mendès France, for details.

SHOPPING HOURS

Regular stores in Lille open at 9 or 9:30am, close for lunch, and reopen at 2 or 2:30pm. Some stores open at 10am and stay open all day until 7 or 7:30pm. Stores in Lille are closed on Sunday. Many are also closed Monday morning, but open at 2pm.

Factory hours are different and often specific to the factory; check before you drive out of the way. Factories and outlets stay open on Monday mornings.

SHOPPING NEIGHBORHOODS

For years, I found Lille difficult to grasp—it's not on a grid system, and I have trouble with medieval streets that interconnect and sometimes change names. In the city, you can pretty much wander, get lost, be found, and have a great shopping day. Just head for the Grand Place.

GRAND PLACE   Like every Grand Place, this one has stores, cafes, banks, and everything else you want from a Grand Place. You'll see a branch of **FNAC**, a **Sephora**, and my discount jobber favorite, **Fantastik.**

RUE NATIONALE   This spoke from the Grand Place is home to **Au Printemps** and the big commercial stores. Au Printemps has been renovated and prices are often given in both euros and sterling; it offers a tax-back plan and a tourist discount card.

RUE NEUVE   This spoke from the Grand Place has many real-people stores, such as **Pro Mod, Electre,** and **Pimkie;** it's sort of the teen and tween shopping area.

RUE FAIDHERBE   This is the main street through the center of town, leading from the core of town directly to the Flandres train station. There's a large branch of **Tati,** the discounter.

RUE PARIS   This spoke from Grand Place runs next to Faidherbe and is the street where the Hôtel Carlton is located, so it will help you get your bearings. There's more shopping as you head away from town on rue Paris.

PLACE DU GENERAL DE GAULLE   Yes, de Gaulle was born in Lille. This area adjoins the Grand Place, leads into Old Town, and signifies the beginning of the fancy shopping district. Look for the **Lancel** shop at the edge of the Grand Place and then follow your nose (that's a de Gaulle joke, get it?).

VIEUX LILLE (OLD TOWN)   From the place du Lion d'Or, check out the rue de la Monnaie for vintage shops and other nice clothing, shoe, and home-design stores (owned by those who couldn't quite pay the higher rents a block away). Then cut back around the Cathedral Nôtre Dame de la Treille for more backstreets with a few jobbers and some antiques shops. The streets run together here and don't really need names. This is a pedestrian-only area located behind the Grand Place between rue Esquermoise and boulevard Carnot (though not including Carnot). You'll find C&A, Camaieu, NafNaf, Zara, and more. The best shopping streets in the Old Town are rue Esquermoise, rue des Chats Bossus, rue du Curé St-Etienne, and rue Basse.

Lille Resources A–Z

ANTIQUES

The part of town with the most antiques shops is right near the Cathedral Nôtre Dame de la Treille, although I did not go nuts for antiques in these stores. Better to wait for the flea market on Sundays or the Braderie in September.

BATH & BEAUTY

MARIONNAUD
Grand Place.

This is a chain of beauty and perfume stores organized by a Frenchman to compete with Sephora; it's not as fancy as Sephora, and the prices and selection are a little more middle-class in order to appeal to locals rather than tourists.

NOUS SAVONS TOUT
45 rue Esquermoise.

And you didn't know the French had a sense of humor? The name of this soap store takes the cake, as far as I'm concerned. It's also a fun shop filled with a variety of bath products.

SEPHORA
Grand Place.

This is not the largest Sephora you will ever see, but it's still a perfectly good example of the beauty supermarket that has become an international chain and shopping icon. It carries everything from designer products to some U.S. brands to its own line to dime-store brands to professional makeup to animal-shaped bath beads. If you meet the *détaxe* requirement, the discount will be applied to your purchase immediately.

BIG NAMES

In Old Town, you can find most of the world's big names: Anne Fontaine, Cartier, Façonnable, Gerard Darel, Hermès, Kenzo Homme, Lancel, Laura Ashley, Longchamp, Sonia Rykiel, Versace Jeans, and Zara. Remember that most Lille stores don't have numbers posted and the Old Town streets wind around—you'll have to hunt around.

CHEESE & OTHER FOODSTUFFS

AUX BONS FROMAGES
13 rue du Curé St-Etienne.

This shop specializes in cheeses from the northern parts of France.

LES BONS PATURAGES
54 rue Basse.

Totally different in feel from Philippe Oliver (see below), this is almost a cute deli-style store with some ready-made food along with wine and cheese. The food items are mostly cheese-based.

PHILIPPE OLIVER
3 rue Curé St-Etienne.

This small but well-known cheese shop also makes the regional specialty, *Flamiche au Maroilles,* which I call the smelly cheese tart. If you're a fan of strongly flavored (and scented) cheese, this is a winner.

DEPARTMENT STORES

AU PRINTEMPS
45 rue Nationale.

This branch of the Paris-based department store is large, well stocked, and chic—a pleasure to shop. There's a 10% discount offered at the Welcome Desk (just show your passport) and an additional 12% tax-back refund if you spend 175€ ($201) in the store in a single day.

TATI
Rue Faidherbe.

There are two different Tati stores next door to each other, so don't miss any of it, if you can cope with bins of junk piled high.

DISCOUNTERS

EURODIF
Rue de la Bourse.

I never know if I should call Eurodif a discounter or a department store; technically, it probably isn't a discounter—it just seems like one to me. This is a fit-all-your-needs multi-level store that sells great stuff (clothes, home style, gifts) for not much money. Eurodif is owned by Bouchara; in most stores, the wares are combined under one roof—only in Paris are they two different resources. This shop stays open on Mondays and during lunch.

FANTASTIK
Place de la République.

This store will not appeal to the tender shopper. It truly is just bins and bins of stuff, everything all very hit or miss. There are three floors of merchandise, and although it's organized into men's, women's, kids and teens, and home, you do have to poke around. My best find? Designer sunglasses for 8.70€ ($10).

PASS BY COLETTE
2 rue St-Jacques, place du Lion d'Or.

This fancy store in the heart of Old Town sells mostly over-stock. The clothes are new, not used; they come from every big designer name in France and Italy; and they have a color-ful and sometimes ethnic feel. Closed Sunday and Monday.

FACTORY OUTLETS

BELGRAND
20 av. de Dunkerque, Cambrai.

This is a large Rodier outlet that sells men's and women's things as well as accessories. The prices are low, but the real giveaways are the sale items—they often go for 10€ ($12) per piece. Bel-grand is about 5 minutes from the Porthault factory; you will pass it automatically. The phone number is ✆ 03-27-72-72-77. Hours are Monday through Saturday from 9:30am to 6:30pm. In July and August, the store is closed on Mondays.

MAGASINS D'USINE
228 av. Alfred Motte, Roubaix.

Rather yucky, crowded, hard to shop, devoid of charm, and a jumble of fun if you like this kind of thing. I do; most don't. It's mobbed on Saturdays and a parking space is always hard to find. You can take public transportation to Roubaix and then a taxi to get here, but you won't think it's worth it. Open Monday through Saturday from 10am to 7pm.

MARQUES AVENUE COTE D'OPALE
Bd. du Parc, Coquelles.

This new 80-store outlet mall is not worth the extra drive from Lille, but if you're in the Calais area anyway, you can make a stop. Marques Avenue has very smartly put itself right near the mouth of Le Shuttle, the tunnel for vehicular traffic to the U.K. From Lille, the beach is about 30 minutes north of the city. If you're coming from Calais, you can get here by bus, train, or car (take the A16 autoroute to exit 12). Closed Sundays. For more information, go to www.marquesavenue.com.

McArthur Glen
44 mail de Lannoy, Roubaix.

This American-style outlet mall in the heart of downtown Roubaix is the stuff of retail legends. I would write a dissertation on it if I ever got my official degree in shopping. The mall is built right on city streets as part of an urban reclamation project. It is not the best outlet center in Lille, but it has plenty of name brands and is both easy to get to and easy to shop. Lacoste, Nitya, Adidas, Nike, and Leonard (glass and tabletop) all have stores here, as do some of the bed-linen people. (The best of the linen outlets is **Sous-Signe,** which has branches both here and at L'Usine.) Parking is located underground. The area has been cleaned up enormously, and the mall is the heart of it all. You can get here easily and directly from Lille by tram or Métro—get off at the Eurotéléport stop. Closed Sundays.

Porthault
19 rue Robespierre, Rieux-en-Cambrésis.

The Porthault factory is about an hour outside Lille; it's not hard to get to, but if you drive, you should be used to driving in France. It is in the middle of nowhere, and you might lose heart while driving because the factory itself is not marked. You should speak some French and have a phone or phone card on you so that if you do get lost, you can call the factory for directions.

What's available in terms of selection is very hit or miss. Prices are laughably low, running from 10% to 50% of the regular retail price. I think the pillowcases are the best buy, but I have also stocked up on robes, towels, baby gifts, and even *gant de toilette.*

Porthault accepts credit cards and has a toilet you can use. If you get there and the outlet—which is in a gatehouse—is closed, go to the offices and ask them to open up for you. Also ask to get on the mailing list, and you'll be notified of the dates of the outlet sales. Hours are Monday through Thursday from 10am to noon and 1 to 4:30pm. Closed in August.

Here are basic directions: Head south from Lille on Autoroute du Nord, A1. Connect to N43 in the direction of Cambrai. In Cambrai, take N44 to the left for Rieux-en-Cambrésis. You will not notice that this is a factory or that it is Porthault, as it's unmarked. Look for the factory chimney and the ironwork at the gates. Drive into the tiny courtyard and park. At the reception desk, ask to visit the shop. Expect to get lost. I recommend calling ahead (✆ 03-27-82-22-33) and telling them when you're coming.

FINDS

N DE B
6 rue Jean-Jacques Rousseau.

This local hatmaker is the fabulous, creative winner of many national design prizes. The N is for the first name of the creator, Nathalie Sarazin. Closed Mondays.

TERRE DE BRUYERE
39 rue Lepelletier.

This shop has a mother store in Paris's 6e, but it is not well known, even in Paris. The specialty is fashion handbags made like fishing or hunting bags. It's a weekendy look that is chic and sophisticated yet casual. Bags are very well made; prices begin around 160€ ($184).

HOME STYLE

Lille has many stores devoted to home style; more and more seem to open all the time. All major brands of furniture are here, as are the mass-market linen stores and linen outlets.

Because of the proximity of Great Britain, the English look is very popular. Still, don't miss the **Flamart** shop for a study in French country chic that's both glam and comfy. You'll find high-style but low-cost items at **Bouchara** and **Eurodif.**

Le Prince Jardinier, 66 rue Esquermoise, has expanded from Paris for tabletop, furniture, gifts, and garden/outdoor decorative items. **Geneviève Lethu** is on the same street (no. 84).

MALLS

EURALILLE
Av. le Corbusier.

This is a commercial center in the heart of downtown; it has a branch of the *hypermarché* (modern dry-goods store) **Carrefour** (which opens at 9am) and many other major multiples and brand stores.

BIARRITZ

Biarritz, which was once enormously chic (its heyday was 1890–1930), has been rediscovered by American tourists, many of whom come to see the surrounding Pays Basque—the French and Spanish Basque country and the Frank Gehry–designed Guggenheim museum in Bilbao.

Meanwhile, the British are flying directly from the U.K. and bypassing the rest of France, as if Biarritz were their own personal secret. You can also fly between Paris and Bilbao.

The sprawl of beach and splendor leading from Spain into France has always been known to local aristocracy and royalty, but never really made it to the American tourist agenda—until now. With its famous surf, many promotional events, some world-class hotels with treatment and therapy centers, and the proximity of the Guggenheim, Biarritz is becoming more of a must-do. To Americans, this is a neighborhood that might as well be called Biarritz-Bilbao; they come not for the textiles but for the art and a chance to see Jeff Koons's *Puppy.*

Although Biarritz was put on the map when Napoléon III built his Spanish empress a summerhouse here, what the world doesn't remember is that Biarritz was firmly located on the medieval pilgrim path to Santiago de Compostela. This prime location certainly meant something to the Empress Eugénie, and it also means a lot now, in terms of the centuries of culture and trade that have followed the path you are about to explore.

Biarritz isn't really in the middle of nowhere. It's been in the middle of somewhere since, well, the Middle Ages. Santiago de Compostela is one of the most special places in the world, and while it's a bit far to be considered a day trip from Biarritz, it is part of the hidden layers of secrets that await you in this corner of both Spain and France.

Because of the Schengen Convention laws, the border between Spain and France has "disappeared." You can cross without your passport—no stopping at immigration. In fact, the immigration stalls have been abandoned. *Vaya conmigo.*

Basque Style

Southwestern France has a warm Spanish country tradition. The colors move away from the dark blues associated with seafaring design or the warm blues associated with the Mediterranean and into yellows, golds, and baked earth tones. The fishing influence is found, of course, in everything from espadrilles to striped T-shirts. Think Picasso.

Those espadrilles, berets, and Basque linens are three of the most important stylistic ingredients that have come from the Basque region, where flax and wool have been grown for centuries. They have permeated not only French style but also international chic. If the Pink Panther wears a beret to signify that he's French, it's because the beret has become a virtual visual signature for the Frenchman—despite the fact that few people in Paris wear berets.

Despite globalization and even the unification of nations, most European countries are in their hearts still regions or fiefdoms. To the French, Provence and the Côte d'Azur are nice, but expensive and touristy. In the meantime, southwestern chic has become the new regional style for home and table. The pottery manufacturer Poc à Poc sells a look it calls *l'esprit Catalan*. There's a whole new kind of French design here for you to start shopping for . . . along with a new way of eating and cooking.

Basque Linen 101

For centuries, the agricultural area stretching from Aquitaine north to the Basque country has been linen-producing land. The Basque-style linens have a famed and specific look, available in traditional or contemporary forms (contemporary is a color concept; the style never changes).

The linens are either natural (sort of beige-y) or white (bleached white), and lined with stripes. The number of stripes, the width of the stripes, and the color of the stripes are the variable factors. If you think, *yawn,* stripes, you are so wrong—even the simplest stripes represent a very pure chic, while the bolder designs are almost all colored stripes with little white in between.

Getting to Biarritz

From Paris, you can either fly or take the train (TGV service from Gare Montparnasse). There are 14 trains a day; note that it's a rather long schlep (about 5 hr.). But wait! Here's the big news: The discount airline **Ryanair** (www.ryanair.com) flies from London-Stansted to Biarritz-Parme. The airport will have expanded by 2007; all major carriers are expected then.

I once drove to Biarritz from Cannes, by way of Provence. It's a long drive from the Riviera; do not make the mistake of thinking you can do it in a day or that France is a small country. When you're driving east to west, you'll find that France is a big country with small roads.

The Lay of the Land

Biarritz has always been a resort city, a place for royalty and aristocrats. It's situated at the edge of the rocky Atlantic coast, and although there is a big, beautiful beach, what makes Biarritz so magical are the ragged edges of the rocks, the pounding of the sea, and the rugged land. The Riviera stands for calm seas; Biarritz, in contrast, is all energy and waves.

Many of the people who work in Biarritz live in Bayonne, which is a few miles away. Some of the goods sold in Biarritz are also sold here, at much lower prices. Biarritz is also near the coastal fishing village of St-Jean-de-Luz, which makes a lovely outing. It's not far from the Spanish border, and it's an easy day trip to San Sebastian or Bilbao.

Centre ville in Biarritz has a surprising number of neighborhoods; this is not the one-lane town you might expect. The city has layers and levels, and the main street winds down to the sea. This city was designed for the promenade, so you'll find plenty of wide sidewalks to browse.

You have to love any town that has a big Hermès sign on top of a biscuit-colored stucco villa, a town where you can turn a blind corner and suddenly see the sea shining between the buildings or the enormous wrought-iron gates at the foot of the shopping street. The gates welcome you to the Hôtel du Palais and a town of incredible glamour.

Getting Around Biarritz

Biarritz is easily walked; the Hôtel du Palais is right in the heart of things.

To get to the nearby villages (or Spain), you'll need a car. There is an autoroute, so driving is relatively easy. There is no formal border with Spain.

Sleeping in Biarritz

HÔTEL DU PALAIS
1 av. de l'Impératrice.

You can actually afford the fanciest hotel in France! Because Biarritz is a little away from the swing of things, prices—even for the grandest of life's little dreams—are moderate, and lower than at comparable hotels in Paris, the Riviera, or

Provence. Although this hotel was created out of a palace (hence the name), it has been renovated; an enormous new spa is set to open sometime in 2005.

The Hôtel du Palais isn't inexpensive, but if you consider the fact that you're sleeping in the private home of the emperor and his empress, with the ocean outside your window, and in the resort town that ends all questions about chic, then you actually have a bargain. The average rate in season is 250€ ($288). For all available rates in dollars, call Concorde in the U.S. at © **800/888-4747**. Local phone © 05-59-41-64-00. www.hotel-du-palais.com.

Treatments in Biarritz

It's not unusual for a couple to sign up for a *forfait* (package) that includes hotel, meals, and treatments at any of the *thalassotherapie* (seawater-related spa treatments) centers in Biarritz. More and more men enjoy these treatments, and the weekend, long-weekend, or 1-week cures for "well being" are common (and sometimes paid for by French health care). Sofitel has an entire division of treatment centers, including one in Biarritz. The Hôtel du Palais hopes to knock the world on its hotel slippers with the opening of its new spa in 2005.

Shopping in Biarritz

Biarritz is an unusual town for shoppers. There are plenty of stores and lots of places to roam, because being out and about is part of the local etiquette. Most of the interesting shops are related to foodstuffs or candy or linens. There are some designer shops, but not an overwhelming number. There are no big malls or commercial centers, especially downtown. It's a very low-key kind of place.

You will find a small business in antiques, with shops scattered here and there; a few discount stores (one resale shop, one shop for clothes without their labels), in the main part of downtown; and a very good bookstore. There's a nice New

England feel to the shopping, but there's no pressure to buy and no pressure to be incredibly chic, like on the Riviera. The look is very much jeans, espadrilles, blazers, and Hermès scarves. And very good jewelry. In fact, Harry Winston just opened a new store here.

SHOPPING NEIGHBORHOODS

PALAIS Along the avenue de la Reine Victoria, there are shops on both the left- and right-hand sides. There are more stores on the avenue de l'Impératrice, such as **Cerrutti 1881** and **Alain Figaret,** which is well known to the French for men's ties with a certain type of silk design. Alain Figaret is also known for his dress shirts for both men and women. As you leave Palais and head toward the high street, you'll see more designer shops, like **Sonia Rykiel.**

THE HIGH STREET: AVENUE EDOUARD VII If you didn't know better, you would think this was the only main drag in town. It's where the branches of the big names (such as Hermès) are located. It leads to the place Clemenceau and the center of town, which is anchored by the department store **Nouvelles Galeries,** which has a supermarket in its basement. If you're driving across France, or simply spending time between Biarritz and Bordeaux, this could be your last convenient time to do French grocery shopping, so load up now.

HIDDEN HIGH STREET: RUE GAMBETTA Who would have thunk it? Biarritz has a second high street. This one is not so easily found and is a little more real-people oriented. However, it's laden with enough seaside tourist traps (TTs) and linen shops to make you glad you came on down.

REAL-PEOPLE UPTOWN Leading in and out of town is yet another high street, avenue du Maréchal Foch, which has more shops for real people and a tiny strip mall that houses a few multiples such as Rodier and Cacharel. There's also a *marché* (market) for everyday, plus more food and gourmet shops one street over, on avenue Victor Hugo—including two that are mentioned by foodies the world over: Mille et Un Fromage (no. 8) and Maison Arosteguy (no. 5).

FINDS

AU BUFFLE D'EAU
8 av. Edouard VII.

I think the name of this shop is a pun in French, although none of the leather goods here seem to actually be made from buffalo. They're put together with such elegant style that you won't be able to sleep at night until you've conquered the large-size Kelly bag.

DAURY
2 av. de la Reine Victoria.

This is resort chic at its best: the kind of store that sells beautiful gifts, tabletop designs, and some antiques in such a way as to make you want to move right in. When you get to shop in places like this, where everything is displayed so beautifully, the magic of Biarritz becomes even more real. Whether you buy anything or not, don't miss a trip here. It's almost directly across the street from Hôtel du Palais.

GOTCHA
21 rue Mazagran.

Surf's up, dudes. This shop is owned by the area's premier surfer king; my son insisted I give you the address. Teens and tweens hang here—or hang ten here.

HELENA
33 rue Mazagran.

One of the many linen stores in Biarritz, this one works for me because its color palette is different—Helena has natural linen, which is beige, trimmed with coral. (Most shops sell a hard white trimmed with primary colors.) Prices are also rather reasonable; I paid about 65€ ($75) for a gigantic table-cloth. Other products for sale here include bathrobes, slippers, aprons, oven mitts, and all sizes and shapes of table linens. The staff does not speak English, but is very friendly about opening up the linen and spreading it so you can see the true size. Wash your find in cool water the first time so the color doesn't run.

HENRIET
Place Clemenceau.

Henriet is a local status brand. As funky as Pariès is (see below), this store just across the street is both fancy and for-mal. It sells pastries, homemade chocolates, fruit and nut can-dies, its own candy bars (great gifts at about 1.75€/$2 each), and adorable little chocolate cakes. The price (about 35€/$40) for a kilo of the califruits isn't bad, considering the quality and the subtext that comes with the gift.

PARIES
27 place Clemenceau.

In a town filled with candy shops, this one stands out as my favorite. Pariès is the maker of a local treat called *kanougas*. For those of you who have tasted your way across France, loosen your belt. A *kanouga* is a regional Basque treat, sort of like fudge-meets-taffy, but not as hard or crunchy as nougat. In fact, it's a gooey flavored caramel. I've gone flat bonkers for the chocolate ones, which are made using the shop owner's fam-ily recipe, handed down through the generations.

You can buy *kanougas* in a bag of mixed flavors (the col-ors of the wrapping paper indicate the different flavors), or you can just buy a kilo of the chocolate and get it over with.

The shop also sells candied fruit rinds, traditional Basque candies, and even *tourons,* which are Spanish-style candy loaves, cut to suit. Oh yes, you can also get pastries and local *gâteaux,* (cake) as well as macaroons and other yummies, such as homemade black-cherry jam.

Sandales d'Eugenie
18 rue Mazagran.

Be it the Empress Eugénie, Cinderella, or simply a barefoot contessa, these locally made sandals have been the vogue since the 1930s. The stylish, slip-on espadrille styles would cut the mustard or make waves in any city in the world. This is not peasant or resort wear.

Nearby Local Hero

Jean Vier
Route St-Jean-de-Luz.

Be still my greedy heart! How I love this look, and how I would have bet the farm that this would become the next Pierre Deux. I'd have given anything to own a string of shops from this brand in every mall in America. Alas, there are no stores at all. But this is the factory and its outlet store, located between Biarritz and St-Jean-de-Luz.

Traditional Basque linens are sold from the shop. They're not dirt cheap, but they're the best quality in the world and worth the trip to France.

Real-People Shopping

You can visit branches of **Jean Louis David** or **Jacques Dessange** should you need to get your hair done. **Parfumerie Frimousse,** right in the heart of town, sells the basics. **Nouvelles Galeries** is the local branch of Galeries Lafayette; it's a low-end department store that has a grocery store in the basement, and it carries many health and beauty aids you might need. It's also a place for cheap thrills for the kids.

THE SUBURBS & SPAIN

....

Bayonne

Bayonne is the large city on the other side of the bay from Biarritz; it's where the real people live. The shopping isn't great, but it can be fun and funky. There is a full **Galeries Lafayette** at 23–30 rue Thiers. But I wouldn't drive all the way here just for this department store; besides, Nouvelles Galeries in Biarritz is much the same, only smaller.

St-Jean-de-Luz

This is a small beach community halfway between Biarritz and the border. It will someday be ruined, but for now it's relatively authentic. Sometimes small cruise ships come to call here. If you want to stay overnight, the best choice is town is the **Grand Hôtel** (© 05-59-26-35-36; www.luzgrandhotel.fr), a member of the Concorde chain.

Beyond Those Borders

Since the border stations are deserted or nonexistent, you will breeze into Spain without even sighing about the rain that stays mainly on the plain. Instead, you'll be shocked by the size of San Sebastián (it's not the small fishing village you were expecting) and how much is going on in Bilbao, which was once an industrial wasteland but is now abloom.

Some people make Bilbao a day trip from Biarritz, but you deserve at least an overnight. The city has its own airport, which like many other smaller airports is suddenly getting a lot of flights. Spending the night in Bilbao has gotten a lot more chic—there are scads of new and very artsy hotels, including a **Sheraton** (© 34-94-428-0000; www.sheratonbilbao.com).

Chapter Seven

....

SHOPPING PROVENCE

WELCOME TO PROVENCE

Most of us think of Provence as a series of tiny villages of post-card perfection, made up of colors like ochre, washed turquoise, burnt umber, and geranium red; home of vines and lavender and more soap suds than you can imagine. True, all of it true, but it's the industrial revolution that connects you to these elements—either the TGV train (3 hr. from Paris to Marseille), a flight into a nearby airport (many low-cost carriers head this way), or a cruise right into the port.

No matter which way you arrive, Marseille and Provence are now at your fingertips; despite the fact that Marseille is a very large city—and may not be on your itinerary—it is the gateway to Provence. The train track from Paris to Marseille is the new spine of Provence.

Avignon is a mere 2½ hours from Paris on the fast train, and Aix is 2 hours and 40 minutes from Paris. Whole new parts of Provence—especially northern Provence and the Drôme—are coming into vogue, partly because of the ease now offered by the train. All of France is doing the foxtrot.

The train itself is also a new icon, with or without its designer decorations by Christian Lacroix—it reduces a long journey to a short one and lays the cornerstone for an international train system that will soon connect to Barcelona and then branch in all directions to cover the face of Europe, uniting people not only with euros but also with quick-rail train tracks.

Marseille and Provence are so intertwined that they share an airport and a history, going back to Roman times. Actually, the airport does not go back to Roman history, but you get my drift. For this reason, I begin the city listings in this chapter with Marseille and then proceed in alphabetical order.

Getting to Provence

BY PLANE   Marseille has a fabulous international airport, so you can fly in from many destinations in Europe as well as from Paris. The Marseille airport lies directly between Marseille and Aix, which is why it is officially named the Marseille–Provence International Airport.

The Nice–Côte d'Azur International Airport (NCE) is not a bad choice at all, and it has the benefit of the nonstop Delta flight from New York. Nice is about a 2-hour drive on the autoroute from Aix-en-Provence, 2½ to 3 hours from Marseille. The road is clearly marked as you get on the A8 right near NCE.

There are also a number of smaller local airports; the one in Avignon is quite popular with locals for quick hops to Paris.

Some of the smaller regional airports (Toulouse, Carcassonne) are in the news because they're served by discount airlines that connect them to the U.K. or other E.U. cities. Meanwhile, the city of Marseille has announced it wants a bigger share of the discount-airline pie and is building a special terminal for these carriers, to open in 2006. Marseille is already served by several low-cost carriers.

BY TRAIN   Train travel along the Paris-Marseille route is up 40%, and all anyone can talk about is the impact of the train on everyday life. The Gare St-Charles has been spruced up since the arrival of the TGV Méditerranée; if you're continuing on to Cannes-Nice-Monaco, you might change trains here. (Or you might not; some trains go through. Check your ticket.)

For the most ease, buy your tickets through **RailEurope** (© 888/382-7245; www.raileurope.com) while still in the U.S.,

Provence

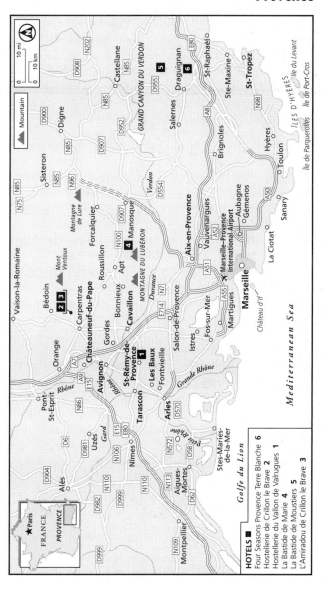

HOTELS ■

Four Seasons Provence Terre Blanche **6**
Hostellerie de Crillon le Brave **2**
Hostellerie du Vallon de Valrugues **1**
La Bastide de Marie **4**
La Bastide de Moustiers **5**
L'Amiradou de Crillon le Brave **3**

as the deals in France are mostly reserved for those who buy 8 or 30 days in advance. You can buy either single-leg tickets or any of a number of multiple-trip passes.

If you speak enough French to carry it off, there are various train rates and promotions for locals—such as discounts for large families, those over 60, those ages 12 to 24, and so on. Many of these require proof of French residence.

Getting Around Provence

BY CAR   You really can't "do" Provence without driving. Well, you can, but you won't get to fight with your spouse or your family or your loved ones. For information on car-rental firms and deals, see p. 20.

Meanwhile, you will need two types of maps: a big one that gives an overview of the area and another that shows details and back roads. If you have not done so before your arrival in the area, get out the bigger map and circle your target cities and make a daily plan. Yes, that's a pun in French, but one that's apropos: A *plan* is a map, and you need a map plan.

Many of the most attractive cities, towns, and villages in Provence are close to one another, but it's hard to know how to get to them all or how to plan how much time you're going to need. Without planning, you might not be able to connect the dots in a sensible way. Furthermore, there's a good bit of spread to Provence, which you might not grasp until you factor in how far apart places are and how difficult the roads can be.

You might also find that a village you read about or dreamed of does not touch you the way you thought it would, or that getting into town and parking are such a nightmare that you are no longer enchanted with that town. After a day or two, you may want to remap your assault and revamp your dreams.

Here are some other tips on driving in Provence:

- Driving in Provence may not be the romantic interlude you dreamed it would be. My late husband and I went on a 2-week driving trip across the south of France; we soon found that getting in and out of the famous towns was grounds for divorce. Getting from the highway into the tourist part of Aix took about an hour and almost caused marital split. We gave up Arles, Antibes, and Nîmes due to traffic congestion and signs that led us in circles. Eventually we took to towns that were easy for us. Easy became more fun; not-so-famous became our finest memories.

- God help those who drive to icon cities in July or August; the traffic is unbearable. You can get from Cannes to St-Tropez in an hour or so off season; in season, it can take 4 hours. Make sure the car you rent has air-conditioning. If you don't want to be stuck in traffic jams, don't leave your resort except by foot.

- Driving is a better sport for two people than for one. You'll have to pull over at times to study the map unless you have someone to call out directions every time you come to a *rond point* (rotary). Or sometimes you just have to drive around the rotary two or three times until you can do it while reading the map.

- When making your map plan, take into consideration the days of the week, since you'll want to hit certain cities on market day. Get to the market early. Those that sell food almost always close by 1pm. There is also more traffic on market day, since there are more people in town.

- You can pay tolls with a credit card. But you cannot buy gas at an automatic-payment pump with a non-French credit card. You can use any credit card at the register or booth, but auto-pay pumps take only French debit cards.

- There are usually bathrooms near the pay stations on the autoroute, and they are clean. They may not be marked, but if you look for the *P*, which means parking, you'll find a pay phone and a toilet.

- French highways are dotted with excellent road stops, all with the word *Aire* in the name. There are basically two kinds. One has an icon of a pine tree (I call this **Aire de Pine-tree**); this kind of rest stop has parking and toilets. Then there's **Aire de Coffee Cup,** marked with an icon of a—you guessed it. These have a gas station with a boutique, very clean bathrooms, and all sorts of other amenities. I'd hold out for the coffee cups unless you're desperate. They come up about every 30km (19 miles).

- Driving around eats money like mad. If you aren't used to driving in France, maybe this is a good time to tell you that pay roads are outrageously expensive and gas prices are frightfully high. Expect to spend 261€ to 435€ ($300–$500) in gas and tolls for a week's driving in the Riviera and/or Provence.

- Remember to gas up at *hypermarchés* (modern dry-goods stores) and to avoid the more expensive stations on the autoroute or in the center of town. The difference between 1€ and 1.15€ ($1.15 and $1.35) is enormous when it comes to paying for a tank of gas. The average small car's tank is 50 liters.

- Please remember that the larger the city, the more roads, the more suburbs, the more ring roads, and the more complications in getting to the center of town. Very often there are so many one-way streets that even if you can remember how you got into town, you can't use the same route to get out. Expect to get lost.

- When approaching a major city, follow the signs to *centre ville*. If you're spending the night in town, have directions to your hotel and an address and phone number handy—not buried in your suitcase. If needed, call for specific directions in English before you arrive.

- A *télécarte* (electronic phone card) will help you call your hotel from a pay phone while you're on the road (if you don't have a cellphone with you). Buy one at a news kiosk.

- Once you've chosen a village for exploration, make sure you understand how to pay for the parking.

- Try this trick: Locate the part of town you want to explore by foot and then, before looking for a parking space, drive around to check it out. This gives you an idea of directions, of street parking, and of parking lots. You'll also know where the shops are, where you want to go, and maybe even how long you want to spend in town. Or you may decide you've seen enough.

- Each day when you leave your hotel for a new hotel and a new city, get detailed directions, preferably marked on a map. Do not waste time with road numbers, as they are rarely marked—and never when you need to make a quick decision. You need city directionals. The only good directions in France are based on city place names; directions such as *east* or *north* are useless.

BY BUS   Provence is pretty well connected by regional buses. You don't do long haul, but you can do short hop. If you find the right hub city, you can do a good bit with buses, although you won't have a lot of flexibility in terms of scheduling.

BY TRAIN   You can buy a France railpass or any of a number of other passes that allow you to hop on and off trains (p. 22). You must get such a pass from **Rail Europe** before you leave the U.S. Passes bought in Europe are similar, but are called **Domino** passes and require proof of E.U. residency.

If you plan a train trip punctuated by 3-day stays, and move across the south of France by train, you will indeed see a lot—and never know the emotions involved with traffic, tour buses, French cars that don't start without a computer code, or signs that point to all directions.

The TGV Méditerranée is building new stations and adding faster tracks—work should be completed between 2005 and 2007. The new station at Les Arcs–Draguignan will make a big impact on visits to both Provence and the Côte d'Azur.

Please remember that many of these new TGV stations bear the name of the town you think you are going to visit, but are, in fact, way out of town. This is now the case in Avignon, Valence, and Aix.

Sleeping in Provence

Even when I have a car, I find myself torn between two different methods of booking hotels: choosing those that are located in city centers, so that I can at least walk around in that town, and choosing those that are romantic and adorable and in the middle of nowhere, but possess great charm and a fair kitchen. Your own preference in this matter will lead you to specific hotel choices and overnight destinations.

You must also decide if you like staying in a different hotel every night and moving on every morning, even if you're moving only 81km (50 miles), or if you prefer to use a certain city as a hub and return to it each night. (No, Marseille is not an appropriate hub.)

I think the easiest way to get around Provence is to pick one or more hub areas with a hotel you can relate to; then stay for a few days (weeks, months, years). Go out on day trips from your hub, even if it means a little extra driving during the days and some doubling back. At least you won't have to pack up your belongings (and purchases) each night.

Note that there are no Hiltons in Provence and few Sofitels. Mostly there's funky, and there's funky grand deluxe. And then there's the new Four Seasons (see below). The places I've chosen as hub hotels are all luxury properties with well-known chefs. They allow you to hole up in comfort and step out into the real world at leisure.

Study your map and your needs before you book. Provence isn't that large, but it's plenty big—and it has distinctly different neighborhoods and areas. Often I don't even return to places I've been before, simply because there's so much to do and you've gotta make choices. By choosing a hub, you begin to choose your shopping destiny.

The hotels listed below are in various districts of Provence, and are presented to help you sort out which cities and shopping experiences best fit your plans. I usually do 2 to 3 nights in an area and then move on; I'm just too old for 1-night stands. However, now that I've been to the Four Seasons in Fayence, I'm thinking about never leaving.

CENTRAL PROVENCE

HOSTELLERIE DU VALLON DE VALRUGUES
Chemin Canto Cigalo, St-Rémy.

Area & Cities: St-Rémy, Tarascon, Les Baux, Salon, L'Isle sur la Sorgue, Aix

Départements: Bouches des Rhône (13), Vaucluse (84)

Despite the fact that I cannot pronounce the name of this hotel (and to this day still call it "That V de V place"), I booked it years ago and considered it my own personal find. To experience the fanciful and sprawling villa, the rooms decorated in Provençal fabrics, and a famous chef is all part of the dream. Although on the edge of town, the hotel really isn't within walking distance of downtown St-Rémy.

The regular rack rate for a double is about 250€ ($288) in season. For reservations, call ℂ **800/553-5090** in the U.S. Local phone ℂ 04-90-92-04-40. www.valrugues-cassagne.com.

EASTERN PROVENCE

FOUR SEASONS PROVENCE TERRE BLANCHE
Château de Terre Blanche, Tourrettes.

Area & Cities: Cannes, Nice, St-Tropez, Moustiers-Ste-Marie

Départements: Alpes Maritimes (06), Var (83)

The Four Seasons is located in the hills nestled between several towns. Locals refer to it as being in Fayence, even though the mailing address for the hotel is Tourrettes. Calling this a hotel is also misleading.

The resort at Terre Blanche is a village unto itself, a getaway from the real world. There's nothing foreign about it, although the styling is rustic and somewhat Provençal. Surrounded by two golf courses with a private clubhouse and a series of little lanes built up with tiny casitas (two apartments per casita), the hotel doesn't feel French at all; it feels more international, speaking the common language of luxury.

Everyone gets a suite, as there are no single rooms. You can also get a whole house, of course. Some have private pools; all have vistas.

Although billed as a golf resort, there is a small spa and a gourmet kitchen. Many of the apartments have kitchens as well. You are in Provence, but just above Cannes and not far from St-Tropez, so day trips are easy.

Note: If it's your first time here, don't attempt the drive in the dark. The hotel will provide directions. It's 45 minutes from the Nice–Côte d'Azur airport, about 3 hours from Marseille.

Rates begin at 400€ ($460) per night. Ask about packages and promotional rates to introduce the property. Call ✆ **800/ 819-5053** for reservations from the U.S. Local phone ✆ 04-94-39-90-00. www.fourseasons.com/provence.

LA BASTIDE DE MOUSTIERS
La Grisolière, Moustiers-Ste-Marie.

Area & Cities: Lorgues, Fayence, Moustiers-Ste-Marie, Manosque, Digne, Forcalquier

Départements: Var (83), Alpes de Haute Provence (04)

La Bastide de Moustiers is higher up in the hills than the Four Seasons—it seems much further from Cannes and Nice. It's on the edge of a very famous shopping town that's filled with stores selling the local *faience* (painted, glazed, monochromatic earthenware). This hotel was the first of superchef Alain Ducasse's country inns. Compared to the Four Seasons, this choice feels much smaller and much more French.

There's a baffling list of choices and prices, each based on weekends and seasons, but figure about 300€ ($345) a night in season. Guests can choose from a few cottages, including the very private pigeon house. Take a look at www.bastide-moustiers.com for photos of each room; they vary in terms of style, use of space, showers or tubs (ask for the Philippe Starck tub), and adjoining space for the kids. Local phone ✆ 04-92-70-47-47.

THE LUBERON

LA BASTIDE DE MARIE
Route de Bonnieux, Quartier de la Verrerie, Ménerbes.

Area & Cities: Ménerbes, Roussillon, Lourmarin, the Luberon

Département: Vaucluse (84)

Yes, Ménerbes is the city that Peter Mayle made famous in his first book about Provence, and yes, this is one of the most plush rustic properties in France. It's been featured in every international design magazine you can imagine and combines the idea of country charm with the capabilities of a small hotel.

La Bastide de Marie is owned by the family that holds La Compagnie des Hôtels de Montagne—which includes a luxury hotel in Lyon and one outside St-Tropez (so don't be fooled by the mountain bit). Created from an old farmhouse and decorated in country chic, this is a feast for all senses as well as an excellent piece of marketing.

The hotel mostly sells by the European plan, which includes breakfast and dinner. Rates start around 400€ ($460), which with promotions often include breakfast and dinner with wine. © 04-90-72-30-20. www.labastidedemarie.com.

NORTHERN PROVENCE

HOSTELLERIE DE CRILLON LE BRAVE
Crillon le Brave.

Area & Cities: Carpentras, L'Isle sur la Sorgue (also easy to get to Avignon or the Luberon)

Département: Vaucluse (84)

This is the hotel that changed my life. On my first visit here, it was smaller and the house next door was for sale. I considered buying it—my first yearning for a house of my own in Provence. Instead, the hotel bought that empty house, enlarging and rearranging it into the spread of the property and redoing all the rooms at the same time.

While the hotel was already very Provençal and luxe, now it has stone towers, enormous bathrooms made from local stone, and other signs of magazine chic. The only thing rustic is the view. One of the most interesting things about this place is that it doesn't feel like a hotel—it's more like a country house or castle owned by very rich people with lots of style.

The Hostellerie is related to the Crillon in Paris in that it's part of the same duke's property; this was the country house built into an old fortress on top of a hill, with views of Mont Ventoux. You can relax in the sitting room with a glass of muscat, listening to opera and nibbling olives stuffed into puff pastry.

The hotel has a pool and gardens and offers cooking lessons in the off season. The staff here even packed and shipped my shopping finds for me. The excellent chef serves in a stone cellar with a roaring fire in winter; there's also a small bistro.

Rates begin at 250€ ($288). For U.S. reservations, call **Relais & Châteaux** (℃ **800/735-2478**). Local phone ℃ 04-90-65-61-61. www.crillonlebrave.com.

L'AMIRADOU DE CRILLON LE BRAVE
Crillon le Brave.

Area & Cities: Carpentras, L'Isle sur la Sorgue (also easy to get to Avignon or the Luberon)

Département: Vaucluse (84)

This is not part of the hotel in Crillon le Brave, but is a private home managed by the same team. It was created especially for groups or families who want every luxury while resting under the same roof. It has air-conditioning, a pool, an elevator serving the three floors, and bourgeois chic decor. Rates vary depending on the season, but begin around 250€ ($288). Book by calling ℃ **04-90-12-89-50**. www.amiradou.com.

Provençal Buys

Local style is about color and comfort and rustic country wares that wear and wear and have the heart of the people and their land in every stitch, curve, contour, or taste. Color and texture are the backbone of the look; handmade and slightly rough hewn—even when done with finesse—add to the value, even in foodstuffs and food packaging.

There are a few designer shops here and there—mostly in Aix or Avignon—but Provence is not the place to really wear or to seriously stock up on your Chanel. The things to buy are foodstuffs, fabrics, and decorative items. What's free to all browsers are ideas and visions that you can take home and translate into your own personal style.

If you insist on fashion accessories à la Provençal, go for the tote bags or backpacks. They're chic and they're sturdy. The bangle bracelets made of plastic-covered Provençal cottons are also nice. In markets, you can buy Provençal-print leggings.

When it comes to gifts for others, be careful. Provençal style may not travel well out of France or have the same cachet to others—who might not know what it means or costs. I bought a 87€ ($100) silk tie in a Provençal print for an American gentlemen who does a lot of work in France. He had no idea what it was or who (or what) Les Olivades was, so the entire gesture was wasted on him. Stick with soap.

The best souvenirs and gifts are inexpensive local products: soaps, jams, jars of honey, olive oil, local candies (a box of callisons for 4.35€/$5 is a winner), or chocolates (see p. 207 for information on zChocolat). Pottery is a great buy, but fragile—and often heavy and hard to pack or carry on.

The Market Day Rule of Shopping

Many villages aren't worth visiting if it's not market day. Sunday is particularly tricky, since most of France is closed on Sundays and on Monday mornings as well. As you decide which towns and villages to visit, mark your map for market days. Specific market days in towns and nearby villages are further delineated later in this chapter. Plan Sundays and Monday mornings with care. Also remember that parking is especially difficult on market days, so get there early.

To find out about antiques fairs or salons, *brocante* day at the local market, or general fun junk shopping, check out the regional and national guides. *L'Incontournable du Chineur* is a tiny computer-printed free guide to fairs in the regions of Alpes-Maritimes, Aude, Bouches-du-Rhône, Gard, Hérault, Pyrénées-Oirentales, Var, and Vaucluse—in short, most of the Riviera and Provence. It includes a calendar of events as well as ads. You can get it at any flea market.

Night Markets

Several villages in Provence have market in the evening and into the night—for food and/or *brocante*. With the heat what it is, you can see the appeal of such an event. These markets usually start around 7pm and go on until 10 or 11pm.

Markets by Region

Bouches-du-Rhone

SATURDAY   Arles

DAILY   Marseille Vaucluse

MONDAY   Bédarrides, Bédoin, Bollène, Cadenet, Cavaillon, Fontvieille, Forcalquier, Goult, Mazan, Piolenc, St-Didier, St-Saturnin-les-Avignon

TUESDAY   Aix-en-Provence, Banon, Beaumes-de-Venise, Caromb, Cucuron, Fontaine-de-Vaucluse, Gordes, Mondragon, Mormoiron, St-Saturnin-d'Apt, Sarrians, La Tour-d'Aigues, Vaison-la-Romaine

WEDNESDAY   Avignon, Buis-les-Baronnies, Entraigues, Malaucène, Mérindol, Monteux, St-Rémy-de-Provence, Sault, Le Thor, Valreas, Violès

THURSDAY   Aubignon, Les Baux-de-Provence, L'Isle-sur-la-Sorgue, Malemort-du-Comtat, Nyons, Orange, Roussillon, Vacqueyras, Villeneuve-lès-Avignon

FRIDAY   Bonnieux, Carpentras, Châteauneuf-du-Pape, Eygalières, Lourmarin, Visan

SATURDAY   Apt, Avignon, Digne-les-Bains, Grillon, Jonquières, Manosque, Monteux, Mornas, Pernes-les-Fontaines, Ste-Cécile-les-Vignes

SUNDAY   Avignon, Camaret, L'Isle-sur-la-Sorgue, Mane, Mormoiron, Sarrians, La Tour d'Aigues

Note: Just because a town has a market or is listed above doesn't mean the market is fabulous or worth the trip. Not surprisingly, markets from town to town can be too similar to please, especially if you pick towns that are too close together. The following markets in Vaucluse are all excellent and different enough to satisfy a daily diet of market and more market:

MONDAY   Bédarrides

TUESDAY   Vaison-la-Romaine

WEDNESDAY   St-Rémy-de-Provence

THURSDAY   Orange

FRIDAY   Carpentras

SATURDAY   Ste-Cécile-les-Vignes (smaller than the others, but nice)

SUNDAY   L'Isle-sur-la-Sorgue

MARSEILLE

Marseille is the gateway to Provence, but it's not really a piece of Provence. It is its own planet; although it's in France, it's also among the stars of the firmament because it is very much its own thing—a city that has evolved because of its location as a major port, because of its proximity to Africa, colonial France, and shipping routes to the Far East. Marseille is a mélange of peoples and cultures, a true melting pot that simmers more happily than bouillabaisse.

You can visit Marseille and not feel you're in part of Provence or the Riviera or even France. You can also visit the region and feel no need to stop in Marseille. Go to Marseille simply because it's very different from everyplace else in France. And curious shoppers want to know.

Everyone in Paris may look alike, but in Marseille you've got everything from African women wrapped in turbans and layered multicolored gowns to Arab traders and North African colonists (called *les Pieds Noir* by the local French) to cutting-edge designers who are proud of the city's multi-ethnic heritage and are out to create a brave new world far from the constraints of Paris. Step this way; Marseille is a brave new French world.

Getting to Marseille

BY PLANE   The Marseille airport is to the north, outside Marseille and halfway to Aix-en-Provence. If you're driving to the airport, it's marked MARIGNANE on road signs. In case you have a difficult connection and need to stay overnight, there's a **Sofitel** (© 04-42-78-42-78) near the airport.

Although most major air travel connects through Paris or Frankfurt, there are a few nonstop flights to other hub cities.

Marseille happens to be one of those cities served by low-cost airlines—for example, you can fly here from Amsterdam on **Basiq Air** (www.basiqair.com) for an incredibly low price. Various other airlines keep adding flights; a new terminal in 2006 will host even more low-cost carriers.

BY CAR   If you are driving into Marseille, get specific directions from your hotel, as there are ring roads and ways to avoid downtown traffic. Note that Marseille is right below the fork of two autoroutes (A7 and A8), which can confuse a first-timer.

BY BOAT   About half a million cruise passengers a year pass through Marseille. There are also ferries from Marseille to Corsica. *Note:* The cruise terminal is not within walking distance of the Vieux Port (Old Port).

Marseille

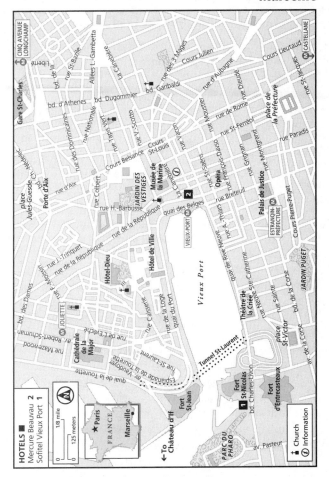

BY TRAIN   The main train station, St-Charles, is north of the Old Port and the primary shopping district. It's not within walking distance of much of anything; you can take a taxi or the Métro.

In 2005, a TGV station will open at the port, which will allow cruise passengers to step from the train onto their ship.

The Lay of the Land

Like Paris, Marseille is divided into *arrondissements* (districts). They are included in specific listings below to help you understand which places are near to others, or to get an idea of distance (for example, your brain should quickly learn that something in the 15e isn't too convenient if you are in the 1er or 2e). The *arrondissements* sort of circle around the Old Port, and the central downtown-business-Bourse and shopping district is the 1er. The higher the number, the further away from center.

Marseille is the second most populous city in France, and the largest physically. You cannot begin to comprehend the sprawl unless you think of Los Angeles. I never totally understood Marseille until I had a car and was able to drive to various parts of the city, to the edges of the big towns, and to the rim of the sea.

Naturally, you get a lot of different neighborhoods and treasures with this much territory. Plus, there's a very long stretch of coastline abutting the city. But Marseille isn't flat, so there are hills to deal with everywhere, most set in rows surrounding the two ports, the Old Port (the center of the shopper's world) and the Port of Marseille (which is where the cruise ships come to port).

The Port of Marseille is on the far side of the Old Port; if you're arriving by cruise ship, you might want to walk into the district called Le Panier (but not at night, please). Le Panier is located on a series of small hills between the Old Port and the new one. It has some fabulous sights and heaps of soul, as well as the city's landmark cathedral and the gorgeous Vieille de Charité (now a museum), but it is not the shopping capital of the city. More serious shoppers may want to take a shuttle into town (marked VIEUX PORT); there will be a TGV station at the *quai* in 2005.

The Old Port is the center of the tourist universe; if you do not have a car, you will stay mostly in this part of town. The Old Port is U-shaped, and the two sides of the U represent other important parts of town: the Panier (as discussed above) and the restaurant and shopping district. If you are standing at the

Old Port, looking at the water, with your back toward the Bourse and train station, then the 2e is to your right, along with the Panier and the cruise docks; and the 4e and 7e are to your left, with restaurant row, Nôtre Dame de la Garde, the Sofitel Vieux Port, and so on.

There are also many, many shopping opportunities and museums outside the center of town; some require a tour bus, a car, or a willingness to pay a lot to a taxi driver.

To really understand the magic of Marseille, you need to step back from the downtown hustle and bustle and see the sea and the effect that 56km (35 miles) of beach has on a community. It also helps to survey the Calanques, a craggy seascape of rocky cliffs that run alongside the beach from Marseille to Cassis, some 25km (16 miles) away. Not only are they breathtaking, but they also hide many little beach coves and pizza places, where you can share some of the moments that become memories when you are forced back into the real world. Sorry, no shopping here.

Marseille is a closed town. It has layers of personalities and secrets; it is not small, nor charming, nor sitting out there in the sunshine, waiting for you to discover it. The only way you can get hold of the soul and essence of the city is to have secret addresses and be ready to delve beneath the surface. Those looking for Camelot should apply elsewhere.

You can find information about Marseille at **www.marseille-tourisme.com**.

Getting Around Marseille

Traffic in Marseille is beyond terrible; it's just plain disgusting. If you must drive, take your car to a central parking lot and leave it for the day. Do not park on the street. Do lock your car and make sure you've left nothing inside it.

The Métro has some, but limited, use for tourists. You can easily get from the St-Charles train station to the Old Port by Métro.

If you're doing a lot of sightseeing, you will need some taxis and very good walking shoes.

Safety Matters

As in any big city, you should be careful about carrying too much cash or flashing it about. On the other hand, it's thought that Marseille is safer than Paris these days. Who knows? You don't want to find out. There are banks and ATMs everywhere; take advantage of them.

Sleeping in Marseille

Your choice of location in Marseille will make a difference in how you see the city and how much shopping you get done. Perhaps the glory of Marseille is not to shop too much, but rather to buy yourself the experience of luxury against a backdrop of the sea.

LE PETIT NICE
160 promenade de la Corniche, 7e.

This is the local Relais & Châteaux property, located in what's almost a little village right on the seaside. From here, you'll have to taxi into central Marseille. But the hotel is drop-dead fabulous and the surrounding area is filled with charm.

You can stay in the small (15-room), bright-yellow villa, which has a gorgeous swimming pool. You can dine on the terrace overlooking the sea and feel totally lost to the real world. The Passédat family owns and runs the villa property, and Gérald Passédat is the award-winning chef.

Rates are about 348€ ($400) a night. Make U.S. reservations through **Relais & Châteaux** (© **800/735-2478**). Local phone © 04-91-59-28-08. www.relaischateaux.com.

MERCURE BEAUVAU
4 rue Beauvau, 1er.

This was the most famous hotel in town at one time; then it got dumpy. Then a miracle happened and the hotel closed for over a year for extensive renovations. It's just now open, with millions of euros' worth of work turning it into the classiest four-star in the Old Port area. There is not a better location in town: The Old Port is out your window, next door is the tourist office, and next to that is the Métro.

Rates start at 110€ ($127). For U.S. reservations, call ℂ **800/MERCURE**. Local phone ℂ 04-91-54-91-00. www. mercure.com.

SOFITEL PALM BEACH
200 corniche John F. Kennedy, 7e.

When I booked into the Sofitel Palm Beach, I knew only that I was getting one of the new hotel experiences in Marseille— I didn't realize that it was some distance from the Old Port. After I accepted that this wasn't going to be the most perfect shopping location, I settled down to enjoy the view.

The location turned out to be perfect, as I had a car and could get to the various spread-out parts of Marseille. Shopping wasn't a problem at all. But the best part was simply gazing out at the sea and enjoying picnics on my own balcony.

The hotel is built into a rocky cliffside that goes down into the water. The place is very modern and luxe without being too expensive; it also has spa facilities, contributing to the resort-like feel. Before you arrive, call the concierge for exact driving directions—if you come from the highway, you can bypass downtown and enjoy a drive along the coast that will take your breath away.

Rates are about 230€ ($265) per night, although numerous promotional deals are available. For U.S. reservations, call ℂ **800/763-4835**. Local phone ℂ 04-91-16-19-00. www. sofitel.com.

SOFITEL VIEUX PORT
36 bd. Charles Livon, 7e.

This high-rise hotel overlooks the Old Port, offering fabulous views and an excellent restaurant. It is within walking distance of town, but it's a good walk. You can also take a bus. The Sofitel hotel is a good compromise in that it gives you a feel for the water without being totally out in the boonies (although the view is likely to be more of the old parts of town than just waves and sea).

There are many different rates and promotions; expect to pay at least 200€ ($230). For U.S. reservations, call © 800/763-4835. Local phone © 04-91-15-59-00. www.sofitel.com.

Eating in Marseille

LE MIRAMAR
12 quai du Port, 2e.

This restaurant is the most famous in town for bouillabaisse, but you can have a perfectly nice meal without going for the big B. A new chef combines the traditional seafaring menu with contemporary and fusion twists, making this the talk of the town. My lunch extravaganza included fish baked in a salt cake, the best fish of my life. If you dine outside, be sure to peek inside at the murals and other decor. To book a table, try © 04-91-91-10-40. It is notoriously hard to get reservations here, but if you walk over and ask, you'll probably get what you want. Closed Sunday and Monday.

LES TROIS FORTS
In Sofitel Vieux Port, 36 bd. Charles Livon, 7e.

Located on the top floor of the Sofitel, this restaurant is best booked for dinner so you can watch the sun set over the harbor and the lights come on all over town. The chef has won awards; this is one of the best tables in town. For reservations, call © 04-91-15-59-56.

Shopping in Marseille

Because Marseille has reinvented itself, the stores sell a far wider assortment than you would ever imagine, and there is a large local selection. You'll see many one-off stores that have no other branches. On the other hand, there's also a Disney store, so this can't claim to be a sleepy town.

In fact, there's a branch (or several) of every French multiple, most department stores, and almost anything that Paris has to offer. You can do anything from fancy-schmancy designer shopping to down-and-dirty discount shopping. Because of the large population base, Marseille has many stores that you will not find anywhere else in the south of France.

Design students flock to Marseille to open their shops; the city has a famous fashion and costume museum and is proud to be host to up-and-coming designers.

While Marseille does abut Provence, and you will find much Provençal influence, you will also find African influence in everyday fashions and lifestyle. This is partly because ethnic is chic now, because imports from India and Africa are cheap, and because a touch of African flair when mixed with the colors of the south actually sells to a non-African population. There are more funky shops here than just about anywhere else.

SNACKING & SHOPPING

The city has zillions of pizza parlors, most of which are great. Restaurant Row is off to one side of the Old Port, which is surrounded by cafes. Look for place aux Huiles, right off cours d'Estienne d'Orves.

LES ARCENAULX
25 cours d'Estienne d'Orves, 1er.

This rehabbed arsenal space is now a fabulous bookstore, gift shop, and cafe. It is charm itself for lunch or snacks.

LES COLONIES
26 rue Lulli, 1er.

This fabulous location, near the Opéra and hidden little shopping streets, serves coffee and chocolates.

LINA'S
Canebière, 1er.

Lina's is a famous Parisian salad-sandwich shop for quick and easy meals. A recent arrival in Marseille, it has plopped down next to the Bourse and near the Fashion Museum, creating a mode theme.

RESTAURANT CAFE BROCANTE
16 rue Lulli, 1er.

This small restaurant also sells *brocante;* its location is near the Opéra and little streets for shoppers.

SHOPPING HOURS

In Marseille, country hours prevail. A very large number of the stores close for lunch. They are also closed all day Sunday as well as Monday morning. Some of the really fancy stores will open up just for you if you make an appointment.

Most stores open at 10am; some small ones open at 9:30am; Nouvelles Galeries in the CC Bourse opens at 9am. Department stores do not close for lunch. Stores that do close for lunch usually reopen at 2pm and stay open until 7pm. However, in the south, they may not reopen until 3pm.

SHOPPING NEIGHBORHOODS

ESTIENNE-D'ORVES   This is a square right next to the Old Port, located in the 4e (to your left if your back is to the 1er). To me, Estienne-d'Orves symbolizes all that is glorious about the new Marseille. I actually heard of an apartment here and was swept away, but friends warned me that it can be very noisy on Saturday nights. Indeed, there are many restaurants, clubs, and bars here; Restaurant Row is around the corner. Meanwhile, you'll also find one of the best stores in town (Les Arcenaulx), as well as some other not-too-shabby stores, like an enormous branch of Agnès b. Years ago, this space was a dump, but now it whispers of magic. Don't miss it.

PANIER It means *basket* in French; to me it's more of a medieval wonderland with a touch of the Corsican chapter of *The Godfather* thrown in. This is the 2e—festooned with medieval alleys and colorful laundry lines, tiny pizza parlors, stairways that will leave you breathless. It's home to the city's main cathedral and the awesome Vieille de Charité, once the poor house and now a museum with cafe and bookstore *(bien sur)*. You won't find heaps of shopping opportunities here, but there are some good ones, including *santon* (figures in a Christmas crèche) makers and the best soap store in town.

CANEBIERE Running through the heart of downtown, creating the core of the 1er *arrondissement,* this street is also called the boulevard de la Liberation. Downtown's main drag is indeed the Canebière, nicknamed "can of beer" by GIs and remembered by tourists that way. This commercial street leads from alongside the train station (St-Charles) to the Old Port and has many old hotels, stores, some Métro stops, and even a museum or two.

The Bourse is located on this street; it is a building that will stun you with its grandeur, the type of architecture you had no idea was beyond Paris. Most of the buildings on Canebière were created by good old Baron Haussmann, who created the Paris we know today. Between the Old Port and the train station are the many side streets of the main shopping district. I have named this area "The Grid" (see below).

THE GRID In an old-fashioned way, the part of town I call the Grid represents what some might refer to as "downtown," the main shopping district. The Grid is located directly behind the Old Port and alongside La Canebière. The main streets run west to east, but the cross streets within the Grid also have good shopping—and many hidden pleasures. Appropriately, the main shopping street is called rue Paradis. However, the rue St-Ferréol is also important for multiples and mass-market names, as are the side streets—particularly rue Grignan, home to many fancy designer boutiques. Don't forget to explore around the Opéra, as the little streets here have some of the best boutiques and represent the hidden aspects of Marseille that I've told you about.

CC BOURSE   The Bourse is a fancy building right on Canebière, but right behind it is a big American-style shopping mall, Centre Commercial Bourse. It's on the other side of the Canebière from the Grid but in the same area, just an adjoining neighborhood. The entrance is rather hidden: You go upstairs and over (or simply walk over 1 block and enter through Nouvelles Galeries).

LA JOLIETTE   La Joliette is the official name of the area of working docks and where cruise ships come to port. Just outside the Old Port, it is in the 2e.

COURS JULIEN   This is an adorable, charming quasi-residential area with a square (flea market once a month, book fair other weekends) and trees and a Métro stop and many small but hip boutiques . . . but not so hip as to appeal only to those under 20. This is in the 6e; it's actually not that far from the St-Charles train station.

Marseille Resources A–Z

ANTIQUES

Because of the traditional spread of wealth outside Marseille, most of the serious antiques dealers are located toward or in Aix. However, a few districts in Marseille are worth browsing.

For *brocante,* locals tend to go out of town. On the last Sunday of each month, there's a *brocante* fair in Aubagne called **La Tourtelle** that features about 120 dealers. (This market is fun, but I don't know that I'd make a special trip unless I had nothing else to do on a Sun.) Call © **04-42-18-18-48** for more information, or call © **04-42-18-18-31** for the exact dates of the fairs.

BARGAIN BASEMENTS

EURODIF
6–10 rue St-Ferréol, 1er.

Eurodif is a discount store, run by the same folks who own Bouchara, a firm that makes fabrics and table linens for the masses. Outside of Paris, the Bouchara and Eurodif businesses are combined into one giant pleasure house of shopping fun. It's borderline junky, with everything from housewares and accessories to kids' clothes, teen fashions, and women's clothes for both regular and plus sizes. Upstairs, you can look at fabric by the yard, trims, and hardware. I've shopped this chain all over France, and I love it. Those who frequent only Gucci will not be amused. Eurodif opens at 9:30am.

TATI
14 rue de la République, 2e.

Tati in Marseille has not yet closed due to the company's financial problems. It isn't as sophisticated as Eurodif, but the prices are similar. The store is one giant bin, which you prowl through hoping to find something decent. Tati's pink-and-white tattersall logo is printed on the bags and is famous all over France. This is not a status shopping bag.

BEAUTY

The department stores are your best bet for a large selection of both big and small brand names—American, French, or international. Pharmacies everywhere sell pharmaceutical beauty brands, and Monoprix, right on the Canebière, sells beauty items as well.

If you need your hair done, try the major French chains in Marseille: **Jean Louis David** (av. Prado) and **Jacques Dessange** (Old Port).

PARASHOP
76 rue Paradis, 1er.

This chain has branches all over France, and you can use its fidelity card at all outposts. It is a *parapharmacie* (large discount drugstore) that sells mostly beauty brands from major French pharmaceutical companies. Parashop discounts items by 20% to 25%.

SEPHORA
56 rue St-Ferréol, 1er.

This is a large branch of the beauty supermarket Sephora.

BIG NAMES

Following are some of the big-name designer boutiques and multiples in Marseille.

AGNES B.
31 cours d'Estienne d'Orves, 1er.

CACHAREL
68 rue Paradis, 1er.

CARTIER
32 rue Grignan, 1er.

CHACOK
47 rue Paradis, 6e.

CHARLES JOURDAN
55 rue Paradis, 6e.

FAÇONNABLE
25 rue Grignan, 1er.

GERARD DAREL
36 rue Paradis, 1er.

HERMES
27 rue Paradis, 1er.

KENZO
67 rue Paradis, 1er.

LONGCHAMP
21 rue Paradis, 1er.

LOUIS VUITTON
22 rue Grignan, 1er.

Marina Rinaldi
74 rue Paradis, 1er.

Max Mara
37 rue Paradis, 1er.

Mont Blanc
22 rue Paradis, 1er.

Tod's
99 rue Paradis, 1er.

Ventilo
28 rue Montgrand, 1er.

Wolford
18 rue Haxo, 1er.

Yves Saint Laurent
104 rue Paradis, 1er.

Zara
57 rue St-Ferréol, 1er.

Boutiques

Make
67 rue Francis Davso, 1er.

Make sells fashion, tabletop, decorative items, home style, gifts, and T-shirts made of camouflage and leopard prints—plus other cutting-edge materials for the teen and tween set.

Marianne Cat
53 rue Grignan, 6e.

I don't care if you buy anything or not—any fashionista worth her espadrilles will come here just to gawk, and to take lessons in how high style is mixed, matched, blended, and reworked to include a makeup bar, an art gallery, and plenty of expensive designer clothes in a euro-funky vein of classic chic.

CHILDREN'S CLOTHES

Most of these are multiples, so the addresses below are not necessarily the only locations.

DU PAREIL AU MEME
7 rue Grignan, 1er.

FLORIANE
40 rue Paradis, 1er.

JACADI
2 rue Grignan, 1er.

JOK
10 rue Sainte, 1er.

LA COMPAGNIE DES PETITS
16 rue Paradis, 1er.

PETIT BOY
1 rue Grignan, 1er.

TOUT COMPTE FAIT
54 rue St-Ferréol, 1er.

DEPARTMENT STORES

GALERIES LAFAYETTE
40–48 rue St-Ferréol, 1er.

Right in the heart of the downtown shopping district is Galeries Lafayette's large store, complete with a Provençal souvenirs section. This is perhaps the largest branch store in the south of France, and it's better than the one in Nice.

NOUVELLES GALERIES
CC Bourse, 2 rue Bir-Hakeim, 1er.

A division of Galeries Lafayette, Nouvelles Galeries is located in CC Bourse and has a fabulous supermarket right inside its door (ground floor). Although it's not quite as large as Galeries downtown, it does offer plenty of choices and brands. You'll see a Provençal souvenirs department as you enter; the store has a parapharmacie as well.

ETHNIC LOOKS

BIASA
43 rue Francis Davso, 1er.

This small shop sells a very particular blend of south of France meets ethnic, with a touch of Africa melted in. It is not a contrived look, though it does remind me of American fashion lines, such as Blue Fish, and even of Eileen Fisher (which isn't ethnic at all). The clothes are artsy and often baggy, funky without being too costumey. Prices are moderate.

EXPOTAMIE
CC Bourse, 1er; 20 rue Montgrand, 6e.

This fashion/home-style chain has stores only in the south of France and sells a rather African-inspired southern look that is sort of Pier 1 goes to town. It has its own lines, but also carries some brands that are ethnically styled. Prices are low to moderate; the selection is fun. The store in CC Bourse is much better (and larger) than the other location.

MIA ZIA
49 rue Francis Davso, 1er.

See "Finds," below.

FINDS

LES ARCENAULX
25 cours d'Estienne d'Orves, 6e.

This is a bookstore, gift shop, tearoom, spiritual place of being, . . . a space created out of rehabilitated warehouses and the city arsenal (hence the name). Walk into the series of stone salons, and you'll be transported to another world. Some people think this is the 4e and others the 1er; it's right in the Old Port area, next to Restaurant Row.

MANON MARTIN
10 rue de la Tour, 1er.

This hatmaker master wizard has a shop in Paris (19 rue de Turenne, 4e), but he does a wonderful business in Marseille, mostly for weddings and special events but also for those going up to Chantilly or Deauville for the horse races—or for those who simply need hats. The hats are made of all media and range from funky to fantastic and very fabulous. They are also carried in most department stores in France. Manon Martin even does custom orders. Prices can get a tad high for the over-the-top stuff, but then, why not?

MIA ZIA
49 rue Francis Davso, 1er.

Now a small chain (with stores in Geneva and St. Barths as well as Paris), this boutique sells an ethnic lifestyle look that's inspired by North Africa but not costumey or cheap. It's pure luxe and elegance in earth tones. The stores themselves are also gorgeous, like terra-cotta jewel boxes. Prices are high.

UNIVERS DE CHRISTIAN LACROIX
6 rue Sainte, 1er.

In case you haven't noticed, most Lacroix stores have closed (they're often made over into Emilio Pucci stores). Lacroix has launched a whole new concept store, which began in Tokyo, went to Bangkok, and then came to France via Marseille.

FOODSTUFFS

BATAILLE
18 place Nôtre Dame du Mont, 6e.

I've died, gone to heaven, and returned here to the city's premier *traiteur* to smell the cheese, gaze upon the produce, pine for a taste of everything in the cases, and become a very fat but happy angel. You can eat at one of the few tables or you can buy picnic fare to go.

CHOCOLATERIE DE PUYRICARD
155 rue Jean Mermoz, 1er.

This is one of the most famous chocolate shops in France. Even though this brand was founded only in 1967, it boasts an international reputation. There are now several branches in various cities in the south. Check out the seasonal molded chocolates—chicks and fish for Easter, and the like. Another local specialty is the chocolate pralines made with almond pâté.

DROMEL AINE
6 rue de Rome, 1er.

Although this is a chocolate shop, the real specialty is covered almonds, which come in a variety of sizes and are called *dragées,* a traditional item for good luck at weddings (white ones) or for babies (pink or blue). We threw them at my son's bar mitzvah. The business was founded in 1760; the tradition of offering sugared almonds began in the court of Louis XIV. This is the status *dragée* source in France.

FOUR DES NAVETTES
136 rue Sainte, 7e.

This is the oldest bakery in town, going back to the late 18th century. The name of the shop relates to a specific local specialty, a cookielike, bread-stick thing called a *navette,* named after a small boat. Every bakery in town makes them, but this is the most famous source. The story of the *navette* is more charming than the eating: This is the boat that the three Marys arrived in. The bakery is open every day, and you can even shop online at www.fourdesnavettes.com.

MAISON DU PASTIS
108 quai du Port, 2e.

I guess it's my job to report what's here, not to tell you that I like it. Besides, my opinion of pastis, as a drink or flavoring in other products, is X-rated. This is right in the Old Port—you can't miss it.

NOUCHIG
45 rue Vacon, 1er.

This is another source for *dragées,* but it's chic and fancy, and there's nothing old-fashioned about it at all. It also sells chocolates and other candies and is most famous for its wraps and presentations; a real status gift.

GENERAL STORES

MONOPRIX
36 La Canebière, 1er.

This branch of Monoprix is right in the heart of town and has two levels, with a full grocery store upstairs. It's one of the most complete Monoprix stores I've ever been to, and it's perfect for picking up health and beauty aids, anything you left at home, whatever you might need for beach play or the kids, and so on. Monoprix has very good clothes for not much money; I'm especially fond of the children's lines. This is also a good place for inexpensive gifts. Oh yes, it opens at 8:30am.

RESONANCES
CC Bourse, 1er.

This store began in Paris's Bercy Village as an experiment, and was so successful that additional branches have opened in both Paris and other major French cities. For an American shopper, Résonances looks and feels something like Pottery Barn, but it specializes in small items and gifts, books and cooking gear. Not all of the merchandise is French, but there is a great selection of gifts including soaps and olive oils. One of the best stores in town.

GIFTS

Also see "Soap," below, and "General Stores," above.

LA MAISON MARSEILLAISE
38 rue Francis Davso, 1er.

This store sells tabletop, home style, and gift items in a contemporary space; the items have some whimsy and humor to them, with clean lines and high style—nothing cutie-pie here or even Provençal.

LES COMPTOIRS DE PROVENCE
40 rue Francis Davso, 1er.

This is your dream store for local scents, aromatherapy, and Provençal herbs and spices. It features products by Durance and Florame, two small French lines that are not found all over; they offer a full range of treatments and home products. One of the best stores in town.

MALLS

CENTRE COMMERCIAL BOURSE
Rue Bir-Hakeim, 1er.

Located right behind the Bourse (hence the name), this is the town's large American-style mall, which happens to be not only air-conditioned but also the home of a very nice museum. The mall has one of just about every French multiple, as well as an **SNCF** train ticket office (expect a long line). Most of the stores open at 10am, but the department store **Nouvelles Galeries,** a division of Galeries Lafayette, opens at 9am. (It has a huge and wonderful supermarket.) There's also **FNAC** for CDs, books, and electronics; **Habitat** for home style; **Loisirs et Création,** a crafts store; and several cafes between the usual mall suspects. Perhaps the fanciest and chicest tenant is **Réso-nances,** a gift source. You can get a lot done in this mall, so don't knock it.

MARKETS & FAIRS

Options range from daily fish markets in Old Port to a very nice food market at rue Longue des Capucins, near the Canebière. This is where you can buy all the ingredients for fresh bouillabaisse. Also check out the heaps of spices, dried fruits, and many exotics. Aux Capucins is open daily from 7am to 2pm and from 4 to 8pm for the after-work crowd (Métro: Noailles).

There's a flower market every Monday morning at place Felix Baret and on Tuesday and Saturday morning in the allées Meilhan.

A Provençal market that sells regional specialties is held every day at the place Castellane. There's also a fresh food market, Le Marché du Prado, that's extremely lively and very ethnic.

Brocante is sold at the flea market at Porte d'Aix, which is not the most glamorous neighborhood. Expect a lot of broken Edith Piaf records. There's a daily book market at Le Cours Julien.

On weekends, a gallery called Les Puces de la Madrague (4 rue Neuve Ste-Catherine, 4e) is open. The big weekend flea market is called Le Marché aux Puce de Marseille, and it's open Sunday from 9am to 7pm (chemin de la Madrague-Ville, 15e). There are about 200 dealers at the flea market, but the specialty here is African food, arts, and crafts. The market is rather far out in the 15e; you can get there on the no. 35 bus.

The second Sunday of each month, there's a *brocante* fair at the Cours Julien. This isn't a huge market, but it's a charming district of Marseille and worth doing if you hit it on the right day.

Note that most locals drive into the heart of Provence for flea markets, and L'Isle sur la Sorgue is not too far away (p. 208).

The city of Marseille has a famous Santon Fair, held from November to February in the allées Meilhan. A Garlic Festival runs from mid-June to mid-July, and there's a pretty big (and somewhat fancy) antiques salon each October. Check the tourist office (4 La Canebière, right at the Old Port) for other shopping events.

PROVENÇAL CRAFTS

ARTERRA
1 rue du Petit Puits, 2e.

This maker of *santons* has a small shop in the Panier district; the *santons* are not as bright as usual and therefore considered very sophisticated. Arterra makes the *santons* for the biggest names in Provençal style.

ATELIERS MARCEL CARBONEL
47 rue Neuve Ste-Catherine, 4e.

Carbonel is one of the most famous makers of *santons* in France. The shop is open Monday through Saturday; on Tuesday and Thursday, you can watch him at work. Small *santons* start around 12€ ($14). Closed in August.

FAIENCERIES FIGUERES
10–12 av. Lauzier, 8e.

I don't care if you steal a car, hail a taxi, or hire a driver: Do what you must to get to this slightly out-of-the-way location, where *faience* is a misleading term. Yes, Faienceries Figuères makes the squiggles and colors on white porcelain, but its claim to fame is the incredible non-edible selection of porcelain fruits and vegetables that are disturbingly lifelike. My favorites are the trompe l'oeil platters with half-eaten cookies or candies. The olives in a dish are also fun.

The shop is on the factory premises; hours are Monday through Friday from 8:30am to noon and 1 to 6:30pm,

Saturday from 8:30am to 12:30pm. Check it out online at www.faiencerie-figueres.com. Note that the shop is on the far eastern side of Marseille, not far from the Musée de la Faience.

LES OLIVADES
102 rue Paradis, 1er.

This is a small branch of the famous fabric and design firm.

SOULEIADO
117 rue Paradis, 1er.

This is a large and airy shop from the famous fabric firm that brought the look to the U.S.

TERRE E PROVENCE
19–21 rue Montgrand, 6e.

This is a small chain of pottery stores that has branches in most of the tourist towns in Provence. The prices are a tad high, but the wares are nice—and Terre è Provence ships.

SOAP

LA COMPAGNIE DE PROVENCE
1 rue Caisserie, 2e.

Soap, soap, soap: Did someone scream soap? This is the best soap source in town and one of the best in France. Yes, it sells the famous square block of traditional 72% Marseille soap, but there are so many other things here that you may want something more exciting. You might even want to buy a candle that looks like the block of soap (fooled me!). Take a look at the little gift packs here: Three paper-wrapped scented soaps tied with string and sealed with an old-fashioned wax seal go for 10€ ($12). The store sells all sorts of bars and gift packs and bath mats and tubes and scents and yummy things. La Compagnie de Provence products are also sold at Bergdorf Goodman and Barneys in the U.S.

LA SAVONNERIE DU SERAIL
50 bd. Anatole de la Forge, 15e.

This is a real-live Marseille soap factory with a factory store. It's in the middle of nowhere; I came on a tour bus. The factory is interesting, but the shopping isn't great. If you visit the store, buy only the original Marseille soap (72%), as the scented soaps are not the best in France. The soap tour is offered once a month by the tourist office and costs about 10€ ($12). I'd take a bath instead. Open Monday through Friday from 8am to noon and 2 to 6pm (5pm on Fri).

L'OCCITANE
20–22 rue Haxo, 1er.

Everybody's favorite soap and Provençal gift store, L'Occitane sells all sorts of scents as well as its own makeup, skin care, men's line, home lines, and so on. I go through little tins of cannelle-orange oil, which I dab on my carpets and bedspread to scent my home.

TEENS

Most of these are multiples, so the addresses below are not the only locations.

H&M
29 rue St-Ferréol, 1er.

MANGO
17 rue St- Ferréol, 1er.

PIMKIE
27 rue St-Ferréol, 1er.

PRO MOD
52 rue St-Ferréol, 1er.

BEYOND MARSEILLE

Marseille has zillions of suburbs that seem as close to metro Marseille as some of the arrondissements, so it's confusing to understand where the city begins and ends. The confusion is compounded by the fact that many malls (called commercial centers) with large chains and department stores are actually in these 'burbs.

Perhaps the two most famous outlying towns are **Cassis** and **Aubagne.** Cassis is on the water; it's one of the most picture-perfect fishing villages in France. It's also mobbed in nice weather. Aubagne takes a little knowing—it's the home of Marcel Pagnol and is known as one of the ceramics cities. It's not chockablock with cutie-pie ceramics shops, although the **Ravel** factory is worth a trip if you want big pottery planters. I'd save Aubagne for one of the ceramics fairs—most of which are held in August (call the tourist office at ☎ **04-42-03-49-98** for dates).

The rest of this chapter addresses Provence towns in alphabetical order.

AIX-EN-PROVENCE

Everyone just calls it Aix, pronounced like the letter of the alphabet: *X.*

Aix is a very large city, not the sleepy little sun-splashed fountain that you think is representative of the town. Even the city center has a few parts to it, so if you're driving, you'll need to study a map and drive around a little to take it all in and get oriented before you park.

This city center is not on a grid system. The reason you need to grasp the lay of the land is that you won't find a parking spot on a market day, and you might get lost finding downtown even when it's not market day.

The Lay of the Land

Although the Aix you're dreaming of is small and *intime,* the city in fact is not. It takes quite some time to get from either the autoroute or the TGV station into the Cute.

The main drag of the *centre ville* is called cours Mirabeau. This is the street with the biggest stores and multiples (yes, there's a **Monoprix**). The tree-lined boulevard was rebuilt recently and brought from four to two lanes of traffic, which means it's even more crowded in summer and on market days. More trees were planted, sidewalks were widened, and the ambience is much improved.

Aix has positioned itself as the capital of Provence and has been attracting tourists for thousands of years; there are tons of students around because of the local language school, as well as tour groups galore. There's a small street of fancy-schmancy designer stores (rue Marius Reinaud) and a second fancy street with more big names (rue Fabrot). Aix just may be the shopping capital of Provence.

There's a touristy street (rue Espariat) with a combination of affordable shops and cute tourist traps (TTs). I'm also partial to the back area around place des Chapeliers that's filled with multiples such as **Orcanta** (no. 2 bis) for lingerie, as well as some real-people shopping.

Aix has plenty of designer shops, ranging from **Sonia Rykiel** and **Hermès** to **Yves Saint Laurent, Escada, Christian Lacroix,** and even **Robert Clergerie,** the shoe maven. There's also **Souleiado** and **Les Olivades,** as would be expected, and then there are some bridge designer lines that you may know of only if you shop in Paris, such as **Nitya** (11 rue Marius Reinaud), an Indian-inspired line with its flagship store on the rue St-Honoré in Paris. On side streets you'll find **Rodier** and most other multiples.

You'll find that everything interconnects and weaves together in a maze, leading to an amazing number of stores. Many are TTs and branches of famous French multiples, such as **Geneviève Lethu** (13 rue Aude) and **Sephora.** Rue de l'Ancienne hosts branches of **Lacoste, Laurèl,** and **Descamps.**

Sleeping in Aix

HOTEL DES AUGUSTINS
3 rue de la Masse.

Everyone needs to find a hotel created from an old convent. This one is well located and not too expensive (rooms start around 100€/$115). There is, however, the problem of the bells, bells, bells. Local phone ✆ 04-42-27-28-59.

VILLA GALLICI
Av. de la Violette.

This just might be the most perfect hotel you will ever visit. It also joins the ranks of hotels featured in novels—it was a character in a John Grisham book. To add to that, it's been featured in every design magazine in the United States and continental Europe, and it just starred in a multiple-page layout in *Town + Country.* It's drop-dead gorgeous and also located within walking distance of town, fulfilling all needs.

It has recently changed hands and is now part of Group Baglioni; the restaurant has gone fancy. Prices are about 261€ to 609€ ($300–$700) per night. For U.S. reservations, call **Relais & Châteaux** (✆ **800/735-2478**). Local phone ✆ 04-42-23-29-23. www.villagallici.com.

Eating in Aix

The town is filled with cafes, pizza parlors, ice-cream stands, and creperies—you'll have no trouble grabbing a bite in between shopping excursions.

One of the best tables in town is the one-star **Le Clos de la Violette,** 10 av. de la Violette (✆ **04-42-23-30-71**; fax 04-42-21-93-03), which is located in an old house with gardens. The luncheon menu is about 35€ ($40); you'll need a jacket. Sit, enjoy, and forget the tourists . . . and dinner.

At the place de l'Hôtel de Ville is **La Cour de Rohan,** a tearoom and tiny restaurant with a patio; open daily.

The most famous bistro in town, right on the main street for staring at people, is **Les Deux Garçons,** cours Mirabeau; but a lot of visitors are now returning to **La Rotunde,** 24 place Jeanne d'Arc, which was closed for a *relooking*. It's now a restaurant, bar, cafe, and meeting place.

Shopping in Aix

Aix has a lot of shops besides Souleiado and Les Olivades that specialize in Provençal cute; they sell mostly fabric and clothing. Other vendors offer clay pots, earthenware, garden furniture, and sundials. You get the drift. Take a look at **Terre è Provence** (6 bis rue Aude) for a big hunk of the local look and more pottery than you've ever dreamed of (this is a chain). You're gonna go nuts for one of the newest stores in town, **Le Faubourg** (5 rue Aude)—a home shop that has moderate prices and Provençal styling that works outside of Provence.

One block over, on the rue Fauchier, there's a branch of **L'Occitane** (no. 10), which sells its own line of bath and soap products as well as other brands. You can also buy soap from stalls in the market . . . or at the new branch of **La Compagnie de Provence,** a Marseille soap source (63 rue des Cordeliers).

There's a good branch of the makeup kingdom **Sephora** located right inside the **Passage Agard** but with the street address 12 rue Fabrot—the passage is one of the alleys leading from the place Verdun to cours Mirabeau. Don't miss it for architectural cuteness and charm galore.

The best antiques are found on the rue Jaubert and the rue Granet, both of which are on the other side of the Palais de Justice from the marketplace. Check out **Le Paris d'Helene** (4 rue Jaubert) for the fancy stuff. There are some junky antiques and *brocante* stores on the rue David, which leads right into the market square.

SHOPPING HOURS

Most stores open at 10am and close for lunch at 12:30pm. Antiques dealers and factory shops open at 9am or even earlier. Stores reopen at 2pm and stay open until 7pm. **Monoprix** does not close for lunch. Most stores are also closed on Monday morning, though TTs stay open Monday morning and during lunch. Aix is not totally dead on Monday, which is a blessing.

FINDS

CHOCOLATERIE DE PUYRICARD
7 rue Rifle-Rafle.

Come here for chocolates from the nearby village of Puyricard, with a national rep as among the best in France. Almost 100 different types!

LES OLIVADES
15 rue Marius Reinaud.

The same but so different in terms of Soleiado and *les tissus Indiennes* (Provençal fabrics made from woodblocks first brought from India)—more vibrant, more trendy fashion oriented, with touches designed by Christian Lacroix. The line is now sold through Pierre Deux stores in the U.S.

SANTONS FOUQUE
63 rue Gambetta.

Within the town of Aix, but outside the immediate tourist downtown, on the rue Gambetta—which is a main artery leading into and out of town—is this *santon* maker which you might want to track down. The shop is open from 8am to noon and 2 to 6:30pm; also open some Sundays in late November and into December, for the Christmas season. Call © **04-42-46-33-38** for an appointment.

SOULEIADO
8 place des Chapeliers.

A stunner: This is one of the largest Souleiado stores in the region, selling both clothes and home style.

UN ETE EN PROVENCE
2 rue Jaubert.

A fancy TT that specializes in local pottery and *boutis*—French bed quilts that can be hand- or machine-made, a differential in their cost and value. This shop has a nice selection of hand-made *boutis*.

MARKETS, FESTIVALS & FAIRS

Market days in Aix are Tuesday, Thursday, and Saturday. The market is a complicated thing, with various parts to it: fruits and veggies to one side, *brocante* to the other. The flower part of the market is half a block away, and dealers selling new clothes and cheap imports from India spill onto cours Mirabeau on Saturday. If you approach town this way and see these vendors first, you will wonder who in the world ever thought this town had a special market. You might even miss the good part of the market, near the Palais de Justice, because it is rather well hidden.

There's a big antiques salon in November and a *santon* fair in December.

OUT OF TOWN

The village of **Puyricard,** outside Aix, is interesting because it's home to the famous chocolate factory of the same name as well as the tile factory, **Carocim.** Carocim makes modern versions of old-fashioned cement tiles. You can make an appointment to see the showroom by calling ✆ **04-42-92-20-39;** check it out online at www.carocim.com.

APT

This is not the cutie-pie village you might think it is—the town is more like a city and is large enough to get lost in. There is an excellent market on Saturdays, but it's mobbed in season. Get there early, or forget it until September.

ARLES

Arles and Nîmes are considered twin cities, although they do not rest on opposite sides of a river, like Buda and Pest or Minneapolis and St. Paul. Nîmes is the real-people town and Arles is more touristy; both have Roman ruins, but Nîmes has much more shopping (p. 214).

Art historians think of Arles and say "van Gogh," while fashion victims scream "Lacroix"—the fashion designer who comes from Arles and is so well known for his Provençal touch that he designed the decoration on the TGV Med trains.

Either way, Arles stands for color and pattern and a splash of heat mixed with much passion. Arles is much more touristy than Nîmes, and it's also smaller. As for shopping—well, this isn't where you do any major shopping; it's more where you wander around and see some tiny shops or craftspeople or possibly luck into something you've been searching for.

Good News/Bad News

The good news first: Lots of stores are open on Sundays during fair weather. Now the bad news: There is a terrific **Monoprix,** handily located right at the place Lamartine where barges come to port—and it's closed on Sundays.

Getting Around Arles

You can enjoy a stroll and see it all, but we're talking a big stroll. You may want to try the Petit Train, one of those tourist trains that stops at all the highlights.

Shopping in Arles

SHOPPING NEIGHBORHOODS

MAIN DRAG   The boulevard des Lices (which becomes the av. Victor Hugo) is the main street through the heart of town, passing the Jardin d'Été before stretching itself out into real-people land. Behind this very nice garden (especially fun on Sun for a very French feel) lie the Théâtre Antique and, beyond that, the Roman Amphitheater.

CUTIE PIE   At a perpendicular angle to the boulevard des Lices lies the smallish rue Jean Juarès, which is the main retail street for name brands, of which there are only a few.

REPUBLIQUE   The town hall is at the place de la République, from which the rue de la République stretches off toward the river, with some mom-and-pop and French brand retail along the way. This is a pedestrian street.

MAYOR'S DRAG   Right around the town hall is the rue de l'Hôtel de Ville, a pedestrian-only street for shoppers. If you follow this street away from boulevard des Lices and toward the river, you'll be parallel to the famed place du Forum.

PLACE DU FORUM   Pushed back into the middle of nowhere, somewhat hidden between shopping breaks, is this adorable square with the two most famous hotels in town (do have a look-see: Le Nord-Pinus and l'Hôtel Forum) as well as the Café Van Gogh. Stores are all around.

AMPHITHEATER   There are scads of TTs in a row encircling the Roman Amphitheater—if you're wandering these back streets, follow the rond point des Arènes (the street that goes around the building) and look for signs to THEATRE ANTIQUE and place Bornier. This will lead you past many shops selling fabrics and pottery, plus a few that offer specialty foods from the area (you have loaded up on bull sausage, haven't you?).

FINDS

LES ETOFFES DE ROMANE
10 bd. des Lices.

This looks like a TT (and it is), but it's got great items made from Provençal-style fabrics—and the prices are the best in the south. This store is also larger than most, and while the fabrics are not of the quality of the big names in *tissus Indiennes,* they do not all look cheap or tacky—as can happen. Open Sundays.

SOULEIADO
4 bd. des Lices.

This branch of Souleiado had items I couldn't find in Nîmes— I got the bed linen I wanted. The staff couldn't be nicer and pulled things down from high shelves for me. Open on Sundays in season.

AVIGNON

This is the part of the book where we all burst into song: *"Sur le pont d'Avignon, l'on y danse . . ."* You, too, will be dancing when you get to Avignon, but not on the bridge. In fact, you may not know that it's not really a bridge—it's half a bridge. It just sort of juts out into the water and ends. People walk to the end, look down, and then walk back and tell their relatives they've been there and done that.

Getting to Avignon

Avignon has two train stations: **Avignon Centre** and **Avignon TGV**. There is shuttle-bus service between the two. If you take the TGV Méditerranée here, you will arrive at Avignon TGV, a very architecturally interesting station that looks like half of a flying saucer. Note that the Avignon TGV station has two fronts, marked North and South; if you're meeting people here, you'd better agree ahead of time exactly which door, as it can be confusing.

Trains to both Avignon stations leave Paris from the Gare de Lyon. However, the train to Avignon TGV takes just under 2½ hours, while the train to Avignon Centre takes almost 4 hours.

The Lay of the Land

The town of Avignon is bigger than you think and has many parts to it; in fact, Avignon is the hub city of this part of Provence. But that's for real people. Tourists and visitors will be most interested in the city that lies within the old walls, *centre ville*—the cutie-pie part.

If you're driving, head for the walls and enter the city through any of the gates. Like all medieval cities, Avignon has true walls and is built in concentric circles. There are no grid streets whatsoever, and only the teeny center of the circle has any kind of sense to it. The whole city within the walls is a warren of tiny streets that are all one-way—*bonne chance*. The bigger rental cars won't even make some of the corners. I know from experience.

If you're lucky, you'll enter town through the Porte de la République (across the street from the main train station). By entering through this gate, you're on the cours Jean Jaurès, which becomes the rue de la République, the main shopping street. It dead-ends into the place de l'Horloge. Park as soon as you are able, even if it means paying for a garage.

Sleeping in Avignon

HOTEL D'EUROPE
12 place Crillon.

This is a great choice, right in the center of town. The restored old hotel is decorated with tapestries and offers two wonderful terraces for meals or drinks—your choice of view. There are 44 rooms and 3 suites; prices average around 261€ ($300) per night. There's also a nice restaurant on the property. Local phone ✆ 04-90-14-76-76. www.hotel-d-europe.fr.

LA MIRANDE
4 place de la Mirande.

Oh me, oh my, where's the camera, where's the *Architectural Digest* crew? This is one of the most magnificent properties in France; you can sleep, eat, sip, snack, go to cooking classes, or just shop in the owner's little boutique in the basement. Try all, but not at the same time.

Each guest room is different, but all are decorated with the Provençal charm you were hoping for. The kitchen is also famous, so you might want to save up for a meal even if you aren't staying here. You can eat in the dining room or on the terrace; there is also a sunroom where tea and snacks are served. The full lunch for two people, along with a glass of wine and some iced tea, was about 100€ ($115) last summer . . . and worth every penny. Room rates begin at 250€ ($288). Local phone ✆ **04-90-85-93-93.** Fax 04-90-86-26-85.

Eating in Avignon

LE CLOÎTRE DES ARTS
83 rue Joseph Vernet.

This is a two-part establishment: part gastronomic restaurant and part quick-bite joint. It's very Starck-meets-medieval, quite spectacular and splendid. For reservations, call ✆ **04-90-85-99-04.**

NANI
Rue de la République (at rue Théodore Aubanel).

This is the perfect soup-and-sandwich kind of cute local cafe, right off the main shopping street. You can eat upstairs or on the street level. Choose from salads, quiches, potato tarts, and local fare. No credit cards.

Shopping in Avignon

The fancy shopping street in town is rue Joseph Vernet, which veers off to the left from the rue de la République, right across the street from the tourist office. It is to your left if the tourist office is to your right, and the "old" train station is behind you.

Your basic multiples are on the main street, rue de la République: There is a newly refurbished **Monoprix** (what more does any shopper need?), as well as branch stores of those essentials like **FNAC, Zara,** and **Sephora.** There are also some crepe stands and tourist traps. The big stores are open during lunch; Monday mornings are not totally dead. The best store in town is located in the basement of La Mirande (see above): It's the hotel gift shop, so it has no official name, but it sells style by the yard, the house brand of olive oil, children's clothing, tabletop and decorative items, and other things of whimsy the owner finds.

Among the stores you'll find on the rue Joseph Vernet are **Laurèl, Georges Rech, Cacharel, Ventilo,** and **Façonnable.** There are also assorted boutiques for everything from jeans to Japanese droop. The big names are concentrated on the part of the rue Joseph Vernet that is almost directly parallel to the place de l'Horloge; get there via the rue St-Agricol, which has become the fanciest street in town. There are several other shops here, including a renovated branch of **Hermès** (no. 7).

All the little streets clustered around rue Joseph Vernet—including rue de la Petite Fusterie, rue Limas, and place de Lunel—have charming and wonderful stores. Many of them are antiques shops; rue de la Petite Fusterie seems to concentrate on home style. When you see the local matrons walking around with their fabric swatches, you'll think of every Judy Krantz book you've ever read; this part of Avignon feels a lot like Beverly Hills.

On the other side of the place de l'Horloge, leading toward place Pie, is rue Marchands, the town's second-tier leading shopping street. You'll find **Les Olivades** here, as well as assorted other real-people shops, including **Foot Locker.** This is a pedestrian area where you can amble and browse.

Surrounding the place du Palais de Papes are several TTs, some of which are rather fancy and good fun. I like **Avignon Souvenirs** (7 place du Palais) because it has very classy giftwares.

MARKETS, FESTIVALS & FAIRS

Every day except Monday, there's a market, Aux Halles, at place Pie. There's also a supermarket there, in a small mall called Les Halles, as well as a public parking lot.

On Saturday morning, there's a *brocante* market at place Crillon. On Sunday morning, there is a flea market at place des Carmes, which is within walking distance of Aux Halles, but a little off center. Check your map.

Avignon is famous for its summer theater festival. There are also numerous big antiques salons and *brocante* fairs during the year. The annual pottery fair attracts some 30,000 visitors; it's hard to say which is more fun—the wares or the fact that you're shopping in the shadow of the Palais des Papes.

OUT OF TOWN

On the other side of the river, which you can reach by a whole bridge (not the famous half-bridge), lies the suburb of **Villeneuve-lès-Avignon,** which has a flea market on Saturday morning. You can get there by bus if you don't have a car.

In **Le Pontet,** a northern suburb, there's a giant commercial center that has all the big stores you would expect of an American suburb, including the *hypermarché* **Auchan** (the French version of Home Depot), **Leroy Merlin,** and many discounters, off-pricers, and outlet shops. There's a nice home store called **Alinéa** that has good prices on pottery and tabletop goods. It's not a charming shopper's heaven, but if you have a house or rent one, this is where you can load up.

DROME PROVENÇALE

The Drôme is a *département* of France, directly north of the Vaucluse yet somewhat south of Lyon. Most of the other sections in this chapter list individual cities, but the Drôme covers several towns that are all near one another (within an hour's drive) and make up a secret portion of Provence.

The part of this *département* closest to Vaucluse is called the Drôme Provençale. This is a great find: Few tourists know about it, yet the area is filled with wonderful castles, fields of lavender, great pottery towns, lots of *brocante*, and more olives than you can count.

You can get here via the A6 autoroute (exit for Nyons) or simply by continuing on past Vaison-la-Romaine (p. 226) in your travels—the border is just past Vaison, and the town of Nyons is a mere 10km (6 miles) from Vaison.

The villages below happen to be in alphabetical order, but are also, by coincidence, listed from north to south. I have not included the city of Montélimar in the listings because it is large and not one of those charming little villages you want to know about, as the others are. Well, actually, there are parts of Montélimar that are charming.

Nougat freaks, however, may want to go to Montélimar for visits to various nougat factories. Nougat is also sold at stores and highway rest stops throughout this region.

DIEULEFIT   One of the most famous pottery towns in Provence, Dieulefit also has a few good antiques fairs throughout the summer. They're listed in any of the monthly antiques guides. Most people come here to visit the various pottery shops that dot the road into town.

GRIGNAN   This town is most famous for its castle, whose mistress (the countess of Grignan) was the daughter of Mme. Sevigne, the woman who wrote her daughter detailed letters describing life at court in Paris in the mid 1700s. As a result, there is an annual Festival de la Correspondance each summer as well as a museum of letters. Grignan is the tiny, adorable, picture-postcard village you've dreamed of finding.

There are various other events throughout the summer, including two evening markets in which the artisans who attend are dressed in costume. The party goes on until 2am. These evening markets are held on Friday nights, usually one in mid-July and one in early August. For exact dates, contact the tourist office (© 04-75-46-56-75; ot.paysdegrignan@wanadoo.fr).

The town of Grignan is not large and can be walked; you can climb up to the château and shop your way there. This is a circular village, but most of the stores are easy to find and include all the artsy little boutiques you could want, along with purveyors of *brocante,* pottery, and even some fashion. Market day is Tuesday; there's truffle market from November until March.

NYONS   Nyons is perhaps the most commercial of the villages, in that there's a well-known American cook, **Lydie Marshall** (www.lydiemarshall.com), who owns a château where you can stay and cook. There are also other small guesthouses, some of which do promotions based on the seasons—such as a truffle weekend or even a well-being weekend (go to www.uneautremaison.com or call © 04-75-26-43-09). The truffle weekend includes three truffle markets, two nights' stay, two dinners, and one truffle hunt with dogs, all for 400€ ($460).

The part of Nyons you'll be interested in is the Old City. It is easily walked, although the area has more sprawl to it than you might think. Don't miss the area alongside the river named promenade de la Digue, which has an olive-oil mill called **Les Vieux Moulins à Huile** (no. 4), a lavender mill called **Distillerie Bleu Provence** (no. 58), and some TTs (tourist traps). The scent of the lavender as it is being distilled will fill your soul.

Market days are Thursday throughout the year and Sunday from April until September. Sundays are mobbed, as this is one of the best Sunday markets in the area.

For real-people needs, there are two excellent supermarkets right in the heart of town as well as a branch of **Monoprix** (which has no grocery store).

FORCALQUIER

Forcalquier is not far from Manosque in eastern Provence. Comparisons end there—this village is everything I wanted Manosque to be, and it's one of the most perfect little dream towns of Provence. It is also the headquarters of **Oliviers & Co.**, the olive-oil firm, and **zChocolat,** the Internet firm that distributes handmade chocs.

Note that this town is more "up" than others and is in the Alpilles. Forcalquier is small, but it's big enough to have an upper medieval city (enter by the obelisk; you can walk). If there's no market (every Mon morning) or crafts fair going on in the main square, you'll want to go into the old town for shopping.

The town is very real and yet has great stores, including a branch of **Oliviers & Co.,** several fabric and home-style shops, and two branches of the home store **La Terraio,** one of which is the cutest store in town. The town of Mane, just outside Forcalquier, is where the O&Co. offices are located; there's a mill there, too. Also check out **La Boutique,** for country textiles— many are heavy canvas or linen for home furnishings.

Finds

HENRI BARDOUIN/DISTILLERIES ET DOMAINES DE PROVENCE
Forcalquier.

This is not quite a factory outlet, but you can call it a factory-owned store. It sells all the brands of pastis and liqueurs made by Henri Bardouin, which is one of the more famous lines. The store is on a side street; you can see the still outside. The decor is cute and the store obviously caters to tourists, who've come to buy the distilled tastes of Provence.

OLIVIERS & CO.
Av. de la Burlière, Mane.

This is the mother *moulin* for the Oliviers & Co. business, although there is no factory-outlet store because O&Co. does not discount olives or olive products. It still makes a great visit.

zCHOCOLAT FACTORY
www.zchocolat.com.

zChocolat has no store, so you can order online and just enjoy or you can call ahead and make an appointment. *Born to*

Shop (and Bonjour Paris website) readers are invited to tour the factory and buy directly while there.

Now then, about the product: The chocolates are not made at the factory but at several places around the region. Each maker makes only his specialties, which the execs at Z have tasted, tested, and voted on. I did a taste test and was knocked out by the quality. You get a very unique range of tastes of Provence, including a lavender chocolate and a local almond chocolate that is not found elsewhere.

Visit www.zchocolat.com to see for yourself. To get directions and make an appointment, e-mail zchocolat@zchocolat. com. If you are not going to show for the appointment, be kind enough to cancel. The phone number is ✆ 04-42-91-43-65.

L'ISLE SUR LA SORGUE

If it's *Dimanche* (Sunday), this must be L'Isle sur la Sorgue, so *bon dimanche,* everyone, and welcome to the best Sunday in Provence.

Note: This is a Sunday that needs to be carefully planned, as French towns that are open on Sunday are few and far between, and you wouldn't want to sleep late and miss all the action. Things do dry up by around 1pm. L'Isle sur la Sorgue has a flea market and food market on Sunday only; on Saturday and Monday, the antiques dealers are open, but there are no markets. It is hard to understand the difference until you see it all in action . . . and read the following:

- Parking in this town is very difficult; get there early and use the **Spar** (a local supermarket) parking lot. You'll be charged 2€ ($2.30) to park, but it will be worth it.
- If you're planning on grocery shopping, don't forget to bring a tote bag or your own little French string bag. This is France, remember? Each package will be wrapped in its own small fashion, but you will not be given any carrier bags.

- Not all toilets are up to American standards. Have tissues in your handbag and be prepared for stand-up bathrooms (that is, wear a skirt).
- Learn your shipping options early in the game.
- Carry a notebook and pen, take notes, and memorize this phrase: *Je suis marchand.* It means "I am a buyer" and it entitles you to an automatic 20% to 25% discount off the asking price. Taking notes is the most convincing part.
- Speak some French; it's not essential, but it makes everything work better, including discounts.

The Lay of the Land

For a village you've never heard of, L'Isle la Sorgue is surprisingly big and stretches along the banks of the Sorgue River—hence the name. It is also a bit confusing at first.

The high street for antiques dealers runs alongside the river. The village is on the other side of the river from the main road, so you really have two parts of town right there. You might do a drive-through along the main drag first, although finding parking will be hard—you may want to grab any available space. Trust me.

The main part of the flea market is the *brocante* market, which is held every Saturday and Sunday, no matter what the weather, and lies at the far end of town along the riverbank. There are about 50 dealers. But don't fret. Antiques shops, some cafes, and some antiques warehouses line the high street on the nonriver side. The name of this street changes frequently but is most often written as avenue des 4 Otages. There are some 200 dealers in permanent digs. Many are in buildings that are behind buildings or in little villages set up over tiny bridges on or around a courtyard. The scene is far deeper than you can imagine at first glance, and the shopping is also far more serious than you can imagine.

The *centre ville* lies on the other side of the river from the antiques shops. The main shopping street of the inner village is called the rue de la République. A fruit, vegetable, and food market runs along the quay side, on the *centre ville* side of the river on Sundays; this is called the quai de Jean Jaurès.

Numerous bridges—some for cars, some for pedestrians—connect the two parts of town. The river is not very wide.

Eating in L'Isle

There are scads of cafes along the river and even on the sidewalk; several markets also have restaurants or cafes. If it's market day, you can picnic; otherwise, you might want to try **Le Café du Village** (village des Antiquaires de la Gare, behind the Spar market).

Shopping in L'Isle

ABOUT SHIPPING   There are several shipping agents in town; just wander in and have a chat. Essentially, it's easy but expensive—price is determined by cubic measurement, not weight, so you can buy a large piece of furniture and fill it with stuff, and it will cost no more to ship than it would to send only the large piece of furniture. That's the good news. The bad news is that prices begin at 435€ ($500) per 1 cubic meter, and that does not include packing, insurance, or clearing U.S. Customs, let alone getting from the port of entry into your dining room. My advice? Take excess baggage on the plane, which costs less. Or buy a house nearby.

SHOPPING HOURS   Things get going around 9am on Saturday and Sunday. Dealers start to set up at 8:30am, but that first hour is sort of lazy, so there's no need to rush. Just about everything in town is open on Sunday morning. The food market closes at 1pm on Sunday, as do most of the local shops, but the dealers and the flea market go on until 6pm.

Note: The *brocante* market is on both Saturday and Sunday, but the food market in the streets runs only on Sunday.

I wouldn't bother with this town anytime except the weekend, and then maybe I'd come for a whole weekend. You can spend Saturday with the regular dealers (many of whom are open only on weekends), and Sunday with the market and the dealers you missed or want to visit again.

If you're in town just for a Sunday, arrive by 10am and shop all day, but plan to buy your Sunday dinner as a picnic before the market closes at 1pm. They'll put your rotisserie chickens in hot-bags for you. Just store in your car, as you will make many trips to the car during the day anyway.

While you're roaming the streets, choose your luncheon spot and reserve a table so that you can return by 1 or 1:15pm. You'll probably want to stop by your car to drop off groceries and other loot before you sit down to lunch. Many places have regulars who know the drill. (I was belittled in French for not knowing the routine at the place I chose for lunch once.)

Dealers are open on Monday. And many are open *sur rendez vous,* which means you call ahead and make an appointment for a time and date other than when the store is open. You need to speak French.

MARKETS & FAIRS   *Brocante* markets are Saturday and Sunday. Market days are Thursday and Sunday (mornings only). There are two big antiques fairs during the year: one at Easter and the other during the few days around August 15, which is a holiday in France (Feast of the Assumption). You can contact the fair organizers (© **04-94-03-40-72;** fax 04-94-31-27-25) for exact dates.

FINDS   Many of the dealers in town are famous and sought after by buyers from all over the world. Perhaps the most famous is **Michel Biehn** (7 av. des 4 Otages), who is an expert in textiles and Provençal fabrics and costumes. Biehn's shop is in a freestanding house. It is one of the best stores in France and sells far more than regional textiles. Francine, of **La Boutique de Francine** (1 rue Julien-Guigue), is also big on fabrics and lace.

Numerous buildings are marked as if they are *brocante* fairs unto themselves. Take a look at **Brocante 11** (11 av. des 4 Otages). Also check out **Isle Aux Brocante** (nos. 7 and 4), where you can shop and eat lunch.

LOURMARIN

Lourmarin has a fabulous, fabulous, fabulous market on Fridays. It's very crowded, but with items you might not have seen before. Count on lots of walking because of the inability to park your car in the actual village. The town itself is another one of those picture-postcard perfections: small, quaint, cutie-pie. It's not far from Roussillon, Apt, and the heart of the Luberon area.

MANOSQUE

I had heard about Manosque and expected it to be delish to look at and marvelous to shop. I was quite annoyed to find that it is a large city, its medieval core is cute but not very cute, and the shopping is less than so-so. With that understanding, this is a pinpoint on the map, not a destination, and it is near many places you'll want to be.

Finds

LE MOULIN DE L'OLIVETTE
Place de l'Olivette.

This olive oil has won many awards. The *moulin* itself is a rather dressed-up TT, but it's still fun. The location is perfect; you'll have to pass by anyway on your way to Forcalquier. The shop sells oil on tap to locals and in bottles for tourists; it also carries soap, books, gifts, pastis, and other goodies. The shop is open Monday through Saturday from 8am to noon and 2 to 6pm. From April through September, the afternoon hours are 2:30 to 6:30pm.

L'Occitane Factory Store
ZI St-Maurice.

Before you wet your pants with anticipation and toss down this guide to book a shopping tour, there are a few things you need to know about this factory shop.

First off, it's very cute and easy to shop, it gift-wraps for free, and it has tons of stuff. But the discount is from 10% to 25%—and that's off French prices, not U.S. prices, which is not my idea of a real bargain.

Second, this outlet is a true factory store, located right on the factory grounds. It's in an industrial park (ZI, *zone industriel,* in French). Although the address reads Manosque, the shop is actually in the greater Manosque metro area, across the river, so you have to make a special driving trip to get here to save little money.

Third, all the tags say FACTORY STORE on them, so you can't pass off gifts to others as anything but a discounted product.

Hours are Monday through Friday from 9am to 6pm, Saturday from 9am to 1pm. For information, you can try e-mailing trecouvret@loccitane.fr. To get here, take the A51 north to exit 18, Manosque. When you get to the roundabout, turn right onto D901. Cross the highway; at the next roundabout, look for the sign to ZI St-Maurice. Finally, after you've made the turn to the ZI St-Maurice, the road forks: Go to the right. If you go left, you will come up to the rear of the factory, think it's closed, and be mad at me.

MAUSSANE-LES-ALPILLES

This town is simply known as Maussane and is near enough to St-Rémy that they are often visited (and shopped) together. **Boutique Jean Martin,** 8 rue Charloun-Rieu, sells local foodstuffs, while **Moulin Jean-Marie Cornille,** rue Charloun-Rieu, is a local olive-oil mill. Jean-Pierre Démery, of the family that founded and until recently owned Souleiado, now has a small restaurant in town called **Centre Ville.**

MÉNERBES

....

This is one of those adorable villages that makes you love the world a little bit more—it's also the original village that Peter Mayle wrote about in his first book and is the home of the Truffle Museum, this being one of the truffle market cities in wintertime. To add to that, Ménerbes is the location of **La Bastide de Marie** (p. 163), one of the fanciest hotels in the area. I call Ménerbes the Beverly Hills of Provence, as it has a superficial layer of perfection to it that isn't very rustic, but rather is distilled to weed out reality.

NÎMES

....

Nîmes and Arles are quite close to each other; Nîmes serves as much more of the commercial shopping area of the two. There is a branch of every major French multiple in Nîmes, and the town has many different shopping districts.

The Lay of the Land

Nîmes has a local airport as well as a train station (beware, it's hard to get taxis at the station!) and is actually the French gateway to Barcelona—a mere 3 hours away. The Spanish influence comingles with the Provençale, and before you can say *olé*, you notice that this part of France is somewhat different from others—even from other parts of Provence.

In fact, Avignon—which is not that far away—is considered the heart of one part of Provence, while Nîmes often claims it's located in southwestern France. Go figure. You'll see the differences reflected in local merchandise. (No bull!)

If you're driving and looking for the real world and the big-box stores, take the Nîmes Ouest exit on the autoroute.

Carrefour is open from 9am to 10pm—and has good prices on gas.

Getting Around Nîmes

Walk, but don't dismiss a taxi or a tour if offered—just for the opportunity to see the various parts of Nîmes and how they connect (especially if you're staying for a few days). Even the city center is larger than you think: There could be a fabulous flea market just 2 blocks from your hotel in an odd direction that you won't know about unless you really get out there. (*Hint:* The Sat flea market is held 2 blocks from the Hotel Imperator.)

Sleeping in Nîmes

HOTEL IMPERATOR CONCORDE
Quai de la Fontaine.

One of the nicest hotels in town, this one is within walking distance of many shopping destinations; there's a big flea market in the other direction that's held each Saturday. You can dine outside in season. Rates begin around 100€ ($115). For U.S. reservations, call **Concorde Hotels** (© 800/888-4747). Local phone © 04-66-21-90-30. www.hotel-imperator.com.

Shopping in Nîmes

SHOPPING NEIGHBORHOODS

MAIN SHOPPING   The main drag in town is rue Général Perrier, where the mass brands such as **Sephora** (no. 1) are located. Running perpendicular is the rue du Grand Couvent at one end and the rue de l'Aspic toward the other. The side streets are home to more upmarket brands and lead into the hidden parts. The mall is also on Perrier.

HIDDEN SHOPPING   There's a medieval maze of streets between Monoprix and the Maison Carrée. Most of the stores are small, but there's a niche area of luxe, with such brands as **YSL.** The rue de la Madeleine is another back street, very picturesque and running crosstown from the place aux Herbes.

CLOCK   To explore the streets weaving around the place de l'Horloge, find the rue des Marchands for one end of the area . . . and use the rue de l'Horloge as another spoke.

PLACE DE LA MAISON CARRÉE   This is the center of the tourist universe and brand-name shopping, including **Les Olivades** (no. 4) for Provençal style.

BOULEVARD SHOPPING   Alongside the Maison Carrée (on the outside) lies boulevard Victor Hugo, which has some good shopping near the tourist areas, including a nice branch of **Souleiado,** no. 40.

FINDS

BOUTIQUE DES PASSIONNES
5 rue Jean Reboul.

This is right near the arena: an everything-bull shop.

LES INDIENNE DE NIMES
2 bd. des Arènes.

Head here for regional clothing designs. Closes at lunch.

MARKETS

FLEA MARKET   Saturdays, at the Jardins de la Fontaine and boulevard Jean-Jaurès.

SPICE MARKET   Outside, facing the street, under the eaves of FNAC at La Coupole des Halles.

LES HALLES   A main-street mall with a fresh-food market on the ground floor and mall above. The market is open from 6:30am until 1pm, 7 days a week. The mall keeps regular store hours.

FLOWER MARKET   Mondays, at Stade des Costières.

OUT OF TOWN: NEARBY OUTLETS

CACHAREL
Av. Maréchal Juin.

You need a car for this; you should also call ahead (℡ **04-66-02-01-38**) to verify. And yes, this was a big textile producing area: That's how denim *(tissus de Nîmes)* got its name!

PERRIER
Vergèze.

Located on the RN113 between Nîmes and Montpellier, the Perrier factory has different hours depending on the season, but is open year-round and 7 days a week. Tastings are free.

ROMANS

Do not confuse Romans with Vaison-la-Romaine (p. 226), although obviously both owe something to Rome. But Romans is much more of a shopping capital—it is not only the home of all the shoe factories for the major French brands (yes, they have factory stores), but also the location of one of the Marques Avenue outlet malls.

Romans is one of those towns that is divided by a river (all commerce needs a river), so some of the shoe outlets are in the town of Bourg-de-Péage, just across the bridge.

To get here from Lyon, exit the A7 autoroute for Romans (exit 13); after you pay the toll, curve right to connect onto the D532, which will lead right into town. Note that it's not too far from the Valence TGV station if you prefer to come by train and then rent a car. Romans is also about a 1-hour drive south of Lyon.

Romans is set off the highway for a rather boring 15- to 20-minute drive, so relax. When you get to town, you will not be knocked out by its charm. Never mind. You didn't come for the charm. Oh yes, there is a shoe museum, too (2 rue Ste-Marie).

On your way into town, you will pass a *hypermarché* named Hyper U; this is a good place to fill the tank with low-cost gas. Note that Romans has several different shopping areas, so don't underestimate the area to be shopped or the need for a car.

If you come from the Valence TGV, you will work in reverse, arriving first in Bourg-de-Péage via the A49. The sources listed below are in order of discovery if you are coming from Lyon.

Finds

CHARLES JOURDAN
Parc Affaires espace Mossant, Bourg-de-Péage.

To get to this large Charles Jourdan store, which is in downtown Bourg-de-Péage, follow signs out of Romans, across the river Isère, and voilà, look to your left immediately.

With McDonald's next door, it's hard to know what more you could want. The selection here changes, as the line is in flux—Patrick Cox has moved in as design director. The store sells men's and women's shoes as well as a few handbags, small leather goods and belts, and some leather clothing—suede shirt-jackets and shearling coats were on sale during my last visit.

JACQUELINE DHERBEYS
12 côte Jacquemart, Romans.

There are a few sources for sheets, towels, and domestic linens at Marques Avenue, but while in the area you might want to pop into this jobber, which sells the Laura Ashley and Dorma brands. The store is right near the Tour Jacquemart, a landmark from the 15th century.

MARQUES AVENUE
60 av. Gambetta, Romans.

This is an American-style mall in that it resembles a village, although not a cutie-pie fake one—it simply has walkways that take you past all the stores. Among my favorites here is the Amor Lux outlet, which sells the colored fisherman's striped T-shirts I like so much, but at half-price. There's also a Souleiado outlet and many fashion brands such as GR (Georges Rech), Apostrophe, Ines de la Fressange, Ventilo, Tara Jamon, and Regina Rubens.

To get to this mall, you most likely will have to drive past it and then circle back at the next roundabout. Facilities include a large free parking lot and clean bathrooms; there is a small cafe for snacks but nothing grand.

Hours are Monday from 2 to 7pm, Tuesday through Friday from 10am to 7pm, and Saturday from 9:30am to 7pm. Closed on Sundays.

ROBERT CLERGERIE
Rue Pierre Curie and av. Duchesne, Romans.

As you drive into town, you'll see a large sign for this outlet, so don't panic by the lack of street address. The factory takes up the entire block and therefore has no exact address.

This is a real factory store in a real factory, selling the Robert Clergerie brand for women and the J. Fenestrier brand for men. Most shoes cost around 90€ ($104), with handbags closer to 150€ ($173). Everything is half-price and to swoon for. Women's sizes go up to 40½; men's to size 45.

For more shoes, head to the street called **côte des Cordeliers,** where there's another Clergerie shop and different factory stores (try no. 6 and no. 18) for brands such as Paraboot and Hardrige.

STEPHANE KELIAN
Espace Mossant, Bourg-de-Péage.

This store is in the same strip center as Charles Jourdan and a few other off-price stores. The line is now designed by Alain Tondowski, who has worked for several big names and launched his first collection in spring 2004.

ST-ETIENNE-DU-GRES

Forget about town—you're here for **Les Olivades** factory shop (chemin des Indienneurs, St-Etienne-du-Grès; ✆ **04-90-49-19-19**), a freestanding building at the rear of the factory that makes all the sensational *tissus Indiennes* prints for this famous firm; there is parking in the rear as well.

The outlet is open on Monday morning, which totally shocked (and delighted) me; hours are Monday through Thursday from 9am to noon and 2 to 6pm. The factory shop accepts Visa, wraps gifts, and can fetch an English-speaking salesperson if needed.

The selling space is compact, neat, and filled with color and merchandise of all sorts and prices. The best bargains are in a few bins and baskets with things crumpled into them.

There is no question that you should shop here rather than at the Souleiado factory outlet.

Note: Once a year Les Olivades has a whopper of a sale— the staff closes the factory store and opens all the warehouses and factory spaces. Boxes overflow with bathing suits, racks are hung with clothes, bolts of fabric are piled into a corner. Prices are as low as 30€ ($35) for a dress, 20€ ($23) for a bathing suit. Call to ask the date of this annual sale; it's usually mid-July and falls on a weekend, with Sunday shopping hours of 9am to 1pm and 3 to 7pm. Yes, they'll still close for lunch.

ST-REMY-DE-PROVENCE

St-Rémy is a unique town in Provence because although it's almost perfect, it doesn't have the fake feel that some villages in the Luberon have adopted. It *is* touristy and could be ruined soon, but at this point, it's one of the few places in greater Provence that has some soul left. This small town offers just the right combination of real-people funk and cute perfection.

It also has one of my favorite chocolatiers in France (Joël Durand), so I drool at the very thought of St- Rémy.

Walking around the town, window-shopping, poking in and out of Souleiado, touching this and that, and buying postcards is a dream because you have the sense that, at last, you have found your own village . . . even if Princess Caroline found it first.

The handful of stores that are good are really good and really different and really able to touch you in a way that no TT can ever do; this is also a good town for foodies.

The Lay of the Land

Like many medieval towns, St-Rémy is built in a circle. Once you're inside the circle, the town has a semblance of a grid system, but there are still blind curves, dead ends, and alleys to nowhere. Fun, huh?

Most of the shopping, especially the more obvious and touristy stuff, is on the boulevard Gambetta, the rue Lafayette, the avenue de la Libération, and the boulevard Mirabeau. The best store in town is possibly **Le Grand Magasin,** 24 rue de la Commune (see below). **Souleiado,** 2 rue d'Résistance, is on one of the main drags of the grid. **Les Olivades** is located at 28 rue Lafayette. The circle that encloses the town is small, so you can just park and ramble. The street that forms the circle is named boulevard Victor Hugo; it has a surprising number of excellent shops on it.

Shopping in St-Rémy

FINDS

EBENE
38 bd. Victor Hugo.

My friend Valerie from Carpentras sent me here for "Le Look": home furnishings and high Provençal style. Ebène is a photo op (it's in an old mill) and a chance to really understand what French style is all about—and how to make it work for you.

FLORAME
34 bd. Mirabeau.

This is the new gal in town—a brand with distribution throughout France along with its own store. You'll find aromatherapy products to make you smile . . . in and out of the bathroom.

HUILE DE MONDE
16 bd. Victor Hugo.

This shop is in a mansion, set back from the street and a little forbidding-looking, but don't be stopped—it's great fun and worth the extra few steps. Each salon of the mansion's ground floor is filled with oil and olive-oil products from producers from, yep, all over the world. Do not confuse this store with Oliviers & Co., although it does sell some of the O&Co. products, along with many other brands.

JOEL DURAND
3 bd. Victor Hugo.

I dream of Joël Durand. To be more precise, I dream of Joël Durand's lavender-and-chocolate concoction, which is now known as the letter *L* ever since he switched from a numerical system to an alphabetical one. All the little squares of his chocolate look alike, but each has a letter of the alphabet on it. You are welcomed into the shop, given a chart, and invited to choose a candy to taste. If you want to taste all 26, you can buy a box that contains one of each kind.

Meanwhile, besides the chocolate squares, the store sells chocolate bars, sauces in jars, *confitures* (jams), biscuits, and other delights. If you can't go on any longer without a fix, Joël will FedEx you whatever you crave.

Note that the shop is very, very air-conditioned. It's open daily: Monday through Saturday from 9:30am to 12:30pm and 2:30 to 7:30pm, Sunday from 10am to 1pm. There is a second shop in St-Paul-de-Vence, in the hills above the Côte d'Azur (p. 295). Durand speaks English.

LE GRAND MAGASIN
24 rue de la Commune.

This is one of my favorite stores in France. It seems to sum up not only my own personality but also a piece of my soul. It's hard to actually categorize what the store sells other than to say "style," but in a fun way: You can find everything from bracelets to drinking cups to Christmas lights to decorative tin boxes to toys. There are little nooks and crannies in the rear of the store, so you can browse for quite some time. Don't drool on the stuff; it's rude.

By the way, don't let the name of the street throw you; it branches right off boulevard Victor Hugo, where all the good stores are; it's almost next door to the cookie shop.

LE PETIT DUC
7 bd. Victor Hugo.

Don't eat too many chocolates when you visit Joel, or you will have no room for old-fashioned cookies, candies, and other baked goods from this fabulous little pastry shop that uses old-fashioned methods and recipes to re-create the lost tastes of grandmother's kitchen. If grandmother were French, of course. Le Petit Duc is a photo op, eating op, and gift op.

LILLIMAND
5 av. Albert Schweitzer.

This is a famous old French source for candied fruits. If you get too sticky on your visit, you can be hosed off. (Visitors often claim their feet stick to the sugar on the floor in the very old factory.) The firm was founded in the mid-1860s and is famous throughout France for its product.

POIVRE D'ANE
25 bd. Victor Hugo.

This is another of the classy lifestyle stores that do the Provençal look with a deft touch.

MARKETS & FAIRS

The St-Rémy market is held on Wednesday and Saturday mornings. There's a local arts-and-crafts fair on the last weekend in July, as well as a big celebration on August 15, which is a holiday in France (Feast of the Assumption). A small *brocante* market is open Tuesday through Sunday afternoons only, from 3 to 7pm, from the last weekend in November until Easter; it's held on the boulevard Gambetta (no. 19).

OUT OF TOWN

Galerie de la Gare, route St-Rémy, Molleges Gare, is an antiques place (a happening that is too elaborate for me to call a store) on the outskirts of St-Rémy in an old train station, hence the name. You will drool the minute you pass by: The front yard is home to old bathtubs, statues, and pieces of style. The inside contains large pieces of furniture and everything else you can imagine. I find some prices high; still, you'll have a ball just looking and touching. It's open daily from 10am to noon and 3 to 7pm.

Olive-oil freaks may want to hunt down the **Moulin de Calanquet,** on the Old Arles road (vieux chemin d'Arles) but well outside downtown St-Rémy (about 5km/3 miles). Open daily from 9am to noon and 2:30 to 7pm.

Les Olivades has a factory shop right outside St-Rémy; see the section on St-Etienne-du-Grès, above.

SALON-DE-PROVENCE

I cannot send you to Salon-de-Provence with any more than a giggle and a warning. As a town, well, there is nothing here to write home about. I went in search of the best soap factory in France, **Savonnerie Marius Fabre** (148 av. Paul Bourret), which we found because my friend Karen refused to give up. I would have quit an hour beforehand.

Because this soap is sold all over France (and in many parts of the U.S.), I see no reason for you to go through all this just to shop at the factory store, where prices did not appear to be significantly lower than usual. However, if you want a soap tour, this is the best one in the region, and I know—I've done them all.

Visiting hours are Monday through Thursday from 10 to 11am. Boutique hours are Monday through Friday from 9:30am to noon and 1:30 to 4:30pm. Group tours can be arranged on request. Local phone ✆ 04-90-53-24-77. www.marius-fabre.fr.

TARASCON

Serious shoppers have already marked Tarascon on their maps, secure in their knowledge that they have only one life to live and that they want to see the Souleiado factory before they die. Well, welcome to my honest opinion of Tarascon.

I love Tarascon. I love the Démery family—creators of the Souleiado prints (even though I don't know them, I love them). Their little museum on the premises of the factory is indeed worth seeing before you die. They have sold the company, but the museum ticks on.

The factory shop, however, is outrageously expensive, and the people who work there are notoriously rude. I cannot welcome you to shop there. But I do welcome you to browse. Then you can go to the museum, where you'll spend your money far better than you would on anything you can buy in the shop. The museum is open Monday through Friday from 10am to 3pm. The entrance fee is 5€ ($5.75) per person.

Note: Souleiado has a relatively new design director, Luc Vincent, who is making the line a little more mode and a little less what-I-wore-to-the-Provençal-fair. Each year, he hires a new designer to give the old fabrics a twist. There's both fashion and home style. There are still Souleiado stores in most major Provençal cities, so coming to Tarascon is more for the museum than anything else.

The Lay of the Land

You will probably enter town via the N99 and find yourself on the main shopping street for real people. (See that Monoprix? Don't you feel better now?) It's called cours Aristide Briand before it becomes the avenue de la République. This main street curves around the city and hits the water, and then you'll see a bridge. Don't cross the water unless you want to leave Tarascon. Park. Walk.

The main cute area is a cobbled pedestrian street called Les Halles. The tourist office is located here, as are a few real-people shops, such as the grocery store, the bakery, and Super Drug. Some of the stores are open on Monday morning (as is Monoprix, 2 blocks over).

Like all medieval towns, the city center here is a warren of squares that dead-end into nothing. Get a map.

Attention, Crafters

If you are seriously interested in the art of making a *boutis* (French quilt), there is a special class held in association with the museum. The package includes hotel, dinner, museum fees, and working in the atelier with embroidery experts. The price is about 300€ ($345) per person; call ☎ 04-90-59-49-36 for info.

VAISON-LA-ROMAINE

Vaison-la-Romaine is famous to the world because it has the largest unearthed Roman village in France; many Americans know it because the cookbook author and foodie Patricia Wells lives here and gives cooking classes from her château. I know it because I live here, too, but not in a château. In fact, my house is so tiny it's really an apartment—but what a view: I live next to the Roman ruins.

Vaison itself is not the most charming town in France or even one worth visiting, except for the ruins. One of the many good things about it, however, is that you can get the feel of real life in Provence. Because it's not overly cute, it's very real. And therein lies much of the charm.

One of the things I like about Vaison is that it functions like a city—so there's much of interest, ranging from shopping streets to several squares to an ancient Roman bridge to an upper and lower village and scads of ruins. On the edge of town, there are vineyards for tastings and all the côte du Rhone vines you can gaze lovingly at.

Vaison makes a good base for exploring the area, for wine tastings, and for taking in assorted Roman cities from here to Orange and beyond. The town has enough shopping opportunities to keep anyone happy—and there are two supermarkets. The Tuesday market, from 8am to 1pm, is becoming one of the largest in the area, and it sells absolutely everything. Get there early—it's hard to find parking.

Vaison is also quite close to the Drôme; Nyons is a mere 10km (6 miles) away (p. 206).

The Lay of the Land

One of Vaison's charms is that it is *atypique*. It is not a circular village, nor is it adorable. The city is divided into two parts by a river and a hill—the medieval city is up the hill and is very cute but closed to vehicular traffic, so wear your best walking shoes. There is not much shopping up there—just a few art galleries, cafes, and some chances to wonder what it would be like to live there.

Below, a Roman bridge leads into the heart of the real town, which is a series of streets backed up around place Montfort, the main square. One of the delights of Vaison is that the main square is not in the heart of town . . . or it's not the only heart of town. The square is lined with cafes on one side, shops on the others, and a nearby pedestrian street called rue Grande offers yet more shopping.

Moving away from the square and the river, you'll come to the line of Roman ruins, divided into two portions cut apart by the post office and the tourist office. The tourist office has a store and even sells the local wines.

As you head away from town, you'll see a supermarket called **Super U;** past that a mile is a larger supermarket called **Intermarché,** which is a good place for cheap gas. Both of these markets carry more than food—they have health and beauty aids, garden supplies, clothes, books, maps, and more.

Finds

ALAIN ET ANNICK BERTHEAS
Mas Belair, route Séguret (between Vaison and Séguret).

Although the south is filled with potters and it's not hard to fall in love with every pot ever thrown, I think you'll find Alain et Annick Bertheas's wares more sophisticated than most—and better able to make the transition from souvenirs to serious pieces.

Prices seem fair to me; I keep buying pieces as gifts and then keeping them for myself. The average for a good-size item falls between 26€ and 43€ ($30–$50). Business is so good that Alain no longer appears at many of the local pottery events, although he is in Séguret for the annual show there at the end of August. Note that Alain does not speak English and does not ship, though he will pack each piece in bubble wrap and box everything for you.

The atelier is well marked (POTIER) and lies halfway between Vaison-la-Romaine and Séguret. If you're driving from Séguret toward Vaison, look for the sign right after you pass the roundabout with the fake Roman arch in the center. The phone is ☎ 04-90-46-15-58.

HADRIEN 2000
Rue la Mexique, Vaison-la-Romaine.

This small gallery is in the heart of downtown Vaison, a block from place Montfort, the main square. All the wares are inspired by the Roman ruins; they're subtle, sophisticated, and worth every euro of the asking price. Unfortunately, the asking price is high (the good stuff costs about 1,000€/$1,150) and the items are so heavy that shipping could cost a fortune. Still, you should stop by just to stare.

LIBRARIE MONTFORT
40 Grand Rue, Vaison-la-Romaine.

This excellent bookstore carries a large concentration of cookbooks and volumes on local color.

PLEIN SUD
24 av. Jules Ferry, Vaison-la-Romaine.

This store makes me think of Barneys in New York—not that it sells clothing or has anything to do with Barneys save the same elegance in display and style. While most local antiques shops look like either a jumble or grandmother's sitting room, this one feels light and stunning and chic. The sign outside the door says *objects trouves* (found objects), which defines the style. Closed for lunch from noon to 3pm, and all day Sunday and Monday.

POTTERIE DE CRESTET
Route Malaucène, Le Crestet.

This is mass-produced pottery, and it comes in amazing colors at such low prices, you'll consider booking a freighter to send yourself a container. This is a casual kind of market roadside stand/store, with wares laid out on the lawn and some tacky kitsch mixed in with the gems.

It's possible that this factory also makes the goods for the famed Emile Henry line of French cookware; more than half the stock is stamped Emile Henry—which sells at ABC Carpet for 20 times the price. I bought large blue mixing bowls for less than 8.70€ ($10) each.

The shop is open daily from 9am to noon and 2 to 7pm; it makes for great Sunday shopping. To get here, drive out of Vaison away from Ségerut, past the Point P hardware store, toward Malaucène.

Chapter Eight

....

SHOPPING THE RIVIERA: ST-TROPEZ TO NICE

WELCOME TO THE RIVIERA

....

The French Riviera isn't just a location—it's a state of mind. A few minutes among palm trees, blue seas, sparkling skies, mountain air, and topless beach bunnies, and nothing else seems real, let alone some of the amenities on those bunnies.

The Riviera is where the concept of Beverly Hills was born. It's where glamour was born. It's where resorts, in season, and postcards were born. The idea of having a suntan came from Cannes. It was none other than Coco Chanel who made being tan the in thing.

If we didn't have the Riviera, Coco Chanel would have invented it. Indeed, it was Chanel and Picasso and Gerald Murphy (whose motto was "Living well is the best revenge") and Scott and Zelda Fitzgerald who resurrected the Riviera, reclaimed it from its posh Victorian past, and made it the playground of the Western world.

For over 80 years, the Riviera has been about red-carpet treatment for the nouveau riche, not only for stars and starlets, but also for anyone who can pay the tab. And these days, the bill may be discounted enough to enable just about anyone to revel in the field of dreams.

Naturally, where there's money and glamour of this caliber, there's also good shopping. You might say this is where the born-to-shop were born. Styles and trends are often born on the streets, or beaches, here; just where do you think it was that topless sunbathing came into fashion?

An evening stroll becomes a fashion show on the catwalk of life. Everyone makes a public appearance in the south of France—that's part of the attraction. What's worn on the streets is as exciting as what's shown on the mannequins. And what's not worn is more exciting still.

Step into the *douche autobronzant* (a shower that sprays you with fake tanning oil); fasten on your sandals. Take off your top during the day and pull out Le Wonderbra by night. And don't forget to visit the spa, drink lots of healthy water, apply bust cream, and use your cellulite spray. In between, we're going to shop and eat and promenade—and be French. Okay, so we'll fake the last part. That's part of what the Riviera is all about, too.

Getting to the Riviera

FROM THE U.S.   Nice–Côte d'Azur International Airport (NCE) is the second busiest airport in France. I'm not sure if it was created to make my life better or just to boost Delta's bottom line, but if you are a south-of-France or Provence person, this airport was made for you and yours. Delta flies a daily nonstop to and from New York.

Delta has special winter promotions that include Nice—one of the few places where the weather is still balmy even when Europe has its off-price season. I got some "Starving Artists' Fares" coupons that made a round-trip ticket from New York to Nice a mere $399.

While technically you can also use the Marseille airport to get to the Côte d'Azur, it's not as convenient as Nice.

FROM PARIS   You can travel to the Riviera through the Nice or the Marseille airport by booking a connection through

The French Riviera

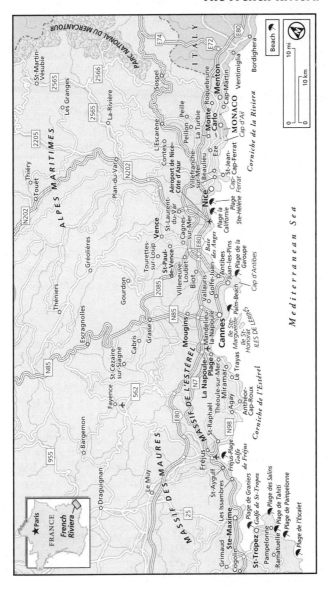

Paris. This can be costly if you want to come in or out of one city and in or out of the other. If you're writing a through ticket, however, the add-on is not as expensive, but you probably don't get a layover in Paris and you do have connecting times and terminals to keep you in line.

You can also take the train from Paris; the TGV Méditerranée will get you to Marseille in 3 hours, and then you can go on to St-Raphaël (closest train station to St-Tropez), Cannes, Nice, or Monte Carlo.

FROM THE U.K.   The boom in low-cost carriers has created scads of flights into southern France from various U.K. airports. Most of these are alternative airports, so know what you are doing and where you are going.

FROM ELSEWHERE IN THE E.U.   Amsterdam is an additional hub for Air France/KLM these days, now that the two have married (financially, at least)—so you may want to price changing planes in Amsterdam, rather than Paris, en route to the south of France. Just a thought.

Getting Around the Riviera

BY RENTAL CAR   Driving the autoroutes is fun and pretty easy, as long as you remember that these guys go fast. There has, however, been a new effort to cut speeds (and highway deaths), so watch out for radar and try to stick to the 130kmph (81 mph) speed limit on highways.

The biggest problems occur in small towns and during the summer. Parking can be a nightmare, but if you get a parking ticket, pretend you're French: Toss it away. There are a few tricks you will quickly grasp, like following signs that say OTHER DIRECTIONS and going around the roundabout a few times because you can't figure out which way to go.

BY PRIVATE TRANSPORT   If being lost in the hills is not your thing, you might need some help. Enter my old buddy Piero Bruni, who now runs **E.T.S.** (© **04-92-98-06-29;** fax

04-92-98-98-58; PBruni@compuserve.com), which stands for Executive Transport Service. Piero and his wife, Martine, are my heroes: They provide all manner of airport transfers and transportation as well as complete tours of the Riviera (and Provence) from offices in Cannes. Piero speaks fluent English and spent years as a hotelier, so service is his business. E.T.S. has cars, limos, and vans; it does day trips and overnights to Italy and around Provence; and there's a special *Born to Shop* transfer rate from the Nice airport to Cannes (p. 248).

VIP Riviera Service (© 04-93-44-22-33; fax 04-93-37-49-93) handles transportation needs in Monte Carlo, Nice, and Cannes for groups or for individuals, and it even does airport pick-ups. The office is open daily, 24 hours a day.

Markets & Fairs

The south of France is one big market. There are regular flea markets and then special events and salons, especially in Cannes and Monte Carlo. The happiest news is that there are terrific flea markets even on Monday—a day that can be totally dead for shoppers in many parts of France—every week, in and out of season.

For *brocante,* there's the **Marché Forville** in Cannes on Monday, with about 75 dealers. Also on Monday is the **Cours Saleya** in Nice, where some 250 dealers congregate. Brocante is sold in Grasse on Wednesday.

On Saturday in Cannes, there's a different flea market at the **Allées du Liberté,** right across the street from the Palais du Festivals in the heart of town. You'll find a few dozen *brocante* dealers at the Saturday market in St-Tropez. And *brocante* is sold on Thursday and Saturday at a teensy market in Antibes and on Sunday in Villefranche, which has two separate little markets—a perfect Sunday browse.

For a list of brocante in the towns you will visit, check out any of the magazines with listings—*Alladin* in the best known, but there's also *Chiner* and *Antiquites.*

Eastward Ho!

Note that the following sections in this chapter are arranged in roughly geographical order, starting with St-Tropez and heading east toward Nice.

ST-TROPEZ

Hang on to your bathing-suit top and welcome to St-Tropez, which got its reputation as the tony beach of the rich and famous in the early 1950s. St-Trop is the opposite direction down the beach from Monaco and actually has a very different kind of shopping from Monaco and Cannes . . . this is the funky kind of shopping.

St-Trop attracts so many tourists that the number-one sport here has to be staring at all those people and what they think passes as fashion. Okay, let me concede the point: Maybe the number-one sport is looking at the topless women and wondering why the ladies who should least go without a top are always the ones who are topless. But I digress. This is the village where being a little bit more outrageous than the next guy is part of a fashion statement, and where trends are set and reset with the changes in the tide.

If you're looking for more than a superficial thrill, head for the hills. If you want to get away from the parade, all you need do is head off on your own. First, get away from the port and those expensive cafes: Work your way through the winding warren of medieval streets in the Old Town, and then wander into the cute parts of the city flats. Venture even farther to the edges of town, where locals shop at the *hypermarché* (modern dry-goods store) and tourists rarely dare to go. Better yet, book yourself into a resort and never leave (try the Villa Marie).

Real Francophiles will want to go to the *hypermarché, mais oui,* but they will crave much more. That's because St-Tropez is in Var, and Var really does reach into Provence.

The area surrounding St-Tropez represents some of the best of the real France. Salernes? Did someone say tile factories? Lorgues? You want a real market? You want to eat? And for heaven's sake, can we head for Gassin now?

Don't forget that once you've gotten yourself to Salernes, you're halfway to Moustiers-Ste-Marie, which is the home of the tiny inn owned by superchef Alain Ducasse (p. 162). But I don't want to push too hard on the Provence button; there are plenty of people who will do St-Tropez as a day trip from Cannes—the contrast between the two is worth experiencing, especially during the film festival.

To sum up, St-Tropez is a place unto itself, a different state of mind. There are Cannes people and there are St-Tropez people, sort of like Martha's Vineyard people and Nantucket people, *n'cest pas?*

Getting to St-Tropez

It ain't easy to get to St-Tropez—and therein lies its fame. For a place to be a genuine haven for the rich and famous, it has to be inaccessible to mere mortals and easy to get to only for those with the ways and means to be the right kind of people. The best way to get to St-Tropez is by yacht—if not your own yacht, then someone else's yacht. Or any of the small but luxurious cruise ships that come to port here.

You can also drive, which is perfect if it's not summer. St-Tropez is only about 1½ hours from the Nice airport. But in summer, that same drive can take 4 hours. You can opt to take a helicopter from the airport or between towns; there is service between Cannes and St-Tropez. If you don't mind regional airports, you can fly right into Toulon.

There is summer ferry service among Nice, Cannes, and St-Tropez, but it's not a reliable form of transportation because it runs only if the sea is calm. Also, the times of the service are meant for day-trippers, not commuters, so you might not find this very useful. There is similar shuttle service by boat *(navette)* between St-Raphaël and Nice, for those using the Nice airport. In season, there is also a maritime transfer from St-Raphaël to

St-Tropez that usually begins in April; it's called the *bateau-taxi* and it leaves from the port. Call ✆ **04-94-95-17-46** for info.

For more direct airport service, you can take a bus, called Aviabus, from the Nice airport to St-Raphaël; you catch it right in front of the airport, easy as *gâteau*.

Hang onto your chapeau, because there is no train track along the Riviera that connects to St-Tropez. This is the meaning of exclusive. The train swerves in St-Raphaël, which isn't enormously far away, but it's not within walking distance. In summer, when the traffic makes the road as slow-moving as cold honey, you'll lose your mind trying to connect on the bus. The bus station is next door to the train station, and if you have a small tote bag, you can easily connect. If you have luggage, however, it could be problematic—made worse by the fact that frequently the connection time between bus and train is a mere 5 minutes. Oh yes, another thing about the train: Schedules change with the seasons.

Ask your hotel if it has a driver and a hotel van that can be hired to get you to the airport or wherever you need to go.

Traffic Warning

I understand that you weren't born yesterday, you are sophisticated, and of course you're expecting traffic. When I go out of my way to talk about traffic, I want to stress that traffic can be so bad that you won't have fun—that, quite simply, you can't get where you are going.

My last visit to St-Tropez was in the month of May—not even the height of the season. The 32km (20-mile) drive to the train station in St-Raphaël took over 2 hours, and we could not get a parking space in any lot (forget the street) in St-Trop on Tuesday—market day.

The traffic is so bad that road rage would be totally understandable. Reconsider bringing a car anywhere near town. Stay at a hotel in town—or stay at a resort and don't leave.

Getting Around St-Tropez

Ha. Good luck!

Sleeping in St-Tropez

HOTEL BYBLOS
Av. Paul Signac, St-Tropez.

Right in the heart of town, the Hôtel Byblos takes up a city block in a sprawl of up-and-down and layers and levels—with a swimming pool at the core. There are several shops here, as well as a nightclub that is the most chic place to boogie in town. There's no cover, but drinks are very *cher.*

Room rates begin at 305€ ($350). For U.S. reservations, call Leading Hotels of the World at ✆ **800/223-6800.** Local phone ✆ 04-94-56-68-00. Fax 04-94-97-40-52. www.byblos.com.

VILLA MARIE
Chemin Val de Rian, Ramatuelle.

Ramatuelle is not in St-Tropez—it's the next town over. Nor is this hotel in downtown Ramatuelle, but out on a plain, not too far from the beach, pushed into a wall of pine trees and lavender.

As you walk in from the car park to the multi-level villa set around a patio and pool, you can actually smell the lavender. One of the Compagnie des Hôtels de Montagne family of hotels, this one is as plush and luxe as the others, with a full spa and dining program so that you truly can make the real world go away. The Fermes de Marie line of beauty products is provided in the bathrooms and sold in the spa. This is the kind of destination you pick when you want to plunk yourself down and escape.

The hotel is open only from April to November. Rates begin at 200€ ($230). ✆ **04-94-97-40-22.** www.c-h-m.com.

Eating in St-Tropez

One of the best-known shops in town is a bakery, **Patissier Senequier** (quai Jean Jaurès), which is behind a cafe of the same name. This is the most famous cafe in town for hanging out, seeing, and being seen. Around the corner is **Carmen et Dominique, Epicurie du Marché** (7 place aux Herbes), where you can buy fresh local cheeses and other goodies.

The surrounding hills are dotted with wineries where you can pop in for free tastings. I've always had doubts about how many of these places you can take (and still be sober enough to drive), and whether the quality of the local wine is worth the time and trouble.

For a sit-down-and-be-part-of-the-scene lunch, no place else will do save **Spoon Byblos,** at the Hôtel Byblos, avenue du Maréchal Foch (© 04-94-56-68-20).

Shopping in St-Tropez

Let's face it: You don't come to St-Tropez just to shop. And it's not a place people go to be seen *in* their clothes—the converse is true. But while you're here, you might as well browse. You'll do your big-name, big-time shopping in Cannes, or even Aix. St-Tropez is for funky little shops, for boutiques filled with specialty resort wares, and for home-style Méditerranée.

Don't get me wrong, there is a very good, big perfumery in town (**Parfumerie Berton,** 19 quai Suffren) and there are a handful of designer shops; but that's not really the shopping action in St-Tropez. Sure, there's everything from **Hermès** to **Sonia Rykiel,** with **Soulieado** as well. But the fun is not in the nationally known brands.

St-Tropez is very much about the beach—especially two famous beaches, **Pampelonne** and **Tahiti.** It's common practice to have your own beach for your crowd, and to go only to that beach. You also eat at your own cafe or club there. After you order lunch, you pop up and shop at the beach shacks, which sell outrageous bathing suits and wraps and other beachy things. Vendors also come directly to you, carrying their wares.

SHOPPING HOURS

Stores usually open around 10am and close at 12:30pm for lunch. They reopen at 2:30pm or later, depending on the type of store and the season. They stay open until 7pm out of season and 9pm in season. Real-people stores tend to open at 9am; pharmacies are open during lunch. Most stores close for the midday break, although a few tourist traps (TTs) stay open nonstop.

The season is July and August; some of the stores close when the season is over. Of those that close, about half will not return the next year. There will be end-of-season sales in September, but the big sales are actually in November.

Saturday and Sunday are both big days for retail; this is one of the few towns in the Riviera where the stores are wide open on Sunday. *Bon dimanche.*

SHOPPING NEIGHBORHOODS

THE PORT   Yes, the port is where the boats are and isn't actually the best of shopping neighborhoods. It's more a shipping neighborhood. But, as in most port towns, the main street facing the water is the high street. In St-Tropez, the name of this street is quai Suffren. It not only hosts the big perfume shop Parfumerie Berton, but also has a ton of artists' stands and stalls on the water side. There are also quite a few TTs selling T-shirts, sweats, sunglasses, and hats.

OLD TOWN   If your back is to the quai Suffren and you are facing the port, the right-hand side of the port U is called quai Jean Jaurès. It is strung with famous cafes. Behind those cafes and to your right is the Old Town, identified by two landmark towers, Tour du Portalet and Tour Vielle.

Be sure to check out the tiny little arcade that is the fish market. Even though it smells, it's covered with tiles and fishy country charm. The little street leading away from the Old Town is rue de la Ponche, which is where all the fancy shops are found.

LA CITADELLE   Two of the good shopping streets in town are at odd angles and aren't where you'd expect shopping streets to be, so watch for them. If the Old Town and the water are to your back, then the rue de la Citadelle is to your left and curves a bit, and then it straightens out.

GAMBETTA: MAIN STREET The main shopping street in terms of regular retail is rue Gambetta, which leads away from the Old Town and out yonder toward the Hôtel Byblos. Rue Gambetta is sort of a cross between a real-people street and a tourist street. There are a number of multiples here, as well as a small grocery store, a toy store, and an ice-cream shop in the area closest to the port. As Gambetta moves out of town, it becomes avenue Maréchal Foch. As Gambetta moves into Old Town, its name changes to rue des Commerçants. You can also cut through some of the medieval maze by using Passage Gambetta, a mall, as your tunnel; shop until you come out the other side.

ALLARD: PORT & CENTER If you stayed on Gambetta thinking it was the only main shopping street in town, you goofed. Rue Allard, which veers off from behind the quai Suffren and to one side as it leads away from town, has its own share of high-rent retail. In fact, this is really the town's high street.

There's lots to see and buy here, much of it local, with only a few big-name French multiples. You'll also find ice-cream cones and chocolates and even a very good art-supply store. The rue Allard becomes the rue Leclerc as you head out of town toward St-Raphaël.

LOUIS BLANC: EDGE OF TOWN Farther from the madding crowd and therefore more used by locals, this street is packed with home furnishings and design studios. Don't miss **Fred Prysquel** (no. 34–36) for the rustic country look of your dreams; **Pierre Basset** (no. 11) for tiles; and **La Maison Marine** (no. 2) for tabletop designs.

CLEMENCEAU: CUTE & CENTER This street is truly the heart of the cute retail in the center of town. It's sort of halfway between Gambetta and Allard—Gambetta runs parallel and Allard curves around to become almost parallel.

Photo ops galore. **Rodini** (no. 16) is one of the most famous makers of sandals in the local style and is considered an icon. The other big name for *tropézienne* sandals is **K. Jacques** (no. 13). Failure to wear sandals from one of these two places immediately places you in jeopardy of being discovered as an American, and a tourist at that. Failure to know what a *tropézienne* is could also be detrimental to your social standing, so here goes: It's a thong-style sandal with a wide, bird-wing strap that goes across the toes, anchored by the tiny leather bit that fits between the big toe and the second toe.

RUE SIBILLE: SIDE & CENTER   This is a little bit of a side street that's right off the place des Lices and runs all the way to the waterfront. It's one of the more chic addresses for locals in the know. **Versace** is located nearby. **Claire L'Insolite** sells a mélange of big-name Italian designers, including Max Mara and Genny.

Big Names

Following are some of the big-name designer boutiques and chains in St-Tropez.

AGATHA
56 rue Allard.

ALAIN MANOUKIAN
Rue Georges Clemenceau.
Rue Allard.

BLANC BLEU
1–3 rue Allard.

CERUTTI 1881
Rue de la Ponche.

DIEGO DELLA VALLE
Passage du Port.

DIOR
1 rue Gambetta.

EMILIO PUCCI
28 place de la Garonne.

FAÇONNABLE
Place de la Garonne.

HERMES
Place Georges Grammont.

LACOSTE
42 rue Allard.

LA PERLA
20 rue Allard.

LONGCHAMP
19 rue Allard.

MANRICO
Place des Lices.

SONIA RYKIEL
Place des Lices.

SOULEIADO
Rue Allard.

FINDS

BLVD. DES RUES
Rue de la Ponche.

One of the most unusual shops I've found in France, this tiny boutique sells items made from street signs and can also make up your name into a French-style street sign. Prices begin around 26€ ($30); a must-do.

FABIENNE VILLACRECES
15 bd. Louis Blanc.

Head here for fashion and home style, all incredibly chic and worthy of magazine layouts.

KIWI
34 rue Allard.

This boutique sells resort wear and clothes that are simply perfect for the Riviera without being glitzy, gold lamé, covered in rhinestones, or tacky.

K. JACQUES
16 rue Seillon.

One of the most famous makers of *tropéziennes* has a new decor and an old rep for the local look in sandals.

LE BYBLOS
Hôtel Byblos, av. Paul Signac.

This is one of the best hotel logo shops I've ever encountered. It has classy merchandise you would want to have that does not seem cheapened by the hotel logo. The little terry-cloth travel pouches are fabulous.

PHARMACIE MOUTON
9 rue Allard.

Yes, of course it's a regular pharmacy, but it also has its own house line of products, which is unusual. I buy the house brand of bubble bath in assorted aromatherapy and natural scents; I like lavender, vanilla, and the woodsy pine scent. It's one of the best lavenders I've ever bathed in. Because the plastic bottle is imprinted with the name and address of the pharmacy, I consider this a fabulously seductive gift-cum-status symbol for around 8.70€ ($10).

MARKETS & FAIRS

If you want a real French market, you'd better get out of town. The St-Tropez market is a marvelous affair, almost theatrical in character, but very showbiz.

This is sort of a hippie, dippy market; it does not feel like France to me, but it's busy and energetic and filled with a wide selection of wares—there's even *brocante* in the rear, although there are no bargains, believe me. The market is not one of those things merely set up to fleece tourists. It's a genuine market, with everything from local products, fabrics, and spices to foodstuff and baskets. There are two market days in St-Tropez: Tuesday and Saturday. Market is better in the summer, but it's also more crowded with tourists then.

Many of the vendors seen in St-Tropez rotate from town to town, and, of course, locals know them and their merchandise. Without the local crowd, the market would be totally bad Disney. As it is, it's small-time, but if you keep expectations low, you'll find it charming.

Unfortunately, some of the sellers who show on Saturday don't come back on Tuesday. *Quel dommage.* My fabric vendor sells in Lorgues on Tuesday and in St-Tropez on Saturday. This is the guy I've been buying Provençal prints from for many years.

On Wednesday, you want Cogolin; Thursday, it's Les Arcs; Friday, Cuers; and Sunday, Le Muy.

Brocante is sold in the place des Lices market in St-Tropez, as well as in all the other markets. For information on specific events or *brocante* fairs, you can contact **L'Union des Brocanteurs du Var** (© 04-94-59-56-13). There is usually a printed schedule available for each season.

On summer Sundays, there's a farmer's market in the parking lot of **Petit Village** (La Foux, Gassin; © 04-94-56-32-04).

OUT OF TOWN

The town of **Gassin** is so close to St-Tropez that it's almost a suburb. Some people go just to look at the view. I go for the jam shop. Honest.

I don't want to ruin **Maison des Confitures** (route de Bourrian, Gassin) for you by offering too much hype, but I can't think of a more perfect French experience in all of France than to spend a half-hour in its delightful stone cottage shop. It carries more than 250 varieties, from the regular to the unusual. (The labels are in French, so you may need a dictionary.) There are some unique flavor combinations that will leave you drooling—I couldn't resist the chocolate-and-cinnamon jam. You can buy gift baskets, low-sugar selections, and even some antiques. No credit cards, folks.

Thierry Derbez (route D98) is a farm-stand-cum-garden-cum-nursery-cum-real-people-gourmet, where you can load up with goodies that are good enough to please serious foodies.

Ramatuelle is a little medieval walled city not far from St-Tropez (just past Johnny Hallyday's house) where everything appears to be perfect. There's not really any serious shopping here, but you will see the usual tourist places that sell pottery and printed fabrics.

FAYENCE

If you think you've heard of Fayence, you're probably thinking of the term *faience,* which is a type of hand-painted pottery. This Fayence is a town some 20km (12 miles) from Cannes. It's close to the Riviera, but is really considered part of Provence—so read about it, and its new Four Seasons Resort Terre Blanche, in chapter 7.

CANNES

Yes, there are parts of Cannes that are glitzy or even silly, but there's so much going on and so many types of things happening that it's the heartbeat of the Riviera to me. I particularly like Cannes out of season and hope you'll plan a winter trip here, carefully avoiding holidays and conventions . . . and other tourists.

Cannes is the perfect hub not only for enjoying the local scene, but also for getting out and about and up the hills and over to Monte Carlo and off to Provence. But, wonderfully, Cannes is also a real city and a walking town, so you don't need a car. If you stay in a centrally located hotel, you can dash in and out without ever having to worry about revving up the car or tipping the bellboy.

Cannes is still the best shopping town on the Riviera. Every store and brand is here, from **Zara,** the Spanish ready-to-wear firm, to **L'Occitane,** the Provençal soap and suds maker, to **Sephora,** the perfume store, and even **FNAC,** for CDs. Shopping is hot, hot, hot in a town that has known how to simmer ever since it recovered from World War II.

Cannes isn't funky like St-Tropez, or small-town like Eze, or tourist-trappy like Vallauris. The real Cannes has several personalities because it's actually a very big city that spreads and sprawls, and there are real people who live here. What you come to Cannes for, aside from the very famous conventions and the film festival, are the sun, the sand, and the shopping. Believe it or not, Cannes has added on a shopping festival, which the city hopes will become as famous as its film festival.

Getting to Cannes

BY PLANE   The easiest way to get to Cannes is to fly into the Nice–Côte d'Azur International Airport. From there, you can now get a helicopter transfer to Cannes. Or you can take a bus, which costs about 17€ ($20) one-way; it departs from the front of the Nice airport every 20 to 30 minutes and takes you to downtown Cannes.

If you take a taxi from the airport, note that prices from Nice to Cannes are fixed; they don't go by the meter, so ask and try to negotiate. There is also a surcharge for each piece of baggage. Be prepared to pay as much as 100€ ($115) from Nice to Cannes. I do not tip on such rigged prices. A taxi from Cannes to the Nice airport is less expensive, as the local politics are different (don't ask).

Your hotel will gladly arrange a car-and-driver pickup at the airport for you (about 150€/$173); better yet, get my friend Piero—or his wife, Martine—at **E.T.S.** (© 04-92-98-06-29; PBruni@compuserve.com). Transfers from the Nice airport to Cannes cost 80€ ($92) for one to four people in a sedan, 120€ ($138) for five to eight people in a van.

Cannes

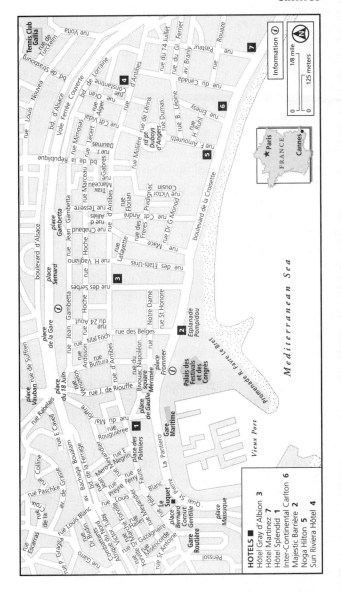

HOTELS ■
Hôtel Gray d'Albion 3
Hôtel Martinez 7
Hôtel Splendid 1
Inter-Continental Carlton 6
Majestic Barrière 2
Noga Hilton 5
Sun Riviera Hôtel 4

Information *i*

1/8 mile

125 meters

Mediterranean Sea

Vieux Port

FRANCE
★ Paris
Cannes

If you plan on doing any driving around the area, pick up your rental car at the Nice airport. The airport is right on the highway; simply take the A8 and get off at the Cannes/Mougins exit. This is by far the best plan, and you will feel like a genius for having saved the round-trip taxi fare.

BY BOAT   Numerous yachts, sailing vessels, and even the big luxury cruise ships call at the port of Cannes. The bay is too shallow for really large ships to come to the pier, so they send passengers to shore via tender, which land right at the Maritime Center next to the Palais des Festivals on La Croisette. The cruise lines that have shallow drafts can come right up to the dock. In many port towns, the pier is in a weird place, but in Cannes, it's right where you want it to be: in the heart of everything and directly across the street from the city's Saturday flea market. Who could ask for anything more?

The Lay of the Land

To get around town, you need to know only these few things:

- The upper city is mostly for real people, and fills in the tiers from the pay road to the sea. You will more than likely just drive through it—or never see it.
- The old city is located around yet another hill, Le Suquet, which rises alongside the old harbor (Le Vieux Port, or Old Port). Wear walking shoes.
- The new money is on La Croisette. By new, I mean post-1834, which is when Cannes suddenly became fashionable due to a cholera epidemic in Nice. Ever since then, the beach area and promenade in Cannes (bd. de la Croisette) have been the in places to be seen in your tight bustle, tight hoop skirt, tight cloche, or tight little Pucci.
- The real-people shopping street is the rue d'Antibes, a block behind La Croisette and running parallel to it.
- The train station is in the heart of town, so if you don't drive, you can easily walk to and from the station from just about any hotel or store.

Getting Around Cannes

Walk. Even if you have a car, don't drive in town if you can help it. Traffic is not as bad as in St-Tropez, but finding a parking space can take longer than the errand you want to run.

Sleeping in Cannes

The hotel situation in Cannes is tricky; here are a few general tips for the smart consumer:

- Because Cannes has imported sand at its beaches and, therefore, has the best beaches in the area, the demand to stay in Cannes and use it as a hub city for the Riviera is high. Consequently, rooms in this town should be booked as far in advance as possible. Although you can get lucky at the last minute, this is not a last-minute kind of town.

- Cannes is not only a beach town but also a convention town—more shows than you can imagine play at the major convention facilities at the Palais des Festivals and the Palais de Croisette. If there's a convention in town, forget about a discount, and possibly forget about a room altogether.

- Forget about getting a room in a palace hotel during the Cannes Film Festival.

- "Festival" is a season in Cannes and no longer refers to simply the famous (or is that infamous?) film festival in May. Festival is the highest rate on the books at palace hotels and is charged anytime a huge convention is in town and rooms are in short supply.

- August is the next most expensive month; it has deals, as most of the other times of the year do, except at festival.

- Out-of-season package deals can be so low that you won't believe you're booking Cannes. These packages provide room, breakfast, and usually other perks as well.

- Hotels that are very similar to one another can have amazingly different prices. Trickier still, their promotional deals might sound similar, but the product each is offering at that price may not be the same.

- The same hotel room at the same time of year may be marketed differently to different nationalities or in different parts of the world. Also note that some promotions require a minimum stay.
- Oceanview rooms always cost more than other rooms and are rarely included in promotional prices.
- Breakfast may be included with your room rate, but find out if it's a continental breakfast or a full breakfast—this makes a big difference, unless you happen to eat like a French bird. Breakfast for two people can easily cost 43€ ($50), so look for hotels in which a full American breakfast or a breakfast buffet is included.
- While you're checking if breakfast is included, find out what else is included. Often a hotel will have several promotions going on at the same time. You'll discover that the hotel with more things included comes out to be a better value.
- If you're choosing a hotel for its beach club, understand that you usually pay 25€ ($29) per person per day for a chaise longue. However, most of the palace hotels have specific summer promotions that include a chaise longue with the room. Ask! Few will volunteer to point out the inconsistencies of the various plans available.
- Of course, your dog can stay in the hotel, too. That's possibly another 25€ ($29) per night, but he's family, *non?* Usually the car fee and the dog fee are equal. Dogs do cost more than children; kids up to the age of 12 or 16 (it depends on the hotel) are usually free if they stay in your room, although there is a charge for an extra bed—and that can be very steep.

THE PALACE HOTELS

Cannes, like all other cities in France, has no five-star hotels, but it does have four four-star deluxe hotels (written ****D) that are classified in the French manner as "palace hotels."

HÔTEL MARTINEZ
73 bd. de la Croisette.

As a member of both Concorde Hotels and Leading Hotels of the World, the Martinez is possibly the most glam of the palace hotels and yet offers a large number of spiffy promotions, including rates frozen in U.S. dollars (sometimes).

It's located at the far end of the shopping district, but when you get Annick Goutal amenities in the bathroom, it's worth the walk. You'll feel as though you're on a 1930s ocean liner, you'll sink into all the Art Deco, and you'll just melt from an overload of swanky. The hotel has just added a spa, an MGM suite, a Ze Beach venue on the sand, and various deals so that you can dine chez Christian Willer, the many-star chef. You can even eat in the kitchen, if you book way in advance.

Note: As much as I adore this hotel, I must confess that it's an apples-and-oranges kind of place: Because it is the largest hotel in town (more than 400 rooms) and because it was built in the late 1920s, it has a number of small and bad rooms— more than most of the other palace hotels. So although you can get a great promotional rate here, you might not get a great room.

Rates begin at about 174€ ($200) out of season with special promotions and go up from there; the summer price I usually pay is about 261€ ($300), which includes the chaise longue on the beach. For U.S. reservations, call © 800/888-4747. Local phone © 04-92-98-73-00. www.hotel-martinez.com.

INTERCONTINENTAL CARLTON CANNES
58 bd. de la Croisette.

The Carlton has been featured in numerous movies and even in a recent automobile ad. None of this fanfare comes cheaply, and the bargain promotional rate advertised in print may be hard to nail in reality. The Carlton does get included in Inter-Continental promotions, although there are few low-cost rooms in season. Even if you don't stay here, I insist that you do lunch on the terrace of the Cafe, preferably during the film festival. There is no better definition of Cannes.

Promotional rates can deliver a room for about 225€ ($259), but the norm is, of course, much higher; during the season, it's more like 500€ ($575) per night. For reservations from the U.S., call © **800/327-0200.** Local phone © 04-93-68-91-68. Fax 04-93-06-40-25. www.cannes.intercontinental.com.

MAJESTIC BARRIÈRE
14 bd. de la Croisette.

Recently renovated and brought up to par with the other palace hotels, the Majestic is more of an insider's place. The chef, Bruno Oger, has stars, and a branch of the famous bistro Fouquet's has come to the lobby. The convention crowds consider this hotel a must-do, and the stores out front make the location ideal. You can dine around the pool, or sit half the day in the lobby bar and simply stare. Of the four palace hotels, this one is often the least expensive. What more could you want?

Rates vary with the season, but begin around 190€ ($219). In the U.S., call © **800/223-6800.** Local phone © 04-92-98-77-00. www.lucienbarriere.com.

NOGA HILTON CANNES
50 bd. de la Croisette.

Location is this hotel's best claim to fame. The property is built into the Palais de Croisette, so if you're going to a convention, you're in the right place. It also has its own small shopping mall. As for the hotel itself, it has a few choice secrets—such as a good chef; a fixed-price gourmet formula; menu service at the beach cafe rather than just buffet service; various promotions, including Hilton rates and local deals; and a house full of rooms that were created to be equal, so they are all the same size—there are no bad rooms.

There are 45 suites and some 200 rooms that have either ocean or city views. Prices are usually competitive with those at the Martinez, although you can sometimes latch onto a Hilton promotion for a room as low as 198€ ($228) per night.

As a special courtesy to *Born to Shop* readers, the hotel's general manager is pleased to offer a room upgrade, which will be granted based on availability. He cannot fax back a confirmed upgrade, but if he's got the space when you arrive, you've got a "suite" deal. From the U.S., send a fax directly to Richard Duvauchelle, General Manager, Noga Hilton Cannes, fax **33-4-92-99-70-15**.

For reservations from the U.S., call ✆ **800/HILTONS.** Local phone ✆ 04-92-99-70-00. www.hilton.com.

THE FOUR-STARS

HOTEL GRAY D'ALBION
38 rue des Serbes.

You can't get a better shopping hotel than a place located in the best mall in town, right in the core of the best shops. The Hôtel Gray d'Albion shares the same owners as the Majestic, but it is more modern and less expensive. Out-of-season rates begin at 145€ ($167). Local phone ✆ **04-92-99-79-79.** www.lucienbarriere.com.

HOTEL SPLENDID
4–6 rue Félix-Faure.

This hotel is actually a three-star, but the location is truly splendid—and closer to McDonald's than any of the palace hotels. It's not fancy, but it has a lot of charm and a super setting in the heart of everything—basically across the street from the Palais des Festivals and 2 blocks from Le Suquet. It's almost on top of the Saturday flea market, and it's deep in the heart of shopping land. Some rooms have kitchenettes; some have sea views (more expensive). This place is a real gem for those who love funky charm.

There are only about 60 rooms, so book early. Rates begin at 103€ ($118) out of season. For U.S. reservations, call ✆ 800/462-7274. Local phone ✆ 04-97-06-22-22. accueil@splendid-hotel-cannes.fr.

SUN RIVIERA HOTEL
138 rue d'Antibes.

This hotel is smack dab in the middle of the Cannes shopping district, a block from La Croisette—but it still has charm and even a small swimming pool. It's a member of Châteaux & Hôtels de France. It closes out of season, but just from the middle of November until New Year's. Rooms begin at 115€ ($132). To book from the U.S., call ✆ 800/553-5090. Local phone ✆ 04-93-06-77-77. www.sun-riviera.com.

Eating in Cannes

If you're just out for a quick bite in Cannes, there are plenty of choices. Ice-cream stores are all over town, even in the high-rent districts. I am almost certain that it is against the law to walk the streets of Cannes without an ice-cream cone in hand; ice-cream vendors are everywhere, but certain ones are known for their exotic flavors made with local ingredients. Try **Curly**, right on La Croisette, between the Majestic and Noga Hilton.

The rue d'Antibes, Cannes's main real-people shopping and strolling street, is crammed with ice-cream parlors (even **Häagen-Dazs**), tearooms, and fast-food joints. Near the Maritime Center, at the Allées de Liberté, there's a **McDonald's** (called McDo in French slang), with **Planet Hollywood** a few doors away.

All the hotel beach clubs have restaurants on the beach, just down the stairs from La Croisette. If the weather is fine, dining alfresco can be part of the pleasure of Cannes—just check to see which restaurants have a la carte service, since some only serve a buffet at a flat price.

Inside the hotels, there are often bistros with fair prices and a chance to see how the other half lives, if you're not a regular.

La Croisette is also lined with streetside cafes that feature average food at high prices, but allow you to be part of the parade. **Felix,** between the Carlton and the Martinez, has just been renovated with a sleek new look; pizza and pasta run about 50€ ($58) per person.

Although the cafes are more of an evening ritual than a day-time and shopping-break thing, they are open for business and less crowded during off hours. **Caffe Roma,** across from the Palais des Festivals, is the hip in spot for the young, Lycra-clad Eurotrash crowd. My fave is **Le Farfalla,** also on La Croisette across from the Palais. From the street it looks very average, but once you're inside and into the scene, you can enjoy a hot, young crowd and these adorable waitresses with lighters on their uniform sleeves—yep, they flick their Bics for you. The scene, especially late at night, is truly outrageous. The food's okay, too, with enormous portions. It's just great fun and very much part of what Cannes is all about.

CAFE CARLTON
Carlton Hotel, 58 bd. de la Croisette.

If you want to enjoy an affordable lunch or snack, let down your hair and set down your packages, be part of the "in" crowd, and feel the special Cannes magic, then head for this coffee shop–cum–breakfast room in the front of the Carlton. If weather permits, dine on the terrace. It's heaven.

FOUQUET'S
10 bd. de la Croisette.

Now for the French lesson: For some reason, you say the final *t.* Located in the Hôtel Majestic, Fouquet's has recently come to town and in short order become an "in" spot thanks to its famous name and great location.

LENOTRE
63 rue d'Antibes.

Lenôtre is one of the most famous (and chic) names in Paris in terms of chocolates and takeaway foods. The meals are light: salads, quiches, or a yummy tomato *tarte* with chevre. You can get breakfast, lunch, a snack, a pastry, chocolates, ice cream, or takeout here.

RELAIS MARTINEZ
Hôtel Martinez, 73 bd. de la Croisette.

From the name you can guess that this place is in the Hôtel Martinez. The rest of the good news: It's open 7 days a week, has a fixed-price menu at about 40€ ($46), and offers tastes of chef Christian Willer's recipes.

Shopping in Cannes

BEST BUYS

Are there any good buys in a resort town where the rich and famous hang? Yeah, as a matter of fact, there are. What follows is an overview of the good, the bad, and the ugly. Also note that if you come during the Shopping Festival, which is in January during the French national sale period, you get discounts and gifties as well as sale prices.

DESIGNER CLOTHES   If you're seriously shopping for serious clothes and you are not headed for Paris, Cannes gives you a better selection of big names than any other city on the Riviera, including Nice and Marseille. Best buys on designer clothes are those items (on sale!) that still qualify for a *détaxe* refund. The savings are even more dramatic if you buy from a *dépôt-vente* (resale shop).

FOODSTUFFS   This is a great town for buying gourmet foodstuffs. Olive oil is a fabulous souvenir. Buy yours in the **Marché Forville** or the tiny store **Cannolive**. However, you will have many other opportunities to buy olive oil, so just warm up to the notion here or start tasting and learning. Meanwhile, try **Boutique des Landes,** right across from the market, which sells homemade *confiture* (jam), complete with the gold medal it won printed on the label.

SHOPPING HOURS

Regular business hours in Cannes are from 9am to 7pm. Many stores open at 9am, although the majority of name boutiques open at 10am.

A large number of stores close for lunch from 12:30 to 2:30pm. Those that do not close for lunch often have the word *nonstop* posted, or the slogan *sans interruption.*

Most stores are closed on Monday mornings, but the glorious thing about Cannes is that Mondays are not dead. During the summer, some stores stay open on Monday mornings. During school vacations or holidays, almost everything is open on Mondays. And, of course, there's a *brocante* market at Forville on Mondays.

Most stores are closed on Sundays, although there is a small amount of Sunday-morning action. Cannes is not nearly as dead as many French towns: Marché Forville is wide open on Sundays, and about half of the shops on the food street, rue Meynadier, stay open on Sunday until noonish. By late afternoon, most of the stores on Le Suquet open and stay open until midnight.

SHOPPING NEIGHBORHOODS

The basic Cannes shopping neighborhoods all interconnect and can be walked, although if it's hot or you are wearing stiletto heels (isn't everyone in Cannes?), this will be more difficult.

LA CROISETTE   The main drag along the waterfront is called boulevard de la Croisette, or simply La Croisette. The beach itself is actually below the promenade, so you must go down steps to get to the sand. All the major hotels and many of the major shops are lined up at attention facing the sea, stretching from the Palais des Festivals to the Hôtel Martinez. The major hotels' lobbies usually have a few shops as well; Noga has a minimall attached to it.

GRAY D'ALBION   Gray d'Albion is a large building, a mall, a shortcut through town to bring you from La Croisette to rue d'Antibes, and a local legend wrapped into one. Oh my, I forgot to say it's also a hotel.

There are in fact two buildings that make up the complex, so if you're shopping, note that you enter, exit, and enter and exit again, before you end up at rue d'Antibes. Once considered the best address in town if you couldn't get the Croisette, the mall houses many big-name shops, including **Hermès** and **La Perla.**

RUE D'ANTIBES   Moving one street back from the sea, you've got the rue d'Antibes, which runs parallel to La Croisette. Although it isn't the low-rent district by any means, it has more real-people shops, more branches of famous French multiples (such as **Kookai, Pimkie,** and **Descamps**), and fewer big international icon names (such as **Lalique** and **Lancel**). Many of the stores have given themselves face-lifts; part of the street has become a pedestrian mall. This street has a neighborhood feel, it has life at night (La Croisette has too much life), and you'll enjoy strolling and just looking in windows. La Croisette is for looking at other people; rue d'Antibes is for shoppers. The central portion has just become a pedestrian thoroughfare.

MIDDLE ETATS-UNIS   This is the name I have made up for the neighborhood of streets that connect La Croisette with the rue d'Antibes. The streets are in the center of town, in between the Palais des Festivals and the Majestic. These streets are only about 2 blocks long, and each is crammed with stores. Many of them are upscale; some even bear designer names.

The central street of this neighborhood is rue des Etats-Unis. Rue des Serbes and rue du Commandant André are also excellent side streets for browsing, prowling, and ruining your credit rating. Most of the stores in this cross-street grid are not big names, although you will find **Sonia Rykiel, Chacok,** and others, as well as shops like **Oliviers & Co.**

ROND POINT DU BOYS-D'ANGERS   Directly behind the Noga Hilton, about a block away, I direct your attention to a tiny, isolated group of shops that you would have never found unless you were lost or someone had given you directions to one of the stores.

FOOD TOWN   There is no part of Cannes that is actually called Food Town, yet what I call Food Town is located behind the Old Port and consists of several parts: Marché Forville (coral stucco; you can't miss it); the rue Félix-Faure, where the market is located; the rue Meynadier, which juts off at an angle from the Félix-Faure; and Allées de la Liberté, where the flower market is held most days. All these elements make for a neighborhood that is more than just a string of gourmet and real-people food stores and candy shops.

The rue Meynadier is filled with gourmet food shops. More important, if your idea of France is not all topless beaches and Chanel sunglasses, you will find what you are looking for in these back streets and byways. That it could also be chocolate is an added plus.

Please do not think that Food Town sells only food. The rue Meynadier is one of the main shopping streets in town, and it's filled with TTs and other stores that service both tourists and real people. Prices are lower here than at Versace.

LE SUQUET   The oldest part of town and the part that most looks like a charming village, Le Suquet is also the place to eat, if we're talking fun or funky, not multiple Michelin stars. There are also some stores around here, but they tend to be either TTs or antiques shops. Many shops sell the inexpensive Provençal fabrics, so they look cute.

Mostly this is an eating street, with dozens of cafes in a row. You simply march up the hill and decide which one you like. I've tried a variety of them and have no favorites. They do tend to be touristy. To get here, walk along rue d'Antibes

---

Cannes Prestige

A majority of the high-end shops in Cannes belong to an association called *Cannes Prestige,* which you can identify by its
logo: a *C* with a feather. Cannes Prestige publishes a guide
of its member shops, which agree to certain bylaws in order
to offer the best service possible. Among the amenities they
offer is at least one member of the sales staff who speaks English. Look for the logo when you shop.

---

in the downtown area until you pass the Old Port. Look for
a tiny pedestrian street called rue St-Antoine, which is mobbed
and lined with cafes. It has recently been repaved with smooth
cobblestones, but it's not the place for high heels. This is an
evening parade, so forget it as a regular shopping district. The
stores stay open late, sometimes until midnight in the summer.

MARKETS & FAIRS

Cannes has plenty of market action just about every day of
the week. Although the Marché Forville is not quite as spectacular as the fruit-and-flower market in Nice, it's not at all
bad, and you can spend many happy hours there. In fact, you
can spend many happy months there. The fruit-and-flower market is open every day except Monday. (Sun is a great day to
come.) This is a morning event, so people tend to pack up by
1 to 2pm. On Monday, the Marché Forville sells *brocante.*

There is a small daily market at place Gambetta, which is
directly behind the Noga Hilton. It isn't much of a market, but
it is open on Monday—and I find it hilarious. It sells dry
goods (cheap shoes, cheap clothes, fake sunglasses), as well as
fruits and veggies, and has a very small-town, neighborhoody
feel to it. I wouldn't go out of my way to get there, but it does
have a quiet charm and a funky flair.

On Saturday, there is a flea market with antiques at les Allées
de la Liberté, across from the Old Port, where La Croisette

becomes La Pantiero. It's right next to McDonald's, so if you need directions, ask for McDo. During the week, a few vendors sell flowers; some guidebooks go so far as to call this a flower market or a sight worth seeing. Vendors also sell flowers in Forville, which is good enough for me, or you can wait for Nice.

CANNES SHOPPING FESTIVAL

Inspired by the success of the shopping festival in Dubai and by its own 50-plus years as creator of festivals, the city of Cannes last year began its own Shopping Festival, held for 3 weeks in January each year.

The timing of the festival was planned in coordination with the national sale dates, and involves various discounts both on hotel rooms and in stores. Stores stay open on Sunday; fashion shows are staged; and rooms in palace hotels go for 115€ ($132) per person. (Four-star rates are 55€/$63 per person.)

For more information on dates and promotions go to www.cannes.com.

Cannes Resources A–Z

ANTIQUES & AUCTIONS

You can't in your right mind consider Cannes as a source for serious antiques, but if you like junk and flea markets and poking around, you'll be surprised not only by how much this town has to offer, but also by the fact that prices are beyond fair—they can be among the best in France. I do not even step foot inside any of the formal antiques shops in Cannes; forgive me, but I'm not interested in formal antiques, and I go by the old rule of thumb that antiques shops in resort cities are always expensive.

Nonetheless, for those who like serious antiques and big-time dealers, there's a biannual show called **Salon des Antiquaires à Cannes,** held every winter and every summer for 2 weeks in the Palais des Festivals. For specific dates, write the **Association des Antiquaires de Cannes** (Pascal Moufflet, 13 rue d'Oran, 06400 Cannes; ✆ **04-93-38-13-64;** fax 04-93-68-99-79).

Note that the hours of formal antiques shows all over France, not just here, are rather unusual by American standards. Shows may not open until 11am or noon, and they stay open until 9pm or so. Sometimes shows are held only in the afternoon, beginning at 3 or 4pm and lasting until 10pm. Perhaps this is so Madame can bring her husband and his checkbook.

If the kind of antiques you prefer are what the French call *brocante,* Cannes is a great place to shop. On Monday morning, beginning at 8am, the **Marché Forville** is filled with dealers—it's fun and funky and quite affordable. Monday is also the big day for *brocante* in Nice—don't miss it if at all possible—so you can start in one town and finish up in the other. Doing the two markets together in one day will make your trip and fill your home.

On Saturday, the Allées de la Liberté (near McDonald's) is filled with dealers; this is also great fun, although it's much more upscale in feel than the Monday show. The dealers are not the same, so don't feel like you've seen it and done it. Note also that this location is directly across from the ship terminal (Maritime Center), so if you're on a cruise ship and you come to port on a Saturday, voilà—*les marché aux puces.*

If you have a car, you can hit *brocante* markets in nearby villages on just about every day of the week. On Thursday, it's *brocante* day at the *marché paysan* in nearby Mandelieu. This is a very low-end affair on blankets in a parking lot, but if you have transportation, you might enjoy it; prices are quite low and this is the real thing, sans tourists.

On Saturday and Tuesday, Antibes has a tiny but yummy little flea market in the street, right off the old port. There are also dealers on the roads that reach outside of Cannes and into the nearby villages—head off toward Grasse and Mougins or toward Antibes and just find 'em.

As for real antiques shops in Cannes, well, along the boulevard de la République, a real-people street in downtown Cannes, there are a few dealers not too far from one another.

These are serious dealers, not funky junk stores. Start with
Lucienne Lai (99 bd. de la République).

Those interested in antiques should also know that Nice has
a big antiques community and that Monaco has some fancy
shops and a very big-time show. There are also auctions in the
winter season. For information on specific auctions or events,
check the local newspaper.

BIG NAMES

For years, there's been a trend in this town toward a handful
of fancy-schmancy boutiques that are named after their owners and that carry several designer lines. Sometimes these stores
have a theme—only Italian designers, for example. I have listed
this type of shop under "Boutiques," below. More and more
designers are opening freestanding shops in Cannes, so this type
of store may eventually die out or move farther away from the
tourist real estate and into the realm of local shopping. What
follows is a list of freestanding, big-name designer stores:

ALMA
67 La Croisette.

BULGARI
14 La Croisette.

CARTIER
57 La Croisette.

CELINE
24 La Croisette.

CERRUTI 1881
15 rue des Serbes (men).
65 rue d'Antibes (women).

CHANEL
5 La Croisette.

CHARLES JOURDAN
47 rue d'Antibes.

CHRISTIAN DIOR
38 La Croisette.

CHRISTOFLE
9 rue d'Antibes.

DUNHILL
14 La Croisette.

EMPORIO ARMANI
52 La Croisette.

ESCADA
15 rue des Serbes.

FERRAGAMO
34 La Croisette.

FRED
21 La Croisette.

GERARD DAREL
119 rue d'Antibes.

GIANFRANCO FERRE
67 La Croisette.

GIANNI VERSACE
9 rue St-Honoré.

GUCCI
17 La Croisette.

HERMES
17 La Croisette.

JEAN LOUIS SCHERRER
17 La Croisette.

JOSEPH
116 rue d'Antibes.

KENZO
96 rue d'Antibes.

LALIQUE
87 rue d'Antibes.

LANCEL
34 rue d'Antibes.

LA PERLA
Gray d'Albion, 17 La Croisette.

LAUREL
123–125 rue d'Antibes.

LOUIS VUITTON
44 La Croisette.

MAX MARA
79 rue d'Antibes.

PIERRE CARDIN
9 La Croisette.

SONIA RYKIEL
15 rue des États-Unis.

UNGARO
55 La Croisette.

VAN CLEEF & ARPELS
61 La Croisette.

VENTILO
121 rue d'Antibes.

YVES SAINT LAURENT/RIVE GAUCHE
44 La Croisette.

BOUTIQUES

ALEXANDRA
Rond Point du Boys-d'Angers.

This is the leading light in the biggest French and Italian names, the most famous of the specialty boutiques, and the last word in chic. I don't need to tell you that we're into expensive garments and high style. But of course, darling. Now you're a member of the club. We must have lunch.

REUSSNER
4 rue Commandant André.

Reussner is another of those small, special shops for those in the know. This one has the cutting edge: Alexander McQueen, Ann Demeulemeester, Dries Van Noten, and so on. Top drawer.

VIA VENETO
91 rue d'Antibes.

The good news is that this is a string of three fabulous shops that have all the big, hip Italian designers and some of the French ones, too. If you love fashion, you will adore these boutiques, where the service-oriented staff is used to a very with-it customer. The bad news is that the Versace jeans I thought I couldn't live without cost 152€ ($175). Still, much fun just to touch everything and dream about the look. Certainly Cannes is the place to wear it.

CHILDREN'S CLOTHES

For affordable kids' clothing, I shop at **Monoprix.** For rich grandmas or those who never look at price tags, a stroll through both parts of the mall at Gray d'Albion will knock your socks off—there are numerous fancy-schmancy boutiques here for kiddie style, including shoe shops and designer clothing shops.

CATIMINI
Gray d'Albion.

Catimini is an absolutely adorable, reasonably priced shop for designer kids' wear.

DOMINIQUE
7 Rond Point du Boys-d'Angers.

This adorable shop is filled with old-fashioned smocking for infants and young girls along with traditional baby items. It's a block behind the Noga Hilton.

FLORIANE
60 rue d'Antibes.

Floriane sells fun, colorful, traditional clothes, with enough of an updated look to not be out of style—very upscale French middle class. It's at the back end of the Gray d'Albion mall.

CRAFTS

At the far end of Allées des Liberté, there are a few crafts vendors who sell their wares from tables; Saturday is the biggest day.

DEPARTMENT STORES

GALERIES LAFAYETTE
6 rue du Maréchal Foch.

If you're thinking about the Galeries Lafayette in Paris or even the store in Nice, try to calm down now. This particular branch is nice but not as big as the Nice or Marseille stores, nor is it particularly complete or satisfying.

MONOPRIX
9 rue du Maréchal Foch.

Monoprix isn't really a department store; it's what an American would call a dime store. It's one of my favorite places to shop. There's a grocery store upstairs, which makes a fine browse and a good place to buy mustard and various foodstuffs for gifts. It's also the best place for postcards.

DISCOUNT, DEGRIFFE & DEPOT-VENTE

CONTREPARTIE
Rond Point du Boys (at rue de Lérins).

This is a *dépôt-vente* that sells gently worn clothes. We're talking Chanel suits for 609€ ($700)—which is, by the way, almost exactly the same price you will pay for used Chanel in New York. This small, packed store is directly behind the Noga Hilton. It has shoes and handbags as well; the best stuff is in the windows and up front. There is a separate men's store.

FILM FESTIVAL SOUVENIRS

If you happen to be in town during the film festival, don't think you have to be invited to walk the red carpet in order to play. Although there are three official screenings a day, the 7:30pm screening is the biggie, and everyone comes all dolled up beginning around 6:30pm.

Freelance photographers stand near the red carpet to take photos, which will be on sale the next day. You need not have tickets or passes to the festival in order to get your photo taken. There is sort of a system to it: Some photographers pop out in front of you, snap a few shots, and hand you a card. Others don't say a word. You can also ask a shooter to take your photo and ask for his card. The next day after noon, you go to the address printed on the card or go to the boards under the tents alongside the Palais, where you look for your photo. The proofs are on the boards—you mark the number, pay, and wait for the print. Prices vary from around 8.70€ to 35€ ($10–$40); the time it takes for the print can be from 10 minutes to 4 hours. In my case, the photos from one of the sources had to be mailed to me—I didn't think they'd ship to the United States, so I left a local contact, my hotel concierge. The hotel forwarded the photos to me.

For high-class souvenirs as well as other items, there's a chain of stores called **Davis,** with one shop right on La Croisette across from the Palais and one shop at the back end of the mall Gray d'Albion.

Souvenirs are also sold in the streets (I found a great tote bag for less than 13€/$15), as well as in official booths under tents at the Palais. The souvenirs with the proper date of the festival come out 2 weeks beforehand and then stay on the shelves for the year—so it could be the year 2005, but up until May 1, you'll see 2004 festival stuff for sale.

Aside from the director's chairs, my favorite souvenir is the T-shirt, which comes packaged in a tin reel can (another 13€/$15 or so). These kinds of things are sold up and down rue Meynadier.

FLOWERS

MELONIE
80 rue d'Antibes.

Melonie sells (and ships!) Provençal-style dried arrangements of lavender, roses, grasses, and so on.

OWO
7 rue Lafontaine.

This tiny, incredibly chic shop sells cut flowers and does arrangements, and its dried concoctions are the best in town. It's located on a street off rue d'Antibes, not far from the Noga.

FOOD & WINE

There's no lack of fine food in Cannes. If you aren't into checking out specific addresses, then merely browse rue Meynadier, which is crammed with specialists and has a branch of the **Champion** grocery store. This isn't the best grocery I've been to, even in the area, but it's there and you're there, so why not?

Monoprix has a small supermarket upstairs; for gift items, this may be all you need. I buy coffee and mustard here. I also found my little wheelie red nylon market cart here. (I don't recommend the cheapie house brand; it's too short for a tall person. Splurge for a more expensive one with a longer extension handle.) You can get picnic items or just browse around enough to feel that you're French.

Remember that there's one fabulous fruit-and-veggie market (Marché Forville) and one small market (place Gambetta). Also note one of the tricks my friend Pierre, the executive chef at the Noga, taught me: The stands in the Marché Forville are ranked. The chefs buy wholesale from dealers who surround the market but are not under the market roof. If they want something special, they go to the area where the top vendors are located, which is in one specific far corner—the prices are higher here than at the other stands, but the quality is better. Almost all markets in all towns have a secret like this to them.

I don't really think you need a map of the *marché* (market), since it's square, but take a look around as you arrive so that you understand the layout. The market is held on the place called place du Marché (so simple, these French). Surrounding the market and facing it are more suppliers; these are mostly wholesalers. Vincent, the fruit broker that Pierre uses, is here. There's a dry-goods store across the way that sells everything, including a wide variety of market baskets, which may come in handy. (I keep mine at the Noga, waiting for me for each trip.) Any store with the address "place du Marché" is in the circle that surrounds the market square.

If you're standing under the arch at the market that says PORTE FORVILLE, your back is to Vincent, the wholesaler, and the covered market is to your left. In the near corner of the top right of the market is the niche where the best-quality goods are sold.

Most food shops open relatively early in the morning but close at 12:30pm; some close for lunch, while some close for the day. Those that reopen do so at 2 or 2:30pm. Many are open Sunday morning. Some close in November. Hours during the summer season and school holidays—when tourists are in town—may be more liberal than usual.

CAVE DE FORVILLE
3 Marché Forville.

This local wine shop also sells some hard liquor and much champagne. You'll have a ball here. You can pick up some gourmet foodstuffs for picnics, too.

CHEZ BRUNO
50 rue d'Antibes.

Perhaps this store considers itself the rival of Maiffret (they are virtually across the street from each other), but I find it very different. There's something funky and friendly about Maiffret, whereas this store, with its very proper packages of just the right candies for gifts and entertaining, is formal and stiff. It's a local status symbol, though.

LA BOUTIQUE DES LANDES
13 place du Marché Forville.

This is a small, sometimes dark, unassuming shop in the area around Marché Forville. It sells canned and packaged French foods, such as duck and mushrooms, but the specialty of the house is the gold-medal confiture, which comes in a variety of flavors. The shop is open on Sundays.

LA FERME SAVOYARDE
22 rue Meynadier.

The most famous cheese shop in Cannes is also one of the most famous in France and has been recognized with honors from the French government. It flies cheese to various luxury hotels around the world, supplies the local big-name chefs, and has been cited by many food writers as the place to worship the cow or the goat or the sheep. Three generations of the Ceneri family run the shop. You can spend weeks here. My favorite is the cheese rolled in raisins.

MAIFFRET
31 rue d'Antibes.

This is a branch of the famous Parisian candy maker. The specialty in the south of France is *fruits confits* (candied and dried fruits), but you can also find many chocolates, various hard candies, bonbons, and things for kiddies. Very high-status gift items. Maiffret also sells cakes and a variety of regional goodies—enough to make a true foodie go nuts. Forget the diet. Note that the store is very deep, so keep walking back to find more and more selections.

OLIVIERS & CO.
4 rue Macé.

This is a branch of the store that's famous for olives, olive oil, and other great stuff.

SCHIES CHOCOLATIER
125 rue d'Antibes.

This chocolatier is toward what I call the uptown end of rue d'Antibes. I went here during Carnaval one year to find that it was making wafer-thin chocolate masks! Divinely French.

HAIR SALONS

CARITA
21 rue Commandant André.

Carita is well established in Paris and rather new in Cannes. This is the place where you'll never go wrong. To book, call ✆ 04-92-99-22-00.

JACQUES DESSANGE
Galerie Noga Hilton, 50 La Croisette.

I've been going here for years, partly because it is in the Noga Hilton. The employees don't speak too much English, but style is universal. It costs about 43€ ($50) for a cut and a blow-dry. For an appointment, call © **04-93-99-00-30.**

JEAN LOUIS DAVID
21 rue des États-Unis.

No appointment needed here. It's not too expensive and you won't get the world's best blow-dry, but it just might be good enough.

HOME STYLE

DESCAMPS
111 rue d'Antibes.

This store sells the famous brand of French bed linen, along with some home accessories, robes, and the like. It's all in a soft, very chic palette of colors—the Armani feel.

MIS EN DEMEURE
Gray d'Albion, 17 La Croisette.

Walk through the first part of Gray d'Albion and then outside. Now head into the second part of Gray d'Albion (this will make perfect sense when you're actually standing there) and look to your left. There is Mis En Demeure, which is sort of like a very tony Pottery Barn—only a little more French and more creative, definitely snazzier than Habitat, but not weird and not Philippe Starck. It sells linen and some furniture.

LINGERIE

EVE
Gray d'Albion.

This is really a cultural lesson in what French lingerie should be. First of all, like all good French lingerie shops, it sells bathing suits as well as underwear. Second, it carries extremely expensive goods so that Americans can faint dead away when they see the prices. It also has pantyhose and bodysuits in stock. Even if you buy nothing, just watching the women who shop here is a real treat.

LOCAL HEROES

CANNOLIVE
16 and 20 rue Vénizélos.

I cannot in good conscience list this store as a tourist trap, although the undiscerning eye might question me on this. Cannolive is a celebration of local goods, items from the Riviera through Provence. One store is devoted mostly to foodstuffs (olive oil can be tasted and poured from a spigot here), while the other store, a few doors away, sells fabrics, *santons* (figures in a Christmas crèche), trays, and gift items. I could spend hours here.

Now, let's talk about the address. This is the correct address. The street is only called this particular proper name for 1 block, and, in fact, you are on this street (which is virtually unmarked) as you walk from Monoprix toward rue Meynadier. The stores are only 50m (164 ft.) from Monoprix—hidden in clear sight.

CORDONNIER BOTTIER
51 rue Meynadier.

If you're looking for a pair of honest espadrilles, not the ones they sell at Hermès, this is the source. The shop looks so much like the local shoemaker that you wouldn't think to enter, but check it out.

MENSWEAR

ANDRE GHEKIERE
69 La Croisette.

André Ghekiere is preppy, but with a touch of the beach and a serious touch of the yacht crowd. It sells bathing costumes with matching robes and that sort of thing.

CLAUDE BONUCCI
Noga Hilton, 50 La Croisette.

Primarily a menswear designer, Bonucci is one of the last couturiers in the Riviera and certainly the most famous to locals who have the big bucks. He makes some women's clothing and sells handmade, ready-made clothes off the rack as well as bespoke (made-to-measure).

Aside from the fact that every known musician, cinema star, and festival-goer wears his clothes, his genius is for original elegance translated into the very distinctive rock 'n' roll of the Côte d'Azur. We're talking resort elegance, which is a hard thing to do without looking like you died and went to Palm Beach. This is the only man in France who can cut a men's suit in pale turquoise and make it work.

Although the clothes are expensive (870€/$1,000-plus for a silk blazer), Bonucci has a classic finesse that actually makes them worth the money. I've got to tell you, I was a skeptic at first, but after a fashion show and a serious browse through his stores, I'm hooked. Now I just need to win at the tables.

Next time you tour with your rock band, break the bank at Monte Carlo, or need to look absolutely with the team à la the local luxe, this need be your only stop.

TRABAUD
48 rue d'Antibes.

Trabaud sells a modified version of Bonucci, but not handmade and not glitzy. This is where you come for those chic-er-than-thou linen blazers in just the right color of the season. The clothes have a preppy touch without being conservative: It's Ralph Lauren goes French resort.

MULTIPLES & CHAIN STORES

CHACOK
7 rue Commandant André.

Chacok has wild patterns and bright colors, good for resort wear.

ET VOUS
84 rue d'Antibes.

This is the Ann Taylor of France.

KOOKAI
18 rue d'Antibes.

Teen angel, can you hear me?

L'OCCITANE
14 rue du Maréchal Joffre.

This is a branch of the famed bath-goods store.

MARITHE ET FRANÇOIS GIRBAUD
Gray d'Albion.

$150 for a pair of jeans?

PIMKIE
42 rue d'Antibes.

Low-cost teen angel, can you hear me?

SEPHORA
53 bis rue d'Antibes.

Sephora has more makeup and scent than an airport.

ZARA
32 rue d'Antibes.

MUSIC

Musical recordings, be they records, tapes, or CDs, are usually frightfully expensive in France and aren't a tourist's best buy. However, if selection—not price—is the issue, you will be in heaven. There are scads of recordings that never come to the United States; there is also a bit of a business in bootleg tapes that were illegally recorded at events and then made into "real" CDs.

FNAC
83 rue d'Antibes.

This is everything you expect FNAC to be: music, tickets, and even computer supplies. It has books and a cafe, too.

PARAPHARMACIES

ANGLO-FRANÇAISE PHARMACIE
95 rue d'Antibes.

This is a good place to warm up to the notion of a *parapharmacie* (large discount drugstore), and it's not far from the Noga. It doesn't carry a huge selection, but the store is spacious, so you can see everything and begin to learn brand names.

PARALAND
22 rue Meynadier.

This is a small shop but has become sort of my regular because it's part of my ritual stroll from Marché Forville into town. I just wish it would open on Sunday. I stock up on my basics here: Lierac's Teint Lift Transparent and Galenic Orphycée Creme de Renovation Cellulaire.

PARA PLUS PHARMACIE
113 rue d'Antibes.

This is a small *parapharmacie* located in the heart of town. It offers discounts on every purchase.

PERFUME, MAKEUP & SOAP

If you're going to Paris, wait 'til you get there for perfume, makeup, and soap—you'll find better prices at discounters like Catherine (see chapter 4). Otherwise, rue d'Antibes has several perfume shops; in the past few years a lot of them have merged into the **Marionaud** family, which discounts slightly for locals and tries to compete with Sephora (but doesn't have as many brands).

BOUTEILLE
59 rue d'Antibes.

Bouteille has earned the reputation among locals as the best shop in town. It not only carries more luxury brands than any other shop, but also gets exclusive items and provides the kind of service and knowledge that you won't find in American supermarket-style stores.

Bouteille has the expected full range of designer names in fragrance and skin care, as well as some of the hard-to-find ones (like the special-edition releases and the collectors' bottles and groups). It carries Annick Goutal (which is not carried at Sephora), as well as Sisley and Bobbi Brown and, yes, Oh My Dog. It also offers fragrance for the home and scented candles from big designers such as Canovas and Rigaud, as well as scented madeleines for your drawers. It has recently started selling big, chunky, fabulous ethnic-style necklaces and accessories.

Bouteille is old-fashioned in its approach to service. Sephora is young and modern and American, but the salesgirls don't know a lot about skin or product. They're cute and they've been trained well, but they aren't experts who have a career in skin care. At Bouteille, they really know something and can give you treatment and product advice, which is especially important if you are over 35.

Bouteille is open on Monday, and it stays open during lunchtime. Of course, it does *détaxe,* too. And it gives out tons of little samples when you buy stuff.

BY TERRY
99 rue d'Antibes.

Terry's makeup has been a cult fave for years; those who can afford it know this, and the rest? Well, they don't even count, do they? You can get custom-created colors, of course, but there is also an off-the-rack selection—*cher,* but not as costly as the couture.

L'Occitane
14 rue du Maréchal Joffre.

L'Occitane is one of the most famous Provençal brands in the world, with global distribution and stores everywhere, including Paris, London, and the United States. It's been expanding like mad the past few years, and it now has a freestanding shop in Cannes. The line is enormous; you can go stark raving nuts with the touching and the sniffing of everything. This store is on the corner of the small part of rue Meynadier and the rue du Maréchal Joffre, between Monoprix and the regular pedestrian street rue Meynadier, a small 1- block offshoot of rue Meynadier.

Sephora
53 bis rue d'Antibes.

Sephora is a rather large chain, with stores all over the place— all of those branches are bigger and better than the one in Cannes. But if you've never been to a Sephora or you aren't going to another city, then well, well, well, have you got a treat in store.

Real-People Shopping

French pharmacies are designated by a neon green cross and carry most items you could need, including condoms. In fact, right on the rue d'Antibes, there's an outdoor condom machine in front of the **Lienhard Pharmacie** (no. 36). There are many nail salons, which do tips and what they call American-style manicures, but few are good. The best one I've found is **OngleStar,** 4 rue Chabaud (℡ 04-93-38-73-02), which also does beauty treatments and waxing (a bikini wax is called a *maillot,* after the word for bathing suit in French). It's closed on Mondays, but otherwise open from 9am to 6:30pm; appointments are suggested.

You can buy feminine supplies at pharmacies, supermarkets, drugstores, and places like Monoprix. For some reason, the big hotels do not seem to have little sundries shops that sell these emergency items.

If you need inexpensive items—everything from pantyhose to sand buckets, beauty aids to picnic supplies—head for that one-stop-shopping haven: **Monoprix,** 9 rue Maréchal Foch, which also has a grocery store upstairs.

The **Cannes English Bookshop,** 11 rue Bivouac-Napoléon (near the Palais des Festivals), is in the heart of town. It's run by a lovely British man, so most of the English-language works are British; you'll have no trouble finding beach or travel pleasures.

There's a branch of **American Express** at 8 rue des Belges, right off La Croisette. There are ATMs all over town and exchange booths in most hotels.

If you need a liquor store and your hotel minibar just won't cut it, try **Sunshine,** 5 rue Maréchal Joffre, an excellent wine-and-spirits shop right in the heart of town with everything from favored vintages to Scotch single malts.

SHOES & LEATHER GOODS

Of course you know about the big names such as Hermès, Gucci, Vuitton, and all that; even Chanel has handbags and shoes. These options are more specialty-related.

CHARLES JOURDAN
47 rue d'Antibes.

Welcome, Patrick Cox! This Canadian designer reached shoe fame in London and has now taken over Charles Jourdan. Look out, Gigi!

JACQUES LOUP
21 rue d'Antibes.

This is the best place in town for shoes, with a roundup of every line including Prada (which is not sold at bargain prices, despite the fact that Italy is just an hour away). Excellent selection for men and women makes this good shopping for any need, from sandal to silk. Jacques Loup now has three shops in a row.

LANCEL
34 rue d'Antibes.

This is one of the fanciest boutiques on rue d'Antibes offering a terrific line of leather goods, from handbags to luggage. Items cost considerably less in France than in the United States. I like the fact that it often has unusual colors—I got an olive-green bag for fall and a honey-colored hemp bag for summer.

L'ETRIER
51 rue d'Antibes.

This is a rather average handbag shop with a few absolutely fabulous copies of big-name bags. This is the kind of store you might walk by without paying notice. Don't. A very good Kelly bag goes for about 174€ ($200).

SOUVENIRS, TTS & NOVELTY GIFTS

There are scads of TTs all over town. A few unusual stores sell gimmicky silly gifts that I guess you can only call souvenirs, although they may not have CANNES emblazoned on them. **Bathroom Graffitti**, 52 rue d'Antibes, is a chain of gift shops, and **Davis**, 1 La Croisette and Gray d'Albion, is an original kind of place that offers film-festival souvenirs, unusual items that you've never seen anywhere else, and all sorts of gadgets. Davis is open on Sunday.

I'm into kitsch and love the junky stores on the rue Meynadier that sell everything from lavender sachets to Provençal-print toilet-paper holders to snow domes made of plastic frogs.

If your idea of a souvenir is a memory you hold forever, perhaps you want to avoid the junk and sign up for a cooking class. **Ecole Lenôtre** has opened in Cannes, offering various workshops on myriad types of foods—not just chocolates. For information, call © 04-97-06-67-67.

SPECIAL SIZES

MARINA RINALDI
15 rue des Serbes.

This small shop carries a selection of Italian maker Max Mara's casual, business, and dress-up line, in sizes 42 to 56.

GRASSE

....

Now that I've fallen in love with chef Jacques Chibois, I welcome you to Grasse with new enthusiasm. I used to have a love-hate thing with Grasse. I mean, I can't imagine that you would come this close and miss the opportunity to visit a town that represents the perfume business. But I am sad to send you to the mostly touristy places that make up the town, and I am appalled at how much the city has changed in recent years in order to accommodate the tour buses.

But here's the good part: When I know I can also send you to eat (and even sleep) chez Chibois, my heart sings. I also think I need a drink, as Jacques has gotten me hooked on a local brew, *vin cuit,* that is heaven in a glass. Plus, the *brocante* market held on Wednesday is wonderful.

If you've been to Grasse and have memories of it, or if you're perusing an old guidebook, forget anything you know about the old system wherein the many perfume houses in town sold copycat fragrances. Nowadays there are no copycat fragrances, no charts saying "If you like Chanel No. 5 you will like . . . ," and no little vials of anything that smell suspiciously like the real thing. So the Grasse I welcome you to is far different than it used to be or than you imagine it to be.

Getting to Grasse

If you haven't got a car, you can take public transportation from Cannes. I took the bus once—great fun. If you're driving, follow the signs for **Monoprix**—in so doing, you'll get a tour of the town and know which fork to take every time you have a choice of roads. Then you can park in the Monoprix parking lot and explore the heart of the old town on foot.

The Lay of the Land

Grasse is located a little more than 15km (9 miles) from Cannes, perched in the hills slightly to the north. It is the industrial and emotional heart of the perfume industry.

There is a sort of downtown Grasse, even a cute street in Old Grasse. However, most of the center of Grasse is neither cute nor charming; it's just vertical. It sprawls up and down and around and feels like the kind of place where you can get lost without having fun being lost.

You don't come to Grasse for the cute; you come for Chibois and the perfumes. So if you have fantasies about fields of poppies or the smell of flowers in the air or friendly worker bees in cute native dress with baskets on their heads, you can think again. Picture instead TTs, tour buses, and zillions of schoolchildren wearing name tags.

Shopping for Scent

Grasse is not one enormous duty-free shop, nor is it nearly as much fun as any branch of the French makeup chain Sephora. You don't come to Grasse to get discounts on designer perfume or to find a bigger or better selection of designer anything. In fact, Grasse is not a designer fragrance town as far as tourists are concerned.

The big names don't allow you to enter their factories or to sniff their poppies. Even though Chanel keeps its own fields to grow its own flowers in order to ensure their purity and that of their essence, Chanel does not appear to be represented to the public in any form.

What Grasse does have are a few renovated mansions that have been turned into museums and shops selling their own brands. What Grasse does have are a lot of tour buses. Power to the petals.

GRASSE ON TOUR

Grasse is included in an enormous number of package tours, including shore excursions offered by cruise lines that come to port along the Riviera. Like most package tours, these are marriages between one perfume house and the firm offering the tour.

You will not be able to cope with more than one factory tour—how perfume is made is fascinating only once. (Sort of like the "How Wine Is Made" speech.) Note that tours at all of the big factories are free and are offered in a variety of languages.

THE BIG THREE

Grasse has three big names in the tourist perfume factory business. Two of these names have factory shops in other parts of the Riviera. I have ranked the big three according to my opinion of their charms.

MOLINARD
60 bd. Victor Hugo.

There's no question that Molinard is the classiest of the big three. If you're going to only one of the three houses, this is the one to pick.

The villa in which the showroom is housed is gorgeous; the costumes in their museum arcades are gorgeous; some of the scents are even gorgeous.

The house has a full range of lines, most of which are sold at Bergdorf Goodman in New York and a few other fancy-dan shops. Most Americans are not familiar with the perfume house itself or any of its brands. Not to worry.

Perhaps its most famous scent is Habanita, which comes in a very distinctive (and highly collectible) Lalique bottle. This is the kind of scent you either love or hate. My favorite part of the collection is a complete line called Les Senteurs, which is a range of *eaux de toilette* made from natural flowers, spices, or herbs, such as vanilla, lime, orange, and cinnamon.

There is even a baby scent, Les Cherubins, for the baby who has everything.

Molinard conducts a perfume-making workshop, usually booked by small groups and arranged ahead of time, whereby you can create your very own scent. To arrange your perfume workshop, fax **04-93-36-03-91**.

FRAGONARD
20 bd. Fragonard.
Les 4 Chemins, route de Cannes and Eze village.

Fragonard sort of owns Grasse; it has two shops/factories in Grasse, one downtown and one on the road from Cannes. There are two other retail factories: one in Eze village and one in Paris near American Express on rue Scribe.

Fragonard's main headquarters is in a magnificently restored villa in the heart of town; its museum and tour are excellent. I just don't happen to like the products very much.

Pick up the free literature distributed in hotels or tourist venues, and you'll likely find a discount coupon for 5% off your purchases here.

GALIMARD
73 route de Cannes.

Galimard has a little-old-lady type of showroom in downtown Grasse and a big factory-style outlet on the road outside town. There is also a shop in Eze.

JUAN-LES-PINS

Time stopped in Juan-les-Pins: It's still 1962, and this lazy little village with the big-time chef and razzle-dazzle Deco hotel is one of the few authentic towns left on the French Riviera. What's so amazing is that this town is not a secret, yet it has remained unspoilt.

Maybe unspoilt is not the right word. Deliciously spoilt but not overly touristy might be the right description. After all, this is the town that is a small but vital character in the book *Bergdorf Blondes,* which provides the inside scoop on the jet set and how many pairs of shoes they can buy in only a few minutes in Juan-les-Pins.

If you have ever lamented the traffic, the out-of-towners, the sweaty kids being towed along, the crassness of the boom-town Riviera cities, I welcome you to the last hurrah, the last small-town big-time city where the glamour is real and the emotions are almost unreal because it all feels so fresh. Grab an ice-cream cone and let's promenade.

Welcome to Juan-les-Pins, which is slightly off the beaten path and therefore has preserved its charm. Welcome to a suburb of Cannes, hidden before Antibes, and nestled against the sea in its own little world.

Part of the reason for this town's success as a glam zone is that it is not far from the Hôtel du Cap in Antibes, which is celebrity headquarters—and has been since the time of Scott and Zelda. Think Great Neck, mid-60s.

Hmmm, no—remember the summer of 1960 when I stayed with Grandma Jessie in Miami Beach—waaaaay before Miami Beach became what it is today? That's the feel: beach town, in soft focus yet seductive.

Secret Flash

Just as you are to know without being told that the Hôtel du Cap (called simply "du Cap") only takes cash, you must know how to pronounce Juan-les-Pins. If you're thinking of the Spanish pronunciation of Juan *(Wan)*, cut it out. This is France. You pronounce the *J*, so say *Ju-wan-le-Pan.*

Getting to Juan-les-Pines

You will miss Juan-les-Pins if you don't look for it. Forget cruising on the autoroute A8. Instead, from Cannes take the (free) coastal road N7 east—the Route 66 of France—and follow signs toward Antibes until you get to a fork marked Juan-les-Pins. This is a small sign and easily missed.

Juan is not the next obvious coastal slash of beach huts and condos (that happens to be the town of Golfe Juan). A little further along, you'll see a full-fledged town with one-way streets, a casino, and just the right amount of scruffy charm to it.

But silly me, giving you directions. Your chauffeur knows the way. (As the driver also knows, Juan is 20 min. from the Nice airport.)

Oh yes, there is actually a train, so you can also come and go as a day trip. But that's beside the point. The point is to hide behind your shade and never leave. The train station is at the edge of town, but is easily within walking distance of the shops and the sea.

The Lay of the Land

The entire town is tiny, but in no way a one-street gig or anything boring. The beaches are 200m (656 ft.) from the center of town; often you can get a hotel room with a beach view. The beach is also the end of the shopping promenade, so you can shop to see and sea. Urrgh, excuse me. I get carried away here. Sea drunk.

To make it more interesting for you, the town has many curving streets and alleys, places to explore, and shopping just about everywhere. If you have feet (all those shoe stores) or eyes (time for window-licking, as the French say), you won't be bored.

Sleeping in Juan-les-Pines

HOTEL JUANA
La Pinède, av. Gallice.

First, the warning: The La Pinède in the address is a part of town, near the pine-tree area for which the town is named. Do not mistakenly attempt to check into the hotel called La Pinède, as I did. How I could check into any other hotel is beyond comprehension, but the Juana was hidden by some pine trees, and the wrong hotel was pretty cute in a funky way.

After three phone calls, the concierge rescued me, I drove around the casino and the pines, and I immediately fell in love with this midsize yellow villa with Art Deco trim. I'd booked here not only because of the fame of the kitchen (Alain Ducasse started here), but also because the hotel had just undergone a face-lift and is now as sleek as a Deco ocean liner. For more on the chef, see the review of La Terrasse, below.

Now then, the hotel—one of those secret leading small boutique places with a multi-star Michelin chef. It's been home to celebs like Bill Cosby, Ray Charles, Johnny Depp, and the like. But forget those stars—instead, think of the chef and the new beach club.

In the main hotel, the rooms are sleek, moderne, air-conditioned (of course), and Deco-ed up to magazine-page perfection. The charming cage elevator is enclosed in glass; the flowers are inventive and sophisticated—a true homage to floral arts and not just your average hotel bouquet. Dining options include the famous restaurant, La Terrasse, and a little bistro.

The 40-room hotel is open year-round; rates vary with the season, but begin at 230€ ($265) per night. Local phone ✆ 04-93-61-08-70. www.hotel-juana.com.

LE MERIDIEN GARDEN BEACH
15–17 bd. Baudoin.

I'm sure this is a nice hotel; I'm a big fan of Le Meridien hotels worldwide. This one is located next to the casino and over-looking the beach. It's modern and glitzy on the outside, and looks a little out of place. Once inside, though, you can eas-ily forget all that.

Rates vary with promotions, but start around 250€ ($288). From the U.S., call ✆ 866/559-3821. Local phone ✆ 04-92-93-57-57. www.lemeridien.com.

Eating in Juan-les-Pins

You can snack and shop your way through town, as there are plenty of pizza places, crepe joints, and ice-cream stores. But part of the point of this town is to not snack, but seriously eat.

La Terrasse
Hôtel Juana, av. Gallice.

He looks like Salvador Dali, but he cooks like the Wizard of Oz: Christian Morisset has been the talk of the Côte d'Azur for going on 20 years as he just keeps on earning his two Michelin stars. You can dine inside or out, at lunch or dinner—but you must be dressed and ready to be seen while acting like you don't give autographs.

In between bites, you can sneak a peak at the foodies who come to worship and the smart shoppers who know there's a fixed-price lunch at under 50€ ($58) per person. The souvenir of your trip south just may be the clay plaque that comes with the saddle of Pauillac lamb, which the chef bakes in Vallauris clay—sort of like the number on your duck at Tour d'Argent in Paris.

Obviously, reservations are imperative. In season or during the film festival, book as far in advance as possible by calling ✆ 04-93-61-08-70.

Les Pecheurs
10 bd. Maréchal Juin.

Enjoy beachside eating in this gourmet restaurant at the Hôtel Juana's beach club. You can have lunch or dinner on the glassed-in terrace year-round, or sit outdoors between June and September. Reserve through the Hôtel Juana, above.

Shopping in Juan-les-Pines

The point here is to roam around and shop as you go. The city is big on fashion for young women (with cigarette-slim bodies), shoes and sandals, bathing suits, accessories, and home style. There's a large TT (Librairie du Casino) that sells books in many languages as well as real-people needs such as sunglasses, toys, beach stuff, office supplies, and postcards. There are two supermarkets in the heart of town for picnic needs. You'll see plenty of beach-pail stores, as expected, but these kinds of things are less costly at the supermarket, if you care.

There are perhaps a handful of freestanding, big-name boutiques—most of which are known for young and casual clothes or beachwear, such as Diesel, NafNaf, Blanc Bleu, Reminscense, and Villequin. All of these brands also have stores in Cannes and in most other French Riviera towns.

Mostly, you'll find tiny shops that sell a few brands or others that provide their own version of the look. Designers come here to copy that look. This is a town where shops have names like Spicy, Cappuccino, and Pam-Pam.

ANTIBES

I welcome you to Antibes if you come out of season. I welcome you to Antibes in summer if you come by yacht. Okay, you can come by train anytime. Otherwise, watch out, I don't think you want to even be welcomed here—you won't find a parking place, and the traffic may make you nuts. If you're game and don't care about the crush, any day is a good day. But the best and most crowded days are Thursday and Saturday, *brocante* days.

On Thursdays, there are actually two markets in Antibes: antiques and Provençale. The latter sells foods as well as some local crafts and souvenir-type items; it is held under a covered market roof. The antiques market is small, outdoors, and runs along the street, just a few yards from the covered market.

On Saturdays, there are also two markets, but of different sorts (antiques and real-people needs). The real-people market is along the waterfront; the antiques market is in the center of the old town. They're not far apart, but they do not merge and no neon signs indicate that there are two types of venues for your shopping pleasure.

The real-people market, where new merchandise is sold, is right on the waterfront and rambles through a parking lot or two. Here you can find a few pieces of *brocante,* but mostly new household and clothing items. A few tables sell factory overruns. One dealer has fake Hermès-style handbags.

The real flea market, held at a midpoint in the Old Town, consists of just a few dealers who lay out their wares on the pavement. The thing that disappoints me about this flea market is there are so few dealers. I will add that in all my research in all of the flea markets that I scoped out in France, this market had the lowest asking prices on traditional French merchandise.

If you arrive in Antibes by yacht or cruise ship, you will tie up at the Port Vauban, which has just been jazzed up and has two new *quais.* From here, you can walk directly into Old Town. This is the best way to enjoy Antibes.

BIOT

There is some discussion as to how to properly pronounce the name of this small town—some pronounce all the letters including even the final *t,* while others say "B.O.," dropping the final *t.* Regardless, you'll find most shoppers come here for the glass factory, which is not in the heart of town.

Downtown itself is only about 2 blocks long. Although the main street is lined with TTs, they are exactly the kind of places you expect to see and actually want to see. Several TTs sell locally made monochromatic pottery. There's also an abundance of Provençal fabrics, sold by the bolt or made up into table items, clothing, and accessories—everything from glasses cases to toilet-paper holders. Several cafes are here as well.

The glass factory, **La Verrerie de Biot** (Chemin des Combes, right outside Biot center), has been made famous to Americans because its bubble-encrusted glassworks are often featured on tables set with Pierre Deux or Souleiado linen. There's no question that the glassware is nice, but it is also very expensive. The store ships, but shipping will double the prices (already high) and subject you to additional American duty. To complicate matters, the store does not ship items bought from the bargain corner, where you can actually find some true bargains. So if you get lucky with a bargain, be prepared to schlep it.

Final note: You can buy much less expensive bubble glass—even in colors—at various home-style shops in the U.S. and throughout France. Within France, check out sources such as Geneviève Lethu, Pier 1, Alinea, and Casa.

VALLAURIS

Years ago, I would have extended a warm welcome to Vallauris, a city I have enjoyed. I would have welcomed you to the place where Picasso got into the lay of the clay, where studios selling locally made dishes dished out their wares, where the name Studio Madoura meant something. Today: Phooey. Yankee, go home.

The town is loaded with tourists, the TTs are overwhelming, and the soul of the city has been destroyed by crass commercialism. Yuck. Or tee-hee yuck. Last time I was in town, I ate at McDonald's.

If you insist on visiting Vallauris, I can tell you that there are plenty of places to shop. Few of them are charming, but here and there you'll find a few special resources.

The main drag is avenue Georges Clemenceau; check out the part with the higher numbers (like 65 bis) rather than the lower numbers, which tend to be more touristy.

My favorite shop from years ago is still open and wonderful: **Foucard-Jourdan,** 65 bis av. G. Clemenceau. You'll have to look hard to find it, even though it's in plain sight, because

of all the junky stores that have been built up along the way.
I also like **Potterie Provençal**, 54 av. G. Clemenceau.

Because of the overwhelming number of TTs, all with merchandise spilling out of their stores and piled high on the
curbs, you'll be tempted to do some of your souvenir shopping here. Compared to elsewhere in France, prices on souvenir items in Vallauris are actually quite good. Have lavender
sachets, will travel.

ST-PAUL-DE-VENCE

Welcome, welcome, and again welcome to St-Paul-de-Vence,
a tourist town that knows how to get it right. This is the kind
of place where the shopping is so adorable that you know it's
all been created for tourists, not locals—but you almost don't
mind simply because it's all so beautiful.

On the whole, the shopping scene within the walls of this
medieval town is what you would expect—lots of TTs selling
everything from postcards to plastic swords and armor. There
are some art galleries with high prices and a handful of very
nice boutiques dotted here and there, so even a person with a
real sense of style can get a sense of well-being when out
strolling and window-shopping the rue Grande.

What seems to make the difference here is the level of taste:
This is a town for rich tourists with good taste. There's nothing tacky about it. Chocolatier **Joël Durand** (3 bd. Victor
Hugo) has opened a shop here, immediately changing the taste
level to higher than yummy. A few stores sell cheap tricks, but
the good fabric houses are in place, and the overall quality of
the goods and the storefronts seduces the visitor into thinking
that this is not an ordinary tourist town.

Les Olivades (1 rue Grande) and **Souleiado** (17 rue Grande),
the two biggest names in quality Provençal fabrics, have boutiques on the cobbled main shopping street. **L'Air du Sud** (56
rue Grande) is an extraordinary store—a local dollop of design,

crafts, color, and the look of the south of France in tabletop and gift items.

But wait, I forgot to tell you that St-Paul is open—and I mean wide open—on Sunday!

Out of Town

MAISON DES ARTS
10 rue Maréchal Foch, La Colle sur Loup.

If you've dreamed about an arts-and-crafts camp for grown-ups, search no more: The find of your dreams is located right outside St-Paul-de-Vence, in the village of La Colle sur Loup. There are painting workshops, cooking workshops, and ceramics workshops. You can stay with the hosts on a bed-and-breakfast deal or you can make your own hotel arrangements. Classes last 1 week; there are in- and out-of-season prices, but the resident fee for a single room in high season is about 1,000€ ($1,150), which includes everything. Oh yes, the hosts and professors are British, so don't expect too many language problems. ✆ 04-93-32-32-50. www.maisondesarts.com.

MOULIN DE LA BRAQUE
2 route de Châteauneuf, Opio.

A movie set couldn't look better than the Moulin Huile Michel, also known as the Moulin de la Braque (it's owned by Roger Michel, hence the two names). The mill makes olive oil and sells a varieties of olives, olive oil, and olive-oil products such as soap. It also sells some fabric, some touristy items, and a few gifts. But you come for the olives.

The oil is sold in any number of tins, and can also be tasted, tested, and bought straight from the vat. If you bring your own container, it costs less. If you were so silly as to leave your container at home, you can pick from a number of types, sizes, and packages. (Remember that tins are easier to pack than glass bottles.) Hours are 9am to noon and 2 to 7pm. ✆ 04-93-77-23-03.

NICE

....

Welcome to a town where you can indeed have a very Nice day, or several. Even if you just come to Nice on a day trip or a shore excursion, I think you're going to like it. The better part of Nice can be seen in a day.

To best enjoy the town, don't focus on shopping—just let it happen. Although rue Paradis is the main pedestrian shopping street, I don't find it paradise at all. I think it's sort of limited, in fact. Cannes has better big-name shopping than Nice, so don't shrug and wonder where paradise has gone. True paradise is around the corner, in Old Nice. Step this way.

I must also say at this point that my 25-year-old son Aaron, who reports for these pages, thinks the teen-tween shopping in Nice is better than elsewhere in the Riviera because the prices are more real-people, there's not so much glam and hype, and there are plenty of big stores with large stocks of mid-price, non-designer names.

Getting to Nice

You can fly directly to the Nice–Côte d'Azur Airport from New York, via Delta.

To get to Nice from Paris, there are regular shuttle flights via Air France called La Navette (the shuttle), departing from both Paris Orly and CDG. At press time, EasyJet also serves Nice, but so many low-cost carriers have gone out of business that you'd better check the website (www.easyjet.com) for the latest info.

Many other carriers serve this airport, so Nice can be used as a hub city for getting around the Mediterranean basin. I use Nice for easily getting to Morocco and Tunisia. Libya isn't yet on my must-do list, but you never know.

You can also get here by train, which is called a TGV though not all of the fast track is yet in place. The ride, at its swiftest, is 5 hours 33 minutes from Paris—and is likely to be longer.

Nice is also a train hub for overnight trips—this is a gateway for Italian cities and many in the new Europe.

Finally, you can arrive in Nice from Corsica by ferry, which comes to dock right near a candy factory.

Getting Around Nice

Warning: Taxi fares are outrageously expensive and controlled by some higher deity. There is little competition and not much room for bargaining. A taxi from the Nice airport to a hotel on the Promenade des Anglais—about a 7-minute drive—will easily cost 30€ ($35). There are supplemental charges for baggage, dogs, and night-time service.

I think the trick to getting around Nice is to stay in a well-situated hotel so you can walk everywhere. Even if you have a car, you might find that parking is hard to get. (Although, I found that parking tickets were easy to get.) Expect overnight parking in a covered lot to cost 30€ ($35) per night, or more.

For some shopping parts of Nice, like the antiques neighborhood, you'll need to drive or take a taxi. Otherwise, everything is accessible on foot.

Sleeping in Nice

The biggest excitement in town is not related to the opening or re-opening of any one store—although the arrival of the second Lafayette Maison, after the first store opened in Paris, is considered a big deal. The news is about hotels.

First of all, there's the **Palais de la Méditerranée**, 15 promenade des Anglais (© 04-92-14-77-02; www.lepalaisdela mediterranee.com), which is under the same ownership as palace hotels like the Hôtel de Crillon in Paris and the Hôtel Martinez in Cannes. This new luxury hotel has been created directly behind a landmark Art Deco facade, sitting smack dab on the promenade des Anglais. Don't miss a chance to gawk. Rates begin at 245€ ($282).

If you are indeed a hotel junky, as I am, you might also want to look in on the **Hi Hôtel**, 3 av. des Fleurs (© 04-97-07-26-27; www.hi-hotel.net). It's one of those new-fangled boutique hotels that offer cutting-edge chic and open bathrooms. Rates start at 145€ ($167).

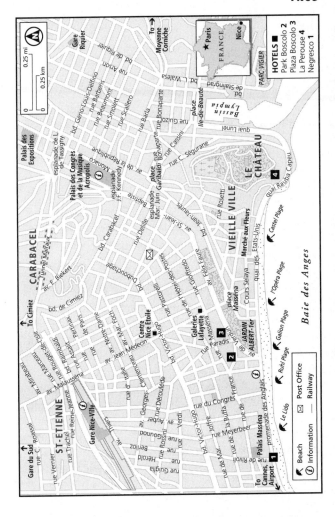

On the edge of the Old Town, the **Hôtel Beau Rivage,** 24 rue St-François de Paule (© **04-92-47-82-82;** www.nicebeau rivage.com), has been redone—after being closed for a year— and is now very modern and boutique-hotelish with a great location. Rates start at 140€ ($161).

HOTEL LA PEROUSE
11 quai Rauba-Capéu.

This is not a great shopping location if you aren't a walker, but the hotel is perched above Old Town, with a stairway leading up and down. It's also perched right over the sea, so the views are incredible. This is the funky luxury hotel of your dreams. Rack rates start at around 245€ ($282). From the U.S., contact Yellin Hotels (www.yellinhotels.com). Local phone © 04-93-62-34-63. www.hotel-la-perouse.com.

HOTEL NEGRESCO
37 promenade des Anglais.

Although Cannes has an international reputation for its Belle Epoque sugar-plum hotels, Nice has one or two left, too. The most famous of them is the Hôtel Négresco, which is downright sumptuous inside and out.

Located right on the promenade des Anglais and overlooking the sea, the Négresco is within walking distance of everything and is considered the place to be. Every star in the world has stayed here, and Richard Burton even accidentally left Liz's 69-carat diamond on the bar one night. The Beatles wrote a hit song here.

Rooms begin around 250€ ($288) per night, but they come with gold-sparkle bidets. Honest. There are also promotional rates. Staying here is one of the world's best treats because the decor is so over the top and the mixture of old-world grandeur with modern art so stunning—and silly.

If you just stop by to stare, have a drink in the English-style bar. Go to the ladies' room; you've never seen a bathroom like this, I promise. There are some stores in the lobby; use them as an excuse to poke around. The hotel shows its devotion to mixing neoclassical architecture with modern art with a Niki de Saint Phalle statue of a jazz player outside on the curb.

For reservations from the United States, call Leading Hotels of the World at © **800/223-6800.** Local phone 04-93-88-39-51. www.hotel-negresco-nice.com.

HOTEL PARK BOSCOLO
6 av. de Suède.

Another Boscolo hotel and one whose renovation has been totally completed, the Park is around the corner from the Plaza and across the street from one of my favorite restaurants in Nice, La Cigale. Better still, the rooms are large, some have ocean views, and rates are even lower than at the Plaza (starting at around 175€/$201). The Park is smaller than the Plaza and has a more boutique-hotel feel. From the U.S., call © **888/626-7265.** Local phone © 04-97-03-19-00. www.boscolohotels.com.

HOTEL PLAZA BOSCOLO
12 av. Verdun.

I've been staying at this hotel for over a dozen years and seen it change management and styles. As we go to press, I beg you to insist on (and confirm) a renovated room if you book here— or else wait for word that all rooms have been renovated. The lobby is now spiffy moderne; the renovated rooms are large and well done, many with ocean views. The location couldn't be more perfect: steps from the rue Paradis, around the corner from Galeries Lafayette, and an easy walk to Old Town and the promenade des Anglais.

The hotel is now owned by Boscolo, an Italian group of hoteliers with four-star and four-star-deluxe hotels around the world. I've seen so many properties that this has become a group that I believe in. The best deals depend on availability, of course, but can be booked online for about 185€ ($213) per night; otherwise expect to pay about 250€ ($288). From the U.S., call © **888/626-7265.** Local phone © 04-93-16-75-75. www.boscolohotels.com.

Eating in Nice

FENNOCHIO
15 rue Droite, place Rossetti, Old Town.

This is the most famous ice-cream shop on the French Riviera. Try the lavender or the tomato-basil flavor.

LA CIGALE ORIENTALE
7 av. de Suède.

This is perhaps my favorite new restaurant concept in France—
a restaurant-cum-store-cum-takeaway department. The menu
is Mediterranean but with a twist—it concentrates on foods
from areas like Lebanon, Egypt, and Greece. You can walk in
off the street, but reservations are better: Call © 04-93-88-60-20.
There's a second location in the Cap 3000 mall on the edge of
Nice (p. 303).

LA MERANDA
4 rue de la Terrasse, Old Town.

No credit cards, no reservations—and no phone. Stop by in
the morning on your way to market and reserve for lunch or
dinner. Two-star chef Dominique LeStanc gave up the big time
to open this teeny-weeny bistro serving local fare. Closed
weekends, school holidays, and the month of August.

LE CHANTECLER
Hôtel Negresco, 37 promenade des Anglais.

Part of the new story of the rotating chefs in the south of France:
Alain Llorca has left Chantecler to move to Mougins, while
Michel Del Burgo, from Taillevant in Paris, has moved in. *Ooh
la la* never tasted so good.

Shopping in Nice

BEST BUYS

Although my son says this town is great for mass-market
French brands for the under-30 set, I think the best buys are
more related to local lore—and food at that. I'd go for olive
oil, *fruits confits,* rose or jasmine jam, or even the local wine,
named Bellet.

SHOPPING NEIGHBORHOODS

NICE AIRPORT For a small airport, this has very good shopping. Half of the stores are located near the gates after you've gone through immigration. The other half are located before the immigration gates, so even if you don't go through immigration because you're on an intra-Euro flight, you can still shop. The offerings include a tiny **Hermès** boutique (where I've found things at fair prices), a newsagent, a duty-free store, a shop that sells Provençal fabric–style souvenirs, and a gourmet grocery for fresh cheeses, olive oil, and so on.

Right near the airport (which is technically not in Nice, but in St-Laurent-du-Var) is a large regional mall called **Cap 3000** (say *Cap trois mille*). While this American-style mall may bore you to tears, it can be a great way to see a lot of French brands in the comfort of air-conditioning. There's a new **MAC** store here as well as a branch of **La Cigale** in the Lafayette Gourmet (see p. 302 for a review of La Cigale Orientale). **Lafayette Maison,** a home-style store also owned by Galeries Lafayette, has just opened.

COURS SALEYA You can have the rest of Nice, I'll keep the airport and the cours Saleya, the main square in the heart of the Old Town, where a flower-and-vegetable market is held every day (yes, Sun, too) except Monday, which is *brocante* day.

I cannot tell you that this is the cutest town square in France or that the Old Town is adorable and worthy of a postcard. The fact that the area is real and not perfect explains some of the charm.

The visual here is color, from striped awnings to gorgeous fruits and flowers. Several cafes that line the way make for the perfect opportunity to stop, have a coffee, stare, and wonder at the fact that this is a way of life for some people.

In the market stands, you'll find a variety of prices for seemingly the same things. Don't buy until you've surveyed the lot. This is one of the best fruit-and-flower markets in the south of France; go out of your way to get here.

Old Town (Vieux Nice) is adjacent to the market, so be sure to allow time for both.

VIEUX NICE This is the Old Town, comprising a small warren of streets surrounding the cours Saleya. You do the two together. Again, I won't tell you that this is the most picturesque old town in France or even on the Riviera. It's actually kind of gritty. But therein lies the charm. You can believe.

With any luck, you're staying at a hotel on the promenade des Anglais or right in the center of town, so you can walk to this area. There's something fabulous about strolling along the ocean side of the promenade and then cutting into the Old Town and coming upon these old-fashioned little stores and TTs as if you were in a dream.

If you're driving and arrive for the day, look for the municipal parking right at the cours Saleya. A computerized sign above the lot tells you how many spaces are available. If the lot is full, the sign will say *complet*. If you park here, do take time to wander over 1 block to see the ocean and the promenade.

QUAI DE LA DOUANE This is the antiques neighborhood. On a map it looks like it's an easy walk from the cours Saleya. However, because of the size of Le Château, on a mountain between the two parts of town, you'll be happier if you take a taxi. Ask for Le Marché Aux Puce du quai de la Douane, and you will be dropped where you need to be. The *marché* has about 18 stalls and isn't impressive, but there is a candy factory next door (**Confiserie du Vieux Nice**, 14 quai Papacino), plus many more warehouses of antiques around the corner. So don't panic. The candy factory is small, but it gives tours and sells samples. It makes chocolates and *fruits confits*; upstairs is a rather large shop with free tastings and great products to take home for gifts, including items such as jasmine jam.

Don't panic that addresses seem strange here; there are 3 blocks that run alongside the tiny boat harbor, and each block has a different name. But don't bury your nose in a map; sniff the air and look around. This is a part of town that's virtually unknown to tourists.

Walk alongside the quay for antiques shops and cafes (ignore the karaoke bars), and then turn left onto rue Antoine Gautier for a 2-block stretch filled with warehouses of used furniture and antiques. Most of the places here will ship your purchases; few dealers speak English. The specialty in these warehouses is large pieces of furniture. Prices, even with shipping added, are at least half of what you would pay for similar pieces in the U.S. Prices are listed, but the more you buy, the more flexible the dealer will become. The warehouses all keep more or less the same hours: Monday through Saturday from 9am to 12:30pm and 2:30 to 7pm.

PARADIS The main fancy shopping street of Nice is called rue Paradis. I don't know how to break this to you gently, but if you think this is paradise, you have come to the wrong book. Don't get me wrong; there's nothing wrong with the rue Paradis or with the stores that are on this 2-block stretch of upper-class French mall. It's just that when a street has a name like that, one has hopes. But this street is boring, filled with the usual suspects: Chanel, Sonia Rykiel, Montblanc, Façonnable, and so on.

VERDUN Forget the battle, and remember your brand names—everything from Gerard Darel to Escada with many others along the way, all in a row surrounding the Hôtel Plaza.

REAL-PEOPLE MASSENA Rue Paradis is a short little street in the greater pedestrian shopping cluster of downtown that branches off away from the main shopping thoroughfare. Place Masséna, with **Galeries Lafayette,** is the anchor of this shopping area. However, the bulk of the neighborhood is off to one side, past rue Paradis and snuggled behind a portion of promenade des Anglais. Note that one of the perimeters of this shopping district is the rue Verdun, which becomes avenue Félix-Faure, another main drag. Check a map to see how the streets converge and intersect.

Some of the stores here are branches of real-people shops that sell cheap shoes and sportswear. Most of them are TTs, cafes, and pizza places. I just love it back here because it's very real. But you will never confuse it with Cannes.

On the surface, all this looks tacky and cheap. That's because most of the good stuff is hidden. On the very side streets that sell the T-shirts, and along the boring rue Paradis and rue Masséna, there are a few addresses that will knock your socks off once you get inside.

As is the tradition in many places in France and Italy, local boutiques sell many of the bigger names. Check out spots like **Pink** (rue de France), **Jelly** (place Magenta), and **Claude Bonucci** (rue Massenet), which sells Claude Bonucci made-to-measure clothes from a very small and discreet shop. Bonucci, with additional shops in Cannes, makes old-fashioned, finely tailored togs for rock stars, movie stars, and the Riviera elite.

REAL-PEOPLE MEDECIN A spoonful of shopping makes the Médecin go down, even if the shopping has very little glamour and represents the basic multiples and real-people resources. Avenue Jean Médecin is where you'll find the chain stores **FNAC** (which sells CDs, tapes, and books), **Zara, Sephora, La Redoute,** and **Monoprix;** these branches are larger than the ones in Cannes. The train station is right off this main thoroughfare. You can easily walk along it, shopping your way to the rue Paradis, the place Masséna, the cours Saleya, and everywhere else.

FINDS

ALZIARI
14 rue St-François-de-Paule, Old Town.

If I had to pick just one store, one place that best captures the soul of what shopping in the south of France should be, I would send you to this hole-in-the-wall little mill, where you can buy olives, olive oil, and olive-oil soap. The olive oil, famed for the design and colors of its royal-blue can, is sold outside Nice in gourmet stores for two to three times what it costs here. If you can't get to the mill in the Old Town, note that the gourmet-food shop in the Nice airport sells two sizes of the olive oil. It's not cheap, even in Nice, but it does make a very special souvenir.

AUER
7 rue St-François-de-Paule, Old Town.

This ice-cream parlor and sweets shop looks like a movie set. It will enchant you as you study the storefront and then again when you step inside. You can have tea or get an ice-cream cone or do what generations of tourists before you have done: Send off some local sweets to your friends back home. Check out the mailing labels.

BLANC D'IVOIRE
Rue de la Préfecture, Old Town.

This home-style store sells newly made quilts to look like the old French *boutis* (bed quilts). Very chic: You get a touch of Provence without going too over-the-top.

CUSTO BARCELONA
23 rue de la Préfecture, Old Town.

Custo, the cutting-edge maker of T-shirts from Barcelona, has had international distribution through department stores for years; now it has opened its first shop in France, right in Nice's Old Town. Besides the iconic T-shirts, there are clothes and accessories for men and women.

LE MOULIN DES CARACOLES
5 rue St-François-de-Paule, Old Town.

Of the several TTs in a row in this part of the Old Town, this one is my favorite because I like the shop, the merchandise, the display, the wrap, and even the business cards. This is where I buy packaged olives (airtight; they can legally be brought into the U.S.) as well as some gift items.

L'OLIVE
7 rue St-François-de-Paule, Old Town.

This spiffy shop is so chic that you will easily grasp the fashion statement now made by designer and prestige olive oils. Open Sunday mornings but not Monday mornings.

MARGAUX
10 rue de la Liberté.

Margaux is a small shop that sells only white and black blouses, T-shirts, and tops—a la Anne Fontaine, but less expensive.

MOLINARD
20 rue St-François-de-Paule, Old Town.

This is the newest showroom of the perfume house from Grasse.

YVES DELORME
Centre Commercial Nice Etoile, av. Jean Médecin.

This large shopping mall has branches of many big name brands, but is particularly useful as a way to shop for bed linens from Yves Delorme, a French brand with little distribution in the U.S. and a nice selection of luxury linens and duvet covers. Remember, French bed sizes do not match American bed sizes, but duvet covers will work just fine.

MARKETS & FAIRS

Nice has a plethora of markets:

- **Fruits and flowers:** Daily except Monday, cours Saleya, from 7am.
- *Brocante:* Monday, cours Saleya, from 7am. More than 200 dealers. Year-round.
- **Antiques:** Daily except Sunday, quai de la Douane, from 11am to 7pm. About 18 stalls. Year-round.
- **Used and old books:** First and third Saturday of each month, place du Palais du Justice, from 8am to 5pm. The first Sunday is old books; the third Sunday is postcards and ephemera. Some 24 stalls. Year-round.
- **Carnaval:** Carnaval is organized by Roy du Cinema. Assorted Carnaval gear—noisemakers, plastic hats, confetti, masks, paper parasols—is sold from tables along the main drag of

Nice (avenue Médecin). However, the most important ingredient for Carnaval is foam string, which is sold in atomizer cans and which you spray until you have lost every care in the world. String battles with total strangers ensue at the drop of a plastic hat. String sells for about 2€ ($2.30) a can.

Nice Resources A–Z

ANTIQUES

There is an entire district of antiques shops in Nice, as well as a regular (but very small) flea market and a wonderful *brocante* market on Monday mornings. Larger pieces of furniture are well priced here, so if you're shopping for shipping, you may hit pay dirt.

BIG NAMES

Following are some of the big-name designer boutiques and multiples in Nice.

CACHAREL
18 rue Paradis.

CHANEL
6 rue Paradis.

CHRISTIAN DIOR
6 rue Paradis.

EMPORIO ARMANI
1 rue Paradis.

ESCADA
8 av. de Verdun.

FAÇONNABLE
7–9 rue Paradis; 10 rue Paradis.

HERMES
8 av. de Verdun.

KENZO
10 rue Paradis.

LACOSTE
6 av. Gustav V.

LANCEL
Centre Commercial Nice Etoile, av. Jean Médecin.

LOUIS VUITTON
6 rue Paradis.

SONIA RYKIEL
3 rue Paradis.

VENTILO
8 bis rue du Congrès.

ZARA
10 av. Jean Médecin.

DEPARTMENT STORES

Galeries Lafayette has a rather large store at place Masséna; the discount card you can get at your hotel entitles you to a 10% discount on all purchases. You must present the discount card before payment. This is not the *détaxe* refund, which at Galeries Lafayette comes to an additional 12%. **C&A,** the Dutch department store for low-cost clothes and things, has a branch at Nice Etoile.

FOODSTUFFS

Most of the stores listed in the "Finds" section (p. 306) offer olive oil and food. There is also a grocery store (a small one, but nice) in the basement of **Galeries Lafayette,** place Masséna.

FLORIAN
14 quai Papacino, Old Town.

This old-fashioned candy factory specializes in candied fruits but also makes jams. Great gifts. Sign up for the tour.

LAFAYETTE GOURMET
Cap 3000, St-Laurent-du-Var.

This gourmet supermarket is located in a nearby Nice mall.

HOME STYLE

CEDRE ROUGE
6 av. de Verdun.

Although Cèdre Rouge is a chain store, it's got high style, nice bistro-style silverware, and good pottery.

HABITAT
Centre Commercial Nice Etoile, av. Jean Médecin.

Habitat, the U.K. chain, is slightly more upmarket than Ikea. This branch is a possible source for tabletop items and gifts.

LES OLIVADES
8 av. de Verdun.

Les Olivades is home to classy Provençal-style printed fabrics, some made into tabletop or home linens. It's located next door to Hermès.

VOYAGE INTERIEUR
115 rue des Ponchettes, Old Town.

This gallery-like space features chic elements from around the world, with a North African twist—lots of natural woods.

ZITA VITO JARDIN
Galerie de la Victoire, 58 av. Jean Médecin.

Here's more North African chic, this time with Zen-inspired lines in earth tones and beige-y browns. The gallery is at the upper end of this main shopping drag, with an interior courtyard filled with merchandise and swagged with crystal chandeliers.

MATERNITY WEAR

FORMES
8 rue Alphonse Karr.

Formes is a French multiple selling chic maternity wear.

MULTIPLES & CHAIN STORES

APOSTROPHE
8 av. de Verdun.

Here you'll find clean lines and very chic clothing—it's really a bridge line and not like a multiple at all.

COTELAC
3 rue Alphonse Karr.

Head here for a younger look—a little more slashed and distressed, but very trendy.

DU PAREIL AU MEME
44 rue Pastorelli.

Du Pareil au Même sells adorable kids' clothes.

PIMKIE
Centre Commercial Nice Etoile, av. Jean Médecin.

This store carries hot teen cheapie looks.

SECRETS DESSOUS
4 rue Masséna.

Secrets Dessous has lingerie in all price brackets.

SEPHORA
8 av. Jean Médecin.

You can shop for makeup forever.

REAL-PEOPLE SHOPPING

FNAC
Centre Commercial Nice Etoile, av. Jean Médecin.

FNAC is right near the train station, on the main shopping street in the big mall in the center of downtown. It's a super source for books, CDs, computer needs, and so on. Open Monday through Saturday from 10am to 7pm.

PARASHOP
5 rue Masséna.

This is a branch of the new modern chain of *parapharmacies*. It carries most brands in a clean, well-lit, open space that's easy to use. Fidelity cards (for frequent shoppers) are available.

INDEX

FROMMER'S® COMPLETE TRAVEL GUIDES

Alaska
Alaska Cruises & Ports of Call
American Southwest
Amsterdam
Argentina & Chile
Arizona
Atlanta
Australia
Austria
Bahamas
Barcelona, Madrid & Seville
Beijing
Belgium, Holland & Luxembourg
Bermuda
Boston
Brazil
British Columbia & the Canadian Rockies
Brussels & Bruges
Budapest & the Best of Hungary
Calgary
California
Canada
Cancún, Cozumel & the Yucatán
Cape Cod, Nantucket & Martha's Vineyard
Caribbean
Caribbean Ports of Call
Carolinas & Georgia
Chicago
China
Colorado
Costa Rica
Cruises & Ports of Call
Cuba
Denmark
Denver, Boulder & Colorado Springs
England
Europe
Europe by Rail
European Cruises & Ports of Call

Florence, Tuscany & Umbria
Florida
France
Germany
Great Britain
Greece
Greek Islands
Halifax
Hawaii
Hong Kong
Honolulu, Waikiki & Oahu
India
Ireland
Italy
Jamaica
Japan
Kauai
Las Vegas
London
Los Angeles
Maryland & Delaware
Maui
Mexico
Montana & Wyoming
Montréal & Québec City
Munich & the Bavarian Alps
Nashville & Memphis
New England
Newfoundland & Labrador
New Mexico
New Orleans
New York City
New York State
New Zealand
Northern Italy
Norway
Nova Scotia, New Brunswick & Prince Edward Island
Oregon
Ottawa
Paris
Peru

Philadelphia & the Amish Country
Portugal
Prague & the Best of the Czech Republic
Provence & the Riviera
Puerto Rico
Rome
San Antonio & Austin
San Diego
San Francisco
Santa Fe, Taos & Albuquerque
Scandinavia
Scotland
Seattle
Shanghai
Sicily
Singapore & Malaysia
South Africa
South America
South Florida
South Pacific
Southeast Asia
Spain
Sweden
Switzerland
Texas
Thailand
Tokyo
Toronto
Turkey
USA
Utah
Vancouver & Victoria
Vermont, New Hampshire & Maine
Vienna & the Danube Valley
Virgin Islands
Virginia
Walt Disney World® & Orlando
Washington, D.C.
Washington State

FROMMER'S® DOLLAR-A-DAY GUIDES

Australia from $50 a Day
California from $70 a Day
England from $75 a Day
Europe from $85 a Day
Florida from $70 a Day
Hawaii from $80 a Day

Ireland from $80 a Day
Italy from $70 a Day
London from $90 a Day
New York City from $90 a Day
Paris from $90 a Day
San Francisco from $70 a Day

Washington, D.C. from $80 a Day
Portable London from $90 a Day
Portable New York City from $90 a Day
Portable Paris from $90 a Day

FROMMER'S® PORTABLE GUIDES

Acapulco, Ixtapa & Zihuatanejo
Amsterdam
Aruba
Australia's Great Barrier Reef
Bahamas
Berlin
Big Island of Hawaii
Boston
California Wine Country
Cancún
Cayman Islands
Charleston
Chicago
Disneyland®
Dominican Republic
Dublin

Florence
Frankfurt
Hong Kong
Las Vegas
Las Vegas for Non-Gamblers
London
Los Angeles
Los Cabos & Baja
Maine Coast
Maui
Miami
Nantucket & Martha's Vineyard
New Orleans
New York City
Paris

Phoenix & Scottsdale
Portland
Puerto Rico
Puerto Vallarta, Manzanillo & Guadalajara
Rio de Janeiro
San Diego
San Francisco
Savannah
Vancouver
Vancouver Island
Venice
Virgin Islands
Washington, D.C.
Whistler

FROMMER'S® NATIONAL PARK GUIDES

Algonquin Provincial Park
Banff & Jasper
Family Vacations in the National
Parks

Grand Canyon
National Parks of the American
West
Rocky Mountain

Yellowstone & Grand Teton
Yosemite & Sequoia/Kings
Canyon
Zion & Bryce Canyon

FROMMER'S® MEMORABLE WALKS

Chicago
London

New York
Paris

San Francisco

FROMMER'S® WITH KIDS GUIDES

Chicago
Las Vegas
New York City

Ottawa
San Francisco
Toronto

Vancouver
Walt Disney World® & Orland
Washington, D.C.

SUZY GERSHMAN'S BORN TO SHOP GUIDES

Born to Shop: France
Born to Shop: Hong Kong,
Shanghai & Beijing

Born to Shop: Italy
Born to Shop: London

Born to Shop: New York
Born to Shop: Paris

FROMMER'S® IRREVERENT GUIDES

Amsterdam
Boston
Chicago
Las Vegas
London

Los Angeles
Manhattan
New Orleans
Paris
Rome

San Francisco
Seattle & Portland
Vancouver
Walt Disney World®
Washington, D.C.

FROMMER'S® BEST-LOVED DRIVING TOURS

Austria
Britain
California
France

Germany
Ireland
Italy
New England

Northern Italy
Scotland
Spain
Tuscany & Umbria

THE UNOFFICIAL GUIDES®

Beyond Disney
California with Kids
Central Italy
Chicago
Cruises
Disneyland®
England
Florida
Florida with Kids
Inside Disney

Hawaii
Las Vegas
London
Maui
Mexico's Best Beach Resorts
Mini Las Vegas
Mini Mickey
New Orleans
New York City
Paris

San Francisco
Skiing & Snowboarding in the
West
South Florida including Miami
the Keys
Walt Disney World®
Walt Disney World® for
Grown-ups
Walt Disney World® with Kids
Washington, D.C.

SPECIAL-INTEREST TITLES

Athens Past & Present
Cities Ranked & Rated
Frommer's Best Day Trips from London
Frommer's Best RV & Tent Campgrounds
in the U.S.A.
Frommer's Caribbean Hideaways
Frommer's China: The 50 Most Memorable Trips
Frommer's Exploring America by RV
Frommer's Gay & Lesbian Europe
Frommer's NYC Free & Dirt Cheap

Frommer's Road Atlas Europe
Frommer's Road Atlas France
Frommer's Road Atlas Ireland
Frommer's Wonderful Weekends from
New York City
The New York Times' Guide to Unforgettable
Weekends
Retirement Places Rated
Rome Past & Present

THE ████████

"I'll pay you ba███████████████████████ Mattie said tartly. "And i███████████████████████

"Of course you ███████████████████████ tone. "Although the less we have to do with each other in Cripple Creek, the easier it will be for both of us."

Remembering his passionate lovemaking, Mattie raised her chin and gave him a cool smile. "Don't you trust yourself around me? Or do you fear being helplessly seduced once more?"

"No, I simply would prefer not to get in the way of a blushing bride and her eager groom." He turned on his heel and marched over to the door.

Mattie took a step toward him and felt something beneath her foot. It was his silver pocket watch.

She scooped it up and held it out. "I believe this is yours, Lord Cameron."

"Keep it, my dear," he said, opening the door.

"No, please. I wouldn't want to be accused of taking more from you than I already have."

"Not at all. Let it be a reminder that I have no time to waste on opportunists—not even one as lovely as you. Good night, Miss Crawford."

The door shut an instant before Mattie hurled the watch at him, its silver workings shattering in a dozen pieces against the heavy, unyielding oak.

STOLEN HEARTS

Sharon Pisacreta

LEISURE BOOKS   NEW YORK CITY

To Barry and Emma,
who both stole my heart long ago.

A LEISURE BOOK®

April 1998

Published by

Dorchester Publishing Co., Inc.
276 Fifth Avenue
New York, NY 10001

ISBN 0-8439-4375-0

ACKNOWLEDGMENTS

A big Thank You to Margaret Mims
Friend, critique partner and fellow crab.
I couldn't have done it without you, Peg.

And thanks to the late Mabel Barbee Lee.
Her first-hand account of Gold Rush Colorado
in *Cripple Creek Days* was simply invaluable.

STOLEN HEARTS

To Wonnie,

Enjoy!

Shawn

Pisacick

Chapter One

New York City, 1893

The young woman closed her eyes and let out a bloodcurdling shriek.

Mattie Crawford stepped back and frowned. "One more tug and you'll swoon, Miss Evelyn. Remember what happened last Sunday."

"That had nothing to do with my corset." Evelyn gasped for breath. "I fainted due to the stifling air in Adelaide Wilson's salon."

"It's too tight," Mattie warned.

Evelyn glanced at herself in the mirror. "Measure me again. And you'd best pray it reads nineteen inches, because you're not leaving this room until it does."

It was futile to argue. Fifty years of extravagant good fortune and wealth had transformed each of the Sinclairs into petty tyrants, and the youngest of the family had a mean streak in her. Mattie had never forgotten the day she'd seen

Evelyn slap the parlor maid for accidentally stepping on the hem of her cashmere wrapper.

Evelyn looked anxiously at Mattie. "Well?"

With an air of barely concealed satisfaction, Mattie announced, "Twenty inches."

"It can't be! You must be reading it wrong. This is absolutely disastrous!"

Mattie fought back a grin. Amazing what the well bred and well fed considered disastrous. "The silk will fit just fine, miss. I've given the bodice a full front and back, with a broad Empire girdle besides. That would make any woman appear slender, even one as large as Mrs. O'Toole."

"I don't enjoy being compared to our Irish cook." Evelyn frowned. "Please refrain from being so vulgar in my presence."

"What's this about vulgarity, my dear?" An older woman entered the bedroom in a great rustling of lavender taffeta.

Evelyn gestured toward Mattie. "She claims that even Mrs. O'Toole would look quite the belle in this dress."

"I only meant that—"

Evelyn cut Mattie off. "Aunt Julia, please tell her that I've never appeared in public with a twenty-inch waist and I don't intend to start today."

Julia Sinclair sat down on a nearby divan, her plumed bonnet concealing the expression in her eyes. "You *will* be celebrating your twentieth birthday next week, Evelyn."

"I don't care what *Godey's Lady's Book* says. It's a preposterous notion that an unmarried woman's waistline should match her age. Does that mean that if I were thirty-five and a spinster, I should be content to have a waist nearly three feet around?" She gave a pointed glance at her silver-haired aunt's ample figure.

"You're overwrought, my dear, and with good reason," Julia said in a conciliatory tone. "It's never pleasant for a young lady to see her friends marry before her." She sighed. "I remember it all too well. It was a cross I hoped you'd never have to bear."

"And whose fault is that?" Evelyn shot back sharply. "Not mine."

"You certainly cannot blame me," Aunt Julia said. "I've told your father dozens of times that he must see about acquiring a proper husband for you."

Mattie's heart sank. If the two Sinclair women started quarreling about *that* again, she'd never get her mistress dressed in time for the wedding. And the blame would fall on her.

"Well, I had a future husband in my pocket until you and Father spoiled everything. So here I am having to attend yet another wedding, and with a twenty-inch waist, too. Abominable."

"Miss Evelyn, you'll look lovely in the new gown," Mattie said quickly before the argument could continue. "Besides, to risk suffocation for a tinier waist is foolish."

"We do not require instruction from *you*." Aunt Julia rapped her purple silk parasol on the floor, her arthritic fingers sparkling with jewels. "If my niece wants her waist cinched tighter, do so. Unless you'd prefer outfitting the kitchen help from now on, Tillie."

Mattie bit back a sarcastic retort. After six months, she was accustomed to the Sinclairs' disdain. But every time one of the family called her "Tillie" it sent her blood boiling. The Sinclairs refused to call her by her given name, "Mathilde"; that was the late Mrs. Sinclair's name, and the idea of a lowly servant being addressed in the same manner was apparently distasteful to them. So they had dubbed her "Tillie," which was probably better than hearing them use the name she had always been called by those who loved her: Mattie.

Still, she longed to speak her mind, to stand proudly and be treated like an equal among these peacocks. But no matter. Tomorrow she would be gone. Mattie smiled with relief.

"Do you find amusement in my niece's predicament?" Aunt Julia asked coldly.

Mattie quickly assumed an expressionless demeanor. "Oh, no, I was just—"

11

The older woman shook her head. "Continue in this vein, Tillie, and you'll find yourself a needlewoman on the East Side once more."

"Yes, Miss Sinclair." If her silly niece wanted to have the breath crushed out of her, so be it.

After she finished cinching Evelyn, she wondered how the young woman could even manage to swallow. But she did indeed meet the demands of that season's fashion, thanks not only to her wasp waist and carefully dressed hair, but to the elegant India silk gown Mattie had sewn for her. Pleased with her latest creation, Mattie hummed softly as she fanned out the Empire puffs on the sleeves. She noticed the approving look that Evelyn gave herself in the mirror and felt a surge of triumph. If Mattie could satisfy a society miss as demanding as Evelyn Sinclair, she should have no problem designing gowns for Madame Victorine's pampered clients.

"I hope you like it, Miss Evelyn." Mattie pulled at the soutache braid that decorated the garment's wrists. "I know you favor blue, but with your chestnut hair, red is really much more striking." Indeed, the bands of red silk ornamenting the ivory-colored skirt and the red bolero sewn onto the bodice did warm Evelyn's pale complexion, deepening the brown of her eyes.

Evelyn fussed with the aigrette feathers adorning her small hat. "It will do," she said curtly.

"I must talk to your father about loosening the purse strings." Aunt Julia frowned. "The daughter of Ward Sinclair should be wearing a Worth gown, not this sorry creation."

Sorry indeed, thought Mattie wryly. She glanced over at the dizzying array of seed pearls and lace decorating the older woman's gown. Not all the stock bonds in New York could buy Julia Sinclair an ounce of taste.

"Father is punishing me," Evelyn said, taking a pair of gloves from Mattie. "I laughed at that dreadful Italian fresco he purchased, so now to spite me, he's ordered his agent in

Florence to buy three more, and with my clothing allowance, too.''

''Your father spends far too much money on his picture galleries. It's time he bought you a husband. And not one of those foreign specimens either.''

Mattie dared to turn a disapproving face in Julia's direction, but, surprisingly, Evelyn laughed.

Aunt Julia pursed her lips. ''Don't dismiss my advice unless you want to turn into an old maid like me. Oh, I've my own money and life, but true status and freedom comes only with a well-connected husband.'' She got to her feet stiffly. ''These knees will be the death of me.''

''Never fear, Aunt,'' Evelyn said. ''My plans do not include spinsterhood.''

''Good.'' Aunt Julia nodded. ''After all, you don't want to end up alone and unwanted like our Tillie here.''

Amused, Mattie couldn't resist answering. ''I'm only twenty-four, Miss Sinclair. Hardly ready for the rubbish heap yet.''

Both Sinclair women looked offended by her statement.

''Even among domestics, your best years are behind you. Working as you must, it will only be a matter of time before you look a washed-out drudge.'' Aunt Julia waved a hand at Mattie's dark blue uniform, as though affronted both by its simplicity and the voluptuous curves it covered. ''Although I should think you'd be grateful for those gaudy red tresses to finally turn mercifully white. Either way, you're sure to miss the happiness of being a bride.''

Brushing back a stray red curl, Mattie only shrugged. No need to tell them she'd already been a bride *and* a widow.

''Well, Tillie's marital status has nothing to do with me, Aunt,'' Evelyn said impatiently.

''Indeed it doesn't. That's why I've been making inquiries on your behalf, and I've learned that Mr. George Braddock will be in Newport this season.'' She raised her eyebrows. ''He's the youngest son of Ephraim Braddock, the gentleman who owns the department store in Boston.''

''The younger son?'' Evelyn pronounced the phrase as

though it were an oath, and Mattie struggled not to smile. "I think I deserve better than a 'younger son.'"

"His older brother is said to be in poor health, something with which I can sadly commiserate."

"Don't trouble yourself with either younger brothers or shopkeeper's sons." Evelyn shook her head. "After all, if both you and Father weren't so stubborn, I could have been the wife of the next Marquess of Clydesford."

The old woman turned on her heel with a snort. "Totally unsuitable gentleman," she harumphed as she walked to the door. "And I use the term *gentleman* advisedly."

"You told me you liked him," Evelyn said.

"That was before I learned of the disgrace and scandal surrounding him."

"He's the handsomest man I ever saw," Evelyn said plaintively, and in that moment, Mattie felt a surge of sympathy for the young woman.

"As too many women have thought, to their ruin."

"He didn't try to ruin me. He asked me to marry him, as proper as can be."

"To his shame, he asked you in secret, and to your shame, you accepted." The old woman lifted up her parasol and pointed it at her. "Luckily you had enough prudence to inform your father and me about this distressing engagement in time."

"But he's so young and dashing. And his estates are said to rival even a duke's."

"Yes, and they are all as bankrupt as his reputation," Aunt Julia said with great exasperation. "Now listen, my dear, British lords in want of heiresses are as plentiful as figs in Italy. Ever since those shameless Jerome sisters, American girls have been throwing themselves at any half-witted pauper with a title to dangle in front of them. It's disgraceful. You don't want to be swooped up by one of those decadent aristocrats. It's become so—so common. Bad enough Bradley Martin's girl married the Earl of Craven last month, but I've just learned that Adele Grant is to become the wife of the seventh Earl of Essex before Christmas.''

''Adele is marrying an earl?'' Evelyn grew so pale that Mattie stepped forward in alarm. ''It isn't fair. I told Father that all my friends are marrying British lords, all the best families, even the Vanderbilts. It's humiliating. It should be me getting married today in Grace Church, and not that simp Ellen Garrett. Imagine, I'll have to address her as Lady Holgrave from now on.''

''More fool her for not marrying a wealthy American businessman, someone who'd let her live in her own country.''

''Who cares about living in America with some businessman? I'd much prefer attending Ascot with the Prince of Wales and having people consult their *Debrett's Peerage* whenever I come to tea.'' Evelyn kicked at the Ming vase near the fireplace. ''Department stores in Boston, really. I swear I'll marry the next English aristocrat who smiles my way, regardless of his reputation.''

''Evelyn, you don't mean that,'' Julia said worriedly.

''Yes, I do, even if he's Jack the Ripper himself!''

That seemed to silence the old woman, although Mattie couldn't resist a grin. The notorious Whitechapel murderer might meet his match in Evelyn.

Julia Sinclair sighed. ''If you won't listen to reason, my dear, then perhaps your father and I shall have to discuss this again. It might be possible to find an English lord who is acceptable.''

''Lord Cameron was quite acceptable to me,'' Evelyn said sulkily.

''Lord Cameron should be the farthest thing from your thoughts.''

''He keeps writing me. What can I do?''

''You don't answer the rogue?''

''Oh no. After I read his letters, Tillie destroys them for me.''

The old woman turned to Mattie. ''Is this true?''

Mattie nodded.

"I can't imagine why you even bother to read them. The man has no shame, none. Appalling enough that he tricked you into a secret engagement; now he's off pretending to look for gold out west."

"He still wants to marry me. I received another letter just a few days ago. I don't know why you won't overlook his past. His father is gravely ill, and Lord Cameron could be the next marquess any day now." Her voice rose. "I could be a marchioness. A marchioness! I would outrank Ellen Garrett."

Aunt Julia drew herself up, her thick rope of pearls swaying majestically. "Imagine what Ellen Garret would say if she knew you wanted a man who was turned out of every drawing room in New York and London. You'd be a laughingstock."

Evelyn bit her lip. "I'm sorry, Aunt. It's just that I'm tired of watching all my friends go off to England with their fancy lords and their titles."

"I promise you, my dear, that we shall arrange a good match before the year is out—and to a British lord, if your heart is so set on it."

Evelyn beamed. Mattie thought she looked like a cat who had swallowed not only the canary, but the gilded cage in which it lived.

"As for Lord Cameron, you will ruin your chances of marrying a respectable English aristocrat if you continue to associate yourself with that rascal. Do you understand?"

"Yes, Aunt Julia," she said meekly.

"Good then; we have this settled. Be quick about the rest of your toilette. Your father is in a bad humor this morning. You know how he dislikes weddings, as do I. And the air will be stifling in the church. I shall probably grow quite short of breath. Thank heavens I leave soon for one of my cures. Now hurry and meet us downstairs."

As soon as Aunt Julia left the room, Evelyn laughed softly. "I knew I'd get them to come round."

Mattie cleared her throat. "Will you be wearing the cameo this morning, miss?"

16

"A pity I won't be able to have Lord Cameron," Evelyn continued. "Although I can't really blame them. Lord Cameron does have an appalling past."

Mattie said nothing. She could imagine the Sinclair's horror if they learned about her own unhappy background.

"It's just that I wanted so much to be a marchioness. It sounds almost as fine as 'duchess,' don't you think?"

"I suppose. Shall I get the cameo, miss?"

Evelyn ignored her. "And he can't have been all that gently reared. Even after I rejected his suit, Lord Cameron still has the bad manners to write me." She turned to a small box on the dressing table and pulled out a thick letter. "No doubt it's another plea for me to come out to Colorado and marry him." She flung the letter to the floor. It was an intimidating gesture often employed by Aunt Julia, but in someone as young as Evelyn, it looked only petulant. "As though I would run off to the wilds of Colorado to be married. What does he take me for—some dismal mail-order bride?"

Mattie picked up the letter and felt a twinge at the familiar handwriting. "But you haven't opened it. Don't you want to at least see what he has written?"

Evelyn sighed. "Oh, I know all too well what that gentleman has to say. That he is no longer the reprobate the world knows him to be, and that he will soon make his fortune in Colorado. Colorado, of all places! Who becomes rich in Colorado? No, do as my aunt instructed and dispose of it."

Mattie slipped the letter into her pocket.

"And bring me my ruby collar."

Mattie looked over in surprise but thought better of saying anything. Fetching the locked velvet-covered case, she handed it over. Evelyn waited impatiently while Mattie retrieved the key.

"I can see by that sour look that you disapprove." Evelyn lifted out the glittering necklace, heavy with gemstones and antique gold.

"It doesn't suit such a dress, Miss Evelyn." She winced

17

as her mistress held the ornate jewels against the delicate silk.

"Hmm, perhaps you're right," Evelyn said after a moment, and tossed the ruby collar back into the case as though it were made of worthless beads. Mattie gratefully closed the case and locked it. Such a necklace would have ruined the effect she wanted the new gown to have.

"And you needn't wait up for me tonight," Evelyn instructed. "Lucy will help me undress. She's been far too careless about ironing my linen and lace; she deserves to lose a bit of sleep."

With a swish of her taffeta petticoats, Evelyn turned to go, but stopped suddenly as she fought to take a breath. After a moment, the color gradually returned to her cheeks and she forged ahead, ominously pale.

As soon as her mistress left, Mattie pulled out the unopened letter and ran her fingers softly over the bold scrawl. It seemed somehow fitting that the letter had fallen to her tonight. Tomorrow she would go to the front parlor and tell Ward Sinclair that she had better prospects elsewhere and would be leaving his employment immediately. After which she would walk out of this overdecorated and unhappy mansion without a backward glance. For there was nothing here she would regret leaving. Nothing except the arrival of Cameron Lynch-Holmes's letters.

With a great yawn, Mattie finished braiding her hair. In the dim gaslight, it gleamed a rich auburn, but she took no pleasure in the sight. Instead she remembered her mother's somber warning: "A red-haired lass brings good luck to no one, least of all herself." When she was a girl, Mattie had laughed at the silly superstition, but the intervening years had proven her mother right. The only luck Mattie had ever known was bad.

But Mattie was about to change her luck, red hair or not. Her bags were all packed, and tomorrow's traveling costume was hung against the door. After six months in the employ of the Sinclairs, Mattie felt like a prisoner escaping from her cell. With a shiver, she remembered what prison was indeed like, and her hands grew suddenly cold despite the warm May night. Don't think of it, she told herself, it's over and done with. Instead, she reminded herself that she had gained her freedom once, and against much more daunting odds. Tomorrow, she would do the same, only this time with the clear hope that she would succeed on her own. She would still serve the wealthy families of New York, but they would pay dearly for the privilege.

Mattie looked over at the unopened letter lying on the washstand. Why hadn't she simply torn it up and tossed it away? After months of hearing Evelyn read aloud his letters, Mattie felt as though they'd almost been written to her. Afterward Evelyn invariably flung the letters at Mattie, expecting her to get rid of them. And eventually she did, but only after she'd read them several more times, pretending this fine young gentleman was asking *her* to marry him, assuring Mattie Crawford that she was the most beautiful and priceless of women. She shook her head. What must it be like to have a man say such lovely things to you?

Her late husband had been a talkative fellow, but Frank would have taken a blow to the jaw before he would have piped up with such gentle, stirring words. Well, Frank was dead—God rest his dishonest soul—and Mattie had never looked at another man in the three years since. She hadn't even thought of a man, except for Cameron Lynch-Holmes. Lord help her, she had even kept a photograph of him, another memento discarded by Evelyn.

Mattie got up now and pulled it from her packed satchel. Why was she taking such a thing with her? It seemed the act of an infatuated schoolgirl. As she gazed at his handsome face, clean-shaven and sensual, she thought that a young woman deserved at least one fantasy. But such a foolish fantasy it was. She would never meet him, never know what his voice sounded like or how easily he smiled. He would always remain a sepia-toned dream, unreachable and elusive. Better to have him fade from memory; she was too old to believe in dreams or in kindhearted, loving men. Mattie

19

took a last long look at that proud, serious expression before tearing the photograph into tiny pieces and flinging them out the open window.

Turning back to the cot, her glance fell on the envelope once more. With sudden resolve, she snatched up the letter. What would it matter if she read it? No one would ever know, and this would be the last time her dream suitor would court her. Before her scruples got the better of her, she tore it open.

The letter was brief, and Mattie laughed at her own disappointment. Sitting on the cot, she raced through the page. Lord Cameron was clearly frustrated, and ready with threats of his own. Still, she couldn't blame the Sinclairs for refusing their daughter to him. Gossip had it that his reputation was positively lurid. And now here he was, foolishly gone off to try to strike gold in Colorado. Mattie shook her head. Another man lost to prospecting fever. Her own father had burned with gold lust his entire life, and all he'd reaped was miner's consumption and destitution for his wife and daughter. Fighting back such melancholy memories, she turned her attention instead to Lord Cameron's closing words.

"I've enclosed a one-way ticket to Colorado, my dear Evelyn," it read. *"If you are not on the train when it arrives, I will assume you haven't a thought for my feelings or wishes. Your absence shall serve as the final refusal of my suit. I have pursued you for nearly two years, and no longer wish to waste my time and heart on a young woman who finds me a nuisance or a disgrace. I thought you had feelings for me—you certainly led me to believe you did on several occasions—yet I realize that my reputation and financial status give you pause. Know that I have lived more righteously than a monk this past year, and having acquired a gold claim, hope to strike it rich very soon. But remember this, Evelyn. Despite my regard for you, if I do not see you alight from the train, I will never contact you again. Nor do I ever wish to hear your name spoken in my presence. With affection and hope, Cameron Lynch-Holmes."*

Mattie drew out the ticket, noting that its departure date

was tomorrow. She would have to show this to her mistress. Proud and selfish as Evelyn Sinclair was, she still deserved to read what was apparently the last letter of her most persistent suitor. *I wonder whom he will turn his attention to next,* she thought with a twinge of envy as she put the letter away. Some other young woman with a prosperous father and a decent pedigree, someone far different from a widowed dressmaker with unhappy memories and slim prospects for anything better.

Yet as she drifted off to sleep, Mattie let herself imagine what it would be like to steam into Colorado Springs—in the shadow of the fiercely beautiful mountains where she had been born—and walk off the train into the impatient arms of Cameron Lynch-Holmes. Some women simply had more than their share of good fortune and besotted men, she thought ruefully, and dreamed that night of a fair-haired English lord bending over her, whispering of his desperate passion.

Startled out of a restless sleep, Mattie awoke to see men standing over her bed. A jolt of terror ran through her as she lay there motionless. The room was dark, and they were only faceless shadows. For a bewildered moment, she thought she must be dreaming.

"She's awake," one of them said coldly just as Mattie let out a full-throated scream.

"Shut your mouth, girl, or I'll have my men gag you." A hand jerked her upright as she stared wide-eyed in fear.

"Who are you?" Mattie asked in a voice as shaky as her hands. "What do you want?"

One of the intruders lit the gas jet by the door, revealing their blue frock coats and round-topped helmets. Not again, she thought in terror, flinging off the restraining hand on her arm.

"No, no, you won't take me! I won't let you!" Bolting from the bed, Mattie ran wildly for the door, and was caught by the pair of policemen standing there.

Struggling like a trapped animal in their iron grip, she

squirmed and twisted, calling out for help. "Leave me alone! I won't go back! I won't!"

The man who had spoken earlier now planted himself before her, his bearded face a callous mask of suspicion. He grabbed her long braid, and yanked her face toward him. "Listen to me, girl, one more attempt to escape and I'll be letting these fellows knock some sense into you. It's no skin off my nose if we bring you into the station house with a few teeth missing."

Babbling with fear, Mattie could barely understand what he was saying. "No, please! What do you want with me? I've done nothing!"

Gripping her arms, the two policemen dragged her over to the rumpled cot and threw her down. She looked up at them with terror. *I must calm down,* she told herself frantically, *I must, I must.* If she'd learned nothing else from her year in prison, it was that if she couldn't control her fear, she would be controlled by others. But dear lord, why had they come for her again? Why?

Sitting up, Mattie clasped her hands together and tried to still her trembling. She dared not speak, for the urge to scream was nearly overwhelming.

"Now that's better, girl," the bearded man said. "No need to bloody such a pretty face as that. We've only a few questions for you. Seems there's been a robbery in the house."

Her head shot up. Not a robbery—anything but that.

"Looking a little pale, aren't you? Well, it's nothing too terrible. Just a necklace that's gone missing, what your mistress calls her ruby collar."

Mattie swallowed hard, dimly aware that the room was still shadowy.

"What time is it?" she whispered.

"Nearly midnight, not that it matters to you. I've been told your name's Crawford. Sounds like a good Scots name. Have you been a thrifty Scotswoman perhaps, and taken your mistress's jewels off to be pawned?"

"What!"

His mouth curled scornfully. "Miss Evelyn Sinclair came back from a wedding ball an hour ago and discovered her ruby collar missing. She's been turning the house upside down looking for it. Says the last time she saw it, the necklace was in your hands."

"But I didn't take it. I didn't!"

"Then who did, Miss Crawford?"

Everyone turned to the doorway, where a tall, balding man in a brown suit stood waiting. Mattie stared in horrified recognition. This must be some hideous nightmare, some black dream that only seemed real.

The uniformed policemen stepped back into the shadows as the bearded man gestured to Mattie. "Tried to run out on us, she did, sir."

"Detective Devlin?" Mattie whispered hoarsely.

The man moved quickly into the room, the gaslight illuminating his small black eyes. "Well, I'll be damned, Seamus. It looks like we've an open-and-shut case here."

"Devlin," Mattie repeated, shaking her head.

"You know this Crawford woman, sir?"

"Crawford?" He planted himself before Mattie. "This woman's taken an alias, boys. If you check the police files, you'll find her listed as Mrs. Mathilde Laszlo. Decided to pass yourself off under another name, eh, girl?"

Mattie swallowed hard before venturing to speak. "Crawford is my maiden name."

Seamus let out a laugh. "A looker like her probably can't remember when she was a maiden, ain't that right, sir."

Devlin ignored the comment. "Your husband's name not good enough for you?"

She stared into those implacable eyes she'd hoped never to see again. "I didn't think it wise to look for a job as Mrs. Laszlo."

He nodded. "I can see how an employer might think twice about hiring a woman who robbed the families she was working for. So I guess that means the Sinclairs don't know about your colorful past?" He raised an eyebrow.

A long moment passed before she shook her head.

"Well, well. You should have kept your skirts cleaner, Mattie. I seem to recall that's what your poor husband called you. What's it been—just three years since you were released from jail?"

"So she did time, eh?" Seamus looked at her with a scornful expression.

"I was innocent. My husband cleared my name before he died."

"Ah, well, that may have convinced Judge Amos—the man has a weakness for redheads—but I've heard too many jailhouse confessions to put any stock in 'em."

"What's the story on her?" Seamus's leering glance traveled over her body.

Mattie grabbed the blanket and held it in front of her.

"Nothing special." Devlin took out a handkerchief and blew his nose loudly. "She and this Bohemian husband of hers were working for a family in Madison Square. After a few months, some things started going missing. A few pieces of family silver, a gold picture frame or two. For the longest time, we thought it was the kitchen staff, every last one of them fit for nothing but the Bowery. When the fancy jewelry got lifted, we knew we were looking at an inside job all right, but it was the pretty little maid and the butler, not the motley staff downstairs."

His sallow face creased in a cold smile. "Apparently she'd conned her husband into helping her. We found the emerald ring and pearl necklace in the pockets of his suitcoat. A fool for sure, but he's not the first man to let his cock rule his brain. No, it was the woman who was responsible for all the thefts, seducing this Laszlo fellow into robbing for her."

"That's not true!"

He ignored her. "But the last robbery went sour. The old lady of the house—a Mary Jenkins—surprised Lazslo in the act and took a blow to the head. She died three days later."

Seamus whistled. "So it was murder, too."

"I never stole a thing in my life. It was Frank. The man was as heartless as he was dishonest. How else could he have harmed poor Mrs. Jenkins? I hope he burns in Hell for that alone!''

''You're a fine one to talk about burning in Hell,'' Devlin snapped.

Mattie looked up at him defiantly, refusing to show the fear trembling through her. ''Indeed, yes, I know a lot about hell. I spent a year in prison for a crime I didn't commit, knowing all along that my own husband lied to put me there. If I had known he was robbing those people, I would have turned him in myself.''

Seamus laughed. ''Sure you would. And my name's J. Pierpont Morgan.''

''Well, it's just hard for me to believe that a sharp girl like you was married to that thief for four years and yet you never noticed how light-fingered he was. That's *very* hard for me to believe.'' Devlin turned toward Seamus. ''When we checked, we found out there'd been thefts at each place the pair had worked.''

''I never guessed. Never.'' What was the use to tell them what her marriage had been like, the trap that she had unknowingly walked into at the age of sixteen. Frank had stolen more than jewels and gold-plate in the years she'd known him. He'd robbed her of trust, innocence and pride.

''Before the jewels were stolen, we'd had a huge fight. I was going to leave him; I told him our marriage was over. That's why he accused me of helping him—out of black-hearted spite!''

She could still feel the outrage and shock, as fresh and piercing as on that terrible morning when the police arrested her. ''And if you were an honest man, Detective Devlin, you'd finally admit that you sent a blameless woman to the Tombs!''

Mattie's anger was getting the better of her, an anger she had suppressed for years, but now it came simmering to the surface.

''The only evidence against me was Frank's word. Even before his deathbed confession you must have suspected that I had been wronged, yet you did nothing.'' Her voice grew as cold as ice. "Of course, you did do something, didn't you? Telling the prison staff that I was violent and unrepentant, encouraging them to use the gag and the shower bath. Enjoying it when they—"

Devlin slapped her hard across the face. Putting a hand up to her stinging cheek, she stared at him with open loathing.

"So you were innocent, were you, Mrs. Laszlo? Is that why you've been hiding behind another name all this time? Is that why a ruby collar has disappeared just at the moment you're employed in the household?" He bent over her. "I put you and your misguided husband away four years ago. It was just bad luck that Laszlo got stabbed in prison and decided to be charitable before he found himself supping with the Devil. No, Mrs. Laszlo, I didn't believe him then, and I don't believe you now. But this time I intend to see to it that you don't wriggle out of prison. This time, I'll make certain that you end your dishonest days behind the walls of the Tombs."

Mattie swallowed hard and said nothing.

Seamus gave a loud whistle. "Hey, sir, will you look at all this?" He pointed to the faded bags piled in the corner. Opening up one of the satchels, he pulled out a cotton stocking. "Seems like the girl is making ready for her getaway. All packed up and ready to spring."

Her heart sank. It felt as though her life was ending, as though every dream she'd ever managed to cling to had now been ripped from her grasp.

Devlin glanced over and smirked. "Innocent? How do you explain being packed up, then?"

"I've taken a position with Madame Victorine's dress shop on the Ladies Mile." Even Mattie heard the defeat in her voice.

"That's a bold-faced lie! Madame Victorine would never hire a person like her." Evelyn Sinclair stood framed in the gaslight by the door, her fists clenched stiffly at her sides.

"Before we took her in, she was sewing in some Elizabeth Street attic. The very idea that a lady like Madame

26

Victorine would employ her is outrageous. It was only due to my father's sense of charity that she was hired here at all. And we've regretted it every day since. She's a born liar and lazy as well! She didn't even wait up tonight to help me get ready for bed.''

''Miss Sinclair, there's no need for you to be here.'' Devlin hurriedly stuffed his handkerchief back into his pocket. ''Let my men take you back to your room. We're almost finished, and you're upset.''

Evelyn waved off the policemen and marched into the room. Her hair was disheveled and her face blotched and tear-streaked. ''Why did you do it, Tillie? Why? Did you really imagine you wouldn't get caught?''

Mattie stood up, still clutching the blanket in front of her. ''Miss Evelyn, I swear I didn't take the collar.''

Her mistress turned to Devlin. ''I wanted to wear my necklace tonight—it looked perfect against my new dress—but she insisted I leave it behind.''

''Indeed?'' Devlin lifted an eyebrow, a satisfied smile on his face.

''And now I see for myself the depth of her lies.'' Evelyn gestured at the baggage. ''She probably planned on running off before dawn. If I hadn't fainted tonight at the reception, I wouldn't have discovered the theft in time—a result, I might add, of her designing a gown that was much too tight. Then there's this outrageous story about working for Madame Victorine. It's the first I've heard of it. Detective Devlin, you must not believe her. It's simply too dreadful!''

''Don't worry, Miss Sinclair. We'll go through her bags, and I'm certain your collar will turn up. And as for this woman, we'll be bringing her to the police station as soon as she makes herself decent.'' The look he gave her implied that he didn't think such a thing was possible.

''Come, Evelyn.'' A voice boomed from the hallway. Mattie shuddered. It was Ward Sinclair. ''You've suffered enough for one night. This is no place for you.''

Evelyn shot Mattie a last accusing glance. As she left, Mr. Sinclair stepped through, dressed impeccably in white tie and tails, his jowled face stern. "I want that woman out of my house as soon as possible. And I want that necklace found. It once belonged to a French queen, and I'll throttle this thieving chit with my own hands if it's broken up or destroyed."

Devlin nodded. "Go with them, Seamus. We need a deposition from everyone."

Mattie ignored Seamus's departing chuckle, but stiffened when the two remaining policemen began flinging open her baggage. It took only moments for her bags to be emptied of her few belongings, the floor strewn with stockings, shoes, and skirts.

"Nothing, sir," one of the men said in a crestfallen voice.

"Same here," the other chimed in. "Probably stashed it in her bed or chest of drawers."

Devlin held up a hand. "Or she's taken another young man to aid her in her crime. The footman, perhaps, or that ruddy coachman downstairs? Well, we'll haul the lot of 'em in for questioning." He turned to the policemen and inclined his head toward the door. "Go on out while Mrs. Laszlo dresses. As soon as she's gone, I want you both to tear this room inside out, even to ripping up floorboards if you must. We've the thief here—make no mistake about it—but to put her away for good, I'll need evidence. Now go."

Mattie took a deep breath as soon as the policemen left. Devlin frightened her, but not as much as her memories of the Tombs. "I did not steal the necklace," she said in a voice as hard as stone. "But my innocence doesn't matter to you one way or the other, does it?"

He stepped closer and surprised her by reaching for her hair. She swiftly moved her head away and the long, thick braid slipped out of his grasp.

"Last time I saw you, your head was cropped closer than a sailor's cap. Too bad you put up such a resistance the first time the matrons tried to cut it. It only made them determined to see that it never grew long again. But you were a proud hellion, weren't you? Too proud and too stupid to submit to prison rules." He smiled, cocking his head to one side. ''I think the staff we've got at the women's prison now will know just how to tame you. Yes, indeed.''

Mattie stood very still as he moved even closer. She could smell peppermint on his breath and see the grease coating his hair.

''I suggest you try to control your fighting instincts this time, tigress. You already have enemies waiting for you in the Tombs. Whether it's sooner or later, we will break you.''

''I'm innocent,'' she whispered.

Devlin straightened, his mocking smile gone. ''Get dressed.''

Mattie slowly lowered the blanket she was holding. ''You intend to watch me?''

''Don't flatter yourself. I've the Sinclairs to attend to. Just get dressed as quickly as you can. I'll have my men stationed outside the door with orders to give you only three minutes—no more.'' Devlin waved toward the narrow window. ''And I don't think you'll be risking a broken neck trying to escape from a fourth-floor roof.''

After the door shut behind him, she allowed herself a second to quiver with relief, but no longer than that. Grabbing up a petticoat, shoes, stockings, a crumpled dress, Mattie stuffed them into an emptied satchel before hurrying over to the window, already open to the spring night. Prepared to hoist herself through, she suddenly froze. Running over to the bed, she pulled out the letter from Lord Cameron; the train ticket was partially visible.

As the guards shuffled just outside the door, Mattie flung her satchel out the window and then crawled out after it. Devlin was right; even in the bright morning light, she would probably break her neck escaping, but in the inky darkness, the odds—as always—were against her.

''It doesn't matter,'' Mattie told herself as she crouched on the narrow ledge. If she let them arrest her, she would never walk out of that dank, horrific prison. This time Detective Devlin would see she suffered a hundredfold for escaping his punishment three years before.

She crawled along the eaves, nearly losing her balance.

A tile slipped from beneath her hand and went clattering down the side of the house. Mattie had no time to hesitate; already she could hear sounds of commotion from her bedroom.

With no thought for caution, she faced forward once more and flung herself recklessly into the night.

Chapter Two

"Well, we'll know in a moment if you've netted your golden bride. Care to wager your share of the claim on it?"

Cameron Lynch-Holmes shot an irritated glance at his friend. The train now steaming into Colorado Springs was an hour late, which only strained his already short temper. "I fail to see why you're so amused by all this, Harry."

"Sorry, old chap, but you just don't understand my fellow countrywomen." The young man tilted back his straw boater. "You'd do better to set your cap on one of these bonanza king's daughters. Their fathers have been too busy mining for gold to hear about your colorful past."

Giving a cursory glance around the train platform, Cameron did indeed see a handful of young women dressed in the height of fashion, giggling and tottering about in opera-heeled shoes, clearly the recipients of newfound wealth. He frowned. Cameron didn't even want to consider having to pursue young Western heiresses. The last three years had been humiliating enough.

"Evelyn may surprise you," he said.

31

Harry Tremont chuckled. "If she shows up today, I'll be struck dumb. From what I observed last year, New York society has turned its collective back on you. I doubt even the most ambitious of mothers would fancy marrying off their little jewels to a reprobate like you."

"Perhaps you underestimate the Sinclair family's ambition." Cameron tightened his grip on his bamboo walking cane. "Just as you underestimate the gravity of my own family's situation."

Harry glanced over at his friend's forbidding expression. "Forgive me," he said in a low voice. "The letter you received this morning from the Clydesford solicitor—was it bad news?"

"Bad enough," Cameron replied tersely. "Either I drastically improve my finances within the year or the estates will have to be sold off. Every last one of them, even the Belgravia address. At this rate my parents and sister will be living in rented rooms in Norwich. I only pray my father dies before having to witness that final disgrace."

An uncomfortable silence followed.

"Only I intend to see that does not happen," Cameron finally said. His jaw tightened. "By whatever means possible."

A piercing whistle halted the conversation and all eyes turned toward the tracks, where the train at last came to a halt. Cameron told himself to stop scowling—this wasn't the proper visage for an eager suitor—yet even as he straightened his gray topcoat and brushed the dust from his linen trousers, he knew that Harry was right. Evelyn Sinclair would not be on the train. He tapped the platform floor impatiently with his cane, telling himself that his last chance to marry for money was now irretrievably lost.

"Probably shouldn't have written that ultimatum to her," he muttered darkly.

Yet beneath his gloom was relief. The role of fortune hunter sat uneasily on his shoulders. Cameron was weary of courting New York's privileged debutantes; all parties involved knew it was only about exchanging an English title for American greenbacks. And now that the latest society belle had clearly thrown him over, he could turn to making money on his own. His mother couldn't complain that he hadn't tried his best to land an East Coast heiress. This would be the first summer in three years that he wouldn't be forced to display himself like a young stallion to the discerning mothers in Newport. Damned fool business. There was gold in the Colorado mountains—stream beds glittering with it—and he was going to forget about pale, cossetted heiresses and turn his hand to ripping a fortune from the rocky earth.

The crowd around him surged forward as passengers began to alight. He noted idly that there were a fair number of elderly women, eager to come to the Springs for its purported health benefits. Along with these wealthy dowagers streamed a line of families eager for a summer holiday, as well as young men, faces aglow with excitement. Gold fever, Cameron thought to himself, certain his own face wore a similar hungry expression. He nodded as the conductors and porters began to unload the baggage. Evelyn Sinclair hadn't come. Good, he thought grimly, although he didn't relish writing home and telling his family of this depressing turn of events.

He took a deep breath. "It looks as though you've been proven correct."

"I wish it were otherwise," Harry said sadly.

"Well, no use standing around here any longer."

About to turn away, Cameron's attention suddenly fell upon a young woman stepping down from a railcar. One glance told him this wasn't Evelyn Sinclair. His first amused impression was that she looked as disheveled and wild as a gypsy. She kept smoothing down her wrinkled brown skirt, while her satchel seemed as worn and dusty as the carpeting in Johnnie Nolan's saloon.

"Is she alone?" he wondered aloud, scanning the platform for a sign of someone waiting for her.

"Who?" asked Harry.

"That red-haired girl over there." Cameron had no more

business here, but he couldn't bring himself to leave. He'd just suffered a serious disappointment, and the best remedy for such things had always been the sight of a beautiful woman. And this one certainly was fine-looking, he decided, admiring the mass of coppery hair pulled back into a loose chignon. But she probably wasn't respectable; not only was she without a hat, she wore no gloves.

Harry shrugged. "I'll wager she's heading for the camps." He raised an eyebrow. "And with that figure, she'll make her fortune in no time."

Just then, she looked in their direction, and Cameron was taken aback. Even at this distance, he sensed she was distressed, possibly in trouble. Regardless of the status of her virtue, Cameron couldn't let a young woman stand there like a woebegone waif. He'd been in Colorado nearly a year. If she needed assistance, he was certain he could provide it. Besides, he just had to see for himself what color her eyes were. Green, he guessed, like the spring grass growing alongside the rivers of gold.

He was as splendid as a god, Mattie thought with disbelief; even his imposing photograph hadn't done him justice. Lord Cameron was tall and broad-shouldered, yet thinner than she'd imagined, and the briefest of glances told her that he was outfitted in his best clothes. Despite the bustle and crowd—and an impending storm—no one jostled or brushed against him. Even on this raucous train platform in the middle of the Rockies, it was as though people sensed he was not quite one of them, a handsome young prince perhaps, although no English prince in recent memory had ever boasted such a remarkable face.

"A fine lord indeed," she whispered to herself, but even his physical beauty paled beside the sight of the great mountains looming overhead. Not until this moment had she realized how much she'd missed these wide restless skies.

"Colorado," Mattie whispered, as though the name itself was a benediction.

She'd never thought to stand once more in the shadow of

34

Pike's Peak, now darkened by a black mass of storm clouds. A crush of emotions and memories swirled about her. Since her mother took her back East nine years ago, her life had been consumed with regrets. If they'd stayed in Colorado, so much might be different now.

Mattie closed her eyes as a wave of dizziness washed over her. For the briefest of moments, she allowed herself to feel safe. After the terror of her escape, she'd hidden in the back alleys of the Bowery for hours until she could use Evelyn's ticket to board the train bound for Colorado. It was a wonder her hair hadn't turned snow white during her journey. She was certain that a suspicious conductor would alert the police, and she trembled at each stop, fearful of spying Detective Devlin's cold black eyes meeting hers through the train window.

Forget Devlin, she told herself. Forget the Sinclairs and even the dashing Lord Cameron, who was now so tantalizingly close. Instead she wanted to savor this lonely homecoming and the sight of these mountains where she had been born. Her stomach growled loudly, reminding her that she'd eaten little more than an apple since leaving New York. The dizziness seemed worse; she struggled to focus her eyes but saw only patches of movement and light.

Dropping her satchel, Mattie tried to steady herself. *I mustn't faint,* she thought nervously, *I mustn't do anything to call attention to myself.* Turning her back on Lord Cameron, Mattie cradled her left arm. She'd injured it while making her escape, and she wished for nothing more at this moment than to lie in bed with a towel of ice wrapped about her wrist. Taking a few deep breaths, Mattie felt the color return to her cheeks, and her breathing grow steadier. But her calm was shattered an instant later when she met the hooded gaze of a federal marshal standing several yards away. Dressed in dusty riding clothes—a star gleaming dully on his leather vest—he seemed deep in conversation with one of the porters, yet he was clearly watching her.

Mattie whipped around, grabbing for her satchel. She had to get out of here. Perhaps the authorities in Colorado

Springs had been alerted to look for a red-haired woman, perhaps any moment she would feel the hand of the law literally on her shoulder. Head bent down, Mattie tried to shield her face from view as she hurried off the platform. She cursed herself for not thinking to bring a bonnet. Intent on escape, she didn't see the two men walking toward her.

"Excuse me, miss," was all she heard before colliding with a strong, hard body. A face with golden hair swam into view before she tripped over and landed in a heap upon the ground.

The wind knocked out of her, Mattie could only stare at the beautiful man speaking to her. Lord Cameron himself.

He knelt beside her. "Are you quite all right?" he asked anxiously.

With a graceful gesture, he lifted off his hat, revealing the full splendor of his thick, smooth hair, which seemed especially golden against his tanned skin.

She nodded mutely as she tried to catch sight of the marshal over his shoulder.

"Please let me help you up." He touched her injured arm, and Mattie let out a small moan of pain. "Oh, but you're hurt." Lord Cameron frowned as he took in her discomfort. "I'm most sorry that my clumsiness has caused you such distress."

"No, it was my fault," she said finally. "I didn't look where I was going."

"The storm is about to hit, Cameron." A young man appeared above them, twirling a straw hat in his hands. Despite his black mustache and beard, he looked amazingly boyish. "We'd best get back to the hotel or at least take shelter in the station."

Mattie sat up. "I'm fine now, but thank you for your concern."

"Nonsense. Your arm is clearly injured." Lord Cameron helped her to her feet, one strong arm gently supporting her waist. "Let me find a doctor to see to it."

With a sinking sensation, Mattie noticed that the marshal

had stopped speaking with the porter and was staring ominously in their direction.

"Is someone meeting you, miss?"

She raised a hand to smooth back her hair, feeling like an ill-mannered hussy to be going about without a hat. About to shake her head, Mattie suddenly realized that a woman traveling alone to a city where she had no acquaintances might arouse a gentleman's suspicions.

"Yes, actually, a—a young man," she stammered.

Cameron looked around the train platform, now empty of everyone but porters wheeling off baggage and that lone marshal. "Perhaps he has been delayed. If you'll tell me what he looks like, I'll ask one of the station employees if anyone answering his description is about."

As he looked at her inquiringly, Mattie could only stare back. "I'm afraid I can't do that."

He raised an eyebrow. "Why not?"

"I've never met him." Taking a big gulp, Mattie searched for a convincing lie. She was back in Colorado now; there must be a clue in that, if she could only remember why a single woman might journey west. Suddenly Evelyn's scornful words came back to her. "What does he take me for—some dismal mail-order bride?" Mattie took a deep breath. "You see, I'm a mail-order bride." Her gaze didn't waver as she met Cameron's startled eyes.

"I see." The two men exchanged amused glances. "I've heard of such things, of course, but you're the first one I've met since coming to Colorado."

The bearded young man chuckled. "That's what *you* should have done, Cameron. Become a mail-order husband. It might have saved you a deuced amount of trouble."

Cameron smiled. "Forgive my friend Harry, miss. He still has his college man's sense of humor. Or what passes for humor at Yale."

Harry raised his hands in mock horror. "Harvard, if you please."

"As I said, I'm quite all right now." Mattie's words were drowned out by a roll of thunder. "You've both been most

37

kind, but I mustn't trouble you any longer." Eager to be off, she unthinkingly reached for her satchel with her injured arm and cried out in pain.

Cameron frowned. "That arm must be looked after. I insist. After all, I'm responsible for your injury."

"No, please. I'm sure it's nothing serious."

His friend nodded. "I think a doctor is definitely in order. You're looking frightfully pale."

"Quite so, Harry. Secure one of the carriages out front."

Mattie bit her lip as Harry strode off into the departing crowd. *I shouldn't be here with Lord Cameron,* she thought nervously. He was a link to the Sinclairs, a link that might lead to her imprisonment. She had to get away as fast as she could, and she struggled to find a way to refuse Lord Cameron's assistance. Yet if she did, what would she do next? She barely had ten dollars with which to make a new start. Certainly she had no money to spare for a doctor.

Taking her satchel, Cameron offered his arm. After a moment's hesitation, she placed her uninjured hand about his elbow. "You shouldn't be troubling yourself. I'm certain that my intended will discover I've arrived. If not, then I'll ask around after him. He's sure to turn up."

"There might be a way to expedite matters." Cameron inclined his head toward the marshal. "Marshal Lee knows everyone in Springs. I'll see if he wouldn't mind asking around after—" Cameron stopped as Mattie suddenly squeezed his arm. "What's the matter? You look as though you're about to faint."

"I'm feeling a bit light-headed. I think you were right. The sooner I see a doctor, the better."

With a worried expression, Lord Cameron ushered her quickly from the train platform, uttering polite reassurances all the while. He didn't seem to notice how improved she became as soon as she settled into the waiting phaeton. As the carriage started up, Mattie sat back with a sigh. One glimpse out the window told her that the marshal was not hot on her heels. She bent her head down and shuddered with relief.

"We should be at the hotel soon, miss." Cameron patted her shoulder nervously. "Don't try to talk. Just sit back and relax. I'll take care of you."

Mattie gave Lord Cameron a gaze filled with both gratitude and something akin to awe. Surprisingly, he turned his own glance aside as though embarrassed. Mattie decided that Evelyn Sinclair was an even greater fool than she'd first imagined.

"Well, I admit she's a pretty filly, but what in the devil are we going to do with her? We have to get back to Cripple Creek. With the strike still on, the mine is just lying idle."

Mattie leaned her head back in the armchair, trying to catch the whispered conversation of Lord Cameron and his friend.

"Be responsible, Harry. I can't just walk away from a young lady whom I've injured. After all, I may be something of a rake, but I'm not a boor. The least I can do is see that she's settled in and her arm properly looked after."

"Putting her up at the Antlers will be a costly proposition."

"Oh, you're a worse miser than your father. No wonder you're so bloody rich."

"Not until I come into my trust fund, which means I've got to watch my expenses as closely as you do. We need every dime just now to buy equipment. Even we shouldn't be staying here."

"I may be bankrupt by Christmas, but I can still afford to stay at a decent hotel and look after a young lady in trouble."

A rueful laugh followed. "Yes, I can imagine the sort of looking after you've got in mind, Cameron. I thought you'd been exercising too much self-control lately. I don't blame you for your interest, but we've got enough problems right now without worrying over some—"

"Miss, if you'll please bend your head forward a bit, I'll place this around your neck." The portly doctor stood before her, a makeshift sling dangling from his hands.

Mattie did as he asked, her wrist now tightly bandaged and her eyelids drooping. She should have refused the tea laced with laudanum that the good doctor had pressed upon her. It dulled not only the pain in her wrist but her panic, and she had to keep her wits about her.

"Now I hope that makes you a bit more comfortable." He gathered up his bag and gestured to Lord Cameron and his friend.

It seemed hardly credible to Mattie that she found herself sitting in the plush salon of the Antlers Hotel, her feet resting on a velvet ottoman while the huge head of a grizzly stared down at her from the wall. She was vaguely aware of other well-dressed ladies and gentlemen moving in the background, and an occasional clink of china or glass.

Lord Cameron came into view. "How is she, Dr. Amory?"

"Oh, just a sprained wrist, nothing too severe. If she keeps it bandaged and uses the sling, it should be back to normal in about two weeks." The doctor's watery blue eyes took in Mattie's drugged state. "And the dose of laudanum I've given her should control any pain she's having. Although I measured it out with a careful hand, it seems to have had quite an effect on her." He tapped her knee. "When did you last eat, young woman?"

"Apple," she said in a slurred voice.

He shrugged. "Well, no use speaking to her now. At any rate, she'll not be troubled by pain tonight." The doctor pulled at the cuffs of his serge coat. "If she requires anything further, I'll be at my office. Of course, I can't guarantee any more house calls. The season is starting up and I've three cases of dyspepsia to attend to later this afternoon."

Lord Cameron nodded. "I appreciate your coming over on such short notice."

"My pleasure, sir. Perhaps you wouldn't be averse to a bit of pigeon shooting at the club later in the week."

"Sounds capital, but I've business to attend to in Cripple Creek."

"Ah, Cripple Creek. If I were twenty years younger, I'd be up there myself. Instead I must struggle to make my living from the health seekers coming to the Springs."

Mattie caught sight of his pearl-studded cufflinks and guessed he probably hadn't struggled a day since setting up his practice.

"Well, good day, gentlemen." Dr. Amory patted her hand as though she were a child. "Drink as much spring water as you can, young lady. No better tonic in the world."

Mattie tried to speak, but her tongue felt as heavy as her eyelids. By the time she murmured a reply, the doctor was gone.

"I've taken a room for you in the hotel." Lord Cameron's voice seemed to come from a great distance. "While we ask around after your young man, you'll need a place to stay, and the Antlers is the best Colorado Springs has to offer."

Even in her stupor, Mattie felt a jolt of alarm. "I—I don't have any money."

Harry smiled kindly. "It's been taken care of. After all, you wouldn't have been hurt if you hadn't collided with this clumsy oaf here, Miss—?" He looked at her expectantly. "I'm afraid we don't know your name."

Mattie wanted to close her eyes and sleep. Each moment found her more drained of energy, less concerned with the real world. "My name?" she asked stupidly.

Lord Cameron frowned. "Actually, I should have introduced myself first. How rude of me."

"You've been in America too long," Harry said. "Any day now I expect you'll be rubbing bear grease in your hair and yelling 'dang.' "

He bowed his head. "My name is Lord Cameron Lynch-Holmes and this sorry fellow is Harry Tremont."

"I could have introduced myself." Harry inclined his head politely. "Pleased to make your acquaintance, Miss—"

"Crawford," she said dreamily. "Mattie Crawford." Some part of her brain warned her that was the wrong response—she should conceal her real name—but she couldn't remember why.

"May I ask where you're from, Miss Crawford?" A hint of a smile played about Lord Cameron's lips, as though he guessed she wasn't quite herself.

"Colorado." She closed her eyes. "I've come home."

She heard one of them clear his throat. "How much baggage did you bring along with you, Miss Crawford?"

Mattie forced her eyes open. "Baggage?"

Lord Cameron gestured toward her dusty satchel, looking ludicrous sitting atop a polished mahogany side table. "We'll send someone down to the station to collect your things. If you could tell us how many bags you've brought with you, it would facilitate matters considerably."

All she wanted to do was sleep. Why were they bothering her with questions? "Just that," she mumbled, flopping a drugged hand in the satchel's direction.

"Ridiculous," Harry said. "She must have brought more."

"Excuse me, Miss Crawford, but if we don't clear this up quickly, your bags may be lost."

Closing her eyes again, Mattie wished they would go away. "What? Yes, the bags were lost," she repeated.

"Lost? Where?"

"Days ago." She sighed. "I lost everything." Her head fell back against the plush chair.

She'd been asleep only a second, it seemed, when she felt herself being pulled to her feet. Lord Cameron and Harry propped her up between them, and she cursed herself for drinking the laudanum.

With a great effort, she tried to clear her head. "I can manage."

Their hold on her waist loosened, but neither man released her.

"We'll escort you up to your room." Lord Cameron snapped his fingers and a uniformed man rushed to open the salon door. "You really must lie down, Miss Crawford."

"You're both too kind," Mattie murmured.

"We can assist you further if we know the name of your husband-to-be. Harry and I have been in Colorado since last October. Perhaps we know him."

Both men stopped walking, and she shrank from the expectant expressions on their faces. His name? She was making this up second by second, and in her present state of mind, she wasn't certain of what she was saying.

"Miss Crawford?" This time she thought she discerned a note of suspicion in Lord Cameron's voice. "You do know his name, don't you?"

"Of course."

At that moment a white-jacketed waiter passed by carrying a tray. Her nervous gaze fell on the tall bottle of whiskey it held.

"It's Mr. Daniels."

"And his Christian name?" Lord Cameron prodded gently.

"Jack," Mattie said with a gulp.

"Jack Daniels?" A chuckle escaped him. "Well, what do you make of that, Harry?"

Harry joined in his friend's laughter. "I hope that's not indicative of your prospective groom's habits, Miss Crawford."

"I—I don't know," she said weakly. She had said something foolish, but she was too tired and confused to puzzle it out. All she saw were their laughing faces and the carpeted stairs looming in front of her. "I'm very tired."

Her words trailed off. She sagged against Lord Cameron, who instantly picked her up in his arms.

"The laudanum," he muttered to Harry.

Mattie was too weary to care about appearances any longer. She only knew that the strong and capable Lord Cameron was carrying her up the stairs. It was like the fantasy she'd harbored ever since Evelyn had first read his letters to her, and now the handsome English lord was indeed sweeping her away. To her bedchamber, she thought happily, and wound her arms about his neck. She felt his face

43

turn in her direction. Closing her eyes, Mattie let her head fall to his shoulder.

"Watch yourself," Harry said. "She's a husband waiting for her."

Through a haze, she heard the reply, "Does she? I don't think so."

She must have fallen asleep once more, for when she opened her eyes, Mattie found herself staring at a polished walnut dressing table with a basin and pitcher centered neatly upon it.

"Have the maid turn down the bed." She recognized Lord Cameron's voice. "She needs to sleep."

Too tired to raise her head, Mattie was content to nestle in his arms while the sound of rustling cloth filled her ears. This was so nice, she thought dreamily, as he finally laid her down on a cool bed. Someone pulled off her shoes, and then a sweet-smelling blanket was smoothed over her. Her eyes fluttered open. Lord Cameron's face was all she could see. She smiled sleepily.

"Beautiful," she murmured.

"The bed? Yes, I suppose it is."

"No." She shook her head. "You."

Lord Cameron gently touched her cheek. "Go to sleep, Miss Crawford."

Mattie whispered something, but her fantasy prince didn't seem to understand. He bent even nearer. "What did you say?"

"Will you kiss me?" This was a marvelous dream, she thought happily, better than any of the other dreams she'd had before about Lord Cameron. Why, she could see the pulse beating in his throat, and feel the smooth linen of his jacket against her face.

She closed her eyes and sighed. "Kiss me."

For a moment, she thought he was going to refuse, which didn't seem right somehow. After all, it was *her* dream. But then she felt his lips brush against hers, and she felt a thrill of pleasure. What strong lips they were, yet gentle, barely brushing against her own. Mattie felt him start to move away

44

and she flung a hand out from under the covers to draw him back.

This time her lips fell open before his, eager for his mouth to press hard against her. She felt no shame. How could she? This was a dream, and only she would ever know how wantonly she behaved. As though sensing her desire, her fantasy lover kissed her with even greater passion, and she shivered to feel his tongue dart hotly into her mouth.

"Cameron, don't you think we should go?" A masculine voice rudely broke in.

She wanted to protest when Lord Cameron pulled away from her. She wanted to say that this was not what she had in mind, that her dreams carried on much longer. But her eyes were heavy.

"Kiss me," Mattie murmured as she nestled under the blanket.

A smile on her face, she was sound asleep before the two men closed the door behind them.

Chapter Three

Cameron smoothed down his white duck trousers for the third time in as many minutes.

"You look fine, old chap." Harry clipped the ends of the cigar he was holding, then held it up to his nose for a delighted sniff. "Besides, yesterday she seemed quite taken with you."

"What in blazes are you talking about?"

Not until Harry had lit up and was contentedly puffing away did the young man bother to answer. "Our titian-haired beauty, of course. She seems to have fallen prey to your charms."

Cameron reached for the *Colorado Springs Tribune*. "Sometimes that celebrated wit of yours seems as thin as this mountain air."

"Then allow me to assume a more serious note." He leaned back in his chair and blew out a series of smoke rings. "Miss Crawford has come here to get married."

"So she says." Cameron loudly rustled the paper and held it up before his face.

46

"I don't know why you persist in doubting her story. The state's bursting with all sorts of dreamers: miners, cowboys, speculators. Not to mention young bloods like us."

"And mail-order brides?" Cameron lowered the paper and shot his friend a cynical glance. "Come now, why would a beauty like Miss Crawford be willing to marry some grubby prospector she's never even met?"

"Probably for the same reason that the Marquess of Clydesford's son is prepared to marry the first rich woman who'll accept him."

"Don't be ridiculous. It's not the same thing at all."

"Of course it is. You're marrying to secure your family's future, and Miss Crawford is marrying to guarantee her own. We've both seen sourdoughs sell off their claims for a measly five or ten thousand dollars. To someone with only a satchel to her name, it must seem a king's ransom."

"So you don't believe she lost her baggage either?"

Harry shrugged. "I've no way of knowing if she has or not. But I do think our pretty lady is down to her last nickel, which is why we should treat her to a hearty meal and then be on our way. Her injury has been looked after, she's resting in the finest hotel Colorado has to offer, and you've even been gallant enough to present her with a new wardrobe." He took a cautious look around. The Antler's reading room was filled with elderly men dozing in wingchairs and young gentlemen smoking cheroots or reading the financial page.

"Which, by the way, you can ill afford," he continued in a low voice. "Another week of expenses like this and we'll be forced to sell our claim as well. Look, Cameron, I came here to achieve financial independence, and I thought you wanted the same. Wasting time and money on a young woman who's promised to another man is both absurd and dangerous. Remember, this is the Wild West. Keep waltzing around Miss Crawford's skirts and you may find yourself facing Mr. Jack Daniels himself, aiming a six-gun at you."

"Jack Daniels." Cameron raised a scornful eyebrow.

"You can't believe she's engaged to a man with a name like that."

"Why not? I met a fellow in Fremont last month who went by the moniker Dirty Balls Johnson." An exasperated sigh escaped him as he tapped out his cigar. "Be realistic. This is mining country, Cameron, not Boston's Back Bay. Oh, I know I sound like one of your stuffy Oxford dons, but we have serious business to attend to in Cripple Creek. Now that your suit's been rejected for the last time by the Sinclairs, I'd hoped we could just concentrate on the mine. Don't take out your frustrations by dallying with a young woman who's come here to make a respectable marriage. It's not fair to either of you."

"And here I thought I'd only done the gentlemanly thing by assisting a lady in distress. But since I'm the notorious Lord Cameron Lynch-Holmes, clearly I must have a lascivious motive."

"That's not what I meant. Look, I don't want—"

"I knew I'd have the ghosts of my past coming between me and any prospective wife, but I thought you knew me better than that. Apparently the poisonous gossip that passes for dinner conversation on Fifth Avenue has influenced even you."

"Damn it, you know that's not true. I'm only looking out for your best interests."

"Now you sound more like my mother than an Oxford don." He pulled out his silver pocket watch. "Well, I think I'll stretch my legs a bit before tea. Maybe when I return, you'll have recovered that college boy's view of the world."

"Cameron, I'm not a boy any longer." Harry looked at him with mingled sadness and affection. "And neither are you. I know you well enough by now to recognize when you're frustrated. I think it disturbs you that you can't consider love when it comes to choosing a wife."

Cameron stood up and straightened his flannel jacket. "I've told you a dozen times, well-bred Englishmen never marry for love. That's why so few of us divorce."

"Joke if you must, but don't deny that you'd prefer to

marry a woman you genuinely cared for.'' Harry shook his head. ''Such a damned pity it was Lady Philippa who pierced that lordly facade of yours.''

Cameron stiffened instantly. ''If you value our friendship, never mention that lady's name again,'' he said in a cold voice. ''Otherwise you can add anger to the frustration you claim I am feeling. Now excuse me. The air in here seems a trifle stale.''

Not bothering to wait for Harry's reply, Cameron stalked out into the spacious lobby of the Antler Hotel. The last thing he wanted to hear was a lecture on morality from young Harry. Damnation, but his friend's accusation stung. In the three years he'd been courting the debutantes of New York, only Harry's lighthearted friendship had made the distasteful endeavor bearable. Not that he was a stranger to innuendo and gossip. Rumors had swirled about him ever since he had been sent down from Oxford, and he'd grown accustomed to being regarded as a devilish rogue. It had never hurt his standing in society; indeed it gave him a certain allure. Not until the tragic affair with Lady Philippa had he realized that the one thing a grown man couldn't dispense with was an honorable reputation.

Pulling out his kid gloves, he slapped them against his open hand as he looked back at the smoking room. He could have forgiven Harry for his meddling, but not for bringing up Lady Philippa. Anyone who had even a passing acquaintance with him knew enough not to touch on the memories of that long-ago romance. He frowned. Harry was wrong, though. He didn't harbor any foolish notions about falling in love again.

And he's wrong about my interest in that Crawford woman, he thought resentfully. Yes, he'd been struck by her good looks and shapely figure. But he genuinely wanted to help Miss Crawford, and after injuring her wrist—well, only a cad would have walked away from such a wounded bird.

Cameron walked over to the long, winding staircase, leaning upon a polished bannister to gaze upstairs. The stairs up which he had carried Miss Crawford yesterday afternoon.

She'd felt good in his arms: soft and voluptuous, snuggled against him like a woman satiated from a night of love. And in the bedroom he'd felt a sharp excitement when he laid her down only to see her sleepy eyes looking up at him with unabashed desire. When she asked him for a kiss, Cameron had felt a wave of lust *and* tenderness. Looking back, it was a good thing Harry and that maid were there. A year of monkish living warranted a visit to the Homestead when he got back to Cripple Creek. Maybe then he wouldn't be so susceptible to a pretty girl's charms.

Yet it still didn't explain why this red-haired woman was disturbing him so. A beauty she was, but he'd seen more angelic creatures in the drawing rooms of London and New York. No, there was something else about her. Something he recognized the moment he helped her to her feet at the train station. It came to him suddenly. In those dark green eyes, he'd glimpsed a desperation that matched his own. That was what Harry didn't understand when he accused Cameron of being merely frustrated. The next Marquess of Clydesford was now desperate—desperate to save his family from ruin, desperate to regain his reputation, desperate to know some peace and stability in his life. And he sensed that Mattie Crawford was desperate, too. For what, he didn't know. Maybe it *was* for a husband. She certainly looked like a lady in need of a strong man at her side.

"Leave her be," he said softly. "Whatever problems she may have, you've too many of your own to bother with hers."

About to turn away, Cameron's eyes widened as the lady in question appeared at the top of the stairs. If not for the lustrous red hair pulled back into a chignon, he might not have instantly recognized her. Gone was yesterday's confused young woman stumbling about in a threadbare jacket and skirt. The lady standing above him could have graced a Sargent portrait.

She saw him too and smiled politely before starting down the carpeted steps. With her crisp white shirtwaist tucked into a green-and-white-striped skirt, and a pert straw hat atop her head, Mattie Crawford managed to look both saucy and refined. She was more than a beauty, he thought as she came closer. She had style, a real presence, and he wondered if she weren't perhaps an actress.

Her smile grew warm as she finally stood before him, smelling of sandlewood, and he noticed for the first time that she had a faint sprinkling of freckles along her nose. He felt himself grinning back like an idiot.

"I don't have to ask how you are today, Miss Crawford," he said with a small bow, relieved that he'd recovered his composure so quickly. "You seem vastly improved." *Indeed*, he thought, *you seem as alive and ravishing as a mountain valley in spring.*

"Scented bath salts and a new wardrobe would revive any woman." She looked down at her outfit. "I don't know how I can ever repay you."

"Nonsense. A young woman on her way to be married must have something decent to wear." He noticed that her gaze didn't waver when he said this. "I hope your groom won't resent my having bought these things for you."

Mattie shook her head and laughed. "I'll tell him that a good Samaritan purchased my trousseau. And he'd best have the good manners to turn up soon. After all, with such a fine wardrobe, I might find myself with more marriage proposals than I can handle."

Cameron felt off-balance. He was close enough to kiss those full, moist lips once more, yet he couldn't discern a trace of confusion or deceit in her expression. Indeed she seemed remarkably serene and self-possessed. Had he only imagined yesterday's fevered desperation? Was she really what she claimed: a mail-order bride who'd lost her belongings?

"Here's hoping we find the gentleman quickly, then. What was his name again? A Mr. Daniels?"

"Mr. Jack Daniels." She met his piercing gaze with aplomb. "My guess is that a whiskey-loving father christened him." A small sigh escaped her. "I don't really know much more about him, Lord Cameron. You see, I received his letter through an agency back East, and unfortunately I lost that along with my trunks.'' She gestured toward the wide doors of the hotel. ''Do you mind if we take a stroll outside? I'm longing for a bit of sun and fresh air.''

''Certainly, although the sky seems to be threatening rain again.'' Still thrown by her self-assured pose, Cameron escorted her through the lobby. ''Does your arm still pain you?''

''Only when I'm trying to dress. As it is, I've tried to make the injury as unobtrusive as possible.'' Cameron followed her gaze and saw that the utilitarian sling used by the doctor had been replaced by one made of delicate Brussels lace. ''I took this off one of the hats you had sent up. I hope you don't mind.''

''Of course not, Miss Crawford. The clothes are yours to do with as you like. I only wish I could do more.''

As he held open the heavy glass-paned door, she turned to him with an almost chiding look. ''Then I have but one more favor to ask. You see, I grew up in Colorado and everyone here knew me only as Mattie. It would make me feel like I'm really home again if you would call me that as well.''

''Certainly, Miss—I mean, Mattie.'' Thoroughly puzzled, Cameron could only follow her out the door, shielding his eyes from the unexpected dazzling sunlight.

Mattie hadn't felt this much tension since she was interrogated by Detective Devlin four years before. Strolling along the broad thoroughfare shaded by cottonwood trees, she listened for any sign that Lord Cameron doubted her story. He was unfailingly polite and gracious, but her instincts warned that he might be as fine an actor as she was. At least she felt better prepared than she had been yesterday; she'd worked over her story while bathing and dressing, and her years since prison had taught her how to dissemble. She could only hope that a time would come when the past lay far behind her, and she could answer innocent questions without evasion.

"It isn't wise to stray so far."

"Excuse me?" Mattie glanced warily over at Lord Cameron.

He gestured toward the bank of clouds now obscuring the sun. "It might rain again. The weather here is quite infernal. Just as you think the roses are about to bloom, it snows. But you must know this country far better than I do, Miss Crawford. Colorado is your home, isn't it?"

She bit her lip. "Mattie, please." Bad enough she'd revealed her real name. Now the only way to rectify that error was convincing everyone to call her simply *Mattie*. That might make it more difficult for Devlin to track her down.

"Then I insist you call me Cameron. None of this 'Lord' business."

"If you like." Actually, Mattie had no intention of lingering in his presence. The wisest thing would be for them to part company soon, but it was essential she answer any questions Lord Cameron had. She couldn't risk anyone who knew the Sinclairs harboring suspicions about her.

"To answer your question, yes, Colorado is my home." Mattie turned back in the direction of the Antler, its imposing facade now hidden by trees and elaborate riding gigs.

"Then you're familiar with the Springs?"

She peeked at him from beneath her lashes. A worldly man like Lord Cameron would certainly sense that she wasn't accustomed to the refined society of Colorado Springs. "Only a passing acquaintance; it was always too rich for our blood. I was born in Black Hawk."

"Black Hawk?"

"It's a mining settlement north of Denver. I hear it's fallen on bad times, but my father took the family there during the Gregory Gulch gold strike. Of course we didn't stay long. Soon enough my father moved us on to Eureka, Apex, Central City, Leadville: wherever he thought he had a chance of stumbling upon a vein of gold or silver."

"And did he?"

"Sometimes." A note of sadness entered her voice. "But as you've probably learned, just finding precious metals is no guarantee of riches. It takes a very resourceful man or a very rich one to get the metal out.''

That comment seemed to make Lord Cameron thoughtful. ''I wonder if Harry and I are wasting our time here. We have a claim in Cripple Creek, but I've no idea if it will pan out.''

Mattie wasn't sure if he actually expected a response but felt compelled to say something. ''Only a first-rate assayer can tell you that, but if you do have a worthwhile claim, I suggest you go to Denver. It's the moneyed investors who are the real bonanza kings here. The harder a man works for his gold, the less likely he is to see any profit from it. Look for a gentleman whose hands have never known a callus, and you'll find the best person to invest in your claim.'' She gave him a knowing look. ''Believe me, I know. I'm a miner's daughter. My father was robbed by the best-dressed men in the state.''

Cameron gently touched her shoulder. ''Harsh words, Mattie, yet you don't sound bitter.''

''It's only gold,'' she said simply. ''There are more important things to suffer for.''

He shook his head, his expression clearly indicating that he didn't agree. Cocking his head to one side, he scrutinized her face so closely, she felt herself blush. ''I wonder if your Mr. Daniels realizes how fortunate he is.''

''You're too kind,'' she murmured. ''And far too generous.''

His gaze remained fixed upon her. ''Actually, I'm neither of those things, I'm afraid.'' He held up a hand to still her protest. ''But I do pride myself on recognizing an extraordinary woman when I see one. You're the first person I've met in Colorado who doesn't consider the pursuit of gold to be paramount.'' He gave a rueful laugh. ''And unfortunately, that includes both Mr. Tremont and myself. Which is why I must take leave of you soon. Harry and I will be leaving tomorrow for Cripple Creek. We have business that cannot wait, but I do wish I could remain with you until your groom shows up.''

Cameron paused, and for one thrilling instant, she thought he was going to kiss her.

"But perhaps that wouldn't be prudent," he continued. "Several more days in your company, and I might be quite jealous of any man taking you off into the hills."

Despite the warmth of the late afternoon, Mattie shivered. Neither fear nor laudanum was fogging her senses now. She could see clearly how splendid a man he was. His deep-set eyes were of a hue seen only on sapphire mornings in the mountains, while his surprisingly dark lashes accentuated their beauty. *Beauty* was the only word she could use to describe Lord Cameron, yet despite his well-tailored clothes, there wasn't a hint of the effeminate or the dandy about him. His fine suit couldn't conceal the lean strength of his body or the athleticism of his movements. Mattie suddenly remembered how strong and hard his arms had felt as he laid her down in bed yesterday. Her eyes darted to his mouth, now curled in an enigmatic smile, and she recalled their sweet but intense kiss. What would it feel like to make love to such a man? she wondered. Now that might be something to struggle and suffer for, she told herself wryly, remembering the four endless years she'd had to submit to her late husband's insensitive demands. She tore her attention away from Lord Cameron's sensual mouth.

Straightening her straw hat, Mattie inclined her head toward a shiny black phaeton pulling away from the train station. "I believe that gentleman is trying to catch your attention."

Cameron turned and tipped his hat at the gray-haired man in a plaid jacket who was waving a hand in their direction. "It's Ethan McCutcheon. He owns the mining exchange on Grove Avenue. I see that his wife's cousin has finally arrived. She's supposed to be suffering from gout, but she looks remarkably well to me. Her taste in hats seems rather unhealthy, however."

Mattie glanced over just as the open phaeton rolled past. The carriage's two passengers had turned their attention elsewhere, but Mattie's gaze remained riveted on the woman sporting a yellow leghorn bonnet. She felt her hands grow icy and bile rise in her throat.

It was Julia Sinclair.

Chapter Four

It was the most expensive meal Mattie had ever eaten, but every bite stuck in her throat. Oblivious to the different courses, she glanced down at her bowl in surprise when Harry asked her how she liked her turtle soup. Luckily neither Lord Cameron nor Harry seemed to notice her agitation. Conversation was brisk and frequently amusing—thanks to Harry—but through it all she kept throwing discreet glances around the hotel dining room. If only there were fewer chandeliers, she thought worriedly, and fewer well-heeled diners. Fortunately Lord Cameron had chosen a corner table, but she was certain that at any moment Julia Sinclair would appear, and the nightmare would begin afresh.

A glittering movement caught her eye. It was only a diamond brooch gracing the silk bodice of a buxom matron. A Worth gown, no doubt. Mattie was chagrined to see how many wealthy couples were staying in the hotel. When she was a girl, the Springs had been frequented primarily by Englishmen and those Americans who were newly made gold and silver kings. Now it seemed that Eastern society had found another place to while away the summer besides Newport. So far she hadn't recognized anyone but Evelyn's aunt, but Mattie knew she had to leave Colorado Springs as soon as possible. It would only be a matter of time before another acquaintance of the Sinclairs appeared, and her red hair already made her too visible.

She looked over at Lord Cameron sitting across from her. A Dresden basket filled with irises partially blocked her view, but he seemed to be barely touching his food. That worried her. He'd been watching her closely all through the meal, and her mind raced as she wondered if she'd somehow made a faux pas. Having served in wealthy households for years, Mattie had a good idea of how one behaved in polite society. Still, she wasn't accustomed to supping with English lords, any more than she was accustomed to wearing an embroidered satin gown. Aware that she might never have the opportunity to wear such a beautiful dress again, Mattie had removed the sling before she came down to dinner. Her injured hand now rested in her lap, and she marveled at the costly cream-colored satin beneath her fingers.

"Would you like more champagne, Mattie?" Cameron gestured toward the sommelier, who stood waiting. "Or perhaps you'd prefer sherry or Madeira?"

She shook her head. Actually she would have loved to have gotten rip-roaring drunk, but she needed a clear head if she was going to keep Lord Cameron from going to visit Julia Sinclair. While she was having tea with Lord Cameron and Harry this afternoon, an invitation had come from Ethan McCutcheon. Her heart in her throat, she waited while the two men debated whether they should accept. Only their guilt over leaving her alone for the evening prevented them, although Harry made a halfhearted suggestion to bring Mattie along. Still, she wouldn't breathe easy until Lord Cameron left tomorrow morning for Cripple Creek. Julia Sinclair had seen Mattie dozens of times; the older woman only lived a few blocks from the Sinclair family and was an almost daily visitor. Certainly she had learned of the robbery before leaving New York, and of the identity of the runaway thief.

No, while Julia Sinclair and Lord Cameron were in the same city, Mattie had to find a way to keep him occupied and at her side—no matter what it required.

Cameron knew he was drinking too much. His face felt flushed and his eyes were straying far too often to Mattie's bare arms. *Well, you've only yourself to blame for this tempting spectacle,* he thought darkly, noticing once more how deliciously the satin gown clung to her womanly curves. Why hadn't he told the dress shop to send over only prim shirtwaists and calico wrappers? But thanks to him, the infernal woman looked as stylish and provocative as Lillie Langtry.

He drained his goblet of champagne, cursing himself for arranging this interminable twelve-course dinner. Not that it wasn't a gracious way to say farewell, but he hadn't counted on being confronted with the luscious swell of her breasts, her full hips and bare, smooth arms. Arms along which he would have enjoyed planting kisses before nuzzling that spot on her neck right below the lone tendril of rich auburn—

"Well, Cameron, it seems a shame that this delightful lady wasn't with us when we arrived in Colorado last October," Harry said jovially. "She knows a far sight more about mining than we do. I'm sure she would have caught on to that first scam we fell into." He leaned back in his chair while the waiter ladled Cardinal sauce over his red mullet. "Two fellows sold us a claim along the creek that they'd salted with a half-dozen pieces of pyrite." He laughed. "Oh, we were the greenest dudes these mountains have ever seen."

Refusing another helping of asparagus and peas, Mattie smiled. "You must have been if you couldn't tell the difference between fool's gold and the real thing."

And which are you? wondered Cameron, thinking over the hours they had spent together this afternoon. What sort of a woman was Mattie Crawford?

He watched how politely she listened to Harry ramble on, while delicately picking at her food. Cameron had been raised in society; he understood its tribal customs and hidden language. Mattie Crawford was behaving most correctly. She used the proper soup spoon, knew how to make clever conversation, and had even arranged her hair in the latest fashion, but it didn't come naturally to her. She's acting, he decided. And she's damn good at it. But why bother with this pose? After all, she was supposedly a mail-order bride come to marry some unwashed sourdough. Why even pretend to be a city-bred lady?

Cameron pushed his plate aside. Blasted champagne. He couldn't think straight. Maybe he didn't want to believe her a lady because then he could consider taking her to his bed. Damn, but it had been a long time since he'd felt this much raw sexual attraction. And he had only his single-minded fortune-hunting to blame. If he'd indulged himself more this past year rather than worrying about gossip reaching Evelyn, maybe he wouldn't now be looking at Mattie Crawford like a stallion in heat. Thank God Harry and he were leaving at dawn.

"You're not hungry?" Mattie was looking at him with those large dark eyes that always seemed a different shade of green, as elusive as the lady herself.

He shook his head. "I've never been fond of the chef here. He has a heavy hand with the salt."

"You should have accepted the invitation to dine with the McCutcheons then," Harry said, giving an approving glance at the oyster pâtés being brought to the table. "I hear his wife has hired a Frenchman who formerly cooked for the Vanderbilts. Although if you had gone, you'd be forced to endure the dinner conversation of Julia Sinclair, so I doubt it would have been worth it. Only a gourmand like myself would find the trade-off acceptable."

"Julia Sinclair?" Mattie asked softly. "Was she the lady you pointed out in the carriage today?"

"Yes, the one wearing that large yellow hat."

Cameron couldn't disguise his grimace. As though it wasn't bad enough that Evelyn had scorned his marriage proposal, her exasperating aunt had to turn up in the Springs at the same time he was here. Not that he was surprised.

Aunt Julia was celebrated as much for her mysterious ailments as for her ugly limestone mansion on Fifth Avenue. The fact that such a professional invalid would turn up in a health resort like Colorado Springs should have been a given. Still he couldn't deny the dismay he'd felt when he recognized her this afternoon. It brought back the unpleasant months spent wooing the debutantes of New York: all the contemptible toadying, the hypocrisy, the cold-blooded bargaining that occurred on both sides of the marriage business.

"That's another reason to be grateful her niece turned down your marriage proposal," Harry said cheerfully, ignoring Cameron's disapproving look. "Otherwise think of all those family meals you would have been forced to sit through. Intolerable prospect. I pity poor Ethan McCutcheon. He's probably trying to slog through his roast pheasant while Julia delights the table with an account of her latest gastronomic disorder."

"I fear I will have to make an appearance nonetheless," Cameron said wearily. "I sent back word that I would try to stop by for brandy and cigars."

"Must you?"

He glanced over in surprise at Mattie's plaintive question. She looked genuinely troubled.

"Yes, I must. It would be exceedingly rude not to pay my respects, especially since I'll be leaving tomorrow."

Mattie fumbled for her champagne glass and took a long sip. "That's why I was hoping to spend this evening with you." She glanced over at Harry. "With both of you. After all, I don't know when or if we shall ever meet again, and I do so want to thank you for all you've done."

Cameron could see her take a deep breath, the swell of her rounded breasts becoming more pronounced.

"Besides, when you both leave tomorrow, I'll feel quite alone. I'd rather postpone that for as long as possible." She gave Cameron a shy smile. "I know I have no right to make such a request. You've already done far too much."

Cameron sat back in his chair while Harry uttered some comforting nonsense. This latest pose wasn't as successful as the others, he thought shrewdly. Playing the girlish co-quette didn't suit her. Mattie Crawford was all woman, in looks and demeanor. Despite the mystery surrounding her, she usually presented herself in a forthright manner, without hesitation or apology. Maybe that was what he liked about her; she was different from the society misses he'd been pursuing for three years. She was just as lovely and polite, but upper-class young ladies were schooled in manipulation. Not that he held it against them. The marriage game was played for very high stakes and it was understood that a cool, calculating mind was essential if both sides were to make a good match. But right now Mattie was clearly trying to manipulate him, and she wasn't anywhere near as adept at it as those Eastern debutantes.

Cameron refolded the linen napkin on his lap. Maybe she wasn't so different after all. Maybe she was just as taken by his title and looks as every other young woman. Well, he no longer had any interest in playing flirtatious games, not even with someone as delectable as Mattie Crawford.

"And I'm certain that any day now your prospective groom will turn up, arms open wide," Harry was saying.

"But will he turn up in such a fancy town as this? I think not." Mattie's expression grew serious. "Mr. Daniels is a prospector; he's probably never even visited Colorado Springs. Maybe I misread his letter. He might be expecting me to meet him in Cripple Creek."

"Is that where he's living?" Cameron narrowed his eyes, discerning a slight flush as it rose to her cheeks.

Mattie took another sip of champagne before answering. "He only mentioned he was caught up in the gold strike in the Cripple Creek district."

"Him and about ten thousand other men." Harry leaned over and patted her hand. "I sympathize with your impatience, but you don't want to go to Cripple Creek alone. It's a morass of mining men and not so respectable ladies. I'm certain your gentleman never meant for you to meet him there, Miss Crawford."

"Mattie, please," she said with more force than Cameron thought necessary.

"Well then, Mattie, I can only assure you that you'll be far happier—and safer—waiting for Mr. Daniels here. Once we get back to Cripple Creek, Cameron and I will ask around after your young man. As soon as we hear anything, we'll send word."

"I can't afford to remain in the Springs, Harry," she replied, her chin lifted in defiance. "And I certainly won't accept any more charity from either of you. No, I've been thinking about this all day. I have enough money to purchase a ticket to Cripple Creek, so why shouldn't I leave tomorrow with both of you?"

Harry choked on his oyster pâté. "With *us?*"

"Cripple Creek is not a place for an unchaperoned woman," Cameron said firmly. "And Harry and I will be much too busy to look after you."

"I hardly require chaperones." Mattie gave him an amused look. "You seem to forget that I was born and raised in mining camps."

"Be that as it may, I would still feel responsible for you." Cameron didn't add that he would also feel an almost uncontrollable desire to bed her. He pulled out his silver pocket watch and flipped it open. "Now I really must try to hurry this delightful dinner along if I am to pay my respects to Miss Sinclair tonight."

"I cannot persuade you to remain here?" she asked.

Cameron shook his head. "I'm afraid not. One of the drawbacks of being an aristocrat is that one is often expected to display a semblance of good manners."

"I can attest to that," Harry said. "Sometimes he makes me feel quite the boorish Yankee."

Mattie nodded, her eyes cast downward. After a moment, she raised her head, and Cameron was surprised to see a bright smile on her face. "Then let us eat our dessert quickly and send you on your way."

"I beg your pardon." Harry held up his fork. "A Tremont must not be rushed through a meal."

"Oh, hurry up, Harry," Cameron muttered good-naturedly. Secretly he didn't mind lingering. This candle-light dinner was probably the last time he would ever see Mattie Crawford, and he experienced a sudden wrench at the thought. Not for the first time, he felt a surge of jealousy over this Jack Daniels she was supposedly off to marry.

Why the hell did he have to be born a bloody English lord anyway?

Mattie felt Cameron's gaze on her as they climbed the stairs. She gave a slight swing to her hips—subtly, she hoped—hearing the rich satin swish behind her. He wanted her. She was certain of that. Her heart beat quicker as she considered the plan she had formed during dinner. Lord Cameron was intent on seeing Evelyn's aunt tonight. Nothing she'd said had made the slightest difference. Even the discreet flirtatious glances cast his way had not moved him. That left her no other choice but to be painfully obvious.

And what if he refused her outright? Such a man was accustomed to fine ladies, the cream of the upper class. The advances of a common mail-order bride might seem laughable to him, if not downright unappealing. A small sigh escaped her. It would have been so much easier if he had decided to retire early, as Harry Tremont intended. Why did he have to be so socially correct? Wasn't he supposed to have a scandalous reputation? Maybe she didn't understand society behavior as well as she thought she did.

At the top of the stairs, Mattie took a deep breath, discreetly tugging at her bodice. Corseted as tightly as she was, the movement revealed her decolletage even more. Another tug like that, and her breasts would spill out of her dress entirely.

While Harry finished up a humorous account of his Harvard days, Lord Cameron offered her his arm. Trying to appear calm, Mattie wordlessly wrapped her fingers about his sleeve. In his formal evening clothes, Lord Cameron looked devilishly handsome, his blond hair in striking contrast to his black frock coat. Perhaps he did desire her, but not enough to risk any involvement, she thought nervously, as they started down the long hallway. When they finally reached the door to her room, Mattie felt as though they'd walked ten miles rather than ten steps.

"I have so enjoyed making your acquaintance, Mattie," Lord Cameron said in that clipped British accent she found endlessly seductive. "And if we do discover your Mr. Daniels, I shall be certain to sing your praises." He leaned closer, and she feared he would hear how loud her heart was pounding. "I only hope I can conceal my deep envy at his good fortune."

"Hear, hear," Harry chimed in. "As soon as we get our gold mine safely underway, I think I'll send off for a mail-order bride of my own." He gave her a wink as he bent over her hand. "If that agency has another lady half as delightful as you, Mattie, I'll be the most satisfied groom in Colorado."

Her thoughts in a turmoil, she could barely bring herself to engage in the polite bantering necessary to making their farewells. When Lord Cameron brushed his lips against her outstretched hand, she returned the gesture by squeezing his fingers tightly. He wore a questioning look when he straightened up again.

Mattie drew a key from her chatelaine bag, waiting silently while Lord Cameron unlocked her door. She turned toward both men. "Good night and thank you again. I am eternally in your debt."

They were still murmuring farewells when Mattie slipped inside and shut the door behind her. Leaning against the thick carved oak, she waited breathlessly while they walked several doors down the hall. She heard Lord Cameron say good night to his friend. Mattie flung her bag and key aside and raised a nervous hand to her hair. It was her only chance. If he called on Julia Sinclair tonight, Mattie knew she'd have to leave immediately. But where could she go? Her ten dollars would barely take her to the mining district. And she'd have to avoid Cripple Creek for fear of running into Lord Cameron. After a conversation with Miss Sinclair, he might easily guess he'd been supping with a known felon.

She heard him walk past her door. Did she only imagine he paused a brief moment before moving on? *You want me, my fine English lord,* she told herself, *hide it all you want with your lovely manners.* And what did she want? Never to set foot in the Tombs again, to be free, to have a chance at a happy life. If that meant she must play the whore, so be it. If Devlin caught up with her, he would subject her to far worse humiliation.

But was it humiliation? she asked herself as she softly opened the door. Wasn't Lord Cameron the man she had dreamed about for months, wasn't his proud photograph the inspiration for countless thrilling and scandalous dreams? *I've had to do so much in life that I dreaded,* she thought, *so why should seducing Lord Cameron bother me?*

Perhaps what bothered her was that she wanted it very much indeed.

Cameron heard a rustle of satin. Turning around, he was surprised to see Mattie standing in front of her door, the light from the hallway sconces giving her upswept hair a burnished sheen.

"May I speak with you a moment?" she said, glancing behind her as though worried they might be seen.

"Of course." Straightening the sleeves of his frock coat, Cameron walked over to her, his interest piqued.

"This is rather embarrassing." She bit her lips and gave him a tremulous smile. "You see, I foolishly told the maid not to come up later tonight."

"I don't understand."

"It's my sprain." She glanced down at her injured wrist. "I forgot I was going to need help getting undressed. Silly of me. After all, that's why I didn't wear gloves tonight; I knew I couldn't pull them on and off without assistance."

"Well, this can be easily remedied. I'll just go down to the front desk and have them send up a girl." Cameron was somewhat disappointed. For a moment, he'd thought she wanted to say a private farewell. He bit back a self-mocking grin. Maybe even ask him for a kiss, as she sleepily had done yesterday.

"Oh no, please." She laid a firm hand on his sleeve. In the flickering hallway light, her eyes seemed a dark, mysterious sea green. "I'm quite spent and have no wish to wait for a maidservant to find the time to come up to my room. I'll be asleep long before then."

He took a deep breath. His experience with women warned him that a proposition was imminent. So he hadn't misread those coy glances she'd been throwing his way all evening. Although flattered that the attraction between them was mutual, Cameron wasn't certain whether he was pleased by the idea. This young lady continually surprised him, and that made her difficult to control. The graceful image of Lady Philippa rose before him, and he recalled once more her tragic death.

Gazing regretfully at Mattie's voluptuous figure, he shook his head. "I don't know how I can be of service then."

She stepped back toward the door, her hand gently tugging at his sleeve. "I fear I may shock you with my boldness, but I was wondering if you could unfasten my dress for me. It will take but a moment, and save so much time and trouble."

"Mattie, I don't think that's wise." He gestured to the elderly couple farther down the hall. "Someone may see us and, innocent or not, it would damage your reputation. Even in Colorado, a lady can't dispense with that." God, he sounded like a deacon. "And you wouldn't want gossip to reach your Mr. Daniels."

"Mr. Daniels is not here. If he were, I'd ask *him* to help me out of this gown." She dropped his arm and shrugged. "If you won't assist me, then perhaps I'll see if Harry will oblige."

Cameron couldn't read her expression. Was he making too much of this? Perhaps she did only want to get undressed and off to bed. Or perhaps she was as eager for his touch as he was for hers. She began walking toward Harry's room, her slim waist catching his eye, as did the creamy skin of her exposed back above the satin. He couldn't deny he'd like to unfasten that dress and glimpse even more of that curvaceous, sweet-smelling body.

"Very well, Miss Crawford," he said curtly, holding open her bedroom door and gesturing inside.

Pausing a moment to give him a searching look, she picked up her train and gracefully swished her way to the door. "I thought we agreed on Mattie," she said in a low, throaty voice.

What was this blasted woman about? Following after her like an obedient puppy, he hadn't felt this uncertain since he was fifteen and found himself being seduced by a friend of his mother's. Of course, this rustic bedroom in the Antler Hotel was far different from the perfumed boudoir where he'd lost his innocence. And Mattie Crawford was a far cry from the thirty-year-old duchess who had taken it from him. Cameron felt his breathing grow short as she reached up to adjust the gas lamp. Instead of increasing the light, she dimmed it. Damn, he'd been right about her. He could always spot an adventuress.

Mattie looked at him over her shoulder. It was the look of a woman offering herself to him: hungry, nervous, excited. Neither spoke for a long moment, and Cameron felt himself grow hard. She was a magnificent-looking woman, no doubt about it. Earlier this evening he had regretted not buying her a piece of jewelry; compared to the other ladies in the dining room, she seemed remarkably unadorned. But now he could see that her vibrant dark eyes and fiery hair were ornamentation enough. And he'd not seen a lady on either side of the Atlantic who could have filled out that satin gown so provocatively.

"Turn around, please, and I'll unfasten the dress." Cameron was surprised that his voice sounded so steady.

Coming to stand before him, Mattie very slowly turned her back to him. His eyes fell first on the stray tendrils of auburn hair curling against that long lovely neck. Controlling the impulse to take down her hair, he instead began to undo the tiny fastenings running along the back of her dress. Despite their number and small size, Cameron had the gown completely undone in seconds; he'd lost count of how many women he'd helped disrobe over the years. Despite this, he was amused to see his hands shake slightly. *Oh, it has been too long for you, Cameron, old man,* he told himself mockingly.

And he couldn't resist a sigh of appreciation as the gown fell open, revealing the white lace camisole beneath. "Can I do anything more for you?" he asked in a teasing voice.

Despite his misgivings, Cameron Lynch-Holmes was a red-blooded male. If such a beautiful young woman was this determined to take him to her bed, he felt forced to oblige. *I'll be gone by dawn,* he told himself. Mattie Crawford wouldn't have the time to complicate his life.

She turned around to face him. The movement caused the heavy gown to fall to her waist, but she made no move to cover herself. Her eyes remained fixed on him, and her mouth was slightly open, as though she was having trouble breathing. "Yes, there is," she whispered.

Cameron stepped closer, until they were only inches apart. He raised his hands and slipped the lace camisole off her shoulders. Her skin felt as smooth and silky as he'd imagined, and he caressed her shoulders for a few moments, his eyes never leaving hers.

"Your skin is so soft," he murmured appreciatively.

Mattie took his hand and placed it between the curves of her breasts. She gazed at him so intensely, he almost looked away. Her body trembled as though she were in the throes of a fever, and her heart was racing. Cameron slowly caressed her, reveling in her warmth, her obvious excitement. So he wasn't the only one out of control. How could he have ever mistaken her for a lady? he thought, feeling both relieved and slightly disappointed. She was a woman accustomed to a man's touch, eager, hungry for it. He should have known from the first. A woman who looked like she did—as lush and enticing as summer fruit—was made for adventure and passion. Only a boy like Harry would take her for a respectable mail-order bride.

Daring to go further, he moved his hand beneath her camisole. Her heart seemed to beat even faster, feeling like thunder beneath his palm.

"It's even softer here," he whispered.

Cupping her breast, Cameron felt his own heart pound when she gave a small moan. He wasn't certain he could go as slowly as he liked. He preferred his lovemaking leisurely and creative, but being without a woman for nearly a year had left him too hungry, too desperate for release. Cameron gritted his teeth as he began to untie the laces of her camisole, stifling the urge to rip it away.

When he finally pulled the camisole off her, she leaned closer and planted a kiss on his neck. His self-control fast ebbing, he pulled her roughly to him. Her mouth was open when he pressed his lips against hers. He crushed his arms around her, delighting in the sensation of her tongue meeting his own. Cameron wasn't certain how long they kissed, or who was the most insistent; he was only aware that everything began happening at a feverish pace. She tugged off his coat while he plunged his hand into her hair, spilling out the pins that kept it bound. When that lustrous mane came tumbling down around her shoulders, he grabbed a fistful of it and breathed in its fragrance.

Even with an injured wrist, Mattie managed to pull open his shirt and run her hand over his muscled chest. Her touch inflamed him and he could barely restrain himself enough to unhook her corset. Finally he took a step back and pulled off the rest of his clothes, not saying a word as Mattie shook off her gown and petticoats. When he stood naked before her, he wondered briefly if his gaze burned as hotly as hers did. He smiled at the open desire on her face and the sight of her chest rising and falling. Panting like a mare waiting to be mounted, he thought with a thrill of triumph. *Waiting for me.*

"Come here," he said hoarsely.

Looking dazed, Mattie walked up to him. Cameron gazed

possessively at her ripe, full breasts and murmured, "I'm pleased."

He leaned down, laving one nipple and then the other, feeling her trembling against him. Cameron pressed her closer, his mouth moving over her flesh with increasing urgency and force.

Sinking to his knees, Cameron hooked his fingers around the waist of her silk drawers and slowly began to pull them down. First he exposed her smooth, flat stomach, his mouth planting hot kisses along her damp flesh.

"I didn't know it could be like this," he heard her whisper. "I didn't know."

Cameron closed his eyes to prevent himself from climaxing that very moment. Taking a deep breath, he pulled her drawers completely off and slid his hand between her legs. She was already wet, he thought excitedly, wet for him. As his fingers probed her moistness, she moaned and leaned heavily against him. With one arm wrapped about her thighs, Cameron supported her while he caressed her hidden nub with his fingers, knowing all too well how to bring a woman to ecstasy. He could feel her grow still, aware only of his insistent intimate touch. She opened her legs wider, letting out a soft moan. Her breathing grew more shallow and he was vaguely aware of her tightly clutching his shoulder. Suddenly she grabbed him so hard, he nearly flinched. A long, hoarse cry left her lips and he felt her spasm in pleasure. She was still limp from his touch, but Cameron could not give her any time to recover.

Without a word, Cameron picked Mattie up and carried her to the bed. When he tossed her down, she looked up at him with half-closed eyes. Cameron cried out as he slid himself into her hot wetness. She felt as wild and exciting as any woman he'd ever bedded. God, the pleasure she gave him, the fiery heat. Almost pulling himself out of her moist sheath, Cameron paused only to savor the satisfying thrill of slowly plunging in again . . . and again and again.

* * *

She wasn't certain how long they'd slept. The grandfather clock down the hall woke her and she counted three chimes. Cameron lay drowsing beside her, his arms moving slightly. He would be awake soon, and she didn't know whether to be pleased or nervous. But one thing she did feel in abundance was relief. Regardless of the consequences, she had kept Cameron from visiting Julia Sinclair. And that was all she wanted, wasn't it? He would be leaving for Cripple Creek at dawn; there would be no time to exchange pleasantries with Evelyn's aunt. Besides, Mattie meant to leave with him. He wouldn't dare object after what they had shared tonight. They'd made love two more times after their first explosive encounter, and the last had left them both exhausted.

Mattie ran a hand over her breasts, her nipples swollen from Cameron's fierce kisses. So this is what passion feels like, she thought in amazement. It had been delirious and frightening to be taken in such a way. And she'd responded as wantonly as any street girl, wrapping herself about him, matching his cries, his rhythm, his mounting excitement. Mattie had barely recognized herself. Her dreams of being loved by Lord Cameron had been scandalous, but not a moment of her fantasies could match the thrilling reality. Although Mattie had known she was missing something all those years with Frank, she'd had nothing with which to compare him. Little wonder Cameron was regarded as a great womanizer. Here, indeed, was a man almost worth one's reputation.

Quietly slipping out of bed, Mattie pulled on a cotton wrapper. If she was to leave in a few hours, she had to finish packing. Most of these fancy dresses would be of little use in mining country, but she had come away from the fittings she'd undergone with one treasure. Mattie patted a well-stocked sewing basket that had instantly caught her eye; the shrewd tailor had demanded two of her new silk tea gowns in exchange, but to Mattie it was worth far more than that. Now she was confident of surviving on her own. With her new sewing basket, she could ride into any town in the West and make a fine living for herself.

Trying to be as quiet as possible, Mattie had just finished folding up her cream satin gown when she felt someone watching her.

"It's an odd time to be cleaning up, isn't it?" Cameron asked in a remarkably alert voice. "The maids will do that in the morning. Come back to bed."

The sound of his voice sent a thrill through her. Not once in her marriage had she experienced this level of pleasure. She wondered if any man would ever again take her to such heights, or if she would ever have the courage to give herself with such abandon.

Mattie finished closing the horsehair trunk before turning to him. Sitting up in bed, the sheet flung carelessly over one leg, he looked too splendid to be real. His body was smoothly muscled and gracefully proportioned, just like the marble statues of Greek gods that Ward Sinclair collected. And the severity of his proud, straight profile was softened by his blue eyes and dimpled smile. Had she been Evelyn Sinclair, she would have defied every society family in New York to marry him.

"If I'm to leave for Cripple Creek this morning, I have to finish packing," she said shyly, preferring to keep a safe distance between her and the naked man on the bed.

No matter how much she might desire this English lord, it was madness to keep company with him much longer. Once they got to Cripple Creek, she could begin to earn the money that would enable her to move on. She had to get far away from the Sinclairs and anyone who knew them. Only then would she feel safe.

A frown replaced his sleepy smile. "I thought we'd discussed this last night at dinner, Mattie. Cripple Creek is no place for you."

"Neither is Colorado Springs." She began picking up his clothes, which were strewn over the bedroom floor. "Besides, that's where I'll probably find Mr. Daniels."

"I think you can drop the charade, my dear. We both

know there is no prospector waiting to marry you.''

Mattie froze. ''What do you mean? Of course there is.''

Cameron shook his head. ''You're no more a mail-order bride than I'm President Cleveland. Why don't you tell me what you're really doing here in Colorado?''

Recovering her composure, she scooped up his silk cravat before laying his clothes on the settee. ''I can't imagine what you mean. I only wish I still had Mr. Daniels's letter to show you.'' She bent over to fold his white shirt. ''You'll feel very foolish once we get to Cripple Creek and set eyes on the man himself.''

''I told you, you're not going to Cripple Creek.'' He cursed and flung the sheet aside. ''And stop fussing with my things like a bloody chambermaid.''

Mattie stiffened at his tone. Too many men in her life had made unreasonable demands, too many men had been unkind. She turned to him, hands on her hips.

''I do not need your permission to go to Cripple Creek, m'lord,'' she said sarcastically. ''Nor do I have to answer insulting questions. I don't owe you a thing.''

As soon as she said that, she wished she hadn't. Cameron's rueful chuckle made her heart sink even more.

''That's rather an odd thing to say, considering I've fed, clothed and housed you from the moment you arrived in the Springs.'' He got up and walked over to his clothes on the settee.

Mattie deliberately turned away while he dressed. ''And I've thanked you for it many times. Nevertheless, as soon as I can put aside some money, I will repay my debt.''

''I think you already have,'' he muttered.

''What does *that* mean?''

''Isn't it clear to both of us? You're down on your luck and came to the Springs, where rich men can be found behind every cottonwood tree. I'm sorry that you mistook me for a possible benefactor, but I have neither the time nor the funds to keep a mistress just now.''

''I wasn't looking for a benefactor! I told you why I came here.''

"Not that I think less of you, Mattie," he went on as if she hadn't spoken. "On the contrary, I know how difficult it is to court the wealthy, to try to win their favor and their interest. I can appreciate your single-minded purpose. I only wish you more success than I've enjoyed." He tapped her shoulder. "Only you must refine that story of yours. It won't wash with any male over the age of twenty, and rich men are a notoriously cynical lot."

"Then you must be very rich indeed." She flounced off to stand by the window. Outside, it was still dark, and a cool breeze blew through a crack.

"I was once, but England has changed, and so have my circumstances." He started to fuss with the buttons on his shirt, then gave up with a sigh. "Look, Mattie, you're right. I have no business questioning you. But after what we shared tonight, I'd rather you said nothing than continue on with these silly lies."

"They're not lies," she said dully. "I'm a mail-order bride."

"I doubt there's ever been a mail-order bride with your special skills."

Her head shot up. "What does that mean?"

He raised an eyebrow. "Not that I'm complaining, but you clearly weren't a blushing virgin, my dear."

"Oh, I see. So that must make me—"

"An adventuress," he put in quickly. "Undeniably exciting, delightful and beautiful, but an adventuress nonetheless." He gave her a penetrating look. "Do you deny that you meant to seduce me tonight?"

Mattie only stared back at him, wishing he would stop smiling so smugly.

"Of course, I should have put up more resistance. My life is not my own at the moment, and I should only be involving myself with women who ask for no more than an hour of my time and perhaps a pretty dress or two." He shrugged into his frock coat. "I thought *you* were such a woman, but it appears you mean to trail after me, hoping for more. Well, I must disappoint you, Mattie."

75

"You're wrong," she murmured.

"What did you say?"

"You're wrong," Mattie said in a louder voice. "I'm not an adventuress. I'm a widow. My husband died three years ago and—"

Cameron held up a hand. "Please, no more embarrassing tall tales. After all, neither of us can complain of being ill-treated. I've outfitted you quite nicely for your next conquest, and you ended a long dry spell of abstinence, to my great satisfaction and relief. So let's call ourselves even." He peered down at the rug. "Now have you seen my silver pocket watch anywhere?"

"I'm going to Cripple Creek," she said warningly.

He straightened and gave her an irritated look. "I can't prevent you. Just remember that I can do nothing for you after we leave here. My energies will be completely devoted to running my gold mine, and if I have the urge for a woman, I'll take myself to the Homestead." He made a step toward her, but the look on her face stopped him. "And I don't expect to be repaid for the clothes. Consider it one of the few gestures of aristocratic largess I can still afford."

"I'll pay you back, make no mistake about that," she said tartly. "And in gold coin, too."

"Of course you will," he said in a dismissive tone. "Although the less we have to do with each other in Cripple Creek, the easier it will be for both of us."

Remembering his passionate lovemaking, Mattie raised her chin and gave him a cool smile. "Don't you trust yourself around me? Or do you fear being helplessly seduced once more?"

"No, I simply would prefer not to get in the way of a blushing bride and her eager groom," He turned on his heel and marched over to the door.

Mattie took a step toward him and felt something beneath her foot. It was his silver pocket watch.

She scooped it up and held it out. "I believe this is yours, Lord Cameron."

"Keep it, my dear," he said, opening the door.

"No, please. I wouldn't want to be accused of taking more from you than I already have."

"Not at all. Let it be a reminder that I have no time to waste on opportunists—not even one as lovely as you. Good night, Miss Crawford."

The door shut an instant before Mattie hurled the watch at him, its silver workings shattering in a dozen pieces against the heavy, unyielding oak.

Chapter Five

Even though the afternoon sun shone brightly on the sagebrush and ponderosa pine, the interior of the lumbering stagecoach held little warmth. Cameron shifted uncomfortably, his right arm numb from the cramped space. He couldn't wait until the narrow-gauge railroad to Cripple Creek was completed. Until then, the last leg of the journey required being squashed into a Concord coach. And squashed was indeed the perfect description, he thought, gazing resentfully at his fellow passengers: a three-hundred-pound blacksmith, a half-drunk prospector and a tall salesman wearing a gaudy plaid jacket. And, of course, Harry and Mattie Crawford.

"Would you consider controlling your tobacco chewing, at least until we disembark?"

Cameron looked over to see Harry once again addressing the mud-stained prospector.

"As you may have noticed, there is no place for your expectorations to land but on our feet." Harry bent over with his handkerchief, attempting to wipe off his patent leather shoes. ''And if you must continue with your indelicate habit, I suggest you try aiming for the window.''

''Dang city slickers,'' the prospector muttered as he let out a spittle of juice that landed about an inch from the feet of the blacksmith sitting between him and Cameron.

''Watch yourself, old man,'' the mountainous fellow growled. ''I paid me a nice penny for these boots and I don't need no damn sourdough dirtying 'em up.''

The grizzled prospector turned an uneasy color and quickly threw his wad out the window.

''I hope you'll excuse my language, ma'am.'' The large man bowed his head apologetically in Mattie's direction. ''I forgot there was a lady on board. We see so few of them in these parts.''

Cameron nodded. ''Indeed. Once Cripple Creek's male population learns of the arrival of a lovely young woman like you, you'll be more popular than Pearl DeVere.''

Harry gave his friend a disapproving look. ''Really, old boy, I believe you forget yourself.''

''Who's Pearl DeVere?'' asked Mattie.

The blacksmith cleared his throat and leaned forward. ''No one a lady such as yourself need concern herself with.'' Crossing his arms, he sat back, deliberately elbowing the English lord in the chest.

''My apologies,'' Cameron murmured, grimacing from the jab to his ribs. He didn't know what had come over him. Raised to behave impeccably at all times regardless of the circumstances, he had just uttered the most boorish insult to a young woman—and in public, too. It was insupportable. His mother, the imposing Lady Irene, would have his head if she knew.

''Well, now you've aroused my curiosity about this scandalous creature.'' Mattie grinned impishly. ''I'll have to seek her out when I arrive in Cripple Creek and discover her secret for myself. I've quite a fondness for colorful characters.''

Cameron felt an even bigger fool as Harry and the blacksmith both sighed audibly. ''I shouldn't have said anything.

It was quite rude of me.'' He hunted for the right words. ''Pearl DeVere is a woman who—well, she manages a—''

''Tell the lady straight out, why don't you? She'll find out soon enough when she gets there. Ma'am, Pearl runs the finest sporting house in Cripple Creek.'' The prospector shook his head. ''Ain't a man in the camp who don't know that soiled dove. I reckon more gold flows through that house of hers on Myers Avenue than reaches any bank in Denver.''

''That's enough, you old coot,'' the blacksmith grumbled.

The prospector rubbed his hand across his face, muttering beneath his breath.

Harry picked a speck of dust off his twill trousers. ''I'm certain you'll never meet the woman in question, Mattie, so don't give it a second thought. The Old Homestead is in a part of town you're not likely to frequent.''

''So her establishment is called the Old Homestead, is it?'' Mattie gave Cameron a half-smile. ''That name sounds familiar. I believe a gentleman mentioned it in my presence recently.''

Cameron squirmed in his seat, remembering his angry avowal to her the night before about going to the Homestead if he had need of a woman again.

Surprisingly, the man in the plaid jacket chose that moment to join the conversation. ''Well, if he spoke of such an establishment in your presence, ma'am, then he was no gentleman.''

Mattie nodded and sighed dramatically. ''Oh, I'm afraid you're right, sir. He's clearly anything *but* a gentleman.''

A high-pitched wail startled Mattie awake.

''Calm down, little lady,'' she heard the blacksmith drawl. ''Probably just some cougar what's pounced on her dinner.''

A murmur of agreement rose up from the rest of her companions, even Cameron, who wouldn't have recognized a cougar if it were gnawing on his fancy walking cane.

Mattie peered out the window of the stagecoach. They

should be in Cripple Creek soon. She took a deep breath, inhaling the strong scent of pine. A cool wind blew against her face as she caught the dying rays of the sun striking the mountaintops.

"I trust you had a restful nap."

She started at the sound of Cameron's cultured voice across from her. "Yes, I did," she said curtly.

Mattie was not inclined to engage Cameron Lynch-Holmes in conversation. He had been unceasingly rude and insulting ever since he'd left her bed last night. After the breathtaking intimacy they'd shared, Mattie had been startled at how quickly their passion had cooled. Yet she shouldn't have been surprised. After all, there were no gentle feelings between them, no real regard. She had behaved so shamelessly only to prevent him from calling on Julia Sinclair, and as for the lusty Lord Cameron . . . well, he had simply been hungry for a woman—any woman. Still, Mattie couldn't deny that both her pride and her feelings were hurt.

She wished again that the coach were more spacious. It was difficult sitting with her knees pressed against the man who had given her so much pleasure the night before. A man whom she had been dreaming about for months, too. If only for a few wanton hours, her romantic fantasy had seemed to come true. She should have known better. Men were not sentimental or kind. Her years with Frank Laszlo had taught her that. It was easier this way, she told herself, glancing over at Harry, who was snoring loudly beside her. Let Cameron believe her an adventuress off to land a rich man. If he thought the worst of her, she'd be left alone to earn some money and then be on her way. In another month, he would have forgotten her, and she could start life under a new name far from the gold mines of Colorado.

Another wail—almost a hoarse scream—rent the air and Mattie stiffened. That was no cougar, and this time no reassuring voice spoke up to comfort her. She sat back in the coach as it took a steep turn, Harry falling against her with the movement. As soon as they righted again, the coach lurched violently to a stop; loud voices were shouting outside.

"Cussed varmints!" swore the man in the plaid jacket as he tore off his pocket watch and stuffed it into his high-laced boot. "Best hide your valuables, ma'am, and be clever about it."

"What in the world is going on?" Cameron watched curiously as the prospector tried to shove gold nuggets into the band of his hat, while the blacksmith pulled off his turquoise ring.

"We're about to be robbed," Mattie said in a matter-of-fact voice.

"Robbed?" Cameron sat forward. "Impossible. We're almost at Cripple Creek. No one would have the nerve to rob us this close to town."

Harry let out a strangled snore before his drooping head shot up. "Robbed, you say? Who's being robbed?"

As though in answer to his question, the door to the coach suddenly flew open. The flickering light of the coach lantern revealed a masked man holding a six-shooter aimed straight at them. "Everybody out with hands in the air! Come on, men. Quicker this is done, the faster you'll be on your way again!"

Huddled in the farthest corner, Mattie opened her pocketbook and stared woefully at the single greenback inside. As the other passengers climbed out, she shoved the greenback beneath her wool jacket. It was all the money she had left in the world, and she wasn't going to give it up without a fight.

"I said everybody out!"

The enormous blacksmith was having difficulty leaving the coach, which gave Mattie time to realize that Harry and Cameron were probably carrying far more than one greenback on them.

"Hurry, you two," she whispered urgently. "Give me your money and I'll try to hide it. But not everything. They'll think it too suspicious if fancy slickers like you aren't carrying valuables."

Wide-eyed with alarm, Harry pulled out a money pouch and pressed it into her hands. She counted out five gold pieces and gave them back to the nervous young man. Swiftly unbuttoning her jacket and blouse, she shoved the pouch down between her corset and camisole.

"Yours too," she hissed at Cameron.

"Absolutely not. You must be mad." He sat back, wearing an agitated expression. Mattie only then realized that a good deal of her bosom was on display.

"Suit yourself. I only warn you that you'll arrive in Cripple Creek without a dime." Giving a shrug, she proceeded to cover herself up, adjusting her jacket so as to conceal the slight bulge of gold beneath the wool.

Cameron grabbed her shoulder and yanked her toward him. "Give Harry back his money right this minute. If these ruffians discover you're trying to cheat them, you'll be shot."

"He's right," Harry agreed. "You mustn't endanger yourself just for a few gold pieces."

"What nonsense. Haven't you two ever been in a stage that was held up?" Mattie was genuinely surprised at their alarm. Stages were always being waylaid in these mountains, especially going to or from a mining camp. One of her earliest memories was traveling to New Mexico on a stage that was held up by a lone gunman who wore gleaming silver spurs. She'd found the whole thing quite exciting, but then she'd been only six.

The blacksmith had nearly completed his laborious exit, and Mattie thought it wise if she got out next. Brushing Cameron aside, she gave him a warning look. "Now don't play the hero. Just keep your head and do what they say. These are thieves, not killers."

Cameron swore under his breath. "You naive little fool. What do you know of either thieves or murderers?"

Giving a last pat to the money under her bodice, Mattie only shook her head. *I could tell you a great deal about violence and deceit,* she thought bitterly, remembering her terrible year in prison. Instead she took a deep breath and stepped to the door, ignoring Cameron and Harry's frantic whispers.

An appreciative whistle greeted her appearance. The robber standing before her shoved his pistol into his holster and said softly, "Ain't that the prettiest hair I ever seen."

Before she could respond, Mattie found herself lifted into the air by the masked man, who swung her to the ground with a flourish. With her hands still pressed against the coins hidden in her bodice, she could only stand helpless within his grasp.

"Looks like we got a pearl among all this swine," he announced to the others, his hands boldly clamped about her waist.

"Well, see if she's got any real pearls on her," another thief shouted back.

Mattie glanced over at the other three masked men, who were brusquely ordering her fellow passengers to empty their pockets. The sounds of coin and jewelry being dropped into an open satchel filled the air.

Mattie looked up at the man who held her, her gaze unblinking. She could easily have pulled the black bandanna from his face. Instead she gave a small smile, nonplussed at the sight of gray eyes that seemed to glitter like cold quartz in a mountain stream.

"I'll thank you to take your hands off me," she said quietly.

The thief chuckled and leaned closer. Even through the bandanna, she could feel his breath, warm and smelling of tobacco.

"You're holding me too tightly." She fluttered her lashes. "You're very strong, you know."

If she dared to flirt with him, he might become too distracted to search her person. Mercifully, his grip loosened, and he leaned back, letting his gaze roam lustfully over her body. Of course, if she was too provocative, he might end up enjoying far more than the gold pieces hidden beneath her jacket.

"There ain't too many men as strong as me." His hands

began to caress her back. "Strong as a bull, my mama used to say."

Mattie put on her most helpless expression. "I'm sure your mother taught you to be gentle with those lacking your strength." She blinked furiously, hoping to bring tears to her eyes. "And to protect young women who might fear such strength."

"So I scare you, do I?" She could feel the young man straighten up, as though preening himself. "Well, don't worry, pretty lady. Even if I am set on robbing this stage, I ain't going to harm a hair on your—"

"Release Miss Crawford this minute!"

With a sinking heart, Mattie recognized Cameron's haughty tones.

"What in tarnation have we here?" the robber muttered, turning his attention to the blond gentleman jumping down from the coach.

A moment later, Harry's head popped out, and Mattie sighed as he too demanded, "Unhand that young woman!"

The robber holding Mattie only laughed. "Neither of you boys got any call to be giving orders around here. Just put your hands up and keep your mouths shut."

Ignoring the warning, Cameron strode up to them and foolishly pulled Mattie out of his grasp. She tried to get between the two men, but the thief was too fast. The masked man whipped out his six-shooter and cocked it ominously.

"I told you not to play the hero," Mattie said with mingled anger and frustration.

"I won't have him manhandling you. Now be still." Cameron stared back defiantly at the man holding the gun. "If you insist on being a bully, then direct your attentions to me or one of the other men. I won't have you laying your disgusting hands on Miss Crawford."

"You're awful close to getting those blue eyes shot out, pretty boy." With his free hand, the masked man pulled Mattie to his side once more.

Cameron made a move toward them, and a shot rang out

at his feet. Shouting in alarm, Harry ran over to stand by his friend's side.

"Don't do another thing, please!" Despite her exasperation, Mattie couldn't help admiring the way Cameron stood there, immobile and expressionless, as though disdainful of the loaded gun pointed at him. She glanced over at the thief, whose index finger was stroking the trigger. If Cameron persisted in this foolish gallantry, he could wind up dead. "Just keep quiet, Cameron. You're making everything worse."

"That's right, listen to the lady." He cocked his head at Mattie. "This your wife or something?"

"Absolutely not," she answered quickly. "I only met this gentleman two days ago while staying in the Springs."

"Well, he sure is acting like you belong to him."

"He's—he's an Englishman," she stammered. "The English have funny ideas about women. They're very polite."

The masked man seemed to seriously consider this nonsensical statement. "Someone should tell him he ain't in England no more."

"Yeah, lookit them fancy duds," one of the other robbers hooted. "I never seen a man wear shoes like that."

Indeed, Mattie had to agree that Cameron's white oxfords were woefully out of place, as were his striped socks, white flannel trousers and dark blazer. Harry only accentuated their tenderfoot status by sporting a green velour fedora. It was a wonder these two had survived even a month in a rough mining district like Cripple Creek.

"They're both concerned that I might be hurt. I tried to tell them that women and children are treated gently by men in the West, even by the wildest desperadoes." Mattie attempted to soften this comment with a demure smile.

"That sure is the truth, miss." Surprisingly he released her arm, even bowing his head, although she suspected he meant to mock her. "Not many ladies travel these hills."

His shrewd glance swept over her, taking in her expensive lilac outfit and ribboned hat. In this store-bought getup, she knew she looked like the daughter of a bonanza king. The coins shoved beneath her bodice slipped slightly, and she squirmed at the thought of being searched.

Mattie opened her mouth to speak but stopped as the man took a step closer. She heard Cameron mutter under his breath. Despite her outspoken certainty that she wouldn't be harmed, she grew uneasy. Still, she dared not move for fear of jarring loose the hidden coins.

"Well, what's the pretty redhead got?" One of the other robbers shouted over at them. "Someone dressed so fancy got to be carrying more than her hatbox."

The masked man nodded. "Sorry to hurry our conversation, miss, but I got a job to do."

"I'm afraid you're wasting your time." She wished his cap wasn't pulled so far down over his face. The lantern hanging from his belt only revealed his steely eyes. "I don't have anything you want."

"I don't know about that." He raised his hand and brushed one finger against her cheek. "There's a couple of things I'd sure like to take from you, Red. Like that soft pretty jacket of yours." His hand snaked down to her neck. "Maybe see if you're hiding anything valuable."

Mattie held her breath as he slowly moved his hand lower. If he got any closer, Mattie was certain she could get the gun from him. As if he read her thoughts, the robber moved nearer, his body pressed against hers. Out of the corner of her eye, Mattie could see the six-shooter dangling loosely in his other hand.

"This certainly feels pretty valuable to me," he breathed hotly as he cupped her breast and squeezed it.

"Damn you, get away from her!" shouted Cameron as he suddenly lunged at them.

A gunshot went off as both men hit the ground, wrestling and cursing in the dirt. The fight lasted no longer than the blink of an eye before the other thieves raced over and quickly pulled Cameron to his feet. To Mattie's horror, they began pummeling him with their fists, one of them wielding the butt of his gun.

"No, please, don't hurt him!" she cried as they flung a

half-conscious Cameron against the stagecoach.

The masked man he'd attacked lay sprawled on the ground at her feet, his bandanna askew, though it still concealed most of his face. While he shook his head as if in a daze, Mattie suddenly spied his revolver lying a few inches away. She grabbed for it an instant before he did. Cocking it expertly, she straightened up and aimed it right for him.

"Leave him alone!" she shouted to the men beating Cameron. "Or I'll shoot the ears and nose off this one."

"Git that damn gun away from her," someone shouted.

Mattie pulled the trigger. Her bullet grazed the outstretched hand of the robber on the ground. He cursed violently. "And I thought you were a lady," he muttered.

"So I am. And a lady doesn't appreciate watching an unarmed man getting beaten to a pulp." She gestured to the three thieves clustered around Cameron. "Back off now. You lay one more blow and your friend will find himself in a sorry way."

In the light from the coach lantern, she could discern both their angry expressions and their uncertainly. Except for the fellow who had pistol-whipped Cameron, the others still had their guns in their holsters. She swallowed hard as one of the thieves started inching his hand toward his revolver. Mattie was afraid her bravado wouldn't sustain an actual showdown with an outlaw. Her father had taught her to be a crack shot, but she hadn't handled a gun in years. She heard someone move to her side, relieved to see it was the bearlike blacksmith.

"Drop it, mister," she yelled at the armed man. "Throw the gun over this way, or you'll be making a pine box for your friend."

"Do what she says!" shouted the man at her feet.

After a round of muttering, the three thieves finally let Cameron go. As he slumped to the ground, one of the fellows tossed over his revolver. It landed about a yard away from Harry, who made a clumsy grab for it.

"Give the gun to this gentleman here, Harry," Mattie said quickly. An armed Harry Tremont was a frightening prospect. Only when the blacksmith had the revolver in his hands did Mattie begin to relax.

"All right, everyone else throw down your guns as well," the blacksmith boomed out.

The stagecoach driver and the prospector scurried over to retrieve the remaining weapons. "Dang, this is better than a Saturday night in Nolon's gambling saloon," the old man cackled.

"Move away from the gentleman," she ordered. Muttering threats, the three robbers reluctantly moved off to the side. "Harry, see to Lord Cameron."

"I'm fine, damn it." Waving off Harry's hand, Cameron pulled himself to his feet. His knees were wobbly and his face streaked with blood, but he didn't seem as hurt as she'd feared. Blood suddenly gushed from his nose.

"Harry, take him inside the coach and try to stop that bleeding." It's his pride that has been done the real injury, she told herself as Harry helped an unsteady Cameron into the stage. Well, if he'd kept his head, none of this mess would have happened.

"You're a mighty spirited woman, Miss Crawford."

She glanced over at the blacksmith. "Having a man as strong as you beside me definitely lifts my spirits, Mr.—"

"Roy MacDuff, ma'am."

Mattie permitted herself a small grin. "I should have guessed you were a fellow Scot."

The robber at her feet made a sudden move and she cocked her revolver. "That wouldn't be wise, sir. Now why don't you join your friends over there and be on your way."

Pushing himself to his feet, he slapped the dirt off his pants. "Best keep your skirts in Cripple Creek, Miss Crawford. We catch you on another stage and you're going to be giving us a lot more than gold coin or a bracelet."

"Don't be threatening her, you filthy cur," Roy said sharply, "or we'll be having a little wrestling match of our own."

Mattie and Roy kept their eyes trained on the four outlaws until they had all ridden off into the night. With a sigh, she finally lowered her gun. "I'd hoped for a quieter arrival in Cripple Creek."

The blacksmith looked over at her with a worried expression. "I fear you've made some dangerous enemies."

She looked down at the revolver, which suddenly seemed so large, cold and lethal. "It won't be the first time."

Cameron felt mortified as the lights at the mines came into view no more than twenty minutes after they reboarded the stage. To think they'd been so close to the outlying tarpaper shacks and tents of Cripple Creek. He crumpled a blood-soaked handkerchief in his fist. Bad enough he'd been beaten in front of Mattie, but far worse was the sight of this lovely young woman aiming a six-shooter at a band of outlaws. He'd never seen any female with that much courage, and damned few men either. The humiliation of it all. To think that just last night he had taken her so manfully, and today she had rescued him as though he were a schoolboy being taunted by toughs. He would never be able to look her in the face again.

"We're almost there, Cameron," she said in a soothing voice. He grimaced and bit back a reply.

"That's right, old man. Soon as we arrive, I'll hunt around for a doctor."

"Harry, I'm fine. Please don't fuss over me like a mother hen." He took a deep breath. "You too, Mattie. You're both carrying on in a most embarrassing manner."

"Well, them boys were whupping you pretty good," piped up the prospector. "I wouldn't be surprised if that nose of yours was broken. Can you wriggle it, or does it feel like it's been whacked with a shovel?"

"Keep quiet," Roy muttered.

"It doesn't seem broken." Mattie gently touched his nose and Cameron flinched. "I'm more concerned that you might have a cracked rib or maybe a sprain."

Cameron was grateful for the darkness in the coach. It concealed the shame on his face. It was humiliating that Mattie had defended him so ably with a sprained wrist of her own. Even worse was the realization that this was all due to a display of stupid jealousy on his part. Why had he gotten upset to see her being touched by that damn outlaw? Had he lost his mind? She was nothing to him. In fact, he had no intention of ever seeing her again. Still, now that she'd rescued him, he couldn't treat her dismissively, even if she were an adventuress.

"Mattie, I—I want to thank you again for what you did," he stammered awkwardly. He was unaccustomed to making apologies. "Not that I think it was a wise or necessary thing to do, but I must acknowledge your bravery. Most commendable."

"Dang right. Scaring off those gunmen got us our gold back." The prospector leaned over and tapped her on the knee. "Here's a gold nugget for your trouble, ma'am. Now don't protest. I got me a bucket of 'em jest sitting in my tent."

"Please, I can't accept this." She waved off the other passengers' offers to pay her as well. "Save it for your next stagecoach trip. You'll probably need it."

Cameron cleared his throat. "As these gentlemen have said, by disrupting the robbery, you saved all our valuables. I am clearly in your debt, Mattie."

"And I in yours."

"Then let us consider both debts amply repaid."

"If you insist." Although he couldn't read her expression, he suspected she was smiling.

As the coach lumbered across the flats, Cameron wondered if he'd judged her too harshly. Perhaps she wasn't quite the opportunist he'd suspected. Maybe last night's passion had surprised her as much as it had him. Earlier, when she'd explained her circumstances to their fellow passengers, the men seemed to accept her story of being a mail-order bride. If Mr. Jack Daniels did indeed ever turn up, Cameron would be eating crow for a week. By the time the stagecoach lurched to a stop in the middle of Cripple Creek, he had almost convinced himself that Mattie Crawford was a respectable young lady.

Even before the driver opened the door, the men in the street were yelling out a familiar chorus of "Welcome to Cripple Creek, tenderfeet", and "Hello, suckers!" To add to the din, random gunshots sent every stray dog into a frenzy of barking.

Cameron turned to Mattie. "Pay no attention to the men out there. They set up the same commotion any time a stage rolls into town."

"Oh, it doesn't bother me at all," she said pertly, alighting from the coach without a backward glance.

By the time their baggage was unloaded, Cameron had nearly lost sight of her among all the shouting men, most of them drunk. He saw her bid farewell to the blacksmith before waving good-bye to the old coot of a prospector. Cameron pushed his way through the men rudely questioning him about his bloody clothes and bruised face.

"Excuse me, excuse me," he said abruptly, trying to make his way toward Mattie.

She was deep in conversation with the stagecoach driver, who nodded once before pointing down the street. Cameron couldn't imagine what he was indicating. He came closer and heard Mattie's closing words, "Thank you so much for arranging to deliver my trunk."

"Least I can do, ma'am. I had near twenty dollars on me today. Waving that gun the way you did kept it out of the hands of those dirty skunks."

He waited until the driver left before tapping her on the shoulder. As soon as she turned to face him, he could see that far from being alarmed by the rowdy atmosphere, she seemed excited by it.

"Quite a change from Colorado Springs, I fear."

"It reminds me of Leadville when silver was flowing out of the mountains," she said happily. "Some things never change." Mattie picked up a large basket that he'd noticed earlier. "I know that Harry will take good care of you, so I'll make my farewells now."

"I don't know where in the world you imagine you can go at this time of night." He pointed to the Continental

Hotel behind them. "Let me get a room for you here, and tomorrow I'll ask around about a decent boardinghouse."

"Thank you, but no. I've taken more than enough charity from you already. Anyway, I have other plans, and the driver is having a boy take my trunk up the street."

"I fear you've been misinformed about Cripple Creek. There is nowhere else you could possibly stay on Myers Avenue."

Mattie smiled. "Of course there is."

"Where you want your things taken, miss?" A tall skinny boy in dirty denims stood before them.

"The Old Homestead, please."

Cameron nearly choked.

The boy grinned and said, "Should have guessed."

"Mattie, you can't be serious. I thought you understood what sort of establishment the Old Homestead is."

"Oh, I do. Perfectly." She took his hand and gave it a firm shake. "Good luck with your gold mine. I wish you Godspeed and good fortune."

"No, wait. See here, I can't have you going to a place like that."

Mattie pulled her hand out of his firm grasp. "As you told me early this morning, you have better things to do than waste your time on opportunists like me."

He frowned. "If you're playing games, Mattie, this is a most dangerous one."

"I don't play games, Cameron, but if I did, it would only be a game I was sure of winning." Mattie stared after the skinny boy dragging her trunk. "I'd best be off before I lose that set of bags as well."

A long moment later, Harry came bounding out of the hotel. "Well, I've got a room for our brave Miss Crawford, and they're sending for one of the camp doctors." The young man scanned the shouting, drunken crowd. "Where *is* Mattie?"

Cameron couldn't bring himself to answer. Instead he kept his eyes trained on the red-haired woman walking so confidently toward Cripple Creek's most celebrated brothel.

Chapter Six

The prostitute glared at herself in the mirror. "I don't like it," she said, stamping her foot. "Bad enough you got me covered up like a parson's wife, but only city brats wear pink."

Her mouth filled with pins, Mattie merely continued her hemming.

"Ain't a whore in the world who would sashay around in this. All these little buttons down the back. How's a gent supposed to get this off before his hour is up?"

"Be still, Hester," Mattie muttered. Another minute and she would be done.

The Old Homestead boasted ten sporting ladies, each with remarkably poor fashion sense, but Hester Lowell was the worst offender. Not even in New York's Tenderloin District had Mattie seen a female so fond of rouge pots and gaudy colors. Garbed now in soft pink tulle with a fresh-scrubbed face and dark wavy hair spilling over her slender shoulders, Hester finally looked like the sixteen-year-old girl she was. Mattie only wished she were altering the dress for a coming-out party, rather than a long night in a Cripple Creek brothel.

The door behind them opened, bringing in a heady fragrance of gardenias. Hester spun around, whipping the skirt out of Mattie's hands.

"Miss DeVere, tell her this gown is all wrong. I need me something with sparkles, something in red or black." She flicked the diagonal row of white silk roses running along the front of the bodice. "And why does she have to put these fancy flowers on it? I ain't going to no dinner party in Denver."

"Stop complaining, Hester. After all, you're not working in a Poverty Gulch crib anymore." Pearl DeVere nodded approvingly at the pink tulle gown. "I'm most impressed, Mattie. She looks far more elegant than me; people will take *her* for the mistress of this establishment."

Both Mattie and Pearl smiled at that obvious exaggeration. It would take more than a tasteful dress to turn any of the Old Homestead's denizens into even a pale imitation of their stylish young madam. Despite the torpor of late afternoon, Pearl looked as crisp and turned-out as a Fifth Avenue matron. The only clue to Pearl's less than respectable status was her obviously dyed hair. It was a harsh, dull red compared to Mattie's natural auburn tresses. Still, in a district like Cripple Creek, Pearl managed to outshine even the most prosperous mine owner's wife.

Mattie slowly got to her feet. "I wish I could take credit for the dress, Pearl, but all I did was remove some of the trimming and shorten it."

Hester's young face screwed up into a terrible scowl. "I won't get me no customers rigged out like this, Miss DeVere. Mebbe *you* can get away looking all elegant and ladylike, but not me."

Pearl sighed and sank into the chaise longue by the window. "If all I offered in my house were common whores, the men in town might just as well visit the Myers cribs every night, and for far less money." She idly stroked her pearl necklace. "No, Hester, my girls must look as expensive as the Baccarat chandeliers in my parlor. That's why

I've hired a real lady to costume the lot of you.''

Mattie cocked an amused eyebrow. "Luckily, I came equipped with a nice new wardrobe of my own. But until a greater variety of dry goods becomes available, I fear there's nothing more I can do now aside from mending. I suppose I could turn my hand to sewing for the miners.''

"You can't be serious. In your line of work the profit comes from catering to women. Where else in Cripple Creek are you going to find a female with gold enough to hire a seamstress?''

It was a sentiment with which Mattie reluctantly agreed. Mining towns were not without hardworking wives and daughters, but these respectable ladies were usually forced to make do with homespun calico and a woolen shawl. The occasional mine owner's wife took herself off to Denver or the Springs to replenish her wardrobe, so the only clientele for a dressmaker resided in brothels, saloons and cribs. That was why Mattie had headed straight for the Old Homestead when she arrived.

"Don't look so worried," Pearl added. "You won't be idle for long. The second day you were here, I sent off to Denver for material.''

"Do I got to wear this tonight?" Hester cast a chagrined look at the mirror.

"Yes, you do. And every night hereafter. Now go down-stairs for lunch. And best hurry, or Delilah will eat up the last of the cherry cobbler.''

With amusing speed, Hester stripped off the dress and ran like a hungry child out of the room, slamming the door behind her.

Pearl let out an exasperated groan. "If only I could manage to clean up those manners of hers. I've actually caught her eating aspic of foie gras with her fingers.''

"She's so young, Pearl," Mattie said, disapproval evident in her voice. "Not until I saw her with a clean face and wearing a pretty pink dress did I realize just *how* young.''

"I'm hardly the one who corrupted her. She spent two years in cribs all over the district.''

The younger inmates of the Tombs flashed before Mattie's eyes, some of them little more than children. "It's terrible to think of a fourteen-year-old selling herself like that."

Pearl's lovely face took on a hardened expression. "I was thirteen when I left home and began to make my way in the world. And I wasn't so fortunate as to find a place like the Old Homestead either."

Hearing the bitterness in her voice, Mattie felt a sudden affinity for the poised but cynical madam. They were too young to be without hope or dreams. Mattie had been barely sixteen herself when she'd married Frank Laszlo and had both her illusions and her innocence shattered. What business was it of hers how Pearl or Hester or any of the girls lived their lives? She knew nothing of the forces that had driven them to this dirty mining town in the Rockies, any more than they guessed what had brought her here.

"I was wondering if business had suffered due to the miners' strike." Shaking out the pink tulle dress, Mattie tried to keep her voice casual. "With the men out of work for four months, some of them must have stayed away. Or were most of your customers loyal?"

Mattie hoped she wasn't being too obvious, but she couldn't rein in her curiosity any longer. It had taken great self-control these past two weeks to keep from inquiring about Cameron Lynch-Holmes.

"Business is always good," Pearl said with a smile. "The strike gave the fine gentlemen even more time to amuse themselves, although I'm as grateful as anyone that the men are back to work again."

As though to reinforce her remark, the four o'clock mine whistle pierced the air.

Mattie knew she should let the matter drop, but she had a perverse desire to say his name and hear him spoken of in return.

"On the stage up here, I traveled with an English lord and his friend. I was wondering if you knew of them. Lord Cameron Lynch-Holmes and Harry Tremont."

A low laugh was Pearl's only response.

Mattie whirled around, disconcerted to see her so openly amused. "I just assumed they had visited your house."

"Not yet, but they could be tempted now. Maybe not the rich man's son, but I'd bet a crate of Mumm's champagne that the English lord will make an appearance soon."

"Why do you say that?" Mattie asked a bit too quickly.

"To see you, of course." Pearl shook her head at Mattie's stunned expression. "If you hadn't been so busy these past two weeks sewing in this room, you'd know that all of Cripple Creek is talking about the beautiful redhead who chased off a gang of stagecoach robbers."

Mattie plopped down on a nearby ottoman. "This is so embarrassing."

"The whole town knows every last detail of the robbery—even the ones that are probably false—but what rings through clearly is that the handsome Lord Cameron got beaten up because he couldn't bear to see the outlaws lay even one finger on you. And you—fiery wildcat that you've been painted—you apparently turned a gun on twelve hulking brutes."

She sighed. "It was only four."

"In some versions it's close to twenty, with a gang of renegade Paiutes thrown in for good measure. Anyway, you and Lord Cameron have become local heroes. Sort of like Cripple Creek's version of Calamity Jane and Wild Bill Hickok."

"How terrible."

"I don't see why. You say you're looking for this Jack Daniels fellow to marry. Well, there's not a man in the district who hasn't heard of you now, and probably far beyond. I wouldn't be surprised if they're telling stories about you clear off in Grand Junction."

Good lord, this was perfectly awful. She was trying to hide herself away in these mountains, not become a Wild West legend. With the trail she'd left behind, a blind man would be able to track her down.

"The tale of your stagecoach rescue was too good not to

spread around. You'd probably have to go all the way to Texas to outrun it." Pearl got up gracefully from the chaise longue, fluffing out the velvet bow atop her bustle. "Besides, you don't want to leave before your dashing English lord comes asking for you."

"*My* English lord?" Mattie replied sharply. "What a ridiculous thing to say. I have no interest in him at all."

Pearl shrugged. "Suit yourself, but I certainly wouldn't mind entertaining him, maybe even for free. I haven't seen a man who looked that good since I tumbled in the hay with a green-eyed actor from Duluth." She shot Mattie a shrewd look. "As I said, he's never visited the Old Homestead, so if he makes an appearance now, it can only be because of you."

"I've come here to marry Mr. Daniels." Mattie was bone weary of her mail-order bride charade, but it was far too late to discard the story now.

Pearl shook her head, her face suddenly looking much older than her twenty-eight years. "To think that pretty city slicker risked his life defending you. My, my, where would I be now if I'd ever met a fellow like that?"

Mattie sat back, thinking furiously. "How long before that material arrives from Denver?"

"It should be coming any day now."

"I could stay until I finished just a few more dresses, but then I'll have to move on." She caught Pearl's suspicious glance. "Oh, not too far, in case Mr. Daniels arrives. Maybe just over the hill to Victor. After all, I can't imagine he'll be pleased to find his future bride in the Old Homestead. I've already stayed here too long."

"What are you running away from, Mattie?" Pearl stood by the window, her arms crossed in front of her. "Don't deny it. You're running, and running scared, too. Every girl in my house has an unpleasant reason for being here, and you're no different." She shook her head. "Staying cooped up in this room. Why, you haven't even set foot out of this house since you got here. Is there someone after you? A jealous lover maybe? It's more than just idle curiosity. If I didn't like you, I'd let you spin all the tall tales you want, but if you're in trouble—''

"I'm not!"

"The more I know," she went on, "the easier it will be to help you."

Mattie was briefly tempted to confide in Pearl; beneath the young madam's polished cynicism, there was a deep sadness and a corresponding compassion. She must have seen far worse times than Mattie. What good would it do to add yet another tale of fear and desperation to Pearl's troubled life? Besides, telling Pearl the truth would only open her to charges of harboring a fugitive. The less anyone knew, the better.

"I'm a mail-order bride sewing for her keep until Jack Daniels shows up," she said quietly.

Pearl looked hurt for an instant, but just as quickly recovered her usual demeanor. "Fine then. If I see your Mr. Daniels slobbering over one of my girls some night, I'll send for you straightaway."

"Don't be angry, Pearl. You've already helped by hiring me to sew. I need the money desperately."

Pearl swished over to the door, and then paused with one elegant hand poised on the doorknob. "If you'd come downstairs, I guarantee you'll make more gold in one night than you've made in two weeks with your needle."

With a sigh, Mattie shook her head. It wasn't the first time Pearl had made the suggestion.

"The men know the famous redhead from the stagecoach robbery is here. Not a night goes by that a half-dozen fellows don't ask for you. You could probably set your own price—with forty percent going to me, of course."

"Sorry. I just can't."

Pearl yanked open the door, letting in the sounds of clattering dishes and high-pitched feminine voices.

"Then you're not as desperate for money as you claim," Pearl said with quiet bitterness. "Women who seek shelter in a whorehouse usually have nowhere else to turn. Every female in the Old Homestead has her back against the wall—even me. I guess I was wrong about you, Mattie. You're not like us, after all.''

The door clicked softly behind her.

Mattie felt a sharp pang of guilt. Images of her humiliating year in prison, her flight from the law, and her shameless seduction of Cameron Lynch-Holmes flooded into her mind.

''You're right about that, Pearl,'' she murmured. ''I'm not like you at all. I'm much worse.''

The marshal leaned back in his chair, his feet propped up on the cluttered desk before him. ''I don't hold with hunting down young ladies.''

''She is *not* a lady, Marshal Lee. I thought I made myself clear.'' Devlin cast a scornful glance around the office. The walls were plastered with wanted posters, out-of-date calendars and a faded photograph of Lillie Langtry. ''And if she is in Denver or Colorado Springs, surely the authorities would wish to see her taken into custody.''

''What do I care about a woman who made off with a pretty necklace back in New York? I got bigger fish to fry. We got a gang of stagecoach robbers stirring things up and a mine owner who's already rounded up vigilantes to kill 'em.''

''Then you can leave the robbers to the lynch mob and turn your attention to tracking down Miss Crawford—although I'm sure she's assumed an alias by now.''

The marshal tapped the toes of his shiny black boots. His weathered face was impossible to read. ''Out here, we always have more on our plate than I would expect an Easterner to understand.''

Devlin sighed. His flannel jacket felt stifling in this cramped office, while he himself felt stifled by his own lack of authority. ''As a member of the New York Police Department for twenty years, I can sympathize. We probably have more murders in one week than you see in a year.''

''That might be, but I got horse thieves, cattle rustlers, Injun killers and stagecoach robbers to chase after, as well as the usual vermin that come to a big city.''

Devlin had to restrain a contemptuous laugh. Denver could be described as many things, but a big city wasn't one of them. "I'm only asking for a little assistance in tracking her down. If you could simply spare a man or two. I'm not familiar with Colorado, and without someone who knows the area I may never find her."

Reaching for the tin cup on his desk, Marshal Lee took a long swig of coffee. Despite the morning heat and Devlin's obvious discomfort, he hadn't offered him anything to drink. "I'd be loco to waste any of my men's time on chasing some petty thief from New York. If she'd stolen a herd of Longhorn or held up the Denver-Pacific, then I'd see about making a fuss. But running off with a little necklace? You Eastern boys in blue don't seem to have the sense God gave you. Besides, how do you even know she's here?"

"Because, unlike you, I take my job seriously," he said in a cutting voice, indifferent to the anger that appeared on the marshal's face. This lazy bastard wasn't going to help him anyway. At least Devlin would have the satisfaction of insulting the oaf. "I've done nothing else since she escaped but scour New York for anyone who might have caught a glimpse of her that night. I know she got on a train bound for Colorado."

"People have been known to just disappear in these mountains. Especially now, with a gold rush on. Every con man, crook and liar hightails himself off to a mining camp. Best place in the world to get lost." The marshal narrowed his eyes in Devlin's direction, his dislike plain. "Sorry, I've got more for my men to do than go nosing around after a filly that took a liking to a bauble. And I'm thinking of running for office next year. It wouldn't help my reputation to be hunting down a helpless female."

Devlin stood up abruptly. "I can only warn you, Marshal Lee, that if the law will not work with me in apprehending this fugitive, I will be forced to work outside the law."

"Is that a threat, Mr. Devlin?" His tanned face crinkled in an icy smile.

"Detective Devlin, if you please." He kept his face impassive, hoping this irritating fellow would not wire New York. He'd be turned out of town if the marshal discovered he'd retired from the force two weeks before. "Not at all, but like those vigilantes, I thirst for justice at any cost."

"I've been tempted to cross the line myself when pursuing a lawbreaker, but they were always cold-blooded killers. You sure this woman you're after hasn't done more than steal a necklace? Maybe she dynamited some Wall Street bank or tried to kill the president." Lee took another noisy sip of coffee, and then grinned. "Or maybe she did something even worse. Like break your heart."

"I'm glad you're amused, Marshal. Perhaps you won't think it's so funny when she begins stealing from the rich folks you've got crawling around Denver and the Springs."

He shrugged. "If that happens, I'll look you up. Until then, I wouldn't mind seeing your back, and that's a fact."

Snatching up his derby, Devlin gave him a curt nod. "Thank you so much for all your help, Marshal. I'm certain that with the ambition and sense of duty you've displayed today, you'll go far in this state."

"Just see that *you* don't." Marshal Lee swept his feet off the desk and leaned forward. "I may not get riled about some poor servant girl who ran off with a necklace, but if I find you taking the law into your own hands, Devlin, I'll show you just how harsh Western justice can be."

"Of course. I wouldn't expect anything else." Devlin paused, thinking of Mattie's flight across the rooftops of New York, escaping him once again. But not for long. "Justice is always harsh—especially mine."

Chapter Seven

Mattie stabbed the needle so sharply into the material, it glanced off her thimble and pierced her finger.

"That's what you get for hiding in a whorehouse," she mumbled. Not that it had done her any good.

A buckboard rattled by, and she leaned out the window.

"Rags . . . sacks . . . bottles!"

It was only the junkman. Mattie chided herself for thinking that Lord Cameron would ride up in a lowly buckboard. Indeed, why would he bother to ride up at all? He clearly didn't want to see her again, not after she'd gone off to work in a bawdy house. If only he knew how dull her life was at Cripple Creek's most famous brothel. The days went by without incident at the Old Homestead; the girls got up long past noon, and Mattie was left in peace to sew and mend.

But at night she couldn't think straight. What would she do if one night she heard Cameron's cultured voice out on the landing? Mattie didn't think she could bear to listen to him enjoy himself with one of Pearl's girls—Hester, perhaps, or graceful Verena—not after she'd experienced herself just how demanding and magnificent he was in bed. Sometimes she thought she must have imagined their wordless but urgent lovemaking.

Mattie flung aside the petticoat she was mending and turned once more to the open window. Even with the dust churned up below, the twilit summer air felt good against her face. She had half a mind to put on a straw hat and go sauntering through the streets, losing herself in the brash noise and activity.

At that moment, however, someone knocked on her door five times in rapid succession. Groaning inwardly, she looked about for something to throw.

"Are you in there, my pretty?" Another five knocks accompanied the man's thick Cornish accent.

"You have the wrong room," she called back in exasperation.

Every night—sometimes twice a night—this same Cornish miner came rapping at her door, mistaking her for a whore named Lil.

"Now don't you be trying that on me again, my lovely." The door flew open and Mattie frowned at the ruddy man's reflection in the mirror. "Don't you know I've been saving up all me gold for just another kiss? Sure you do, my Lil."

With an audible sigh, Mattie turned to face the stocky young man.

Dressed in a faded shirt and jacket, the unsteady Cornishman held out a bag. "It's gold dust, to be sure. As much as you want, it's all for the asking, if you'll only be letting me wriggle between your legs again."

"Will you please go?" she said loudly, hoping there was someone in the hall to take him off her hands. Unfortunately, all she could see was the hand-painted wallpaper and flickering gaslights. Pearl's strong man downstairs would have to be summoned.

He took a halting step inside, his nose red from drinking and his breath stinking of beer. Most of Pearl's customers were well-dressed fellows with at least a smattering of manners, but occasionally a rough prospector or miner would turn up, bearing an irresistible amount of gold. This Cornishman's shabby pockets were apparently very well lined.

"I need you, Dan!" she called.

"Come now, my pretty. You remember how you favored old Johnny here, riding me cock like a prize mare. Sure you do." He began pulling off his jacket with one hand, flinging his bag of gold dust at her with the other.

"Stop right now. I am not Lil and I have no intention of even shaking your hand, let alone riding you." Mattie pointed toward the door. "Now get out before I call Big Dan."

"You don't mean that, Lil. Come now, come see what Johnny has waiting for you." He made a move to unbutton his pants.

Mattie threw her hairbrush at his head. It bounced off his temple, but he barely flinched.

"Dan!"

"Come, my pretty. We're wasting time, we are." His pants dropped to his ankles and Mattie's eyes widened. He wore nothing underneath. He lurched forward and grabbed her by the waist.

As he bent over to nuzzle her neck, Mattie shoved him away. With his trousers around his ankles, he couldn't keep his balance. Unfortunately, his grip on her waist was like steel and Mattie fell with him.

As they landed in a heap on the floor, Mattie heard her blouse rip. "You stupid, drunken lout! That's the only shirtwaist I have left."

"All right, Johnny, you've had your fun for tonight. Leave the lady alone."

With giddy relief, Mattie saw Big Dan's bushy yellow eyebrows come into view just as he hauled the Cornishman off her. Next to the tall, burly strongman, Johnny looked comically puny, like a rag doll he'd just picked up off the floor.

"Thank you, Dan," Mattie said breathlessly as she struggled to her feet. Shaking gold dust from her crumpled skirt, she noticed with dismay that her new white blouse was torn from top to bottom.

"Sorry we took so long to get here, but Ruby burned herself in the kitchen." Pearl helped Mattie brush off her skirts, her shoulders shaking gently with laughter. "Looks like you'll be sewing for yourself next."

"Yes, and all because of this stupid, drunken—"

"Customer," Pearl finished for her, one eyebrow raised in warning. "A well-paying customer, too." She turned to the Cornishman next, fluttering her gauze fan. "Although if I catch you upstairs again without one of my girls on your arm, Johnny, I'll be forced to bar my door to you."

"But this is Lil, here. *She's* my girl." The Cornishman tried unsuccessfully to slip out of Big Dan's grasp. "I came up and knocked five times just like she always told me to." He reached out to Mattie. "Isn't that right, my lovely?"

"Take him downstairs and get some hot coffee into him," Pearl ordered. "And when he's as sober as we can make him, put Hester in his lap. That should make him forget Lil."

As Big Dan dragged the Cornishman out the door, Pearl picked up the bag of gold dust lying on the floor. "Although why he should carry on over Lil, I'll never understand. I had to let her go in January, she made so little money. Not only did she have hair the color of a ripe carrot, she had the biggest ears I've ever seen on a woman. In the right light, she was the spitting image of a jack rabbit."

"And, of course, he takes me for her."

"Knowing Johnny, he probably drank a keg of beer at Flynn's saloon before he got here." Pearl winked and gave the bag of gold dust a small toss. "Well, I've business to attend do, and you'd best lock your door." She pointed her fan at Mattie in mock warning. "After all, it's Saturday night. Anything can happen."

Cameron jumped back, narrowly avoiding the man who came careening out of a nickel beer hall. Day or night, Myers Avenue was as raucous and bawdy as a cow-town whore, but Saturday nights were the worst. A younger and more foolish Cameron might have found the violence and crudity entertaining. Now his idea of an exciting evening involved witty conversation, expensive wine and a cultured, beautiful woman. Like Lady Philippa, he thought with a wrench, but instead of her graceful image looming up, the sparkling, green-eyed gaze of Mattie Crawford sprang to mind. *You're a damn fool,* Cameron told himself as he stepped around the drunken fellow now retching over the boardwalk.

The summer sun hung low in the sky. Even so, the red lamp shining beside the front door of the Old Homestead could be seen half a block away. Cameron hesitated before crossing the street. Did he really want to join the trio of well-dressed gentlemen now ambling up the brick walkway to the Old Homestead?

He gazed at the brothel as though it were a dangerous but alluring woman. Enclosed by a wrought-iron fence, the two-story house boasted not only a dozen tall stovepipes but rich-looking burgundy draperies at every window. Freshly painted a buttercup yellow, Pearl DeVere's sporting house stood out like a polished jewel amid the garish saloons and weathered cribs lining the avenue. Well, if Mattie was a soiled dove, he thought sourly, better she sell herself in a place with clean sheets. But despite its sophisticated veneer, it was still a bloody whorehouse and probably reeked of horse manure, sweat and beer, just like the rest of Myers Avenue.

"Why shouldn't I see her?" he asked himself aloud, stepping down into the congested street. If Mattie Crawford's charms were for sale, he was just the man to buy them.

"Watch where you're going, slicker!" yelled a driver of an ore wagon that nearly ran him down.

Angry at himself, but even angrier at Mattie, Cameron marched up to the Old Homestead like a man late for a train.

"No need to push past us, sir," chided an older fellow in a black frock coat. He had a mass of pomaded white hair and a large diamond stickpin glittering on his collar. "The

108

night is nearly as young as you are.'' He smiled as the door to the brothel swung open. ''And the girls are as generous with their time as we are with our gold.''

''How flattering for us,'' Cameron snapped back. The man looked to be sixty if he was a day. The thought of him pawing Mattie only increased his fury. He hoped he wouldn't create a scene.

The old man seemed to have the same thought, for he leaned over to whisper, ''Miss DeVere runs a strict establishment, young man. Best control your temper and your tongue.''

About to make a sharp reply, Cameron caught sight of a red-haired woman swishing through the house. He pushed his way inside only to find a petite maid blocking his way.

''Gentlemen, your hats and gloves, please,'' she said.

As he impatiently stripped off his gloves, Cameron noticed that the walls of the dimly lit foyer were covered with miniature oil paintings. Eighteenth-century hunting scenes, he noted shrewdly: expensive, tasteful, but obvious fakes. Well, that described Mattie Crawford perfectly.

Cameron walked into the main parlor, which was brilliantly illuminated by crystal chandeliers. Although he caught sight of a shabbily dressed miner lolling on the divan—a young brunette perched on his lap—the other men were impeccably outfitted. He was wrong; the stench of Myers Avenue didn't penetrate the Old Homestead's thick walls. Instead, the salon smelled pleasantly of French perfume and summer flowers. Cut-glass vases held large arrangements of irises, gardenias and white roses, their delicate color contrasting with the wine-colored velvet of the draperies. He could only imagine the expense and trouble it required to bring these fresh flowers to Cripple Creek, not to mention the golden oak panelling, Persian carpet and rococo Louis XV furniture.

He suddenly caught sight of the redhead again. Her back was to him as she chatted with the elderly white-haired man boasting the diamond stickpin.

Before she could disappear again, Cameron set off toward the corner of the salon, incensed to see that Mattie was wearing the same satin gown she'd donned the night she'd seduced him in the Antlers Hotel. *It seems I bought her an ideal dress for whoring,* he thought angrily.

"Excuse me, excuse me." He brushed aside a waiter bearing a silver tray, nearly upsetting a half-dozen champagne glasses.

He stopped right behind her, his eyes focused on the fat collar of pearls wound about her neck. Clearly, she'd done very well for herself these past two weeks. And she reeks of gardenias, he thought with contempt. Not only that, but the beautiful auburn hair he remembered now seemed as brassy as a cheap red corset. No doubt he was finally seeing her in her true light, as the money-grubbing opportunist she really was.

Clearing his throat, he assumed his stuffiest English manner. "Well, Miss Crawford, I see that you've settled in marvelously well. Perhaps you'll favor me with a moment of your costly time, although I fear you've gone up in price since we last met."

The older gentleman looked over at him with wide eyes. After a brief moment, the red-haired woman turned around, her hand lazily waving an ivory gauze fan.

"Excuse me, I—I thought you were someone else," Cameron stammered, disconcerted by the woman's amused gaze.

"Obviously."

"This is Miss DeVere," her male companion harumphed at him. "A woman to whom you owe an apology, young man."

She held up a hand. "No need to get upset, Lionel. I believe I know who this gentleman is searching for."

Cameron couldn't believe he'd made such a mistake. This woman was far less voluptuous than Mattie, and stood several inches shorter. And although she had pretty features and a sensual mouth, she didn't possess a tenth of Mattie's loveliness. But what in the devil was she doing wearing that gown? And where was Mattie?

110

As though reading his thoughts, Pearl tapped his shoulder lightly with her fan. "The lady you seek is upstairs." Her gray eyes narrowed at his expression. "Oh, don't worry. I believe she is presently unoccupied, if you know what I mean."

He swallowed both his embarrassment and his anger. "May I see her?"

"Certainly. I've never refused a gentleman's request for any of the females under my roof." She gave him another maddening smile, like a mountain cat who'd just glimpsed her supper. "She's upstairs, the last room on the left."

Cameron bowed his head stiffly.

"Oh, and knock five times on the door." Pearl held up her fan so that it covered the lower part of her face. "She'll be sure to let you in right away."

Chapter Eight

Mattie held up the mended shirtwaist. It looked awful. That fool Cornishman, she thought with irritation. With a resigned sigh, she pressed the blouse to her cheek. Egyptian cotton, as smooth as silk; she'd never find material as fine as this to make another.

"Ah well, it's probably for the best," she murmured. With most of the wardrobe he'd bought her now gone, soon there would be nothing to remind her of Cameron Lynch-Holmes. Except for her memories, and those scandalous dreams that too often disturbed her sleep.

Directly below her, Pearl's scratchy gramophone started up, cranking out the familiar nightly tune. Putting away her sewing basket, Mattie hummed along.

When she heard the five knocks, Mattie shook her head in disbelief. No man could be that stupid. Again five knocks in rapid succession.

"That Cornishman doesn't have the sense of a dead mule," she muttered.

Walking over to the washstand, she picked up the heavy

ceramic pitcher, pleased to see that it was full. *And once I've doused him,* she told herself in exasperation, *I'll smash the pitcher over his stubborn head.*

Positioning herself by the door, she took a deep breath. "Come in," she called out.

The oak door slowly swung open. With a grunt, she heaved the contents of the pitcher.

"What in blazing hell is this!"

Stunned, she could only stare at a drenched Lord Cameron, the now empty pitcher dangling from her hand.

"Have you gone mad?" he bellowed, brushing back the wet hair plastered to his forehead.

"What are *you* doing here?" Mattie said in a shocked voice.

He looked down at his soaked linen jacket and embroidered waistcoat. "I'll be damned if I know. Of all the ill-mannered ways to greet a fellow, this surely is the worst."

Even wet and angry, Mattie thought him the handsomest man she'd ever seen. She winced, however, to see the water dripping onto his shiny spats. "I'm so sorry, Cameron. I—I thought you were someone else. Please forgive me."

Hurriedly putting down the offending pitcher, she held out her hands. "Give me your jacket and I'll lay it near the fire."

Wearing a stern expression, Cameron whipped off his jacket and waistcoat, bypassing Mattie to drape them himself over an ottoman near the small fireplace. Well, she'd craved a visit from the dashing Englishman, and now here he was. Angry and insolent as ever. It might have been better if Cornish Johnny had made a return appearance instead.

"I didn't expect to see you," she said softly.

"And what would you have offered as a greeting if you had?" He peeled off his shirt. "A rabid dog to bite off my leg?"

"I told you, I was expecting someone else." The sight of his bare chest sent an involuntary shiver through her. "I hoped that dousing him with water would either clear his head or drown him.''

''It might be simpler to lock your door, or isn't that allowed in the Old Homestead?''

''I never lock my door.'' Sometimes at night, she imagined she could still hear the echo of her cell door clanging behind her. No matter the possible danger, ever since prison, Mattie had been unwilling to bar her door. She needed the illusion of an instant escape.

''That's foolish. If you keep your door unlocked, you have to expect all sorts of riffraff to find their way in.''

''You've certainly proved that tonight.''

He turned to face her, his wet shirt hanging from his hand. ''How very droll. Is this what passes for humor in the Wild West?''

''Your nose,'' she breathed in dismay, noticing for the first time its bumpy shape. ''So it *was* broken.''

''Yes, something else I have you to thank for,'' he said in a clipped voice.

As much as she'd longed to see him again, Mattie's patience was wearing thin. If one more rude man burst into her room tonight uninvited, she'd go hunting around for a loaded shotgun.

''You can thank your silly heroics for that.'' She tightened the belt of her muslin wrapper. ''Just as it was your coming up here unannounced that got you a soaking. Why in the world did you knock five times?''

''Your little red-haired employer instructed me to.'' Cameron looked down at his soaked trousers.

''My employer?''

''Well, isn't she?''

''Yes, actually.'' Mattie bit back a grin. ''But not in the way you think.''

''Oh, I'm quite certain that nothing about you is just as anyone thinks. Look, do you have a blanket I could wrap around me while I divest myself of these now ruined trousers? I'd hate to ride back to my cabin in the beginning throes of pneumonia.''

With a scornful expression, she walked over to her bed and stripped the quilt from it. "City slicker," she murmured. "Never met a man so proud of his tenderfeet."

"I can hear you over there, muttering away like some half-crazed prospector."

"The last time I heard, you were the one digging in the dirt." She flung the quilt at him. "And none too successfully either."

He wrapped it around himself, and then bent down to kick off his shoes and pants. "Obviously these past two weeks in Cripple Creek have been more profitable for you than me. But then, you've landed in the middle of a seller's market, haven't you?"

"I'm only the daughter of a Colorado sourdough, m'lord," she said sarcastically. "You'll have to speak plainer."

"If I speak plainer, I fear I may seem insulting." He shrugged at her challenging expression. "Very well, then. I only mean to say that you made a shrewd choice in coming here. Clearly you'll make your fortune quicker in Cripple Creek than among the refined circles of Colorado Springs. As you said yourself, you're merely the unschooled daughter of a prospector and unlikely—"

"I never said I was unschooled! Even mining towns have schoolhouses and books. I've had the best education these mountains can offer."

He raised an amused eyebrow. "Exactly."

Mattie stormed over to him, her pleasure at seeing him now gone. "Get out of my room. I don't have to listen to anyone belittle the way my parents brought me up, especially a hoity-toity snob like you."

"See here, I didn't mean to insult your family. You present yourself very well for a person of your background." Although she tugged at his arm, he remained rooted to the spot like a strong tree. "A less sophisticated man might easily take you for a lady." From the room next door came the sounds of loud panting.

She felt her face grow crimson.

He smirked. "Which will certainly stand you in good stead here."

Mattie gave him a shove and he fell backward on the ottoman. Hands on her waist, she stood over him. "What has always stood me in good stead are my brains and my willingness to work hard. Both of which you obviously lack."

"You impertinent chit! Harry and I have worked like slaves this past year: digging, dynamiting, hauling away dirt and ore from dawn to dusk, sometimes until midnight. Even in the dead of winter, we went down into the mine. Harry nearly lost a finger to frostbite in February." He tightened the quilt about his shoulders. "I don't know why I feel the need to justify my behavior to a woman like you. I only came here to see how you were doing, and this is the thanks I get."

"Save the noble story for someone who doesn't know you better. You came here to play the high-and-mighty English lord once more. Hiding behind those fancy clothes, pretending you're a fine gentleman. No wonder you can't find a rich American girl who'll marry you!"

His eyes narrowed suspiciously. "How in the world did you know that?"

She took a deep breath, irritated that she'd let her temper overcome her good sense. "Harry mentioned something about your suit being rejected by New York's debutantes." Mattie lifted her chin defiantly. "Not that I blame them one bit. You're a rude devil."

"I should have a talk with Harry, only it wouldn't do any good. He's almost as exasperating as you are."

Giving a sigh, Cameron gazed regretfully at the woman standing before him. He hadn't seen her in two weeks; all this time, he'd hoped it was his loneliness that made her so desirable to him. But looking at her now—her fiery auburn hair tumbled loose about her shoulders, her large green eyes flashing with anger and her womanly figure hugged by the flimsy white wrapper she wore—he felt his need for her grow even stronger. The sun had finally sunk behind the hills and only the fireplace gave any light. He wished they'd started off better tonight. Perhaps the two of them would now be wrestling in that large tester bed in the corner, enjoying themselves as heartily as the loud couple next door.

"Look, Mattie, I didn't come here to quarrel," he said. "I've made far too many mistakes in my life to start acting like the Archbishop of Canterbury now. However you choose to make your way in the world is your business. To be honest, we all sell ourselves in one form or another. You may as well get the highest price you can. If this is what you want, I'm happy for you." He forced that last sentence out through gritted teeth.

"I see." Mattie looked at him for a long moment before sitting down in a nearby wingchair. She rearranged the folds of her muslin wrapper neatly about her before speaking. "Tell me, did you come here to congratulate me on my success, or to find out if you can afford my price? I warn you, unless you've struck gold, you're wasting my time. I'm shockingly expensive."

His feeble attempt at self-restraint was at an end. "Not only are you a deceitful adventuress, you're an unrepentant, shameless, mercenary—"

"Seamstress," she finished for him. "My grandfather was the finest tailor in Glasgow, like his father before him. Angus McClaren made suits for every shipbuilder in the city, and their sons, too. He taught my mother how to sew, and she taught me. I'm not boasting when I say that with a bolt of fine brocade or silk, and a little Flanders lace, I could create a gown to rival the hand of Charles Worth himself. That's how I earn my keep."

Cameron felt a flicker of relief, quickly overcome by doubt. "I don't understand. You admitted that Pearl DeVere is your employer."

"She is. Who better to want my services than the madam of a bawdy house, especially an elegant one? Pearl has ten girls who must be dressed reasonably well, and here I am with a fat sewing box and a new wardrobe."

Everything seemed to make sense now. "That's why she was wearing your satin gown."

Mattie nodded. "I hope you don't mind, but I had to sell just about everything you gave me. Of course, I've altered most of it to make it appear more—ummm—revealing."

Cameron laughed, the quilt slipping down around his chest. Suddenly he felt warm and almost at peace with himself. "So you've been here all this time sewing. Wait until I tell Harry." He looked at her intently. "I'm glad, Mattie."

She shifted uncomfortably in the dark velvet chair. "You were very kind in the Springs. I would hate for you to always think the worst of me."

"That's not true." Even as he said it, he felt a wave of guilt wash over him.

Mattie bit her lip. "I can't blame you. My behavior in the Springs was dreadful."

"That's not quite the word I'd use," he said in a husky voice.

He suddenly recalled her standing before him in the Antler hotel room, her gown fallen to the floor, her creamy white breasts exposed and waiting for his touch. It pleased him to know that he had been the last man to see such a delectable sight, the last man to pleasure himself with Mattie Crawford.

Beneath the quilt he felt himself grow hard. She had given herself to him eagerly in the Springs; surely her desire hadn't waned since then. Hadn't she saved his life during the stagecoach robbery? And wasn't she now sitting across from him, clothed only in a thin wrapper, her bare feet only inches from his own? And there in the corner waited that large, tempting bed. The firelight cast a warm glow about her figure, making her long auburn hair seem as though it were aflame. Just like the woman herself, he thought. Yes, he would make love to her tonight—long, leisurely, uninterrupted—so that both would have their fill. And he would make certain there were no stupid arguments to spoil their pleasure. Hadn't they already wasted two weeks?

"Mattie, you have no need to apologize for anything that

happened in the Springs.'' He leaned forward, trying to see her eyes in the dim light. ''After all, neither of us has any entanglements to worry about.''

''That's not true. I've come here to marry another man.'' She looked down at her hands, which were nervously twisting the wrapper's belt. ''I lost my head that night. You had been so kind to me.'' She paused. ''But I think the real reason was that I was afraid.''

''Afraid?'' Cameron didn't want her fears or regrets; he wanted the fiery, shameless woman he'd discovered that night at the Antler Hotel. Especially now that he knew she'd not been selling that wanton beauty in Cripple Creek, that she'd been here alone. Maybe she'd been thinking of him as often as he thought of her. Wondering if he'd come calling and repeat that long, urgent night they had shared.

''What in the world were you afraid of?''

Mattie wanted to tell him the truth, that she feared curious strangers and too many sharp questions. Maybe she even wanted to tell him that she feared the way her throat grew dry whenever she saw him, that he was the only man who'd ever made her tremble with desire, with a hot, shameless hunger she'd never even dreamed existed. But she was much more afraid of losing her freedom again, so a lie was all she could give him.

''I was afraid of marrying a man I've never met. After all, I don't even know what he looks like or how old he is.''

''Then why in bloody hell are you doing it?'' he asked in obvious exasperation. ''Being a mail-order bride doesn't make any sense. I could understand it if you were an unattractive woman, or a step away from the almshouse, with a brood of children clinging to your skirts. But your situation doesn't call for such desperate measures.''

Mattie flinched. That hit too close to home.

''It's more than wanting a little security.'' She took a deep breath, something she always needed to do whenever she recalled Frank. ''Ever since my husband died, I've been alone in the world. I'm not begging for sympathy. It wasn't so bad; in fact, it was much better than the years I spent as his wife. But even though my marriage wasn't a happy one, I don't want to believe that all men are deceitful and unkind. I'm willing to try again. It's just that being with you in the hotel that night—well, I wanted to steal a little bit of happiness before getting on with my life. And my marriage.''

Cameron let the silence fall between them like a cloak. Gazing at him, Mattie could see him struggle with himself. Since that first meeting in Colorado Springs, she'd sensed his doubt, his uncertainly about her motives and her stories. But she also knew that he desired her, probably against his will; after all, he was used to refined society females. Still, she could see he wanted to believe her, yet there was something about her story—about her—that nagged at him.

Perhaps he didn't want to believe her a mail-order bride because his motives were less than noble. Maybe he didn't want a prospective husband cluttering up the picture. Maybe he wanted Mattie Crawford in his bed—his bed and no other—at least until the time he settled up his mine or made a proper marriage of his own.

And maybe you want to believe all that even more than he does, she told herself mockingly.

''I hope you understand a bit better now why I'm here,'' she said softly, uneasy about breaking the silence. He seemed so lost in thought. ''It probably doesn't make sense to a man like you. I'm sure you're used to a far more agreeable life.''

He shook his head. ''Actually, life has not been agreeable for quite some time.''

Cameron turned around slightly so that his broken profile was framed by the firelight. He remained silent a moment longer, as though considering whether to go on. Mattie sat patiently across from him, the crackling of the fire blending with the disturbing grunts and groans next door.

''My father is the Marquess of Clydesford,'' he said finally, ''the head of a once important and powerful family. But even he cannot hold back the future. For twenty years, the income from our farms in Kent has fallen steadily, mostly due to the flood of imported foodstuffs. We've lost tenant after tenant, yet our expenses grow by the month. We've tried selling off some of the estates, but finding buyers in the present economic climate is extremely difficult.''

His voice grew low. ''Six years ago, my older brother Arthur—my father's heir—should have been trying to make an advantageous marriage. Instead he took up with the wife of a Tory MP. The fool believed himself to be in love.'' The last word was uttered with great scorn. ''He refused even to consider marriage to anyone else. And to compound his folly, his beloved mistress was also a very Catholic one, so divorce was not a possibility.''

''You can't blame him if he lost his heart.''

''He lost his mind, not his heart,'' Cameron said in a harsh voice. ''And as befits all besotted fools chasing after romantic dreams, he lost his life.''

''How awful,'' she said quietly.

''He was killed in a carriage accident, caused by his driving at pell-mell speed to meet his beloved at their latest rendevous. And so the title of Marquess of Clydesford will fall to me, as does the sorry business of making a brilliant match. I never thought to be the next marquess, never wanted it. I still don't. Before his great romance, my brother had an unblemished reputation. Arthur could have waltzed into any Fifth Avenue mansion and danced out with a rich debutante for a wife.'' He brushed back his damp hair from his brow. ''Not like me. I've had no luck at all since coming to America. If I were a fanciful chap, I'd suspect I was cursed.''

''Perhaps your luck will change,'' Mattie suggested gently. ''Harry said that all signs indicated a vein of gold on your claim.''

''My father suffered a stroke three years ago. His health is as precarious as my family's future. No, I fear he will die in penury long before Harry and I dig our way down.'' Cameron straightened. ''Which means I cannot afford to waste more time playing at being a prospector. We'll probably have to sell cheap, cut our losses and go on.''

"Don't do that!"

He looked up in obvious surprise at her urgent tone.

Mattie leaned forward. "I've watched too many bankers and lawyers walk away with millions in these hills. They let other men do all the work, take every sort of risk, only to come with their insulting offers and rob them of a king's ransom. You can't let them do that. Not again."

"I don't see that we have much choice. We simply don't have the capital to invest in equipment and men."

"Then find a way. Don't you understand? The mountains here are bursting with gold, silver, copper. You'll never forgive yourself if you surrender a claim that may hold the mother lode. It's possible, you know. I've seen it. My own father spent half his life searching this district, a divining rod in one hand and a pick and shovel in the other. When I was nine years old, he struck a rich vein of sylvanite, and worked like a dog to mine and sort it. Then a man from Denver showed up, his pockets filled with greenbacks, and bought his claim for three thousand dollars. Three thousand! That vein turned a profit of three thousand a day for the next two years.

"But that wasn't the worst. Five years later, my father was cheated again, and legally too." Her voice grew bitter. "The rich know just how to bend the law so that it profits them and chokes the life out of us. You fear your father will die penniless. Well, that's how Alec Crawford met his end, with nothing to show for years of struggle except the miner's consumption that killed him."

Mattie shook her head, the anger suddenly drained out of her. "For my father—and for you—gold means freedom." She sighed. "I understand wanting to be free. I understand that all too well. That's why I don't want you to give up too soon. You've worked hard at your mine. Don't surrender it without a fight."

He walked over to her and laid a gentle hand on her shoulder. She was trembling.

Mattie looked up at him. "Don't sell it."

"I'll hold on as long as I can, but my family will be

bankrupt by next year. I dare not wait too long.'' The quilt slipped further and he pulled it down to his waist with one hand. ''I'll have to take myself back East soon and fish the marital waters once more.''

Mattie gave his half-naked body an appraising glance. ''Those debutantes don't know what they're missing.''

He laughed. ''It seems I'm remarkably easy to resist.''

''I wish you were,'' she said softly.

Mattie stared up at him, the firelight making it impossible to read his expression. She felt a warmth suffuse her body and knew it was not only desire she felt, but tenderness. It seemed as though she were stepping onto a high wire, with a strong wind blowing at her back and no net below to break her fall. Suddenly she wanted nothing more than to escape once more. Run away, she told herself urgently, run away from this splendid man, this hot, close room, these soft feelings that disturbed her more than a hundred fevered dreams.

The couple next door had finished their lovemaking, and the room seemed tensely quiet. Cameron knelt down beside the chair, one arm straying to Mattie's knee.

''And I have found you totally irresistible from the moment I saw you step off the train.''

She caught her breath, staring toward the fire behind him. ''Please, Cameron.''

''I'm a lonely man, Mattie. Like you, I crave a last chance to be impractical and happy. I'll be forced to make an marriage of convenience soon, even if I have to go through every Social Registry in America. Before that happens, there's no reason we shouldn't comfort each other, as we did in Colorado Springs.''

''That evening didn't end well,'' she whispered.

''My fault, my fault entirely.'' He reached out and tipped her chin toward him. ''You're a desirable woman, as fiery and spectacular as that red hair of yours.'' Cameron cupped her chin tighter, moving her face closer to his. ''I'm tired of paying court to well-bred, steel-corseted young women, women who only care about my title, women who have

123

never felt the kind of passion that I've seen course through you."

She tried to protest, but he quickly pressed his lips against hers. Mattie gave a small moan, as her hand brushed against his muscled chest. Beneath her hand, his heart pounded, and she felt her desire—and her alarm—grow stronger.

His lips pressed down with greater urgency, while his tongue gently pried open her soft, full lips. Without thinking, she returned his kiss with astonishing force.

"Both of us deserve this, Mattie," he said hoarsely. "After all, you've come here to marry a man you've never even met. What if he can't make you tremble like this, what if you find that marriage is nothing more than a loveless prison?"

She stiffened suddenly. What in the world was she doing? A few warm kisses and she forgot for a moment what was at stake.

"Let me show you what pleasure I can bring you." Cameron tried to take her face in his hands again.

"No, Cameron," she said in a shaky voice. "I forgot why I came to Colorado once already. I can't make that mistake again. My future depends on it."

He released her and sat back on his heels. It hurt to look at the desire and frustration on his face, but Mattie couldn't do as he wanted—as she wanted. Seducing him in the Springs had been necessary, but there could be no excuse for giving in to her desire now. And what would it get her?

Without much effort, she might find herself falling in love. What a disaster that would be, she thought sadly. Cameron could never be hers; he was an English lord who, gold mine or no, would inevitably marry a woman of breeding and money. He had treated her with contempt simply because he suspected her of being a money-hungry adventuress. She could only imagine what he'd do if he discovered she was a former convict fleeing from the police—for stealing from his former fiancée.

She had to keep her own survival uppermost in mind. So far, her mail-order bride story had been useful; it gave her a reason for being in Cripple Creek. As soon as she earned more money, she'd take off for Wyoming or even Montana, only next time she'd take care to assume an alias and a far better story.

"I guess I was wrong," he said ruefully. "I thought you wanted me as much as I want you. I thought we both needed—"

"What I need is a friend," she broke in. "Cameron, I came West to start a new life. My old one wasn't very happy. Won't you be a friend to me and make all this easier?"

He gave her a penetrating look. "And will marrying this Jack Daniels make you happy?"

She took a deep breath, tired of lies. "Happiness is for children, and I haven't been a child in a long time. But I'm determined to make another life for myself, and Jack Daniels will help me to do that."

Cameron nodded. "Very well then." His voice betrayed his disappointment. "I'll be your friend. If marrying Mr. Daniels seems to be the answer you're seeking, then I'll do my best to help you find him."

"No. You've already done far too much."

"I insist. It's the least I can do after subjecting you to my veiled insults and unwanted advances."

"Not unwanted." She smiled and lightly brushed his cheek with her fingers. He closed his eyes. "Just impractical and unwise."

"Well, I've quite a reputation for being both those things back in England, but for you, Mattie, I'll make an effort to—"

Someone pounded five times on the door. Both of them looked over.

"Is that the man you were expecting before?" he asked in an affronted tone.

Fighting back the urge to laugh, she could only nod.

"Well, I'll settle this once and for all." Just as the door flew open, Cameron stood up, forgetting the quilt that now dropped to the floor.

125

The drunken Cornishman stopped in his tracks, his bleary eyes opening wide at the sight of Mattie in her thin wrapper and Cameron standing there in all his naked glory.

"My pretty, have you betrayed me?"

"Get out this minute before I toss you through the window," Cameron barked, taking a threatening step forward.

The Cornishman brandished his fist, yelling, "My pretty Lil has broken my heart! She's broken it in two! I hope to never set eyes on you for the rest of my natural life."

Cameron marched over to him and grabbed him by the arm, giving him a shake. "You ever bother this woman again and I'll serve you up to the coyotes!"

Young Hester burst in just then, clad only in a camisole and stockings. "What are you doing in here, Johnny?" she said querulously. "We haven't even gotten started. You don't need—" She suddenly caught sight of the unclothed muscular Adonis shaking Johnny. "Land sakes, mister, if you ain't a right fine bull. If the dressmaker don't make you happy, you just come to me. I'll have you bucking like a bronco, sweetie. Don't waste it on her."

"That's my Lil," wailed Johnny as he tried to pull himself from Cameron's grasp. "He's been riding my pretty, the bastard!"

Another whore popped her head in. "Is Johnny in here again?"

"Who is this man?" roared Cameron, but his words were lost as Big Dan hurried in, followed by a giggling Pearl. It was sheer pandemonium for a moment. Mattie watched it all from her comfortable seat in the wingchair, trying to keep a straight face.

As Johnny the Cornishman was finally wrestled out of the room, he kept pointing to Mattie and screaming, "Harlot! My Lil is a harlot!"

Cameron slammed the door and turned to Mattie, his face a mask of disbelief. "Can you explain any of this?"

She shrugged, her shoulders shaking. "It's Saturday night."

"What the devil does that mean?"

But Mattie was laughing too hard to answer him.

Chapter Nine

Every time Harry saw Cameron and Mattie together, he
didn't know whether to be touched or alarmed. He had recognized the physical attraction between them from the first.
What else but sexual desire had drawn Cameron to her at
the train station in Colorado Springs? He could still hear
Mattie's sleepy voice begging Cameron for a kiss that first
night. And why else were they all wasting yet another hour
on the picnic lunch Mattie had brought to the mine?

"You gonna eat that egg?"

Harry sighed and wordlessly handed over the hard-boiled
egg to Roy MacDuff.

This was the third picnic basket she'd brought out to the
mine this week. And this time the blacksmith had accompanied her. For the food, no doubt. He glanced over at Cameron, who was wolfing down a huge piece of corn bread.
Since when did his aristocratic friend enjoy eating on the
ground?

Pretending to listen to the blacksmith blather on about
shoeing horses, he watched Mattie and Cameron instead.

Sitting companionably on an Indian blanket spread over the ground, the two of them chatted and smiled together like flirtatious adolescents.

Harry scrutinized Mattie once more, as though her appearance held the key to his friend's behavior. Although she was a bit too robust and animated for his tastes, Harry thought she was a lovely woman. With her voluptuous figure and bold green eyes, she would probably have done well on the stage, he thought. Still, Cameron had seduced scores of beauties in England; the ill-starred Lady Philippa had reputedly been the prettiest woman in the south of England, and the most elegant. As charming as she was, Mattie Crawford just didn't seem refined enough to hold an English lord's attention.

She'd foolishly taken off her hat, and Harry fought back the impulse to warn her against being unfashionably sunburnt. Her titian-colored hair—which even he admitted was breathtakingly beautiful—was not pinned up today, but worn instead in that irritating Western style, pulled into a long rolled curl and flung over one shoulder. Not that he didn't want his friend to find a woman to care for, but this lively redhead in yellow gingham could never be a proper consort for the son of a marquess. Harry sighed and wiped at his damp brow with his bandanna. He liked them both, but he sensed they were entering treacherous emotional waters. If only that blasted Jack Daniels would show up and take Mattie away. But even if he arrived this very moment, Harry feared that things had already gone too far.

"What a sour face, old chap." Cameron laughed. "Was it the cole slaw or the fried chicken?" He turned to the smiling woman beside him. "Harry has a most sensitive palate. Anything that hasn't been prepared by a foreign chef gives him indigestion."

"Well, Ruby may not be a chef, but she *was* born in Canada." Mattie began folding up the cloth napkins and returning them to the picnic basket. "Does that change your opinion of the lunch?"

Before Harry had a chance to answer, Roy reached over

for the last drumstick. "Ain't nothing wrong with this lunch. This here's the finest chicken I've eaten since I sat down in the Brown Hotel in Denver." With a hearty bite, he tore off nearly all the meat. "Dang, but this Ruby girl can cook. It's a shame she's living in the Old Homestead. A female that can whip up a lunch like this would make a mighty useful wife."

"Don't let her current residence bother you, Roy," Cameron said, leaning back on his elbows and stretching out his legs before him. "Finding the right woman is like hunting for gold. Sometimes the most precious metal lies hidden in the muck." He glanced over at Mattie, who was busily packing up. "After all, our delightful Mattie is boarding at the same establishment."

"Well, that's different," Roy said quickly. "Mattie's a real lady. The whole town knows she's only sewing for Pearl DeVere. Besides, she's sure to be married soon and setting up her own household."

"I wish I were as sure of that as you." Mattie offered Roy the last piece of corn bread, which he gratefully accepted. "If Mr. Daniels doesn't make himself known soon, I'll probably move farther west. Cripple Creek is too wild for a young woman alone. Eventually my reputation would suffer, and I'd never make a respectable marriage then."

"I can't think why that's so important to you. Here you enjoy freedom, celebrity and, of course, the amusing company of Harry Tremont." Cameron shot her a dazzling smile, blatantly exerting his good looks and charm. He'd left his faded cotton shirt half unbuttoned, revealing his tanned, muscled neck and chest, now provocatively damp with sweat.

Harry almost choked on his lemonade. He'd seen saloon girls who were less obvious.

"Not to mention my sincere, and I hope not unwelcome, friendship," Cameron continued.

Mattie turned her face away as though wary of that potent, blue-eyed gaze. "I shall miss Cripple Creek, of course. But as soon as I've saved enough money, I will be moving on.'' She shot Harry a knowing look. ''I *must* be moving on.''

Harry nodded. It was just as he thought. Cameron might be foolishly forgetting who and what he was, but Mattie, thank heavens, understood their impossible situation perfectly.

Cameron glanced over at the blacksmith. ''Ah well, I've tried my best. Do you have any suggestions to get her to change her mind?''

Roy shrugged, wiping his mouth with the back of his hand. ''Can't say that I blame the little lady. Mattie here wants to get married, which is just as it should be. Now maybe if you was to offer to walk down the aisle with her, she might decide to stay.'' Tipping his head back to swig down his lemonade, he missed the sudden awkwardness that came over everyone else.

''If I stumble upon the mother lode this afternoon, I might consider it. What do you think, Harry? If we hit a vein today *and* find a rich investor, Mattie and I get married tomorrow. Maybe we can even convince MacDuff here to go calling on the talented Ruby. It could be a double wedding.'' Although Cameron said this with a careless laugh, his old friend knew him well enough to discern the slight edge to his voice.

''Perhaps I'd better leave Cripple Creek this minute then,'' Mattie said with a nervous laugh.

Cameron's expression suddenly turned serious. ''Don't leave,'' he softly. ''Not just yet. Look on it as a selfish request from a friend who cares.'' He paused. ''Perhaps too much.''

Mattie looked up at him. ''Well, if you put it like that, I might remain for a little while longer.'' She squeezed his arm, and Cameron stiffened, as though her touch had seared him.

Harry shook his head. He was wrong. They were both hopeless.

*   *   *

Sometimes Cameron couldn't believe the words coming out of his mouth, nor the feelings surging inside him. Had he openly pleaded with a woman not to leave him? Not that he hadn't tried such persuasion before on coy duchesses or hesitant debutantes, but this time he felt genuinely panicked at the thought of this particular female's departure. For a twenty-eight-year-old man who'd seen quite a bit of the world, there was no excuse for such pitiable behavior. If he didn't get a grip on himself, he'd become a laughable fool like his brother. Well, not that bad surely. Arthur had believed he was in love, and whatever Cameron felt for Mattie Crawford, it wasn't love. Desire, certainly. And, of course, he liked her. He liked nearly everything about her.

Unfortunately, his feelings of friendship warred with his lust. At any other time in his life, he would have used every sexual ploy and instinct he possessed to make her his mistress. But, blast it, he liked her. With an unhappy marriage behind her, Mattie deserved a devoted husband. His conscience wouldn't permit him to seduce her, and he could never offer marriage. Soon enough, he would have to leave and find a proper wife. Weeks ago, he had decided to do as she asked and be her friend.

But it wasn't easy, he thought, finally tearing his attention away from her. One hand shading his eyes, he squinted in the sunlight, making out the approach of a man on horseback.

"We have a visitor, Harry." Cameron stood up, holding out a hand to pull Mattie to her feet. "He sits a horse like a cowpoke, but I swear he's wearing a brocade vest."

"Ah, yes, another city slicker come to see if our mine's worth coveting." Harry tucked in his denim shirt. "What does this make so far this week? Five, at last count."

"Six," Cameron replied grimly. "All of them interested in buying, but none of them willing to invest."

"Of course not." Mattie turned an accusing gaze on the approaching stranger. "To invest would mean they might want to share profits rather than just steal them."

The blacksmith heaved himself to his feet, tossing his

eaten drumstick into the dried grass behind him. "Now, Mattie, if a gent offers a decent price for another fella's claim, you can't rightly call it stealing. It's just good business."

The look she threw him would have frozen a more sensitive man.

"Oh, we've no grudge against a shrewd capitalist," Harry said, ignoring Mattie's muttering. "Make us a reasonable offer and we'll consider it."

"What's the best that's been laid on the table so far?"

Cameron turned a cynical gaze on the blacksmith. "Ten thousand."

The sum brought a sheepish expression to Roy's face. "Ten thousand?" He whistled. "That's one of the lowest I've heard for a claim this size."

"The lower the offer, the lower the man who makes it." Mattie sniffed, taking a challenging step toward the rider. Hands on her hips, she watched him approach like a warrior preparing to meet the enemy.

The men were intent on the new visitor, who expertly reined in his majestic roan stallion before dismounting. Striding toward them, he swept off his broad-brimmed hat, revealing a shiny bald head and a lined, weathered face. At almost the same moment Mattie exclaimed, "Hugh Rawley!"

Cameron turned in surprise. "You know him?"

"Know him?" she repeated hoarsely.

Ignoring Cameron and Harry, Rawley instead inclined his head toward Mattie as a strange smile cracked his expression. "Never thought to see Alec Crawford's girl again. 'Course I'd recognize that hair anywhere. Same color as your mother's."

"Don't you dare speak of my mother!"

Although Rawley didn't even flinch, Cameron looked over at Mattie in shocked surprise. With fists clenched at her sides and her eyes boring a hole into the stranger, she looked as angry as any woman he had ever seen. Her bitter words about the men who cheated her father came back to

132

him, and he sensed that this Rawley probably had had a hand in it.

Hoping to end the confrontation before it began, Cameron held out a hand and quickly introduced both Harry and himself. Behind him, he could hear Mattie breathing as heavily as a bull about to charge.

Rawley only nodded, placing his hat back on his head. "I know who you are. My people have made inquiries into every worthwhile claim in the district, and this one seems more promising than most. I spoke to the assayers myself this morning. They report you've already found good-size pieces of 'float.'"

Harry frowned. "Pardon me, Mr. Rawley, but isn't that a breach of ethics on the assayers' part?"

He shrugged. "Take it up with the assayer's office in Denver, Mr. Tremont. My only concern is ascertaining where the vertical plugs are along these slopes, and this claim is—"

"Get out of here, you lying snake!" Mattie pushed Cameron aside and marched up to Rawley. "Go slither around Cripple Creek until you find another starving miner you can cheat out of his gold. But you'll not get a chunk of dirt out of these fellows here, I swear it."

"I really don't see how this concerns you, Mattie," Harry said with obvious irritation.

Cameron stepped beside her, but she seemed oblivious to anyone but Rawley. "Maybe you should have Roy take you back to town," he suggested gently. "Lunch is over and we've business to discuss."

She whirled about, her eyes flashing fire. "Business? This bastard isn't here to discuss business. He's a thief and a liar, no better than the gang of outlaws who tried to hold us up."

"Yes, I heard about your courage, young lady," Rawley said evenly, only a slight twitch near his left eye suggesting that Mattie's outburst hadn't left him totally unmoved. "No doubt your father would have been proud. But what do you think he would say if he could hear you cursing like a mule driver?"

"It's a pity I can't ask him," she snapped back. "But he died soon after you and your partner stole his claims."

His hat brim concealed his sharp, dark eyes, but Cameron suspected they'd just narrowed. "You've been misinformed." He turned to the others. "Miss Crawford was little more than a child at the time. I doubt her memory is to be trusted."

"Child? I was fourteen and cooking as many hours a day for a team of brickmakers. And I remember very well indeed the day Hugh Rawley and Sam Leland rode into Bonanza looking for poor miners to cheat."

"A pity your temper is still as fiery as your hair. A cooler head might permit you to see the truth." He raised his voice. "Her father had four claims in Bonanza, but unfortunately he couldn't afford the yearly assessments. My partner and I learned of this and offered our own bid."

"You stole his claims!"

Harry glanced over at Mattie's furious expression. "Although I haven't practiced law yet, Mattie, I do know that the state mining code demands annual proof of labor and a yearly assessment. Failure to comply can result in a mine being reclassified as public territory."

"How can you be so gullible?" she replied harshly. "Rawley and his thieving crony made a practice of hunting through affidavits, searching for claims that weren't paid up. Small mines and small claims, easy pickings for vultures with money in their pockets. They nosed around carefully for their victims, trying to sniff out the weakest. And Alec Crawford *was* the weakest, wasn't he? A man sick with consumption, struggling to keep his family from starving; a man who'd lost two children in the fire at Poncha Springs the year before. How can you sleep at night, knowing you got rich from the claims you stole out from under him?"

"Your father was delinquent in his payments. Since he couldn't afford to pay for what he claimed, it was my right—"

Her hand slapped loudly across Rawley's cheek, and his hat flew off, showing an angry face now purpling with rage.

"Don't speak of rights to me, you conniving scum!" Heedless of any risk, Mattie stepped even closer, so that they were only inches apart.

"Losing those claims broke my father. He died knowing that you and Leland were getting fat and rich while he could leave his family nothing but grief."

Cameron pulled her away, his arm tight about her waist. Her whole body seemed as taut as a drawn bowstring. "I think you'd better leave, Mr. Rawley. Miss Crawford is a friend of ours and your presence is clearly upsetting her."

He slowly bent down and picked up his hat. "Well, that is most regrettable since—"

"A man like you knows nothing of regret. All you know how to do is destroy decent lives."

"You Crawfords are all alike," Rawley said scornfully. "Blaming the world for your bad judgment."

"That's enough, Mr. Rawley." Cameron felt Mattie's arm steal around him, as though seeking an anchor. "When there's this much animosity between people, no good can ever come of it. I think you'd best be on your way."

Harry cleared his throat. "We haven't heard his offer."

"Nor shall we." Cameron threw his friend a warning look.

"Perhaps you and I need to talk," Harry replied stubbornly.

"Of course, but only after Mr. Rawley has left."

Mattie slowly drew away from Cameron. "I don't want to cause trouble between the two of you. If you want to listen to this man's lies, Harry, I won't stand in your way."

"Mattie, wait," Cameron called after her.

She quickly marched toward the blacksmith's buggy. MacDuff lumbered after her. Her back was as straight as a board, head held high, but Cameron knew she was trembling with emotion. Rawley's appearance seemed to turn her into that unhappy teenage girl, mourning the loss of her father and all his dreams. His chest tightened as he watched her seat herself in the buggy, eyes cast forward, hands clasped childlike on her lap. If he had only one wish at that moment,

135

it would be to get beside her in that buggy and ride away together into the mountains.

"Did you hear what Mr. Rawley is offering?"

At the sound of Harry's voice, Cameron forced himself back to reality. "What is it?" he asked, watching Mattie and the blacksmith ride away.

"Forty thousand payable in cash." Rawley once more wore an iron expression. "That's for all rights, of course. And the transfer would be immediate. I've got pneumatic drills ready to be shipped up here, and close to a hundred men already willing to hire on."

"You seem pretty certain you'd be able to buy us out."

"I don't have the time or inclination to haggle, Lord Cameron. I need to clear part of the site for a mill stamp, and I'd rather not dance around this sale, which we both know is inevitable."

"Hardly inevitable, I'd say. After all, forty thousand isn't exactly a fortune. My father used to spend that much on the annual care of his polo ponies."

A knowing look came into those hawklike eyes. "And how many polo ponies does your father care for now, Lord Cameron?"

Cameron stared back at him, his jaw set. Now he not only disliked him for Mattie's sake, but for his own. "That was a mistake," he said in a hard voice.

Shuffling his feet nervously, Harry looked away.

"I beg your pardon?" Rawley asked with a hint of uncertainty.

"Your offer is refused."

Rawley threw a glance at Harry, who refused to meet his eyes. "I shouldn't give in to such schoolboy bartering, but as I said, I've already made plans for the mine. So fifty thousand, my final offer."

"And here's my final answer: no." Rolling up his sleeves, Cameron jerked his head toward Rawley's waiting roan. "Now, I suggest you get on your horse. Harry and I have to get back to work."

"And how far will you get with your buckets and your

mules?'' Rawley jammed his hat back on his head. ''The ground beneath your feet holds maybe a million or more dollars in gold, but it will take you nearly a quarter of that to pull it out. And where will you find that sort of money? Not from your family, which by all accounts is a step from bankruptcy court.''

''You'd better go, Rawley, before you try my friend's patience,'' Harry said anxiously.

The older man shot Harry a scornful look. ''And your rich daddy ain't about to give you a red cent either, is he? Shows you what the mighty Jed Tremont thinks of his only son's business sense.''

Harry's face turned scarlet. ''Get the hell out of here. And don't bother coming back.''

Rawley muttered all the way to his horse, swinging into the saddle with a curse. ''You would have sold to me in a minute, if not for that redhead kicking up a fuss. Maybe I should forget about trying to deal with you two jackasses and have a long talk with the lady instead.''

Cameron walked over to him, grabbing the horse's bridle so hard that the roan tried to rear up. ''Listen carefully, Rawley. If you even breathe in the direction of Miss Crawford, I'll see you buried twenty feet lower than my gold. Do you understand me?''

He jerked his horse away. ''I understand enough not to trifle with a man so foolishly in love. Good luck, Lynch-Holmes. You're going to need it.''

Cameron watched the man ride off in silence, not moving until Harry stepped beside him.

''If he was intent on being so unspeakably insulting, the least he could have offered was seventy thousand,'' Harry said in a halfhearted attempt at a joke.

''Of all the ridiculous things to accuse me of!'' Cameron turned an agitated face in Harry's direction.

''What?''

''Saying I'm in love with Mattie.''

Harry looked at him with a pitying expression. ''You are.''

137

Cameron pushed his friend aside and stalked off.

Bloody fools, the lot of them. Couldn't they distinguish friendship from something as pathetic as romantic love? Apparently not. Well, he could, and he knew he was not in love with Mattie.

God help him, he couldn't be.

Chapter Ten

Nervous as a cat, Mattie waited for her first sight of Cameron in two days. The miners, their bare torsos gleaming with sweat, strained to pull the steel-screened cage up the shaft. Harry stood a few feet away, occupied with hauling the last shift out of the mine. Having been raised in mining towns, Mattie had to admit that the operation here was primitive. No freight elevators to take the miners down, no pneumatic drills or hydraulic equipment. No mill stamp waiting to begin processing the ore. Guilt washed over her once more.

She had stood in the way of Cameron getting forty thousand dollars for the claim, and she knew only too well that forty thousand was all he was ever likely to see. *I've ruined it for him,* she thought miserably, *and for Harry, too.* But Harry was a rich man's son. It was different for Cameron; she'd spoiled his best chance so far. And all because of her bitterness toward the scoundrel who'd robbed her father. She'd had no right interfering.

She'd lain awake these past two nights, thinking over her

confrontation with Rawley. Yes, she hated him, perhaps more than ever. He was so clearly prosperous and alive, riding on his fine horse through the valleys of Colorado while her entire family lay cold in their paupers' graves. Yet what had that to do with Cameron? Forty thousand wouldn't save his family from bankruptcy, but it might make things a bit easier for them in the coming year.

With a screech of metal, the pulley stopped cranking and the cage opened, spilling out four dirt-streaked miners. Cameron wasn't among them.

"The boss says he's going to work through supper," one of the miners said to Harry. "Maybe he'll come up when the next shift is sent down."

"I doubt it," Harry muttered wearily.

Mattie hurried over, taking care not to trip on the ore buckets scattered about the ground.

"Let me go down, Harry. I want to talk with him."

"Don't be silly. It's damper than the sea bottom down there, and twice as dark." Harry scratched furiously at the sweat dripping off his beard. "Besides, a mine shaft is no place for a woman."

She rolled up her cotton sleeves. "I've probably been in more mine shafts than you, Harry Tremont. Every Sunday in Bonanza, I'd go down and dig beside my father, and I'm sure it was a darn sight narrower than this."

"Sorry, Mattie, but it's not safe."

"You're not coyoting or blasting right now, are you? All right then, just let me down. I want to talk with him." She marched into the cage, shutting the gate behind her.

Harry crossed his arms in front of him.

"He hasn't been to see me in two days," she said in a softer voice. "I have to talk with him, please."

A moment later, Mattie found herself being lowered into the earth, her feet spread apart for balance on the cage's metal floor. A miner's hat sat heavily on her head, and she gazed upward as the afternoon sky slowly receded from view. As warm as it was above ground in the sunny July heat, within the confines of the shaft there was only damp, chill and darkness. The sound of water dripping mingled with the scraping of the cage against the dirt and rock walls. She winced, thinking of the back-breaking labor it took to get down this far. With the right equipment, Cameron and Harry could have tunneled easily through the bedrock, but without money and the technology it bought, they could only hack away at the earth like desert prospectors, with little more than picks and shovels to aid them.

I'll ask him to reconsider Rawley's offer, she told herself as the cage finally rattled to a halt. He mustn't throw away his only chance at a profit out of this mine. With the ceasing of the cage's movement, the sound of dripping water seemed nearly thunderous. A lantern hung from the timbered wall of the adjacent tunnel, illuminating the tools scattered on the ground. She touched her miner's hat, reassuring herself that the candle was lit. Opening the cage door, she gingerly stepped over to the tunnel. Listening a moment, she heard distant sounds, like someone hacking away at rock.

"Cameron," she called. "Cameron, it's Mattie."

The hammering continued. *He can't have heard me,* she thought, crouching down and staring into the tunnel. It was too small to stand in; she would have to crawl through. Pulling off her skirt and petticoats, Mattie tried not to shiver from the cold damp. Her white pantalets would get filthy crawling on the dirt, but she'd never be able to get through the shaft any other way.

She turned back to the cage, fighting the impulse to signal Harry to pull her up once more. No, she had to see Cameron, not only to change his mind about selling, but just to look on him once more. Was he angry with her? Did he resent her interference? Why hadn't he come to see her these past two nights? The one question she dared not ask herself was why she cared so much.

Cameron worked like a man possessed. Sweat poured into his eyes until they burned, and his arms were scraped nearly raw. Since Rawley's visit, he'd spent almost sixteen hours a day in the mine, hacking away at the rock, desperate to find the vein of gold that remained so tantalizingly out of reach. Rawley's offer had been the best they'd had in nearly a year. Both he and Harry knew that they wouldn't get a better one, and yet he'd turned it down. True, the scoundrel had insulted him. Worse, he'd insulted Mattie. And for the sake of a woman's hurt feelings, Cameron was willing to lose the best profit on the claim they were likely to have. Unless they could find the vein soon.

With a bed of gold staring them in the face, they might be able to snag a bank's interest *and* money. They might be able to persuade a businessman to buy a partial interest rather than take the whole operation outright. But it all depended on a fool's luck, and a fool's dream. He would hack away here in the dark until his muscles gave out. And when he knew it was truly lost, he'd go back to New York. He'd don his pretty clothes and smile at those pampered heiresses, and he'd be a proper fortune hunter once more. He would put all thoughts of striking gold out of his mind, and never look back lest he catch a glimpse of gleaming red hair and bright green eyes.

"Cameron?"

The feminine voice startled him so much that he dropped the pickax he was wielding. Swinging around so his lantern faced the opposite way, he was stunned to see Mattie crawling toward him. She was wearing only a dirt-streaked white blouse and pantalets.

"What are you doing here?" he shouted, then remembered where he was and lowered his voice. "Mattie, who the devil let you down here? I'll have Harry's neck for this."

He reached out and pulled her toward him, forcing her to sit back on her heels. With her hair in disarray beneath the large helmet, and her curvaceous legs outlined by the revealing pantalets, Mattie Crawford was the unlikeliest miner he had ever seen. He gritted his teeth at the sight of her, far too close in this cramped space. And far too stirring.

"Don't blame Harry," she panted, obviously tired from

the effort to crawl through the tunnel. "I insisted. I wanted to talk to you."

"Well, you're going up right now. You and Harry must both be insane. This is no place for a woman. And where in blazes is your skirt?"

"I took it off before I entered the tunnel. I could never have crawled here otherwise, with all those petticoats getting in the way."

He shook his head. Of all the stupid things to do. Mines were always in danger of collapsing, and they'd already tunneled a good way under the bedrock. Even the timbered walls they'd constructed wouldn't save them if there were a cave-in. "Do you realize how far down we are? I thought you of all people would understand the risks of a hard-rock mine."

"Well, it doesn't stop you or any of the other men from coming down here." She rubbed at her cheek with a dirty hand, leaving a wide black mark behind. Somehow it made her more irresistible to him. "And this is not the first tunnel I've crawled through. I even helped my father dynamite a mine once."

"Well, he must have been out of his mind," he barked. "And don't look at me like that, Mattie Crawford. I don't care what sort of rapscallion childhood you led, this is my mine and I set the rules."

"Which includes no unexpected visitors?" she finished pertly, trying to settle herself more comfortably on the rocky floor.

"Which includes *no* visitors, especially young women crawling about in their underwear." He shot her a disapproving glance. "When supper is over and the next shift makes their way down, you're going to be less than pleased to be caught without your petticoats and skirt."

"I'll be gone before then."

"Indeed you will. You're going this instant, even if I have to drag you through the tunnel."

She pressed her hand against his bare chest, pushing him back. They both gave an involuntary shiver. "I have to talk with you, Cameron. Please, it's important. And don't tell me to wait for you aboveground. Harry says that you haven't been coming up till nearly midnight."

Cameron was much too close to her now, both of them agitated, sweaty and half-dressed. He was only thankful that the mine tunnel was so narrow and uncomfortable. Otherwise he'd pull her beneath him this instant and plunge into her as ferociously as he beat against the hard tunnel walls.

"What do you want?" he finally asked in a hoarse voice, looking down at her hand against his chest.

Mattie suddenly seemed to feel awkward as well. She withdrew her hand and sat back. Unfortunately, the movement only accentuated her rounded thighs beneath the thin white material. "I want you to reconsider Hugh Rawley's offer."

"What? I thought you hated the man."

"I do, but that's a matter that concerns only him and me." She took a deep breath. "I can't let you throw away forty thousand dollars because you don't want to upset me."

"Actually, the last offer was fifty thousand," he said wryly. "Once you left, the price went up."

"Fifty!" Her eyes clouded over and for a moment she seemed to be in pain. "You can't refuse such a sum. No one else will make a better offer, and you desperately need the money to save your family from ruin. I've been thinking about this ever since Rawley showed up. Harry was right, it's none of my business. And even though you defended me, I know that you did so only because you were acting as you thought a gentleman should." She paused. "You must regret your gallantry now."

"And how do you know this?" he asked quietly.

"Because you haven't been to town since Rawley's visit." Mattie gaze was steady, but he sensed her nervousness.

"I've been busy here, Mattie. I told you that time was running out, and the vein is so close I dream of it at night. There's gold in this mine, I know it. I feel it. It's here somewhere, buried in the dirt around me. I can't be coming into

town to see you every evening, as much as I would like to.''
Even to himself, that sounded forced, and he saw that she
took it as a rebuke for her behavior with Rawley.

It was better she think that rather than know the truth.
Since Rawley's careless remark, Cameron had done little
else but deny the accusation to himself. He was not in love
with this bold young woman. It didn't matter what Harry or
Rawley believed, Cameron Lynch-Holmes was not a man
who would permit himself such folly. It had cost him too
dearly in the past, and neither he nor Mattie Crawford deserved to suffer for an ill-suited love again.

''I know that you turned down Rawley's offer because
you didn't want to hurt me,'' she said stubbornly. ''That's
kind of you, but I don't deserve it. I've done little else since
coming here except complain about how the miners are always cheated. Even though it's true, there's nothing to be
done about it. Mining is big business now; the idea of one
man panning for gold and striking it rich is nothing more
than a western fairy tale. Only one prospector in a thousand
ever reaps a fortune from the gold he discovers. The men
here know that. They consider themselves lucky if they sell
their claims for enough to buy another stake. Do you remember that silver mine in Leadville that my father sold for
three thousand dollars?'' She took a shaky breath. ''Well,
that money put food on the table for years, and bought us
a cabin in Poncha Springs besides. If Rawley's money can
help your family, please don't let my bitterness stand in the
way. I wouldn't be able to live with myself.''

Cameron felt as though the tunnel walls were closing in
on him. Why did this maddening woman keep surprising
him? From the first moment at the train station in Colorado
Springs, she'd continually kept him off-balance and guess-
ing. He'd never encountered a female who touched so many
emotional chords: friendship, desire, exasperation and affection. Up to now, only Lady Philippa had truly moved him,
but even that graceful temptress hadn't managed to hold his
interest with such intensity.

''I do need the money, Mattie, but fifty thousand would

145

barely cover one year's expense on Clydesford Hall.'' It would take too long to explain how the family estates were handled. To a woman like Mattie, it would seem as though they had spent money as madly as the Roman emperors, and perhaps they had. ''We have a shooting lodge in Scotland, a house in London, another estate in Norfolk, not to mention two Welsh farms we've been trying to sell for a year.'' He shrugged. ''It's not quite as simple as you think.''

Her face looked as puzzled as he'd expected. ''But at least you can save Clydesford. You told me that it was the family seat.''

''Mattie, I have a partner. Harry would receive half of that fifty thousand, so selling would not even pay the upkeep on Clydesford for six months.'' He shook his head. ''Not that it wouldn't be tempting to walk away from this infernal mine. But if we must sell it, I'd rather hand it over to someone less unsavory than this Rawley fellow. After all, he did steal your father's claims.''

Mattie sighed. ''Rawley was correct on one point. It was done legally.'' She looked up at him, her chin jutting out defiantly. ''But it was still theft. There were dozens of unpaid assessments in the San Luis Valley, but Rawley and Leland wanted a miner who wouldn't be able to fight back. Times were bad for us then. Papa joked that it was a shame we weren't part Indian, so we could go to a reservation and be assured of a dish of cornmeal. He was working four claims day and night. To make extra money, he laid bricks on Saturdays. Mama was little help to us. The year before we'd lost my younger brothers in the fire at Poncha Springs, so all she could bring herself to do was sit and cry.'' Mattie shut her eyes, as though driving away the memory.

Cameron said nothing, feeling like a fraud. His childhood had been one of wealth and privilege. The only trauma he remembered while growing up was the day one of their Rubens was stolen.

Mattie looked up at him, her face stoic once more. ''I worked over in Villa Grove, cooking and cleaning at a boardinghouse. Up to then, life here had been happy. As hard as the mining camps could be on grown men and women, for us children, it seemed like one big adventure. Only I turned fourteen in Bonanza, and I wasn't a child anymore. Everything changed that year." She closed her eyes. "Everything ended. From that moment on, life grew dark and cold. Papa died soon after his claims were stolen, and I couldn't bear to watch Rawley and Leland get richer by the day. So Mama and I went back east, but it wasn't any easier for us there. Not at all."

She grew silent, and Cameron reached out, taking her smaller hand in his own.

"If I had the money, Mattie, I'd take you back home with me right now. I'd show you how Clydesford Hall nestles in the Kentish hills like a perfect jewel. Then I'd take you north into Scotland so you could see the heather growing beside the deep blue lochs."

"I'd like to visit Scotland," she murmured, returning the pressure of his hand. "Mama always dreamed of returning home. We used to talk about going back to Glasgow."

For one mad moment, Cameron was on the verge of saying that he would sell the mine to Rawley. Let the wily devil have the gold, and he would sail off to Britain with Mattie by his side. It was a glorious notion, and he wished he could savor it, but he could no more take a poor American seamstress home to Clydesford Hall than Mattie could be presented at Court.

"Maybe I will one day," she continued, her smile just a little too bright.

"Of course you will," Cameron lied.

They looked at each other. If he were five years younger, he'd not hesitate to take her in his arms. Indeed, she would have been his mistress, set up nicely in costly lodgings in London. But that seemed a lifetime ago. He was an older man with responsibilities now. And those responsibilities did not include Mattie Crawford.

"You won't accept Rawley's offer, will you?"

Cameron shook his head. "You say you couldn't live with yourself if you thought you stood in the way of my seeing a profit. Well, I can't accept the idea of handing over a gold mine to the man who stole a fortune from your father."

Mattie's eyes shone with unshed tears. "Thank you," she whispered brokenly; then she hurled herself in his arms.

He embraced her in return, reveling in the softness of her skin, the fragrance of her tousled hair, and in the emotion that made her nestle within his arms like a devoted lover. *I don't love her,* he told himself stonily, aware at the same time of his quickened breathing.

After a moment, he pushed her away. "You have to go back now, Mattie," he said in an uneven voice. "The evening shift will be down soon, and I've work to do."

Turning his back on her, he grabbed his pickax and began hacking at the rock and dirt. Although he didn't look back, he instinctively knew she was still crouched behind him— her gaze burning into his back. *Please go,* he thought furiously, pounding harder and harder at the wall, taking care to control his movements so there would be no chance of striking Mattie. *Go away and take your green-eyed beauty with you.* All Cameron wanted was to lose himself in the back-breaking labor. Again and again, he struck at the wall, splinters of rock flying about him. He would pound until his arms ached and he was too exhausted to dream. He would pound harder and harder and maybe he would forget the feel of Mattie in his arms, and the way his throat constricted when he saw the tears in her eyes. He suddenly shut his own eyes as though to blot out the memory. With blind strength, he struck once more at the wall.

"Stop! Stop, Cameron!"

Cameron opened his eyes and spun around. "What are you still doing here?"

Mattie looked at him with a startled expression. My God, had he somehow injured her?

"Are you all right?" he asked anxiously.

She could only point to where he had been hacking away so maniacally a moment before. He swung around and gave a strangled cry. Glittering in the lantern light was a broad, unmistakable swath of gold.

The barrel of the gun gleamed like black ice in the moonlight. Devlin stared without blinking at the masked man who held the weapon only inches from his face.

"Don't give me that look, like you was a bear about to maul me. Just hand over what's in your pockets, mister."

With a contemptuous expression, Devlin slowly opened up his jacket. The lantern hanging from the robber's belt illuminated only the jacket's gray lining and his faded black vest.

"Do I look as rich as those gentlemen over there?" he asked coldly, cocking his head in the direction of his five fellow passengers. As though to confirm his assessment, the well-dressed lawyers and businessmen began pulling off watch chains and emptying fat wallets into the satchel held by another gunman.

"I don't rightly care if you got only four bits for a plug of tobacco," the outlaw replied. "Whatever you got, it now belongs to us. Ante up or I'll let you get a taste of this cold steel here."

Devlin felt no fear, just exasperation. Everything in the West exasperated him. The wild frontier he'd heard so much about was nothing more than dust-choking streets and ramshackle towns. He disliked the spur-jingling cowboys, the gaunt, bone-weary women and the strutting lawmen who didn't have brains enough to catch a stray horse. Worst of all, without a railroad line linking the smaller towns, it was endlessly difficult traveling through these monstrous mountains. And now he'd had his first taste of what the West called criminals. Laughable. Four men clumsily holding up a stagecoach, and for what? Risking the hangman's noose for a measly pocket watch, or maybe a fistful of greenbacks. All this when gold was pouring out of mines all around them. Fool amateurs. And stupid, too. He disliked giving them even the twenty dollars he had in his wallet. Certainly he would never hand over his money belt, which they were too idiotic to discover.

"I said to hurry it up, old man."

About to retrieve his wallet, Devlin stopped at the snide young fool's remark. Old man, indeed. Devlin wasn't yet fifty. There wasn't an ounce of fat on his lean, hard body, and he didn't doubt he could take this young pup down if he weren't aiming a Colt at him. Still, his month in Colorado had left him in a sour mood. He was no nearer to catching Mattie Crawford than he had been five weeks before, and being robbed by inept bandits didn't improve his temper.

"On second thought, I don't think I'll oblige you." He closed his jacket.

The young bandit turned to his comrades, who were now pushing the passengers back onto the stagecoach. "Do you hear what this old slicker says? He don't think he has to give us anything."

"Well, don't that beat all?" One of the other outlaws holstered his pistol and walked over. "What makes these tenderfeet think they can spit in our eyes like this?" He walked right up to Devlin, shoving his face only an inch away. His breath reeked of tobacco and bad liquor. "You know we'll kill you and leave you for the buzzards iffen you don't give us your valuables."

Devlin lifted his brows in distaste. "You smell worse than a drunken whore."

One of the other bandits hooted. "You tell him, mister. We got to live with this stinking tramp."

"Shut up!" the outlaw snarled. He pointed at the stage, which all the passengers but Devlin had now boarded. "Tell the driver to get a move on. If we decide to let this old coot live, he'll have to make his way to Aspen on foot."

Although the bandits all turned vindictive eyes in Devlin's direction, he refused to show any emotion. He'd worked the beat for ten years in New York's notorious Five Corners. Nothing about these stupid louts could frighten him. But it would be a nuisance to have to walk all the way to Aspen, and in the dark, too.

"All right, you can stop showing off, mister." The first outlaw to hold a gun on him cocked his revolver. "Your audience is gone, so do as we say and hand over your money. No more trouble or else we're going to have to bloody our hands."

"If you ruffians insist, I've a money belt on me." With an audible sigh, Devlin slowly reached behind him, his hands snaking under his jacket. He shot the young man a dark look. "Of course, I'm not giving it to you."

Devlin whipped out a loaded pistol, which he always kept holstered at his back. Before the armed outlaw could move, Devlin had fired one shot, nicking him in the hand so that his revolver spun to the ground. Devlin cocked again. "Throw your weapons down, or I'll shoot this fool's hand off."

The other guns were slowly tossed in a pile at Devlin's feet.

"This ain't right, I tell you. Word gets out about this, we'll be the laughingstock of Colorado. Ain't no gang ever been foiled twice in one month before."

Devlin cast a sardonic look at the young man who had just spoken. "Perhaps you should confine your activities to women and children. That way you might at least be able to steal a sugar teat or feathered hat. But I suggest you leave grown men alone."

"Dang, but it was a woman who turned our own guns on us last time." The bandit with the foul breath stood shaking his head. "I blame her for this. Word about her stopping the robbery has gotten out all over the district. We been made to look like fools."

Another man lifted up his bandanna and spit a wad of tobacco on the ground. "I ever catch that little redhead again, she's gonna have more than our guns to deal with."

Busy kicking the other guns behind him, Devlin jerked up his head. "Redhead?"

"Yeah, some fancy little filly by the name of Mattie Crawford."

Devlin froze, hardly daring to breathe.

"That's right, you old codger." The outlaw with the injured hand glared at Devlin. "Bad as it is you robbing from us, it ain't as bad as having some freckled girl kick us in the ass."

Devlin felt a shiver of excitement course through him. It was like sexual pleasure, only better. "Calm down, gentlemen, I've no interest in your so-called booty. In fact, we both may be after the same quarry."

"What are you talking about?" As though tired of playing outlaw, one of the men pulled down his bandanna, revealing a pale, pockmarked face.

"You seek revenge and I seek justice." Devlin quietly released the hammer of his gun. "With a little assistance from you, I can see that both are accomplished forthwith."

"You're not going to take our money or turn us in?" The foul-smelling bandit pulled off his bandanna as well. His features were as ugly as his rotten teeth.

Devlin shook his head. "Let the authorities in Colorado track you down. Having seen how they operate, I wager you'll all be safe for the next ten years. No, what I want is information."

" 'Bout what?"

"The fancy little filly, as you called her." His voice suddenly grew harsh and urgent. "Mattie Crawford."

Long after midnight, Harry and Cameron were still celebrating. Curled up in a rocker by the stove in their cabin, Mattie was trying desperately to stay awake. For hours, she'd listened to them shout and laugh as they stroked the chunks of gold brought to the surface. Even as she felt herself nodding off, Mattie couldn't resist smiling. It was a broad, fat vein, maybe even leading to the mother lode itself. If they couldn't get investors—and surely they could interest a rich businessman now—the least they could do was sell it for far more than fifty thousand dollars.

Cameron let out an exuberant laugh and she peeked over. Both men were in their shirtsleeves, crouched over the rickety kitchen table, heads together like conspiring schoolboys.

It was the first strike these city-bred gentlemen had ever known, yet they celebrated it as every Colorado prospector had since the day gold was spied in the shadow of Pike's Peak. An empty whiskey bottle lay on the floor, and another had just been opened. She wouldn't be surprised if both of them were rip-roaring drunk by dawn. If she weren't so tired, she might even join them. It brought back memories of Leadville and her early days in the mining camp of Creede. Harry gave another excited yell and clapped his hands together. Mattie chuckled. Her father always said that striking gold for a man was like a woman catching a first glimpse of her baby after the birthing.

Her eyelids closed. She was very happy for them both, especially for Cameron. He'd hugged her so hard when he first saw the gold vein that she feared her ribs were bruised. Still, she hadn't said a word, and when they came to the surface—a bucket of gold chunks held between them— she'd whooped and hollered and danced as wildly as the men. This was what made prospecting worthwhile: not the riches that might result from the finding of the metal, but the dizzying joy, the mad exultation of that first moment. The incredible discovery that it was possible just once to beat all the odds and stand triumphant. She was pleased that she'd been there to share it with Cameron. The men's excited voices started to fade as she drifted off to sleep. Now Cameron wouldn't have to marry some spoiled rich debutante like Evelyn Sinclair.

"She's asleep, so keep your voice down." Cameron glanced over at Mattie.

Her cheeks looked flushed in the light of the kerosene lamp, and her soft, full lips seemed curled into an angelic smile. No wonder she was exhausted. Their little mining camp had been one shouting, madly rushing circus. Shaking off the effects of the whiskey, he got up unsteadily.

"Leave her alone," Harry hissed. "You'll wake her,"

"We can't let her sleep all night in the chair. Bad enough she had to see this broken-down cabin we're living in."

Stepping over to her, Cameron felt his heart swell at the

way her dark lashes swept against her smooth skin. A true Celtic beauty, he thought, and had a sudden image of her laughing beside a Scottish stream, the highland air blowing that rich auburn hair behind her. He reached out a finger and gently touched one of the pert freckles sprinkled over her nose.

Harry cleared his throat.

Without a word, Cameron picked up Mattie as though she were as light as a feather, carrying her to the small room off the kitchen where he normally slept. Laying her on his lumpy bed, he wished he could offer her something as grand as the bedroom suites at Clydesford Hall; perhaps the blue canopied four-poster that Queen Anne herself was reputed to have slept on. As he spread a faded blanket over her sleeping form, Cameron thought Mattie looked every inch a queen herself.

He leaned down and listened to her even breathing. "Thank you, Mattie," he whispered.

If not for her, the mine would now be in Rawley's greedy hands. After three difficult years in America, his luck finally seemed to be changing. He could scarcely believe it. Not only was Mattie a desirable and endearing woman, but apparently she was a good luck charm as well.

"It's decided then," Harry said when Cameron returned to the kitchen. "You stay here and and hire more men, and I'll get on the Denver stage tomorrow. With luck, I'll be on a train heading for New York by the following morning."

Cameron shoved his hands in his pockets, stretching his neck from side to side. "Are you certain you don't want to stop in Philadelphia first?"

Harry poured out another shot glass for himself. He paused, and then with a violent gesture, he swigged the burning liquor down.

"Beastly stuff," he gasped. He looked over at Cameron. "The possibility that I might achieve financial success on my own would only put the old man into an extremely spiteful mood. I wouldn't put it past him to somehow buy the whole thing out from under us. Remember, I've known presidents who stepped back when Jed Tremont entered a room. No, my father isn't the only greedy rich man back East.''

''So our chances appear promising then?''

Harry nodded, stifling a yawn. ''I know a half-dozen bankers on Wall Street who might put money up for this, not to mention a veritable financial wizard in Hartford. I think we can really do it this time, Cameron. It isn't just the promise of riches anymore; the treasure is staring us right in the face like Jason's golden fleece. We have a real bargaining chip now.'' This time he did indeed yawn. ''Give me four weeks. I won't need more than that. Hell, I'll drag this gold nugget through every drawing room and banking office along the East Coast if I must. I promise I'll be back in less than a month with a well-heeled investor or two in my pocket.''

Cameron walked over to his friend as he sleepily rose. The two men clasped hands for one long moment. ''We've struck gold,'' he said softly, the wonder still evident in his voice.

Harry grinned. ''Eureka!'' he replied in a joyous stage whisper.

An hour later, Cameron still sat in the kitchen, Harry's snores sounding from the room in the back. He heard Mattie murmur in her sleep, but she soon quieted. Leaning back in his spindle chair, he propped his feet on the table. Sleep was impossible for him tonight. He'd never been one to need much rest, but after a day such as this, he didn't know if he'd ever shut his eyes again.

Was it possible that he would singlehandedly save his family? Would this gold mine, which was always a last-ditch enterprise for both him and Harry, be their salvation? A cool breeze blew through the open window where to the east, a slight rosy hue began to tint the darkness. East: where Harry would go, all their hopes riding with him. Cameron was glad it was Harry returning to New York. For himself, New York only held bitter memories. To think of the years he'd spent parading through drawing rooms, offering himself discreetly to the highest bidder. He gritted his teeth. And

155

of all the humiliations he'd endured, his secret engagement to Evelyn Sinclair rankled the most.

What would Evelyn think when she heard that the man she'd rejected now stood on the brink of riches that would put her father's wealth to shame?

"What *would* she think?" he asked himself.

The temptation to let her know he'd thrived after her rejection was overwhelming. After all, why shouldn't his former fiancée be informed that he'd just uncovered the biggest pot of gold in the state? It wouldn't make up for all the slights and humiliations he'd suffered in New York, but it would afford him a small amount of satisfaction and vindictive pleasure.

In a burst of energy, Cameron grabbed an inkwell and sheaf of paper from the counter behind him. As soon as he dashed off the brief letter, he'd try to rest. There was a lot to be done at the mine today: security guards to post, more miners to hire. Still, he couldn't resist chuckling as he bent over the paper.

One thing he knew for certain: despite her indifference to his last correspondence, Miss Evelyn Sinclair would lose at least one night's sleep after she received *this* letter.

Chapter Eleven

Someone was watching Mattie. She was certain of it. Whenever she walked through town these past few days, she felt the weight of an intense, invisible gaze. Even here in the Homestead's empty kitchen, she was uneasy. It couldn't be Devlin. If Devlin was watching her, he'd know in an instant he had found his quarry. And she would be on a train bound for prison.

It could be some lovestruck miner. With "Jack Daniels" apparently nowhere to be found, Mattie was fair game for every wife-seeking male in the district. Yesterday, busybody Mrs. Oberlin had tried to set her up with her brother-in-law. A widower with thirteen children!

I have to leave soon, she told herself as she stretched a piece of soiled lace over a towel, then sliced off one end of a loaf of bread. No matter who was watching her, the danger was too great. So why was she fussing over this silly lace trim for her picnic dress instead of packing her trunk?

Yet that would mean leaving Cameron, she thought with a wrench. Well, leaving him was inevitable, wasn't it? Was she so taken with this man that she would risk capture for a few more days of his charm? No, she would not. With a frown, Mattie bent over the lace and began rubbing it with the soft part of the loaf to clean it. I'll tell him at the picnic tomorrow, she decided. Cameron had no claim on her, and she could leave comforted by the fact that he at least had found what he was looking for. Mattie blinked furiously. Then why was she tearing up like some schoolgirl reading a penny romance?

When Ruby opened up the kitchen door, Mattie turned and wiped an embarrassed arm across her eyes.

"I thought you went off to buy strawberries for the pies, Ruby."

The cook was dressed in her market dress, a gunnysack hanging from her arm. "That I was, miss, but standing right out front is the stubbornnest man I ever did see. Blocked my way until I told him where Mattie Crawford was."

Mattie squeezed the loaf so tightly, a shower of bread crumbs fell on the lace. "Well, who is he? What does he want?"

"Only a chance to talk in private, Miss Crawford." Marshal Lee's stern face appeared in the doorway. Ruby gave her a questioning look before leaving them alone.

Mattie felt her heart stop. It was over, her desperate attempt to escape, her hopeless longing for Cameron—it was ending here in this kitchen. Perhaps that brief glimpse he'd had of her at the train station in Colorado Springs had been enough for him to track her down. Were there warrants out for her arrest? My God, was every lawman in Colorado out looking for her?

"Do I know you, sir?" Mattie was amazed at how calm she sounded.

"Marshal Sam Lee, ma'am." He walked into the spotless kitchen, his shiny boots squeaking on the floor. "I saw you a few weeks ago at the train station in Colorado Springs. I believe that's where you bumped into Lord Cameron and his friend."

Mattie and Lee stared at each other for a long, tense moment. "You're prettier than I remembered," he said in a low voice. "When you were living in Bonanza, I thought you skinny as a fencepost."

She couldn't have heard correctly. "We've never met, Marshal," she said nervously. *I would have remembered you,* she thought. This close she could see that Lee's right eye was a different color than his left, while a faded scar ran along his neck. The only man she remembered with those traits was—

She let out a strangled gasp. "Sweet Lord! You're Sam Leland!"

Unwilling to believe her own eyes, she visibly shuddered when he nodded. What in the world was Hugh Rawley's old partner doing masquerading as a federal marshal?

"Is this some sort of trick you and Rawley have put together? No matter what you threaten me with, I still won't help you or your partner buy Lord Cameron's mine. He's a good, decent man, and deserves to profit from his hard work." She was babbling, but she couldn't stop herself. "You're not getting his mine. You're not! So you can stop pretending to be a marshal."

"Unbelievable as it seems, I am a federal marshal. Have been for six years." He spoke far more gently than the Leland she remembered. "Pretty good one, too, I think. At least I've tried to serve justice as best I can. It's one of the ways I've chosen to make amends."

Mattie fell back in a chair. Another moment and her legs would have collapsed beneath her. "Sam Leland and Hugh Rawley know nothing about justice," she said. As frightened as she was, the old bitterness was still there.

He didn't seem offended. "You're right. The Sam Leland you knew was a corrupt, greedy man. But that was ten years ago. A lot has happened since then."

Mattie bent her head down. A lifetime had happened in those ten years.

"I became a rich man after Poncha Springs. Your father's claims were productive ones."

She flinched. "I don't want to hear about your good fortune. Especially since it's been at the expense of my family.''

"Mine, too.''

She looked up, surprised at the desolation in his voice. Yes, she could see why she hadn't recognized him at the train station. He looked twenty years older than the Sam Leland she'd known. His once thick black hair was streaked with gray, and he now went about clean-shaven. How she had hated Leland's bristly beard and handlebar mustache. How she had hated the man himself. She still did.

"Well, I had nothing to do with your misfortune.''

"And I had everything to do with yours," he finished for her.

She didn't bother to nod.

"I'm ashamed to say that your family wasn't the only one destroyed by Rawley and me," he continued. " 'Fraid that Rawley is still the same old lying polecat; even the archangel Gabriel wouldn't convince him of the error of his ways. He and I had a lot of victims, some with stories even sadder than yours. But it wasn't until I lost my own wife and child that I saw just how terrible a man I'd become.''

"Why are you telling me this?" Mattie felt suddenly weary. "Have you come here to ask my forgiveness? If you have, it's too late. Years too late.''

"I've tried to make it up to the families I cheated. As I said, I'm a rich man. If they won't take money from me— and some won't—I try to offer them opportunity. When I saw you get down from that train in the Springs, I thought to myself, could that really be Mattie Crawford, after all these years? I wasn't sure about approaching you, though. Last time I saw you, I recall you saying some terrible things to me.''

She shot him a dark glance.

"All of them deserved, I'm afraid.''

She looked into his lined face and saw only regret and curiosity. *He doesn't yet know I'm a fugitive,* she told herself. For a little while at least, she was safe.

Pretending he left her unmoved, she stood up and returned her attention to the lace.

A long, uncomfortable silence ensued, which he at last broke. "My wife used to do that," he said quietly.

Mattie only rubbed at the lace, wishing he would leave.

"Not that she had much lace to clean in the early years of our marriage. We were dirt poor, with barely a decent pair of work boots between us." He looked away for a moment. "My Ruth took fine care of whatever we did manage to lay our hands on, though. Seeing you working away in this kitchen reminds me of those times. That was before the money started rolling in. Before my wife ran off with a Texas rancher." His voice grew thick with emotion. "Before my boy died in a mining accident."

"I'll spare you my sad story, if you'll spare me yours," she broke in sharply.

He frowned. "I wish you would tell me your story. If I knew what these past ten years have been like for you, I'd know how to help you."

Mattie stopped cleaning the lace. "I don't want your help. I don't need it."

He muttered something to himself, before jamming his hat back onto his head. "Maybe it was a mistake to come here."

Mattie finally flung down the bread, her emotions near to straining. "How dare you come to me now to discuss old times! An apology and a few dollars won't bring back my parents. Did you somehow imagine I would forget what you did to us?"

"No, why should you?" he asked sadly. "I haven't forgotten. I wish I could, though. I wish I didn't dream at night of your mother crying over your pa's grave in Poncha Springs. I wish I didn't remember how thin and hungry you looked the day you both left Colorado."

She closed her eyes. "Please go."

Lee sighed, the lines in his face seeming more deeply etched than ever. "You hate me, then?"

"Until the day I die," she said calmly.

161

"That's a shame. I might have been able to help you."

"You can't help me. No one can." There was a note of startling finality in her reply.

"I don't believe that." He slowly walked to the door, but stopped before leaving. "Don't let hatred control your life, Mattie. I promise you, you'll regret it. You'll regret it very much."

When the outer door slammed, Mattie looked down at her hand, surprised to see how much it trembled. So he hadn't changed after all, she thought. Despite his changed demeanor, he'd left here uttering a threat. Oh yes, she was certain he could make her regret many things. Hadn't he already? Thank God she was leaving tomorrow. She desperately needed to get away from Cameron and Marshal Lee. Both men touched dangerous chords in her that were better left alone.

After another moment of scrubbing, Mattie flung the bread aside. It was hopeless. The lace was too deeply stained with dirt to ever come clean again. She fought back a lump in her throat. Mattie feared the same could be said of her own life.

Cameron didn't think he'd ever been happier. With a wave to his mule driver, he strode through the boisterous crowd. The smell of roasting pork wafted along Golden Avenue where tables and tents had been set up, and set his mouth to watering. American flags and red, white and blue bunting decorated nearly every inch of the town, while over the shouts of the crowd, the loud strains of the Portland Miners Band struck up. Every few steps, he answered a friendly greeting. A younger Cameron might have found such rawness contemptible; now it gave him a feeling of freedom and dazzling possibility.

Scanning the street, he caught a glimpse of fiery red hair.

Cameron straightened his hat, confident he looked as fine as any man could in clean denims, white shirt and new string tie. With the Stetson on his head, he fancied he looked like a cowboy.

As Mattie emerged from the crowd, twirling a blue and white parasol, Cameron smiled. Even in simple gingham she was a delight to behold, but today she was strikingly stylish in a dress of white cotton, its leg-o'-mutton sleeves decorated with bright blue braid. Cameron knew there wasn't a woman in the Rockies who could hold a candle to her.

Sometimes he didn't know how he had controlled himself these past weeks. It was difficult speaking to her sometimes, while images of her naked body trembling beneath him filled his overheated mind. Certainly she couldn't have forgotten that wild night in Colorado Springs. The question was how to convince her to become his lover once more. But he mustn't be crude or obvious about it; after all, he'd agreed to keep their friendship strictly platonic.

Mattie stopped before him, a delighted laugh bubbling out of her. "Where did you get that hat?" she asked as he swept it off with a flourish.

"I bought it from a street vendor yesterday. Crazy Bob Womack told me just an hour ago that I looked just like a cowpoke."

She lifted an amused eyebrow. "That's why they call him 'Crazy Bob.' "

"Impertinent wench," he teased back. He touched an approving finger to her long, lustrous hair, which she'd worn loose today so that it spilled down her back, its auburn beauty held in place by a silk ribbon. "Your coiffure is even lovelier, if a bit brazen for a proper young woman."

Although he'd only spoken in jest, he was surprised to see a frown cross her face. "A gold rush does that to a person. It makes you forget there's a world of rules and order just outside the mining district. I lived for ten years back East, and I should know better."

"I was only joking."

She turned to him, her green eyes serious beneath the shadow of her parasol. "Well, I'm not. I've been here too long. It's time to move on."

He stopped, pulling her beneath the awning of a closed butcher shop. "I thought we'd settled all this. You're to stay

163

while I search for Jack Daniels.'' Although he faithfully posted ads for her missing groom, Cameron had long ago stopped expecting to find him.

"You and I both know Mr. Daniels is never going to show up. It's been too long. He's either dead, or taken off for parts unknown. I only came to Cripple Creek to marry him."

"It's not even been six weeks," he protested.

"I have to go, Cameron."

"Well, I don't see that you do. My claim is sure to pay off before the end of summer. How can you leave without seeing this whole thing pan out?"

"I'm happy for you and Harry. You both worked hard for this chance, and no one deserves it more. But what has any of that to do with me? The mine belongs to you."

"But—but you're my friend. I care about you and I'll worry damnably about you out there on your own. Where do you imagine you're going to go?"

Mattie shrugged and looked off in the direction of Mount Pisgah. "Maybe Cheyenne. My father had a cousin who lived near there. Then again, I might head for New Mexico or even south of the border."

"A young woman off by herself south of the border! What will you do there? Work in some flea-infested cantina? Oh, this is too ridiculous for words."

"I'm sure people in London say the same about the future Marquess of Clydesford, who went all the way to Colorado hoping to strike gold," she said dryly. "Please, I don't want to argue. Let's just say our farewells and part friends."

"You're leaving today?" He felt like a stone was lodged in his chest.

She nodded, turning back to face him. It hurt to see how collected—how resolved—she appeared. "I've already told Pearl I'm going. Thanks to her generosity, I'm not leaving here penniless, and I can turn my hand to dressmaking wherever I go. I'm not afraid." The green of her eyes turned darker, like a troubled sea. "If the truth be told, I'm more afraid of staying here."

"Because of me?"

"In part because of you," she finally said. "That night in Colorado Springs should never have happened . . . for a lot of reasons."

"See here, Mattie, you must know I have feelings for you. I've behaved like a gentleman these past weeks because you asked me to, but I see now I should have been clearer about my intentions."

"Which are romantic, but strictly dishonorable," she finished with a rueful smile.

He didn't want to lie to Mattie; he hadn't so far. "I can be discreet, Mattie. With the money from the mine, you and I could travel, perhaps to Scotland. Afterward, you need only pick the city and I'd set you up in the most elegant lodgings you could desire."

She shook her head. "That might appeal to a Broadway chorine or one of the Homestead girls, but not me."

"I can't marry you, Mattie," he said with genuine regret.

Mattie looked at him with an air of surprise. "Of course not. Any more than I could marry you."

"But you're perfectly willing to give yourself to this Daniels fool," he said in an injured tone.

"I'm prepared to make a new life for myself." She snapped her parasol shut, slamming it down in front of her so that its tip struck the boardwalk. "I believe that even in the hoity-toity circles you normally move in, a respectable marriage is preferred over a tawdry back-street affair."

"Whatever I might offer you, I can assure you it would not be tawdry. Besides, I hardly think getting 'hitched' to some unwashed prospector is going to advance your future."

She bit her lip, whether in irritation or amusement he couldn't tell. "Well, it doesn't matter about the absent Mr. Daniels now. It seems as though he never intends to show up. But there are a lot of men without women in the West: honest, decent men who want to build a solid future. If I stay here much longer, my reputation will be ruined. Soon enough, people will forget I foiled a stage robbery and will only remember me as that redhead who used to work in Pearl's sporting house.''

Mattie stepped off the porch.

Cameron caught her by the arm. "I wish I could offer you marriage," he said softly.

She smiled. "Then do the next best thing. Let me go."

"To marry someone else?" For a terrible second, his voice actually shook.

"If need be."

They stared at each other, mirroring each other's pain and confusion. Somewhere in the distance, firecrackers went off, and they both jumped.

"So here you are, Mattie."

Both of them turned to see Roy MacDuff lumbering over. Following closely behind was a lanky young fellow in a green checked shirt and faded denims.

"I've already been to Pearl's house looking for ya. She said you were at the picnic, so I hurried over as fast as I could." The poor man was beet red and fighting for breath.

Mattie put a hand on his heaving shoulder. "Why all the rushing about? Has something happened?"

Roy could only shake his head, casting a pleading look at the man next to him.

"What's wrong?" she asked, feeling herself tense up. Perhaps word had come over the telegraph about the theft in New York. Maybe there was a wanted poster of her right now in the marshal's office.

"If you have bad news, spit it out, man," Cameron said impatiently.

"It's him!" Roy said in a gasping breath.

Mattie turned wide eyes toward the tall stranger. Her parasol clattered to the ground.

"The name's Jack Daniels, miss." The young man grinned and ducked his head in greeting. "And I come here to marry you."

Chapter Twelve

"The devil you say!" Cameron said curtly. "You can't be Jack Daniels."

Mattie stood speechless beside him.

"Sure I am. If you don't believe me, I got a bill of sale in my pocket that shows I jest sold my silver claim up near Leadville." The fellow promptly fished out a folded paper from his shirt pocket. Handing it over to a stunned Cameron, Daniels bowed his head in Mattie's direction. "You sure are easy on the eyes, miss. It didn't seem possible that any respectable young lady would be willing to marry a sourdough like me, but here you be—and lookin' prettier than a field of mountain daisies. I done struck the mother lode when I sent for you."

Roy's eyes were wide with excitement. "Ain't it grand, Mattie?"

Mattie looked at Roy as though he were speaking gibberish. "What—what did you say?"

"I said, ain't it grand your intended finally showed up?"

This couldn't be happening. Mattie felt so unsteady, she

was certain that even a slight breeze would knock her over. What was she supposed to do next?

"Yes, it's grand indeed." She returned her attention to the young man, wincing at his eager, hopeful expression. "I'm not sure how you knew where to find me, Mr. Daniels."

"It was one of them ads you placed in the *Crusher*, miss. Billy Red Eye—he's an old friend of my pa's—well, he come to Cripple Creek two weeks ago to see how the gold was running. Soon as he read about this order-book woman what was lookin' for Jack Daniels, he hightailed it back to Leadville. You see, he knew that I sent off for a bride back in February. I ain't heard nothing since then, so I thought they jest couldn't find no lady that wanted to come out to Colorado. But then Billy showed me this here ad saying there's a bride asking about a prospector by the name of Jack Daniels. Soon as I seen that, I knew you was the gal I sent for. I sure am sorry I wasn't here to meet you. I moved off to Leadville three months ago and didn't think to tell the order-book people how to reach me. I thought you weren't coming, but if I'd knowed you was on your way to me, I would've stayed put like moss to a pine."

"I must be dreaming." Mattie shook her head. This impossible. Someone was playing an elaborate trick on her. But why was no one laughing?

"That's jest how I feel, miss." Daniels took a tentative step closer. "These past two nights, I been dreaming of angels. Couldn't figure out why, but now that I seen you, I can see I was dreaming of the angel what come to marry me."

Mattie shifted nervously. "I simply can't believe this." She looked at Roy, hoping to see his broad face creased in a joking grin, but he seemed to be taking this much too seriously.

"Nor do I." Cameron lifted his head from the bill of sale. "This piece of paper doesn't prove anything, young man. And if you have no other form of identification, I'm afraid we will not be able to take you at your word."

Both Roy and Daniels looked startled. "Who is this funny-talking fella?" Daniels asked Mattie.

She took a deep breath. "This is a friend of mine, Lord Cameron Lynch-Holmes. He's part owner in one of the mines here."

"Well, meaning no offense, Lord Holmes, but I don't rightly see how this is any of your business. I done sent off for a wife last winter, and here she is. All you should be doing is asking if you can kiss the bride." He gave Cameron a slight grin, which was at odds with the warning expression in his eyes. "I waited a long time for Miss Crawford, and she's been lookin' for me too. It ain't for you to be raising no objections."

Mattie felt as though she were watching some traveling carnival where the most fabulous and absurd things were taking place. "How can this be possible?" she asked softly. "I truly never expected—I mean, after all this time. How can this be?"

Daniels twisted the faded hat he held in his hands. A slight blush colored his cheeks, making him look shy and boyish. "I was afraid a pretty lady like you wouldn't like what she saw. I'm sorry, and that's a fact, but I got this homely face from my grandpa."

"You're not at all homely, Mr. Daniels," she broke in, struggling to get control of the situation.

In truth, no one would find the tall young man unattractive. He had thick, wavy brown hair, clear hazel eyes and a wide, engaging smile. He looked somehow familiar to her, however, and she wondered if he was a relative of a miner her family had known from the old days.

Mattie nodded her thanks to Roy for retrieving her parasol. She'd been so shocked at Daniels's appearance, it was amazing she hadn't crumpled in a heap rather than just dropping her sunshade.

"Excuse me for asking, Mr. Daniels, but how old are you?" She fought to keep her voice calm.

"I'll be twenty-two next January, miss."

Mattie breathed a sigh of relief. She would grab at even

the flimsiest excuse to get out of this marriage, and he had just provided it. "What a shame. I'm four and twenty, Mr. Daniels. If it was a fresh young girl you expected to marry, clearly I won't do. So if you wish to call off the marriage, I perfectly understand."

"Call off? No way, miss. I never gave a thought to how old my bride was going to be. As long as she's a strong, child-bearing woman, I ain't got no complaint. And I sure don't think I could find another lady as pretty as you, no matter how young she was. No sir, you look to be everything I ever wanted when I sent off for a wife, Miss Crawford."

His last words gave her another lifeline to grab onto. "That's another thing I must clear up. You see, this will not be my first—"

"So he showed up after all!" Mrs. Oberlin, the local busybody, burst upon them like an invading swarm of bees. "Land sakes, it's enough to make a body believe in miracles. Word of your Mr. Daniels is spreading through the picnic faster than a spring thaw." She pushed back her bonnet, screwing up her eyes to give Daniels an appraising stare. "You're six weeks late, young man, but it looks as though you'll be worth the wait."

He ducked his head. "Thank you, ma'am. I hope you've all been looking after my intended in the meantime."

"Indeed we have," Cameron broke in. "Which is why none of us are willing to hand over Miss Crawford to any stranger claiming to be Jack Daniels."

"Cameron, let me handle this," Mattie murmured, laying a restraining hand on his arm.

"What's the problem here?" Mrs. Oberlin looked sharply from Cameron to Daniels. "Ain't this the man who sent for Mattie?"

"So he says." Cameron's voice dripped with sarcasm and disbelief.

Daniels held out his paper once more. "Here's a recent bill of sale, ma'am. It shows plainly that my name's Jackson Otis Daniels—'Jack' to my friends."

Mrs. Oberlin read over the bill. "Everything seems perfectly correct, Lord Cameron. Why are you making such a fuss?"

"He's only looking out for my welfare." Mattie shot Cameron a sad smile, all too aware of his growing frustration. She knew instinctively that he always doubted her story of being a mail-order bride; to be suddenly confronted with the groom himself must be almost as shocking to him as it was to her.

"He don't have to spend another second fretting about your future, miss." Daniels straightened up, his chest puffed out with pride. "As you can see from that bill, I am now in the possession of eighteen thousand dollars. I had me a right fine silver mine. All in all, I'd say you and me can start a good life together."

"Eighteen thousand dollars," repeated Mrs. Oberlin. She snuck a peek at Mattie and raised an eyebrow. "If you don't marry him right quick, this fellow will be snatched up by the first girl with a head on her shoulders."

Daniels grinned broadly. "Don't want no other girl, jest Miss Crawford here."

"I'm very honored by your proposal, Mr. Daniels, but there's something you should know."

"She is not going to marry you," Cameron broke in loudly.

Roy leaned forward and took Cameron by the arm. "Why don't we move off and give the young couple a little time to get to know each other?"

Cameron tried to shake off the gargantuan man's grip, but he might as well have been wrestling with a grizzly. "I'm not going anywhere until this business is settled."

"Please go Cameron," Mattie said gently. "This doesn't concern you."

Wriggling out of this marriage was going to be hard enough; she didn't need Cameron making a scene and turning this into an even greater nightmare than it already was. She nodded to the blacksmith, who tugged the protesting Englishman after him.

"But it does concern me," he protested angrily, struggling against the giant who held him. "Miss Crawford is my friend."

"Friend or not, she ain't your woman," Daniels shouted back.

"Well, she's not yours either!"

Mattie bit her lip to keep from yelling out that she *was* Cameron's woman. She certainly felt as though she belonged to Cameron, and God knows she wanted to belong to him body and soul.

"She is not your woman!" Cameron repeated, his face purpling with rage.

"Never seen a fella act like that," Mrs. Oberlin said as MacDuff dragged Cameron off. "I always thought them English lords had manners, but I guess you can never tell with a foreigner. Well, don't you two pay him no mind. Mr. MacDuff is right. A young couple about to get married needs a bit of privacy. You get to know each other, and I'll rustle up Reverend Haller."

"Whatever for?" Mattie's voice came out in a squeak.

"Why, to get you two hitched. That's what you came to Colorado for, ain't it?"

Things were moving much too fast. "Yes, but—"

"No sense in wasting any more time. The sooner you two are man and wife, the faster Lord Fancy Pants there will back off. Oh, I had a few notions about matching you up with my brother-in-law, but I got to admit Mr. Daniels here is much younger and handsomer than Ben. *And* he's got himself eighteen thousand dollars to boot." She straightened her skirt, as though preparing to march off to battle. "A wedding should turn this day into the biggest party Cripple Creek ever saw."

"But you can't get the preacher. Please, Mrs. Oberlin!" Mattie watched helplessly as the woman hurried off into the boisterous Fourth of July crowd. "This is simply awful."

"I thought you wanted to get married, miss," Daniels said softly.

She jumped. Her thoughts were in such a turmoil, she'd

almost forgotten the young man standing patiently before her. Mattie felt miserable. Of all the luckless things to come to pass. Why hadn't she chosen a more unusual name than Jack Daniels for a prospective husband? Still, this all seemed like an impossible coincidence. Was he indeed Jack Daniels, a man who had sent off for a wife earlier this year? She knew how scarce marriageable young women were in the West, especially in mining districts. Mail-order brides were not uncommon; her mother's best friend in Villa Grove had been a mail-order bride herself. But for him to turn up now!

She shielded her eyes from the sun. If he was telling the truth, then he must think her a baffling young woman. After all, what reason could she have for balking at their marriage? For six weeks, she had stated constantly that all she wanted was to discover the whereabouts of Jack Daniels so she could become his wife. She had even let Cameron run ads on her behalf. Well, here he was. Now what was she going to do with him?

"I'm sorry, Mr. Daniels. I must seem like a fool for behaving like this."

"I'd be pleased if you'd call me 'Jack,' miss."

She sighed. "That's what I've been trying to tell you . . . Jack. I'm not really a 'miss.' You see, I was married before. I've been a widow for over three years."

"Don't matter to me none."

"It might if you knew that my husband died in rather shameful circumstances." Mattie met his questioning look. "Frank was killed while serving out a prison sentence."

Daniels shrugged.

"He was in prison for robbery and murder." She dared not reveal much more about her past, but she hoped this was unsavory enough to give Daniels second thoughts about marrying her.

"I can't see how that has anything to do with you, miss. After all, you weren't the one in prison."

If her safety didn't depend on it, Mattie would have told

him everything right then and there. Barring that, she didn't know how to dissuade him.

"I should also tell you that I've been staying at the Old Homestead since I arrived." She looked away, pretending to be embarrassed by the admission.

"The blacksmith there told me you'd only been sewing for the girls." He leaned forward and spoke in a near whisper. "And to tell you true, miss, even if you'd been a calico queen, I'd still be wanting to make you my wife. You see, I've been by myself since I was fifteen, working to put some money in my pocket. Well, it's been mighty lonely these past few years; there were times when I wanted to chuck it all, and forget about striking it rich. But I had this dream of making enough money so's I could go off to Montana and buy a big piece of land. Always wanted to be a rancher; I'm tired of hacking away at rock and stone. Well, now I got me enough greenbacks to buy me a sheep ranch, and all I need is a young woman to work by my side and give me a houseful of children."

Mattie groaned inwardly. She hated to hurt people, but she didn't know how to reject this man otherwise. Suddenly she was grateful for Cameron's jealous behavior. Her reputation would be in tatters afterward, but she would be leaving Cripple Creek anyway. So what did it matter?

"You are clearly a decent, upstanding gentleman," she said. "That's why I fear that I don't deserve you. No doubt you've been wondering why Lord Cameron was so upset about me marrying you."

"I know a jealous man when I see one. Don't blame him neither. A pretty lady like you, I'd bet every dollar in my pocket that every man here in Cripple Creek would rather you were marrying them instead of me."

She held out her hands in frustration. "Won't you believe me when I say that I wouldn't be a good wife for you? I know I came to Colorado to get married, but I've had second thoughts."

He put his hat back on his head. "Nah, it's just bride

174

jitters. You'll be fine once we're standing before the preacher.''

Mattie took a deep breath, steeling herself for the young man's hurt and disappointment. "I'm very sorry, but I simply can't marry you. I know that I came out here with every intention of doing so, but since then, things have—''

"Well, it seems congratulations are in order." Marshal Lee bowed his head in Mattie's direction, while extending a hand to Daniels. "Glad I was able to stay in town for another day. I sure am pleased your young man turned up, Miss Crawford. The folks hereabouts told me how long you been looking for him. Makes me rest easier, knowing that you've got a little bit of happiness coming your way.''

Mattie felt her heart race at Lee's unexpected appearance. His marshal's star glittered in the summer sun, and she turned her head aside as though the sight of it was blinding. Clutching her parasol, she looked up the street, wondering if it was possible to escape on foot. "Hopeless," she murmured.

"Excuse me, miss?" The marshal cleared his throat, forcing her to meet his piercing gaze. "You said something?"

Before she could reply, Daniels kicked the dirt at his feet and sighed. " 'Fraid Miss Crawford's got wedding jitters. Says she don't want to get married now.''

"Is that so?" The marshal raised an eyebrow in her direction. "Now that *is* surprising.''

"Not really," she forced herself to say calmly, while her heart pounded. "After all, even if I am a mail-order bride, I'd like to know something about the man I pledge to spend the rest of my life with.''

"Tell you anything you want to know," began Daniels, who stopped when the marshal held up his hand.

"I think I know what's troubling the lady. It's like asking for references when a person comes looking for a job." He nodded. "Seeing as how I'm a federal marshal, I'm certain I can set Miss Crawford's mind to rest if you're both willing to wait a few days. I'll just make some inquiries." His eyes narrowed, his gaze even more penetrating. "It will be no problem. It's my job to uncover deception and fraud.''

Ignoring Daniels's protests, Marshal Lee only straightened his leather vest, one finger touching his lawman's badge. ''Do you have any objections to my asking about your intended, Miss Crawford?''

''Now look here, I don't rightly understand what the law's got to do with any of this. I only came here to get married.'' Daniels's disappointment was replaced by self-righteous anger. ''She's the one who advertised for me.''

''Now settle down, boy. If it will make you feel better, I'll look into Miss Crawford's background as well.'' He bowed his head in her direction, ignoring her stricken expression. ''Not that I believe there's anything criminal to uncover, but this way you can both start off the marriage on an equal footing.''

If anyone had touched Mattie at that moment, she would have felt as cold as a frost-covered window. She recognized a lawman's trap; hadn't she fallen into it twice before? Did he somehow suspect her of being dishonest, had he already heard rumors of a red-haired thief from New York? He was already too curious about how life had treated her these past ten years. If she ran off tonight, as she planned, he would be more determined than ever to look into her past. How difficult could it be to discover that she was wanted for theft back East? And with Lee nosing around, he was sure to run into Devlin. The specter of having both men hot on her trail almost made her break the parasol she was clutching in two.

Glancing over at Daniels, she let out a deep sigh. It was Mattie the marshal wanted to investigate, not this gangly, overgrown boy. But he was a boy who wanted to take her off to Montana. *I could get lost up in Montana,* she thought with a numbing sensation. Once there, she could make her way to Seattle, or even head for Alaska and the Klondike. It would be a sin—a terrible one—marrying someone under false pretenses. *But I have no choice,* she told herself stonily. *I have no choice.*

''Well, I don't know why there's got to be all this trouble.

All I wanted was to marry the lady.'' Daniels jammed his hat on his head

"You're right, Mr. Daniels.'' Her voice was surprisingly calm. "I mean, Jack. Please forgive me. I guess I panicked for a moment. As you said, a bride's entitled to a few jitters.''

Stepping out into the street, she opened her parasol with a flourish. Turning back to the two men, she forced a smile on her face. "If you'll give me your arm, Jack, we can see if the Reverend Haller is ready for us.''

"You mean, you *are* gonna marry me?'' The young man's voice nearly cracked with disbelief.

"Of course I am.'' Mattie smile grew even wider as she returned Marshal Lee's startled look with defiance. "And the sooner the better.''

Cameron flung his Stetson against the watering trough. Of all the asinine, insane things to have happen. After six weeks, who could have imagined that this jackass Daniels would actually turn up? Looking over at the crowd of revelers gathered under the tent, he grimaced to see Mattie among them. To think that Mattie was going to marry this gangly beanpole—and right this minute, too.

"I wonder if they'll let me be the maid of honor,'' a feminine voice purred beside him.

Cameron jerked around, his eyes meeting the amused gaze of Pearl DeVere.

She smiled at his angry expression. "Ah, perhaps not. Even for Mattie I couldn't pretend to be a maid.'' She tapped his chest lightly with a gloved finger. "Come now, Lord Cameron, if our friend has decided to go through with this circus, then we should lend our support.'' Pearl lifted a careless shoulder. "Although I was as surprised as you when Mr. MacDuff showed up at my place with Mattie's intended in tow. I never believed there was such a fellow as the erstwhile Mr. Daniels. I guess I assume every woman is as conniving as I am.'' She gave a mirthless laugh. "It seems I was wrong.''

"I'd bet my share of the mine, he's only some lying young bull who wants to get under Mattie's skirts."

"At least he's doing it legally." Her voice grew hard. "Any man willing to make even the smallest compromise for a woman is to be commended."

"She doesn't want to marry him," he said through clenched teeth. "Any fool can see that."

Pearl turned in the direction of the tent, where Reverend Haller was clapping his hands for attention. "Well, I don't see a gun pointed at her, Lord Cameron, and she clearly looks like a woman about to get wed. She even has the good luck to be wearing a white dress today."

Cameron's face twisted into a frown as the preacher began. "She can't go through with this. I won't let her."

He made a move toward the open-sided tent but was stopped by Pearl's warning voice.

"Don't upset her life, Lord Cameron, unless you have something better to offer her."

To his irritation, Pearl refused to leave his side. Both of them pushed into the mass of people crammed under the flapping tent. Cameron was taller than most of the onlookers, and thus had a clear view of Mattie's ramrod-straight back as she stood before the preacher.

If only he could catch sight of her face, he thought; if he glimpsed even a hint of acceptance for this mad thing she was about to do, he would leave her be. She could tie herself forever to some awkward stranger, and go riding off into the mountains like a trapper's woman. As much as it would pain him to see her leave, he would accept it—he would— but first he had to see her face.

The reverend piped up, "If any man here has just cause why these two should not be joined together, let him speak now, or forever hold his peace."

Mrs. Oberlin swiveled around and shook a finger in Cameron's direction.

She was going to do it, he told himself with a sinking heart. She really had been a mail-order bride all along, come

West only to make a home for herself. But what of the night they'd shared back in the Springs? What of all that had passed between them these past six weeks? Maybe it had all been unspoken, but Cameron knew enough about women to recognize desire and affection—and something more.

"Do you—what was your name again?—Jackson Otis Daniels, take this woman to be your lawfully wedded wife from this day forward, for better or worse—"

"From the looks of his clothing, I'd guess worse," Pearl whispered in amusement.

Cameron cursed under his breath as Daniels agreed to take possession of Mattie.

"And do you, Matilda Crawford, take this man, Jackson Otis Daniels, to be your lawfully wedded husband . . ." the preacher droned on.

Mattie turned her face to Daniels. Her profile riveted Cameron as it had from the first moment he'd seen her step off the train in Colorado Springs. It was an impertinent nose, and he'd teased her a dozen times about the freckles sprinkled lightly across it.

"Leave me alone," he said to Pearl, who was hissing at him to keep still.

Mattie glanced over at the sound of his voice and he groaned at her expression. She looked trapped and unhappy. Her green eyes appeared as troubled as a stormswept sky, and her sunburnt face held an unhealthy pallor. She doesn't want to marry him, he thought with growing conviction. He felt certain it was not just his own jealousy speaking now.

"Don't marry him, Mattie," he said aloud, drawing gasps from the assembled crowd.

A look of fear and something he hoped was relief spread over her face.

"Well, I'll be damned," swore Daniels as he spun around to face him. "You again."

"I beg your pardon, sir," the preacher stammered, peering at him over his spectacles.

"This marriage is absurd," Cameron stated fiercely, his eyes never leaving hers. "She doesn't love him."

179

"Of course she don't love him," Mrs. Oberlin shouted back. "She don't rightly know him yet. And she never will if you don't keep your nose out of what doesn't concern you."

Several other voices rose up in agreement, but Cameron ignored them, pushing closer to Mattie. He vaguely heard Pearl murmuring her disapproval behind him. Well, damn them all.

"This does concern me." He stopped inches short of Mattie.

"You ornery bastard." Daniels stepped between them, but before he could get another word out, Cameron grabbed him by the collar and yanked him forward.

"This is my woman, boy," he growled, sending up titters and hoots throughout the tent. "If you interfere once more, I'll tear you apart with my bare hands." He glanced over at the preacher, who stepped back at Cameron's glowering expression. "And in front of the reverend, too."

Oblivious to the consternation erupting around him, Cameron kept his gaze leveled at Mattie. Her eyes were still troubled, but he thought a touch of color had risen to her smooth cheeks.

His voice came out surprisingly low and gentle. "Tell them you're not getting married."

Mattie stared back at Cameron. Had she ever seen such a penetrating, demanding gaze? "Why not?" she finally asked in a bewildered voice, as though only he held the answer.

"Because you don't love him." Cameron shoved Daniels aside. His voice grew louder. "You love me."

He doesn't know that for certain, she thought, but he wants it to be true. Seeing how tense and agitated he was, Mattie felt her heart turn over with more emotion than she'd allowed herself to feel in years. "I do?" she asked, a tentative smile curving her lips.

"Mattie, you don't have to let this fancy lord tell you what to think." Mrs. Oberlin peeked around Cameron's broad shoulders. ''You just say the word and we'll send him packing.''

Two bearded fellows appeared on either side of Cameron, taking him firmly by the arms. He took no more notice of them than of Pearl whispering in his ear, or the quiet cursing of Daniels, now standing a safe distance away.

''Tell them the truth, Mattie,'' he said calmly.

A wave of fear swept over her. The truth? Mattie longed to tell the truth, to shout out the pain and desperation she had endured since her father died in a miner's shack. But the truth had never helped her before. To be honest now would only shatter Cameron's affection for her. She clutched her hands together. Even worse, the truth would destroy her hard-won freedom. No, the one thing she could never give Cameron was the complete truth.

Another figure moved into view, distracting her for a second. It was Marshal Lee, his sober face revealing nothing other than avid curiosity. The star on his vest shone duller under the shade of the tent, and she shut her eyes at the sight of it. How long was she going to live in fear of the law? How many times would her life be blighted and controlled by these men out for cold justice?

''Mattie?''

She opened her eyes at the sound of Cameron's quiet plea. Every instinct she possessed screamed at her to turn this beautiful, exasperating man away. Her future did not lie with Lord Cameron Lynch-Holmes—it couldn't. To join her fortune with such a respectable gentleman would only destroy both their lives. Yet at this moment she thought him the most endearing, irresistible human being she had ever encountered. Or was ever likely to.

Don't be a fool, she told herself. Her mind raced as Cameron continued to gaze at her, naked pleading in his eyes. *You'll regret this forever. He'll regret this, too, and hate you for it.* Mattie winced.

''Miss Crawford, would you like me to proceed with this marriage?'' Reverend Haller leaned cautiously toward her.

She took a deep breath. ''No, I would not.''

181

"Tell them why, Mattie." Cameron spoke with an urgency that told her that he needed to know the answer far more than anyone else sweltering under this tent.

Mattie stepped forward, the crowd moving back as though she were an actress onstage.

"Because I love you, of course."

"Well, I never heard such a thing in all my born days," Mrs. Oberlin cried over the shouts of the crowd.

The men holding Cameron released him, but he didn't move.

Mattie walked over to him and took his hand, surprised to find he was trembling. She looked down at her own hand, which was steady as a rock. *I've probably destroyed my chances for escape,* she thought. *Maybe I've even destroyed him.*

"Let's go." Cameron pulled her without protest through the crowd. She suddenly felt a hand on her shoulder and looked over to see Pearl.

"Are you certain you want to do this?" Pearl asked.

Mattie nodded as Cameron led her away.

They didn't speak until they'd walked clear of the tent, past the stacked melons and barking dogs.

Cameron squeezed her hand. "I couldn't let you marry him."

"I know."

"My wagon is just down here." Suddenly he stopped and whirled her around to face him. "Did you mean what you said back there?"

"Yes," she said softly.

Cameron took a deep breath, looking off to the horizon. After an awkward moment, they began walking once more, trying to ignore the townspeople calling after them.

"I suppose you're wondering if I love you, too."

She smiled. "I know you do."

They looked at each other. Cameron gave a barely perceptible nod, and then squeezed her hand. "I may have destroyed your chance for a decent marriage."

"Most likely."

"Damn it all, Mattie, can't you say something more? I mean after what I've just done—acted quite a boor, stopped your wedding in front of the whole town even though we both know I can never marry you. You can't be happy about all this."

"But I am happy." Mattie was astonished that it was true. Despite her misgivings and the certainty that she'd made a foolish decision, she *was* happy: unreasonably, ridiculously, terrifying happy.

Cameron pulled her to him, his hand cupping her chin so that their faces nearly touched.

"So am I," he breathed before claiming her lips.

As soon as they kissed, a raucous cheer went up from the crowd now milling around them.

"Well, it looks like Lord Cameron finally won his little lady," someone shouted drunkenly.

He won me a long time ago, Mattie thought as she and Cameron broke apart. *Before I ever met him.*

She would have given a Worth gown to kiss him once more, but dozens of curious townspeople suddenly surrounded them. As though to emphasize everyone's excitement, a string of firecrackers exploded loudly in the street, drowning out their words. And the fevered beating of Mattie's heart.

Chapter Thirteen

Devlin hated saloons. The smell of stale vomit and cheap beer reminded him of his father, a drunken Irishman of no use to anyone but the barkeep. John Patrick Devlin, however, was as abstemious as a Quaker missionary, and just as zealous. His adult life had been devoted to ridding society of liars and felons: people like his father, and those damned stagecoach robbers. And Mattie Crawford.

He glanced at his pocket watch, knowing instinctively that those fools had failed. As though to confirm his suspicion, a gangly young man pushed open the saloon's swinging doors. Devlin glared at the fellow as he made his way through the hurdy-gurdy girls and drunken miners weaving over the sawdust floor. Curse these lowlife scum. Not only couldn't they rob a mountain stage, they couldn't even lure away one lone female.

The young man stopped before Devlin's table, his right eye twitching nervously. '' 'Fraid I got some bad news for you, Devlin.''

''Let me guess: The Crawford woman is still traipsing about free in Cripple Creek.''

"It ain't my fault. She was all set to get hitched to me, just like we planned. But it was that fancy English fellow that threw a hammer into everything. I told you she saved his life when we was robbing that stage they were on. Ain't likely he was gonna just hand her over to me. Stopped the wedding ceremony, he did, and walked off with her." His eye twitched again. "Don't blame me, blame him."

"I blame you both, Andy," Devlin said, his voice quiet and threatening. "If you'd stood up to the Englishman—which I'm sure you didn't—maybe she would have gone through with it. Now he'll be sticking to that little thief like a duck to water. The whole purpose of you pretending to be Jack Daniels was to get her far away from any innocent bystanders or lovers."

"Well, he's probably taken her back to his cabin." Andy sat down in the chair opposite Devlin. "If you want her that bad, me and the boys can nose around there tonight and grab her then. The whole town's getting drunker than muleskinners, and with all them firecrackers going off, no one's gonna pay attention to the sound of a few guns being fired." He grinned. "Besides, the Englishman's got a heap of gold out there."

"I know. And he also keeps two armed guards at the mine entrance. Not to mention a Colt revolver by his side." Devlin hadn't spent the last two weeks nosing around Cripple Creek without discovering everything about both Mattie and Cameron Lynch-Holmes. He reached for his hat. Today wasn't the day, after all.

"That's only three armed men. Me and the boys make six," Andy said. "What say we go there after dark, you take the girl and we'll help ourselves to a few gold nuggets."

"Shut up," Devlin said and pushed himself up from the table.

He should have known better than to put his trust in these buffoons; still, it was the best chance he'd had so far. After two weeks of shadowing Mattie, he'd at last had the foresight to read one of the town's weekly papers. The ads posted for a Jack Daniels seemed sent by heaven itself. If she was trying to masquerade as a mail-order bride, that meant she would be willing to go off with whomever claimed to be her erstwhile groom. If it was handled publicly—as planned—then chances were good Mattie would be forced to flee Cripple Creek or go through with the wedding. Either way, she would have fallen into Devlin's hands. He hadn't taken Lord Cameron seriously, however. Trust an Englishman to ruin things.

"For a little extra, we'll put a bullet in him right quick," Andy said eagerly, his hand up to prevent Devlin from leaving. "That way you can take the girl without fretting over that pretty gent of hers."

Devlin felt his insides tighten. It galled him to ask assistance from these lowlifes. "I have no intention of harming an innocent man."

"You saying you ain't gonna pay us?" His boyish face turned sullen.

"Keep your voice down," Devlin said coldly. "You get paid when I have the girl."

"So let's go get her."

Devlin could barely keep his fury in check. "I came here to bring a criminal to justice, you stupid bastard, not help you steal another man's gold or put a bullet in him." He straightened up to his full height. "I'm a lawman."

"You ain't no lawman," Andy said with a sneer. "If you was, you'd just go up there and put her in handcuffs. Don't be acting like no Texas Ranger just 'cause things didn't turn out like you planned."

Fighting the urge to put his fist through the young man's teeth, Devlin pushed his way out of the saloon. How long was this Crawford woman going to best him? Even worse, the idiot was right. Devlin wasn't a lawman, not anymore. Not since that damnable bitch escaped over the roof right out from under him. The shame of his forced retirement was still so great that his face purpled at the memory. His superiors had told him he'd gotten too old, had grown careless and soft in his middle years. Better for all concerned if Lieutenant John Patrick Devlin—a policeman of over twenty years' standing—was put out to pasture like a broken-down dray horse.

No, he needed to get Mattie alone if he wished to subdue her and put her on a train bound for New York. Only then could he reclaim his reputation and the respect of the Department. Only then could he get on with the rest of his life. Until then, he was bent on destroying hers.

Cameron dusted off the spindle-back chair with his handkerchief. "Sorry the cabin is in such a state," he said, a sheepish expression on his face. "With Harry gone, I fear I've let our humble domicile fall into ruin. For a rich man's son, the dapper Mr. Tremont has quite a way with a scrubbing brush and broom."

A mouse scuttled past Mattie's feet, squeaking loudly.

Mattie sat down in the chair he'd cleaned for her. "I was born in a mining shack with no windows and a dirt floor. This is a step up for me."

An uncomfortable silence followed. After the emotional scene staged at the wedding tent, both of them seemed suddenly embarrassed to find themselves alone together. Had they really confessed their love for one another? Mattie thought nervously. If so, why were they acting as if this was merely a social call?

Cameron looked at the unpainted walls decorated only by a small shaving mirror and a calendar. "I rather like it. You can see Beacon Hill from the back porch. Of course, if you compared it to Clydesford Hall, you'd conclude I've quite come down in the world."

"It doesn't bother you, does it?"

He shot her a friendly glance. "Actually, no. I like not having to wander through two dozen chambers just to get to the breakfast table. From the moment we came West, I've felt like a boy playing truant from school, despite the back-breaking labor. It's a bit of a strain on Harry, though. I do hope we can find investors." He paused. "For both our sakes."

Mattie played with the smooth handle of her parasol. "Otherwise, you'll be back in the marriage game again?" She knew what the answer would be, and felt pained.

"Yes, I fear I will. I'm the future Marquess of Clydesford. With my brother gone, and Cornelia unmarried, someone has to see the line doesn't die out."

"Or the family fortune."

With an impatient gesture, Cameron flung his soiled handkerchief onto the kitchen counter. "I've not lied to you, Mattie. You know that I can never make you the next marchioness."

"I probably find that even more absurd than you do." Mattie laughed with genuine amusement.

"So you don't think I'd make a proper husband?"

Mattie was struck by the note of injured pride in his voice. "Never for an instant have I imagined we could marry. Harry would cart you away if he thought there was the slightest chance you had serious intentions toward a person like me."

"Nonsense," he replied a bit too quickly. "Harry regards you highly."

Mattie twirled her closed parasol. "Do you know, this is the first parasol I've ever owned? Oh, I've had my share of sturdy rain umbrellas and secondhand sunshades, but never a useless, pretty little thing such as this." Her voice grew wistful. "Your sister no doubt has a dozen parasols in every possible color and material."

Cameron frowned. "Cornelia may have a taste for frippery, but she's no empty-headed, spoiled girl, if that's what you're implying."

Mattie shook her head. "I'm certain that Cornelia is as generous and kind as her brother, but both of you are accustomed to things that I've never allowed myself even to dream about."

His defensive stance changed to one of gentle pity. "My dearest Mattie, I'll give you more parasols and gloves than you can imagine.

We're sitting atop a mountain of gold. Anything you've

ever longed for—the sweetest, more pleasurable life—I can give that to you now. And it's not just money I'm offering, although I want you to learn the freedom that gold can bring. Let me cosset and pamper you, let me take care of you.'' He took a deep breath. ''Let me love you, Mattie.''

So they weren't going to be all that sane and civilized, after all. Mattie shut her eyes. If he was unable to be practical or strong, then she must.

He dropped into the chair opposite her, his strong hands clasped before him on the table. ''I deeply regret that I cannot take you as my legal wife, but in every other way that matters, you and I shall belong to each other.''

''Please stop,'' she whispered.

''We don't have to stay in Cripple Creek. Once this mine business is wrapped up, we can go anywhere you like. Anyplace at all, even Europe. I'll buy you the fanciest house, or set you up in the most elegant suite of rooms.'' He stopped. ''Perhaps I've misread your intentions. I thought you loved me.''

''I do,'' she said softly.

He visibly relaxed. ''If you have misgivings about creating a scandal, I can only assure you that I can be most discreet, despite my reputation.''

She took a deep breath. ''I stopped worrying about such things long ago. But my life is too complicated right now for any . . . entanglements.''

His calm veneer suddenly shattered. ''Yet you were willing to marry that Daniels fool.''

''That would have been a terrible mistake. No matter what happens, I'll always be grateful that you stopped me. I almost let my fear get the better of me.''

''Fear? What do you have to be afraid of?''

Mattie realized she'd said too much. Now was not the time to let down her guard, especially before a man who moved her so. ''What any reasonable woman has to fear,'' she said. ''Poverty and loneliness. Silly of me to think that marrying a total stranger would better my life. After all, there's no reason why I can't prosper on my own. I'm a skilled needlewoman. It's far better if I rely only on myself. Trusting other people always leads to disaster."

"You must know that you can trust me."

Mattie wished he didn't look so hurt. "I've learned it's not wise to trust any man."

"Even a man you claim to love?"

She lifted an eyebrow. "*Especially* a man I love." Mattie slowly got to her feet. "I think it's best if I go. Coming here was a foolish thing to do."

"Leaving now would be far more foolish. It took us nearly three hours just to shoo away all those busybodies and get to the wagon. My dear, you walked away from your own wedding after boldly admitting that you loved me. And the entire town was there to witness it. If you thought you were celebrated before, I've no doubt Cripple Creek will name a street after you now. Between the gossips and the drunks, you won't get a moment's peace."

She shrugged. "Let them do what they like. I'll be gone before daybreak."

"You can't leave me now," he said harshly. "Not after what happened today. If ever a woman proclaimed herself as mine, it was you. Blast it all, don't you know why I brought you back to the cabin?"

Mattie felt a thrum of desire course through her. "I know," she said in a breathless voice.

Kicking his chair behind him, he crossed over to her in two strides, grabbing her by the arms. "I admitted that I loved you, damn it. I've never told any woman that, even the single other time it was true."

She struggled to get her breathing under control. "Do you still love her?"

"Lady Philippa is dead," he snapped, his blue eyes seeming as dark as jet. "The only thing I allow myself to feel for the dead is pity."

A wave of melancholy swept over her. Suddenly it wasn't Cameron staring at her so imploringly, it was the face of her late husband. As cruel and deceitful as he'd turned out to be, there had been moments when even Frank had looked at her with urgent longing. She'd loved only two men in her life; both times brought only regrets and disappointment. Apparently Cameron had fared just as poorly in romance. Not even his tight-lipped denial could mask the pain he still felt over his lost English lady.

She reached up and laid a gentle hand against his cheek. "You still miss her," she said in a voice barely above a whisper. "And love her."

Cameron stepped back so that her hand remained poised in the air. "I may have loved her once, but no more." He shot her a dark glance. "Any more than you still love your late husband."

Mattie sighed, letting her arm fall back down to her side. "I love the memory of how Frank treated me in our first months together," she said, noticing how Cameron's eyes darkened even more. So he was jealous even of a dead man.

"You said it was a dreadful marriage." His eyes looked at her now with suspicion. She could read his thoughts. He feared she was lying to him again, dancing around the truth like an imp sent to madden him.

"Not in the beginning." She looked away, as though seeking comfort in the grass and rubble outside the window. "Things were different in the beginning. Frank was just nineteen when I met him, and I was smitten in the first five minutes. I believe we both were."

"How romantic," Cameron muttered.

"I'm sorry I married him, of course. He brought me much grief and pain. But what good would it do to deny that I once loved him?" Mattie fidgeted with her parasol; if it weren't dusk, she would have started walking back to town this minute. The air seemed thick with tension and too many secrets. "After all, pretending you didn't love Lady Philippa hasn't eased *your* pain."

"I don't want to talk about her," he said in a clipped voice. "It was your brute of a husband we were discussing."

"My marriage is none of your business." Mattie walked

over to the door of the cabin, which was slightly ajar to let in the summer breeze.

"It *is* my business, damn you." Cameron blocked her way, slamming the door just as she reached for the handle. "I'm in love with you, and I'm willing to take care of you for the rest of your life."

"A gilt-lined prison," she murmured.

"Hardly that." He leaned back against the door. "Is it poetry you want, impassioned pleas as I kneel before you? What must I do to convince you that I can't allow you to walk out of my life?" His voice shook. "Tell me!"

Mattie felt suddenly weak. Everything about him seemed overwhelming: his golden physical beauty, the melodious tones in his voice that always thrilled her, the lust he was barely keeping in check. Her mind whirled. Why did she have to stumble upon such a man at this point in her life? With Devlin hunting for her, with a dark prison cell awaiting if she lost her head for a moment, with Marshal Lee watching her every move.

Yet even if she were free of the law and prison, she balked at the idea of becoming his mistress. No doubt they would share a few fevered and blissful months, but then what? No matter how fancy the suite of rooms he might lodge her in, she would only be his pampered whore. Eventually—deny it though he might—circumstances would demand he take a proper wife and carry on the family name. Mattie had endured the sweatshops of New York, the poverty-stricken death of her parents; she'd endured betrayal by her husband and an agonizing year in prison, but she didn't know if she could survive seeing another woman bear Cameron's children and share his bed. It was hopeless. So why had she come with him to the cabin?

She raised her eyes to meet his. Because of the memory of that wild night in the Springs, perhaps. Perhaps she wanted a snippet of pleasure for herself, something to ease the long months or years of lonely running that awaited her. Mattie felt her palms grow wet at the thought of wrapping herself about him as he whispered words of love.

"Let me go." Her voice sounded weak and unconvincing to her own ears.

Cameron seemed to hear the yearning as well. He moved closer. "I can't. You've embedded yourself in my soul, Mattie. You're as deep in me as any vein of gold that lies hidden in these mountains."

"You don't understand. I can't stay with you." She shook her head helplessly as he stepped up to her, his breath warm against her upraised face.

"You belong here with me." He reached down and took the parasol from her, dropping it to the side. "It's no use denying it any longer. You've told all of Cripple Creek that you're mine."

She stared up at him, her lips slightly parted. "But I didn't mean that we should be together. I truly didn't. It can never work between us."

"You left your young groom standing before the preacher and let me take you away." Cameron bent over and gently kissed the hollow of her neck. "You came willingly to my cabin, to where you know I intend to take you to my bed. That time in the Springs was too brief for both of us. Starting today, Mattie, I will give you such pleasure, such delight, that any thought of skinny young boys or old loves will be burned away." He nuzzled her neck more passionately now, then planted hot kisses along her flushed face. "We'll burn each other, darling." His kisses became more urgent, his hands caressing the swell of her breasts.

Mattie shivered, and she heard his sharp intake of breath as he recognized her imminent surrender. "Cameron, please."

He straightened so that his intense gaze met hers. "Please what?" he said softly.

She could only stand speechless, gazing into those blue eyes that seemed to blot out the late afternoon sun—and her last shred of reason.

Chapter Fourteen

Cameron kissed her so fiercely, she almost cried out in pain. A moment later, Mattie found herself clinging to him, moaning, clutching at him as though he were her only lifeline. If this man stopped touching her, she would die. When he finally did pull away, she gasped for air like a woman struggling for breath. Cameron traced her cheek gently with his hand. Mattie closed her eyes, savoring his touch. *This is surrender.* The thought sent a shiver of fear through her.

"My fiery love," he murmured, mistaking her trembling for passion.

Mattie flung her arms about his neck once more, pressing her mouth against his. He returned her embrace, his strong arms circling her so tightly she could barely breathe. If only she could lose herself in him, if she could give him everything he might ask of her: love, desire, honesty. The rest of her life. His wonderful mouth—so experienced and knowing—seemed intent on devouring her. Her tongue eagerly met his own as it darted in and out of her mouth, both of them reluctant to end the kiss.

Her heart fluttered like the wings of a startled bird. She couldn't walk away from him no matter how much her reason screamed at her to end this embrace. She couldn't.

"I do love you," she said, letting her head fall back as he rained soft kisses along her face.

Pressed against him, Mattie felt his hard arousal and knew he was as out of control as she was. She sank her fingers into his thick golden hair, forcing him to look at her. His blue eyes, now smoky with desire, seemed to pierce her to the soul. He had looked at her with many expressions—suspicion, lust, amusement, exasperation—but she had never seen him like this. That proud, chiseled face now appeared boyish and pleading. Had Lord Cameron ever permitted any woman to see him this vulnerable, this open? She instinctively knew the answer.

Mattie drew his face close, pressing her cheek against his. A wave of tenderness swept over her, and she wanted to weep. She loved him so. It would be the ruin of her, and perhaps of him. His grip loosened now as his hands caressed her back, stealing down to cup her buttocks. Now her trembling was indeed one of desire.

Ever since Evelyn Sinclair first displayed his photograph, Mattie had regarded Cameron as a romantic vision too beautiful—too masculine and proud—ever to exist in the real world. Especially her world. Mattie nuzzled his neck; he smelled of cinnamon tonic and the hot summer day. Yet, he did exist. The man she had dreamed about for months was holding her, frenzied with desire. Desire for her. She clung to him as he whispered of his love.

Mattie felt fevered, her movements languorous, her senses heightened. As his hands roamed over her body, caressing her waist, stroking her breasts, she hungered to touch him as well. Mattie awkwardly undid his shirt while Cameron continued his assault on her senses. She had desired him on that reckless night at the Antler, but not like this. Her feelings then seemed wan and lifeless compared to the torrent raging within her now. Back in Colorado Springs, Cameron had been little more than a dashing stranger, a romantic fantasy, and her seduction was prompted more by desperation than desire. But Mattie loved him now. She was deeply, perilously in love.

She moaned as Cameron grabbed her hand, placing it inside his unbuttoned shirt. Her fingers found his nipple and she rubbed it slowly, eliciting a moan from him. With a teasing caress across his chest, she squeezed his other nipple, marveling at how a simple touch could have such effect.

His hot gaze held hers as he stopped her hand, both of them barely breathing. Some part of her mind was still alert enough to warn her that this might be only desire on his part; healthy, yearning lust from a man experienced in bedding women. Mattie stood very still as Cameron unfastened her blouse, his impatience with the tiny buttons causing him to rip one off. She didn't move to help him; she wasn't certain she could. Did she even have a will of her own at this moment? She hadn't realized how warm she was until he pulled the thin cotton blouse off her shoulders. When he bent to kiss the swell of her breasts above the corset, Mattie felt how damp her flesh was. And how very willing.

Her skirt fell away next, leaving her standing within the circle of his arms wearing only her lacy undergarments. As she stood watching him with heavy-lidded eyes, Cameron quickly tore off his own shirt. Her breath grew short at the sight of his smooth, powerful chest.

They met again in a tight embrace. Mattie let her hand roam down that glorious bare torso before coming to rest on his swollen manhood. She sought his mouth, eager to feel his hot tongue. His kiss this time was so deep, so probing, that her hands fell away from his body and she could only stand helplessly in his arms. If he had asked her for anything at that moment—anything—Mattie feared she would have given it to him.

I love him, I want him. God help me, she thought. *Let what happens, happen.*

As though sensing her fevered submission, Cameron ended his kiss, wordlessly taking her by the hand into the adjoining bedroom. The small window next to the bed looked out over the back porch, letting in a grass-scented breeze. In the distance, the explosion of firecrackers sounded.

''I'm so warm,'' Mattie said in a dazed voice, vaguely aware that Cameron had stripped off his trousers and boots and stood before her naked. She put out a hand to his waist, circling it gently, conscious of his erect manhood between them.

Cameron didn't answer but only unbuttoned her damp camisole and flung it behind her. She wanted to help him unfasten her corset; it felt so heavy, so hot, and she wanted—she needed—to be free of it, to feel those tanned, strong hands cup her breasts and take them into his mouth. But she had given him control at this moment and so she only stood there, eyes half-closed, as he stripped her of the corset, then her pantalets and petticoat. Stepping out of her shoes as he knelt before her, Mattie felt as though she were on fire. As hot as she'd felt before, she was aflame now.

''I love your womanly smell,'' Cameron said hoarsely, kneeling before her. He slid his hand between her legs and Mattie moaned.

Mattie felt Cameron's fingers steal inside her moist crevice. Helpless, she bent over his shoulders, hanging on to prevent herself from falling to the floor. She opened her legs further, welcoming him inside her most private place. She wanted him to drive her insensible, wanted to be free of all the caution and reserve she'd wrapped herself in for so long. His fingers—so expert, so maddening—sent her into some quiet world where nothing existed but this sensual ecstasy. With closed eyes, she let herself drift away on a wave of desire, growing ever stronger at Cameron's incessant and delightful touch. Her feminine scent seemed as strong as musk. Her body trembled and Mattie almost went over that exquisite precipice she'd glimpsed only once before. But Cameron paused just at the moment before climax, as though he wanted to draw her only so far into those hot depths. Instead, he started to slowly caress her thighs, while she cried out his name in frustration. As she stood aching for release, his fingers again found her hidden nub. It was as though he knew he could drive her insensate with pleasure, as though he reveled both in her panting submission and in the control she had given over to him.

His fingers began a maddening vibration inside her. She groaned, closing her eyes, aware only of her ragged breathing and Cameron's intimate touch. She grew still as once more she felt herself on the edge of release, but again Cameron stopped.

"No, please," she cried out.

With one swift motion, Cameron stood up, pushing her back on the bed. She lay there waiting for him, wet and aching with desire. Mattie flung an arm over her eyes, wondering dizzily if she should beg him to touch her.

Before she could speak, she felt Cameron's hard, smooth body stretched out on hers. His bare flesh was hot and hard, as though molten gold flowed through his veins. When she opened her eyes, she saw she had no need to beg. The hunger and love on his face was overwhelming. Had she ever seen any man as exposed as he was now?

Spreading her legs, Mattie moaned with pleasure as Cameron grasped her thighs. Poised above her, he slowly plunged himself into her and she cried out. Wrapping her legs around his back, Mattie thrust herself toward him, his shaft rubbing tightly against her wet sheath. As they moved together, each gasping with every thrust, Cameron suddenly grabbed her waist, and Mattie found herself lifted off the bed as he expertly switched positions with her. Sitting astride him, Mattie arched her back in pleasure, feeling her hair come undone and tumble about her shoulders.

Her hands caressed his erect nipples and Mattie gasped as his fingers once again sought her damp nub. She tried to ride him, pushing down on his shaft, but his fingers had found her. She held herself still as his fingers vibrated within her . . . until finally the still summer air seemed to explode into light and fire and her fevered cries. At almost the same time, she felt Cameron convulse, his drawn-out yell filling the silence as hers died away. She fell exhausted across his chest, feeling his seed spilling hotly within her.

Yes, it was surrender. Each of them had yielded completely to the other.

Cameron gazed at the woman beside him, filled with awe and tenderness. The setting sun gave a fiery sheen to her tousled hair, making her look like a flame-haired goddess. For weeks he had longed to have her once more in his bed, and dreamed of it, cursing himself over his loneliness. And now here she was, her soft voluptuous body lying next to him, his hand cupped possessively over one full breast, her clear green eyes only inches away.

He had known many women—both wantons and unawakened virgins—and had given and received a fair amount of pleasure. But what he had shared with Mattie today was something unique. It was fire, yes, hot and urgent, but beneath it all there was a haunting tenderness, and a different sort of longing. He'd felt this way only once before, during the early days of his liaison with Philippa Courtland. As attractive and engaging as she had been, however, she still hadn't shaken him like this red-haired beauty. From the moment he'd laid eyes on her at the train station, Mattie had disturbed his thoughts and his sleep. Despite his Casanova reputation, he knew he'd never met a woman so unaffected, natural and courageous, so vibrant and sensual. God help him, but he loved her to distraction. Was this how Arthur was undone? He felt the first glimmer of sympathy for his late brother.

"You're wrong, darling," he said softly. It was the first thing either had said since making love.

She cocked her head quizzically.

"I am not in love with Lady Philippa," he continued, pressing her close to him. "I haven't been for a long time."

"It doesn't matter." Mattie kissed him.

She had given herself completely to him this afternoon, yet beneath the satisfied languor, Cameron discerned an air of sadness. He didn't think it was the melancholy that had plagued Philippa, finally destroying their love—and her. But he doubted Mattie would tell him what was troubling her. If only he could convince Mattie to trust him. It was that bloody husband of hers, he told himself angrily. No doubt she was wary of any male who tried to steal his way into her bed and her heart.

"You must realize now how completely I love you," he said. "And I believe you love me just as desperately."

She only nodded, that elusive sadness appearing in her eyes.

"I'm grateful for that Daniels idiot finally coming to town. It brought things to a head, darling, made us both understand how right we are for each other." He brushed her forehead with his lips. "It would be madness to think of living apart."

Mattie took a deep breath. "I can't be your mistress."

He hurriedly covered her lips with his hand. "Don't say that like it was a curse. I love you more than I've ever loved any woman; I'll treat you always like the precious jewel you are. You need not worry about wagging tongues. Don't imagine that the rest of the world is as crude as Cripple Creek. Gentlemen have had lifelong liaisons with beautiful women, liaisons that were stronger in many cases than any marriage blessed by a minister."

She took his hand away. "No, Cameron."

Cameron lay back on the pillow, staring in despair at the ceiling. He felt as though he were being torn in two.

He needed to make a good marriage, a proper, respectable marriage to a woman of his social standing. He would be the next marquess. How could he carry the family line through an American maidservant, a brash young woman who thought nothing of turning a gun on an outlaw or living among whores? He had despised his brother as a coward. Perhaps Arthur was the one who had the real courage . . . courage to follow his heart regardless of the cost. It gave Cameron a wrench to realize he was unable to do the same.

"Mattie, if it's marriage you want, it's not as simple as you think. I have obligations, financial and personal, to my family. I can't marry whom I please."

"I'm not looking for a husband anymore."

"Then what *do* you want?" he asked in a desperate voice, praying it was something he could offer her.

"My freedom."

"But you'll be free if you stay with me. I'll not make any demands, except that you love me." God, he sounded like a desperate boy.

Mattie propped herself up on one elbow, her mass of auburn curls falling over her shoulder. "If I could stay with you, I would. I swear it on my mother's grave. But I have obligations as well." She paused. "To myself."

Cameron couldn't speak, a lump rising in his throat.

"Please don't make this harder for me than it already is. Do you think I want to leave you? The thought of never seeing you again—" She couldn't finish the sentence. Mattie turned her head aside, but not before he noticed the tears in her eyes.

He hated to see women cry. It was a practiced feminine trick, but it always affected him. Perhaps because he had never seen his own elegant mother in such a weakened state. And up till now, Mattie had shown similar fortitude; the fact that he had broken down that steely resistance made him feel even worse. Cameron stroked Mattie's head, reveling in the silkiness of all those curls. He wondered if a child born to her would also have such glorious hair. He stopped stroking her head as a dreadful thought struck him.

"Dear lord, Mattie, I might have got you with child today," he said. "I didn't mean to spill my seed within you. That night in the Springs I was careful not to. This is unforgivable of me, but I was just—" He didn't need to finish the sentence. They both knew he had been as wildly out of control as she.

"It doesn't matter." Mattie lay back on the pillow. "I was married to Frank for four years and never conceived. I was sorry at the time, but looking back I realize it was a blessing." Her voice grew softer. "I don't think I can have children."

Or it could have been that scoundrel of a husband who was at fault, he thought nervously. If she left him only to later find herself pregnant, Cameron feared she wouldn't come back. Not his proud, stubborn Mattie. Fool, to have not controlled himself better or used precautions. The thought of Mattie and his child struggling in some shanty-town put his teeth on edge.

"Are you always so considerate to your women?" she asked.

Cameron was surprised to see her smiling. He didn't feel at all amused. "I've no wish to leave a trail of fatherless children behind me. It's not fair to them or their mothers."

"Considerate and wise." Mattie squeezed his hand.

He pulled his hand away, uncomfortable with the loving approval he saw in her eyes. "I certainly wasn't where Philippa was concerned. I was selfish and unkind."

"And you blame yourself for her death?"

A long silence followed. Cameron felt the old pain steal into his chest, the weight of guilt and remorse, and yes, self-hatred. He never spoke about Philippa—not to his family, not even to Harry. She was like a phantom who haunted his heart and mind, all the more powerful because he kept her shrouded in secrecy.

Cameron looked over at Mattie. She made him feel young and vulnerable again, as though the world was once more a place of reckless passion and love. The very least he could give her in return was the truth. Suddenly he wanted nothing more than to be free of that awful burden of guilt and self-hatred he'd been carrying.

"Philippa committed suicide five years ago," he said in a low, flat voice. "She killed herself because of me."

He expected Mattie to gasp or move away, but all she said was, "Go on."

"We'd been lovers for nearly a year." Cameron swallowed hard, hoping he could get through this confession with some dignity. "The longest time I had ever been faithful to any woman. I was notorious for cutting a swath through London's fine ladies: most of them married, rich and very bored. I had no qualms about seducing other men's wives. Society expects a certain degree of discreet infidelity, especially from a young blood. And often the women approached me, although Philippa didn't. She was recently widowed and concerned about appearances, so I must bear the blame for initiating the affair.''

He watched Mattie closely, certain he'd see disapproval in her eyes, but she only nodded.

''We became lovers, meeting at the country estates of discreet friends, occasionally daring to visit each other at our respective homes in London. She'd never loved her husband; he'd been thirty years older than she, and an avaricious dolt into the bargain. What she felt for me—'' He paused. ''What we felt for each other took us quite by surprise. It was the worst possible time for such a liaison, and not only because her husband was barely cold in his grave. As I told you before, my older brother had just set up house with the Catholic wife of a cabinet minister. The scandal ruined Arthur's political career and caused Father to disinherit him. Until the day he died, my mother refused to speak his name.''

''He sounds like a brave fellow.''

Cameron frowned, wishing she hadn't echoed his own recent thoughts. ''At the time, I considered him foolhardy and stubborn. And his defiance only made things worse for Philippa and myself. For me also to bring scandal down on the family would have been unconscionable. Besides, I was just twenty-three years old with no intention of settling down yet, least of all with a woman who began to show signs of emotional instability.''

''She was ill?''

''Melancholia ran in her family; two aunts tried to kill themselves in her youth, and her father died under mysterious circumstances. Even so, I think I could have tolerated her sad moods, but not the hysterical scenes.'' Cameron shook his head at the memory. ''In the beginning she'd been the one most concerned with being discreet, but after a few months, that changed. Philippa grew impatient with our furtive meetings, and with the pretense of being a grieving widow. Drawn by my presence, she began to make appearances at events no young woman in mourning should.''

The embarrassment of those encounters at the Henley Regatta and society dinners still made him cringe. She'd hung on to his arm possessively, caressing him in public as though she were a lady of the streets. When he admonished her, she became overwrought and often had to be led away by mortified friends.

"By November both our reputations were in tatters. My sister was to be presented at Court the following season, and my parents were fearful that my escapades with Lady Philippa would spoil Cornelia's coming out. So I broke it off." He knew that brief statement couldn't possibly convey the agony of his last meeting with Philippa.

Cameron stared up at the ceiling. For so long he'd tried to keep those terrible memories at bay, but Philippa's sobs and pleadings always whispered to him in his dreams. Young and callow he may have been, but he had loved her. And yet he'd never told her that. His passionate, tender Philippa died for him, but he was too proud—too sophisticated—to give her a simple "I love you." Cameron would have done anything to prevent being seen as a lovesick fool like his brother, and so he told her she was ravishing, a delight, his sweet beauty, but never would he let her see how much he truly cared. And he couldn't forgive himself even now for that heartless omission.

"I loved her," he finally said, "but not enough to defy my family. So I walked away."

He heard Mattie's quiet breathing and knew she was waiting patiently for him to speak. Long moments went by before he did. "It all came to a head at the Duke of Sunderland's Boxing Day supper. About twenty of us were in the salon listening to some Italian woman play the piano. There was a bit of a stir, and I looked about to see Philippa standing in the doorway. She was dressed in a dark cloak, her black hair piled high on her head. She looked gorgeous and pale and quite mad."

Cameron shut his eyes. "A servant came to take her cloak. Only then did we see that she was wearing only a red corset and black silk stockings. She announced that she was Lord Cameron's scarlet woman, and that everyone knew it, so why shouldn't she dress the part.'' He felt Mattie lay her head against his shoulder. ''Everyone was dumbstruck; three members of the House of Lords were there that night, one of them a cousin of her late husband's. I was shocked—and so frightened—for both of us. I couldn't move. When the duchess tried to go to her, Philippa screamed and fell into hysterics.''

Mattie sighed and clutched him closer.

''She hanged herself the next morning. A farewell note was discovered on the dressing table. In it she declared her love for me and—and the news that she was carrying my child.'' He had to force himself to say it aloud, no matter how it tore at him, even all these years later.

''May God forgive me,'' he whispered, fearful of Mattie's silence.

Outside the singing of mountain jays mingled with the sizzle of fireworks. Speaking about those London memories in such a setting made it seem unreal, as though some other man had watched his mistress scream and overturn tables in a plush London salon. He turned to Mattie suddenly, desperate to feel her breath upon his face, feel her heart beat beneath his. Desperate for the touch of a woman who had the terrible power of making him feel again after all this time.

''Stay with me,'' he whispered.

Cameron thought he heard a sob catch in her throat, but when she raised her head to look at him, no tears marked those beautiful freckled cheeks.

''I would give anything if that were possible. But it isn't.'' Mattie smoothed away a tear that had fallen shockingly from his own eyes. ''Please trust me. If I were to remain with you, it would be doomed to end within a few months. I'm still a prisoner of the past, too.''

A disturbing thought occurred to him, one that sent a tremor of jealousy through him. ''Is someone looking for you, Mattie? A man? I thought you said your husband was dead.''

''Frank is long dead.'' She bit her lip. ''If I remain silent, it's to protect both myself and you. Please don't ask me any more questions, or I'll get up this minute and leave. I swear it, Cameron.''

He didn't doubt it. That stubborn expression on her face was familiar to him now. Even though he had a million questions, a million pleas, he didn't own her. She wasn't his. He doubted any man could lay claim to such a proud, strong woman.

''All right, Mattie. I'll do as you like, no more questions, and I'll let you leave Cripple Creek without any more of my unwelcome demands.''

''Not unwelcome.'' She smiled sadly. ''Just impossible.''

He grabbed her hand and held it tightly against his chest. ''I ask only one thing of you, and I hope you love me enough to grant it.''

She looked at him warily.

''Stay with me until I know you are not carrying my child.''

''Are you saying you intend to keep your distance in the meantime?'' she asked, a note of skepticism in her voice.

''Of course not. While you're with me, I want you in my arms and in my bed, every minute of every day.''

Mattie started to protest, but he silenced her with a kiss.

When they were both breathless, he raised his head. ''There are ways to prevent conceiving, my darling. This isn't a ruse to keep you here indefinitely, I promise.''

''Cameron, please, this is no use. I've never conceived before, so it's unlikely to happen now. Putting off my leaving for a couple of weeks will only make it harder on both of us.''

He pulled her to him, and when he spoke his voice was ragged with emotion. ''If you leave tonight or a year from now, it will still tear me apart. I'm reconciled to that. At least if I know you're not pregnant, I won't have to mourn both your loss and my child's.''

''I must be a fool to agree to this.'' Mattie closed her eyes. ''I deserve whatever happens.''

Chapter Fifteen

"So when is your English lord going to take you away from all this?"

Mattie looked over at the woman sitting beside her in the buggy. "Pearl, I told you that I'll be leaving Cripple Creek any day now." She straightened the folds of her muslin skirt. "Alone."

Pearl flicked the reins against the smooth backs of her two high-stepping black geldings. "You've been singing that tune ever since you got here. I didn't believe it then and I don't now. Neither does anyone else, especially after that exciting little scene at the wedding that you and Lord Cameron played out for us."

"I was going to leave that afternoon," Mattie said, "but things just got out of hand."

She waved at Mrs. Oberlin. The older woman frowned, turning her face away. Mattie sighed. Ever since she'd walked out on Jack Daniels three weeks before, the glances thrown her way had been decidedly chilly.

Noticing Mattie's crestfallen expression, Pearl called out

a loud greeting, "Good morning to you, Mrs. Oberlin. Give Mr. Oberlin my best. He's such a lively little man."

As they drove past, Mattie caught the anger on Mrs. Oberlin's face. "You really shouldn't tease her," she said. "It won't restore my reputation. Setting up house with Cameron has put me beyond the pale."

"I can't say I blame them. They expected you and your handsome lord to marry the very next day, and you've cheated them out of a fancy shindig."

"You never thought that, did you?"

Pearl shook her head. "Respectable men don't marry women like us. I'm only surprised Lord Cameron hasn't taken you off to the Springs and bought you a fancy new house. Holing up in that moldy cabin of his is hardly my idea of being a rich man's woman."

"I'm not his woman," Mattie said wearily. "Honestly, you seem to think a female is no better than a china doll that men can play with whenever the fancy takes them."

"That's the way of the world. Anyway, being his mistress seems to suit you. You look as giddy as a girl after her first tumble in the hay."

"What nonsense," Mattie grumbled, but she knew it was true.

"Nonsense, is it?" Pearl laughed. "I know enough about women to recognize one who's been fool enough to fall in love." She shook her head, causing the willow plume on her hat to bounce wildly. "After all, I'm as female as the rest of you, or do you think I keep company with Mr. Stone only because he lets me win at roulette?"

Mattie reached over and squeezed her friend's hand. The whole town knew that the notorious madam was the mistress of Bradford Stone, owner of the most popular gambling hall in Cripple Creek. To the outside observer, it seemed a perfect match of two prosperous sinners. What they didn't know was how desperately Pearl loved him. Mattie ached for her, for she knew after her first conversation with Stone that he regarded Pearl as nothing more than the most expensive object for sale in the city. She suspected that having Pearl pleased his vanity.

"I've been here too long," Mattie sighed. "I should have left as soon as I had the money."

"The same can be said for me," Pearl said. "I'm as frightened to leave Brad as you are to leave Cameron."

"I'm not afraid," Mattie protested.

"Well, I am."

Mattie looked over as Pearl blinked back tears.

"I love him, even though I know he doesn't care for me. Oh, he tells me all sorts of pretty things, and he treats me like a princess, but we both know I'm just a whore. He'll toss me over as soon as someone younger and more exciting comes along. But I won't give him the pleasure of rejecting me. I went through that a long time ago, I won't do it again. I can't." She whipped the horses as the road steepened. "As soon as I gave myself to Brad, I paid a visit to Griff Lewis's Pharmacy."

"I don't understand."

Pearl lifted her chin defiantly. "I bought a large bottle of morphine. The largest one he had. The day I sense I'm losing him, I intend to drink it all down." Her voice grew hard. "Every last drop."

"You can't be serious!"

"Why not? If Brad leaves me, what have I left? To continue as Cripple Creek's richest madam? There's no joy in that—and no future. Oh, don't shake your head in disapproval. You're no different. If Cameron kicked you out tomorrow, you might be asking me for a draught of morphine yourself. Don't deny it."

"You're wrong, as wrong as you can be. I was in love once before, too. Even worse, I was fool enough to marry him." She took a deep breath, as though she were about to walk out along a precipice. "My late husband was caught stealing. He lied and accused me of being his accomplice. I spent a year in prison before the truth came out. But as much as his betrayal hurt me, I never considered killing myself." She clenched her fists. "I entertained a fancy or two of killing *him,* but never myself. A man who betrays you doesn't deserve any consideration, least of all your life. Don't mention such a terrible thing again!''

Pearl clicked at her horses. ''I shouldn't have told you,'' she said. ''That's the second time I've made the mistake of thinking we were the same.''

Mattie didn't bother to protest. Clearly the only things the two women shared were red hair and a scandalous reputation.

But was she really much better than Pearl? These last three weeks, she'd let her guard down, allowing her heart to rule her head. Perhaps if Marshal Lee had remained in Cripple Creek, she would have grown nervous enough to move on, but the lawman had left the morning after the aborted wedding, and there had been no word of him since. She didn't know whether that was good or bad, but she did know that she was courting disaster to remain any longer.

The tombstones of the Pisgah graveyard came into view, sinking her spirits even further. Maybe she hadn't consciously entertained thoughts of suicide, but by staying here she had behaved just as self-destructively. She loved Cameron, but she loved her freedom more. The thought of living without Cameron sent a wave of pain through her, but spending the rest of her life locked away from the fresh air and the light would kill her faster than any poison.

Mattie took a deep breath, her decision made. She would leave Cripple Creek tomorrow. Even though her monthly flux hadn't yet started, he didn't have to know that. It was highly unlikely she was pregnant, so there was no need for this charade to continue any longer. All she needed was to tell him her monthly course had begun. The idea of deceiving him once again made her wince. It seemed she had been lying to him from the first moment they met. But this was one lie that was necessary. And she hadn't lied about what was most important, after all. She did love him. Dear lord, how she loved him.

Saying good-bye to Cameron would break her heart, but her heart had been broken before. The one thing that had

never been broken—the one thing no man could ever do—
was break her spirit.

Cameron was so excited he could barely pause long
enough to tie his donkey to the hitching post in front of his
cabin. He'd hoped to see Mattie in town, but when he'd
stopped by the Homestead, Ruby had said the two women
had just left. It was nearly four o'clock and she wasn't home
yet. The kitchen table still hadn't been set, and carrots and
tomatoes lay unwashed on the cutting board. She would
have to return soon if they were to have supper at a decent
hour.

Hang supper, Cameron thought, as he flung the mail down
onto the table. He'd get dressed in his fanciest broadcloth
suit—even his silk top hat—and take her to the Continental
Hotel for the most lavish meal this mudhole had to offer.

After weeks of receiving no word from Harry, two letters
had arrived today regarding investors for the gold mine. The
offers seemed not only legitimate, but quite impressive.
Damn it all, but he'd been so wrapped up in Mattie, so
painfully aware of her constant exciting presence, that he'd
nearly forgotten why he was in Colorado in the first place.

He scooped up a dipper of water from the bucket by the
door. It was hot and brackish, but he swallowed it as though
it were Mumm's champagne. Which was what he hoped
they would all be drinking soon, Mattie included. He looked
out the front door again, relieved to see Pearl DeVere's
fancy buggy round the corner.

It had been three weeks since that fateful Fourth of July,
and every day he waited anxiously for Mattie to inform him
that she knew for certain she wasn't pregnant. For the first
time in his scandalous life, he hoped that he had gotten a
woman with child. Unscrupulous as it might be, he was
prepared to use any means at his disposal to keep her with
him. He wouldn't let her leave if she was pregnant; Mattie
was a stubborn woman, but not even her pleas and logic
would dissuade him. Cameron Lynch-Holmes never gave up

anything that was his, and that included the woman who would bear his child.

He snatched up the letters once more. Cameron didn't like to get his hopes up; that was a mistake only boys and drunkards could afford to make. But if either of these offers panned out, he and Harry could not only buy mining equipment to extract the gold, they were looking at a million dollars—perhaps more—in profit. Enough to save Clydesford Hall, enough to make Harry independent of his father. He heard Mattie call a farewell to Pearl as she stepped onto the porch. Maybe enough so that he could refuse to marry, and instead spend his life with the woman who had captured his heart. But would Mattie agree? Probably not, unless she had to take an unexpected pregnancy into consideration.

The door opened and he looked forward to his first glimpse of her all afternoon. Every time he saw her, it was just as unsettling as that initial meeting at the train station. Walking into the sunny kitchen, Mattie seemed to bring the color and warmth of summer with her. Her face was tanned and freckled beneath the jaunty straw bonnet, her hair tied back with a yellow ribbon so that a wave of coppery curls cascaded down her back. She looked as fresh and lively as a schoolgirl playing truant—but far more desirable. If things were different, here indeed was the woman Cameron would have chosen for his golden bride.

"You look pleased with yourself," Mattie said with a grin.

As though to confirm this observation, Cameron caught her up in his arms and kissed her thoroughly.

"Do that again and supper will be even later than usual," she said when they finally came up for air.

"Doesn't matter. I didn't bring you here to be my household drudge." Then he kissed her again, drinking in the feel of her ripe woman's body and the moist lips pressed against his.

After a few moments of nuzzling and caresses, Mattie laughed softly and raised her head to look at him once more.

"Has something happened? Was there another vein discovered at the mine today?"

"Better." Cameron stepped back, holding up the two letters. "I went into town as soon as I heard the stage was due with the mailbags."

"You've finally heard from Harry!"

He handed over the letters to Mattie, who dropped into one of the kitchen chairs.

As she read them over, Cameron sat across from her. "It's been nearly six weeks since he left, and not a word since that telegram informing me he'd arrived in New York. The next time I go looking for a business partner, remind me to choose one who takes pen to paper occasionally."

"But this is wonderful! He's found a wealthy investor, a man willing to be partners rather than buying you out." She glanced up at him, relief written all over her face. "I'm so happy for you, for both of you. Now you won't have to sell the mine."

"Well, we'll see. I wish Harry was a bit more forthcoming. He doesn't even mention the man's name, although knowing Harry's Ivy League connections, it's probably the father of some old Harvard chum. As you can see, he's bringing the gentleman to Colorado; they should be arriving in Denver tomorrow."

"Why does he want you to meet them there? It would seem more practical for Harry to bring the investor to Cripple Creek to look over the mine."

"You don't know Harry like I do. The dear boy regards anything west of Philadelphia as a wild and uncouth wasteland. No doubt he wants to put the man up at a suite at the Brown Palace and slowly acclimate him. If he's as staunch an Easterner as Harry, the stagecoach ride alone might make him forget about the whole thing, regardless of the potential profit." Cameron sat back. "Besides, going to Denver will work out perfectly. The other letter is from an attorney in the city. Apparently his client is also very interested in investment. He proposes a six-figure amount."

Mattie scanned the letter quickly. "He doesn't mention

his client's name either. I don't understand the need for all this secrecy."

"Discretion, my dearest. Any man willing to invest this kind of money prefers to keep it under his hat, at least until the deal is completed. Well, going to Denver seems inevitable. Harry will be there tomorrow, and this attorney—a Mr. Lawrence Hill—says his client will be back in the city in four days and would like to meet with me then."

Mattie looked down at the letter, slowly folding it up. "This works out for the best, Cameron. I can leave knowing that you've found a way to save both your mine and your family."

"What are you saying? You'll come with me, of course. Harry will love to see you again."

She raised her eyes to his; they were distressingly calm. "My monthly course began today."

A long silence followed. The smell of dying lupines filled the air as a hot August wind blew through the window.

"I'm not pregnant, Cameron."

He shook his head. "I don't believe it."

She sighed. "Yes, you do. It was inevitable. I'm not carrying your child."

"What are you saying?" He knew he was being deliberately obtuse, but he wasn't going to make this easy for her. Why should he?

"I'm leaving, Cameron. I made my farewells to Pearl this afternoon, as a matter of fact." The stubborn tilt of her chin defied him to doubt her. "I agreed to stay until this moment occurred. We both agreed. Now that there's no unborn child to fret about, I can finally take my leave of Cripple Creek." She took a deep breath. "And you."

"You say that so easily!" Cameron felt the anger and frustration explode inside him. "As though what we've shared was no more than a long steamy night at the Homestead. Good God, woman, does ice water run in your veins?"

"We agreed on this, Cameron," she said, anger evident

in her voice as well. "Why do you have to make everything so difficult?"

"Well, I'm not letting you go. Do you hear? You're not going anywhere!"

Mattie stood up. "I'm leaving on the first stage. You can make our farewell pleasant or ugly. It's up to you."

He slammed a fist on the table. "I love you, Mattie," he said. "Does that mean nothing to you?"

She closed her eyes and didn't speak for a long moment. "If you really loved me, you'd let me go," she finally said in a low voice. Mattie opened her eyes, and this time he saw genuine pain in their green depths.

"To stay with you any longer would destroy me, just as surely as it destroyed Philippa."

He flinched. The thought of harming another woman he loved was unthinkable. As empty as he would feel once she was gone, he could probably live with her absence—but not her destruction.

Mattie saw his reaction and knew that she had won. It was unkind to remind him of Lady Philippa, but she needed to make her escape. It might already be too late. Who knew how persistent Devlin had been these past weeks? The best she could do was try to outrun her past and find a measure of peace. But she knew that without Cameron, she would never find happiness.

"Very well, my dear. If you feel you must leave me, then I won't stand in your way." Cameron ran a hand nervously through his hair. "Being out here in Colorado, I seem to have lost any semblance of manners or sense. I've never forced myself on a reluctant woman before; now is a damnable time to start."

"I do love you," she said, knowing it was unfair and unwise to say such a thing at this moment. "I love you more than you'll ever realize."

"Will you at least come with me to Denver tomorrow?" he asked, ignoring her last comment.

She began to protest, but he held up his hand. "You can say good-bye to Harry. And since you're determined to vanish into the horizon, better to take the train than a stage-coach. I'll even pay for your ticket.''

''I can pay for my own ticket.''

''You agree then?'' His face looked heartbreakingly hopeful. ''You'll come to Denver with me?''

''Why not?''

Indeed, she couldn't see the harm in it. Denver wasn't Colorado Springs, filled with idle, rich Easterners. The chance of running into high society during her brief stay in Denver was practically nonexistent. Besides, leaving on a train was faster than taking the stage. And safer, too, as the memory of the botched robbery came to her.

''I'll go with you, Cameron,'' she said.

His face showing emotional strain, Cameron nodded. He abruptly got up and started for the door, then changed his mind and walked over to her. He took her in his arms without a word. She trembled so much she could barely return his embrace.

You cowardly, selfish fool, she told herself. She'd given herself a little more time with the man she adored. Probably just enough time for her besieged heart to break into a million pieces.

Chapter Sixteen

For the first time in three weeks, Mattie woke up alone.

She forced herself to sit up in the huge bed, feeling lost under the embroidered silk coverlet. They'd traveled most of the day yesterday, arriving exhausted and tense last night; too late to see if Harry had arrived yet. She was grateful. The emotions churning inside her seemed as wild and daunting as the mountain scenery they'd rumbled over. But she had to hold on just a little while longer; she mustn't break down, mustn't allow the grief to flood over her. Once she was safely away, once Cameron could no longer look at her with that tight-lipped smile, she could let herself feel the loss. But not quite yet. Her ticket lay on the table beside her bed. It was a one-way ticket for a ten o'clock departure on the Denver-Pacific train bound for Cheyenne, Salt Lake City and San Francisco. The names sounded meaningless; she hadn't the faintest idea where she was heading next.

Mattie forced herself out of bed, feeling just as tired as when she lay down. It had been a sleepless night, her throat tight with unshed tears, the large ornate room dwarfing her without Cameron's presence. If her bedroom was any indication, the Brown Palace was indeed Denver's finest hotel. Cameron had considerately arranged for them to share a suite, each with their own bedroom. Somehow that kind gesture made her feel a hundred times worse. It was so clear that both of them were preparing themselves for what the day would soon bring: their last sight of each other.

Slipping into a cotton wrapper, Mattie hunted through her bags for a brush and slippers. She had packed so hurriedly yesterday in Cripple Creek, she had no idea where anything was. Finally discovering a comb, Mattie struggled to get it through her tangled hair. She took a deep breath before opening the door. *You'll be gone soon*, she told herself, *in a matter of hours.*

"You're up, then?" Cameron was sitting in a carved walnut chair by the window, a newspaper in his hand. He rose as she stepped into the sitting room. He was fully dressed, his white duck trousers and shirt almost too bright in the sunlight. Mattie noted a spot of blood on his clean-shaven face; were his hands unsteady this morning? She looked down at her own hands, nervously twisting the comb.

"I thought it was best to make an early start of it," she said, trying to smile. "I'd like a bath, but I'm afraid they've not put out any towels."

"I'll ring for the maid." Cameron walked over to the bellpull. He turned a composed face to her, but she could see his jaw was rigid, as though he was forcing himself to remain calm. "Perhaps I can order breakfast for us as well. We could have a table set up here, if you like."

"No, please." Mattie couldn't keep the alarm out of her voice. "I mean, I would rather eat in the dining room." *And not alone here with you,* she thought fearfully. "Then I can leave straight for the station."

Cameron nodded. "Of course."

The tension in the room was unbearable. How could two people who had been so intimate now stand apart like frightened strangers? Mattie blamed herself. She should never have allowed things to have gotten so out of hand. She was the hunted fugitive; she had no right to allow any man to love her, no right to fall desperately in love herself. Trying to breathe calmly, Mattie walked over to the chair Cameron had been sitting in. She sat down, her legs wobbly beneath her. The cushions still felt warm from the heat of his body, and she wished it was his arms holding her, chasing away the cold and the fear.

"Mattie, are you all right?" Cameron stood a safe distance away. "You look pale."

I'm sick with the prospect of losing you, she wanted to scream. Instead, she only sighed and gave him a wan smile. "I'm feeling a bit light-headed," she said. "Bouncing for hours in a stagecoach never did set well with my stomach. I'll be fine once I've had a bath and eaten."

An uncomfortable silence followed. Despite his dapper, well-groomed appearance, Cameron looked wretched, like a man about to go to his doom. What could she say to him? The truth, perhaps—but then he would despise her. She'd lied to him from the beginning; what would he say if he learned she'd once worked for his former fiancée, that she'd stolen the ticket he'd sent to Evelyn? Mattie clutched the comb so tightly, one of the teeth broke in her hand. As soon as he learned she was wanted by the police for stealing from the Sinclairs, he would realize why she'd seduced him that night in Colorado Springs. Not out of desire, but out of fear that he'd call on Evelyn's aunt. *He would hate me,* Mattie told herself. And she wasn't strong enough to face both his hatred and their parting.

He took a deep breath. "Mattie, there's something I have to say."

"I'd rather you wouldn't," she said quickly, her voice tight. Her chest burned from the effort of trying not to cry. She should have stayed in her room and never have come out here where Cameron waited so quietly and so unhappily. Tears rose up in her eyes, and she blinked to keep them back.

"My darling Mattie." He took a step closer.

"Please don't say anything," she whispered. "Please."

A sudden rapping at the door made them both jump. Cameron put his hands on his hips, looking down at the floor for a moment as though to gain composure. "It must be the maid," he said.

As Cameron went to open the door, Mattie huddled within the chair, pressing her fingers against her eyes.

"Cameron, you devil. Why didn't you come up to my room last night when you got in?"

Peeking around the side of the chair, Mattie was surprised to see Harry Tremont stride into the room. He looked as well turned out as Cameron, dressed in a navy blazer, oyster white trousers and pale oxfords.

The two men embraced. "What happened to that beard?" Cameron asked with a laugh.

Harry rubbed his clean-shaven cheeks. "The mountain man look doesn't go over too well on the croquet lawns of Newport, old fellow."

"Newport? Is that where you've been trolling for investors?"

"Oh, I've been quite the society explorer these past six weeks. Newport, Saratoga, the Jersey shore. I should get an extra share of our mine just for spending part of the summer in Manhattan. The place is an inferno."

Cameron gripped his friend's shoulder. "It's good to see you again, Harry. I do wish you'd written, though. For a while I thought your father had kidnapped you and taken you back to Philadelphia."

"I've been much too busy to write. You know as well as I do what an effort it is to shake the gold out of those old moneybags back East. But I think I've hooked a big one this time. I've got him all stowed away in a suite even fancier than this one, and he's eager to buy into our mine. I'm hoping to close the deal during breakfast, which is at half-past eight in the private dining room. By the way, I'm putting on quite a display, so be prepared to pay for all the champagne and aspic of foie gras I've ordered."

Both men smiled at each other. "We've done it, haven't we?" Cameron asked softly.

"I think so."

"Can I know this gentleman's name? Or do you feel compelled to turn everything into an orchestrated surprise?"

Harry whistled as he flicked off a speck of lint from his sleeve. "Oh, I'm just full of surprises. Wait until you see what I've—"

He stopped abruptly as he turned in Mattie's direction. She was still huddled in the chair by the window, only her head peeking out. From behind Harry's shoulder, she glimpsed Cameron's face. Clearly he'd forgotten about her in the excitement of seeing Harry again.

"Mattie!" Harry's jaw dropped. "What are *you* doing here?"

Cameron stepped around. "We came on the stage together from Cripple Creek."

Harry stared at her as if she were a Gila monster or desert snake.

Mattie stood up, clutching her thin cotton wrapper about her. "It's nice to see you again, Harry," she said, feeling a twinge of pain at the expression on his face. Although she knew he disapproved of Cameron's interest in her, she had hoped they were friends. Apparently not. This above all should prove that her world and the one Cameron and Harry inhabited were too wildly different ever to co-exist.

"But—but what are you doing here in Denver?" Harry scanned the sitting room as though the answer lay hidden in the gilt mirrors or Hepplewhite tables. Mattie stiffened as his gaze fell on the open door of her bedroom, the large unmade bed visible in the sunlight. Cameron's trunk sat just outside the bedroom door, Mattie's parasol propped beside it.

He turned to Cameron. "What in the world do you think you're doing? This is hardly the time to revert to your womanizing ways."

"I don't believe this is any of your business," Cameron said, a warning note in his voice. "And I strongly suggest you think very carefully about what you say next." He gestured in Mattie's direction. "Or need I remind you there's a lady present."

Mattie felt her cheeks flush. The distance between her and the bedroom seemed immense, and she'd have to walk past Harry and Cameron to reach its safety.

"Need I remind *you* what's at stake?" Harry said sharply. "Damnation, Cameron, I work for weeks like a toadying fiend to secure an investor while you're back here carrying on like the Prince of Wales."

"How dare you come into my room and play the deacon! Perhaps if you had more of a real life yourself, you'd not be so interested in my private affairs."

"Your private affairs have the power to wreck our public business." Harry's face flushed crimson. "And as for my lack of a 'real life', I'll have you know that I—"

"Please stop, both of you!" Mattie cried out.

One hand clutching the collar of her wrapper, she stepped forward, her chin held high. Harry glanced down at her bare feet. She cursed herself for not finding her slippers, although that would have helped little. She was dressed only in a thin robe, her long hair tumbling about her shoulders. Although Cameron and she hadn't spent the previous night together, no one would believe it.

"Mattie, I mean no offense," Harry said. "I like you; I always have. But Cameron should know better than to engage in a dalliance at this time. Particularly with a woman—" He glared at Cameron. "With a *lady* such as yourself."

"And you should know better than to meddle in my private life," Cameron shot back.

"I won't have the two of you quarreling over me." Her voice rang out in the room, hard and loud, making both men look at her warily. "Whatever passed between Cameron and myself is our concern, not yours. Unless you like to gossip, Harry, it need never leave this room."

She continued in a quieter voice, "I'm scheduled to leave this morning on a ten o'clock train bound for Cheyenne. And I won't be coming back. So you needn't worry about your friend 'dallying' with me while you're trying to conduct business.''

Harry looked away, a sheepish expression on his face.

''I don't want to talk about this any longer. I'm going to get dressed and leave for the station. We might as well say our farewells now.''

''I'm taking you to the station, Mattie,'' Cameron said stubbornly. ''Don't imagine you can just slip out of my life that easily. I don't care what this fool says.''

''Let her go without a scene,'' Harry hissed at his friend. ''Listen to Mattie.''

''Yes, will you please listen to me without an argument? Honestly, I've never met a man so determined to—''

Mattie broke off in midsentence as the door to the suite swung open. A young woman in a heather blue gown stood there, her face wreathed in smiles. ''Cameron,'' she cried before flinging herself in his arms.

Mattie looked over at Harry. He put a hand over his eyes and groaned. What was going on? She turned her attention back to Cameron, who was now clutching the beautiful blond woman, his face wearing a stunned expression.

''Cornelia, what in the world are you doing in Colorado?'' Mattie heard him say.

Cornelia? Mattie walked up to Harry, pulling at his arm. ''His sister?'' she whispered.

With his hand still covering his eyes, Harry nodded.

''Was this one of your surprises?'' Cameron raised his head and stared accusingly at his friend.

Harry sighed. ''I'm afraid so.''

Mattie's heart sank. She felt as trapped as when Devlin and the police had burst into her room in New York. Bad enough for Harry to have discovered them in such an intimate setting, but the unexpected presence of Cameron's young sister made her feel as great a whore as Pearl DeVere. She had to get away from here as soon as possible. She darted toward the bedroom only to be stopped by Cameron's voice.

''Come here, Mattie. I want you to meet my sister.''

"Not now, Cameron," she said curtly, her eyes cast down. "I'm not dressed properly."

"Yes, let the woman dress, Cameron," a cultured voice rang out. "Or at least give her the chance to cover her feet."

Mattie looked up to see a tall, elegant woman enter the room. The stranger's deep blue eyes remained riveted on Mattie; not even Devlin's cold gaze had frozen her like this.

"Mother!" Cameron said as he finally released his sister. "This is an unholy surprise if I ever saw one."

"Clearly," she replied, shutting the door behind her.

Clutching the wrapper so tightly she feared it would tear, Mattie stepped toward her room, prepared to run if necessary.

"Might I know your name before you scamper off, young woman?"

Such peremptory tones demanded obedience. Mattie swallowed hard and gathered up her pride. After all, they were the ones who had come barging into her room; why should she feel mortified and ashamed? But she did. If she'd been caught stark naked on Fifth Avenue, she couldn't feel more embarrassed.

"This is Miss Mattie Crawford, Mother," Cameron said smoothly, his face betraying none of the agitation Mattie was certain he was feeling. "Actually, it's Mrs. Crawford. I forget sometimes that she's a widow."

"You've had that problem before," his mother said as she came closer. She seemed to glide as she walked, as though she wore skates under her summer gown rather than shoes.

Mattie saw Cameron flinch. He came quickly to her side, his hand resting lightly on her back. Mattie had a sudden impulse to hide behind him; then she wanted to laugh at herself. She'd faced prison matrons and an unforgiving judge, why should she quail before a rich Englishwoman? *Because she's the mother of the man you love,* she told herself, *and you see now how ridiculous—how doomed— that love is.*

"This is my mother, the Marchioness of Clydesford."

224

Mattie managed to meet the woman's eyes, inclining her head slightly. "I'm pleased to meet you," she murmured.

Cameron's hand tightened around her waist. His mother seemed aware of the intimate hidden gesture and lifted an eyebrow.

Standing only a few feet away, Mattie could smell the heliotrope scent Cameron's mother wore, and glimpse the silver streaks in her upswept mass of blond hair. She was a formidable beauty; Mattie could see where Cameron got his perfect profile, generous mouth, and blue eyes. A pity his mother's eyes held no corresponding warmth. Just now that steady gaze traveled over Mattie's wrinkled cotton wrapper.

She straightened defensively. Nothing in her possession was as expensive as the beige silk gown the Marchioness wore. She might as well have been a beggar girl brought before the Queen.

"Mother, why don't we let her dress?" Cameron's sister appeared beside her mother. She was shorter and slighter than the Marchioness, but no less beautiful. If Mattie had believed in angels, she would have wanted them to look just like Cornelia, with her cornflower blue eyes, sylphlike figure and gentle voice. Just now she regarded the young woman as angelic indeed, for she allowed Mattie to make her escape.

"Thank you. I do think I would feel more comfortable wearing something else," Mattie said quickly before the Marchioness could respond. "Excuse me."

Before she fled into her bedroom, Mattie had the small satisfaction of seeing a frown cross Irene Lynch-Holmes's majestic face. As intimidating as the older woman was, Mattie wasn't going to be ordered about as though she were a Clydesford scullery maid. But leaning against the closed door, she suddenly felt worthless and ashamed. How could she even dare to take such a man as Lord Cameron into her bed?

A wave of nausea and grief swept over her, and Mattie trembled until it passed. Ten o'clock couldn't come too soon. She glanced over at the clock on the mantel. Two hours more and she would be gone. A sob burst out of her and she clamped a hand over her mouth. Hurrying to the bed, she threw herself down and buried her face deep in the covers. She would smother to death before letting anyone in that sitting room know she was crying. She would die first.

It felt like she already had.

"Now that we've humiliated the young lady, perhaps you can tell me why you and Cornelia are here?"

Cameron straightened the cuffs of his shirt, walking away from Mattie's door. He could hear muffled sobs, and it took all his will not to run in after her. But that would only feed the flames of his mother's scorn and deepen Mattie's shame. Instead he walked to the far side of the room, where his white flannel jacket lay draped over a chair. As expected, his mother followed him. He breathed a sigh of relief. At least she wouldn't have the satisfaction of knowing she'd made Mattie cry.

"Since we haven't seen each other for the better part of two years, even a minimal display of filial affection wouldn't go amiss." The Marchioness glided over to the chair recently vacated by Mattie, sighing as she sat down. "But then, my sons have always boasted the most reprehensible manners."

Cornelia took a shy step forward. "We wanted to surprise you, Cameron."

"That you have. Is there some reason I wasn't informed that you were traveling all this way? Perhaps there are more surprises in store for me." Cameron stood before his mother, his expression stony. "Is Father also lurking somewhere in the hotel?"

A strange expression came over his mother's face.

"Father's back at Clydesford Hall," Cornelia said. "He seems to be recovering from the stroke. I wanted him to come with us, but the doctors said a transatlantic trip was out of the question."

Cameron kept his attention on his mother; something about her made him definitely uneasy.

He felt Cornelia touch his arm. "Father is so much better. I can't wait until you see him again. He's been asking for you."

At that Cameron looked at his sister in shock, but she only nodded and pressed her cheek against his shoulder. "It's true, he's speaking again."

Overcome by a welter of emotion, Cameron took his sister in his arms. "I thought to hear of his death any day," he said softly.

"And we thought to hear of your impending marriage." Irene steepled her fingers and gazed at him.

He sighed, pressing his sister closer, reluctant to give up her sweet warmth for the chill his mother exuded. "I wrote to you about Evelyn Sinclair. We became secretly engaged last July, as you know. I would have preferred everything aboveboard from the beginning, but the girl wanted time to convince her father of the match. Unfortunately, the family never came round, although I believe she did harbor genuine feelings for me."

"I'm not surprised it failed, then. Romantic trysts never end in marriage—at least not profitable ones," his mother said sharply. "Or have you understood nothing of what I've tried to teach you?"

"Oh, I've learned many things from you, Mother." He gently put Cornelia aside. "But practiced charm and the promise of a title does not always reap an heiress. No one could have courted these American debutantes more assiduously than I, but a scandalous past is as damning here as in Britain. Or have you forgotten the demise of Arthur's political career?"

"I don't need to be reminded of your brother's failings, any more than I need to go over your own," Irene said. "I find it difficult to believe that your boyish pranks and misadventures are cause for your inability to marry well."

"Boyish pranks!" he said in disbelief.

"You've always been a stubborn, irresponsible young

man," she went on. "Being so far away from the family, I suspect your courting has been halfhearted at best. And after that terse cable you sent announcing the end of your engagement to Miss Sinclair, I knew I had to take matters into my own hands. I hoped at least one of my sons would have the ability to prosper in the world without my assistance, but I see now I was wrong. A few clumsy attempts at courtship, and then you run off to dabble in gold mines." Her eyes narrowed in disapproval. "As though that wasn't distasteful enough, I see you've also managed to disfigure your profile. Harry told us you were set upon by ruffians. You look quite frightful, I'll have you know."

"No, he doesn't, Mother," Cornelia piped up loyally. "I think Cameron looks even more dashing now, like a—a Roman general."

Cameron couldn't resist smiling at his little sister, but his mother's voice sobered him once more. "Well, I am here to see there are no more broken noses *or* broken engagements," she said.

He laughed, but the sound held no mirth. "Do you honestly imagine that having my mother at my side will convince these businessmen to give up their daughters to the womanizing, disreputable Cameron Lynch-Holmes?"

"Try presenting yourself as the future Marquess of Clydesford instead," she said pointedly. "And disregard lingering gossip. I am tired of hearing whispers about a certain young woman who chose to make a tragic spectacle of herself. Our family has paid far too much for that pathetic remnant of your misspent youth."

Cameron felt the blood rush to his head. "I think it's best if Harry and Cornelia leave us alone," he said in an icy voice.

With an expression of relief, Harry offered his arm to Cornelia.

She took it reluctantly, her young face creased in a frown. "I do wish you wouldn't quarrel," his sister said. "I was hoping that things would have changed between the two of you. It's been so long since we've all seen each other. Can't we be as other families, happy to see one another after such a long absence?''

Cameron tried to force a smile but failed. ''I am always happy to see you, Neely. And don't imagine our family is the only one to carry on in this fashion. Harry has nearly as interesting a relationship with his father as I do with our dear Mama.''

Glaring at his friend, Harry led Cornelia out of the room. As soon as the door clicked shut, Cameron turned back to his mother. ''Now see here, I won't—''

''They're engaged to be married,'' she broke in serenely.

''What? Harry and Cornelia?''

''They both swear it's a love match, children that they are.''

''But they barely know each other,'' he protested. Cameron shook his head. ''I am damnably tired of being the last one to know these things.''

''It happened very quickly. Love at first sight, I fear.'' A sarcastic smile graced her beautiful face. ''They met five weeks ago at a lawn party in Newport, where Harry was diligently singing the praises of your little mine.''

''And where you were diligently scouting out another marriage prospect for me,'' he said bitterly.

Were he and his mother that mercenary, that cold-blooded and ambitious? The image of Cornelia and Harry riding off in a bridal carriage saddened him suddenly. It didn't seem fair. Harry needed money just like Cameron, yet here he was marrying a beautiful young woman he apparently loved. Why did things have to be so different for him? Because he carried a bloody title?

''Actually, I have no objections to the match. Lovely as your sister is, without a dowry she has no prospects in England.'' She smoothed down her silk skirt, which gleamed in the morning sun. ''Our solicitor was most impressed by Mr. Tremont's portfolio. Harry's father is by all accounts monstrously rich.''

''And a monstrous sort of man as well, if Harry is to be believed.'' He walked closer to his mother, forcing her to

229

crane her neck to look up at him. "Harry will not reconcile with his father, so I wouldn't look for our estates to be rescued via that route."

"We shall see what young Harry intends, especially after he's set up house and has a family on the way. It doesn't matter, though. Our estates are to be saved by your efforts, my son."

He gazed at his mother for a long moment, trying to find a hint of sympathy or tenderness in her expression. It was useless. "I've come to Denver to meet with two investors," he finally said. "If they buy in, the chances are good we'll be able to extract a fortune from the mine. Perhaps millions."

She shrugged. "Perhaps. But if you marry well, the marriage contract will guarantee just as large a fortune. That's why I'm here."

Cameron stiffened. "You've found someone?"

The Marchioness nodded. "A rich young woman you will be most pleased with, I assure you."

In all his twenty-eight years, he had never felt as ashamed or humiliated as he did at this moment. A grown man listening to his mother announce he was about to be married—sold off—to the highest bidder, and to a woman he hadn't even met. A slave sold on the auction block couldn't feel any more debased. Had he really gone along with this mercenary scheme for three years? He wanted to cry out in pain that he'd wasted so much energy in such a base and futile exercise.

"I should have married Philippa," he said ruefully.

"What a bizarre thing to say." She stood up abruptly, as though affronted by the idea. "Not only was the lady unstable, her income would barely have paid the annual salaries of our land agents."

"Are you so obsessed with money that you can think of nothing else?" he exploded. "Good God, that makes us all little more than whores! Is this the sort of cold-blooded bargain you struck with Father? If so, no wonder your marriage has been such a chilly sight to behold. If I were you, I would hardly want my children to repeat such a dismal coupling.''

She bit her lip, visibly shaken. "Not even your brother dared speak to me like that.''

"Perhaps he should have, instead of giving up all rights to the Clydesford title and lands. But even his disgrace and disinheritance weren't sacrifice enough for you. No, you demanded he also give up the lady he loved. Thank God he had the courage to refuse.''

"She was no lady. She was a—''

"She was the woman he adored.'' Cameron stepped toward her. "And if her husband had ever seen fit to grant her a divorce, she would have been Arthur's wife and your daughter-in-law.''

"Then it's a blessing my son died before that could happen.''

Cameron felt too shocked to respond for a moment. "Not even you could be that callous,'' he said finally in disgust.

His mother returned his angry gaze without blinking. "Sometimes one must be callous—cruel even—to ensure a greater good. I would no more have accepted that immoral woman into my family as I would that bit of baggage you have locked away in there.'' She pointed to Mattie's closed bedroom door.

Cameron took a deep breath. "That 'bit of baggage,' as you call her, is the finest lady I have ever met.''

His mother clasped her hands tightly before her. "So this is why you're unmarried after three years of fortune hunting,'' she said. "You've been too busy wallowing in the mud—sniffing after any silly chit's skirts—to be mindful of your obligations back home.''

"Lower your voice,'' he said, hoping Mattie couldn't hear the two of them fighting like fishmongers. "That's a grossly unfair charge. I've done little more than prostrate myself up and down Fifth Avenue. There's no man in London more adept at insincere smiles and empty flattery. And I've no doubt it would have worked long ago, despite our bankrupt estates, were it not for the persistent story of Lady Philippa hanging from the rafters.''

He clenched his fists at the haunting image. "And the gossip has been embroidered since then. In some versions, I'm lolling in bed while she hangs herself in front of me. But no matter how it's told, I come out a cad and a coward, spurning the love of a widow I chased after, leaving her to kill herself with grief." He fought for control, his chest heaving. "*And* carrying my bastard child. There are dozens of penurious English lords fighting to wed rich Americans, Mother. And most of them with far less sordid gossip attached to their names."

"Well, I've found one who will have you, sordid gossip and all." Her unwavering gaze told him she was speaking the truth.

Cameron felt exhausted suddenly, as though he'd just scaled a mountain only to find himself slipping down the other side. "Things have changed this past year," he said, knowing he wore a guilty expression. "I'm no longer of a mind to marry."

Irene stared at him, her elegant features seemingly frozen in place. "You will let the family be destroyed then, overrun with creditors, broken up by the auctioneer?"

Cameron sighed. "Things cannot be that dire. I need just a bit more time to make the mine profitable. I'm certain the banks will hold off. After all, Father is not without influence."

"Your father is dead."

He didn't know which shocked him more, the harsh announcement or the impassive expression on his mother's face. "Cornelia just said he'd made a recovery, that he's even regained his speech!"

"A few slurred words your sister chose to interpret as coherent conversation. In reality, the doctors said it was only a matter of weeks before the end came. That's why our departure was so precipitous and unannounced. I wanted to get Cornelia away before it happened, else she would have been quite distraught, and I would have been forced to remain in England to take care of her." She took a deep breath, seemingly oblivious to the lone tear that coursed down her cheek. "When we docked in New York Harbor, I received the telegram informing me that he'd passed away in his sleep the night before."

Cameron groped for a chair. "You left Father knowing he was soon to die?"

"A bedside vigil would have accomplished little, aside from satisfying convention. Had he been more aware, I know your father would have agreed with my decision. Given the condition of our finances, the moment his death was known, the legal onslaught would have begun. Instead, I chose to come here and see that a profitable marriage was arranged before the financial raptors closed in. I won't leave these shores until the contracts are signed and you and your bride are shaking the rice from your clothes."

She straightened, although she already seemed to be as upright and unmoving as a steel bar. "I know you would prefer me to wallow in grief and sentimentality, but I chose to save this family from ruin instead."

He felt numb. "So Cornelia doesn't know yet?"

"When I feel the time is right, I shall tell her."

"What a wretched family we are," he murmured, covering his eyes with his hand. "Poor Father."

"Oh, I weary of all my children—romantic, useless fools." She turned away and walked slowly toward the door, her usual gliding motion replaced by a hesitant gait.

"Mother, I will not let the family go bankrupt," he said solemnly. "I give you my word. But I will do it in my own way."

With one hand on the doorknob, she turned a disbelieving expression on her son. "Are you so naive, Cameron, that you think you must pay no price for security? While I have been busy looking out for your welfare, you have been playing the callow youth once more. Do you not think it is time to put aside selfish luxuries, even if they do have pretty red hair and a fine figure?"

He knew that his mother would never understand what he felt for Mattie; he was only beginning to understand it himself. "I'm very much in love with her, Mother."

The Marchioness flinched, her face growing white. She murmured something to herself before opening the door.

"I wish you could try to understand my feelings, Mother," he called out.

She paused, keeping her face turned resolutely away from her son. "If your father had lived, you could have asked him if he has known happiness with me. You might have been surprised at the answer."

"Mother, I've tried hard to be what you wanted, but you expect too much from me. I'm no better than Arthur. I'm just a man, after all."

"No," she said with finality. "Now you are the eighth Marquess of Clydesford."

The silence after she left was deafening. Cameron dropped his face in his hands. The Marquess of Clydesford, he thought in despair.

It sounded like a death sentence.

Chapter Seventeen

Mattie didn't think it was possible to feel worse, but the raised voices coming through the door plunged her spirits even lower. So in those rarefied circles not even death counted for much. Not when money weighed in the balance. She walked over to the door. Silence. Instinctively she knew that Cameron was now alone—more alone than she had ever realized. At least she had known the warmth and love of a family; as desperate as her future appeared, she had memories of gentler, sunnier times. All Cameron possessed was a calculating mother and obligations that dared him to try for happiness. She didn't think all the manor houses or gold mines in the world were worth it.

Opening the door a crack, she saw Cameron slumped against a table, his hand covering his eyes. A wave of sympathy and love swept over her.

"Are you all right?" she asked, afraid to speak above a whisper. He didn't move.

Mattie rushed over to him. "Cameron, are you ill?"

Only when she laid her hand on his shoulder did he finally

respond. But it was merely to lift his head and laugh. The bitterness in that sound made her shiver.

"I couldn't help overhearing." She winced at his bleak expression. "I'm so sorry about your father. It must be a shock for you to hear it like this."

He only shook his head.

She squeezed his shoulder. "I remember the night my father died. We'd been expecting it all winter. Yet when it finally came, we were crushed. Ma wailed like the wind in a dust storm." Mattie bit her lip at the memory. "It was terrible."

"I hadn't seen my father in two and a half years," Cameron said wearily. "He'd just had his second stroke and couldn't speak, so I did the talking. All nonsense, I realize that now." He heaved a great sigh. "Telling him I was going to America to seek a rich wife, and that I'd bring my bride back by Easter. I even had the audacity to go over the ledger books as I sat next to him, detailing how we'd use the money to pay off bank debts or repair the stables. Damn empty promises, every last one of them."

"But you discovered gold," she said softly. "You've even found investors to help you."

Cameron turned away. "He's dead now, so it matters little. He died thinking both of his sons were failures." A pause followed. "And he was right."

"But you have a gold mine worth a fortune, and as for marrying—" Mattie hesitated. "I heard what your mother said about finding a wife for you." He whirled around to face her. "It seems you'll soon have both investors and your golden bride."

His gaze was piercing. "What a fortunate chap I am. I give up a woman I love in return for a bulging stock portfolio and a society wedding at Grace Church."

"I have nothing to do with this. I'm leaving in less than two hours, Cameron, and I'm never coming back. What good would it do either of us for you to refuse a marriage that will benefit your family?" Mattie spread her arms. "You and I can never share more than we already have."

"Why not?"

She turned away in frustration. Cameron clutched at her instantly, forcing her to face him.

"Damn you! You've said it yourself, I've a fortune lying beneath my feet back in Cripple Creek. And now I've got investors banging on my door. What need do I have for any New York heiress now? Why shouldn't I marry you?"

"Marry?" she asked, stunned.

"Yes, why shouldn't we marry? I'm the Marquess of Clydesford now, and I'm about to save the entire family from ruin. The least I should be able to get in return is a chance at happiness with you."

"It's impossible! We can't marry. Think what you're saying."

"I am. It's all so clear to me now. How could I have been so thickheaded, thinking I must marry not only wealth but social status, as though I were a bloody English monarch."

"Cameron, I can't marry you," she said, shaken by the intensity in his expression and voice.

"Yes, you can," he said. His fingers dug into her shoulders, but she was too shocked to cry out. "You can marry me and save me from dying alone like my father did. Do you really imagine that any woman who loved her husband—truly cared for him—would leave him with only servants to hear his dying breath? I don't want that, Mattie. I want to know I'm sharing my life with a woman who would never leave me, even if it meant a hundred fortunes lay in the balance."

"Cameron, please," she murmured. It was his grief talking—grief and fear.

"Marry me, Mattie." He shook her again, as though he could force an agreement out of her. "Marry me. Don't let me enter into a marriage as bleak as the one my parents shared. Stay with me always."

Mattie thought of a dozen logical reasons why they could not remain together, but she wanted only to gaze into those dark blue eyes. Feeling his hands on her, knowing that he, indeed, did love her enough to make foolish statements. Hopeless statements.

"I love you, Cameron," she began, and found herself crushed in an embrace. His heart thundered against her. "I'll always love you, but I must leave." She threw her arms about his neck, clinging to him. "And you must marry this rich and willing young lady."

"Never," he whispered.

The ormolu clock above the fireplace chimed the half hour. For a long moment, Mattie nestled in Cameron's embrace, savoring the feel of his strong arms straining to hold her close, breathing in his scent, the silkiness of his thick hair, letting her heartbeat race as wildly as his own. *I'll never love any man like this again,* she thought with wonder and grief. That she had stumbled onto such a love was miracle enough. It was far too much to expect it to last.

With great effort, Mattie finally opened her eyes and raised her head. "It's getting late, Cameron. My train will be leaving soon."

A shudder wracked him, and she steeled herself for the disappointment and sadness in his eyes.

"You won't stay," he said dully. It wasn't a question.

She took a step back, freeing herself from the circle of his arms. Already she felt the chill of that loss. "I can't."

He bent down his head, as though he'd been felled by a great blow. Mattie felt the tears flood her eyes, and she had to dig her nails into the palms of her hands to keep them from spilling over. If she cried now—God forbid, if either of them cried—neither Cameron nor she would be able to bear it.

"You must leave, too," she said in a tight voice. "Didn't Harry say the breakfast for the investor was planned for half-past eight?"

Cameron took several deep breaths, his hands on his hips. He seemed to be fighting for composure as desperately as she. "Yes, he did."

"Then you should leave now."

He stared at her for a long moment. "Will you at least

let me take you to the station in an hour? I'm not up to a good-bye at just this moment.''

"I understand," she whispered.

They gazed at each other, separated by a foot of air that seemed as vast as a mountain valley.

"Good luck with the investor." Mattie forced a smile to her lips.

Without answering, Cameron turned on his heel and snatched up his jacket. He paused at the door for one final look at her. "Wait for me."

After he'd gone, Mattie walked over to the door Cameron had just shut and leaned weakly against it. If only her heart was as hard as that polished oak.

"Good-bye, Cameron," she whispered.

Nothing mattered anymore. As he paced outside the private dining room, Cameron felt like a jungle cat about to be cornered by hunters. And who could he blame but himself? The memory of those wasted years maddened him; not just the ones devoted to securing an heiress, but all those self-indulgent, cynical years of his youth and young manhood. He didn't want to dwell on his childhood, which was little more than a procession of stern nannies and icy schoolrooms.

What could he look back on with pride? he wondered. He might have redeemed himself where Philippa was concerned, but instead of giving her his loyalty and love, he'd behaved like a coward and let her die alone. Alone, he thought darkly, just like his father. He was no better than his mother, abandoning people for the sake of convention and gold.

A waiter went past him, carrying a covered tray. A least he'd had the heartbreak and the joy of loving again. For he did love Mattie, so much that it left him shaken and weak.

"Forgive me, Arthur," he murmured. "I understand now. I really do."

"What did you say, Cameron?"

He turned around to see Cornelia beaming at him, her

arm tucked through Harry's elbow. He thanked God that Mother had been unable to change her. She seemed radiant, happy, at peace. Maybe that was the reward for sweetness of spirit and a gentle heart.

"It seems congratulations are in order," he said.

"I wanted to tell you myself," Harry said, a guilty expression on his face.

"Oh, I knew Mother couldn't wait." Cornelia laughed. "It is wonderful news, isn't it? To think all this time when you wrote us about Harry and the gold mine, I was actually listening to you describe my future husband. Life is so odd." She squeezed Harry's arm, exchanging a smile with him. "I fully expected you to wed a brash American, but I never thought to marry one myself."

"I love her very much, Cameron," Harry said solemnly, covering Cornelia's hand with his own. "And I'll take good care of her, I promise."

Cameron nodded. Seeing his sister married to a good man like Harry was the only solace he had at the moment. "I know you will."

"I wrote to Father as soon as we became engaged," Cornelia said with a smile. "I can't wait for him to meet Harry. He'll be so pleased for us, don't you think?"

"Of course, Neely." He forced a smile in return. Now was not the time to tell her about Father, but soon, very soon . . . How could his mother dare to play with other people's lives like this? It was unconscionable.

Harry cleared his throat and took a step closer. "I trust there will be no one else joining us for breakfast."

Cameron shook his head.

Cornelia tugged at Harry's arm. "I think we should tell him. He doesn't deserve any more surprises."

"Nothing could surprise me, my dear," Cameron said with an air of resentment. "Not after this morning."

"I wouldn't count on that." Harry looked decidedly uncomfortable. "You see, your mother has arranged a marriage for you."

"I know," he said. "Apparently dear Mama has con-

vinced some rich young woman that I'm a sterling catch.
More fool she.''

"She's here, you know," Cornelia said softly.

Cameron felt as though he'd just been dashed with a
bucket of cold water. "You don't mean to say Mother has
dragged this lady to Colorado? What a lunatic thing to do!"

"Keep your voice down," Harry warned. "She's in the
private dining salon waiting for us."

"I can't believe I'm hearing this." Cameron began to
pace once more, swearing under his breath. "What in the
devil is this strange lady doing at a business meeting? This
is no time for polite chatter and flirtatious lies. Doesn't
Mother realize what's at stake? If she ruins this deal for us
by her infernal matchmaking, I swear I'll let the bankers
turn her out onto the streets."

"None of this will ruin your business transactions," Cornelia said. "You're getting upset for nothing."

"Neely, you're a sweet girl, but you know nothing of the
intricacies of conducting business. Potential investors want
to hear only about profits and costs, not wedding plans."

"But this investor will be interested in both," Cornelia
replied.

He whirled around to face her. "Why ever should he
be?"

"Because she's his daughter," Harry said, looking nearly
as wretched as Cameron felt. "I told your mother we should
have written. This is going to blow up in our faces, I know
it.''

If he'd had his mother in front of him at that moment,
Cameron feared he would have wrung her neck. To have
worked so hard, first at wooing debutantes and then at digging the mine, only to have his mother step in and take over!
The resentment boiled up inside him, warring dangerously
with his grief over losing both Mattie and his father. And
now to learn that this so-called investor was apparently trad-
ing not only money for a share of the mine, but his daughter
as well! Suddenly the whole deal smelled rank and suspicious.

Cameron straightened his jacket, forcing his voice to remain calm and not betray his agitation. They had all miscalculated where he was concerned. He was no longer that wayward, callow young man, willing to sacrifice honor and love for a sack of gold. He no longer had the stomach for this cold manipulation of his life.

"If the deal hinges on my marrying this man's daughter, then I advise you to book him a return ticket immediately," he said sharply. "Two tickets. I came here to sell a share of the mine, not myself. So tell this fool to pack up his bankbook and his old-maid daughter and clear out."

"Well, I'd hardly call myself an old maid," a lovely feminine voice trilled behind him. "But perhaps girls marry straight out of the cradle in the Wild West."

Cameron felt he must be dreaming. It couldn't be. This was impossible. Fearing the worst, he slowly turned to face the young woman.

Evelyn Sinclair smiled at him.

Devlin hunched over in the overstuffed armchair, trying to peer through the rubber plant. The lobby of the Brown Palace seemed busier than Grand Central Station and, despite its pretensions, was nearly as loud. Damned mine owners and western lawyers. Money or not, they didn't have the manners of a bunco artist in the Tenderloin.

He pulled out his pocket watch, the third time in the last minute he'd done so. Past eight-thirty, and no sign of her yet. But she'd have to appear soon. Devlin had taken the afternoon stage out of Cripple Creek as soon as he'd heard that Lord Cameron and Mattie had gone off to Denver. A few bribes spread around the train station and hotel told him the rest. He'd spent the night in a room just down the hall from their cozy little suite, and for a five-dollar bill, one of the valets had discovered that the Englishman had bought his lady friend a ticket bound for Cheyenne. She was leaving this morning at ten o'clock—alone. It was as though the fates had at last conspired to place Mattie Crawford Laszlo in his hands.

He'd be on that train this morning, make no mistake about
it. But he didn't dare leave the hotel until she did. She'd
slipped out of his grasp twice before, once after she'd been
put safely behind bars. That red-haired baggage had more
lives than an alley cat, but he had her this time. He had her
good. Devlin didn't stop to think what he would do once
he got her away from the leering protection of Cameron
Lynch-Holmes or the busybodies of Cripple Creek. All he
knew was that his quarry was almost within reach.

The doors of the Brown Palace opened, and Devlin settled
back in his chair, trying to blend in with the other guests in
the onyx-paneled lobby. As he unfolded his newspaper, he
caught a glimpse of a tall blond woman gliding past him.
She's a rich one, Devlin thought. Dressed in lace and silk,
a gemstone larger than a cherry glittering on her finger. On
the streets of New York, she'd have it snatched off before
she walked a block. 'Course that kind never walked. Hoity-
toity matrons drove about in black-wheeled carriages, a
mink wrap covering their delicate knees, protected from the
stares of fellows like him.

Not that he wanted to stare at them. Devlin scanned the
tiny newsprint as the lady and her male companion walked
past him.

"I fear our little stroll has caused us to be ten minutes
late," she said in a clipped English accent. "I only hope
Cameron is still in a good humor. My son is notoriously
punctual and hates to be kept waiting."

Devlin's head shot up.

"Don't worry," the gentleman replied. "I'm sure Evelyn
will keep him amused."

"What?" Devlin said aloud, startling an elderly lady
snoring in an armchair behind him.

He stood up, brushing aside the thick rubber leaves to get
a better view of the well-heeled couple. Damn if that wasn't
Ward Sinclair himself. Even though he caught only a passing glimpse of the man as they disappeared through the
crowd, Devlin recognized that florid face, that thick neck
threatening to burst out of his collar. What in the world was

243

Ward Sinclair doing in Denver? And with his daughter, too, apparently. He thought back over the snatch of conversation he'd overheard. So the blond woman was Lord Cameron's mother. What a devil's brew this was.

Devlin threw down the newspaper. He had no need to trail after Mattie now, no need to beg for assistance from lazy marshals or idiot stage robbers. All he had to do was present that thieving hussy to Ward Sinclair, like a piece of meat thrown to a hungry lion. With a rich and powerful man to verify that she was indeed an escaped criminal, Devlin could return home with Mattie in tow, bound and gagged if need be, back to where justice awaited them both. Only it would be a very cold, unforgiving justice for her.

For the first time in weeks, he felt a lightness in his heart, a lifting up of all the bitter frustration, the humiliation he'd endured because of that woman. Soon it would be over. Out of nervous habit, he reached for his pocket watch, then laughed before looking at it. What need to check his watch? He knew exactly what time it was. Time to bring Mattie down.

Chapter Eighteen

The bright morning sun made the silver service gleam, setting afire the tiny orange baskets garnished with strawberries. Crystal stemware sparkled as richly as the gemstones worn by the Marchioness of Clydesford, while expensive perfumes mingled pleasantly with the aroma of baked ham and country sausage. Cameron was oblivious to both the lavish breakfast and the aesthetic beauty set before him, however.

If there was a worse morning in recent memory, he couldn't conjure it up. All night he'd tossed in bed, aching to go to Mattie, knowing with chill certainty that she would be leaving him soon. He suspected Mattie would not wait for him to take her to the station, that even now she could be gone from the hotel. And his life. How long before he would adjust to that loss, not to mention the loss of his father?

He glanced over at the sound of polite laughter. His mother was conversing serenely with Evelyn Sinclair. No one at the table would suspect she was newly widowed.

Hiding one's thoughts and feelings was admired in his circle; it was a mark of pride to remain impassive, controlled, superior. Cameron suddenly saw it as bitter failure, moral cowardice.

And that's what I've been for most of my life, he told himself. *A coward, sitting calmly at the table while the person I love most in the world vanishes from sight.*

"But I don't agree at all. I think your son looks quite well indeed." Evelyn leaned in Cameron's direction. "The Marchioness is dismayed that you've broken your nose. I, however, find your new profile most attractive." She gave a low laugh. "Even if it does make you look a bit like a pugilist."

Cameron couldn't summon up even the pretense of a smile. What in hell was he doing here?

"I'm afraid we've taken Cameron totally by surprise," Evelyn continued. "He's not uttered more than three words." She smiled at Irene. "Or perhaps your son doesn't care for too much conversation over breakfast."

Cameron cleared his throat before his mother could reply. Everyone at the table turned to look at him.

"I fear I'm not in the proper frame of mind for either breakfast or conversation, Evelyn," he said, pushing aside a plate heaped with sweetbreads and oysters. "At least not polite conversation."

His mother shot him a warning glance. "I must apologize for my son. Being marooned in this mountain wilderness for nearly a year has apparently stripped him of his manners. I'm certain that once he's taken in the fact that we've traveled so far just to be with him, he'll act a bit more civilized."

He could feel the blood pound at his temples. "Do not presume to speak for me, Mother, or I shall be forced into quite an uncivilized display."

"Harry was right; we should have warned Cameron we were coming," his sister said, her eyes beseeching him to behave.

"Quite," Cameron said tersely.

"But some surprises can be most pleasant." Evelyn turned in his direction, a sweet expression on her face. "That's how I viewed the visit of your mother and sister last month in Newport. My father and I agreed that it was the most enjoyable summer we've ever spent at the cottage." She threw him a coy look. "Except for last summer, when we met you, of course."

Cameron stared back at her, remembering how he'd once kissed that soft, bow-shaped mouth and enjoyed the tremulous quality of her voice. The ivory and red gown she wore accentuated her rosy complexion and brought out the bronze highlights in her brown hair. She was a pretty young woman: poised, clever and teasingly sensual. A year ago he'd expected to marry her, his duty done and not without pleasure. Yet the idea of spending his life with Evelyn Sinclair now left him cold. As she sat next to his mother, he suddenly discerned a similarity between the two women. Of course, the Marchioness was far more dignified, imposing and confident. Yet both ladies looked at him with a cool shrewdness that was at odds with their gracious smiles. Neither woman loved him, he realized with a jolt. They never had and they never would.

Cameron sat back in his chair. "Pardon me for being blunt, but both you and your father seemed remarkably resistant to my charms last summer. My friend here can vouch for that. What exactly was it Mr. Sinclair called us at the croquet match, Harry? I believe you were dubbed a stupid spendthrift, but I can't remember if I was accused of being a murderous fortune hunter or an immoral fool."

Harry anxiously signaled to the waiter for more biscuits. Cornelia bit her lip and whispered, "Cameron, please."

Irene sat as still as a statue, her face revealing nothing.

"Now see here, young man, what happened last summer has nothing to do with my being in Colorado today," Ward Sinclair began.

"Father was only concerned about my welfare," Evelyn broke in. "After all, we did become engaged without his permission. It was foolish of us to expect him to be pleased when we deceived him in such a manner."

Cameron didn't bother to remind her that it was she who'd insisted on keeping it a secret. "Oh, I don't blame him. What father wishes to marry off his only daughter to a bankrupt English lord with a bad reputation?"

"And bad manners," his mother put in sharply. She carefully adjusted the lace at her throat before speaking again. "As soon as I heard of this ridiculous secret engagement, I knew I had to come to America and try to put things right. If I couldn't convince Mr. Sinclair to accept you as his son-in-law, the least I could do was apologize for your appalling behavior." She inclined her head in Sinclair's direction. "Which I have done, most profusely."

And not without result, her expression clearly said.

"Father has reconsidered his hasty decision about our engagement, Cameron," Evelyn said, a triumphant smile on her face.

"So it was my mother's gracious pleas that finally convinced you of my worth." Cameron held up his fluted champagne glass to the light. "Or was it the news that I've struck gold?"

Ward Sinclair looked decidedly uncomfortable as he gulped down his sausage. He had always been a ruddy fellow, but now his jowled face looked beet red. Cameron could almost feel sorry for him, but not for his pretty daughter, who threw him an impatient glance. Yes, all too much like his mother.

Yet he couldn't blame her; he couldn't blame any of them. After all, he'd been playing the marriage game for nearly three years now. To save the Clydesford estates and future, he'd been resigned to marrying even a cold-hearted shrew as long as she boasted a fat inheritance. He could hardly hold it against any woman for shying away from a prospective husband hounded by creditors.

And to give Evelyn her due, she had agreed to marry him last year; it was only when her father withheld his consent that she'd quite sensibly backed down. Evelyn Sinclair had been raised to marry well and behave accordingly. She wouldn't disgrace him as his Marchioness, and would probably make an agreeable bed partner. Why was he balking and making things unpleasant for everyone? It wouldn't bring Mattie back to him. With her gone, it didn't really matter whom he married. He could never love another woman as he loved her. And he would always love her.

"I won't deny that the change in your financial prospects has played a part in my coming here," Sinclair said, his fingers drumming on the linen tablecloth. "When Evelyn got your letter a few weeks back, we had a very long discussion. She convinced me that perhaps I'd been a bit precipitous in rejecting you."

Cameron let out a short laugh. He'd forgotten that he'd sent off a boasting letter to his former fiancée on the very night he and Mattie had discovered the vein of gold. It had been an exaggerated account, marked more by his hurt feelings at being rejected by Evelyn than by the truth. And look where such idiocy had gotten him. Exactly where his mother, Harry and the Sinclairs wanted him. Exactly where he deserved to be.

"Being out here all these months," continued Sinclair, "working as you have, obviously you're not merely some blue-blooded layabout content to live off his wife's money. You've shown real initiative, young man, and it's paid off in a big way. This is how Americans make their fortunes; we go out and sweat for it. You should be proud of yourself." He tugged at his collar, as though embarrassed to go on. "I am proud of you, as is my daughter. We would both be pleased to welcome you into our family. If there are any hard feelings over some of the things I said last summer, I only hope you'll overlook them."

Evelyn patted her father's arm, while Cameron stared at the older man in amazement. Ward Sinclair had never been anything but disagreeable and rude in his presence. For the wealthy stockbroker to almost condescend to an apology was worth a concession or two. Cameron took a deep breath and glanced around.

Harry tapped a fork against his plate, refusing to meet Cameron's eyes. He knew how much this gold mine meant to Harry. It was a chance to be free of his tyrannical father, a chance at believing that he could succeed on his own. If Cameron walked away and spoiled that dream, his friend would sink further in his own estimation, perhaps never to recover. And a self-confident Harry would only increase his sister's chance at happiness.

Cornelia wasn't looking too happy at this moment. She stared at her brother with a puzzled expression, as though she only now sensed just how much he did not want to be at this table. Dear gentle Neely, so strikingly different from the elegant woman who sat next to her. One glance at his mother's face was all he would permit himself. It was the face of duty, of reason. It was the only face he had ever obeyed, but glancing at it now made him think of the Medusa. If he stared too long, his heart would turn to stone—as hers had.

"I'm glad you've changed your opinion of me," he said finally, feeling a lessening of tension at the table. The salvation of his family was being laid out before him and everyone knew it.

He folded his hands in his lap, ready to talk business. "So you're interested in buying into our mine?"

Sinclair visibly relaxed. "That I am. Harry has shown me the assayer's reports, and I'm most impressed. The Senate is going to scrap the Sherman Act any day now, and I've far too much tied up in the silver market. With free silver coinage gone, the price of gold will shoot sky high, with no end in sight. Your Cripple Creek mine is the best investment I'm likely to see in my lifetime. Of course I want to buy in. The future of this country is gold."

"And that's what our future will be," Evelyn put in, clearly as pleased as her father that Cameron was going to come around. "Golden."

Irene lifted her champagne glass for a sip.

"It's going to take a sizable investment to get things up and running." Cameron wasn't up to playing the suitor at this moment, not while Mattie was still so near.

"Of course," Sinclair replied.

"We need to buy heavy mining equipment immediately," Cameron went on. "Compressed air drills, surface steam engines, pistons, dynamite. We've only a dozen fellows digging for us now, and we need to hire teams of men to work in rotating shifts. Skilled workers, too, preferably Cornishmen. No better miners in the world."

Sinclair nodded. "Certainly."

"And if this vein is as rich as the assayer suspects, investing in our own stamp mill would probably be wise."

"Perhaps we shouldn't try to do too much at first," Harry said. "After all, with just one investor—"

"Possibly two." Cameron told them briefly about the letter he'd received from the Denver lawyer. "With two investors willing to stake us, it shouldn't be too deadly a risk." Indeed, the only deadly risk he saw was vowing to spend the rest of his life with a woman he didn't love. "There's a tremendous amount of work to be done."

"I hope you won't have to oversee everything personally," Evelyn said with a smile. "I was counting on a leisurely honeymoon in Europe. Your mother has told me so much about Clydesford Hall, it sounds a virtual palace."

Cameron straightened. He hadn't yet said the engagement was back on. It was bad form for Evelyn to speak as though a wedding was imminent.

As though noting his discomfiture, the Marchioness sat forward. "Clydesford Hall will wait until after we've glimpsed this glorious gold mine we've heard so much about."

"Oh, of course," Evelyn replied eagerly. "After all, it's going to make possible the restoration Clydesford and your other estates require. The least I can do is pay one visit to Cripple Creek in return. But I don't think either Cameron or I can sit still for a long engagement. Not after the separation we've endured."

"As you can see, my daughter is not only impatient but rather headstrong." Sinclair patted Evelyn's hand. "I fear

I've indulged her since her mother died. My suggestion to her future husband is to do likewise. It will make the marriage far more agreeable.''

An uncomfortable silence followed as all eyes turned toward Cameron. He knew that they were waiting for him to say something definite about the wedding. He felt like a man about to stick his head through the hangman's noose.

"I don't blame you for wanting to see Clydesford Hall," Cornelia finally said. "It's in the loveliest part of Kent, with fields as green and lush as any in Ireland. I already miss it dreadfully and I've only been gone a few weeks. I don't know how Cameron has been able to stay away from home so long.''

"I've had work to do, Neely," he reminded her gently. First, fortune hunting and then gold mining. It had been a busy three years, often unpleasant and frustrating, but he hadn't realized until this moment that he'd never once longed to go home. Not if Clydesford Hall was home. "Besides, I've taken quite a fancy to Colorado. It suits me.''

"I can see that it does." Evelyn seemed bewildered by his obvious sincerity, but he knew she wouldn't dare argue. Not now, not when she wasn't yet certain of him. "You're nearly as brown as an Indian, and you and Harry look remarkably healthy. That's what mountain air will do for you. Aunt Julia always told me I should go to the Springs one summer instead of Newport. I'm not surprised you've enjoyed your stay here.''

"I'm glad you understand, Evelyn, because I don't think I'll be leaving Colorado for some time.''

Harry cleared his throat. "Cameron, once the equipment is in place, neither of has to remain here. That's what mine superintendents are for. We can shift some of the responsibility onto a few capable and trusted employees.''

"And you've responsibilities back in England," Evelyn said in a gentle voice, as though he were a cranky toddler she was trying not to upset. "You're the future Marquess of Clydesford; you can't forget that.''

"I've never forgotten that." Cameron paused. "I've never been allowed to forget it."

Evelyn glanced at his mother.

Irene seemed composed, but Cameron knew her well enough to glimpse the anger in her tight smile. "Perhaps my son feels that you aren't prepared yet to take on the duties of Marchioness. He may be right, my dear. Life among the English aristocracy demands more from its females than a male heir and a talent for riding. An extended stay in America might do you both a world of good."

"Besides, Evelyn, neither you nor Cameron has to worry about running Clydesford for a long time." Cornelia couldn't keep the happiness out of her voice. "With Father making such a surprising recovery, it could be years before you have to worry about being the Marchioness."

Cameron bit back a groan. He would have to tell his sister the truth soon.

"Still, one never knows what the future will bring." Irene gazed down into her empty champagne glass.

"Of course, I hope such an eventuality doesn't take place for many years," Evelyn said. "But were Cameron to become the Marquess tomorrow, I believe I am quite prepared to step in as his wife." As Evelyn said this, she exchanged a glance with the Marchioness.

Cameron dropped his hand to the table with a thud. It was an exchange between equals, he noted with alarm, a look of both conspiracy and respect. Evelyn *knew* that his father was dead; it was as obvious as the fact that his sister—the Marquess's youngest child—did not.

The rage built up in Cameron like a cold winter storm. He should have known that his mother would tell Evelyn before she informed her own children of their father's death. For them, his death only meant mourning and regrets, insignificant things that could be handled later at a more convenient time. But telling Evelyn that she would become the Marchioness of Clydesford the moment she married her son—that was the real bait needed to hook his golden bride.

He suddenly knew how Philippa must have felt on the

evening she'd burst into the Duke of Sunderland's party. At the time, it had seemed the act of a madwoman, but now he realized it was the only reasonable way to respond to having your love and pride stripped from you.

"There's only one problem, Evelyn," Cameron said, his voice as smooth and forbidding as an icy cliff.

His mother arched a suspicious eyebrow.

"And what is that?" Evelyn didn't yet have the instincts of his mother; her smile was still foolishly eager.

"I have no intention of taking you as my wife."

Cornelia's spoon clattered to her plate, while Sinclair choked on a biscuit. Neither Irene nor Harry said a word.

Evelyn's mouth dropped open. "I don't understand. For months you wrote, asking me to come to Colorado and marry you."

"Yes, I did. Letters which you no doubt tossed aside with your discarded dance cards and fans." He saw her flinch. "I was even foolish enough to send you a train ticket to come out and join me, but at least I had the sense to include an ultimatum with it. Apparently you didn't take it seriously."

"Train ticket?" Evelyn shook her head. "I haven't the faintest idea what you're talking about. I never received a train ticket *or* an ultimatum from you."

Cameron snatched up his napkin and threw it on the table. "Clearly you didn't bother even to read my letters before tearing them up."

"That's not true," she said hotly, her poised facade slipping. "I read all of them, even the ones that were tiresome and ridiculous."

"It doesn't matter." Cameron stood up, pushing back his chair. "You and I will not be marrying, and if your investment hinges on such a marriage, Mr. Sinclair, then I accept the fact that I've just lost one of my investors."

Sinclair's old steeliness was back. "What game are you playing, Lynch-Holmes? Have you already made a deal with this other interested party? Are you trying to cut me and perhaps even your friend Harry out of the lion's share?"

Cameron shook his head. "At this moment, I don't give a tinker's dam if anyone invests in the mine." He shot Harry a rueful look. "Sorry, old chap, but that's how I feel."

Although he looked pale and miserable, Harry only nodded. "It's your decision, Cameron."

"There's another woman, isn't there?" Evelyn stood up now as well, glaring at him across the table. "You've stumbled onto another wealthy young lady here in Colorado, the daughter of a rich mine owner, no doubt. That's why you don't care if Daddy invests in your mine!"

Cameron didn't answer, but something in his face must have told her she'd struck home.

"It's true, then," she breathed in disbelief. "You've found someone else."

The Marchioness started to speak, but Cameron held up his hand. "Yes, it's true."

While Evelyn let out a cry of dismay, her father swore loudly. "Damn it all, do you mean to say we've been brought here under false pretense! If you think I'll stand still for being duped by any of you English bluebloods, you've got a nasty surprise in store. Both you *and* your mother."

"My mother knew nothing of this woman," Cameron said coldly. "And if anyone had had the presence of mind to write to me of your arrival, all of this could have been avoided."

"Who is she?" Evelyn demanded, her face screwed up like a little girl about to cry. "Are you going to marry her?"

"Let it go, Evelyn," Sinclair said in a disgusted voice. "Don't make a fool of yourself. If he wants to play the cad, then let him."

"Cameron!" she whispered brokenly.

Perhaps she cared for him a little, he thought sadly, regretting having to hurt her now. But he knew she cared far more about being an English marchioness, a titled lady with a place at Victoria's court. He had no doubt that by next spring she'd be engaged to a Wall Street lawyer or the son of an industrialist.

"I'm sorry, Evelyn," Cameron said. "But I can't help the fact that I've fallen in love."

"You said that you cared for me only a few months ago." She stamped her foot in frustration.

"And so I did," Cameron said in a gentle voice. "But I *love* her. There's the difference."

"You're a dreadful man," she cried tearfully, flinging her napkin at him. "All those terrible things they said about you were true. You *are* a cad, and a womanizer, and a liar. I'm not surprised that English lady hanged herself over you. I'm not surprised at all!"

With that, Evelyn ran out of the dining room, nearly colliding with a waiter bringing in the coffee. Irene made a move to follow, but Sinclair motioned her down again.

"Let the girl be." He glared at Cameron. "I think she's had more than enough of the Lynch-Holmes family."

Cameron sat down once more, refusing to look away from his mother's accusing stare. In the bright sunlight, he could discern fine lines around her eyes and mouth. She seemed suddenly older, her beauty fading, her indomitable will diminished. This terrible morning had taken its toll on both of them; he only prayed there were no more unpleasant surprises remaining.

"Yes, Mother, I'm just as bad as Arthur," he said wearily.

She shook her head. "I'm only grateful that your father isn't alive to learn of your latest folly."

"What did you say?" Cornelia cried out.

Cameron closed his eyes. He was wrong. The morning had just gotten worse.

Mattie waited nervously for the porter, keeping one eye on the double doors leading into the dining room. It was nine o'clock and Cameron was undoubtedly in there right now talking business. A passing gentleman in a plaid suit tipped his hat, obscuring her view. Mattie turned away. Why in the world was she staring at the doors anyway? Was it because she longed for one last glimpse of him? Or because she dreaded it?

"Is this everything, madam?" The porter, thin as a whippet, gestured to her bags.

She nodded. "I need a carriage to the train station, please. As soon as possible. I have a ten o'clock departure."

"Wait here and I'll take care of everything."

As the porter hustled out the door with her bags, Mattie picked up her sewing basket. She could have let the fellow carry this for her as well; the wardrobe she'd made for herself didn't require more than a carpet bag and one small trunk. Still, the basket gave her a sense of security. She could lose everything else—it felt as if she already had—but with this basket she could make her way in the world. Besides, it reminded her of Colorado Springs, and those first days with Cameron.

She looked back toward the dining room once more. She was sorely tempted to peek inside; just a glimpse of his profile would be enough. Let him go, she told herself. He had his gold mine, his investor, even his rich bride-to-be. Mattie was no more than a diversion, passionate yet hopeless. Now they both had to get on with their lives.

She had to devote her energies to slipping farther from the authorities' grasp. For now, it was taking all her will just to force herself to leave the hotel. In order to block her view of the dining room, Mattie sat down in a chair facing the opposite way, an enormous rubber plant dangling above her.

Almost as soon as she sat down, she felt a frisson of fear. Someone was watching her. The same cold certainty had afflicted her in Cripple Creek. Beneath the wide brim of her bonnet, Mattie looked about discreetly, but the lobby seemed filled only with bustling businessmen and respectable matrons. *It doesn't matter,* she thought, *I'm leaving now. And there'll be nothing and no one to hamper my escape from this point on.*

From behind her, she heard the dining room door crash open. She held her breath, fearing it was Cameron rushing out to find her. After a breathless second, Mattie dared to peek around the rubber plant, her view partially obscured by a trio of bellhops. Apparently it was a woman who had fled the private dining salons. She could see an ivory-colored skirt swishing about behind the bellhops as though the woman was pacing.

The porter swung open the heavy door. "The carriage is waiting, madam."

She stood up, giving a tug to her suit jacket. Bending down to retrieve her sewing basket, Mattie caught a better look at the woman. Her back was turned toward her, but Mattie's discerning eye automatically took note of the lady's fashionable gown. It seemed to be made of India silk, just like the one she'd designed for Evelyn back in New York. Remarkable coincidence, even to the broad Empire girdle and bands of red trimming the flared skirt.

The woman turned just then, and Mattie gasped. Dear merciful Lord, it was Evelyn!

Mattie turned her back so quickly, she nearly toppled over. What was Evelyn Sinclair doing in Denver? She didn't have time to worry about it; it was about twenty steps to the hotel entrance. Taking a deep breath, Mattie started for the door, eyes down, her hand clutching the basket so tightly, it shook in her fingers.

Her heels clicked on the parquet floor. Three more steps, that was all, and then she would be free. Free at last of Cameron and Evelyn and—

"That's far enough, Mattie."

She froze. That terrible voice. Mattie looked up, stunned to see Devlin blocking her way. He looked just as he appeared in her nightmares, black-eyed, unsmiling and cruel. There was no time to scream, although a wail began rising in her throat. *Run,* she said to herself, *I must run.*

Numb with fear, Mattie backed away from him, her eyes darting for escape, salvation, a miracle. Where could she go, with Devlin before her and Evelyn behind? Devlin took a step toward her, his hand moving inside his jacket.

He had a gun. He was going to kill her, shoot her right

there in the middle of a Denver hotel lobby. As she turned to run, Mattie flung her sewing basket at him. It struck his shoulder and burst open, sending spools and needles flying about. Pushing and shoving through the crowd, she ran wildly for the stairs. A bearded gentleman grabbed her elbow.

"See here, young woman, you shouldn't be crashing into people like this," he grumbled.

"Leave me alone," she cried, vainly trying to twist out of his grip. Out of the corner of her eye, she saw Devlin march through the crowd, his revolver drawn and pointed at her.

"Stop right there, Mattie, or I'll shoot you for sure," he said loudly.

Several ladies screamed. One of them was Evelyn.

"Tillie, is that you?" Mattie heard her shout. "Oh my God, it is! Daddy, come quick! Lieutenant Devlin's caught Tillie!"

Mattie stopped struggling. It was over. The urge to fling herself at Devlin was overpowering. Let him shoot her here and now and spare her the torment of what was to come. Devlin came closer, a hint of a smile on his lined face.

"You won't be escaping this time, Mattie," he said in a calm voice. "Dead or alive, I'm taking you back to New York."

She stared back at him, too horrified to speak.

The gentleman holding her arm seemed startled by Devlin's gun. "I don't know what you imagine you're doing, sir, but drawing a gun on a helpless lady—"

"She's no lady and she's not helpless—just outmatched." Devlin's cool, triumphant gaze raked over her. "I'm Detective John Devlin, and this woman is wanted by the New York police."

The bearded fellow dropped her arm and stepped back. Mattie was vaguely aware of the buzz and excited cries around her. She was a prisoner once more, she'd lost her freedom, her hopes. Mattie shut her eyes. For the first time in her life, she wished she was dead. Long dead and buried.

"See, Daddy, I told you. It *is* Tillie!"

Mattie opened her eyes. Evelyn, flushed and breathing heavily, clutched at her father's sleeve. The two of them stared at her in wonder and shock, as if she was a gorilla caught wandering in their midst.

"Damnation, but it is you." Ward Sinclair took a step closer, Evelyn still gripping his arm. "You miserable, lying thief! I'll have you put away for the rest of your worthless life, I swear it."

Mattie didn't blink an eye; she was too overwhelmed, too devastated to conjure up any sort of response. They could have carved her into pieces at that moment and she wouldn't have been able to make a sound.

As though disappointed by her stoic demeanor, the older man turned to Devlin. "And what are *you* doing here, Devlin? I thought you'd been kicked off the police force."

"Yes, thanks to you, Mr. Sinclair, and this red-haired scum," Devlin said coldly. "But even your arrogance won't stand in the way of my seeing that justice is done. I've tracked this woman for three months, without pay and without a thought of reward. All I ask is that—"

"What's going on here, Evelyn?"

Mattie stirred to life. Not Cameron. She couldn't bear to have Cameron see her now. Her heart raced and her breathing grew shallow as Cameron pushed his way through the press of the crowd. Spots appeared before her eyes, and she suddenly prayed she would lose consciousness. Or fall down dead.

She saw Cameron catch sight of Devlin first, his eyes widening at the drawn gun. A second later, he saw Mattie. He rushed over to her, his body blocking Devlin's view.

"Mattie, are you all right?"

She dared not look at him. Instead she helplessly sagged against his chest, wanting to bury herself forever in his embrace.

"Step away, Lord Cameron," ordered Devlin. "This woman is a fugitive from justice."

"Cameron, what are you doing?" Evelyn cried out. "Get away from her."

Cameron whirled around. "Have you all gone mad? Put that gun down or I'll turn it on you myself. You make one move toward Mattie and I'll—"

"Mattie?" Evelyn pointed an accusing finger at Mattie. "That is Tillie Crawford, my maidservant. Three months ago she stole my ruby and diamond collar. The police came to our house to take her off to jail, but she escaped over the roof."

"I don't believe it!"

"It's the truth, Cameron," Sinclair put in.

"If you don't believe us, ask Lieutenant Devlin here." Evelyn's cheeks were aflame. "He was the man who arrested her."

Mattie could feel Cameron trembling with anger. He would despise her for the rest of his life. If he even bothered to remember her.

"I'll have every one of you locked up in jail myself if you dare make one more accusation against this innocent woman." Cameron's voice seemed as deadly as Devlin's gun. "I'm well acquainted with Mrs. Crawford, and I can assure you that you're making a mistake. She's a widowed seamstress who came to Colorado as a mail-order bride."

Devlin waved his gun. "She's Matilda Crawford Laszlo, and that's a fact. I put her away four years ago for burglary and attempted murder. And in May we had her to rights for the theft of Miss Sinclair's jewelry."

"You're lying!" Cameron moved toward Devlin, who quickly cocked his pistol.

"Stay back, Lord Cameron. I'm going to bring this thief to justice even if I have to spill that blue blood of yours. Just step away and let me take her into custody."

Mattie moved swiftly beside Cameron. "Leave him alone, Devlin," she said. Her voice sounded cracked and hoarse. "Just take me and get it over with. There's no need for anyone to get hurt."

"Mattie, what are you doing?" Cameron asked angrily.

"Don't be afraid of him just because he has a gun."

"Listen to her," Devlin cautioned. "I know the two of you have been nice and cozy up in Cripple Creek, but you don't want to be risking arrest or a bullet just because you've got an itch for her."

"What!" Evelyn stormed up to Cameron. "Don't tell me you've been involved with my maid?"

"Not now, Evelyn," he said, pushing her out of the way.

Evelyn turned her eyes in Mattie's direction. "So you're a harlot as well as a thief."

"Bloody hell," Cameron said sharply. "This is the woman I love and I won't stand for one more insult flung her way, do you understand?"

"You love her!" Evelyn's voice came out in a squeak.

Cameron was looking at Mattie with a heartbreaking expression, an expression that showed plainly his love—and his fear that they were telling the truth. She reached out to him, then let her hand fall. Better he should turn his back on her.

"Is this the woman you've fallen in love with? You turn down marriage to me for this—this servant, this criminal!" Evelyn shook her head in disbelief, her gaze taking in Mattie's fashionable traveling costume. "Deck her out as a lady all you like, but she's still a low-born, cunning wench. And you've been fool enough to care for her." She clenched her fists at her sides. "I can't believe it. My own maid! Tillie, how could you do this to me?"

Mattie took a deep breath. "I didn't mean for this to happen, Evelyn. Not any of it."

"How dare you call me 'Evelyn,' you—you whore!" Evelyn reached back and slapped Mattie soundly across the face.

The blow made her ears ring, but Mattie barely felt the stinging pain. She was too distraught over the expression on Cameron's face.

"So it's true?" Cameron asked brokenly. "You worked for the Sinclairs?"

Mattie nodded, her heart aching at the horror in his voice.

He turned his face away. She didn't protest or even flinch when Devlin handcuffed her.

"We've had enough dramatics for one day," he said. "It's off to jail with you."

"Mattie," Cameron murmured, but she kept her head high and refused to look back.

"I hope the judge is merciless," Evelyn hissed. "I hope they hang you."

So do I, thought Mattie as Devlin led her away. *So do I.*

Chapter Nineteen

The afternoon sun streamed through the barred window. Striped shadows fell on Mattie as she sat on the cot, oblivious to the buzzing flies and the sound of drunken swearing down the hall. Caged again, like an animal at the zoo. She knew it was only a matter of time before visiting hour commenced. Starting no doubt with Lord Cameron Lynch-Holmes.

Mattie listened to the voices in the outer office with indifference. Did it matter if there was one last agonizing farewell with the man she loved? She had already resigned herself to losing him. What she couldn't endure was the thought of being imprisoned once more—locked away from the fresh air, from birdsong, from the sound of children laughing.

I'll never see the mountains again, she thought numbly. Or sleep with the window open to a balmy night. Or have a second of privacy or dignity. Or love. Could she bear it? Mattie dared not move. If she sat very still, perhaps she could dredge up a shred of courage, a tiny remnant of the persistence and determination that had kept her alive once before in the Tombs. An involuntary shudder ran through her, and she clenched her hands tightly on her lap. But that terrible year had nearly stripped her of every ounce of will and endurance. Even worse, she knew now just how nightmarish an existence yawned in front of her.

This time she would die in prison. And no one would care when she did.

To think that just a few short hours ago, her only concern was saying good-bye to Cameron. Well, she had no need to worry about him casting aside any marriage opportunities for her sake now. No doubt he'd gotten a bellyful from the Sinclairs since her arrest this morning. All that remained was an inevitable final visit. She only wished he would come soon. Then everything would be finished, his love for her and her doomed obsession with him. Pearl was right about loving a man too much. Staying in Cripple Creek had been foolish and dangerous, one of the few times she'd allowed her heart to rule her. She couldn't have been more self-destructive if she'd swallowed a bottle of morphine.

Keys jangled loudly, and the door leading into the marshal's office creaked open.

"I don't rightly know if I should be allowing you in here, Lord Cameron," the deputy marshal said. "Marshal Lee don't usually let no visitors into the cells. Can't see why you just don't talk to her through the bars. It ain't safe to get too close to any of 'em. Even a pretty gal like her."

"I only require a few moments."

Mattie took a deep breath at the sound of Cameron's voice. She kept her gaze riveted to the floor.

The deputy grumbled. "Sure wish the marshal would get back. I don't like dealing with all you rich greenhorns, and I sure don't like that red-faced feller ordering me around like he done. I ain't no criminal. I'm a lawman same as you got back East."

"I wouldn't take it personally," Cameron replied. "Ward Sinclair treats everyone with the same lack of consideration.

No doubt he'd dare to rail at Prime Minister Gladstone himself.''

"Who?"

Their footsteps shuffled to a stop before her jail cell. "Hello, Mattie," Cameron said softly.

Raising her eyes, she fought to keep her expression impassive. The sight of Cameron standing there, looking splendid and strong as always, brought a lump to her throat. She must seem like the lowest of wretches, locked up in a dingy Denver jail while a drunken man bellowed curses down the hall.

"Hello, Cameron." Her voice was surprisingly calm, her gaze level. "You've no need to be here. This has nothing to do with you. I wish you'd leave." She hesitated. "Please."

Cameron merely gestured to the deputy to unlock the door. The cell was barely six by ten feet, and once he entered it seemed even smaller. She glanced at the deputy, hoping he would at least stay to keep guard. Instead he only muttered under his breath as he walked off, leaving her locked in with Cameron.

His gaze was far too intense and somber, yet she risked staring back at him.

"Are you all right?" Even though Cameron spoke gently, he noticed how she flinched at his voice.

"Please go," she said dully. "I don't want you to see me like this."

He walked over to the cot and sat down beside her. Mattie sprang up and walked to the bars, the farthest away she could get from him. Damn it, what was it about this woman? She was the one who had lied to him; why did he feel as though he were guilty of something?

"What do you want?" she asked, her back turned toward him.

Cameron noticed how tightly her hands gripped the iron bars. "The truth."

A long moment passed. The deputy could be heard yelling at the drunken prisoner. Cameron wouldn't rush her, but he would have an answer, some understandable reason as to what sort of game she had played from the beginning. The minutes ticked by, and finally Mattie turned around to face him. He winced at the sight of her pale face and her bright red hair coming down from its pins. She looked emotionally drained and exhausted. He didn't want to cause her further grief, but he had to know the truth. He had to know if these past few weeks had all been a sham—a way to hide from Devlin and the Sinclairs—or if she had felt any flicker of affection for him.

"You've talked to the Sinclairs." Mattie crossed her arms in front of her. "And Lieutenant Devlin. I'm sure they've told you the whole story."

So they were to keep their distance from each other, he thought ruefully. So be it. He bent forward, nervously twirling his hat in his hands. "I've heard their version. Now I want to hear yours."

"They accused me of stealing a necklace." Mattie jutted out her chin stubbornly. "I didn't."

"Devlin says you were imprisoned four years ago for theft," Cameron said, resisting the impulse to go to her, take her by the shoulders and either shake the truth out of her—or embrace her tightly. "And as an accomplice to murder."

She looked at him with a hurt expression. "If you believe that, we have nothing more to say to each other."

"Sweet Jesus," Cameron snapped, not caring that she jumped at his abrupt tone. "I've had enough of your lies and evasions, Mattie. I want to hear the truth from *you,* not Ward Sinclair or that weasel of a police detective. Are you even capable of telling the truth?"

"Get out," she cried, the color finally returning to her cheeks. "Go back to your own kind and listen to their well-fed lies. I don't need you here, I don't want you here! I'm tired of defending myself, tired of having no one believe me."

"And why should anyone believe you? Haven't you lied to me from the beginning?" He stood up, nearly crushing his straw boater in his hands. "Telling me you were a mail-order bride come here to marry Jack Daniels. I should have known. The whole thing sounded ludicrous from the start. Jack Daniels indeed!''

''What did you want me to say? That I was running from the law, that I needed to hide in the mountains and keep my real identity a secret? All that mattered was getting as far away from New York as I could.'' She looked away. ''And Colorado Springs, too. It wasn't safe for me there. I'm sorry I had to involve you, but—but I had no choice.''

The mention of Colorado Springs reminded Cameron of the first time he had seen her, looking like a windblown gypsy girl as she stepped down from the train. He should have sensed she was trouble from the beginning, should have realized she was lying from that lovely first kiss she had sleepily demanded from him to her bold seduction of him in the Antlers Hotel. A hurtful pang coursed through him as he suddenly remembered what he had planned to do on that night—before Mattie drew him into her room.

''Why did you take me to your bed in Colorado Springs?'' he asked in a tense voice. ''I want the truth, Mattie.''

For the first time, a look of guilt crossed her face. ''I had to stop you from meeting with Julia Sinclair.''

God, that statement hurt. So he had been used, and from the very first moment.

Mattie seemed to sense his pain. ''Evelyn's aunt visited often; I saw her on the day of the theft. I couldn't risk the two of you talking together. She might have mentioned something about Evelyn's red-haired maid running away, and it might have made you too curious or suspicious.'' She broke off, looking miserable. ''I simply had to keep you with me until we left for Cripple Creek. I had to.''

''Of course. Perfectly understandable.'' Cameron tried to get his temper and hurt feelings under control. ''So you knew from the first about my relationship with Evelyn.''

Mattie bit her lip. ''I started working for the Sinclairs two months after you'd gone to Colorado. Evelyn read your letters aloud to me. It was her way of bragging that an English lord was courting her, even if she'd broken the engagement. Afterward, she always handed them over for me to destroy. One of those letters included a photograph, so I knew what you looked like.''

He frowned. Although he'd suspected Evelyn didn't love him, it was disheartening to realize just how little she cared. Had no woman ever loved him but poor Philippa?

''How convenient that one of my letters also included a ticket to Colorado Springs,'' he said.

Mattie nodded, her face mirroring the dismay in his voice.

''You did tell me that gold rushes were a haven for rogues and runaways. I should have listened.''

''I didn't steal the necklace,'' Mattie said sharply. ''I've never stolen anything in my life.''

''You stole the train ticket.''

Her cheeks flamed nearly as red as her hair. ''Your last letter arrived just before Evelyn's necklace went missing. She was rushing off to a wedding that day and didn't even bother to open it. When I finally did later that night, I discovered the train ticket. I had every intention of giving it back, but then the police burst into my room, and—and everything turned upside-down.''

Mattie leaned her head against the bars. ''I was so close to making a fresh start. I was going to leave the next morning for a position as dressmaker at Madame Victorine's. I hated being in service, hated living in cramped, smelly rooms, listening to insults without ever being able to talk back. I hated not being free.'' She closed her eyes. ''Sometimes it was almost as bad as the year I spent in the Tombs. But I knew I could work my way out of the sweatshops and the Fifth Avenue mansions. I spent three backbreaking years doing just that. Then, as I was about to make a decent life for myself, another rich woman gets her jewelry stolen, and I'm back once more protesting my innocence.'' A bitter laugh escaped her. ''Of course, in the eyes of the law, the poor are never innocent.''

''Then who stole the necklace?''

''How should I know?'' she said wearily. ''I'm not the

police, although I couldn't do worse than they've done."

Cameron stepped beside her, cautious not to get too close for fear she'd shy away once more. "Devlin claims you should still be in prison for robbing another employer four years ago. Apparently it was only your husband's deathbed confession that got you released."

She shot him a cynical glance. "Which Devlin doesn't believe, of course. Any more than you do."

"Damn it, I want to believe you!"

"Why? Why is it so important to believe me? It won't make any difference to our lives." She shook her head, her face twisted with grief. "It doesn't matter to anyone what I say—it never has. Why should it matter to you now?"

"Because I love you, that's why," he thundered back, grabbing her by the arm. "Or have you already forgotten that I asked you to marry me just this morning?"

She stared up at him, her eyes suddenly swimming with tears. "I'll never forget, but it's best if you do. As quickly as possible."

"Damn you, Mattie," he said hoarsely. "I don't know what you expect of me. I learn that all this time you've been lying to me, pretending to care when all you sought was a refuge from the police."

"Cameron, please." She looked down at his hand. "You're hurting me."

His grip loosened. What sort of arrogant fool was he? Railing at her for trying to save her life. Hadn't he played dozens of women false, and with far less reason? This close to her, he saw how tired and vulnerable she was—a far cry from the vibrant, resourceful woman he'd known up till now. Despite his hurt feelings and sense of betrayal, the woman he adored was on her way to prison. If the prospect seemed nightmarish to him, he could imagine what it meant for Mattie.

"Why couldn't you tell me the truth?" he asked. "I would have tried to help you. You must know that. I want to help you now. Let me hire someone to look into this case. Better yet, I'll speak with Ward Sinclair about dropping the charges. What's a measly ruby necklace to a moneyed fellow like him? I'll pay him what the bloody thing is worth, if I must.''

Mattie looked at him for a long moment. Despite what he now knew, Cameron couldn't keep his heart from softening.

A sad smile briefly touched her lips. ''You don't have that much money, my darling.''

''Not now perhaps, but very soon. Certainly, I can get a loan on the basis of the mine if all else—'' He stopped as her whispered endearment finally sank in. ''You've no need to flatter me, Mattie. I'll help you regardless, so please don't pretend to care.''

Mattie flung her arms about him. After a startled moment, he embraced her in turn, savoring her familiar warmth and the delightful feel of her womanly body pressed against him. Even if it had all been a sham, he couldn't deny the happiness he had known with her, the piercing satisfaction and joy.

''It wasn't a lie,'' she said, her voice muffled against his shoulder. ''Long before I met you, I dreamed of you at night. I reread your letters for weeks, and I kept your photograph under my pillow like a schoolgirl.''

''Mattie,'' he breathed softly, kissing the tousled hair that even now smelled fresh and sweet. ''My beautiful Mattie.''

She straightened and gazed into his eyes. ''Cameron, it's true I wanted to keep you with me that night in the Springs, but not just because of Julia Sinclair. I had been yearning for you for months, imagining your arms about me and your mouth kissing mine. For just one night, I wanted to pretend that my dream lover desired me as much as I did him.'' Mattie leaned her head against his. ''And you were so much better than my dreams, so much better. When I got to Cripple Creek, I knew I should steer clear of you, I knew it wasn't wise. But I couldn't. After you stopped my wedding to Daniels, I realized I loved you. That ended any hope of escape.''

The deep sadness in her voice caused him alarm. He put a hand under her chin and made her look at him once more.

"Dearest, I promise I'll get you out of here."

Mattie shook her head. "They won't let you." Her eyes clouded over. "*He* won't let you."

Cameron brushed back her hair. "Sinclair may be an arrogant braggart, but enough gold will convince him to listen to reason."

"Not Sinclair." A shiver ran through her. "Devlin. He'll never let me go free a second time. He'll see me dead first, I know it."

He kissed her softly. "Devlin's just a policeman. He can't do anything if the charges are dropped."

She took a step back. "Hate can make a man do nearly anything, and Devlin hates me."

"I don't understand. You can't be the only prisoner of his who's tried to run off. Devlin's professional pride may be bruised, but I hardly think he's going to turn this into a personal matter."

"But it *is* personal between us." Mattie rubbed her forehead, as though it ached. "I don't know why he seems so bent on destroying me. It seems crazy, unreasonable. He wasn't even the officer in charge when Frank was arrested. But once Frank confessed and lied about me being involved, Devlin took over." She shuddered. "He came for me at night, just like he did at the Sinclair's."

Cameron took her in his arms once more. "What kind of cowardly bastard was your husband that he would drag you into prison with him?"

Mattie sighed. "I found out that Frank was the one who'd stolen some rare coins at the last place we worked. We had a terrible fight about it, worse than you can imagine. He admitted that he'd been stealing from every employer we'd had since we got married . . . and long before. Then he told me how he was set to rob old Mrs. Jenkins, and since I finally knew everything, there was no reason not to help him. I refused, of course, and said I was leaving him. He told me he'd beat me within an inch of my life if I tried."

Cameron held her even tighter, anger boiling up inside

him. If Frank Laszlo hadn't already been in his grave, he would have been happy to put him there.

"Don't stiffen so, darling." Mattie looked up at him. "A girl raised in frontier towns knows how to take care of herself. Frank knew how bad my temper was, and just stormed off cursing." She frowned at the memory. "Later that night, he tried to rob the old woman and nearly killed her in the attempt. Poor Mrs. Jenkins died later from her injuries, may she rest in peace."

"So he implicated you out of spite?"

"Spite, fear. I don't know, maybe even a twisted kind of love." She stepped out of his embrace. "Frank must have felt something for me. Guilt, if nothing else. After all, he didn't have to confess that he'd lied all along about me. Thank heaven the authorities believed him."

"But not Devlin."

She shook her head. "He came to look in on me at the prison, like I was some wildflower he'd planted in a garden of weeds. I think he took pleasure in seeing how much worse I was every month. Getting thinner and paler, sometimes coughing like a consumptive, other times covered in bruises."

"Dear God," murmured Cameron. "What sort of hell was that place?"

Mattie looked at him with dread. "Nothing I can say will make you understand what being in prison is like. I've spent three years trying to burn it out of my memory, but now they're taking me back. Back to the damp cells, back to the rats and moldy bread. And back to those matrons. They shaved my head and—and sometimes put me in with prisoners who seemed mad." She pressed her hands to her mouth, as though to stop a cry from escaping. "If I go back, I'll lose more than my freedom, Cameron. I'll lose my sanity. My life!"

Her shoulders began to quake with sobs. "Please don't forget me when I'm gone. I have to know that someone remembers me when I'm in that hell. Please don't forget me, no matter how happy you are with Evelyn, spare a thought for me.''

''You little fool.'' Cameron grabbed her hands, clutching them to his chest. ''I could no more forget you than stop breathing. I love you. Don't you understand? I love you, only you. Do you honestly imagine I'm going to marry Evelyn now?''

''But you have to,'' she sobbed. ''You have to save Clydesford Hall, your family.''

''The hell with Clydesford Hall. I've sacrificed enough for it, as did my father. And what did it reap either of us but loneliness and pain? No, Mattie, I'm not going to marry any woman merely for the sake of gold. That sort of marriage would seem as much a prison as the one you have known. I want my freedom as desperately as you do, dearest. I need it.'' He kissed her. ''I need you.''

''I've no more strength left to fight,'' Mattie said in a quiet but terrible voice. She looked as though she were standing a foot from the gallows. ''I'll die if I go back to the Tombs.''

Cameron framed her face tenderly with his hands. ''I swear on my father's soul that you won't have to.''

''How?'' she whispered, her body trembling.

He took a deep breath, hoping his own fear didn't show. ''Don't worry, Mattie. No matter what it takes, I'll see that you're set free.'' He pulled her into his arms once more, unwilling to look at her sweet face, now so fearful and stricken.

''I'll take care of everything,'' he said soothingly.

If only he knew how.

Chapter Twenty

"Do you take me for a fool, Lynch-Holmes?" Ward Sinclair banged the brandy decanter down on the tray. His walrus mustache seemed to bristle with righteous indignation, as did his voice. "This woman has stolen from my family. And after I was charitable enough to hire her out of an abysmal sweatshop in the Bowery."

Cameron sat down in a nearby wingchair. "I didn't come here to debate Miss Crawford's innocence."

Sinclair snorted. "I should say not. What's there to debate? She's as guilty as a fox caught in an empty henhouse."

"You've no proof whatsoever that she stole from you." Cameron tried to control his own growing anger. "No one has turned up the necklace itself."

"Proof! Haven't you heard one damn thing Devlin and I said? Miss Crawford spent a year in prison after robbing her last employer, an unfortunate woman who lost her life due to that scheming liar and her husband."

"Clearly a miscarriage of justice. She was released as

soon as her husband admitted he falsely accused her.''

Sinclair downed his brandy in one gulp, wincing as the burning liquor went down. ''They must breed damned gullible men back there in England if you believe anything Tillie's thieving husband said.''

''No proof exists showing Miss Crawford has stolen anything.''

Sinclair sat down on a velvet sofa, one arm thrown casually along the rosewood trim. ''If she was innocent, why did she bolt over the rooftops when the police tried to question her?''

''She's terrified of going back to prison,'' Cameron said in a low voice. ''Good God, she'd already been imprisoned once for a crime she didn't commit—and at the tender age of twenty. By all accounts, the Tombs is as fearful a place as its name indicates. I don't think we can blame the woman for trying to avoid spending the rest of her days there.''

''She should have thought of that before she stole my daughter's necklace. A necklace she probably sold somewhere between New York and Colorado.'' Sinclair's eyes narrowed. ''I know you're not thinking clearly about this, young man. From what I hear, you've been playing house with this little thief for nearly the whole summer.''

Cameron straightened. ''Miss Crawford and I have grown quite close these past few months, which is why I am convinced of her innocence.''

''Well, I never doubted that redhead had hidden talents,'' Sinclair said sarcastically. ''But let that hot blood of yours cool, and you'll realize she's nothing but a thieving slut.''

Cameron stood up, his determination to remain calm now broken. ''I'll not tolerate that sort of talk about Mattie Crawford. She's as fine a lady as any of your kind has laid eyes on.''

''My kind, indeed. Have you forgotten where our respective wealth and positions place us on the social scale? At the top, Lord Cameron, which is as it should be. I'd heard your reputation suffered in England due to a woman, but at least she was a titled lady. It would be a tragedy were you to disgrace yourself in America over a mere servant. You'd not be able to show your face in any drawing room from here to Paris.''

''My standing in drawing rooms is of no consequence to me.''

''Well, it might be to your future wife.'' Sinclair pointed a reproving finger at him. ''You may regret being a social pariah when you've a woman at your side, sharing your name and reputation.''

''I doubt Miss Crawford will give a damn if anyone accepts us into their hallowed drawing rooms,'' Cameron replied stiffly.

''What the devil is that supposed to mean?''

Cameron cleared his throat. ''I've asked her to be my wife.''

Sinclair's normally ruddy complexion grew sallow. ''Merciful heavens, boy, you've thrown it all to the dogs, haven't you?''

''I know this may appear rash—''

''Rash?'' Sinclair let out a harsh laugh. ''You're nothing but a mad, lusty fool who's let himself be seduced by a pair of green eyes and a tasty young body.''

''I'm in love with her, Sinclair.''

''A few months ago you were proclaiming your love for my daughter.''

''My affections,'' Cameron corrected quickly. ''I was fond of Evelyn—I still am—but I never pretended to either of us that it was love.''

Sinclair stared at him for a long, uncomfortable moment. ''You've some brass, Lord Cameron, I'll say that. You reject my girl, then take up with the hussy who robbed her. Well, after she's been in prison a few months, your lust for her will die down. When you're thinking clearly again, you'll thank me for locking her away before she ruined your life.''

''I don't believe that for a minute.'' He fixed Sinclair with an icy stare of his own. ''Any more than I believe you would actually send a poor innocent girl to prison.''

"You're right. I'm not sending an innocent girl to prison. I'm sending Miss Crawford."

"Sinclair, I've come here to ask you to drop the charges."

"Don't be absurd."

Cameron shoved his hands into his pockets, balling them into fists. "If it's the price of the necklace you're grieving over, then I'll pay you what it's worth."

"It was worth quite a lot," he replied coolly. "and not just in monetary terms. That necklace was crafted for Marie Antoinette. I doubt any amount of greenbacks can replace such a treasure."

"So you're that rare man without a price," Cameron said bitterly.

Sinclair paused. "Oh, I didn't say that."

Taken by surprise, he scrutinized the older man to see if he was serious. "What do you want in return for Miss Crawford's freedom?"

Instead of answering, Sinclair stood up and walked over to the fireplace. "Do you recognize this?" He ran a finger lightly along the frame of the oil painting that hung above the mantel.

"It looks Dutch. Seventeenth century." Cameron stepped closer to the seascape. "Seems a bloody fine painting for the Brown Palace to be hanging for its guests."

"It's mine," Sinclair said softly. "I refuse to spend a night away from it. Your vice may be women, but mine is collecting objects of art. Both vices have their dangers, but I've no doubt mine provides far deeper pleasures."

"What has all this to do with Miss Crawford?" he asked impatiently.

"I'm a collector, Lord Cameron. I work on Wall Street unceasingly, taking enormous financial risks, only that I may acquire the means to indulge my vice. Flemish paintings, Chinese vases, twelfth-century manuscripts, the gems of a doomed French queen: all fodder for my passion. I collect because I must. I can no more resist a priceless acquisition than you can resist a woman with hair the color of fire."

278

His hand stroked the gilt frame of the painting as if it were the face of a lover. "Not that I don't appreciate the weaker sex, of course. Evelyn's mother boasted skin as smooth and pale as marble, and in the candlelight her eyes were as blue as a Limoges enamel. But women sicken and die; their beauty fades." His voice dropped to a near whisper. "Marble statues, however, never lose their majesty, a Virgin painted by an Old Master is forever young and pure."

Cameron felt uneasy. It was the first time Sinclair had lowered his brusque, unfeeling mask. He felt as though he were watching a bull turn into a swan. "I'm not sure I understand."

Suddenly it dawned on him. "It's a gold mine you're looking to add to your collection, isn't it? In exchange for a ruby necklace, you demand a mine worth a hundred such necklaces, maybe more." He smirked. "Who's the thief now?"

"You misunderstand. I am first and foremost a collector. As is my daughter. Evelyn has had her heart set on acquiring only one thing since she was twelve."

"And what is that?"

"An English lord." Sinclair finally tore his gaze from the painting.

"Are you saying she wants to 'collect' me?" Cameron laughed, but it had a hollow sound.

"She wants to be a titled lady and bear aristocratic sons." He shrugged. "It's a banal wish, I know. Still, I've grown accustomed to indulging her, and she does have my sympathy. I know what's it's like to hunger after an acquisition, only to have it snatched away."

"I seem to recall that you were the one who disappointed her. You were quite adamant in rejecting my offer of marriage last autumn."

"At the time, I hoped she could do better. No need to settle for a Huydens when there's a chance of getting a Rembrandt." Sinclair gave him a thin smile. "Even you must admit that your reputation was appalling. That messy business with Lady Philippa, quite sordid. Being the future

279

Marquess was an asset, of course, as were the rumors of the Clydesford art treasures. And Evelyn was more than pleased that you brought a handsome face along with the title of Marchioness. But your circumstances still left much to be desired in my eyes.''

''I didn't have a gold mine then, did I?'' Cameron finished coldly.

''Exactly. As satisfied as Evelyn would have been with the situation, a bankrupt son-in-law—no matter how much ermine he's entitled to wear—is still a liability. As I said before, collecting has its perils, and one of them is the risk of financial ruin. With a strike as rich as yours promises to be, that need not be a fear of mine again.''

''So now I'm in a position to offer both you and your daughter what you want.'' Cameron's voice rang with contempt. ''How convenient for the pair of you. And how romantic.''

The older man seemed oblivious to Cameron's scorn. ''As for matters of romance, that's best left to my daughter. No doubt she'll be quite grateful at being made a Marchioness.'' He paused. ''Grateful *and* enthusiastic, if you take my meaning.''

''Only too well, I'm afraid,'' Cameron said coldly. ''You must be demented if you think I'll agree to this nasty little bargain.''

Sinclair shrugged. ''Promise to marry Evelyn and I'll drop all charges against Miss Crawford. Otherwise, she'll be put on a train bound for the Tombs within the next twenty-four hours, and in chains, too, if I can manage it.'' He smiled again, a chilling sight this time. ''Which I'm certain I can.''

''You're really quite despicable, aren't you?''

''Not at all. I'm merely a conscientious father who wants to make his daughter happy. Just a few months ago, you were more than willing to become my son-in-law. In fact, you seemed not only eager, but desperate to sign the marriage contract. I hardly think you have reason to protest now that I'm finally giving you what you came to America begging for.''

Cameron frowned in distaste at the memory.

"Now there's an added incentive," Sinclair said quietly. "Your little red-haired mistress won't have to dodge the police for the rest of her life. At least until she gets herself in trouble again. You've had your romantic fling, Lord Cameron. Now it's time to act the man and take up your responsibilities. You can't seriously imagine you could marry a woman like that. It would have been a disaster for both of you. Do the right thing, my lord. Satisfy all of us. Marry my daughter, and let the resourceful Miss Crawford go free.''

Cameron turned away, revolted by Sinclair's smug expression. So he was being acquired as though he were little more than an Aubusson rug. He closed his eyes, remembering the fear in Mattie's voice, her deathlike pallor, the chill certainty and doom in her gaze. He couldn't let her go back to prison; he would do anything to prevent it. Better to resign himself to being the titled captive of the Sinclairs than let Mattie be locked away in that hellhole. He'd known so little freedom as it was; the memory of it, and his love for Mattie, would have to last him a long time.

"I want your assurance that all charges against her will be dropped immediately," he said in a deadly calm voice. "*Written* assurance. I don't care if your bloody necklace ever turns up. She is not to be implicated in any way with it in the future. Is that understood?"

When only silence greeted him, Cameron swiveled around. Sinclair gazed at him with a proprietary air. Cameron felt disgusted by the sight.

"I said, do we understand each other?"

Sinclair finally moved, one hand outstretched. When Cameron refused to take his hand, the older man lifted an eyebrow in disapproval. "Come now, let's at least be civilized about this.''

Cameron glared at him.

Sinclair lowered his hand with an indifferent shrug. "I'll

give you all the written assurances you want, but I insist on some of my own. Namely that Miss Crawford leave Denver tomorrow, and that she is never to have any contact with you again. That also means no last tearful good-byes or farewell love notes.''

"Perhaps you would like me to be branded as well," Cameron snapped back.

"One more thing." Sinclair's face had resumed its normal ruddy color, as though he had been enervated by the transaction. "The marriage will take place as soon as possible, *before* we leave Denver. I never rest easy until a deal is closed and the merchandise is firmly in my possession."

Instead of replying, Cameron looked once more at the Flemish seascape over the mantel. "I believe I was wrong about the quality of that painting. On closer inspection, it appears rather second-rate." He picked up his hat and gloves. "Like its owner."

She was free. Mattie stared unbelievingly out the stagecoach window, as though expecting the fragrant vista of pine and sagebrush to suddenly transform itself into the iron bars and stench of the Denver jail. Free. It had been hours since her release, but she still couldn't comprehend it. All charges dropped, the deputy marshal had told her as he unlocked her cell at dawn. She was free, no longer a fugitive on the run.

But recalling how she was hustled out of Denver, Mattie couldn't shake the feeling that she was escaping once more. Run out of town; there was no other word for it. She'd been put on the first conveyance leaving Denver—a narrow-gauge train bound south—with instructions to stay on the train until it ran out of track in the high country. After that she transferred onto a stagecoach headed for the Rio Grande. Like a solitary gypsy, she thought. Or a woman running for her life.

The deputy marshal made it clear that she was to get herself out of Colorado as fast as she could. "Go to Texas," he advised with a frown, "Or better yet Mexico. And when you get there, change your name and lie low. You got some mighty powerful enemies.''

Not that she wasn't grateful for his gruff advice. It didn't matter where she ended up as long as it wasn't in another jail cell. She trembled with relief at being in the open air, no longer under lock and key, shut away and despised.

The man across from her sneezed.

''Would you like me to lower the window covering, sir?'' she asked.

The man had spent the entire trip shivering, with the collar of his jacket turned up.

''If you would, miss,'' he said. ''I'm a city fellow and this healthy mountain air doesn't sit too well with my lungs, I'm afraid.''

Mattie glanced over at the other passengers to see if they would object to having the fresh summer air cut off. The only other female on board was snoring quietly.

She turned to the two men beside her. ''Do either of you gentlemen mind?''

The passenger boasting a white canvas duster and a handlebar mustache merely shrugged, but the old fellow gave a harsh laugh.

''Dang greenhorns,'' he said, stretching out his legs so that his mooseskin boots scraped against the city slicker's shiny spats. ''Used to be a time when all you could find out here were Injuns and buffalo skinners like me. Now there ain't nothing in these mountains 'cept for lawyers and businessmen.'' He ran a weary hand over his empty cartridge belt and buckskin shirt. ''Shut the window, little lady. It don't matter none to me. The Rockies have been bought and sold, and there ain't a free man left between here and Laredo.''

In the uncomfortable silence that followed, she reluctantly lowered the oilcloth over the coach window; the interior of the stage grew glum and tinged with a dirty yellow light. Mattie fought back a moment of panic as the lumbering walls of the coach suddenly seemed to close in on her like a moving prison. Calm down, she told herself. Despite the old buffalo skinner's bitter pronouncement, she *was* free. No one would ever lock her away again. Yet the thought of her freedom brought no joy. Somehow she still felt a prisoner, shackled by feelings of doom, of uncertainty, and a crushing, unbearable loneliness. The rocking of the coach brought on another wave of dizziness, and she leaned her head back and breathed deeply. What was the matter with her? She was free, wasn't that all she had ever wanted? Why was she behaving like a girl with the vapors, tremulous and weak?

She turned her face to the side of the coach and stifled a sob. Yes, she was weak—weak and foolish and utterly lost. More than anything in the world she wanted to be back in Denver at this moment, even if it meant being locked up once more. Cameron was in Denver. Dear God, did that mean Cameron was more important than her freedom? Impossible. Nothing was more important than being free. Nothing. But why hadn't he come to say good-bye? she asked herself for the hundredth time. At the least he could have said good-bye. Yet hadn't they been saying their farewells for a long time? *You knew this day would come,* she told herself sternly. *We both knew.*

She took some comfort in believing that Cameron was the one who had brought about her release from jail; it had to have been him. There wasn't a soul in the world besides him who cared about her happiness. Happiness. The word echoed hollowly. With every turn of the wheel, she was being driven farther away from the only happiness she'd known as an adult. She felt as though she'd been thrown out of Paradise. The weeks spent with Cameron in Cripple Creek had been filled with passion, gentleness and love. She'd known all along it was too sweet, too beautiful to last. But she hadn't expected the pain at being parted from him to be so overwhelming. It felt as though a stone were lodged in her chest, threatening to crush her.

"Goodbye, Cameron," she whispered, reveling in the sound of his name.

She sat up straighter as the dizziness worsened, accompanied this time by nausea.

"You feeling all right, miss?" the city slicker asked solicitously.

"Actually, no," she said in a weak voice. What in the world was the matter with her?

"You want us to ask the driver to stop again?" The buffalo skinner tapped her gently on the knee.

She was mortified. Twice already, she'd had the coach stop while she went off to be sick in the bushes.

"I don't think that will be necessary." She tried to smile. "It must be the rocking of the stagecoach that's upsetting me."

"Are you certain of that?" the older woman said in a sleepy voice. She'd been napping on and off for hours. "Last time I remember being sick in a stage, I was expecting my last young'un. Lots of women in that condition can't bear all this shaking."

Mattie shook her head, fighting back her nausea and alarm. "That's impossible."

"You sure about that?" The woman yawned and adjusted her shawl.

"Leave the girl be," said the buffalo skinner. "If she says she ain't in the family way, then she ain't. Probably just had a bad pot of stew before she boarded."

The city fellow cleared his throat. "I hardly think this is a proper topic of conversation for mixed company."

"Who are you to be telling us what's proper and what ain't?" The woman in the shawl was now fully awake and ready to scrap.

Mattie paid little attention to the quarrel erupting around her. So much had happened these past two days, she'd forgotten about her monthly course. She *was* late, but was that so unusual? Circumstances had been trying; surely that had upset her cycle. She couldn't be carrying a child. Four childless years of marriage had convinced her she was barren. How could a few weeks with Cameron have produced the baby she had so hungered for when she was younger? If she was pregnant, it was nothing short of a miracle. Cameron's child. For a moment, she felt such joy, it nearly obliterated her heartache. If it was true, she would have something to remind her of their love, a child who might look at her with dark blue eyes and a noble brow, a little boy or girl with soft golden hair and a dimpled smile. Cameron's child.

Yet this wouldn't be the first time for Cameron. Her joy suddenly vanished. Lady Philippa had also been carrying Cameron's baby, and the loss of both her and the unborn child had nearly destroyed his capacity to love. How terrible that once again Cameron would be cheated of both the woman he loved and his child.

"It can't be true," Mattie cried out, startling the other passengers into silence. "It can't."

As though to reinforce her despair, a mournful wail rent the air. It reminded her of the moments leading up to the stagecoach robbery in June. The nausea was worse than ever, and even though the evening air was cool, she felt overheated. In another moment she would be sick again.

"Shouldn't we have reached a halfway house by now?" she asked anxiously. "Don't the horses have to be changed?"

"They been having problems on this line," the buffalo skinner said with a grunt. The old fellow slumped down, crossing his arms on his belly. "Too many young hotheads holding up the stage. I hear they been closing some of the stations."

"Good lord," the city man said. Even in the gloom she could see him shiver. "I didn't think anyone was still holding up stagecoaches. It would seem far more lucrative to rob trains, wouldn't it?"

Mattie felt too sick to reassure him. Besides, something wasn't right. Why had she been put on a narrow-gauge train heading deep into the mountains? Was it simply because it was the first train leaving Denver, or did someone want her traveling on a lonely stagecoach far from curious eyes or civilized life? Was this merciful "release" merely another trap laid for her? What if Sinclair and Devlin had promised

Cameron she would go free, but instead planned to have her taken out of Colorado under guard?

She glanced nervously at the men in the coach. That cowboy in the duster hadn't said a dozen words all day. She bit her lip, wishing she'd packed a pistol on her person. And the old buffalo skinner looked as though a few gold dollars would buy his silence and his services. Any of the men in the coach could have been hired by Sinclair to see that she got out of town, even the city slicker. Mattie edged toward the door, lifting up the oilcloth. Dusk fell swiftly in the mountains, and she could barely make out the passing trees. They were slowing now. Was it the result of the steep grade, or was this another trap? Was she going to be transferred for a stage bound east? She felt her face go white. Dear God in heaven. It was possible that she was even now being carted off to New York—and the Tombs!—like an unknowing fool. Only this time it wasn't only her going off to prison, it might be her child as well.

"Sir, could you stop the coach?" she yelled out the window at the driver. "Sir, could you please stop?"

The city fellow sat up in alarm. "What's wrong? Did you see something outside? Are we being attacked by bandits?"

"Relax. She's just gonna be sick again." This came from the normally taciturn cowboy.

The buffalo skinner reached up and banged twice on the ceiling of the coach. The driver could be heard shouting to his team, and the coach creaked and heaved as it was suddenly brought to a halt.

"Thank you," she replied. Mattie gathered up her skirts and opened the door. She'd barely jumped down to the ground before she leaned over and was sick in the grass. Straightening up a moment later, she felt weak but somewhat restored. She leaned against the wheel. The coach lantern hadn't been lit yet, and the trees were only swaying dark shadows. Something scurried off into the nearby brush.

Mattie peered up toward the driver. "I'm sorry for making you stop so often."

"No need to apologize, little lady," the driver said as he

swung down. In the gloom she saw him fumble with the lantern. It blazed up and she turned her face away from the sudden brightness. "We were set to stop soon anyways."

Turning back, Mattie was about to ask him how much farther to the halfway house. Instead, her mouth fell open. "You—you tried to rob us before," she stammered out. "On the stage to Cripple Creek."

"Yeah, and you pointed my own Colt at me, too," the man sneered. "The boys really had a time with that." With practiced ease, he pulled out another Colt revolver. "But I promise you now, you ain't gonna lay a finger on this one without me blowing it off."

"What are you doing driving this stagecoach?" Mattie backed away, clutching her drawstring purse to her as though it were a bronze shield.

"Me and the boys figured it was a lot easier robbing a stage if one of us was driving it."

She bumped into someone and whirled about. The buffalo skinner and cowboy had gotten out of the stage as well.

"What in hell's going on out here?" the cowboy growled.

"Shut up and toss your weapons down," the robber said with a sneer.

The cowboy glared for one heartstopping second, and then slowly unbuckled his holster. Just as he threw the holstered gun to the ground, he made a move for his boot. Before he could pull his knife free, the robber fired a shot. Mattie yelled a warning too late, and the cowboy fell to his knees. Swearing profusely, he clutched his wrist.

"Do that again and I'll blow your hand off," the robber said coldly. "And tell the woman in there to stop that caterwauling."

The buffalo skinner leaned toward the stage, trying to calm the hysterical lady inside.

Mattie looked about, but the darkness was too thick for her to see more than a few feet in front of her. Was he the only one they had to contend with, or were his partners on the way?

As though reading her mind, the bandit grinned. "We

weren't supposed to stop for another hour. The plan was to get off this steep grade, but you had to be such a nuisance—'' he gestured at the cowboy—''everything got moved up. The gunshot told them the robbery's begun. My partners will be here in a few minutes. And I'm sure they'll be pleased as fed hogs to see we got hold of *you* again.'' He smiled at Mattie, his teeth gleaming yellow in the lantern light.

''What are you going to do to me?'' she demanded hoarsely.

He stepped close and ripped the purse from her hands. ''First off, I'm going to rob you.'' His fingers closed around the drawstring bag. ''And it seems right heavy, too. I heard you was holed up with Pearl's whores in Cripple Creek. Guess there are some fellows who don't mind bedding a sassy redhead.''

''Leave the lady alone,'' the cowboy said from behind her.

The robber cocked his gun. ''You ain't in a position to be giving me warnings. Now git those two fools inside the coach to come out, otherwise I'm going to give them something to really wail about.''

While the city gentleman and the woman tearfully disembarked, Mattie nudged her foot toward the knife the cowboy had dropped onto the ground.

''Don't try it.'' The robber took another step closer, pressing the barrel of his gun to her temple.

''You knew I was on this stage, didn't you?'' she asked. He nodded.

Despite her fear, the sense of betrayal was even stronger. So it *had* been a trap. Obviously Sinclair had paid these thieves to abduct her, not caring who they robbed or hurt along the way. No matter how hard she fought, how desperately she struggled, how much she sacrificed, she would never be free.

The gun at her head slowly lowered, but she was barely aware of it. It didn't matter. She'd been trapped again. From behind her came the thunder of horses, nearly drowning out the wails of the other female passenger.

"Well, you've already taken my money," she said in a voice cold with anger and betrayal. "Now what do you plan to do with me?"

The robber with the gun didn't answer. Instead he stepped back so that his face was in shadow.

A voice cut in, however, loud and triumphant. "I'm going to bring you to justice."

She gasped and turned around.

It was Devlin.

Chapter Twenty-one

Mattie stared at Devlin in disbelief.

He ignored her stricken expression as he pushed aside the other passengers. Behind him, Mattie could see three other horsemen come into view, guns pulled out, faces disguised by bandannas or hoods. Devlin's face was brazenly uncovered—and he was gloating.

"Get away from me," she said hoarsely as the dark reality of him swept over her. As always, he smelled of peppermint drops and tonic water, and she knew all too well that slight wheezing sound he made when he was agitated.

One of the other horsemen rode closer and pulled down his bandanna. "Ain't you got a kind word for your intended, Mattie?" he asked, and then hooted with laughter.

"Jack Daniels!" She looked around wildly at the other outlaws, all of them chuckling and making obscene comments. So it hadn't been a coincidence that a man called Jack Daniels showed up in Cripple Creek. It had all been a lie, a terrible trick to deceive her.

"You can call me anything you like, honey, as long as

you treat me like a sweet bride should." Another round of coarse laughter erupted.

"Shut up, all of you!" shouted Devlin. "And cover your face, you stupid jackass. Every one of you deserves to hang. Which I've no doubt you will one day."

In the tense silence that followed, Devlin turned his attention back to Mattie. "Get in the coach." The revolver in his hand gleamed in the lantern light.

"Haven't you had your fill of tormenting me?" she cried out in frustration.

Devlin shook his head slowly. "No, I haven't."

"Hey, if you're going play any games with this filly, me and the boys are gonna watch," complained the bandit who'd driven the stage. "After showing us up outside Cripple Creek, the least she owes us is a show of them legs."

"Shut your mouth." Devlin barely spared him a glance. His attention was riveted on Mattie. "This woman is mine. Any idiot who interferes will find a piece of lead in his belly."

Mattie stood frozen between the two men, searching for an avenue of escape. There didn't seem to be one. The other thieves were ordering the passengers off to the side, yanking at the older lady's satchel and snickering at the city fellow's trembling hands. Devlin's hand was steady, however, and he was pointing his gun at Mattie's heart.

"Don't forget where you are, lawman," the bandit sneered. "Them's my boys over there, and we outgun you four to one. We didn't mind letting you ride along with us, specially since you was paying, but don't start giving any orders. You make me mad, and I'll take down you *and* the girl." He shouted to his friends. "Ain't that right, boys? This son of a bitch deserves a little lesson in—"

He never finished the sentence. Without blinking, Devlin shot a bullet dead center into the thief's right arm. Mattie let out a strangled gasp, while the man bellowed like a downed bull. Mattie stared in horror as Devlin calmly turned to the others. "Anyone makes a move and I'll finish him off."

For one uneasy moment, Mattie was certain the other

thieves were going to open fire. They cursed and cocked their revolvers. In response, Devlin pointed his gun at the wounded thief's right shoulder and fired. This time, Mattie's yell matched his own.

"You crazy murdering bastard!" screamed the thief, blood running down his arm, his face contorted in pain. "I'll see you in hell."

Devlin only cocked his gun again. "If you don't want to see your friend's face blown off, I suggest you all divest yourselves of your weapons. Now!" He gave the bandits a cold glance. "It's nothing to me if another crook lies dead. I'm a lawman and you're breaking the law. This is justice, boys—Eastern style. Now stick those guns in that bag and toss it over."

The flickering lantern cast an eerie glow over the white faces of the other passengers. It was a nightmarish scene made worse by the moans of the wounded man and the violent oaths of the bandits as they threw down their weapons. In the center of it all stood Devlin, implacable, seemingly unstoppable.

When the bag of guns was tossed at his feet, Devlin ordered everyone back. "Not you," he said to the old buffalo skinner. "Get up there and drive."

The old man peered at the revolver trained in his direction, and then shrugged. "You got the gun, so I guess you're the foreman," he said as he climbed up.

"Once we're inside, you start up the team and ride on."

"Any place in particular we're headed?" He untied the reins and clucked to the restless horses.

"Just keep going forward, old man. Don't stop until I tell you, or you may hear a few more gunshots, you understand me?"

The buffalo skinner looked straight ahead and nodded.

Devlin turned his attention back to Mattie. "Help him inside." His voice was calm and steely. "Then get in there with him."

Mattie stared at him, as though seeing a monster even more horrifying than she'd feared.

"Move!" he shouted. As Mattie struggled to get the wounded man into the coach, Devlin turned back to the gang. "Any of you boys think about following me, I'll finish off your friend."

When Devlin shut the door behind them, Mattie felt as though she'd been sealed in her tomb. Beside her, the wounded man was still cursing, but his breathing was ragged. In another minute, he'd probably faint from loss of blood. Or die.

"Damn your soul to hell," she said as the coach started up with a lurch.

"At least I have a soul, Mrs. Laszlo." With his free hand he struck her chin, sending her sprawling back onto the seat.

Dazed, Mattie fought to keep from going under, but it might have been better if she had. Trapped in a stagecoach with a man who wanted to kill her, she could only hope he wasn't going to prolong the torture, like a malicious cat toying with a mouse.

"If you've a soul, it's a black one," she said, struggling to pull herself upright. Her chin ached, but she barely felt it. "You're a devil and you have the devil's own luck."

"Then you must finally be sharing some of it with me." He cocked his pistol again. "Three times I've caught you, and at the last moment—like a blasted dark angel—you found a way to fly off." His wheezing was so heavy, he seemed on the verge of choking. "Not this time, though."

"If you're going to shoot me, have done with it," she said flatly. "No matter what you threaten me with, it can't be worse than prison. I warn you, I'm not going back."

Devlin snickered. "Don't see why not. A cage is the best place for a wild animal like you."

"I'm not going back," she said in a louder voice, sitting even straighter. She hadn't gotten this far to surrender meekly now. In a moment, she was going to rush him, fling herself on the gun. If it went off and one of them died, so be it. But it would all end here and now in this dust-choked stagecoach. By heaven, it would end.

"Don't get any funny ideas, woman."

"Why not?" Suddenly she felt a great calm, a feeling that nothing more could hurt her. She was at the end of a long, tortuous road, with death the destination. "If I fight you for the gun, one of us will die. Unless two bullets go off, and there's the finish of us both. I just don't care anymore."

Mattie stopped suddenly as a wave of dizziness washed over her. Dear lord, she'd forgotten she might be pregnant. If she *was* carrying Cameron's child, she owed it to him and the baby to survive. As terrible as the prospect of prison was, at least the child would have a chance; to die here in the mountains would mean the end of everything. She couldn't let Devlin have such a total, black victory as that.

Devlin seemed to sense her hesitation. "Oh, I think you care about your worthless life very much," he said scornfully.

"Not as much as you care for yours," she shot back. "You want to take me back to New York like a prize stag you've brought down. You want to move up in the police department on the backs of innocent men and women. No, you don't want to die just yet. Not when there are lives still to be ruined."

Devlin sat back, his grip firm on the gun. "You've already cost me my career. For that alone, I could kill you. But what I really hate you for is your dishonesty."

"Dishonesty?" Mattie shook her head. "You're crazy as well as evil. I'm the one who spent a year in prison for a crime I didn't commit. I was beaten, starved, molested—"

"No more than what you deserved."

She ignored him. "And when I was finally released, I had to change my name and find work without references. You know as well as I do, Devlin, that in New York my only choices were the sweatshops or the brothels."

"Tried them both, did you?" His face was in shadow, but she could hear the sneer in his voice.

"It might have been better if I had."

"How touching. So instead the noble Scots lass sews her way out of the Bowery. That's right, I've looked into your grubby past. I know how you hid when you got out of prison, pretending to be a respectable working girl. But all along you were just waiting for your chance. As soon as you got yourself hired into another fancy household, I suspected those talented little fingers of yours couldn't keep from lifting what didn't belong to you." He leaned forward, the light from the swaying coach lantern outside illuminating his black eyes. "Oh, you're a shrewd bit of goods, more clever than half the con men I've locked away. I might even show a bit of respect for you if only you'd come clean. But I can't stomach hearing you protest your innocence. You robbed people who trusted you, spat in the face of the law and killed an old lady for her pearls."

Mattie's temper flared again. "It was my husband Frank who did all that. Two judges believed Frank's deathbed confession; why won't you? I don't know who's caused me more grief: you or that lying rat I married!"

Devlin suddenly jumped at her, pressing his gun against her throat. This close, she could feel his heart pounding through his jacket.

"Shut your mouth about Frank," he hissed at her. "It's because of you he's dead."

"What are you saying?" Mattie gasped, both Devlin's weight and the gun pressing at her throat choking the air out of her.

"I'm saying you're responsible for his death." Devlin eased back an inch and looked down at Mattie with implacable hatred. "If it weren't for you, Frank would still be alive."

"You knew Frank Laszlo?" She could barely get at the words. "Before prison?"

The detective pushed himself away from Mattie. "If it weren't for you, he'd never have been in prison," Devlin said, ignoring her question. "But he had the foul luck to marry a thief like you."

Something in Mattie seemed to snap. All the unhappy years spent as Frank's wife seemed to sweep over her once more, stifling her with the hurt, the betrayal, the bitterness. "A thief like *me?* You despicable fool! I only hope one day you're accused of something you didn't do, and I hope you suffer for it a hundredfold the way I did.''

"Shut up," Devlin said in a menacing voice, his voice lower than ever. "Don't push me."

Mattie sat up straight, meeting him eye to eye. Her jostling caused the bleeding man next to her to groan in pain. "Or what? You're going to make me pay? Well, I've paid, Devlin. I've been paying since I said 'I do' to my late husband. Between the state of New York and Frank Laszlo, there's not much left of me to tear apart. I guess that's why they sent a vulture like you to hunt me down."

Devlin stared at her, his hold on the gun seeming to grow even tighter. "No one sent me, Mrs. Laszlo. I came because I had no other choice, because it's my nature to punish the wicked, and see that vermin like you don't corrupt innocent young men."

Mattie shook her head. "The only innocent man I ever knew died nine years ago in a Colorado shack, cheated by scum who used the law like a knife." She gave him a bitter smile. "Just like you."

"Oh, I tried to use the law to lock you away. For all the good it did me. A year after we had you in the Tombs, I found out that you were to be released, set free as a bird, and all because Frank was too softhearted to let you rot as you deserved." He shut his eyes for an instant, as though the memory was too painful too bear. "Even at the end— even after you'd cost him his life and his freedom—Frank couldn't let you suffer for your sins. That's the sort of lovesick fool he was. With his dying breath, he lied to save you, insisting that you were innocent all along."

"I was!"

"Still lying, aren't you?" Devlin spat out. "Lying even with a gun pointed at you!"

"If you were any kind of a policeman, you'd have looked into our backgrounds and seen who was the thief. What was I before I met Frank but a girl who'd done nothing but cook and clean and sew for her keep? But Frank had been on the streets since he was a child, running numbers, stealing from

297

pushcarts and snatching purses. Or don't you know that he spent two years in a reformatory for nearly beating a pawn-broker to death?''

''You're the wanton who led him astray,'' he whispered with hatred. ''You destroyed a fine, decent boy who had his whole life ahead of him.''

''Frank Laszlo was a deceitful, violent man,'' she cried out in exasperation and anger. ''Instead you speak about him as though he were your son.''

''He was!'' Devlin shouted back.

Mattie felt as though he'd struck her again. ''What? You can't mean that!''

''He was my son and you're responsible for his death.''

''That's not true. It can't be. Frank said his father died before he was born.'' She searched her memory frantically. ''His father was Bohemian, a cigarmaker.''

''His mother was Bohemian,'' Devlin corrected icily. ''Anna Laszlo, a dark-haired little thing who could barely speak 'Englishka,' as she called it. She lived in a tenement by the East River and spent her days wrapping cigars. I was walking a beat in the neighborhood; it was a dirty rathole filled with drunks and ash-barrels stinking of tobacco leaves. The only decent thing in the whole place was Anna.'' His mouth twisted in a bitter smile. ''But she let me have my way with her, so I guess she wasn't so decent, after all.''

''You got her with child,'' Mattie breathed with con-tempt. ''You fathered a son, and then abandoned him, didn't you?''

''What did you expect me to do? I was already married with three daughters, not that I've known a drop of pleasure from any of them. My wife looked down on me as shanty Irish till the day she died, but it was only marrying into her family that got me a place on the police force. I certainly wasn't going to give up my job and my reputation for the sake of some slum girl. Still, Frank was my only son. I tried to keep tabs on him while he was growing up—from a dis-tance, of course. It wouldn't have helped either of us if I'd admitted the truth.''

Mattie was too shocked to reply. So this monstrous man was her father-in-law! She shuddered, her expression clearly showing her revulsion.

Devlin frowned at her response. "Don't like the fact that we're related? Well, I'm the one that's been disgusted ever since Frank took up with you. Shows you how innocent my Frank was, marrying a girl good only for the sweatshops or the streets. I knew it was only a matter of time before you dragged him down to your level."

"If you'd been looking out after Frank all that time, then you must have seen how wild he was," Mattie protested, aghast at this man's stubborn refusal to see the truth. "All the trouble he got into running with the Rag Gang, then beating up that poor old man."

He shrugged. "Growing up where he did, I figured he'd get into a few scrapes. But he never tried anything on respectable folk until he married you. My son was too smart for that. It took a pretty face like yours to egg him on. All those thefts at the house the two of you worked for—I knew it was you behind them, but I couldn't do anything without dragging Frank into it. I can see now I should have hired someone to get rid of you. It would have spared Frank and me a lot of grief. But I was a fool. I believed in working within the bounds of the law then. And all it got me was a son dying in prison for a crime he didn't commit."

"That's not true!"

Devlin lurched forward, pressing the barrel of his gun to her temple. "I talked to Frank after he was arrested. I finally told him I was his father. He didn't take it too well, not that I blamed him. I hadn't done my duty by him, but I wanted to make up for it. He was being accused of a crime he wasn't responsible for. I told him I knew it was his little red-haired wife who put him up to it, and all the other thefts, too. As soon as he saw I knew about you, he started singing like a bird. Not that it was going to save him from doing prison time, but at least the truly guilty party wasn't going to go free. And by confessing, he got a few years shaved off his sentence.'' A note of grim satisfaction entered his voice. ''Years that were added to yours.''

Mattie felt the pressure of both the gun at her head and the weight of those long-ago memories. She didn't know which felt more terrible. ''So it was you who gave him the idea of accusing me. It's your fault I went to prison. Why, you're worse than Frank. At least he couldn't bear to die with me on his conscience and finally admitted the truth. But you—'' She shook her head, feeling the metal barrel scrape against her. ''You're not even honest enough to admit that it's your guilt that's behind all this.''

''My guilt?'' He pressed the barrel even harder. ''Talk about the pot calling the kettle black.''

''You hate yourself for deserting your son, leaving him to fend for himself in the slums. Those two years he spent in the reformatory were probably as painful for you as for him.''

He breathed heavily, slowly sitting back a bit so that a few inches appeared now between her and the gun. ''Not as painful as seeing him sentenced to prison.'' His voice shook slightly. ''Not as painful as hearing he'd been stabbed to death by some half-witted inmate.'' He seemed to rouse himself. ''And not as painful as watching the woman responsible for my son's death walk free.'' His voice rang out with conviction. ''Nothing matched the hell of that moment, Mattie Laszlo. Nothing!''

It was no use reasoning with him. ''You've been following my progress ever since I was released, haven't you?'' she asked softly, chilled at the thought that this man's evil gaze had been riveted on her. ''All these years you've been waiting, hoping I'd slip up somehow and give you the chance to pounce.''

He nodded. ''Three years and not a hint of dishonest behavior. I never suspected you possessed such patience. But when the Sinclairs hired you out of the sweatshops, I knew it would happen soon. I knew you'd fall back on your old ways and start pinching the family silver, or find some idiotic man to act as your accomplice.''

''Then Evelyn Sinclair's necklace turns up missing.'' Mattie sighed. ''What a happy night that must have been. It made things so easy for you. Unfortunately, I didn't do it.''

''I know you didn't steal the necklace.'' Devlin suddenly went very still; in the darkness he seemed like a breathing shadow. ''I did.''

''What?'' Mattie's hands felt cold as ice. When it seemed as though this man's malice had no bounds, he amazed her yet again. ''*You* stole Evelyn's necklace?''

''I was tired of waiting, tired of wasting my energies and my final years on the force just to see you slip up. I knew you would steal something eventually—it was only a matter of time—but I didn't *have* the time. They were pressuring me to retire; things hadn't gone well since Frank died. If they took me off the force, I would lose the opportunity to nab you red-handed, lose the deep hot pleasure of leading you off to jail in handcuffs.'' His noisy breathing filled the dark stagecoach. ''So I arranged for a light-fingered fellow I know to break into the house the day of the society wedding and make off with it. He's not going to talk, unless he wants to see the inside of prison again. Meanwhile I have you right where I want you.''

''All this time I thought you were just too pig-headed to believe I was innocent. But you actually know that I'm innocent and you don't care.''

''You're innocent only of this latest crime,'' he snapped back. ''A crime I have no doubt you would have committed within the year. How was I to know you'd climb over the rooftops and get away at the last minute? But there'll be no escaping this time. Not from me.''

''So Ward Sinclair arranged this whole thing. He lied when he told the deputy marshal I would go free.''

Devlin shook his head. ''Sinclair is nearly as big a fool as that Englishman. Hang all these rich, fancy gentlemen. I couldn't believe it when Sinclair called me in last night to say he was letting you go, dropping all charges. I wanted to wring his fat ruddy neck, but you never get anywhere with a fat cat like that. Got to go behind their backs, and that's just what I did. I knew which train you were leaving on, and that your only choice after that would be the stage heading for Texas." He gestured to the unconscious man slumped next to her. "Getting this buffoon to switch places with the stagecoach driver was child's play. That whole gang of robbers are nothing but stupid kids. If I'd been marshal, they would have all been swinging from a tree by now."

Mattie looked over at the young man. She could feel the wetness on her sleeve and knew it was his blood. "You've probably killed him, or don't you care?"

"He's a criminal. I just executed justice a bit early."

She turned her attention back to Devlin. "Like you're going to do with me?"

Devlin nodded. "I have to give you credit; you almost got away with it all. The thefts back in New York, my son taking the fall for you. You even nabbed that pretty English lord right out from under Evelyn Sinclair's nose. I always pegged you for a harlot, I just didn't know how strong those charms of yours were. Although I'm sure the memory of them will quickly fade once he gets his manicured hands on the marriage settlement." He saw her start. "That's right, Mrs. Laszlo. The wandering lord has gone back to his lady, although he doesn't seem too happy about it. You must have given him quite a show in bed."

Mattie felt as though the life had been snuffed out of her. "Cameron and Evelyn are going to be married?" she asked hoarsely.

"As soon as possible. Maybe even tomorrow. That was the bargain struck between Sinclair and the Englishman. He drops all charges and lets you go free, and Lord Cameron marries his daughter immediately." Devlin gave a hard, mirthless laugh. "Sinclair's taking no chances. Seems your Englishman said he loved you, wanted to marry you! That's why you were hustled out of Denver like greased lightning. The Sinclairs are afraid of you, afraid you'll lure their fancy lord away again. You show your nose anywhere around them or Lord Cameron and the deal's off. You'll be hauled off to prison before you can even flash your petticoat." Devlin aimed his revolver. "Not that there's any chance of that happening. It's time for my brand of justice now—and from my justice there is no escape."

Mattie looked straight at the barrel of the gun, the gun Devlin was about to fire. Her mind was a swirl of grief, anger, fear. It was terrible enough that she'd been tricked both by her husband and then his father. But now to learn that Cameron had sacrificed his freedom and happiness for her! Even worse, his sacrifice would be for nothing. He would never find out she had died in the foothills of Colorado. Devlin would see to that. The injustice of it all sent a terrible resolution through her. Her instincts warned her that he was about to pull the trigger. She had nothing more to lose. If he was going to kill her, then by heaven she would not make it easy for him.

With a hoarse cry, Mattie flung herself on top of Devlin. The gun went off, the bullet striking the roof of the coach. Like the wild animal he accused her of being, Mattie struggled frantically with him, biting down hard on his arm so that his revolver clattered to the floor.

He might have been stronger, but Mattie was filled with rage. She fought him like a banshee, kicking, scratching, clawing. The coach rocked wildly and she fell against Devlin, ignoring his fists, pummeling him with her own. Cursing and grunting, neither one was aware when the coach lurched to a halt. When the buffalo skinner yanked open the door, he was met with a flurry of fists.

The old man tried to break up the fighting; wedging himself between them, he managed to pry them apart. Devlin landed a blow on his face, but the wiry old fellow backhanded him. With a great effort, he pulled Mattie out of the coach. Once outside, she continued to struggle, caught up in a feverish quest for revenge, wanting to go back and strike at Devlin again and again.

"You'll both die, I swear it!" Devlin yelled. The detective scrambled for the gun he had dropped.

"Looking for this?" a weak voice rasped.

Devlin looked up. The coach lantern afforded a brief

303

glimpse of the wounded outlaw. He was holding Devlin's gun. "Give me that, you—"

Mattie struggled free of the buffalo skinner just as the gun went off. Both she and the old man froze, staring at the open door of the coach. A moment later, Devlin appeared, bleeding from his mouth, his clothing wildly askew, his face scratched. She took a deep breath, prepared to attack him once again.

Devlin raised a hand. It was only then she saw the scarlet stain spreading over his stomach. His hand reached out to them as though accusing them of the crime. Devlin's eyes opened wide and he looked as though he were about to say something. Instead he fell forward onto the ground like a rotten tree collapsing from its own weight. Mattie stared at his fallen figure, fearing he would come to life again.

The buffalo skinner pushed her aside. Kicking Devlin's body over, the old man cautiously laid a hand on the detective's chest. Then he peered into the stagecoach before turning back to Mattie.

"Seems they're both dead, miss," he said with a grunt. "And not a minute too soon either, the way I look at it."

For one hysterical moment, Mattie feared she would burst out laughing. Devlin was dead. He could never haunt her again, never steal up on her, poisoning her dreams and killing her future. He was dead and she was free. Then she remembered that Cameron was being forced to marry Evelyn Sinclair, and that she was powerless to prevent it. If she returned to Denver to stop the wedding, she would be arrested and sent back to prison.

With dawning horror, Mattie walked over to Devlin's motionless body. Her knees buckled and she collapsed on the ground, her hands covering her face. So the nightmare wasn't over—not for her and not for Cameron. While the world believed her guilty, neither she nor Cameron were truly free.

And the only man who could prove her innocence now lay dead.

Chapter Twenty-two

Although Cameron didn't expect happiness from marriage, he never thought to feel so appalled on his wedding day. He pulled at the snug coat that felt as cumbersome as a suit of armor. Out in the chapel, he could hear low murmurs, restless sounds from a small gathering of uneasy guests. Witnesses to an execution, he thought bitterly. The execution of his self-respect, his dream of an honest and satisfying life.

A year ago, he would have felt pleased with himself to be standing here, waiting for Evelyn Sinclair to come down the aisle. He turned away in defeat. A year ago, he hadn't known the freedom of making his own way in the world. He hadn't experienced the exultation of pulling a fortune out of the hard, resisting ground. A year ago, he hadn't known Mattie.

Cameron closed his eyes, imagining her riding through the mountains she loved so well, the wind blowing that bright coppery hair, riding away from him—toward freedom. Mattie deserved to be free far more than he did. She was honest and strong, defiant and passionate, just like this country he had grown so fond of. If his marriage allowed her to be free, then it would be worth it.

"As long as one of us is happy," he said aloud.

"Somehow I suspect it isn't you."

Cameron whirled around. Behind him stood Marshal Lee, a puzzled expression on his face.

"I thought you were out of town, Marshal." He thought a moment. "Your deputy Zeke said something about a trip back East."

"I've been gone nearly a month. High time I got back. I got off the train just an hour ago, and I have to admit that I was mighty surprised to hear about you getting married to this Sinclair woman. Seemed like you and Mattie Crawford had an understanding back in Cripple Creek." He held up a hand as Cameron started to protest. "And then I learn from Zeke about the little lady getting arrested." He frowned. "Guess I stayed away too long."

Cameron cleared his throat. "Mattie is free now. I've seen to that. The charges against her were blatantly ridiculous, but nonetheless it took some hard talking to convince Ward Sinclair. Anyway, that doesn't matter. The young lady was released from jail with all charges dropped." His voice grew tight with emotion. "She's far away from here now. And safe at last, thank God."

"Depends on what you call 'safe.' "

"What does that mean?"

The Marshal looked down for a moment at the black Stetson in his hand, as though considering whether to go on. "Let's just say there's some unfinished business involving Miss Crawford," he said finally.

"See here, Marshal, I made certain that all charges against Mattie were dropped permanently. She's a free woman, as free as you or I!"

Lee looked up at him with a knowing expression. "Maybe more?"

Cameron stiffened. "I won't permit anyone to harm her again, not even you. She's suffered enough from the law and men like Devlin and Sinclair."

"Where *is* Lieutenant Devlin?" The older man's voice now held an edge. "According to Zeke, he disappeared around the same time as Miss Crawford left town."

"I just assumed he went back to New York once Sinclair dropped the charges."

"I don't think he headed East. At least he hasn't yet."

"Is Mattie in danger from this infernal policeman? Please tell me, Marshal. If Mattie is still in trouble, I must know. I have to do something."

"It seems like you've already done a great deal," Lee drawled, taking in Cameron's black tail coat and white silk vest. "Or was it Miss Sinclair you wanted to marry all along?"

"I have no intention of answering that." Cameron straightened his white cravat. "My marriage to Evelyn is irrelevant to this discussion. My only concern is for Mattie's welfare. I'll do anything to keep her safe."

Lee nodded. "Exactly as I thought."

"Damn you, is Mattie still in danger from this policeman?"

He paused. "I intend to find out."

The door opened, and a tall man in a surplice peeked in. "We'll be starting the service in about ten minutes, Lord Cameron."

Lee gaped at the minister. "Reverend Haller is marrying you and the young lady?"

Cameron colored slightly. He'd been mortified to discover that the officiating minister at his marriage was the same fellow who had presided over the aborted wedding of Mattie and Jack Daniels in Cripple Creek.

"It seems Reverend Haller marries all the best families in Colorado," he said stiffly.

"And in Cripple Creek, too." Haller smiled. "Don't look so uneasy, Marshal. I have been assured by both the groom and his bride that this ceremony will not suffer any interruptions. After all, this is Denver, not Cripple Creek. We do things a mite differently here."

"I hope you're right," Lee mumbled. When Haller closed

the door behind him, he grabbed Cameron by the arm. "Look, this here wedding just doesn't smell right to me."

Cameron shook off his hand. "It's none of your business."

"Yes, it is. I've known Mattie Crawford since she was a girl. She's gone through more trouble than any ten women ought to. I know because I was the cause of some of it. Well, I tried to make it up to her and to others by becoming a lawman. And once I saw that she'd come back home, I was determined to pay her back somehow for what I did to her father."

"What are you talking about? What did you do to—"

"It doesn't matter now," he broke in. "All that matters is seeing that Mattie finally gets a fair shake around here. When you spirited her away from her own wedding, I knew right then and there it was you that could make her happy. And that girl deserves to be happy. So I decided to do what I could to bring it about. That's why I went back East."

"Back East? Marshal, what's this all about?"

"It's about setting things right and letting the truth come out." He stepped closer to Cameron. "It's about not making any more bargains with the devil. Any fool can see that you're only marrying this rich girl because her daddy set Mattie free."

"I repeat, my marriage is none of your bloody business."

"Maybe so, but I was prepared to make it my business as long as Mattie was here to reap the benefits. You understand that I was prepared to invest in that mine of yours?"

"You? Excuse me, Marshal, but I hardly imagine that your government salary is enough to warrant serious investment in anything."

"Don't let appearances fool you. I made a fortune years ago in these mountains, and not always in a legal fashion, if you get my meaning. But a mansion on Poplar Avenue in Denver didn't keep my wife from running off with another man, or save my son from dying in a cave-in. My gold has done nothing but bring me grief. I thought maybe this time I could use some of it to help one of the people I hurt. I thought you and Mattie were set to get hitched, and I knew you were itching for investors. Helping you to keep your mine would be a way of setting things right with Alec Crawford's daughter. But now you've gone and ruined all my plans."

So it was Marshal Lee's lawyer who had summoned him to Denver. It seemed no matter what he did, things were not destined to turn out. "Sorry for ruining your plans, but I had more important things on my mind—like seeing that the woman I love didn't rot in prison. Maybe you would have handled things differently, but I didn't see any options. I still don't. Now, if you don't mind, I'd rather not discuss this any longer. I'm about to be married."

"You're making a mistake," Lee said grimly.

Cameron turned away. "I've made so many mistakes, Marshal. I hardly think another one will crush me."

"This one might," Lee said in a low voice.

Only Cameron's sudden flinch indicated that he'd heard the whispered warning. Then the organ music sounded and he walked into the church to meet his bride.

Mattie was so exhausted that she thought she would collapse onto the dusty boots of the man holding her arm. "We're almost there," she murmured, catching sight of the sandstone walls of the Trinity United Methodist church. A few more steps and she would be inside.

"You sure you want to go through with this?" the man beside her asked again. "We can just turn around and go to the train station. Once you're safely gone, I'll mosey over to the marshal's office and tell him about the robbery and shooting. Let the lawmen clean up this mess, not a little lady like you."

"But this is my mess to clean up, Ben. I have to stay. I never should have run away in the first place." She managed a smile at the old buffalo skinner. It had been nearly two days since Devlin had abducted their stagecoach. Making their way back to Denver, Mattie had grown more certain with each turn of the wheel that she was doing the right thing. Only fear had made her leave: blind, selfish terror.

Trying to save my own skin, she thought glumly, leaving Cameron to pay an all-too-heavy price for her freedom.

"I won't let him down," she said to Ben as they reached the steps of the church. "It's time everyone knew the truth."

"I've had my run-ins with the law, too," Ben muttered. "It don't always seem that being honest gets you any favors. You could be sitting in jail again before sundown."

"I know," she said in a calm voice. Mattie stopped and shook off his hand. The church loomed above them in the late morning sun, its Victorian Gothic walls looking almost garish against the blue mountain sky.

The shaky strains of a lone organ reached her ears from inside.

"Sounds like they started already," Ben said with an upraised eyebrow. "You sure you're ready?"

"I'm ready, Ben," she said. And she was. Even if she walked out of the church an hour later in handcuffs, never to know a second's freedom again, it would be worth it. At least Cameron wouldn't be forced into a marriage as cold and calculating as the one his parents had shared. All she had to offer Cameron was the truth—and her love. It might not be enough to save her, but it would be enough to save him.

That was all that mattered.

Cameron stood unmoving and expressionless beside Evelyn. In their city finery, he imagined they looked like two elegant dolls atop a wedding cake. And that was what Cameron felt like: a lifeless doll with no will of its own. He cast a sideways glance at his bride. She looked remarkably composed for a young woman who knew her groom was in love with another woman.

The minister cleared his throat and loudly finished his speech, prelude to the exchange of vows. Cameron straightened and took a deep breath.

"Therefore if any man here knows just cause why these two should not be joined together, let him speak now or forever hold his peace." As he spoke, Reverend Haller stiffened. Cameron nearly laughed. Did he actually imagine that anyone in this wedding party would halt the ceremony? Not likely. But the minister did not continue; instead his eyes widened as he stared past both him and Evelyn.

Just as he was about to turn around to see what was causing the minister so much consternation, a familiar voice broke the silence. "Don't marry her, Cameron."

A collective gasp went up as everyone swiveled around. There in the middle of the aisle stood Mattie. Behind her shuffled a grizzled old man.

"Mattie," Cameron cried out. "What in the world are you doing here?"

"How dare you interrupt my wedding!" Evelyn moved to her father's side. "Daddy, do something, please!"

Ward Sinclair looked purple with rage. "I'll see that you're thrown in prison for the rest of your dishonorable life, do you understand me, Miss Crawford? Of all the double-dealing, sneaky things to pull on me and my family. Marshal, arrest this loathsome creature before I strangle her with my own hands."

"Don't sacrifice your happiness for me, Cameron," Mattie said, ignoring the Marchioness's poisonous stare and Sinclair's cursing. "You deserve to marry a woman who loves you."

"You spiteful witch!" Evelyn screamed. "Will someone get her out of here?"

"You need to marry a woman who you love as well," Mattie continued. She took a step forward, and the light from a side window struck her full force. She looked pale and exhausted, Cameron thought, her dress rumpled and stained with what looked like blood. My God, what had happened to her since her release?

"Don't give up your happiness for me," she pleaded, stepping closer.

"Marshal, I told you to arrest this damnable hussy!" Ward Sinclair thundered.

Marshal Lee only sat back in his pew, an expression of relief on his face.

Cameron stared at Mattie, drinking in the sight of her. With

311

her standing just a few feet away, he forgot for a moment that this was his wedding. It suddenly didn't matter that his bride was on the verge of hysterics or that his sister seemed about to faint. Mattie was here once more. His Mattie.

He covered the space between them in only a second, catching her up in his arms as though she were the only thing to keep him from dying. "*You* are my happiness," he breathed, wrapping his arms around her so tightly, he felt they would both shatter. "Only you."

She clung to him in turn. "Better I go back to prison for the rest of my life than have you do this. As much as I want to be free, I want your happiness more."

He pulled back and looked into her eyes. "I won't let them lock you away. I won't. If marrying Evelyn is what is required, then it's a small price to pay."

Mattie shook her head and pressed herself against him. Lord in heaven, she felt good. Would this be the last time he would ever hold her?

"Please don't spoil my last gift to you," he whispered. "Leave me to my fate."

"You won't be happy," Mattie protested. "If you marry Evelyn, you'll be as unloved and neglected as your own father."

"Insufferable creature!" Irene pointed her parasol at the couple as though it were an arrow she wished to unleash. "What sort of country is this where slatterns from the street are permitted to mock their betters?"

"Oh, Mother, don't be such a beastly snob," Cornelia said sharply. "Father would have been mortified to hear you say such dreadful things to anyone, but especially to the woman your son apparently loves. You should be ashamed of yourself."

For a moment, both Cameron and Irene were so shocked at Cornelia's uncharacteristic outburst that neither could respond. Harry quickly moved over to stand beside his delicate-looking fiancée, but she didn't seem to need any support.

"Cameron, if you do indeed love Miss Crawford, then I

don't know how you can in good conscience marry Miss Sinclair,'' she went on, her chin jutting out stubbornly beneath the brim of her black crepe bonnet.

Across the aisle, Evelyn gasped.

"Of course, I love her, Neely,'' Cameron said. "Isn't that obvious?'' He ignored his mother slamming down her parasol onto the pew. "But something more important than my wishes are involved here.''

"Yes, like justice being served finally on this lying baggage!''

Cameron rounded on Ward Sinclair. "If one more person dares to insult Miss Crawford—no matter who he is!—I swear I will pick him up bodily and throw him out of the church. Is that clear?''

"But she stole my necklace,'' Evelyn said tearfully. "Cameron, how can you not see that she's only using you to escape the law?''

"That's not true,'' Mattie protested. "I didn't steal your necklace.''

"Liar!'' Evelyn stamped her foot in frustration. "Marshal, she's a criminal. How can you just sit there and not do anything?'' She flung herself against her father's barrel-like chest. "Daddy, get her away from me, please.''

Ward Sinclair shouted, "Marshal Lee, I insist you arrest this woman.''

Lee slowly rose, his demeanor remarkably relaxed. "On what grounds? Busting up a wedding?''

"Of course not, you dolt. She stole my daughter's necklace.''

"Didn't you drop all charges?'' Lee drawled.

"Well, I'm reinstating them.'' Sinclair turned towards Cameron, who only tightened his arms around Mattie. "Not even a gold mine and a title are enough payment for this sort of humiliation. The marriage is off.''

"Daddy, no!'' Evelyn wailed.

"And that woman you're so besotted with is going to back to prison.''

"Not if I have anything to say about it,'' Cameron shot

313

back tersely, although he didn't know what he could do to save Mattie. He might have no other choice but to become a fugitive himself.

Mattie seemed to read his mind. "No, darling," she murmured. "I won't let you ruin your life for me."

Cameron looked about the church wildly, seeking a quick exit. If they started running, Sinclair wouldn't be able to catch them. But Marshal Lee, unfortunately, always wore an Army revolver.

"I won't let Cameron destroy his future for my sake," Mattie announced loudly. "And I'm done with running away. Even if the truth isn't enough to save me, I won't resort to flight or deception anymore. I refuse to allow circumstances to turn me into a dishonest, self-serving woman. If nothing else, I can deny Devlin that final victory."

"Such noble words from a lying thief!" Evelyn said spitefully.

"I am not a thief, Evelyn," she said. "For the last time, I did not steal your necklace."

"Then who did?" she said, angry tears running down her face.

"Lieutenant John Patrick Devlin," answered Marshal Lee.

Everyone swerved in the lawman's direction.

"What?" Cameron said in shock.

"How long have you known?" Mattie gasped.

The marshal slowly inched his way down the aisle. "Nearly a week. That's why I went back East. I suspected something fishy when I first saw you back in Cripple Creek after all these years, but then Devlin paid me a visit in the summer. Seems he wanted my help in tracking down a New York jewel thief, a red-haired young woman. I thought it was you he was talking about right off, but I didn't cotton to his manner. Seemed a sour, mean fellow any way you looked at it. So I decided to go poking around and find out what I could."

"Then you could have arrested me at any time in Cripple Creek?"

"Number one, I don't work for any big-city policemen. If they're not sharp enough to track down their own crooks, I ain't gonna help them. I have enough to deal with in these mountains without taking up their slack. Second, I figured I owed you a couple of favors after cheating your father out of his claims all those years ago. The least I could do was try and help Alec Crawford's daughter if she was in trouble now."

"Do you expect me to believe that you went back to New York City only to help this criminal?" Sinclair sputtered scornfully.

"She's not a criminal. If you don't believe me, I have a police report from the Fifth Precinct sitting right now in my office verifying the fact that Willie Bass—a three-time convicted burglar and jewelry thief—was blackmailed into stealing your daughter's necklace on the night of the society wedding. Devlin apparently caught him redhanded in a heist back in April. Instead of turning Willie in, Devlin agreed to forget everything if he would lift the Sinclair necklace."

"This is unbelievable," breathed Harry.

Cameron nodded, and laid a steadying arm across Mattie's shoulders. "Did Willie confess?"

Lee nodded. "He got caught two weeks ago breaking into a gem cutter's on the east side. For a fourth offense, he was going to go away for life, so he tried to make a deal: the truth about the Sinclair necklace for a lighter prison sentence."

"Not that I swallow any of this, mind you, but if this Bass person did steal the necklace, where in blazes is it?" Sinclair pushed Evelyn aside, paternal feelings now supplanted by greed. "That necklace was worn by Marie Antoinette, and if the police have somehow lost or misplaced it, I'll sue every—"

"The police found the necklace in Devlin's apartment," Lee broke in impatiently. "I've also got a written statement from the police apprising you of the present location of the necklace." He smirked. "Relax, Sinclair. You'll get your pretty little bauble back."

Mattie slumped against Cameron in relief. "It's finally over."

"This is wonderful, darling," Cameron whispered in her ear. "You're free at last." He took a ragged breath. "We're both free."

"Well, even if this is true, it doesn't explain why this infernal woman ran away on the night of the theft," Sinclair said defensively. "If she *was* innocent—"

"My God, you have written proof from the police department itself and you still suspect her of something!" Cameron shook his head in disgust. "Small wonder she ran away, with a pack of wolves like Devlin and you and your daughter waiting to bring her down."

"That's not fair," Evelyn cried. "I always treated her well, and she rewarded me by flinging herself at you. Maybe she's not a jewel thief, but she's certainly guilty of stealing a man who belonged to me."

"Be quiet, Evelyn," Sinclair said, his expression strained. "Haven't we suffered enough shame and disappointment this morning? After all, he's not the only bankrupt English lord sniffing about for an heiress."

"But Daddy," she pleaded softly, biting her lip when her father turned away.

"What I don't understand is *why* Devlin did this," Cameron said.

Mattie and Marshal Lee looked at each other, and she saw instantly that he knew the complete truth. "Why don't you tell them?" she suggested quietly.

Irene and Sinclair both sat down with a thud while Lee tersely related the long-simmering vengeance of Lt. Devlin against his daughter-in-law. Cornelia clutched Harry's arm, her face revealing her shock.

"Where is this terrible man now?" Cornelia asked when Lee was finished.

"Yes, where is he?" Cameron intoned in a deadly voice.

"He ain't nothin' but food for coyotes," said the buffalo skinner. Everyone but Mattie looked at him as though he were a waxwork dummy come to life. Rubbing an arm across

316

his nose, the old man made his way down the aisle. Evelyn Sinclair put a handkerchief to her face as he drew near.

"Are you saying he's dead?" Lee asked with a frown.

Ben nodded. "Shot clean through the stomach, and not a moment too soon. Otherwise he'd a had the little lady in his sights, and no mistake about it."

While the buffalo skinner began his colorful retelling of the incident, Mattie only sighed and leaned her head against Cameron's shoulder. He brushed the hair away from her cheek and searched her eyes in frantic concern. "Are you all right, Mattie?"

"I am now," she whispered, the joy in her eyes evident even in the dim light of the church.

"No one will ever harm you again, darling. I swear it."

"That's not a promise anyone can keep, Cameron." She smiled. "All I ask is a chance at happiness with you."

"I've disappointed every woman who wanted to share my life," he said with no small amount of trepidation. "I may fail you, too."

"Just you try." She laughed, nestling in his arms.

Cameron didn't think he had ever known such happiness. He'd almost sold his soul to the devil, only to have it rescued at the last moment by a flame-haired angel.

"The Sinclairs were right about one thing," he said softly. "You *are* a thief."

"What!" Mattie's head shot up.

"Well, you did steal my heart, didn't you?" He cupped her face tenderly in his hands. "Stole it clean away."

"It's only fair." Mattie returned his smile, although her eyes were bright with unshed tears—as were his. "You stole mine a long time ago."

The aspens swayed under the autumn sky like blazing beacons. Even though it was only September, the breeze was brisk and smelled of wood smoke. Cameron smoothed back his hair and then tucked in his flannel shirt.

"Hardly standard wedding attire," Harry joked beside him. "I feel a tad embarrassed to be standing up here decked

317

out only in a pair of clean Levi's and a cotton shirt. Even Roy managed to squeeze himself into his Sunday suit."

"Mattie didn't want any frills," he replied with a smile. "Just the company of good friends and an open sky above us."

The sound of a hand organ interrupted the birdsong and quiet chatter. Cameron turned about, pleased at the small sea of smiling faces that greeted him. Cornelia looked luminous despite her mourning attire, Marshal Lee beamed as though he were the father of the bride and Roy MacDuff strained at his high starched collar. They were getting married in a small clearing just outside Cripple Creek, one of the few spots not yet ripped up for gold. He caught sight of Pearl DeVere's plumed bonnet and grinned at the thought of Pearl serving as maid of honor, while an old buffalo skinner gave the bride away.

It was fitting that rough men and fancy women should witness the ceremony. Here in the West each individual got the chance to make himself anew. Such wide-open opportunity could get you a hangman's rope or a fifty-room mansion on Colorado Spring's Millionaire's Row. Or love, he thought, as Mattie and Ben began to make their way across the grass toward him. A fellow in the West might even find a woman as fine as this one. A woman who would soon bear his child. Cameron felt a lump rise in his throat. Mattie had given him so much already, and now there would be a baby as well.

He felt free, freer than he ever had. His mother had left for England immediately after the scene in the Denver church, so her bitter presence wouldn't mar his happiness today. Instead he could celebrate his good fortune with those who had helped him and his bride. Especially Marshal Lee, whose sizable investment in their mine assured Cameron and Harry of a truly golden future.

"You take good care of her, y'hear," Ben warned as he led Mattie up to her groom.

Cameron turned a solemn face to the old man. "I will."

Mattie tucked her hand about his arm. "We'll take good care of each other."

"May we begin?" the minister said in a low voice as the couple turned toward him.

"You look beautiful," Cameron whispered, his gaze traveling over her pale yellow dress and the circlet of mountain flowers atop her flowing hair.

"So do you," Mattie replied with a grin.

Reverend Haller cleared his throat. "Please."

Bride and groom grew silent, their expressions both guilty and amused.

"With your kind permission, I would like to alter the wedding ceremony by asking a question of the congregation," Reverend Haller said, his fingers drumming nervously against his prayer book.

Mattie looked at Cameron and shrugged.

"Go ahead, Reverend," Cameron said.

"Ladies and gentlemen, as you know, we are gathered here to join this man and this woman in holy matrimony." The reverend threw a long-suffering look at the bridal couple. "However, sometimes the Lord—and an occasional bride and groom—work in strange ways, so I must relieve my mind of something immediately."

Haller gazed out over the small circle of wedding guests as though daring them to protest. "Now let's settle this before the ceremony begins," he said in a voice loud enough to be heard in the neighboring town of Victor. "If anyone here—anyone at all—should find just cause why these two should not be joined together, let him or her speak now or forever hold their peace!"

Mattie fought to keep a straight face as Haller, breathing heavily, waited for yet another wedding to be halted. For several moments, only Cameron's laughter could be heard.

"That's more like it." The reverend opened his prayer book with a victorious flourish. "Now let's get these two married."